ENGLISH NOVEL

English Novel Richardson to Hardy

Edited by

FRANK N. MAGILL

Derived from Library Editions
Published by Salem Press, Inc.

SALEM SOFTBACKS
Pasadena, California

LIBRARY OF CONGRESS CATALOG CARD NUMBER: 80-54245

ISBN 0-89356-301-3

Some of this material has appeared previously in
works published under the titles *Masterplots*: Revised Edition, *Cyclopedia of World Authors*, *Cyclopedia of Literary Characters*, and *Magill's Bibliography of Literary Criticism*.

First Printing

PRINTED IN THE UNITED STATES OF AMERICA

PUBLISHER'S NOTE

MAGILL SURVEYS form a series of integrated study guides designed to provide sources for augmenting classroom work in the Humanities. These guides offer ready-reference information about authors and their works and are structured with classroom requirements strictly in mind. Articles include biographical information about authors and their total canon, and, where appropriate, they provide plot summaries, character studies, critical evaluations, and extensive bibliographical references.

Magill Surveys are intended to take the student far beyond the immediate assignment. For example, if the program calls for the study of "a Dickens novel," the appropriate Survey will present to the student half a dozen or more pages on each of several Dickens novels, including a critical biography of Dickens, plot summaries and critical evaluations of the novels, individual character analyses of scores of the characters appearing in these novels, and finally an average of about twenty bibliographical references for *each* of the novels—the latter element a highly valuable resource whether for class work or term papers. Thus, the student may gain extensive background information about the author and his canon while concentrating on in-depth study of a particular work.

The text for this Survey derives from a series of extensive library references in world literature edited by Frank N. Magill, including the following sources: *Masterplots*, *Cyclopedia of World Authors*, *Cyclopedia of Literary Characters*, and *Magill's Bibliography of Literary Criticism*.

All the material drawn from the above sources has been revised and supplemented where necessary to reflect current critical opinion. The text has been arranged to provide convenient access to a great amount of basic information condensed in one handy volume. Elaborate indexing techniques have been employed to assure information retrieval with a minimum of time and effort.

The original material reproduced in *Magill Surveys* has been developed through consultations with and contributions by hundreds of professors and scholars throughout the United States and abroad over a period of years. Its authoritativeness is attested by the thousands of academic and public libraries where the basic works from which this material is drawn will be found. The student who wishes to go beyond his assignment will find here ample means to satisfy his desire.

This collection on the English novel deals with thirty authors and seventy-five representative novels. It provides an overview of important early works of English long fiction and depicts the magnificent growth of this literary form down to the doorway of the twentieth century.

CONTENTS

CONTENTS

Special Consultant

Leslie B. Mittleman

List of Contributors

Walter Allen
Kenneth John Atchity
Nancy G. Ballard
Judith Bloch
Peter A. Brier
Sally Buckner
David B. Carroll
Edward E. Foster
Jan Kennedy Foster
Bonnie Fraser
Patricia King Hansen
Lodwick Hartley
Katharine Bail Hoskins
Muriel B. Ingham
George Burke Johnston

Joanne G. Kashdan
David L. Kubal
Eileen Lothamer
Margaret McFadden-Gerber
Jean G. Marlowe
Leslie B. Mittleman
Catherine E. Moore
Keith Neilson
Fannie Ratchford
Bruce D. Reeves
Edgar F. Shannon, Jr.
Archibald B. Shepperson
Edward Wagenknecht
Carl J. Weber

ENGLISH NOVEL

JANE AUSTEN

Born: Steventon, Hampshire, England (December 16, 1775)
Died: Winchester, England (July 18, 1817)

Principal Works

NOVELS: *Sense and Sensibility*, 1811; *Pride and Prejudice*, 1813; *Mansfield Park*, 1814; *Emma*, 1815 (dated 1816); *Persuasion*, together with *Northanger Abbey*, 1818.

The seventh of eight children of a rural clergyman respected for his learning and literary taste, Jane Austen, born at Steventon, Hampshire, on December 16, 1775, was the second daughter in a vigorous, able, and affectionate family. Two of her brothers followed their father to Oxford and into the Church, and two others rose to be admirals in the Navy. Except for brief schooling in Oxford, Southampton, and Reading, which ended at the age of nine, she was educated at home, where she learned French, a smattering of Italian, some history and, in addition to Shakespeare and Milton, gained a thorough acquaintance with the essayists, novelists, and poets of the eighteenth century.

Always somewhat shy but lively and witty, Jane Austen developed into a young lady of cultivated manners and pleasing appearance, who at balls and assemblies enjoyed her share of masculine attention. A brief but genuine romance with a young man whose identity is uncertain ended suddenly with his death. When she was nearly twenty-seven, she accepted, and the next day rejected, the proposal of Harris Bigg-Wither, a friend of long-standing, whom she realized she did not love.

Aside from writing, Jane Austen devoted her life to domestic duties and household affections, and especially to being the companion and confidante of numerous nieces and nephews, who found her unfailingly kind, sympathetic, and amusing.

Having spent the first twenty-five years of her life in the rectory at Steventon, she removed in 1801, upon her father's retirement, with her parents and sister Cassandra to Bath. After her father's death in 1805 and a sojourn of three years in Southampton, she settled with her mother and sister in a cottage belonging to her brother Edward at Chawton, Hampshire, where she resided until two months before her death. Here, working mainly in the general sitting room, she composed the final drafts of all her major works, hurriedly slipping the small sheets under the blotting paper if a visitor or servant appeared. In 1816 her health began to fail; and in May, 1817, she and Cassandra moved to Winchester for adequate medical attention. Despite weakness and pain, she remained cheerful to the end. Dying peacefully on July 18, 1817, aged forty-one, she was buried in Winchester Cathedral.

Jane Austen's novels, the first published when she was thirty-five and followed by five others in as many years, were the final fruits of an early and painstaking apprenticeship to literature. Three small volumes of juvenilia, *Volume the First* (1933), *Love and Friendship* (1922), and *Volume the Third* (1951), written by the time she was eighteen years old and bearing witness to her youthful talent for mimicry and burlesque, also contain her first serious piece, "Catharine, or the Bower," probably a literary ancestor of *Northanger Abbey*. Her first completed novel, *First Impressions* (the lost original of *Pride and Prejudice*), begun in October, 1796, and finished in August, 1797, her father offered to a publisher without success. In November, 1797, she started *Sense and Sensibility* and in that year and the next wrote *Northanger Abbey*, a revised version of which, entitled *Susan*, she sold in 1803 for ten pounds to the publisher Crosby, who advertised but failed to publish it; finally retrieved in 1816, an amended text appeared posthumously in 1818. *The Watsons* (1871, 1927), a fragmentary progenitor of *Emma*, and *Lady Susan* (1871, 1925), a biting epistolary satire, probably the germ of *Mansfield Park*, have survived in manuscripts written on paper watermarked 1803 and 1805 respectively. Extensively revised or re-written in 1809–1811, *Sense and Sensibility* was published on October 31, 1811. Favorably received, the edition sold out in less than two years and brought its author one hundred forty pounds. *Pride and Prejudice* appeared in 1813, *Mansfield Park* in 1814, and *Emma* in 1815 (dated 1816). *Persuasion* was issued with *Northanger Abbey* in 1818, and by that date *Sense and Sensibility* and *Mansfield Park* had reached a second edition, *Pride and Prejudice* a third. She was engaged upon the rough draft of the early chapters of a new novel, *Sanditon* (1925), only a few weeks before she died.

Far ahead of her time in the techniques of narration, especially in the control of point of view, Jane Austen, through her fidelity to life, her delineation of character, and her ironic insight, produced sophisticated comedy unsurpassed in the English novel. Entertainment, however, was not her sole aim. Primarily a moral writer striving to establish criteria of sound judgment and right conduct in human relationships, she inculcates the related virtues of self-awareness and unselfishness.

Northanger Abbey, the earliest of the major novels in chronological order of composition, while revealing its kinship to the juvenilia by depending for much of its humor upon burlesque of the Gothic novel, offers much more than mere parody. The education of its callow heroine, Catherine Morland, by examples of the discrepancy between appearance and reality, typifies Jane Austen's method and illustrates her penchant for proportion and symmetry in both literature and life. Although *Sense and Sensibility* also contains an element of literary satire—upon the current novel of feeling—it is essentially a paradigm of the proper balance between self-control and emotion. *Pride and Prejudice*, the most scintillating of her novels and long the popular favorite among them, provides in Elizabeth Bennet one of the most delightful heroines of fiction. She and Darcy eventually overcome first impressions (note the original title) distorted on both sides by pride and prejudice. With its high proportion of dialogue and with the ironic commentary shifted from the author to a character within the story (Mr. Bennet), this book represents the apex of her dramatic act. Convinced that *Pride and Prejudice* was too playful, she tended to the opposite extreme with *Mansfield Park*, where her irony is chastened and her censure of worldly values borders on didacticism. *Emma*, Jane Austen's masterpiece and profoundest moral comedy, is a study in the self-delusions of vanity. Unified in time (a cycle of one year) and place (Highbury and its environs), the beautifully concentric action revolves, as the title implies, around a dominant heroine, who, having every advantage in life, is a victim only of herself. *Persuasion*, more patently infused with emotion than is customary with Jane Austen, but saved from sentimentality by the full play of her wit, examines, through the person of Anne Elliot, aged twenty-seven, the author's only mature heroine, the conflicting claims of prudence and true love.

Jane Austen's style—unadorned, concise, flexible, and animated—is the ideal instrument for her art. Her dialogue, without resort to slang or obvious tags, shows a precise ear for individual and revealing rhythms of speech. Her ironic detachment and technical skill have established her reputation with modern critics, but the deftness with which she pleases and instructs has endeared her works to generations of readers.

Bibliography

The definitive edition is *The Novels of Jane Austen*, edited by R. W. Chapman, 5 vols., 1933 (3rd ed.), with a sixth volume added in 1954. The standard biography is W. and R. A. Austen-Leigh's *Jane Austen: Her Life and Letters*, 1913. This work supplements J. E. Austen-Leigh's *Memoir of Jane Austen*, 1870–1871 (reissued 1926). A companion volume to the biography is M. A. Austen-Leigh, *Personal Aspects of Jane Austen*, 1920. Other biographical and critical studies include Geraldine Mitton, *Jane Austen and Her Times*, 1905; F. W. Cornish, *Jane Austen*, 1913; R. B. Johnson, *Jane Austen: Her Life, Her Work, Her Family, and Her Critics*, 1930; Lord David Cecil, *Jane Austen*, 1935; Mary Lascelles, *Jane Austen and Her Art*, 1939; R. A. Austen-Leigh, *Jane Austen and Southampton*, 1949; Elizabeth Jenkins, *Jane Austen*, 1952; Marvin Mudrick, *Jane Austen: Irony as Defense and Discovery*, 1952; and A. H. Wright, *Jane Austen's Novels*, 1953.

A most useful book of Austen studies is R. W. Chapman's *Jane Austen: Facts and Problems*, 1949. In *Speaking of Jane Austen*, 1944, and *More Talk of Jane Austen*, 1949, Sheila Kaye-Smith and G. B. Stern present lively, appreciative table talk on Jane Austen and her art. Recent studies include Ian Watt, ed., *Jane Austen: A Collection of Critical Essays*, 1963; and A. Walton Litz, *Jane Austen: A Study of Her Artistic Development*, 1965.

EMMA

Type of work: Novel
Author: Jane Austen (1775–1817)
Type of plot: Social comedy
Time of plot: Early nineteenth century
Locale: Surrey, England
First published: 1816

In this novel about a headstrong, snobbish, intellectually proud young woman, Austen's genius for ironic comedy is displayed at its peak. The plot involves finding the proper husband for the heroine, but behind the deceptively simple and everyday events lies the author's moral vision of a world in which social responsibility and familial obligation are key virtues, and compromise a necessary response to the irreconcilable opposites encountered in life.

Principal Characters

Emma Woodhouse, the younger daughter of the wealthy owner of Hartfield and the most important young woman in the village of Highbury. Good-hearted, intelligent, but spoiled, she takes under her protection Harriet Smith, a seventeen-year-old girl of unknown parentage, who is at school in the village. Given to matchmaking, Emma breaks up the love affair between Harriet and Robert Martin, a worthy farmer, because she thinks Harriet deserves better, and persuades her to fall in love with the vicar, Mr. Elton. To her dismay, Elton proposes to her rather than to Harriet and is indignant when she refuses him. Next, Emma becomes interested in Frank Churchill, an attractive young man who visits his father in Highbury, and thinks him in love with her; but it develops that he is secretly engaged to Jane Fairfax. Emma had never really cared for Churchill, but she thinks him a possible match for Harriet. She becomes really concerned when she discovers that Harriet's new interest is in Mr. Knightley, an old friend of the Woodhouse family. She now realizes that Knightley is the man she has always loved and happily accepts his proposal. Harriet marries her old lover, Martin, and the matrimonial problems are solved.

George Knightley, a landowner of the neighborhood, sixteen years Emma's senior, and an old family friend. Honorable, intelligent, and frank, he has always told Emma the truth about herself. When she thinks that he may marry someone else, she realizes that she has always loved him and accepts his proposal.

John Knightley, George's brother, married to Emma's older sister.

Isabella Knightley, nee Woodhouse, John Knightley's wife and Emma's sister, a gentle creature absorbed in her children.

Henry Woodhouse, father of Emma and Isabella, kindly and hospitable but an incurable hypochondriac.

Mr. Weston, a citizen of Highbury who has married Anne Taylor, Emma's former governess.

Anne Weston, nee Taylor, Emma's former governess, a sensible woman whom Emma regards highly.

Frank Churchill, Mr. Weston's son by a former marriage. He has been adopted by and taken the name of his mother's family. His charm attracts Emma briefly, but she is not seriously interested. He is secretly engaged to Jane Fairfax.

Jane Fairfax, a beautiful and accomplished orphan who visits her family in Highbury. Emma admires but cannot like her, finding her too reserved. The mystery of her personality is solved when it is learned that she is engaged to Churchill.

Mrs. Bates and

Miss Bates, grandmother and aunt of Jane Fairfax. Poor but worthy women, they are intolerably loquacious and boring.

Harriet Smith, the illegitimate daughter of a tradesman. Young, pretty, and impressionable, she is taken up by Emma Woodhouse, rather to her disadvantage, for Emma gives her ideas above her station. She is persuaded to refuse the proposal of Robert Martin and to believe that Mr. Elton, the vicar, is in love with her. When Elton proves to be interested in Emma, Harriet is deeply chagrined.

After considering the possibility of Harriet as a match for Churchill, Emma finds to her dismay that Harriet is thinking of Knightley. This discovery makes Emma realize how much she has always loved him. After Emma and Knightley are engaged, Harriet is again proposed to by Robert Martin; she happily marries him.

Robert Martin, the honest young farmer who marries Harriet Smith.

The Rev. Philip Elton, vicar of the parish. A conceited, silly man, he proposes to Emma Woodhouse, who has thought him in love with Harriet Smith. Emma's refusal makes him her enemy.

Augusta Elton, nee **Hawkins,** the woman Elton marries after being refused by Emma. She is vulgar, pretentious, and officious.

The Story

Emma Woodhouse, rich, clever, beautiful, and no more spoiled and self-satisfied than one would expect under such circumstances, had just seen her friend, companion, and ex-governess, Miss Taylor, married to a neighboring widower, Mr. Weston. While the match was suitable in every way, Emma could not help sighing over her loss, for now only she and her father were left at Hartfield and Mr. Woodhouse was too old and too fond of worrying about trivialities to be a companion for his daughter.

The Woodhouses were the great family in the village of Highbury. In their small circle of friends there were enough middle-aged ladies to make up card tables for Mr. Woodhouse but no young lady to be friend and confidante to Emma. Lonely for her beloved Miss Taylor, now Mrs. Weston, Emma took under her wing Harriet Smith, the parlor boarder at a nearby boarding-school. Harriet was an extremely pretty girl of seventeen, not in the least brilliant, but with pleasing, unassuming manners, and a gratifying habit of looking up to Emma as a paragon.

Harriet was the natural daughter of some mysterious person, and Emma, believing that the girl might be of noble family, persuaded her that the society in which she had moved was not good enough for her. She encouraged her to give up her acquaintance with the Martin family, respectable farmers of some substance though of no fashion. Instead of thinking of Robert Martin as a husband for Harriet, Emma influenced the girl to aspire to Mr. Elton, the young rector.

Emma believed from Mr. Elton's manner that he was beginning to fall in love with Harriet, and she flattered herself upon her matchmaking schemes. Mr. Knightley, brother of a London lawyer married to Emma's older sister and one of the few people who could see Emma's faults, was concerned about her intimacy with Harriet. He warned her that no good could come of it for either Harriet or herself, and he was particularly upset when he learned that Emma had influenced Harriet to turn down Robert Martin's proposal of marriage. Emma herself suffered from no such qualms, for she was certain that Mr. Elton was as much in love with Harriet as Harriet—through Emma's instigation—was with him.

Emma suffered a rude awakening when Mr. Elton, finding her alone, asked her to marry him. She suddenly realized that what she had taken for gallantries to Harriet had been meant for herself, and what she had intended as encouragement to his suit of her friend, he had taken as encouragement to aspire for Emma's hand. His presumption was bad enough, but the task of breaking the news to Harriet was much worse.

Another disappointment now occurred in Emma's circle. Frank Churchill, who had promised for months to come to see his father and new stepmother, again put off his visit. Churchill, Mr. Weston's son by a first marriage, had taken the name of his mother's family. Mr. Knightley believed that the young man now felt himself above his father. Emma argued with Mr. Knightley, but she found herself secretly agreeing with him.

Although the Hartfield circle was denied Churchill's company, it did acquire an addition in the person of Jane Fairfax, niece of the garrulous Miss Bates. Jane rivaled Emma in beauty and accomplishment, one reason why, as Mr. Knightley hinted, Emma had never been friendly with Jane. Emma herself blamed Jane's reserve for their somewhat cool relationship.

Soon after Jane's arrival, the Westons received a letter from Churchill setting another date for his visit. This time he actually appeared, and Emma found him a handsome, well-bred young man. He called frequently upon the Woodhouses, and also upon the Bates family, because of prior acquaintance with Jane Fairfax. Emma rather than Jane was the recipient of his gallantries, however, and Emma could see that Mr. and Mrs. Weston were hoping that the romance would prosper.

About this time Jane Fairfax received the handsome gift of a pianoforte, anonymously given. It was presumed to have come from some rich friends with whom Jane, an orphan, had lived, but Jane herself seemed embarrassed with the present and refused to discuss it. Emma wondered if it had come from Mr. Knightley, after Mrs. Weston pointed out to her his seeming preference and concern for Jane. Emma could not bear to think of Mr. Knightley's marrying Jane Fairfax, and after observing them together, she concluded to her own satisfaction that he was motivated by friendship, not love.

Mr. Elton returned to the village with a hastily wooed and wedded bride, a lady of small fortune, extremely bad manners, and great pretensions to elegance.

Harriet, who had been talked into love by Emma, could not be so easily talked out of it; but what Emma had failed to accomplish, Mr. Elton's marriage had, and Harriet at last began to recover. Her recovery was aided by Mr. Elton's rudeness to her at a ball. When he refused to dance with her, Mr. Knightley, who rarely danced, offered himself as a partner, and Harriet, without Emma's knowledge, began to think of him instead of Mr. Elton.

Emma herself began to think of Churchill as a husband for Harriet, but she resolved to do nothing to promote the match. Through a series of misinterpretations, Emma thought Harriet was praising Churchill when she was really referring to Mr. Knightley.

The matrimonial entanglement was further complicated because Mrs. Weston continued to believe that Mr. Knightley was becoming attached to Jane Fairfax. Mr. Knightley, in his turn, saw signs of some secret agreement between Jane Fairfax and Frank Churchill. His suspicions were finally justified when Churchill confessed to Mr. and Mrs. Weston that he and Jane had been secretly engaged since October. The Weston's first thought was for Emma, for they feared that Churchill's attentions to her might have had their effect. Emma assured Mrs. Weston that she had at one time felt some slight attachment to Churchill, but that that time was now safely past. Her chief concerns now were that she had said things about Jane to Churchill which she would not have said had she known of their engagement, and also that she had, as she believed, encouraged Harriet in another fruitless attachment.

When she went to break the news gently to Harriet, however, Emma found her quite unperturbed by it, and after a few minutes of talking at cross purposes Emma learned that it was not Churchill but Mr. Knightley upon whom Harriet had now bestowed her affections. When she told Emma that she had reasons to believe that Mr. Knightley returned her sentiments, Emma suddenly realized the state of her own heart; she herself loved Mr. Knightley. She now wished she had never seen Harriet Smith. Aside from the fact that she wanted to marry Mr. Knightley herself, she knew a match between him and Harriet would be an unequal one, hardly likely to bring happiness.

Emma's worry over this state of affairs was soon ended when Mr. Knightley asked her to marry him. Her complete happiness was marred only by the fact that she knew her marriage would upset her father, who disliked change of any kind, and that she had unknowingly prepared Harriet for another disappointment. The first problem was solved when Emma and Mr. Knightley decided to reside at Hartfield with Mr. Woodhouse as long as he lived. As for Harriet, when Mr. Knightley was paying attention to her, he was really trying to determine the real state of her affections for his young farm tenant. Consequently Mr. Knightley was able to announce one morning that Robert Martin had again offered himself to Harriet and had been accepted. Emma was overjoyed that Harriet's future was now assured. She could always reflect that all parties concerned had married according to their stations, a prerequisite for their true happiness.

Critical Evaluation

Jane Austen had passed her fortieth year when her fourth published novel, *Emma,* appeared in 1816, the year before her death. Although *Pride and Prejudice* has always been her most popular novel, *Emma* is generally regarded as her greatest. In this work of her maturity, she deals once more with the milieu she preferred: "3 or 4 Families in a Country Village is the very thing to work on." Having grown to womanhood in her native Hampshire village of Steventon, the seventh of the eight children of the learned village rector, and having spent the remainder of her life, except for brief intervals in Bath and Southampton, in another Hampshire village, Chawton, she was thoroughly familiar with the world she depicted.

The action of *Emma* cannot be properly considered apart from the setting of Highbury, the populous village only sixteen miles from London, its physical attributes presented in such circumstantial detail that it becomes a real entity. London seems far away, not because of the difficulty of travel, but because of the community's limited views. It is a village where a light drizzle keeps its citizens at home, where Frank Churchill's trip to London for the alleged purpose of getting a haircut is foppery and foolishness, where the "inconsiderable Crown Inn" and Ford's "woollen-draper, linen-draper, and haberdasher's shop united" dominate the main street. Emma's view of the busiest part of town, surveyed from the doorway of Ford's, sums up the life of the village:

> Mr. Perry walking hastily by, Mr. William Cox letting himself in at the office door, Mr. Cole's carriage horses returning from exercise . . . a stray letter boy on an obstinate mule . . . the butcher with his tray, a tidy old woman . . . two curs quarrelling over a dirty bone, and a string of dawdling children round the baker's little bow-window. . . .

The novel concerns the interrelationship between such an inconsequential place and Emma Woodhouse, a pretty and clever young lady almost twenty-one who is rich and has few problems to vex her. Ironically, however, her world is no bigger than the village of Highbury and a few surrounding estates, including her father's Hartfield; nevertheless, in that small world, the Woodhouse family is the most important. Therefore, states the author, the real dangers for Emma are "the power of having rather too much her own way, and a disposition to think a little too well of herself."

Moreover, these dangers are unperceived by Emma. Thus, in the blind exercise of her power over Highbury, she involves herself in a series of ridiculous errors, mistakenly judging that Mr. Elton cares for Harriet rather than for herself; Frank Churchill for herself rather than for Jane Fairfax; Harriet for Frank rather than for Mr. Knightley; and Mr. Knightley for Harriet rather than for herself. It is the triumph of Jane Austen's art that however absurd or obvious Emma's miscalculations, they are convincingly a part of Emma's charming egotism. The reader finally agrees with Mr. Knightley that there is always "an anxiety, a curiosity in what one feels for Emma."

Emma's vulnerability to error can in part be attributed to inexperience, her life circumscribed by the boundaries of Highbury and its environs. No mention is made of visits to London, though Emma's only sister lives there. She has never been to the seacoast, nor even to a famous scenic attraction nearby, Box Hill. She is further restricted by her valetudinarian father's gentle selfishness, which resists any kind of change and permits a social life limited to his own small circle, exclusive to the degree of admitting only four people as his closest acquaintances and only three to the second group.

Nonetheless, Emma's own snobbery binds her to the conclusion that she has no equals in Highbury. Mr. Knightley well understands the underlying assumption of superiority in Emma's friendship for Harriet Smith: "How can Emma imagine she has anything to learn herself, while Harriet is presenting such a delightful inferiority?" Emma fears superiority in others as a threat. Of the capable farmer Robert Martin, Harriet's wooer, she observes: "But a farmer can need none of my help, and is therefore in one sense as much above my notice as in every other way he is below it." Her resolution to like Jane Fairfax is repeatedly shattered by the praise everybody else gives Jane's superior attractions.

While Emma behaves in accordance with her theory that social rank is too important to be ignored, she fails to perceive that she is nearly alone in her exclusiveness. Indeed, the Eltons openly assume airs of superiority, and Jane Fairfax snubs Emma. Emma's increasing isolation from Highbury is epitomized in her resistance to the Cole family, good people of low rank who have nevertheless come to be regarded socially as second only to the Woodhouse family. Snobbishly sure that the Coles will not dare to invite the best families to an affair, she finds only herself uninvited. Thus, ironically, she imagines her power in Highbury to be flourishing even as it is already severely diminished.

Emma's task is to become undeceived and to break free of the limitations imposed by her pride, by her father's flattering tyranny, and by the limited views of Highbury. She must accomplish all this without abandoning her self-esteem and intelligence, her father, or society. The author prepares for the possibilty of a resolution from the beginning, especially by establishing Mr. Knightley as the person who represents the standard of maturity which Emma must assume. Emma is always half aware of his significance, often putting her folly to the test of his judgment. There are brief, important occasions when the two, united by instinctive understanding, work together to create or restore social harmony. However, it is not until Harriet presumes to think of herself as worthy of his love that Emma is shocked into recognition that Mr. Knightley is superior to herself as well as to Harriet.

Highbury itself, which seems so confined, also serves to enlarge Emma's views simply by proving to be less fixed than it appears. As John Knightley observes: "Your neighbourhood is increasing, and you mix more with it." Without losing her desire for social success, Emma increasingly suffers from it. She is basically deficient in human sympathy, categorizing people as second or third rank in Highbury or analyzing them to display her own wit. Yet, as she experiences her own humiliations, she begins to develop in sensitivity. Thus, while still disliking Jane, she is capable of "entering into her feelings" and granting a moment of privacy. Her rudeness to Miss Bates is regretted, not only because Mr. Knightley is displeased but also because she perceives that she has been brutal, even cruel to Miss Bates.

Despite her love of small schemes, Emma shares an important trait with Mr. Knightley, one which he considers requisite for his wife—an "open temper," the one quality lacking in the admirable Jane. Emma's disposition is open, her responsiveness to life counteracting the conditions in herself and her circumstances which tend to be constricting. Her reaction to news of Harriet's engagement to Robert Martin is characteristic: she is "in dancing, singing, exclaiming spirits; and till she had moved about, and talked to herself, and laughed and reflected, she could be fit for nothing rational." Too ready to laugh at others, she can as readily laugh at herself. Impulsive in her follies, she is quick to make amends. She represents herself truthfully as she says, in farewell to Jane, "Oh! if you knew how much I love every thing that is decided and open!"

A fully realized character who develops during the course of the action, Emma is never forced by the author to be other than herself, despite her new awareness. Once Harriet is safely bestowed upon Robert Martin, she complacently allows their friendship to diminish. The conniving to keep her father reasonably contented is a way of life. Mr. Knightley, if he wishes to marry her, is required to move into Hartfield. Serious reflection upon her past follies is inevitably lightened by her ability to laugh at them—and herself. The novel is complete in every sense, yet Emma is so dynamic a characterization that one shares Mr. Knightley's pleasure in speculation: "I wonder what will become of her!"

Bibliography

Beer, Patricia. *Reader, I Married Him: A Study of the Women Characters of Jane Austen, Charlotte Brontë, Elizabeth Gaskell and George Eliot.* London: Macmillan, 1974, pp. 49–82.

Bramer, George R. "The Setting in *Emma*," in *College English*. XXII (December, 1960), pp. 335–346.

Drew, Elizabeth A. *The Novel; A Modern Guide to Fifteen English Masterpieces.* New York: Norton, 1963, pp. 792–821.

Duckworth, Alistair M. *The Improvement of the Estate; A Study of Jane Austen's Novels.* Baltimore: Johns Hopkins University Press, 1971, pp. 145–178.

Duffy, Joseph M. "*Emma*: The Awakening from Innocence," in *Journal of English Literary History.* XXI (1954), pp. 39–53.

Edge, Charles. "*Emma*: A Technique of Characterization," in *The Classic British Novel.* Edited by Howard Harper and Charles Edge. Athens: University of Georgia Press, 1972, pp. 51–64.

Hagen, John. "The Closure of *Emma*," in *Studies in English Literature, 1500–1900.* XV (1975), pp. 546–561.

Halperin, John and Janet Kunert. *Plots and Characters in the Fiction of Jane Austen, the Brontës, and George Eliot.* Hamden, Conn.: Shoe String Press, 1976.

Hamouchene, Ulla, Gerd Lemvig and Else Thomsen. "Aspects of Three Novels by Jane Austen, Part Two: *Emma.* Love and Marriage, or How the Rigid Class Division Should Be Mollified a Little," in *Language and Literature.* II, (1973), pp. 56–71.

Harvey, W.J. "The Plot of *Emma*," in *Essays in Criticism.* XVII (January, 1967), pp. 48–63.

Jones, Evan. "Characters and Values: *Emma* and *Mansfield Park*," in *Quadrant.* XII (1968), pp. 35–45.

Karl, Frederick R. *An Age of Fiction; The Nineteenth Century British Novel.* New York: Farrar, Straus and Giroux, 1964, pp. 27–62.

Kissane, James D. "Comparison's Blessed Felicity: Character Arrangement in *Emma*," in *Studies in the Novel.* II (1969), pp. 173–184.

Kooiman-Van Middendorp, Gerarda M. *The Hero in the Feminine Novel.* New York: Haskell House, 1966, pp. 49–59.

Kroeber, Karl. *Styles in Fictional Structure: The Art of Jane Austen, Charlotte Brontë, George Eliot.* Princeton, N.J.: Princeton University Press, 1971, pp. 15–26, 75–79, 151–180.

Lawry, J.S. " 'Decided and Open': Structure in *Emma*," in *Nineteenth-Century Fiction.* XXIV (June, 1969), pp. 1–15.

Leeming, Glenda. *Who's Who in Jane Austen and the Brontës.* London: Elm Tree Books, 1974.

Lodge, David. *Emma: A Casebook.* Nashville, Tenn.: Aurora, 1970.

Mansell, Darrel. *The Novels of Jane Austen: An Interpretation.* London: Macmillan, 1973, pp. 146–184.

Moore, E. Margaret. "*Emma* and Miss Bates: Early Experience of Separation and the Theme of Dependency in Jane Austen's Novels," in *Studies in English Literature*. IX (Autumn, 1969), pp. 573–585.

Pinion, F.B.   *A Jane Austen Companion: A Critical Survey and Reference Book*. London: Macmillan, 1973, pp. 114–122.

Swingle, L.J.   "The Perfect Happiness of the Union: Jane Austen's *Emma* and English Romanticism," in *Wordsworth Circle*. VII (1976), pp. 312–319.

Tomlinson, T.B.   "Jane Austen's Originality: *Emma*," in *Critical Review*. IX (1966), pp. 22–37.

Weissman, Judith.   "Evil and Blunders: Human Nature in *Mansfield Park* and *Emma*," in *Women and Literature*. IV (1976), pp. 5–17.

White, Edward M.   "*Emma* and the Parodic Point of View," in *Nineteenth-Century Fiction*. XVIII (June, 1963), pp. 55–63.

MANSFIELD PARK

Type of work: Novel
Author: Jane Austen (1775–1817)
Type of plot: Social criticism
Time of plot: Early nineteenth century
Locale: Northamptonshire, England
First published: 1814

Mansfield Park *is essentially a "Cinderella story" in which the heroine, Fanny Price, wins happiness after a long and demeaning series of experiences as the "poor relation" at Mansfield Park. Fanny wins the love of Edmund Bertram and the approbation of his family because she embodies those virtues which Jane Austen thought most valuable: charity, loyalty, honesty, self-knowledge, and plain goodness.*

Principal Characters

Fanny Price, the heroine of the novel. Brought up by the Bertrams at Mansfield Park, she is timid and self-effacing and is constantly reminded by her Aunt Norris of her position as a poor relation. She has always loved Edmund Bertram, the second son. Henry Crawford falls in love with her and proposes but she refuses him, for she considers him shallow and worldly. Thus she angers Sir Thomas Bertram, who feels that she has thrown away her best chance for marriage. Later, when both Bertram daughters disgrace themselves, Sir Thomas understands Fanny's real worth. Edmund, who had thought himself in love with Mary Crawford, is shocked by her attitude towards his sisters' behavior and realizes that he actually loves Fanny. They are married at the end of the novel.

Sir Thomas Bertram, a wealthy baronet, the owner of Mansfield Park. He is dignified, reserved, fundamentally kind and just, but too remote from his children to understand them. Though fond of Fanny Price, he is angered by her refusal to marry Henry Crawford; however, when his daughters disgrace him, he realizes that Fanny has a better judgment of people than he and is happy when she marries his younger son.

Lady Bertram, his wife, the spoiled beauty of her family. She is an indolent, self-indulgent, good-natured woman.

Mrs. Norris, her sister, the widow of a clergyman. A stingy, ill-tempered busybody, she is unbearably severe to her poor niece, Fanny Price, but lavish in her flattery of the rich Bertrams. Her flattery does much to ruin the characters of the Bertram daughters. After Maria Bertram's divorce, Mrs. Norris goes to live with her.

Mrs. Price, the third sister, Fanny's mother. She has made the worst marriage, her husband being a lieutenant of marines without fortune or connections. They have nine children and live at Portsmouth on the edge of poverty.

Lieutenant Price, her husband, a marine officer disabled for active service. He is uncouth but good-natured.

William Price, their son, in the Royal Navy. The favorite of his sister Fanny, he gets his promotion through the Crawfords' friendship with her.

Tom Bertram, the older son of Sir Thomas. He is headstrong, worldly, and idle, but a severe illness sobers him.

Edmund Bertram, the second son, a serious young man who desires to take Holy Orders. He fancies himself in love with Mary Crawford until, disgusted by her cynical attitude towards the clergy and by her easy acceptance of his sisters' conduct, he becomes aware that he really loves Fanny Price. They are married and live near Mansfield Park.

Maria Bertram, the older daughter, spoiled and selfish. She marries wealthy Mr. Rushworth but tires of him, runs off with Henry Crawford, and is irretrievably disgraced.

Julia Bertram, the second daughter and equally spoiled. She elopes with Mr. Yates and by so doing cuts herself off from her family.

Henry Crawford, a wealthy young man who flirts with Maria Bertram. He falls in love with Fanny Price, but she refuses him, and he elopes with Maria, now Mrs. Rushworth. They separate after a few months.

Mary Crawford, his sister. She is cynical and worldly but attracts Edmund Bertram. He is disillusioned and repelled when she takes his sisters' conduct so casually.

Mr. Rushworth, the rich but brainless husband of Maria Bertram, whom she deserts for Henry Crawford.

Mr. Yates, a fashionable young man who visits Mansfield Park and eventually elopes with Julia Bertram. The marriage greatly displeases her father.

The Story

Of the three Ward sisters, one had married very well to a baronet, one very badly to a lieutenant of the marines, and one neither too badly nor too well to a clergyman. The fortunate sister, Lady Bertram, agreed at the instigation of the clerical sister, Mrs. Norris, to care for one of the unfortunate sister's nine children. Accordingly, Fanny Price, ten years old, and a shy and sensitive child, came to make her home at Mansfield Park. Among her four Bertram cousins, Tom, Edmund, Maria, and Julia, Fanny found a real friend only in Edmund. The others usually ignored her except when she could be of use to them, but Edmund comforted her, and advised her. He alone seemed to recognize her good qualities—cleverness, grace, and a pleasant disposition. Besides Edmund's attentions, Fanny received some of a very different kind from her selfish and hypocritical Aunt Norris, who was constantly calling unnecessary attention to Fanny's dependent position.

When Fanny was fifteen, Sir Thomas Bertram went to Antigua to look after some business affairs. With him went his oldest son, who was inclined to extravagance and dissipation, and the family was left to Edmund's and Lady Bertram's care. During Sir Thomas' absence, his older daughter, Maria, became engaged to Mr. Rushworth, a young man who was rich and well-connected but extremely stupid.

Another event of importance was the arrival in the village of Mary and Henry

Crawford, the sister and brother of Mrs. Grant, whose husband had become the rector after the death of Mr. Norris. Both of the Bertram girls liked Henry immensely, but since Maria was engaged, he rightfully belonged to Julia. They also became close friends with Mary Crawford, who in turn attracted both Tom, now returned from abroad, and Edmund.

Fanny regretted the Crawfords' coming, for she saw that Edmund, whom she herself loved, was falling in love with the shallow, worldly Mary, and that her cousin Maria was carrying on a most unseemly flirtation with Henry. The less observant, like Mrs. Norris, saw only what they wished to see and insisted that he was paying particular attention to Julia.

At the suggestion of Mr. Yates, a pleasure-loving friend of Tom, the young people decided to engage in some private theatricals and chose for their entertainment the sentimental "Lovers' Vows." Fanny opposed the scheme from the start, for she knew Sir Thomas would have disapproved. Edmund tried to dissuade the others, but finally let himself be talked into taking a part because there were not enough men for all the roles. Rehearsals and preparations went forward, the plan growing more elaborate as it progressed. However, the unexpected return of Sir Thomas put an end to the rehearsals. The house was soon cleared of all theatrical gear, including Mr. Yates, whose trifling, affected ways Sir Thomas had disliked immediately.

Maria, willing to break her engagement to Mr. Rushworth, had hoped her father's return would bring a declaration from Henry. Instead of declaring himself, he announced his departure for a stay in Bath. Although her pride was hurt, Maria resolved that Henry Crawford should never know she had taken their flirtation seriously. She was duly married to Mr. Rushworth.

Julia went to Brighton with the Rushworths. With both the Bertram sisters gone, Henry began an idle flirtation with Fanny and ended by falling in love with her. One of his plans for winning her favor was a scheme for getting her beloved brother William, who had just visited her at Mansfield Park, a promotion in the navy. Although Fanny was grateful for this favor, she refused him promptly when he proposed. In doing so, she incurred the serious displeasure of her uncle, Sir Thomas, who regarded as sheer perversity the sentiments which made her turn down such an advantageous match. Even Edmund encouraged her to change her mind, for he was too preoccupied with his attachment to Mary Crawford to guess that Fanny had more than a cousinly regard for him. Edmund had just been ordained as a clergyman, a step which Mary Crawford had ridiculed, and he was not sure she would accept him as a husband. He persisted in believing, however, that her frivolous dislike of the clergy was only a trait she had acquired from worldly friends, and that her opinion could be changed.

About this time Fanny went to Portsmouth to visit her family. The stay was a depressing one, for she found her family, with the exception of William, disorderly and ill-bred, by Mansfield Park standards. Also, several catastrophes occurred at Mansfield Park to make her long to be helpful there. Tom, the oldest son, had such a serious illness that his recovery was uncertain; Maria, now Mrs. Rushworth, ran away with Henry, who forgot his love for Fanny long enough to commit an irrevocable indiscretion; and Julia eloped with Mr. Yates. The Bertram family, crushed under this series of blows, at last realized Fanny's value and dearness to them, and welcomed her back to Mansfield Park with tenderness that touched her deeply.

Mrs. Norris, as spiteful as ever, said that if Fanny had accepted Henry Crawford as she should have, he would never have run away with Maria. But Sir Thomas gave Fanny credit for seeing Henry's character more clearly than he had, and forgave her for having refused Henry. He blamed himself for Maria's downfall, for he realized he had never taken the trouble to know his children well.

But good came from all this evil. Tom's illness sobered him, and he proved a better son thereafter. Mr. Yates, though not a great match for Julia, had more income and fewer debts than Sir Thomas had anticipated, and seemed inclined to settle down to quiet domesticity. Henry and Maria separated after spending a few unhappy months together. Sir Thomas refused to receive her at Mansfield Park, but provided a home for her in another part of the country. There Mrs. Norris went to live with her favorite niece, to the great relief of everyone at Mansfield Park.

Edmund had finally realized Mary Crawford's frivolous and worldly nature when she treated his sister's and her brother's affair quite lightly. Her levity shocked him, and made it easier for him to give up thoughts of an unsuitable marriage. Eventually he fell in love with Fanny, who had loved him so long. They were married and lived at the parsonage near Mansfield Park.

Critical Evaluation

Despite the centrality of the theme of courtship in Austen's work, *Mansfield Park* is not primarily about a man and woman discovering their compatibility; this is not a novel constructed solely on the premise that "a single man in possession of a good fortune must be in want of a wife," the "universal truth" that launches *Pride and Prejudice*. Rather, *Mansfield Park* is a book about a place (as its title implies), and that place proves to be a touchstone for social and personal values, a haven of comfort and permanence, what Lionel Trilling, one of Austen's most distinguished critics, has called the "Great Good Place."

Fanny is drawn with little charm, but this is done primarily to underscore her outstanding characteristic, which is character itself. Although charm temporarily rules at Mansfield Park, in the wit and grace of the Crawfords and in the mode and spirit of the "theatrical," its beguiling attractions are put in a sober perspective with Sir Thomas' return. Eventually, Fanny's essential honesty and plainness, which initially relegates her to the background at Mansfield Park, become the very traits that identify her with Mansfield Park's values.

Henry Crawford first simply pursues Fanny as a sport, but he eventually is enamored of her plain goodness. Sir Thomas misjudges her and orders indefinite exile, but after his return Fanny seems to him the truest "daughter" Mansfield Park has produced. Edmund is finally cured of his superficiality by the example of Mary Crawford's indifference to his sister's fate, and it is only then that he proves worthy of Fanny. Jane Austen has so constructed the novel that her seemingly passive heroine reverses social fate, produces a change of heart in a Lothario, and indirectly restores intelligence to a weak-minded lover. Evidently, Austen did not believe that the stability of a home had everything to do with charm.

Bibliography

Anderson, Walter E. "The Plot of *Mansfield Park*," in *Modern Philology*. LXXI (1973), pp. 13–17.

Beer, Patricia. *Reader, I Married Him: A Study of the Women Characters of Jane Austen, Charlotte Brontë, Elizabeth Gaskell and George Eliot.* London: Macmillan, 1974, pp. 63–82.

Bush, Douglas. *Jane Austen.* New York: Collier, 1975, pp. 108–135.

Colby, Robert A. *Fiction with a Purpose; Major and Minor Nineteenth-Century Novels.* Bloomington: Indiana University Press, 1967, pp. 66–104.

Draffan, Robert A. "*Mansfield Park*: Jane Austen's Bleak House," in *Essays in Criticism.* XIX (October, 1969), pp. 371–384.

Duckworth, Alistair M. *The Improvement of the Estate; A Study of Jane Austen's Novels.* Baltimore: Johns Hopkins University Press, 1971, pp. 35–80.

Edge, Charles E. "*Mansfield Park* and Ordination," in *Nineteenth-Century Fiction.* XVI (1961), pp. 269–274.

Edwards, Thomas R., Jr. "The Difficult Beauty of *Mansfield Park*," in *Nineteenth-Century Fiction.* XX (June, 1965), pp. 51–67.

Fleishman, Avrom. "*Mansfield Park* in Its Time," in *Nineteenth-Century Fiction.* XXII (June, 1967), pp. 1–18.

————. *A Reading of Mansfield Park: An Essay in Critical Synthesis.* Baltimore: Johns Hopkins University Press, 1970.

Fowler, Marian E. "The Courtesy-Book Heroine of *Mansfield Park*," in *University of Toronto Quarterly.* XLIV (1974), pp. 31–46.

Goldberg, Annemette, Margit Mortensen and Marianne Sorensen. "Aspects of Three Novels by Jane Austen, Part One: *Mansfield Park.* Love and Marriage, or How to Catch a Husband Without Really Trying," in *Language and Literature.* II (1973), pp. 39–56.

Halperin, John and Janet Kunert.   *Plots and Characters in the Fiction of Jane Austen, the Brontës, and George Eliot.* Hamden, Conn.: Shoe String Press, 1976.

Jones, Evan.   "Characters and Values; *Emma* and *Mansfield Park*," in *Quadrant.* XII (1968), pp. 35–45.

Lauber, John.   "Heroes and Anti-Heroes in Jane Austen's Novels," in *Dalhousie Review.* LI (1971–72), pp. 489–503.

Lodge, David.   *Language of Fiction; Essays in Criticism and Verbal Analysis of the English Novel.* New York: Columbia University Press, 1966, pp. 94–113.

Mansell, Darrel.   *The Novels of Jane Austen: An Interpretation.* London: Macmillan, 1973, pp. 108–145.

Nardin, Jane.   *Those Elegant Decorums: The Concept of Propriety in Jane Austen's Novels.* Albany: State University of New York Press, 1973, pp. 82–108.

Pinion, F.B.   *A Jane Austen Companion: A Critical Survey and Reference Book.* London: Macmillan, 1973, pp. 101–113.

Sherry, Norman.   *Jane Austen.* New York: Arco, 1969, pp. 70–76.

Simon, Irene.   "Jane Austen and the Art of the Novel," in *English Studies.* XLIII (1962), pp. 225–239.

Tave, Stuart M.   *Some Words of Jane Austen.* Chicago: University of Chicago Press, 1973, pp. 158–204.

Weissman, Judith.   "Evil and Blunders: Human Nature in *Mansfield Park* and *Emma*," in *Women and Literature.* IV (1976), pp. 5–17.

White, Edward M.   "A Critical Theory of *Mansfield Park*," in *Studies in English Literature, 1500–1900.* VII (Autumn, 1967), pp. 659–677.

Zimmerman, Everett.   "Jane Austen and *Mansfield Park*: A Discrimination of Ironies," in *Studies in the Novel.* I (Fall, 1969), pp. 347–356.

NORTHANGER ABBEY

Type of work: Novel
Author: Jane Austen (1775–1817)
Type of plot: Comedy of manners
Time of plot: Early nineteenth century
Locale: England
First published: 1818

In Northanger Abbey, *Jane Austen parodies the then-popular gothic novel to underscore a favorite theme of her early novels: the confusion in an immature mind between literature and life. Thus, beyond the gothic parody,* Northanger Abbey *is a subtle, lively novel about the maturing of her heroine, Catherine Morland.*

Principal Characters

Catherine Morland, a young girl whose head is filled with "Gothic romances." At Bath she meets the Thorpe and Tilney families. Her brother James is attracted to Isabella Thorpe, and John Thorpe becomes attentive to Catherine. She, however, is more interested in Henry Tilney, a younger son, whose father invites her to his home, Northanger Abbey, under the mistaken impression that she is rich and will make a good match for Henry. Overcome by the thrill of being in a real abbey, Catherine makes several foolish blunders, even thinking that her host must have murdered his wife. The visit ends when General Tilney, learning that Catherine is not rich, asks her to leave and forbids Henry to see her. But Henry's love proves strong enough for him to defy his father, and the lovers are finally married.

General Tilney, the owner of Northanger Abbey. Eager for money, he is polite to Catherine only because he believes her to be rich.

Captain Frederick Tilney, his older son, for whom Isabella Thorpe jilts James Morland.

Henry Tilney, the younger son, a clergyman, who marries Catherine Morland.

Eleanor Tilney, their sister. Her marriage to a viscount puts her father into a good enough humor to permit the marriage of Henry and Catherine.

James Morland, Catherine's brother. He falls in love with Isabella Thorpe but is jilted by her.

Isabella Thorpe, a scheming young woman whom Catherine meets at Bath. She becomes engaged to James Morland but jilts him for Captain Tilney, though without much hope of marrying the latter.

John Thorpe, Isabella's stupid brother, who tries to marry Catherine and who boasts to General Tilney of her wealth. When she refuses him, he takes revenge by telling the General that she is poorer than she really is.

The Story

Catherine Morland, though a plain girl, thought herself destined to become a heroine like those in her favorite gothic novels. She might, however, have spent her entire life in Fullerton, the small village in which she was born, had not Mrs. Allen, wife of a wealthy neighbor, invited her to go to Bath. There a whole new world was opened to Catherine, who was delighted with the social life of the colony. It was at Bath that she met Isabella Thorpe, who became her best friend. Isabella was more worldly than Catherine and took it upon herself to instruct Catherine in the ways of society.

Isabella also introduced Catherine to her brother, John Thorpe. He and Catherine's brother, James Morland, were friends, and the four young people spent many enjoyable hours together. Catherine, however, had in the meantime met Henry Tilney, a young clergyman, and his sister Eleanor, with whom she was anxious to become better acquainted. John thwarted her in this desire, and Isabella and James aided him in deceptions aimed at keeping her away from Henry and Eleanor. After Isabella and James became engaged, Isabella doubled her efforts to interest Catherine in her brother John. Although Catherine loved her friend dearly, she could not extend this love to John, whom she knew in her heart to be an indolent, undesirable young man.

While James was at home arranging for an allowance so that he and Isabella could be married, Henry Tilney's brother, Captain Tilney, appeared on the scene. He was as worldly as Isabella. More important to her, he was extremely wealthy. Catherine was a little disturbed by the manner in which Isabella conducted herself with Captain Tilney, but she was too loyal to her friend to suspect her of being unfaithful to James.

Shortly after Captain Tilney arrived in Bath, Catherine was invited by Eleanor Tilney and her father, General Tilney, to visit them at Northanger Abbey, their old country home. Catherine was delighted, for she had always wanted to visit a real abbey, and she quickly wrote for and received a letter of permission from her parents. Henry aroused her imagination with stories of dark passageways and mysterious chests and closets.

When the party arrived at Northanger Abbey, Catherine was surprised and a little frightened to find that his descriptions had been so exact. Mrs. Tilney had died suddenly several years previously, and in her fear Catherine began to suspect that the general had murdered her. At the first opportunity she attempted to enter the dead woman's chambers. There Henry found her and assured her that his mother had died a natural death. Catherine was almost disappointed, for this news destroyed many of her romantic imaginings about Northanger Abbey.

For more than a week after this event Catherine worried because she had had no letter from Isabella. When she received a letter from her brother James, she learned the reason for Isabella's silence. He wrote that Isabella had become practically engaged to Captain Tilney. Catherine was almost ill when she read the news, and Henry and Eleanor Tilney were as disturbed as she. They knew that only greed and ambition drew Isabella from James to their wealthier brother and they feared for his happiness. They thought, however, that the captain was more experienced with such women and would fare better than had James.

They were right. Shortly afterward Catherine had a letter from Isabella telling the story in an entirely different light. She pretended that she and James had just had a misunderstanding, and she begged Catherine to write to James in her behalf. Catherine was not to be taken in. She wasted no time in sympathy for her one-time friend and thought her brother fortunate to be rid of such a schemer.

A short time later the general had to go to London on business and Eleanor and Catherine were alone at the Abbey, Henry's clerical duties compelling him to spend some time in his nearby parish. One night, soon after the general's departure, Eleanor went to Catherine's room. In a state of great embarrassment and agitation she told Catherine that the general had returned suddenly from London and had ordered Catherine to leave the Abbey early the next morning. Because she loved Catherine and did not want to hurt her, Eleanor would give no reason for the order. In great distress Catherine departed and returned to her home for the first time in many weeks. She and her family tried to forget the insult to her, but they could not help thinking of it constantly. Most of Catherine's thoughts were of Henry, whom she feared she might never see again.

Soon after her return home, Henry called on her and explained why his father had turned against Catherine. When the Tilney family first met Catherine, John Thorpe had told the general that she was the daughter of a wealthy family and that the Allen money would also be settled on her. He had bragged because at the time he himself had hoped to marry Catherine. But when Catherine rebuffed him, and after his sister Isabella was unable to win James again, John spitefully waited for the first opportunity to do her harm. He met the general in London and lost no time in telling him that Catherine had deceived him. Although she had never in any way implied that she was wealthy, the general gave her no chance to defend herself.

After Henry had told his story, he asked Catherine to marry him. Her parents gave their consent, with the understanding that the young couple must first win over the general. Henry returned home to wait.

Eleanor's marriage to a wealthy peer proved an unexpected aid to the lovers. The general was so pleased at having his daughter a viscountess that he was persuaded to forgive Catherine. When he learned also that the Morland family, though not wealthy, would allow Catherine three thousand pounds, he gladly gave his consent to the marriage. In less than a year after they met, and in spite of many hardships and trials, Catherine Morland married Henry Tilney with every prospect of happiness and comfort for the rest of her life.

Critical Evaluation

In all the history of the novel, perhaps no genre can claim more popularity than that of the Gothic novel of the late eighteenth century. Unfortunately, when *Northanger Abbey,* Jane Austen's parody of the Gothic novel, was published in 1818, a year after her death, the Gothic fad was all but over. However, her delightful mockery was actually written when such works were all the rage, about 1797-1798, and sold to a publisher in 1803, but for reasons unknown published posthumously. In her early twenties at the time of the composition, the young author lived in the quiet rectory where she was born, in the Hampshire village of Steventon, her circumstances resembling those of the young heroine of her novel—even to such amusements as poring over Gothic novels. The reader who has never perused Ann Radcliffe's *The Mysteries of Udolpho* (1794), which occupies so much of Catherine Morland's time and thoughts, will find other reasons to enjoy *Northanger Abbey*; but a knowledge of *The Mysteries of Udolpho* or any other Gothic novel will bring special rewards.

At one level, then, *Northanger Abbey* is an amusing parody of Gothic novels, with particular reference to *The Mysteries of Udolpho*. Nevertheless, Jane Austen's satire is not pointed simply at such novels with their mysterious castles and abbeys, gloomy villains, incredibly accomplished heroines, sublime landscapes, and supernatural claptrap. The romantic sensibility of the Gothic enthusiast is also a target. Thus *Northanger Abbey* is a comic study of the ironic discrepancies between the prosaic world in which Catherine lives and the fantastic shapes which her imagination, fed by Gothic novels, gives to that world. Throughout, the author holds up the contrast between the heroine's real situation and the Gothic world she fantasizes.

The prevailing irony begins with the first sentence: "No one who had ever seen Catherine Morland in her infancy would have supposed her born to be a heroine." As she grows up she develops neither the prodigious artistic and intellectual accomplishments necessary for the role nor the requisite beauty, being merely pretty. However, once her adventures get under way, she begins to assign stereotyped Gothic roles to her new acquaintances. Detecting villainy in General Tilney's haughty demeanor merely because in *The Mysteries of Udolpho* the evil Montoni is haughty, she overlooks his real defects of snobbery and materialism, traits which prove far more threatening to her than his hauteur.

Since the central feature of the Gothic novel is the sinister, dilapidated castle or abbey, Catherine's most cherished daydreams center upon Northanger Abbey and its long, damp passages. In reality, nothing is damp except an ordinary drizzling rain, nor is anything narrow or ruined, the Abbey having been thoroughly renovated for modern living. Try as she will, she cannot manufacture genuine Gothic horrors. Instead of dark revelations of murder and madness in the Tilney family, she faces self-revelation, her recognition that she has suffered from a delusion, a desire to be frightened.

If the ridicule of Gothicism and the exposure of false sensibility comprise one major theme, another more inclusive theme, common to all of Jane Austen's novels, is the problem of limitation. Catherine at seventeen is "launched into all the difficulties and dangers of six weeks residence at Bath," the fashionable resort, leaving a sheltered life in her village of Fullerton. She immediately discerns, however, a state of artificial confinement as a way of life in Bath:

> Catherine began to feel something of disappointment—she was tired of being continually pressed against by people, the generality of whose faces possessed nothing to interest, and with all of whom she was so wholly unacquainted, that she could not relieve the irksomeness of imprisonment by the exchange of a syllable with any of her fellow captives . . . she felt yet more awkwardness of having no party to join, no acquaintance to claim, no gentleman to assist them.

Jane Austen, throughout, continues to develop this initial image of an empty, fashionable routine in which each day brought its regular duties. But Catherine romanticizes this reality, her delusions culminating with the invitation to visit the Tilneys at Northanger Abbey, an invitation that delights and excites her. Thus the Gothic parody functions also as a study of one common response to a society circumscribed by empty rituals and relationships—escapism. This theme is resolved when Catherine's visions of romance are shattered by the mundane discoveries at Northanger Abbey, compelling her to abandon her romantic notions and choose the alternative of always acting in the future with common sense.

Nonetheless, in her dismissal of fantasy, she has not yet come to terms with the limitations in reality, the pressures of society which can impose imprisonment. Such experience is melodramatically represented by her expulsion from the Abbey—an order delivered without explanation, the time and manner of departure determined by General Tilney, and Catherine denied either friendship or common courtesy. With no alternatives, in a situation which resists good sense, Catherine is reduced to a passive awareness of the reality and substance of life. When she is shut off in her room at the Abbey, her mind is so occupied in the contemplation of actual and natural evil that she is numb to the loneliness of her situation. Confined in a hired carriage for the long, unfamiliar journey to Fullerton, she is conscious only of the pressing anxieties of thought. At home, her thought processes are lost in the reflection of her own change of feelings and spirit. She is the opposite of what she had been, an innocent.

Catherine has survived the transition from innocence to experience, proving to her mother, at least, that she can shift very well for herself. However, Catherine's maturity is tested no further. The restoration of her happiness depends less upon herself and Henry than it does upon General Tilney. Nor is she finally received by the General on the basis of personal merit. Ultimately, in the General's world, life is defined by money. When the Morlands prove to be a family of good financial standing, Catherine is free to marry the man of her choice.

Concerning the rapid turn of events in her denouement, Jane Austen wryly observes: "To begin perfect happiness at the respective ages of twenty-six and eighteen, is to do pretty well." However, despite the happy ending which concludes the novel, the author leaves Catherine upon the threshold only of the reality of life that her experiences have revealed. The area of her testing has already been defined, for example, in the discrepancy between her image of Henry's parsonage and General Tilney's. To Catherine, it is "something like Fullerton, but better: Fullerton had its faults, but Woodston probably had none."

Thus *Northanger Abbey* is a novel of initiation, its heroine ironically discovering in the world not a new freedom, but a new set of restrictions. Once undeceived of her romantic illusions of escape, she is returned, with a vengeance, to the world as it is, small but decent. As an early novel, *Northanger Abbey* points the way to Jane Austen's mature novels, in which the focus will be upon heroines who are constrained to deal with life within defined limitations.

Bibliography

Beer, Patricia. *Reader, I Married Him: A Study of the Women Characters of Jane Austen, Charlotte Brontë, Elizabeth Gaskell and George Eliot.* London: Macmillan, 1974, pp. 66–77.

Burlin, Katrin R. " 'The Pen of the Contriver': The Four Fictions of *Northanger Abbey*," in *Jane Austen: Bicentenary Essays.* Edited by John Halperin. New York: Columbia University Press, 1975, pp. 89–111.

Bush, Douglas. *Jane Austen.* New York: Collier, 1975, pp. 57–70.

Chard, Leslie F., II. "Jane Austen and the Obituaries: The Names of *Northanger Abbey*," in *Studies in the Novel.* VII (1975), pp. 133–136.

Duckworth, Alistair M. *The Improvement of the Estate; A Study of Jane Austen's Novels.* Baltimore: Johns Hopkins University Press, 1971, pp. 81–85, 91–102.

Emden, Cecil S. "The Composition of *Northanger Abbey*," in *Review of English Studies.* XIX (August, 1968), pp. 279–287.

Fleishman, Avrom. "The Socialization of Catherine Morland," in *Journal of English Literary History.* XLI (1974), pp. 649–667.

Gallon, D.N. "Comedy in *Northanger Abbey*," in *Modern Language Review.* LXIII (October, 1968), pp. 802–809.

Gooneratne, Yasmine. *Jane Austen.* New York: Cambridge University Press, 1970, pp. 49–62.

Griffin, Cynthia. "The Development of Realism in Jane Austen's Early Novels," in *Journal of English Literary History.* XXX (1963), pp. 36–52.

Halperin, John and Janet Kunert. *Plots and Characters in the Fiction of Jane Austen, the Brontës, and George Eliot.* Hamden, Conn.: Shoe String Press, 1976.

Hennedy, Hugh L. "Acts of Perception in Jane Austen's Novels," in *Studies in the Novel.* V (1973), pp. 25–30.

Kearful, Frank J. "Satire and the Form of the Novel: The Problem of Aesthetic Unity in *Northanger Abbey,*" in *Journal of English Literary History.* XXXII (1965), pp. 511–527.

Kiely, Robert. *The Romantic Novel in England.* Cambridge, Mass.: Harvard University Press, 1972, pp. 118–135.

McKillop, Alan D. "Critical Realism in *Northanger Abbey,*" in *Jane Austen: A Collection of Critical Essays.* Edited by Ian Watt. Englewood Cliffs, N.J.: Prentice-Hall, 1963.

Mansell, Darrel. *The Novels of Jane Austen: An Interpretation.* London: Macmillan, 1973, pp. 1–45.

Mathison, John K. "*Northanger Abbey* and Jane Austen's Conception of the Value of Fiction," in *Journal of English Literary History.* XXIV (1957), pp. 138–152.

Nardin, Jane. *Those Elegant Decorums: The Concept of Propriety in Jane Austen's Novels.* Albany: State University of New York Press, 1973, pp. 62–81.

Page, Norman. *The Language of Jane Austen.* Oxford: Blackwell, 1972, pp. 15–20.

Pinion, F.B. *A Jane Austen Companion: A Critical Survey and Reference Book.* London: Macmillan, 1973, pp. 76–83.

Rothstein, Eric. "The Lessons of *Northanger Abbey,*" in *University of Toronto Quarterly.* XLIV (1974), pp. 14–30.

Rubinstein, E. "*Northanger Abbey*: The Elder Morlands and 'John Homespun,'" in *Papers in Language and Literature.* V (1969), 434–440.

Shenfield, Margaret. "Jane Austen's Point of View," in *Quarterly Review.* CCXCVIII (July, 1958), pp. 296, 298–306.

Sherry, Norman. *Jane Austen.* New York: Arco, 1969, pp. 46–56.

Tave, Stuart. *Some Words of Jane Austen.* Chicago: University of Chicago Press, 1973, pp. 36–73.

PERSUASION

Type of work: Novel
Author: Jane Austen (1775–1817)
Type of plot: Comedy of manners
Time of plot: Early nineteenth century
Locale: Somersetshire and Bath, England
First published: 1818

In this last completed novel by Jane Austen, the tone is mellow, the atmosphere autumnal; even the satire is noticeably gentler than in her other works. The story of a love affair which is culminated only after a broken engagement and a separation of eight long and lonely years, Persuasion *has a certain melancholy quality despite its finally happy ending.*

Principal Characters

Anne Elliot, the heroine, second daughter of Sir Walter Elliot, and the victim of persuasion. Although pretty and attractive, she has always been ignored by her family. When quite young, she had been wooed by Frederick Wentworth, then a junior officer in the Royal Navy; but because of her father's disapproval and the advice of her mother's friend, Lady Russell, she had given him up in spite of her love. At the age of twenty-six she meets him again, for his brother-in-law and sister have leased the Elliot property. Wentworth, now a captain and rich through prize money, seems to have forgotten her, although she still loves him. He is apparently in love with Louisa Musgrove. Having joined her family at Bath, Anne receives the attentions of her cousin, William Elliot, whose charm makes some impression upon her. But through an old school friend, Mrs. Smith, she learns of William's cold, calculating, and selfish character. Although happy to be enlightened, she is still distressed by Wentworth's indifference. To her joy, he finally realizes that he is not in love with Louisa and proposes to Anne. Since he is now wealthy and a captain, Sir Walter can no longer oppose the match, and the story ends happily.

Sir Walter Elliot, Bt., of Kellynch Hall, Anne's father. Inordinately vain of his ancestry and his good looks, he is a foolish man who lives beyond his income until he is forced to lease Kellynch and live at Bath. He neglects Anne in favor of his oldest daughter, whom he wishes to marry his heir, William Elliot. He is almost snared by Elizabeth's scheming friend, Mrs. Clay, but is saved by William.

Elizabeth Elliot, the oldest daughter of Sir Walter. She is handsome but cold and selfish. Unable to make a brilliant match, she remains unmarried.

Mary Musgrove, the youngest daughter of Sir Walter and the wife of Charles Musgrove. She is spoiled and selfish.

Charles Musgrove, her husband, a typical sporting country squire.

Captain Frederick Wentworth, R.N., the hero of the novel. When a young and penniless officer, he had fallen in love with Anne Elliot and she with him; but she had given him up because of family opposition and the advice of her friend, Lady Russell. When he meets Anne again after eight years, he seems no longer interested in her; rather he is apparently in love with Louisa Musgrove. But further association with Anne makes him aware of her real worth; he proposes again, and is accepted. Since he is now a captain and a rich man, the Elliots can no longer oppose him, and the marriage can take place.

Admiral and
Mrs. Croft, brother-in-law and sister of Wentworth. They lease Kellynch Hall.

William Elliot, the villain of the novel. Although heir to Sir Walter's title and estates, William, as a young man, takes no interest in his cousins. Instead of marrying Elizabeth, as Sir Walter had hoped, he married the wealthy daughter of a grazier. Being left a rich widower, he becomes interested in his family and cultivates their friendship at Bath. Having charming manners, he makes a favorable impression upon Anne, until she learns from Mrs. Smith of his scheming character. He also selfishly prevents a marriage between Sir Walter and Mrs. Clay, a match which might ruin his prospects, by inducing Mrs. Clay to become his mistress.

Mr. and Mrs. Musgrove, of Uppercross, Charles' parents.

Louisa Musgrove, their daughter. It seems that she may marry Wentworth, especially after she is injured in an accident that he considers his fault. But she marries Captain Benwick.

Henrietta Musgrove, her sister, who marries her cousin, Charles Hayter.

Lady Russell, a widow and an old friend of the Elliot family. She persuades Anne not to marry Wentworth because of his uncertain future.

Mr. Shepherd, Sir Walter's agent, who has the task of persuading him to lease Kellynch Hall.

Mrs. Clay, Shepherd's scheming daughter. She insinuates herself into the Elliot family in order to marry Sir Walter but in the end becomes William Elliot's mistress.

Mrs. Charles Smith, a school friend of Anne. Formerly wealthy, she is now a poor and ill widow living at Bath. She reveals to Anne the true character of William Elliot.

Captain Benwick, a melancholy widower who, after being attentive to Anne Elliot, marries Louisa Musgrove.

The Story

Sir Walter Elliot, a conceited man, vain of both his good looks and his title, lived at his countryseat, Kellynch Hall, with two of his daughters, Elizabeth and Anne. Elizabeth, handsome and much like her father, was the oldest and her father's favorite. Anne, sweet, self-effacing, and quietly intelligent, was ignored, neglected, and underrated by both. Mary, the youngest daughter, was married to an agreeable young man named Charles Musgrove, and lived in an untidy house at Uppercross, three miles from Kellynch Hall.

Living beyond his means had brought financial disaster upon Sir Walter, and on the advice of his solicitor and of a family friend, Lady Russell, he was persuaded to rent Kellynch Hall and take a smaller house in Bath. Anne would have preferred to take a modest house near home, but as usual her father and sister had their way in the matter.

Reluctantly, Sir Walter let his beloved countryseat to Admiral and Mrs. Croft. Mrs. Croft was the sister of a former suitor of Anne, Captain Frederick Wentworth of the navy. Anne and Captain Wentworth had fallen in love when they were both very young, but the match had been discouraged. Anne's father felt that the young man's family was not good enough for his own and Lady Russell considered the engagement unwise because Captain Wentworth had no financial means beyond his navy pay. Also, she did not like or understand Captain Wentworth. Anne had followed their advice and broken the engagement. But it had been poor advice, for Wentworth had advanced and had become rich in the navy, just as he had said he would. Anne, at twenty-seven, had not forgotten her love at nineteen. No one else had taken Captain Wentworth's place in her affection.

With all arrangements completed for the renting of Kellynch Hall, Sir Walter, Elizabeth, and her friend, Mrs. Clay, were off to Bath. Before they departed, Anne warned Elizabeth that Mrs. Clay's was not a disinterested friendship, and that she was scheming to marry Sir Walter if she could. Elizabeth would not believe such an idea, nor would she agree to dismiss Mrs. Clay.

Anne was to divide her time between her married sister, Mary Musgrove, and Lady Russell until Christmas. Mary and her family lived also near her husband's father and mother and their two daughters, Henrietta and Louisa. During her visit to the Musgroves, Anne met Captain Wentworth again, while he was staying with his sister at Kellynch Hall. She found him little changed by eight years.

The Musgroves at once took the Crofts and Captain Wentworth into their circle, and the Captain and Anne met frequently. He was coldly polite to Anne, but his attentions to the Musgrove sisters were such as to start Mary matchmaking. She could not decide, however, whether he preferred Henrietta or Louisa. When Louisa encouraged Henrietta to resume a former romance with a cousin, Charles Hayter, it seemed plain that Louisa was destined for Captain Wentworth.

The likelihood of such a match was increased when, during a visit to friends of Captain Wentworth at Lyme Regis, Louisa suffered an injury while the captain was assisting her to jump down a steep flight of steps. The accident was not his fault, for he had cautioned Louisa against jumping, but he blamed himself for not refusing her firmly. Louisa was taken to the home of Captain Wentworth's friends, Captain and Mrs. Harville, and Captain Benwick. Anne, quiet, practical, and capable during the emergency, had the pleasure of knowing that Captain Wentworth relied on her strength and good judgment, but she felt certain of a match between him and the slowly recovering Louisa.

Anne reluctantly joined her family and the designing Mrs. Clay at Bath. She was surprised to find that they were glad to see her. After showing her the house, they told her the news—mainly about how much in demand they were, and about a cousin, Mr. William Elliot, who had suddenly appeared to make his peace with the family. Mr. William Elliot was the heir to Sir Walter's title and estate, but he had fallen out with the family years before because he did not marry Elizabeth as Sir Walter and Elizabeth felt he should have. Also, he had affronted Sir Walter's pride by speaking disrespectfully of his Kellynch connections.

Now, however, these matters were explained away, and both Sir Walter and

Elizabeth were charmed with him. Anne, who had seen Mr. Elliot at Lyme Regis, wondered why he chose to renew a relationship so long neglected. She thought it might be that he was thinking of marrying Elizabeth, now that his first wife was dead; Lady Russell thought Anne was the attraction.

About that time news came of Louisa Musgrove's engagement to Captain Benwick. Joy, surprise, and a hope that Captain Wentworth had lost his partiality for Louisa were mingled in Anne's first reaction. Shortly after she had heard the news, Captain Wentworth arrived in Bath. After a few meetings Anne knew that he had not forgotten her. She also had the pleasure of knowing that he was jealous of Mr. Elliot. His jealousy was groundless.

Even if Anne had felt any inclination to become Lady Elliot, the ambition would have been short-lived, for Mr. Elliot's true character now came to light. Anne learned from a former schoolmate, who had been friendly with Mr. Elliot before he basely ruined her husband, that his first design in renewing acquaintance with Sir Walter's family was to prevent Sir Walter from marrying Mrs. Clay and thus having a son who would inherit the title and estate. Later, when he met Anne, he had been genuinely attracted to her. This information was not news to Anne, since Mr. Elliot had proposed to her at a concert the night before. She, of course, gave him no encouragement.

Her patience in waiting for Captain Wentworth was soon to be rewarded. Convinced that Anne still loved him as he did her, he poured out his heart to her in a letter, and all was settled happily between them. Both Musgrove girls were also married shortly afterward. Neither of their husbands was as rich as Anne's, much to Mary's satisfaction. Mrs. Clay, sacrificing ambition for love, left Bath with Mr. William Elliot, and went to live under his protection in London. Perhaps she hoped some day to be Lady Elliot, though as the wife of a different baronet.

Critical Evaluation

If Jane Austen's last completed work, finished on July 18, 1816, exactly one year before her death, can be characterized as "Autumnal," it can also be regarded as a novel of new beginnings. Opening in the fall, the action of *Persuasion* concludes in the early spring of 1815 with the marriage of Anne Elliot and Captain Wentworth. Adding to this note of regeneration is the fact that the heroine, a repressed, timid spinster of the landed gentry at the outset, has achieved a new state of independence at the conclusion. This freedom she demonstrates by marrying a man who is outside her own class, a man who was once forbidden to her. Yet her liberty, as Anne realizes, is won at a price—for she must relinquish a certain security to take up the tenuous position of a naval officer's wife, never knowing when another war might begin. Indeed, at the time of her marriage, the peace in Europe was hardly secure and the Battle of Waterloo was still to be fought.

Read in this light, Anne's choice of Captain Wentworth over the future baronet of Kellynch Hall, William Elliot, dramatizes Jane Austen's conviction that the gentry had lost its moral force; that out of a fear of social change it had grown inbred and restrictive, denying its own members, especially the young, a vital existence. In *Persuasion* the upper reaches of the gentry, mean-spirited and socially irresponsible, no longer possesses the creative intelligence of Mr. Darcy of *Pride and Prejudice* or the moral integrity of Mr. Knightley of *Emma*.

Anne's escape from domination by her father and sister preserves her own self, threatened with suffocation by an effete class. Her victory and her happiness in marriage are rendered bittersweet, however, by the loss of long-established connections and an uncertain future. It is in just this alloy that we recognize the autumnal nature of *Persuasion*.

Bibliography

Auerbach, Nina.   "O Brave New World: Evaluation and Revolution in *Persuasion*," in *Journal of English Literary History*. XXXIX (1972), pp. 112–128.

Beer, Patricia.   *Reader, I Married Him: A Study of the Women Characters of Jane Austen, Charlotte Brontë, Elizabeth Gaskell and George Eliot.* London: Macmillan, 1974, pp. 45–82.

Bogh, Kirsten.   "Aspects of Three Novels by Jane Austen, Part Three: *Persuasion*. Love and Marriage, or 'Bad Morality to Conclude With?,'" in *Language and Literature*. II (1973), pp. 72–94.

Bush, Douglas.   *Jane Austen.* New York: Collier, 1975, pp. 169–186.

Collins, K.K.   "Mrs. Smith and the Morality of *Persuasion*," in *Nineteenth-Century Fiction*. XXX (1975), pp. 383–397.

Duckworth, Alistair M.   *The Improvement of the Estate; A Study of Jane Austen's Novels.* Baltimore: Johns Hopkins University Press, 1971, pp. 179–208.

Duffy, Joseph M.   "Structure and Idea in *Persuasion*," in *Nineteenth-Century Fiction*. VIII (1954), pp. 272–289.

Gomme, Andor.   "On Not Being Persuaded," in *Essays in Criticism*. XVI (April, 1966), pp. 170–184.

Halperin, John and Janet Kunert.   *Plots and Characters in the Fiction of Jane Austen, the Brontës, and George Eliot.* Hamden, Conn.: Shoe String Press, 1976.

Kaul, A.N.   *The Action of English Comedy; Studies in the Encounter of Abstraction and Experience from Shakespeare to Shaw.* New Haven, Conn.: Yale University Press, 1970, pp. 237–249.

McMaster, Juliet. "Surface and Subsurface in Jane Austen's Novels," in *Aerial.* V (1974), pp. 15–20.

Mansell, Darrel. *The Novels of Jane Austen: An Interpretation.* London: Macmillan, 1973, pp. 185–221.

Monaghan, David M. "The Decline of the Gentry: A Study of Jane Austen's Attitude to Formality in *Persuasion*," in *Studies in the Novel.* VII (1975), pp. 73–87.

Nardin, Jane. *Those Elegant Decorums: The Concept of Propriety in Jane Austen's Novels.* Albany: State University of New York Press, 1973, pp. 129–154.

Pinion, F.B. *A Jane Austen Companion: A Critical Survey and Reference Book.* London: Macmillan, 1973, pp. 123–129.

Rackin, Donald. "Jane Austen's Anatomy of *Persuasion*," in *The English Novel in the Nineteenth-Century: Essays on the Literary Mediation of Human Values.* Edited by George Goodin. Urbana: University of Illinois Press, 1972, pp. 52–80.

Ruoff, Gene W. "Anne Elliot's Dowry: Reflections on the Ending of *Persuasion*," in *Wordsworth Circle.* VII (1976), pp. 342–351.

Sherry, Norman. *Jane Austen.* New York: Arco, 1969, pp. 83–88.

Simon, Irene. "Jane Austen and the Art of the Novel," in *English Studies.* XLIII (1962), pp. 225–239.

Tave, Stuart. *Some Words of Jane Austen.* Chicago: University of Chicago Press, 1973, pp. 256–287.

Walling, William A. "The Glorious Anxiety of Motion: Jane Austen's *Persuasion*," in *Wordsworth Circle.* VII (1976), pp. 333–341.

Wiesenfarth, Joseph. "*Persuasion*: History and Myth," in *Wordsworth Circle.* II (1971), pp. 160–168.

Wolfe, Thomas P. "The Achievement of *Persuasion*," in *Studies in English Literature, 1500–1900.* XI (1971), pp. 687–700.

Zeitlow, Paul N. "Luck and Fortuitous Circumstance in *Persuasion*: Two Interpretations," in *Journal of English Literary History.* XXXII (1965), pp. 179–195.

PRIDE AND PREJUDICE

Type of work: Novel
Author: Jane Austen (1775–1817)
Type of plot: Comedy of manners
Time of plot: Early nineteenth century
Locale: Rural England
First published: 1813

In this masterpiece, Austen follows an empty-headed mother's scheming to find suitable husbands for her five daughters. With gentle irony, the author re-creates in meticulous, artistic detail the manners and morals of the country gentry in a small English village, focusing on the intelligent, irrepressible heroine Elizabeth. Both major and minor characters are superbly drawn; the plot is beautifully symmetrical; and the dazzling perfection of style shows Austen at her best.

Principal Characters

Elizabeth Bennet, a spirited and intelligent girl who represents "prejudice" in her attitude toward Fitzwilliam Darcy, whom she dislikes because of his pride. She is also prejudiced against him by Mr. Wickham, whose false reports of Darcy she believes, and hence rejects Darcy's haughty first proposal of marriage. But Wickham's elopement with her sister Lydia brings Elizabeth and Darcy together, for it is Darcy who facilitates the legal marriage of the runaways. Acknowledging her mistake in her estimation of Darcy, she gladly accepts his second proposal.

Fitzwilliam Darcy, the wealthy and aristocratic landowner who represents "pride" in the story. Attracted to Elizabeth Bennet in spite of her inferior social position, he proposes marriage but in so high-handed a manner that she instantly refuses. The two meet again while Elizabeth is viewing the grounds of his estate in Derbyshire; she finds him less haughty in his manner. When Lydia Bennet and Mr. Wickham elope, Darcy feels partly responsible and straightens out the unfortunate affair. Because Elizabeth now realizes his true character, he is accepted when he proposes again.

Jane Bennet, the oldest and most beautiful of the five Bennet sisters. She falls in love with Mr. Bingley, a wealthy bachelor. Their romance is frustrated, however, by his sisters with the help of Mr. Darcy, for the Bennets are considered socially undesirable. As a result of the change in the feelings of Darcy and Elizabeth Bennet toward each other, Jane and Bingley are finally married.

Mr. Bingley, a rich, good-natured bachelor from the north of England. He falls in love with Jane Bennet but is easily turned against her by his sisters and his friend, Mr. Darcy, who consider the Bennets vulgar and socially beneath them. When Darcy changes in his attitude toward Elizabeth Bennet, Bingley follows suit and resumes his courtship of Jane. They are married at the end of the story.

Mr. Bennet, an eccentric and mildly sarcastic small landowner. Rather indifferent to the rest of his family, he loves and admires his daughter Elizabeth.

Mrs. Bennet, his wife, a silly, brainless woman interested only in getting her daughters married.

Lydia Bennet, the youngest daughter, a flighty and uncontrolled girl. At the age of fifteen she elopes with the worthless Mr. Wickham. Their marriage is finally made possible by Mr. Darcy, who pays Wickham's debts; but the two are never very happy.

Mary Bennet and
Catherine (Kitty) Bennet, younger daughters of the family.

Mr. Wickham, the villain of the story, an officer in the militia. He had been brought up by the Darcy family and, having a certain charm, attracts Elizabeth Bennet, whom he prejudices against Mr. Darcy by misrepresenting the latter's treatment of him. Quite unexpectedly, he elopes with fifteen-year-old, flirtatious Lydia Bennet. Darcy, who has tried to expose Wickham to Elizabeth, feels responsible for the elopement and provides the money for the marriage by paying Wickham's debts. Wickham and Lydia soon tire of each other.

William Collins, a pompous, sycophantic clergyman, distantly related to Mr. Bennet and the heir to his estate, since the Bennets have no son. He proposes to Elizabeth. After her refusal he marries her friend, Charlotte Lucas.

Lady Catherine de Bourgh, Mr. Darcy's aunt and the patron of Mr. Collins. An insufferably haughty and domineering woman, she wants Darcy to marry her only daughter and bitterly resents his interest in Elizabeth Bennet. She tries to break up their love affair but fails.

Anne de Bourgh, Lady Catherine's spiritless daughter. Her mother has planned to marry her to Mr. Darcy in order to combine two great family fortunes.

Charlotte Lucas, Elizabeth Bennet's closest friend. Knowing that she will have few chances of marriage, she accepts the pompous and boring Mr. Collins shortly after Elizabeth has refused him.

Caroline Bingley and
Mrs. Hurst, Mr. Bingley's cold and worldly sisters. They succeed for a time in turning him against Jane Bennet.

Mr. Gardiner, Mrs. Bennet's brother, a London merchant.

Mrs. Gardiner, his sensible and kindly wife.

The Story

The chief business of Mrs. Bennet's life was to find suitable husbands for her five daughters. Consequently she heard with elation that Netherfield Park, one of the area's great houses, had been let to Mr. Bingley, a gentleman from the north of England. Gossip such as Mrs. Bennet loved reported him a rich and altogether eligible young bachelor. Mr. Bennet heard the news with his usual dry calmness, suggesting in his mild way that perhaps Bingley was not moving into the county for the single purpose of marrying one of the Bennet daughters.

Mr. Bingley's first public appearance in the neighborhood was at a ball. With him were his two sisters, the husband of the older, and Mr. Darcy, Bingley's friend. Bingley was an immediate success in local society, and he and Jane, the oldest Bennet daughter, a pretty girl of sweet and gentle disposition, were attracted to each other at once. His friend, Darcy, however, created a bad impression, seeming cold and extremely proud. In particular, he insulted Elizabeth Bennet, a girl of spirit and intelligence and her father's favorite. He refused to dance with her when she was sitting down for lack of a partner, and he said in her hearing that he was in no mood to prefer young ladies slighted by other men. On future occasions, however, he began to admire Elizabeth in spite of himself. At a later ball she had the satisfaction of refusing him a dance.

Jane's romance with Bingley flourished quietly, aided by family calls, dinners, and balls. His sisters pretended great fondness for Jane, who believed them completely sincere. The more critical and discerning Elizabeth suspected them of hypocrisy, and quite rightly, for they made great fun of Jane's relations, especially her vulgar, garrulous mother and her two ill-bred officer-mad younger sisters. Miss Caroline Bingley, who was eager to marry Darcy and shrewdly aware of his growing admiration for Elizabeth, was especially loud in her ridicule of the Bennet family. Elizabeth herself became Caroline's particular target when she walked three muddy miles to visit Jane, who was sick with a cold at Netherfield Park after a ride through the rain to accept an invitation from the Bingley sisters. Until Jane was able to be moved home, Elizabeth stayed to nurse her. During her visit Elizabeth received enough attention from Darcy to make Caroline Bingley long sincerely for Jane's recovery. Nor were her fears ill-founded. Darcy admitted to himself that he would be in some danger from the charm of Elizabeth, if it were not for her inferior family connections.

Elizabeth now acquired a new admirer in the person of Mr. Collins, a ridiculously pompous clergyman and a distant cousin of the Bennets, who would some day inherit Mr. Bennet's property because that gentleman had no male heir. Mr. Collins' patroness, Lady Catherine de Bourgh, had urged him to marry, and he, always obsequiously obedient to her wishes, hastened to comply. Thinking to alleviate the hardship caused the Bennet sisters by the entail which gave their father's property to him, Mr. Collins first proposed to Elizabeth. Much to her mother's displeasure and her father's joy she firmly and promptly rejected him. He almost immediately transferred his affections to Elizabeth's best friend, Charlotte Lucas, who, twenty-seven and somewhat homely, accepted at once his offer of marriage.

During Mr. Collins' visit, the younger Bennet sisters, Kitty and Lydia, on one of their many walks to Meryton, met a fascinating new officer, Mr. Wickham, stationed with the regiment there. Outwardly charming, he became a favorite among the ladies, even with Elizabeth. She was willing to believe the story that he had been cheated out of an inheritance left him by his godfather, Darcy's father. Her suspicions of Darcy's arrogant and grasping nature deepened when Wickham did not come to a ball given by the Bingleys, a dance at which Darcy was present.

Soon after the ball, the entire Bingley party suddenly left Netherfield Park. They departed with no intention of returning, as Caroline wrote Jane in a short farewell note which hinted that Bingley might soon become engaged to Darcy's sister. Jane accepted this news at face value and believed that her friend Caroline was telling her gently that her brother loved elsewhere, and that she must cease to hope. Elizabeth, however, was sure of a plot by Darcy and Bingley's sisters to separate him and Jane. She persuaded Jane that Bingley did love her and that he would return to Hertfordshire before the winter was over. Jane almost believed her until she received a letter from Caroline assuring her that they were all settled in London for the winter. Even after Jane told her this news, Elizabeth remained convinced of Bingley's affection for her sister, and deplored the lack of resolution which made him putty in the hands of his designing friend.

About that time Mrs. Bennet's sister, Mrs. Gardiner, an amiable and intelligent woman with a great deal of affection for her two oldest nieces, arrived for a Christmas visit. She suggested to the Bennets that Jane return to London with her for a rest and change of scene and — so it was understood between Mrs. Gardiner and Elizabeth—to renew her acquaintance with Bingley. Elizabeth, not too hopeful for the success of the plan, pointed out that proud Darcy would never let his friend call on Jane in the unfashionable London street on which the Gardiners lived. Jane accepted the invitation, however, and she and Mrs. Gardiner set out for London.

The time drew near for the wedding of Elizabeth's friend, Charlotte Lucas, to the obnoxious Mr. Collins. Charlotte asked Elizabeth to visit her in Kent. In spite of her feeling that there could be little pleasure in such a visit, Elizabeth promised to do so. She felt that in taking such a husband Charlotte was marrying simply for the sake of an establishment, as was indeed the case. Since she herself could not sympathize with her friend's action, Elizabeth thought their days of real intimacy were over. As March approached, however, she found herself eager to see her friend, and she set out with pleasure on the journey with Charlotte's father and sister. On their way, the party stopped in London to see the Gardiners and Jane. Elizabeth found her sister well and outwardly happy, though she had not seen Bingley and his sisters had paid only one call. Elizabeth was sure Bingley had not been told of Jane's presence in London and blamed Darcy for keeping it from him.

Soon after arriving at the Collins' home, the whole party was honored, as Mr. Collins repeatedly assured them, by a dinner invitation from Lady Catherine de Bourgh, Darcy's aunt and Mr. Collins' patroness. Elizabeth found Lady Catherine a haughty, ill-mannered woman and her daughter thin, sickly, and shy. Lady Catherine was extremely fond of inquiring into the affairs of others and giving them unasked advice. Elizabeth turned off the meddling old woman's questions with cool indirectness, and saw from the effect that she was probably the first who had dared to do so.

Soon after Elizabeth's arrival, Darcy came to visit his aunt and cousin. He called frequently at the parsonage, and he and Elizabeth resumed their conversational fencing matches. His rather stilted attentions were suddenly climaxed by a proposal of marriage, but one couched in such proud and condescending terms that Elizabeth indignantly refused him. When he requested her reason for such an emphatic rejection, she mentioned his part in separating Bingley and Jane, and also his mistreatment of Wickham. Angry, he left abruptly, but the next day brought a letter answering her charges. He did not deny his part in separating Jane and Bingley, but he gave as his reasons the improprieties of Mrs. Bennet and her younger daughters, and also his sincere belief that Jane did not love Bingley. As for his alleged mistreatment of Wickham, he proved that he had in reality acted most generously toward the unprincipled Wickham, who had repaid his kindness by attempting to elope with Darcy's young sister. Elizabeth, at first incensed at the proud tones in which he wrote, was at length forced to acknowledge the justice of all he said, and her prejudice against him began to weaken. Without seeing him again, she returned home.

She found her younger sisters clamoring to go to Brighton, where the regiment formerly stationed at Meryton had been ordered. When an invitation came to Lydia from a young officer's wife, Lydia was allowed to accept it over Elizabeth's protests. Elizabeth herself was asked by the Gardiners to go with them on a tour which would take them into Derbyshire, Darcy's home county. She accepted, reasoning that she was not very likely to meet Darcy merely by going into the same county with him. While they were there, however, Mrs. Gardiner decided they should visit Pemberly, Darcy's home. Elizabeth made several excuses, but her aunt was insistent. Then, learning that the Darcy family was not at home, Elizabeth consented to go.

At Pemberly, an unexpected and most embarrassing meeting took place between Elizabeth and Darcy. He was more polite than Elizabeth had ever known him to be, and asked permission for his sister to call upon her. The call was duly paid and returned, but the pleasant intercourse between the Darcys and Elizabeth's party was suddenly cut short when a letter came from Jane telling Elizabeth that Lydia had run away with Wickham. Elizabeth told Darcy what had happened, and she and the Gardiners left for home at once. After several days the runaway couple was located and a marriage arranged between them. When Lydia came home as heedless as ever, she told Elizabeth that Darcy had attended her wedding. Elizabeth, suspecting the truth, learned from Mrs. Gardiner that it was indeed Darcy who brought about the marriage by giving Wickham money.

Soon after Lydia and Wickham left, Bingley came back to Netherfield Park, and with him came Darcy. Elizabeth, now more favorably inclined to him than ever before, hoped his coming meant that he still loved her, but he gave no sign. Bingley and Jane, on the other hand, were still obviously in love with each other, and became engaged, to the great satisfaction of Mrs. Bennet. Soon afterward Lady Catherine paid the Bennets an unexpected call. She had heard it rumored that Darcy was engaged to Elizabeth. Hoping to marry her own daughter to Darcy, she had charged down with characteristic bad manners to order Elizabeth not to accept his proposal. The spirited girl was not to be intimidated by the bullying Lady Catherine and coolly refused to promise not to marry Darcy. She was far from certain she would have another chance, but she had not long to wonder. Lady Catherine, unluckily for her own purpose, repeated to Darcy the substance of her conversation with Elizabeth, and he knew Elizabeth well enough to surmise that her feelings toward him had greatly changed. He returned to Netherfield Park, and he and Elizabeth became engaged. Pride had been humbled and prejudice dissolved.

Critical Evaluation

In 1813, her thirty-eighth year, Jane Austen became a published novelist for the second time with *Pride and Prejudice*. She had begun this work in 1796, her twenty-first year, calling it *First Impressions*. It had so delighted her family that her father had tried, without success, to have it published. Eventually putting it aside, she returned to it probably at about the time that her first published novel, *Sense and Sensibility*, appeared in 1811. No longer extant, *First Impressions* must have been radically altered; for *Pride and Prejudice* is not an apprenticeship novel, but a mature work, which continues to be the author's most popular novel, perhaps because its readers share Darcy's admiration for the "liveliness" of Elizabeth Bennet's mind.

The original title, *First Impressions,* focuses upon the initial errors of judgment from which the story develops, whereas the title *Pride and Prejudice.* besides suggesting the kind of antithetical topic which delighted rationalistic eighteenth century readers, indicates the central conflict involving the kinds of pride and prejudice which bar the marriages of Elizabeth Bennet and Darcy and Jane Bennet and Bingley, but bring about the marriages of Charlotte Lucas and Collins and Lydia Bennet and Wickham.

As in all of Jane Austen's novels, individual conflicts are defined and resolved within a rigidly delimiting social context, in which human relationships are determined by wealth and rank. Thus the much admired opening sentence establishes the societal values which underlie the main conflict: "It is a truth universally acknowledged, that a single man in possession of a good fortune, must be in want of a wife." Mr. and Mrs. Bennet's opening dialog concerning the eligible Bingley explores this truth. Devoid of individuality, Mrs. Bennet is nevertheless well attuned to society's edicts and therefore regards Bingley only in the light of society's "truth." Mr. Bennet, an individualist to the point of eccentricity, represents neither personal conviction nor social conviction. He lightheartedly views with equal indifference both Bingley's right to his own reason for settling there and society's right to see him primarily as a potential husband. Having repudiated society, Mr. Bennet cannot take seriously either the claims of the individual or the social order.

As the central character, Elizabeth, her father's favorite child and her mother's least favorite, must come to terms with the conflicting values implicit in her parents' antithetical characters. She is like her father in her scorn of society's conventional judgments, but she champions the concept of individual merit independent of money and rank. She is, indeed, prejudiced against the prejudices of society. From this premise she attacks Darcy's pride, assuming that it derives from the causes that Charlotte Lucas identifies: " . . . with family, fortune, every thing in his favour . . . he has a *right* to be proud."

Flaunting her contempt for money, Elizabeth indignantly spurns as mere strategy to get a rich husband or any husband Charlotte's advice that Jane ought to make a calculated play for Bingley's affections. She loftily argues, while under the spell of Wickham's charm, that young people who are truly in love are unconcerned about each other's financial standing.

As a champion of the individual, Elizabeth prides herself on her dis- criminating judgment, boasting that she is a student of character. Significantly, it is Darcy who warns her against prejudiced conclusions, reminding her that her experience is quite limited. For Darcy is not simply the representative of a society which primarily values wealth and consequence—as Elizabeth initially views him—but he is also a citizen of a larger society than the village to which Elizabeth is confined by circumstance. Consequently, it is only when she begins to move into Darcy's world that she can judge with true discrimi- nation both individual merit and the dictates of the society which she has rejected. Fundamentally honest, she revises her conclusions as new experi- ences warrant, in the case of Darcy and Wickham radically altering her opinion.

More significant than the obviously ironic reversals, however, is the grow- ing revelation of Elizabeth's unconscious commitment to society. For example, her original condemnation of Darcy's pride coincides with the verdict of Meryton society. Moreover, she always shares society's regard for wealth. Even while denying the importance of Wickham's poverty, she countenances his pursuit of the ugly Miss King's fortune, discerning her own inconsistency only after she learns of his bad character. Most revealing, when Lydia Bennet runs off with Wickham, Elizabeth instinctively pronounces the judgment of society when she states that Wickham would never marry a woman without money.

Almost unconsciously Elizabeth acknowledges a connection between wealth and human values at the crucial moment when she first looks upon Pem- berley, the Darcy estate:

> She had never seen a place for which nature had done more, or where natural beauty had been so little counteracted by an awkward taste. They were all of them warm in their admiration; and at that moment she felt that to be mistress of Pemberley might be something!

She is not entirely joking when she tells Jane that her love for Darcy began when she first saw his beautiful estate.

Elizabeth's experiences, especially her discoveries of the well-ordered Pemberley and Darcy's tactful generosity to Lydia and Wickham, lead her to differentiate between Charlotte's theory that family and fortune bestow a *"right* to be proud" and Darcy's position that the intelligent person does not indulge in false pride. Darcy's pride is real, but it is regulated by responsi- bility. Unlike his aunt, Lady Catherine de Bourgh, who relishes the distinc- tion of rank, he disapproves less of the Bennets' undistinguished family and fortune than he does of the lack of propriety displayed by most of the family. Thus Elizabeth scarcely overstates her case when, at the end, she assures her father that Darcy has no improper pride.

Elizabeth begins by rejecting the values and restraints of society, as represented by such people as her mother, the Lucases, Miss Bingley, and Lady Catherine, upholding instead the claims of the individual, represented only by her whimsical father. By the end of the novel, the heart of her conflict appears in the contrast between her father and Darcy. Loving her father, she has tried to overlook his lack of decorum in conjugal matters. But she has been forced to see that his freedom is really irresponsibility, the essential cause of Jane's misery as well as Lydia's amorality. The implicit comparison between Mr. Bennet's and Darcy's approach to matrimony points up their different methods of dealing with society's restraints. Unrestrained by society, having been captivated by the inferior Mrs. Bennet's youth and beauty, Mr. Bennet consulted only his personal desires and made a disastrous marriage. Darcy, in contrast, defies society only when he has made certain that Elizabeth is a woman worthy of his love and lifetime devotion.

When Elizabeth confronts Lady Catherine, her words are declarative, not of absolute defiance of society, but of the selective freedom which is her compromise, and very similar to Darcy's: "I am only resolved to act in that manner, which will, in my own opinion, constitute my happiness, without reference to *you,* or to any person so wholly unconnected with me." Jane Austen does not falsify the compromise. If Elizabeth dares with impunity to defy the society of Rosings, Longbourne, and Meryton, she does so only because Darcy is exactly the man for her and, further, because she can anticipate "with delight . . . the time when they should be removed from society so little pleasing to either, to all the comfort and elegance . . . at Pemberley." Her marriage to Darcy is in a sense a triumph of the individual over society; but, paradoxically, Elizabeth achieves her most genuine conquest of pride and prejudice only after she has accepted the full social value of her judgment that "to be mistress of Pemberley might be something!"

Granting the full force of the snobbery, the exploitation, the inhumanity of all the evils which diminish the human spirit and which are inherent in a materialistic society, the novel clearly confirms the cynical "truth" of the opening sentence. Yet at the same time, without evading the degree of Elizabeth's capitulation to society, it affirms the vitality, the independent life which is possible at least to an Elizabeth Bennet. *Pride and Prejudice,* like its title, offers deceptively simple antitheses which yield up the complexity of life itself.

Bibliography

Anderson, Walter E. "Plot, Character, Speech, and Place in *Pride and Prejudice*," in *Nineteenth-Century Fiction.* XXX (1975), pp. 367–382.

Beer, Patricia. *Reader, I Married Him: A Study of the Women Characters of Jane Austen, Charlotte Brontë, Elizabeth Gaskell and George Eliot.* London: Macmillan, 1974, pp. 47–75.

Booth, Bradford. Pride and Prejudice: *Text, Backgrounds, Criticism.* New York: Houghton, Mifflin, 1963.

Bush, Douglas. *Jane Austen.* New York: Collier, 1975, pp. 91–107.

Dooley, D.J. "Pride, Prejudice and Vanity in Elizabeth Bennet," in *Nineteenth-Century Fiction.* XX (September, 1965), pp. 185–188.

Duckworth, Alistair M. *The Improvement of the Estate: A Study of Jane Austen's Novels.* Baltimore: Johns Hopkins University Press, 1971, pp. 115–143.

Duffy, Joseph M. "The Politics of Love: Marriage and the Good Society in *Pride and Prejudice*," in *University of Windsor Review.* XI (1976), pp. 5–26.

Fox, Robert C. "Elizabeth Bennet: Prejudice or Vanity?," in *Nineteenth-Century Fiction.* XVII (September, 1962), pp. 185–187.

Gooneratne, Yasmin. *Jane Austen.* New York: Cambridge University Press, 1970, pp. 81–103.

Gray, Donald J. Pride and Prejudice: *An Authoritative Text, Backgrounds, Reviews, and Essays in Criticism.* New York: Norton, 1966.

Griffin, Cynthia. "The Development of Realism in Jane Austen's Early Novels," in *Journal of English Literary History.* XXX (1963), pp. 36–52.

Halperin, John and Janet Kunert. *Plots and Characters in the Fiction of Jane Austen, the Brontës, and George Eliot.* Hamden, Conn.: Shoe String Press, 1976.

Karl, Frederick R. *An Age of Fiction: The Nineteenth-Century British Novel.* New York: Farrar, Straus and Giroux, 1964, pp. 27–62.

Kooiman-Van Middendorp, Gerarda M. *The Hero in the Feminine Novel.* New York: Haskell House, 1966, pp. 49–59.

Lauber, John. "Heroes and Anti-Heroes in Jane Austen's Novels," in *Dalhousie Review.* LI (1971–72), pp. 489–503.

McCann, Charles J. "Setting and Character in *Pride and Prejudice*," in *Nineteenth-Century Fiction.* XIX (June, 1964), pp. 65–75.

Marcus, Mordecai. "A Major Thematic Pattern in *Pride and Prejudice*," in *Nineteenth-Century Fiction.* XVI (December, 1961), pp. 274–279.

Maugham, William Somerset. *Art of Fiction; An Introduction to Ten Novels and Their Authors.* Garden City, N.Y.: Doubleday, 1955, pp. 55–78.

Moler, Kenneth L. "*Pride and Prejudice*: Jane Austen's 'Patrician Hero,' " in *Studies in English Literature, 1500–1900.* VII (Summer, 1967), pp. 491–508.

Nash, Ralph. "The Time Scheme for *Pride and Prejudice*," in *English Language Notes.* IV (1967), pp. 194–198.

Orum, Tania. "Love and Marriage, or How Economy Becomes Internalized: A Study of Jane Austen's *Pride and Prejudice*," in *Language and Literature.* II (1973), pp. 3–37.

Pinion, F.B. *A Jane Austen Companion: A Critical Survey and Reference Book.* London: Macmillan, 1973, pp. 92–100.

Rubinstein, E. *Twentieth Century Interpretations of* Pride and Prejudice; *A Collection of Critical Essays.* Englewood Cliffs, N.J.: Prentice-Hall, 1969.

Shapiro, Charles. *Twelve Original Essays on Great English Novels.* Detroit: Wayne State University Press, 1960, pp. 69–85.

Weinsheimer, Joel. "Chance and the Hierarchy of Marriages in *Pride and Prejudice*," in *Journal of English Literary History.* XXXIX (1972), pp. 404–419.

Zimmerman, Everett. "Pride and Prejudice in *Pride and Prejudice*," in *Nineteenth-Century Fiction.* XXIII (June, 1968), pp. 64–73.

SENSE AND SENSIBILITY

Type of work: Novel
Author: Jane Austen (1775–1817)
Type of plot: Comedy of manners
Time of plot: Nineteenth century
Locale: England
First published: 1811

To Jane Austen there were people of sense and people of fine sensibility, but little sense. In this novel of early nineteenth century English life she makes it quite clear that she admires men and women of sense. Although the dialogue of this early novel may seem stilted at times and the characters overdrawn, they combine to give a clear picture of the manners of upper- and middle-class English society of that period.

Principal Characters

Elinor Dashwood, a young woman representing the "sense" of the title. She is much attracted to Edward Ferrars, Mrs. John Dashwood's brother, and believes him attracted to her. His seeming indifference puzzles her until she learns from Lucy Steele that the two are engaged but cannot marry because of Mrs. Ferrar's opposition. Elinor arranges for a living for Edward when he shall have taken Holy Orders so that he and Lucy can be married. Elinor is led to believe that the marriage has taken place but soon learns that Lucy has jilted Edward in favor of his brother Robert, because Edward has been disinherited. Edward is forgiven by his mother, and he and Elinor are married.

Marianne Dashwood, Elinor's younger sister, representing the "sensibility" of the title. She is emotional and impulsive, with highly romantic ideas of love and marriage. Beloved by Colonel Brandon, she considers him too old for her and falls in love with John Willoughby, an attractive young man. But when the sisters visit London, Willoughby ignores Marianne, and this rejection makes her emotionally ill. While stopping at a country estate on her way home, she becomes physically ill also. Willoughby, having heard of the illness, comes to confess to Elinor that his family, incensed at his seduction of Colonel Brandon's ward, had cut off his allowance, and, having no money, he had been compelled to marry a rich wife. Cured of her infatuation, Marianne learns to appreciate Colonel Brandon's good qualities and marries him.

John Willoughby, the villain of the story, a handsome and fashionable but dissipated young man. He encourages Marianne Dashwood to fall in love with him. It is revealed that he has seduced Colonel Brandon's ward and, rejected by his family, been forced into a loveless but wealthy marriage.

John Dashwood, the half brother of Elinor and Marianne and owner of Norland Park. Since he was wealthy both by inheritance and marriage, he had been urged by his father to provide for his stepmother and his half sister; but, being cold and selfish and easily influenced by his wife, he does nothing for his relatives.

Fanny Dashwood, his wife, daughter of the rich Mrs. Ferrars. She is even colder and more selfish than her husband and persuades him not to carry out his plan of settling three thousand pounds on his half sisters and stepmother.

Mrs. Dashwood, stepmother of John and mother of Elinor and Marianne. She is a warm-hearted, impulsive woman, not endowed with much practical sense.

Mrs. Ferrars, mother of Mrs. John Dashwood, Robert, and Edward. She is rich, ill-tempered, and domineering, using her money to coerce her children.

Robert Ferrars, her older son. He marries Lucy Steele.

Edward Ferrars, her younger son. He wishes to take Holy Orders. When young, he had become engaged to Lucy Steele and thus cannot woo Elinor Dashwood, whom he really loves. His mother, learning of his engagement, disinherits him, and Lucy jilts him for his brother. Thus freed, he is able to marry Elinor.

Lucy Steele, a vulgar, mercenary young woman, engaged to Edward Ferrars. When he is disinherited, she marries his brother Robert.

Anne Steele, her equally vulgar sister.

Colonel Brandon, a quiet man of thirty-five, in love with Marianne Dashwood. She considers him too old. When his ward is seduced by Willoughby, Marianne, horrified by the latter's conduct, finally appreciates the Colonel, and they are married.

Sir John Middleton, wealthy and hospitable, befriends his Dashwood cousins.

Lady Middleton, his wife, also kind to the Dashwoods.

Mrs. Jennings, her mother, a kindly but silly old lady.

Mrs. Palmer, Lady Middleton's sister, good-natured and rattlebrained.

Mr. Palmer, her husband, sensible but cold and sarcastic.

The Story

When Mr. John Dashwood inherited his father's estate, it was his intention to provide comfortably for his stepmother and his half-sisters. His wife Fanny, however, had other ideas, and even though she was independently wealthy she cleverly prevented her husband from helping his relatives. When Fanny's brother, Edward Ferrars, began to show interest in John's half-sister Elinor, Fanny, determined to prevent any alliance between them, made life so uncomfortable for the older Mrs. Dashwood and her daughters that those ladies accepted the offer of their relative, Sir John Middleton, to occupy a cottage on his estate.

Mrs. Dashwood, Elinor, and Marianne were happy in the cottage at Barton Park. There they met Colonel Brandon, Sir John's friend, who was immediately attracted to Marianne. She, considering him old at the age of thirty-five, rejected his suit and fell in love with John Willoughby, a young man visiting wealthy relatives on a neighboring estate.

Once, while all the friends were preparing for an outing, Colonel Brandon was called away in a mysterious fashion. Elinor and Marianne were surprised later to hear that he had a daughter; at least that was the rumor they heard. Willoughby seemed determined to give Marianne a bad impression of Colonel Brandon, a fact which did not make Elinor happy. Shortly after the colonel's sudden departure,

Willoughby himself left very suddenly, without giving Marianne a satisfactory explanation. Elinor could not help being concerned about the manner of his departure, particularly since he had not made a definite engagement with Marianne.

A week later Edward Ferrars appeared at the cottage for a visit. In spite of Elinor's attraction to him, Edward seemed no more than mildly interested in her. After a short stay he left the cottage without saying anything to give Elinor hope.

Meanwhile Sir John had invited to his home Miss Lucy Steele and her sister, two young ladies whom Elinor thought vulgar and ignorant. She was therefore stunned when Lucy told her that she was secretly engaged to Edward Ferrars, whom she had met while he was a pupil of Lucy's uncle. According to Lucy's story, they had been engaged for four years, but Edward's mother would not permit him to marry. Since Edward had no money of his own and no occupation, they were forced to wait for Mrs. Ferrars' consent before they could announce their engagement. Elinor, concealing her unhappiness at this news, told Lucy that she would help in any way she could.

A short time later Elinor and Marianne were invited to London to visit friends. Marianne immediately wrote to Willoughby that she was near. Although she wrote two or three times, she had no reply. One day she met him at a party. He was with another young lady and treated Marianne courteously but coolly. The next morning Marianne received a letter from him telling her that he was sorry if she had misunderstood his intentions and that he had long been engaged to another girl. All of her friends and relatives were furious with Willoughby. Even though she was heartbroken, Marianne continued to defend him and to believe that he was blameless. She was comforted by Colonel Brandon, who was also in London.

Privately, the colonel told Elinor Willoughby's story. The colonel had a ward, the young girl believed by some to be his daughter, who was in reality the daughter of his brother's divorced wife. When the colonel had had to leave Barton Park so suddenly, he had learned that his ward had been seduced and then abandoned by Willoughby. Elinor gave this news to Marianne, who received it with such sorrow that Elinor feared for her health. Colonel Brandon continued to be kind to Marianne, and it was obvious to everyone that he loved her.

The girls continued their stay in London, and a little later their brother John and his wife Fanny took a house there. When the Misses Steele also arrived in town for a visit, Edward's mother learned at last that he and Lucy were engaged. Angry, she settled what would have been Edward's inheritance on her other son, Robert, and Edward and Lucy were left with no means of support. He planned to study for the ministry, and Elinor arranged with Colonel Brandon for Edward to become a curate on his estate so that Edward and Lucy could be married.

Before Elinor and Marianne returned home, they visited Cleveland, an estate between London and Barton Park. There Marianne became ill with a heavy cold. Because she was anxious to see her mother, Colonel Brandon went for Mrs.

Dashwood. Before they returned, Willoughby, having heard of Marianne's illness, called at the house. He told Elinor that he had treated Marianne shamefully because he had no money of his own and because his wealthy relative had learned of his treatment of Colonel Brandon's ward and as a result had refused to give him an allowance. Consequently, he had married a wealthy girl and renounced Marianne. He said that he still loved Marianne and wished her to know his story so that she would not think harshly of him.

Marianne recovered from her illness and returned home with her mother and Elinor. There Elinor told her Willoughby's story. Marianne continued to sorrow for him, but she no longer loved him.

After their return Elinor learned from a servant that Edward and Lucy had been married. Soon Edward appeared at the cottage and told the Dashwoods that the unscrupulous Lucy had married his brother instead, after their mother had disinherited Edward in favor of Robert. Edward had come to ask Elinor to marry him, and he had no trouble in gaining her consent, as well as that of her mother. It remained only for him to secure a living. He went to London to seek his mother's forgiveness. Because Mrs. Ferrars also had scorned her son Robert after his marriage to Lucy, she felt a need for affection from one of her children. After much weeping and pleading, which failed to move Edward in his determination to marry Elinor, Mrs. Ferrars gave her consent to the wedding. After their marriage they moved into the parsonage promised Edward by Colonel Brandon some months before.

The colonel continued his quiet and friendly courtship of Marianne. At last she recognized his gentleness and kindness and they were married. When they moved to his estate, the two sisters were near each other once more. Fanny and John were so pleased to be related to the colonel that Fanny even forgave Edward for marrying Elinor. Mrs. Dashwood was delighted at the good fortune of her children, and the families lived in peace and contentment for all of their lives.

Critical Evaluation

Except for the behavior of Marianne Dashwood and John Willoughby, Jane Austen's characters have nearly impeccable manners. They are the upper-middle class whose time is spent in decorous leisure, in visiting, outings, and dinner parties. Voices are modulated, amenities observed, and social station respected. Yet, underneath this exquisite exterior, emotions of the most primitive kind are hidden. From the beginning of the novel, avarice and lust threaten to break through the restraints of the agreed-upon rules and create chaos—a disorder both social and moral.

The plot is set in motion by the greed of Fanny and John Dashwood, leaving his step-mother and half-sisters vulnerable to the likes of John Willoughby. Willoughby himself is forced to deny his real feelings for Marianne because he has no money, and must, therefore, marry into it. Mrs. Ferrars attempts to choose her sons' brides using her wealth to bend them to her will. In short, the passionate lives of the young are smothered by those who hold the purse. Colonel Brandon's ward, seduced and abandoned by Willoughby, is an apt example of what happens to the innocent in a culture whose morality is based on land and money and where class determines identity and value.

Through the prudential efforts of Elinor Dashwood and Colonel Brandon, the social fabric is kept intact, tragedy averted, and the comic spirit permitted to emerge. Still, if sanity and harmony are restored at the novel's conclusion with the weddings of the Dashwood sisters, the resolution barely compensates for the emotional deprivation of Marianne, Willoughby, and even Elinor. The sisters' marriages are certainly ones of sense; yet, they lack a dimension of human experience, a sensibility to the possibilities of passion, which is forbidden by a rigid system of manners, uninformed by love or compassion.

Bibliography

Brown, Lloyd W. "The Comic Conclusion in Jane Austen's Novels," in *PMLA*. LXXXIV (1969), pp. 1582–1587.

Bush, Douglas. *Jane Austen.* New York: Collier, 1975, pp. 78–88.

Cecil, Lord David. *Fine Art of Reading; And Other Literary Studies.* Indianapolis: Bobbs-Merrill, 1957, pp, 149–160.

Duckworth, Alistair M. *The Improvement of the Estate; A Study of Jane Austen's Novels.* Baltimore: Johns Hopkins University Press, 1971, pp. 81–91, 102–114.

Gillie, Christopher. "*Sense and Sensibility*: An Assessment," in *Essays in Criticism.* IX (January, 1959), pp. 1–9.

Gooneratne, Yasmin. *Jane Austen.* New York: Cambridge University Press, 1970, pp. 63–80.

Gornall, F.G. "Marriage, Property, and Romance in Jane Austen's Novels," in *Hibbert Journal.* LXV (1967), pp. 151–156.

Griffin, Cynthia. "The Development of Realism in Jane Austen's Early Novels," in *Journal of English Literary History.* XXX (1963), pp. 36–52.

Halperin, John and Janet Kunert. *Plots and Characters in the Fiction of Jane Austen, the Brontës, and George Eliot.* Hamden, Conn.: Shoe String Press, 1976.

Kooiman-Van Middendorp, Gerarda M. *The Hero in the Feminine Novel.* New York: Haskell House, 1966, pp. 49–59.

Kroeber, Karl. *Styles in Fictional Structure: The Art of Jane Austen, Charlotte Brontë, George Eliot.* Princeton, N.J.: Princeton University Press, 1971, pp. 65–68.

Lauber, John. "Heroes and Anti-Heroes in Jane Austen's Novels," in *Dalhousie Review.* LI (1971–72), pp. 489–503.

————. "Jane Austen's Fools," in *Studies in English Literature, 1500–1900.* XIV (1974), pp. 513–515.

Leeming, Glenda. *Who's Who in Jane Austen and the Brontës.* London: Elm Tree Books, 1974.

Lerner, Laurence. *"Sense and Sensibility*: A Mixed-Up Book," in *Critics on Jane Austen.* Edited by Judith O'Neill. Coral Gables, Fla.: University of Miami Press, 1970, pp. 97–101.

————. *The Truthtellers: Jane Austen, George Eliot, D.H. Lawrence.* New York: Schocken, 1967, pp. 137–139, 160–166.

McKillop, Alan D. "The Context of *Sense and Sensibility*," in *Rice Institute Pamphlets.* XLIV (1957), pp. 65–78.

Mansell, Darrel. *The Novels of Jane Austen: An Interpretation.* London: Macmillan, 1973, pp. 46–77.

Morgan, Susan. "Polite Lies: The Veiled Heroine of *Sense and Sensibility*," in *Nineteenth-Century Fiction.* XXXI (1976), pp. 188–205.

Nardin, Jane. *Those Elegant Decorums: The Concept of Propriety in Jane Austen's Novels.* Albany: State University of New York Press, 1973, pp. 24–46.

Page, Norman. *The Language of Jane Austen.* Oxford: Blackwell, 1972, pp. 20–24.

Pinion, F.B. *A Jane Austen Companion: A Critical Survey and Reference Book.* London: Macmillan, 1973, pp. 84–91.

Rubinstein, E. "Jane Austen's Novels: The Metaphor of Rank," in *Literary Mongraphs.* II (1969), pp. 107–117.

Sherry, Norman. *Jane Austen.* New York: Arco, 1969, pp. 56–63.

Zimmerman, Everett. "Admiring Pope No More Than Is Proper: *Sense and Sensibility*," in *Jane Austen, Bicentenary Essays.* Edited by John Halperin. New York: Cambridge University Press, 1975, pp. 112–122.

THE BRONTËS

Charlotte Brontë

Born: Thornton, Yorkshire, England (April 21, 1816)
Died: Haworth, Yorkshire, England (March 31, 1855)

Principal Works

NOVELS: *Jane Eyre*, 1847; *Shirley*, 1849; *Villette*, 1853; *The Professor*, 1857.

Emily (Jane) Brontë

Born: Thornton, Yorkshire, England (July 30, 1818)
Died: Haworth, Yorkshire, England (December 19, 1848)

Principal Works

NOVEL: *Wuthering Heights*, 1847.
POEMS: *The Complete Poems of Emily Jane Brontë*, 1941.

Anne Brontë

Born: Thornton, Yorkshire, England (January 17, 1820)
Died: Scarborough, England (May 28, 1849)

Principal Works

NOVELS: *Agnes Grey*, 1847; *The Tenant of Wildfell Hall*, 1848.
POEMS (IN COLLABORATION): *Poems*, by Currer, Ellis, and Acton Bell, 1846.

On December 29, 1812, the Reverend Patrick Brontë, incumbent of Hartshead, Yorkshire (originally of County Down, in Ireland), was married in Guiseley Church to Maria Branwell, a Cornish lady then visiting in the home of her uncle, the Reverend John Fennell.

Little more than seven years later, having in the meantime served a ministry in Thornton, he was appointed perpetual curate of Haworth. There he re-moved his family in April 1820. Eighteen months later Mrs. Brontë died of cancer, leaving six small children: Maria, Elizabeth, Charlotte, Branwell, Emily, and Anne, ranging in age from seven years to twenty months. The emergency was solved when Elizabeth Branwell, Mrs. Brontë's eldest sister, came from Penzance to order the house and bring up the children.

In late summer of 1824, the four older girls were entered as pupils in the Clergy Daughters' School at Cowan Bridge. Precocious in mind but shy in spirit and frail in body, they fell victims to the severity of its routine. Maria and Elizabeth, ill of tuberculosis, were taken home to die, Maria on May 6, and Elizabeth on June 15, 1825. Charlotte and Emily were immediately re-called, and thereafter the Parsonage children knew no formal school room until Charlotte, near the end of her fourteenth year, entered Miss Margaret Wooler's school near Roe Head. Branwell was taught by his father, while the girls received training in household arts from their aunt. Left much to their own devices, the children found endless entertainment in creative plays continued from day to day. Shortly after Charlotte's tenth birthday, they launched a new play centering around twelve wooden soldiers, which absorbed all other household plays, and, having taken permanent form as an imaginary world of escape, nourished and shaped the genius of the family. Not only did the heroes of this play perform great deeds, but, turning authors, artists, and publishers, they recorded them in tiny volumes in proportion to their size—histories, biographies, novels, poems, and dramas.

In January, 1831, the Young Men's Play was interrupted by Charlotte's departure for Roe Head, when Emily and Anne took advantage of the break to withdraw from the family group and set up a play of their own called Gondal. Despite Charlotte's revival of the old creation on her return eighteen months later, and its expansion into a farflung empire called Angria, the younger girls stood aloof, and, from that time on the Brontë children played and wrote in pairs: Charlotte and Branwell, of Angria; Emily and Anne, of Gondal.

Through the years, 1832–1835, the game grew and matured with its creators through an astonishing number of "books." Branwell's productions, closely paralleling Charlotte's in characters and plot, betray his corrupting association with "rough lads of the Village" and the society of the Black Bull Inn. It was time for him to prepare for his chosen work of portrait painting. To help with family expenses, Charlotte, in late summer of 1835, returned to Miss Wooler's school as teacher, taking Emily with her as pupil.

The plan worked out badly. Branwell went to London but did not enter the Royal Academy, as had been planned. Charlotte and Emily, torn from their all-absorbing dream world, inseparable from home surroundings, were miserably homesick. Emily fell so ill that Charlotte sent her home and brought Anne to school in her place. Charlotte herself endured for two years until she collapsed nervously. Back home again, and lost in their writing, both regained health and courage to try again earning a living away from home, Emily in a school near Halifax, Charlotte as a nursery governess. Convinced that health and happiness were not for them away from home, the girls laid plans for a school in the Parsonage. To acquire the needed French, they borrowed from Aunt Elizabeth the money for a term of study in Mme. Héger's school in Brussels. Charlotte and Emily entered this school in February, 1842, leaving Anne in a position as governess in the Robinson family at Thorp Green, where Branwell was tutor. They were making satisfactory progress when they were called home by the death of Aunt Elizabeth in October.

The small legacies which they received from her enabled the older girls to finish out the year quietly at home. But in January, 1843, Charlotte returned to the Pensionnat Héger as teacher-pupil. Without Emily she was lonely. Worst of all, increasing weakness of overstrained eyes raised the spectre of blindness and reinforced M. Héger's frowning advice to give up Angria, the only medium she knew of creative dreaming and writing. Life stretched before her in years of unrelieved teaching, which her soul loathed.

Broken for a time in health and spirit, she returned to Haworth on New Year's Day, 1844. In the summer of 1845, Branwell, having conceived an infatuation for his employer's wife, was dismissed from his post. Already a habitué of drink and drugs, he never again rose above the piteous existence of an addict. Anne returned to the Parsonage with him.

At home the girls found alleviation of their distress in their old creative plays of Angria and Gondal. There is evidence that Charlotte tried by this means to bring her brother back to his rightful place in the group, but his manuscripts of the period show how grievously she failed.

The order was broken in the fall of 1845, when Charlotte accidentally came upon a manuscript volume of Emily's poetry, headed "Gondal Poems," which she read with astonishment at their grandeur and power, and the beauty of their "wild, wailing music." Out of this discovery, a joint volume of verse by the three girls was carefully worked out. For it, each drew from her store of verse (chiefly Angrian and Gondalan) twenty-one pieces, and chose a pseudonym to fit her own initials. The small volume was printed at the authors' expense with £31.10s. from Aunt Elizabeth's legacy: *Poems by Currer, Ellis, and Acton Bell*, London, Aylott and Jones, 8 Paternoster Row, 1846. Charlotte records that only two copies were sold. Disappointment turned the girls more determinedly to their novels already in progress, not the usual run of the Angrian and Gondal mills, but novels of realistic setting designed to please a publisher. Charlotte's, *The Professor*, was a skillful and artistic adaptation of portions of the Angrian creation to a Yorkshire-Brussels setting. Emily's, *Wuthering Heights*, showed many recognizable Gondalan features, traceable through her poems. Anne's, *Agnes Grey*, based on her own experience as a governess, had no kinship to her earlier writing. All three retained their previous pseudonyms.

After months of repeated rejection, *Wuthering Heights* and *Agnes Grey* were accepted by Thomas Cautley Newby of London. *The Professor* continued its rounds until it reached the house of Smith, Elder and Company, who returned it, but with such encouraging advice that Charlotte, on August 24, 1847, dispatched for their consideration a second novel, *Jane Eyre*, in characters and plot incidents derived directly from Angria.

Accepted, and published in October following, *Jane Eyre* was an immediate success. Newby now hastened the publication of *Wuthering Heights* and *Agnes Grey*, encouraging the surmise that they, too, were by the author of *Jane Eyre*, the three Bells being actually one person.

In the meanwhile Branwell had sunken so far out of family life that he knew nothing of his sisters' publishing ventures. Through late summer he grew rapidly worse, dying on September 24. Emily, having taken cold at his funeral, passed rapidly into tuberculosis, and followed him on December 19. Anne, already ill of the family scourge, succumbed on May 28, 1849.

Alone in the Parsonage with her father, Charlotte returned to an interrupted novel (*Shirley*) of Yorkshire local color which had been developed through fifteen years of Angrian writing. In November, 1852, she began the refining and naturalizing of yet another group of her beloved Angrians against a Belgian background. The result, *Villette*, was published in January, 1853.

On June 29 of the next year, she married her father's curate, Arthur Bell Nicholls. Her happiness was of short duration; she died on Easter Eve, March 31, 1855.

Bibliography

The Life of Charlotte Brontë, by Mrs. E. C. Gaskell, 1857, is the pioneer biography, but this work should be supplemented by more recent studies, which include Clement K. Shorter, *Charlotte Brontë and Her Circle*, 1896; F. Macdonald, *The Secret of Charlotte Brontë*, 1914; Rosamond Langbridge, *Charlotte Brontë: A Psychological Study*, 1929; E. F. Benson, *Charlotte Brontë*, 1932; Laura Hinkley, *The Brontës, Charlotte and Emily*, 1947; and Margaret Crompton, *Passionate Search: A Life of Charlotte Brontë*, 1955. The best book on Emily Brontë is Charles Simpson, *Emily Brontë*, 1929; but see also A.M.F. Robinson, *Emily Brontë*, 1883, and Lord David Cecil, *Early Victorian Novelists*, 1934. For Anne Brontë see Will T. Hale, *Anne Brontë: Her Life and Writings, Indiana University Studies*, XVI, No. 83, 1929.

More general studies of the Brontë family include Clement K. Shorter, *The Brontës: Life and Letters*, 2 vols., 1908; May Sinclair, *The Three Brontës*, 1912; K. A. R. Sugden, *A Short History of the Brontës*, 1929; Lawrence C. Willis, *The Brontës*, 1933; Phyllis Bentley, *The Brontës*, 1947; Ernest Raymond, *In the Steps of the Brontës*, 1948; Lawrence and E. M. Hanson, *The Four Brontës*, 1949; Margaret Lane, *The Brontë Story*, 1953; Annette B. Hopkins, *The Father of the Brontës*, 1958; Daphne Du Maurier, *The Infernal World of Branwell Brontë*, 1960; Winifred Gérin, *Branwell Brontë*, 1961; John Lock and W. T. Dixon, *A Man of Sorrow: The Life, Letters, and Times of the Rev. Patrick Brontë, 1777–1861*, 1965; and Phyllis Bentley, *The Brontës and Their World*, 1969.

All recent Brontë studies owe a tremendous debt to Fannie E. Ratchford, whose definitive work is *The Brontës' Web of Childhood*, 1941, supplemented by her *Two Poems by Emily Brontë, with the Gondal Background of Her Poems and Novel*, 1934; Introduction to Emily Brontë's *Gondal's Queen*, 1955, with notes; and *Legends of Angria*, edited with W. C. DeVane, 1933. Recent studies include Winifred Gérin, *Anne Brontë*, 1959; Ada Harrison and Derek Stanford, *Anne Brontë: Her Life and Work*, 1959; Muriel Spark and Derek Stanford, *Emily Brontë: Her Life and Work*, 1960; Robert Bernard Martin, *The Accents of Persuasion: Charlotte Brontë's Novels*, 1966; Winifred Gérin, *Charlotte Brontë: The*

Evolution of Genius, 1967; Judith O'Neil, comp., *Critics on Charlotte and Emily Brontë*, 1968; Thomas Vogler, ed., *Twentieth Century Interpretations of Wuthering Heights: A Collection of Critical Essays*, 1969; and Earl Knies, *The Art of Charlotte Brontë*, 1969. Other specialized studies are C. P. Sanger, *The Structure of Wuthering Heights*, 1926; Leicester Bradner, "The Growth of *Wuthering Heights*," *Publications of the Modern Language Association*, XLVIII (1933), 129–146; Martin Turnell, "*Wuthering Heights*," *Dublin Review*, CCVI (1940), 134–149; and Richard Chase, "The Brontës; or, Myth Domesticated," in *Forms of Modern Fiction*, edited by W. V. O'Connor, 1948. See also the *Transactions and publications of the Brontë Society*, various dates; in particular, Hilda Marsden, "The Scenic Background of *Wuthering Heights*," Part 67, XIII, No. 2, 1957.

AGNES GREY

Type of work: Novel
Author: Anne Brontë (1820–1849)
Type of plot: Sentimental romance
Time of plot: Mid-nineteenth century
Locale: England
First published: 1847

    Agnes Grey is a typical nineteenth century sentimental romance in which piety and goodness triumph over arrogance and frivolity. Agnes' pious sentimentality, however, is lightened unexpectedly throughout the story by her cutting observations on contemporary life and by a certain gently but penetrating sarcasm which steals through in remarks about her employers.

Principal Characters

Agnes Grey, the pious, sheltered daughter of a clergyman. She takes employment as a governess when her family's financial situation becomes desperate.

Richard Grey, Agnes' father, a poor parson who loses his patrimony in a disastrous speculation.

Mrs. Grey, Agnes' mother.

Mary Grey, Agnes' sister.

Mrs. Bloomfield, mistress of Wellwood. Agnes' first employer, she is convinced that her incorrigible children, Agnes' charges, are angels.

Tom Bloomfield,
Mary Ann Bloomfield, and
Fanny Bloomfield, Agnes' arrogant, disobedient charges.

Mr. Bloomfield, the stern father of Tom, Mary Ann, and Fanny. He blames Agnes when the children misbehave.

Uncle Robson, Mrs. Bloomfield's brother. His encouragement of Tom's cruel behavior brings forth a protest from Agnes and causes her dismissal.

Mrs. Murray, mistress of Horton Lodge and Agnes' second employer.

Rosalie Murray, Agnes' pretty, flirtatious charge at Horton Lodge. At sixteen, she is interested only in making a good match.

Matilda Murray, Agnes' younger charge at Horton Lodge who is interested only in horses.

Edward Weston, the pious, sincere curate at Horton Lodge. He later becomes Agnes' husband.

Mr. Hatfield, the pompous rector of Horton and the rejected suitor of Rosalie Murray.

Harry Meltham and
Mr. Green, suitors of Rosalie.

Sir Thomas Ashby, the wealthy, boorish owner of Ashby Park with whom Rosalie makes an unhappy marriage.

Nancy Brown, an old widow at Horton visited by Agnes and Edward Weston during the development of their romance.

The Story

Mrs. Grey, a squire's daughter, had offended her family by marrying for love a poor parson in the north of England. She bore him six children, but only two, Mary and Agnes, survived. Nevertheless, the Greys were happy with their humble, educated, pious life in their small house and garden.

Mr. Grey, never wholly at his ease because his wife had been forced to give up carriages and fine clothes in order to marry him, attempted to improve their fortunes by speculating and investing his patrimony in a merchant's sea voyage. But the vessel was wrecked, everything was lost, and the Greys were soon left penniless. In addition, Mr. Grey's health, never robust, began to fail more perceptibly under the strain of his guilt for bringing his family close to ruin. Mary and Agnes, reared in the sheltered atmosphere of a clergyman's household, had spent their time reading, studying, and working in the garden. When the family situation became desperate, however, Mary began to try to sell her drawings to help with the household expenses, and Agnes, the younger daughter, decided to become a governess.

Overcoming the qualms her family felt at the idea of her leaving home, Agnes found a situation and, on a bleak and windy autumn day, arrived at Wellwood, the home of the Bloomfield family. She was received rather coldly by Mrs. Bloomfield and told that her charges, especially Tom, a seven-year-old boy, were noble and splendid children. She soon found that the reverse was true. Tom was an arrogant and disobedient little monster whose particular delight was to pull the legs and wings off young sparrows. Mary Ann, his six-year-old sister, was given to tantrums of temper and refusal to do her lessons. The children were frightened of their father, a peevish and stern disciplinarian, and the father, in turn, blamed Agnes when the children, as frequently happened, got out of control.

Agnes found it impossible to teach the children anything because all her efforts to discipline them were undermined by Mrs. Bloomfield, who felt that her angels must always be right. Even four-year-old Fanny lied consistently and was fond of spitting in people's faces. For a time, Agnes was heartened by Mr. Bloomfield's mother's visit, but the pious old lady turned out to be a hypocrite who sympathized with Agnes verbally and then turned on her behind her back.

Matters became a great deal worse with the visit of Uncle Robson, Mrs. Bloomfield's brother, who encouraged young Tom to torture small animals. One day, after he had collected a whole brood of young birds for Tom to torture, Agnes crushed them with a large stone, choosing to kill them quickly rather than to see them suffer a slow, cruel death. The family felt she had deprived Tom of his normal, spirited pleasure. Shortly after this incident she was told that her services would no longer be required; the Bloomfields felt that she had not disciplined the children properly or taught them very much.

Agnes spent a few months with her family at home before taking up her next post. She found the Murrays, the owners of Horton Lodge, more sophisticated, wealthier, and less bleak and cruel than the owners of Wellwood; but they were still hardly the happy, pious, warm family that Agnes had hoped to encounter. Her older charge, Rosalie, was sixteen, very pretty, interested only in flirting and in eventually making the most suitable marriage possible; her younger charge, Matilda, fourteen, was interested only in horses and stables. Although they treated her with politeness, neither girl had any respect for the learning and piety that Agnes had to offer. If Agnes' work was less unpleasant than it had been at Wellwood, it was equally futile.

After living at Horton Lodge for nearly a year, Agnes returned home for a month for her sister's wedding. During this time, the Murrays had given Rosalie a coming-out ball, after which she began to exercise her charms on the young men at Horton. Agnes was shocked, when she returned, to find Rosalie flirting with all the men and summarizing the marital possibilities of each with such a hardened and materialistic eye. In the meantime a new curate had come to Horton. Edward Weston was a sober and sincere churchman, neither climbing nor pompous like the rector, Mr. Hatfield. Edward Weston and Agnes, attracted to each other, found many opportunities to meet in their sympathetic visits to Nancy Brown, an old widow who was almost blind. At first Rosalie found Weston both dogmatic and dull, but Agnes found him representative of the true piety and goodness which she believed were the qualities of a clergyman. Rosalie, continuing to play the coquette, conquered first the unctuous rector, Mr. Hatfield, and then after Mr. Hatfield had proposed and been quickly rejected, turned her charms on Mr. Weston. Although Agnes was fiercely jealous of Rosalie's flirtation, she never really acknowledged her own growing love. Finally, Rosalie accepted Sir Thomas Ashby; his home, Ashby Park, and his fortune were the largest in the vicinity of Horton.

Shortly after Rosalie's marriage, before Agnes had the opportunity to see much of Edward Weston, she was called home by the death of her father. She and her mother decided to start a school for young ladies in the fashionable watering place of A——. Although Agnes returned to Horton Lodge for another month, she did not see Weston before she resignedly left to rejoin her mother. Although the school began to prosper after a few months, Agnes still seemed weary and depressed, and she welcomed an invitation from Rosalie, now Lady Ashby, to visit Ashby Park. She found Rosalie disappointed in her marriage to a grumbling, boorish man who ignored her and who after a honeymoon on the Continent, had forbidden her the frivolous pleasures of London and European society. Agnes also learned from Rosalie that Weston had left Horton a short time before.

A few days after Agnes returned to her mother and the school, she was walking along the water front one morning when she was surprised by Weston. He had secured a living in a nearby village. He promptly began calling on Agnes and her mother and as time passed gained Agnes' love and her mother's esteem. One day, while walking with Agnes to the top of a high hill, he proposed. As husband, father, clergyman, and manager of a limited income, he was in after years the perfect mate for virtuous and worthy Agnes.

Critical Evaluation

The youngest child of the Reverend Patrick Brontë, Anne Brontë, is the most shadowy figure among the Brontës. Gentle and timid, she stands behind her more famous sisters and notorious brother, yet her two novels have an interest of their own, on their own merits. Although *Agnes Grey* does not possess the vigorous writing of *The Tenant of Wildfell Hall* or the depth of characterization, in its quiet way it is a more solid novel and presents a fuller picture of the life that Anne Brontë knew so well. *Agnes Grey* is a minor book by a minor writer, but it will continue to be read for its gentle humor and the integrity of its realism.

Anne was twice a governess in private houses, so she was all too familiar with the humiliations and difficulties inherent in such a position. The story of Agnes, the governess, is told in the first person, in short, straightforward chapters. The ending of the novel is sentimental, but the narrative along the way is at times sharp and always well-observed. When Agnes and Rosalie discuss the engagement of a sister to a neighboring vicar, Rosalie wonders if he is rich or handsome or young, but Agnes replies, " . . . only middling." Every aspect of the life facing Agnes and the other characters is only middling; the author does not glamorize her heroine's existence. The characters, for the most part, are described without romanticism, sometimes almost mercilessly; their lives are dragged out day by day, duty by duty. Perhaps Agnes is saved at the end by her clergyman husband, but only in a very limited sense. After her difficulties, Agnes is content with a very modest existence; in fact, from the beginning, she is a young woman of slight expectations and no pretensions. Rather like its heroine, this novel is modest and without pretensions, but is pleasantly satisfying.

Bibliography

Bentley, Phyllis. *The Brontës.* New York: Haskell House, 1975, pp. 104–107.

Calder, Jenni. *Women and Marriage in Victorian Fiction.* New York: Oxford University Press, 1976, pp. 30–31, 34, 57, 58.

Craik, W.A. *The Brontë Novels.* London: Methuen, 1968, pp. 202–227.

Gerin, Winifred. *Anne Brontë.* London: Thomas Nelson, 1959, pp. 125–127, 230–233.

Hale, Will T. *Anne Brontë: Her Life and Writings.* Folcraft, Pa.: Folcraft, 1929.

Halperin, John and Janet Kunert. *Plots and Characters in the Fiction of Jane Austen, the Brontës, and George Eliot.* Hamden, Conn.: Shoe String Press, 1976.

Harrison, Ada and Derek Stanford. *Anne Brontë: Her Life and Work.* London: Methuen, 1959, pp. 223–245.

Pinion, F.B. *A Brontë Companion: Literary Assessment, Background, and Reference.* London: Macmillan, 1975.

JANE EYRE

Type of work: Novel
Author: Charlotte Brontë (1816–1855)
Type of plot: Psychological romance
Time of plot: 1800
Locale: Northern England
First published: 1847

The poetry and tension of Jane Eyre *marked a new development in adult romanticism in fiction, just as Jane herself was a new kind of heroine, a woman of intelligence and passion, but one lacking in the charm, beauty, and grace usually associated with romantic heroines. Likewise, the strange and unconventional hero, Rochester, is a new type, who sets the often eerie, moody, or even violently passionate atmosphere of the novel.*

Principal Characters

Jane Eyre, a plain child with a vivid imagination, intelligence, and great talent in art and music. Left an orphan in childhood, she is forced to live with her aunt Reed, who was the sister-in-law of her father. At the Reed home she is mistreated and spurned, and is finally sent to a charity home for girls. Her education completed, she teaches at the school for several years and then takes a position as a private governess to the ward of Mr. Rochester. After a strange, tempestuous courtship she and Mr. Rochester are to be married, but the revelation that his insane first wife still lives prevents the wedding. After each has suffered many hardships, Jane and Mr. Rochester are eventually married.

Edward Fairfax Rochester, a gentleman of thirty-five, the proud, sardonic, moody master of Thornfield. Before Jane Eyre's arrival to become a governess in his household he visits Thornfield only occasionally. After he falls in love with Jane, much of his moroseness disappears. When they are separated because the presence of his insane wife becomes known, Mr. Rochester remains at Thornfield. His wife sets fire to the house and Mr. Rochester loses his eyesight and the

use of an arm during the conflagration, in which his wife dies. Summoned, she believes, by his call, Jane Eyre returns a short time later and the two are married.

Adele Varens, the illegitimate daughter of Mr. Rochester and a French opera singer, his ward upon her mother's death. She is pale, small-featured, extremely feminine, and not especially talented.

Mrs. Fairfax, the elderly housekeeper at Thornfield. She has been extremely kind to Jane and is delighted that she and Mr. Rochester are to be married.

Grace Poole, a stern woman with a hard, plain face, supposedly a seamstress at Thornfield but actually the keeper of mad Mrs. Rochester. Occasionally she tipples too much and neglects her post.

Bertha Mason Rochester, Mr. Rochester's insane wife, kept in secret on an upper floor at Thornfield. She had lied and her family had lied when Mr. Rochester met her in Jamaica while traveling, for she was even then demented. During Jane's stay at Thornfield Mrs. Rochester tries to burn her husband in bed. Finally she burns the whole house and herself, and seriously injures her husband.

Mrs. Reed, an exact, clever, managing woman, the guardian of Jane Eyre. She hates her charge, however, misuses her, and locks her in dark rooms for punishment. At her death she repents of her actions. Her children turn out badly.

Eliza Reed, her older daughter, a penurious, serious girl who eventually becomes a nun.

John Reed, the son, a wicked child who torments Jane Eyre and then blames her for his own bad deeds. He ends up as a drunk in London and dies in disgrace.

Georgiana Reed, the younger daughter, a pretty, spoiled child who later becomes very fat. She makes a poor marriage.

Bessie Leaven, Mrs. Reed's governess, pretty, capricious, hasty-tempered. Before Jane Eyre leaves the Reed house, Bessie has become fond of her.

Robert Leaven, Bessie's husband and Mrs. Reed's coachman.

Abbot, the Reed's bad-tempered maid.

Mr. Lloyd, an apothecary called in when Jane Eyre becomes sick and feverish after having been locked in a dark room. He suggests that she be sent off to school.

Mr. Brocklehurst, a strict clergyman and the master of Lowood School. He forces the girls to wear short, uncurled hair and plain wrappers, and he feeds them on a starvation diet.

Maria Temple, the supervisor of Lowood School, a pretty, kind woman who tries against tremendous odds to make her pupils' lot as easy and pleasant as possible. She is interested in Jane Eyre's talents and is responsible for her getting a teaching position later at Lowood.

Miss Smith,
Miss Scratcherd, and
Miss Miller, teachers at Lowood School.

Alice Wood, an orphan, one of Jane's pupils in the school where she teaches after leaving Thornfield.

Helen Burns, a clever thirteen-year-old pupil at Lowood School, constantly ridiculed and punished by her teachers because she is not neat and prompt. She dies during a fever epidemic.

Miss Gryce, a fat teacher at Lowood School and Jane Eyre's roommate when they both teach there.

Mary Ann Wilson, one of Jane Eyre's fellow students, a witty and original girl.

John and
Leah, the house servants at Thornfield Hall.

Sophie, the French maid.

Mrs. Eshton, a guest at a house party given by Mr. Rochester. Once a handsome woman, she still has a well-preserved style.

Mr. Eshton, her husband, a magistrate of the district.

Amy Eshton, their older daughter, rather small, naïve, and childlike in manner.

Louisa Eshton, the younger daughter, a taller and more elegant young woman.

Lady Lynn, another woman whose family is invited to the Thornfield house party; she is large, stout, haughty-looking, and richly dressed.

Mrs. Dent, another guest, less showy than the others, with a slight figure and a pale, gentle face.

Colonel Dent, her husband, a soldierly gentleman.

The Dowager Lady Ingram, another guest, a proud, handsome woman with hard, fierce eyes.

Blanche Ingram, her daughter, a young woman with an elegant manner and a loud, satirical laugh, to whom Mr. Rochester is reported engaged.

Mary Ingram, her sister.

Henry Lynn and
Frederick Lynn, gentlemen at the party, two dashing sparks.

Lord Ingram, Blanche's brother, a tall, handsome young man of listless appearance and manner.

Mr. Mason, Mr. Rochester's brother-in-law. During a visit to see his sister, she wounds him severely. He halts the marriage of Jane Eyre and Mr. Rochester.

Diana Rivers and
Mary Rivers, daughters of the family with which Jane Eyre takes refuge after running away from Thornfield. They turn out to be her cousins, their mother having been Jane's aunt. At first they do not know that Jane is a relative because she calls herself Jane Eliot.

St. John Rivers, their brother, a complex religious-minded man who wishes to marry Jane but plans to live with her in platonic fashion while they devote their lives to missionary work in India.

Hannah, the Rivers' housekeeper, a suspicious but kind woman.

Rosamund Oliver, a beautiful, kind heiress, the sponsor of the school in which St. John Rivers finds Jane a post. Miss Oliver is coquettish and vain, but she holds real affection for Rivers.

Mr. Oliver, her father, a tall, massive-featured man.

The Story

Jane Eyre was an orphan. Both her father and mother had died when Jane was a baby, and the little girl passed into the care of Mrs. Reed of Gateshead Hall. Mrs. Reed's husband, now dead, had been the brother of Jane Eyre's mother, and on his deathbed he had directed Mrs. Reed to look after the orphan as she would her own three children. At Gateshead Hall Jane knew ten years of neglect and abuse. One day a cousin knocked her to the floor. When she fought back, Mrs. Reed punished her by sending her to the gloomy room where Mr. Reed had died. There Jane lost consciousness. Furthermore, the experience caused a dangerous illness from which she was nursed slowly back to health by sympathetic Bessie Leaven, the Gateshead Hall nurse.

Feeling that she could no longer keep her unwanted charge in the house, Mrs. Reed made arrangements for Jane's admission to Lowood School. Early one morning, without farewells, Jane left Gateshead Hall and rode fifty miles by stage to Lowood, her humble possessions in a trunk beside her.

At Lowood, Jane was a diligent student, well-liked by her superiors, especially by Miss Temple, the mistress, who refused to accept without proof Mrs. Reed's low estimate of Jane's character. During the period of Jane's schooldays at Lowood an epidemic of fever caused many deaths among the girls. It resulted, too, in an investigation which caused improvements at the institution. At the end of her studies Jane was retained as a teacher. When Jane grew weary of her life at Lowood, she advertised for a position as governess. She was engaged by Mrs. Fairfax, housekeeper at Thornfield, near Millcote.

At Thornfield the new governess had only one pupil, Adele Varens, a ward of

Jane's employer, Mr. Edward Rochester. From Mrs. Fairfax, Jane learned that Mr. Rochester traveled much and seldom came to Thornfield. Jane was pleased with the quiet country life with the beautiful old house and gardens, the book-filled library, and her own comfortable room.

Jane met Mr. Rochester for the first time while she was out walking, going to his aid after his horse had thrown him. She found her employer a somber, moody man, quick to change in his manner toward her, brusque in his speech. He commended her work with Adele, however, and confided that the girl was the daughter of a French dancer who had deceived him and deserted her daughter. Jane felt that this experience alone could not account for Mr. Rochester's moody nature.

Mysterious happenings occurred at Thornfield. One night Jane, alarmed by a strange noise, found Mr. Rochester's door open and his bed on fire. When she attempted to arouse the household, he commanded her to keep quiet about the whole affair. She also learned that Thornfield had a strange tenant, a woman who laughed like a maniac and who stayed in rooms on the third floor of the house. Jane believed that this woman was Grace Poole, a seamstress employed by Mr. Rochester.

Mr. Rochester attended numerous parties at which he was obviously paying court to Blanche Ingram, daughter of Lady Ingram. One day the inhabitants of Thornfield were informed that Mr. Rochester was bringing a party of house guests home with him. In the party was the fashionable Miss Ingram. During the house party Mr. Rochester called Jane to the drawing-room, where the guests treated her with the disdain which they thought her humble position deserved. To herself Jane had already confessed her interest in her employer, but it seemed to her that he was interested only in Blanche Ingram. One evening while Mr. Rochester was away from home the guests played charades. At the conclusion of the game a gypsy fortune-teller appeared to read the palms of the lady guests. Jane, during her interview with the gypsy, discovered that the so-called fortune-teller was Mr. Rochester in disguise.

While the guests were still at Thornfield, a stranger named Mason arrived to see Mr. Rochester on business. That night Mason was mysteriously wounded by the strange inhabitant of the third floor. The injured man was taken away secretly before daylight.

One day Robert Leaven came from Gateshead to tell Jane that Mrs. Reed, now on her deathbed, had asked to see her former ward. Jane returned to her aunt's home. The dying woman gave Jane a letter, dated three years before, from John Eyre in Madeira, who asked that his niece be sent to him for adoption. Mrs. Reed confessed that she had epidemic at Lowood. The sin of keeping from Jane news which would have meant relatives, adoption, and an inheritance had become a heavy burden on the conscience of the dying woman.

Jane went back to Thornfield, which she now looked upon as her home. One night in the garden Edward Rochester embraced her and proposed marriage. Jane accepted and made plans for a quiet ceremony in the village church. She wrote also to her uncle in Madeira, explaining Mrs. Reed's deception and telling him she was to marry Mr. Rochester.

Shortly before the date set for the wedding Jane had a harrowing experience. She awakened to find a strange, repulsive-looking woman in her room. The intruder tried on Jane's wedding veil and then ripped it to shreds. Mr. Rochester tried to persuade Jane that the whole incident was only her imagination, but in the morning she found the torn veil in her room. At the church, as the vows were being said, a stranger spoke up declaring the existence of an impediment to the marriage. He presented an affirmation, signed by the Mr. Mason who had been wounded during his visit to Thornfield. The document stated that Edward Fairfax Rochester had married Bertha Mason, Mr. Mason's sister, in Spanish Town, Jamaica, fifteen years before. Mr. Rochester admitted this fact; then he conducted the party to the third-story chamber at Thornfield. There they found the attendant Grace Poole and her charge, Bertha Rochester, a raving maniac. Mrs. Rochester was the woman Jane had seen in her room.

Jane felt that she must leave Thornfield at once. She notified Mr. Rochester and left quietly early the next morning, using all her small store of money for the coach fare. Two days later she was set down on the moors of a north midland shire. Starving, she actually begged for food. Finally she was befriended by the Reverend St. John Rivers and his sisters, Mary and Diana, who took Jane in and nursed her back to health. Assuming the name of Jane Elliot, she refused to divulge anything of her history except her connection with the Lowood institution. Reverend Rivers eventually found a place for her as mistress in a girl's school.

Shortly afterward St. John Rivers received from his family solicitor word that John Eyre had died in Madeira, leaving Jane Eyre a fortune of twenty thousand pounds. Because Jane had disappeared under mysterious circumstances, the lawyer was trying to locate her through the next of kin, St. John Rivers. Jane's identity was now revealed through her connection with Lowood School, and she learned, to her surprise, that St. John and his sisters were really her own cousins. She then insisted on sharing her inheritance with them.

When St. John decided to go to India as a missionary, he asked Jane to go with him as his wife—not because he loved her, as he frankly admitted, but because he admired her and wanted her services as his assistant. Jane felt indebted to him for his kindness and aid, but she hesitated to accept his proposal.

One night, while St. John was awaiting her decision, she dreamed that Mr. Rochester was calling her name. The next day she returned to Thornfield by coach. Arriving there, she found the mansion gutted—a burned and blackened ruin. Neighbors told her that the fire had broken out one stormy night, set by the madwoman, who died while Mr. Rochester was trying to rescue her from the roof of the blazing house.

Mr. Rochester, blinded during the fire, was living at Ferndean, a lonely farm some miles away. Jane Eyre went to him at once, and there they were married.

For both, their story had an even happier ending. After two years Mr. Rochester regained the sight of one eye, so that he was able to see his first child when it was put in his arms.

Critical Evaluation

Charlotte Brontë was always concerned that her work be judged on the basis of its art and not because of her sex. Thus the choice of the pseudonym which she continued to use even after her authorship was revealed, often referring in her letters to Currer Bell when speaking of herself as writer. *Jane Eyre,* her first published novel, has been called "feminine" because of the romanticism and deeply felt emotions of the heroine-narrator. It would be more correct, however, to point to the feminist qualities of the novel: a heroine who refuses to be placed in the traditional female position of subservience, who disagrees with her superiors, who stands up for her rights, who ventures creative thoughts; more importantly, a narrator who comments on the role of women in the society and the greater constraint experienced by them. Those "feminine" emotions often pointed to in Jane Eyre herself are surely found as well in Rochester, and the continued popularity of this work must suggest the enduring human quality of these emotions.

Brontë often discussed the lack of passion in her contemporaries' work and especially in that of Jane Austen, about whom she said, "Her business is not half so much with the human heart as with the human eyes, mouth, hands and feet." Coldness, detachment, excessive analysis, and critical distance were not valued by Brontë. The artist must be involved in her subject, she believed, and must have a degree of inspiration not to be rationally explained. Such a theory of art is similar to that of the romantic poets, an attitude not altogether popular by mid-nineteenth century.

In *Jane Eyre*, therefore, Brontë chose the exact point of view to suit both her subject matter and her artistic theory, the first-person narrator. The story is told entirely through the eyes of the heroine Jane Eyre. This technique enabled Brontë to bring the events to the reader with an intensity that involved him in the passions, feelings, and thoughts of the heroine. A passionate directness characterizes Jane's narration: conversations are rendered in direct, not indirect dialogue; actions are given just as they occurred, with little analysis of either event or character. In a half-dozen key scenes, Brontë shifts to present tense instead of the immediate past, so that Jane Eyre narrates the event as if it were happening just at the present moment. After Jane flees Thornfield and Rochester, when the coachman puts her out at Whitcross having used up her fare, she narrates to the moment: "I am alone. . . . I am absolutely destitute." After a long description of the scene around her and her analysis of her situation, also narrated in the present tense, she reverts to the more usual past tense in the next paragraph: "I struck straight into the heath." Such a technique adds greatly to the immediacy of the novel and further draws the reader into the situation.

Jane Eyre, like all Brontë's heroines, has no parents and no family that accepts or is aware of her. She, like Lucy Snowe (*Villette*) and Caroline Helstone (*Shirley*), leads her life, then, cut off from society, since family was the means for a woman to participate in society and community. Lacking such support, Jane must face her problems alone. Whenever she forms a close friendship (Bessie at Gateshead, Helen Burns and Miss Temple at Lowood, Mrs. Fairfax at Thornfield), she discovers that these ties can be broken easily —by higher authority, by death, by marriage—since she is not "kin." Cutting her heroines off so radically from family and community gave Charlotte Brontë the opportunity to make her women independent and to explore the romantic ideal of individualism.

Jane Eyre is a moral tale, akin to a folk or fairy tale, with nearly all ambiguities—in society, character, and situation—omitted. Almost all the choices that Jane must make are easy ones, and her character, although she grows and matures, does not change significantly. Her one difficult choice is refusing to become Rochester's mistress, leaving Thornfield alone and penniless instead. That choice was difficult precisely because she had no family or friends to influence her with their disapproval. No one would be hurt if she consented; that is, no one but Jane herself, and it is her own self-love that helps her to refuse.

Again like a fairy tale, *Jane Eyre* is full of myth and superstition. Rochester often calls Jane his "elf," "changeling," or "witch"; there are mysterious happenings at Thornfield; Jane is inclined to believe the gipsy fortune-teller (until Rochester reveals himself) and often thinks of the superstitions she has heard; the weather often presages mysterious or disastrous events. And, most importantly, at the climax of the story when Jane is about to consent to be the unloved wife of St. John Rivers, she hears Rochester calling to her —at precisely the time, we learn later, that he had in fact called to her. This event is never explained rationally, and we must accept Jane's judgment that it was a supernatural intervention.

Numerous symbolic elements pervade the novel; most often something in nature symbolizes an event or person in Jane's life. The most obvious example is the chestnut tree, which is split in two by lightning on the night that Jane accepts Rochester's marriage proposal, signifying the rupture of their relationship. The two parts of the tree, though, remain bound, as do Jane and Rochester despite their physical separation.

Likewise, the novel is full of character foils and parallel situations. Aunt Reed at Gateshead is contrasted with Miss Temple at Lowood; the Reed sisters at the beginning are contrasted with the Rivers sisters—cousins all— at the end; Rochester's impassioned proposal and love is followed by St. John's pragmatic proposition. Foreshadowing is everywhere in the book, so

that seemingly chance happenings gain added significance as the novel un-
folds and each previous event is echoed in the next.

Thus, the novel's artful structure and carefully chosen point of view,
added to the strong and fascinating character of Jane herself, make *Jane Eyre,*
if not a typical Victorian novel, surely a classic among English novels.

Bibliography

Aldrich, John W., Margaret Webster and Lyman Bryson. *"Jane Eyre,"* in
Invitation to Learning: English and American Novels. Edited by George D.
Crothers. New York: Basic Books, 1966, pp. 109–117.

Beer, Patricia. *Reader, I Married Him: A Study of the Women Characters
of Jane Austen, Charlotte Brontë, Elizabeth Gaskell and George Eliot.*
London: Macmillan, 1974, pp. 86–126.

Benvenuto, Richard. "The Child of Nature, the Child of Grace, and the Unre-
solved Conflict of *Jane Eyre,"* in *Journal of English Literary History.*
XXXIX (1972), pp. 620–638.

Blom, M.A. *"Jane Eyre*: Mind as Law unto Itself?," in *Criticism.* XV (1973),
pp. 350–364.

Craik, W.A. *The Brontë Novels.* London: Methuen, 1968, pp. 70–122.

Day, Martin S. "Central Concepts of *Jane Eyre,"* in *Personalist.* XLI (Autumn, 1960), pp. 495–505.

Dunn, Richard J. Jane Eyre: *An Authoritative Text, Backgrounds, and Criticism.* New York: Norton, 1972.

Gribble, Jennifer. "Jane Eyre's Imagination," in *Nineteenth-Century Fiction.*
XXIII (December, 1968), pp. 279–293.

Karl, Frederick R. *An Age of Fiction; The Nineteenth Century British
Novel.* New York: Farrar, Straus and Giroux, 1964, pp. 77–103.

Knies, Earl A. *The Art of Charlotte Brontë.* Athens: Ohio University Press,
1969, pp. 171–184, 204–211.

Kramer, Dale. "Thematic Structure in *Jane Eyre,"* in *Papers on Language
and Literature.* IV (1968), pp. 288–298.

Langford, Thomas A. "Prophetic Imagination and the Unity of *Jane Eyre,"* in
Studies in the Novel. VI (1974), pp. 228–235.

Lodge, David. *Language of Fiction; Essays in Criticism and Verbal Analysis of the English Novel.* New York: Columbia University Press, 1966,
pp. 114–143.

O'Neill, Judith. *Critics on Charlotte and Emily Brontë; Readings in Literary Criticism.* Coral Gables, Fla.: University of Miami Press, 1968, pp. 25–31.

Pell, Nancy. "Resistance, Rebellion and Marriage: The Economics of *Jane*

Eyre," in *Nineteenth-Century Fiction.* XXXI (March, 1977), pp. 397–430.

Pinion, F.B. *A Brontë Companion: Literary Assessment, Background, and Reference.* London: Macmillan, 1975.

Riley, Michael. "Gothic Melodrama and Spiritual Romance: Vision and Fidelity in Two Versions of *Jane Eyre,*" in *Literature/Film Quarterly.* III (1975), pp. 145–159.

Sherry, Norman. *Charlotte and Emily Brontë.* London: Evans, 1969, pp. 51–70.

Siebenschuh, William R. "The Image of the Child and the Plot of *Jane Eyre,*" in *Studies in the Novel.* VIII (1976), pp. 304–317.

Solomon, Eric. "*Jane Eyre*: Fire and Water," in *College English.* XXV (December, 1963), pp. 211–217.

Tillotson, Kathleen M. *Novels of the Eighteen-Forties.* London: Oxford University Press, 1961, pp. 257–313.

Williams, Raymond. *The English Novel: From Dickens to Lawrence.* London: Chatto and Windus, 1970, pp. 60–74.

Wilson, F.A.C. "The Primrose Wreath: The Heroes of the Brontë Novels," in *Nineteenth-Century Fiction.* XXIX (1974), pp. 42–46.

Yeazell, Ruth B. "More True Than Real: Jane Eyre's 'Mysterious Summons,' " in *Nineteenth-Century Fiction.* XXIX (1974), pp. 127–143.

Yuen, Maria. "Two Crises of Decision in *Jane Eyre,*" in *English Studies.* LVII (1976), pp. 215–226.

VILLETTE

Type of work: Novel
Author: Charlotte Brontë (1816–1855)
Type of plot: Psychological romance
Time of plot: Nineteenth century
Locale: Belgium
First published: 1853

Published six years after the author's famous Jane Eyre. Villette *is a flawed psychological novel that is nevertheless interesting for its autobiographical material. The author's passion for Constantin Héger is believed to find an echo in this fiction.*

Principal Characters

Lucy Snowe, a quiet, intelligent, hard-working young English girl whose grave demeanor covers a deeply passionate nature. Orphaned at an early age, she spends her childhood in the homes of distant relatives and with her godmother, Mrs. Bretton. Later, through a varied chain of circumstances, she goes to Villette, a city on the Continent, where she becomes a governess in the household of Madame Beck, the mistress of a boarding school for girls. Before long Madame Beck gives her a post as a teacher of English in the school. Eventually, with the help of Monsieur Paul Emanuel, another teacher at the school, she secures a school of her own. At the end of the novel she anticipates marrying M. Paul.

Dr. John Graham Bretton, called **Dr. John,** the son of Lucy's godmother. Now living in Villette, he is the kind-hearted, handsome young physician who attends Madame Beck's children. Lucy had known him earlier in her life as a mischievous boy who had little time for girls. His recognition of Lucy comes when he is summoned to revive her after she has fainted while leaving a church. For a time romance seems about to flower between Lucy and Dr. John, but when Paulina de Bassompierre once more appears in the lives of the Brettons,

Dr. John's heart goes to her. At the end of the novel Pauline and Dr. John marry.

Mrs. Bretton, John's mother and Lucy's godmother. A handsome and vivacious widow, she cares for Lucy after the child has been orphaned. Mrs. Bretton is most attentive to the details of domesticity, and her home and life testify to this interest. In Villette once more she and her son care for Lucy.

Monsieur Paul Emanuel, Madame Beck's cousin, the instructor in music and French at her school. Hot-tempered, passionate, he falls deeply in love with Lucy and hates to see her in the company of Dr. John. At the beginning of his interest in Lucy he constantly admonishes her and tries to draw her out by his discussions. Later his manner becomes less abrupt, and because of the consideration and tenderness he shows she finally falls in love with him. Before he leaves for a three-year journey abroad, he makes arrangements to establish her in a school of her own. The two plan to marry when he returns.

Madame Beck, a cold, dumpy-looking, self-controlled headmistress of a school for girls in Villette who hires Lucy Snowe to teach English. Always in possession of herself, Madame Beck is an outrageously curious person, snooping in Lucy's desk and drawers whenever she feels the occasion warrants it, restlessly prowling, ghostlike, through the school at night. She, together with her relatives, tries to block the romance of Lucy and M. Paul, but her efforts are thwarted.

Paulina Mary Home de Bassompierre, also called **Polly Home,** a beautiful and poised young lady who marries Dr. Bretton. She first appears in the story as a lonely small girl called Paulina Home. Because her father, Mr. Home, is forced to leave her for a time with the Brettons, she falls into a state of depression broken only by the attentions of young John Bretton. She transfers all her affection for her father to the schoolboy and ignores Lucy Snowe's efforts to help her. Later she grows into a charming young woman and marries her old playfellow, who is now known as Dr. John.

Mr. Home, also known as **Monsieur de Bassompierre,** a distant cousin of Mrs. Bretton and the father of Paulina Home, to whom he is completely devoted. Because his wife was a giddy, flirtatious woman who never gave her husband the warmth and love he bestowed upon her, he became very close to his daughter, and he is quite reluctant for her to marry anyone. Finally he is reconciled to her marriage with Dr. John and looks forward to becoming one of their household.

Miss Marchmont, a woman of fortune, a rheumatic cripple when Lucy goes to care for her after living with the Brettons. Miss Marchmont's lover had died when she was young, and the old woman has turned into a firm, patient, sometimes morose person who cares a great deal for Lucy. When Miss Marchmont dies, Lucy is once more forced to go into the world to make her own living.

Mrs. Barrett, the old servant of Miss Marchmont, also fond of Lucy Snowe.

Mrs. Leigh, an old schoolmate of Lucy,

a comely, good-natured woman. Her French maid suggests to Lucy, after Miss Marchmont's death, that there are many English girls living on the Continent and that perhaps Lucy can find a position abroad.

Ginevra Fanshawe, a vain, proud, but attractive girl, Paulina Home's cousin. She is a passenger aboard the "Vivid," the ship on which Lucy crosses the channel, and is a student at Madame Beck's school. She carries on a flirtation with Dr. John while at the same time meeting Alfred de Hamal secretly on Madame Beck's premises. Spoiled and unscrupulous, Ginevra torments Lucy with constant demands for attention. Eventually she elopes with Alfred de Hamal, and the two are married.

Colonel Alfred de Hamal, one of Ginevra's suitors and eventually her husband, a dandified figure in fashionable society. He disguises himself as a nun in order to hold many rendezvous with Ginevra in Madame Beck's establishment.

Mrs. Cholmondeley, Ginevra's chaperone at many parties, a woman of fashion in Villette who has attached herself to court circles and enjoys a prominent place in society.

Mademoiselle St. Pierre, a fellow teacher in Madame Beck's school, a prodigal and profligate woman whose chief achievement is the ability to keep order among the students.

Rosine Matou, the portress at Madame Beck's school, a pretty, airy, fickle young woman afraid of M. Paul's temper tantrums.

Fraulein Anna Braun, a worthy, hearty woman of forty-five; she instructs Lucy Snowe and Paulina Home in German.

Mademoiselle Sauver, Monsieur Paul's ward, who adores him.

Vashti, a complex and beautiful actress

who entrances Lucy Snowe when Dr. John takes her to one of Vashti's performances.

Désirée, the oldest daughter of Madame Beck, a vicious child who smashes things and steals from the servants; she is over-indulged by her mother.

Fifine, Madame Beck's middle child, an honest, gleeful little girl.

Georgette, Madame Beck's youngest daughter attended during her illness by Dr. John. Her sickness introduces him to the Beck household.

Mrs. Sivinc, the whiskey-drinking nursery governess to the Beck children, replaced by Lucy Snowe.

Mademoiselle Blanche,
Mademoiselle Virginie, and
Mademoiselle Angélique, three obstreperous pupils at Madame Beck's school; they plague Lucy Snowe on the first day of her teaching.

Dolores, another unusually willful student whom Lucy Snowe punishes by locking her in a closet.

Madame Walravens, a hideous little woman, the grandmother of M. Paul's dead sweetheart. He supports her after the death of Justine Marie, his betrothed.

Père Silas, the priest who hears Lucy Snowe's confession, a cleric supported by M. Paul because he is a kinsman of the dead Justine Marie. He tries in vain to change Lucy to a Catholic.

Monsieur Boissec and
Monsieur Rochemonte, professors who attempt to embarrass M. Paul by claiming that he has written Lucy Snowe's compositions.

The Story

When Lucy Snowe was a young girl, she went to visit her godmother, Mrs. Bretton, about twice each year. It was a warm, active household, and Lucy loved Mrs. Bretton.

During one of her visits, a small girl, whose widowed father was leaving England for a sojourn on the continent, came to stay with the Brettons. The girl, Polly Home, developed a strange and tender fondness for Mrs. Bretton's son Graham, who was a kind and compassionate boy. Mature and worldly for her years, Polly exhibited an almost maternal attachment toward Graham. Since Lucy shared a room with the young visitor, she became the recipient of the child's confidence. Although Polly's father had originally intended to deposit his daughter at Mrs. Bretton's home for an extended stay, he became lonely for her and returned to take his daughter back to Europe with him.

Lucy's visits with the Brettons came to an end when they lost their property and moved away. After that Lucy lost track of her godmother.

As a grown woman Lucy earned her living by acting as a companion to elderly women. Tiring of her humdrum existence, she went to France. There an unusual chain of circumstances led her to the city of Villette and to a boarding school run by Madame Beck and her kinsman, Monsieur Paul Emanuel. Lucy's calm disposition, ready wit, firm character, and advanced intellect soon led to her appointment as instructress of English.

Attending the school was Ginevra Fanshawe, a pretty but flighty and selfish girl whose relations with Lucy took the form of a scornful friendship. Madame Beck was a clever schoolmistress. She conducted her pension by a system of spying which included occasional furtive searches among the personal possessions of others and also a constant stealthy watching from her window. In spite of her behavior, Lucy felt a firm respect for Madame Beck. Her system was steady and unflagging. Monsieur Paul was a voluble and brilliant instructor. He seemed always to be at Lucy's elbow admonishing her, tantalizing her intellect, attempting to lead her. Often Lucy attributed the peculiar notions of the pair to their Catholicism, which Lucy abhorred.

Dr. John was a general favorite at the institute; he was a handsome, generous young practitioner who attended the children of Madame Beck's school. Lucy, although she did not betray her knowledge, recognized him as the John Graham Bretton whom she had known years before.

In her characteristically scornful and triumphant manner toward Lucy, Ginevra Fanshawe confided that she had a pair of ardent suitors. One, whom she called Isidore, was madly in love with her; the other was Colonel de Hamal, whom Ginevra herself preferred.

One night, in the garden, Lucy found a letter intended for someone in the school. Dr. John appeared in time to assist Lucy in disposing of the missive before Madame Beck, spying, could interfere. The young doctor knew, apparently, the person for whom the letter was intended. Some time later Lucy learned that Ginevra's Isidore was Dr. John himself. Thus the mystery of the nocturnal letter was solved. De Hamal had sent it and Dr. John was attempting to protect his beloved. In discussing his hopeless passion for Ginevra, Dr. John confessed that he hoped to marry the schoolgirl.

During a vacation Lucy, left alone at the pension, was overcome by depression. She had been haunted in the past by the apparition of a nun, and the reappearance of this specter so aggravated the already turbulent emotions of the young teacher that she fled into the streets of the town. There she wandered, driven to despair by her inner conflicts, until she came to a Catholic church. A strange fascination drove her to confession, but she later regretted her action. While trying to find her way back to the school, she fainted. When she regained consciousness, she found herself in a room that contained familiar furnishings. She was in a Villette chateau occupied by her godmother, Mrs. Bretton, and Graham Bretton. Graham, who was giving Lucy medical attention, was the Dr. John whom Lucy had recognized at the pension. For the first time he recognized her as the young girl who had so often stayed in his home in England.

Lucy became a frequent visitor in the Bretton home, and before long she realized that she was in love with Dr. John. The warm friendship between the two young people was constantly put upon by the ubiquitous Monsieur Paul and his sarcastic raillery.

While at a concert one evening with Dr. John and Mrs. Bretton, Lucy noticed

Ginevra Fanshawe in the audience. Ginevra, having located the doctor's party, began to mimic Mrs. Bretton, who was unaware of the young girl. Dr. John was not. At once he sensed the weakness and the selfishness of Ginevra, who could so irreverently make fun of a woman as good as his mother. His infatuation for Ginevra ended in disgust.

Again at a concert with Lucy, Dr. John rescued a young girl named Paulina from a rough crowd of people. Bringing Paulina Bassompierre to his own home, Dr. John discovered that she was in reality Polly Home, who had stayed at the old Bretton house in England. All the old acquaintances were together again.

Repeated meetings between Polly, now called Paulina, and Dr. John fostered the doctor's love for the girl who had loved him since childhood. Lucy, closing her eyes and ears to this grief, believed that Dr. John was lost to her.

Lucy began a new phase in her life at the school. Madame Beck gave her greater freedom in her work, and Monsieur Paul showed a hearty interest in her mind and in her heart. The only flaw remaining in Lucy's tranquillity was the reappearance of the apparition of the nun.

Once Madame Beck sent Lucy on an errand to the home of Madame Walravens. There Lucy was told a touching story about Monsieur Paul. He had loved a girl, Justine Marie, in his youth, but cruel relatives refused his suit and she subsequently died. Filled with remorse, Monsieur Paul undertook to care for Justine Marie's relatives. There survived old Madame Walravens and a priest, the same man to whom Lucy had confessed. The priest, Father Silas, had been Monsieur Paul's tutor; he was anxious to keep Monsieur Paul from coming under the influence of Lucy, a heretic.

Lucy's affection for the truculent professor grew, but suddenly all her hopes toppled about her. Monsieur Paul was leaving France for the West Indies. Madame Beck, always present when Monsieur Paul and Lucy met, kept the distraught teacher from talking to him.

Ginevra Fanshawe eloped with de Hamal. A letter from the runaway girl explained Lucy's ghostly nun. De Hamal had thus attired himself when making nocturnal visits to Ginevra.

But Monsieur Paul refused to abandon Lucy without an explanation of his sudden forced departure. On the eve of his sailing he arranged a meeting with her and explained his recent silence. Surrounded by his possessive relatives, he had occupied his time with secret arrangements to make Lucy mistress of the school. To avoid the temptation of telling Lucy about his plans before they were consummated, he had remained apart from her. Upon his return, in three years, he promised to rid himself of all his encumbrances, so that he would be free to marry Lucy Snowe.

Critical Evaluation

In *Villette,* Charlotte Brontë returns to the first-person narration used so successfully in *Jane Eyre* and continues exploring the problems and consciousness of a lonely, plain heroine. Although Brontë knew well the scene and subject matter here—she had in Brussels experienced a *pensionnat* similar to that in which Lucy Snowe studies and teaches—she reworks autobiographical details to fit the exigencies of her plot and characters.

But *Villette's* first-person point of view differs from that used in *Jane Eyre,* in accordance with the nature of Lucy Snowe's character. One finds much more character analysis, description, and indirect dialogue as well as more use of reflections, and introspections. There are even short "essays" on diverse subjects. Thus, Brontë uses a first-person narrator who employs several omniscient-narrator techniques. There is little of the immediacy of *Jane Eyre,* as the aged Lucy Snowe relates her early adventures. *Villette* always incorporates that double focus on past and present, which the traditional "novels of education" exhibit. In such *Bildüngsromans,* a matured and now-wiser protagonist narrates his growth, education, and—usually—excesses, now able to look back with sympathy and irony. *Villette,* then, belongs to that illustrious sub-genre which includes Dickens' *Great Expectations,* Joyce's *A Portrait of the Artist as a Young Man,* and Austen's *Emma.* While Lucy Snowe's irony is often over-subtle, it does gradually appear as her personality develops, so that we smile at her earlier retiring, self-effacing attitudes.

Lucy as narrator is never so candid and naïve as Jane Eyre, and when she withholds key information from us—that Dr. John is the Graham of her childhood—we learn to doubt her judgment about other matters as well. We distrust her assessment of Ginevra, who clearly has more life than Lucy, and we do not accept her immoderate anti-Catholicism or her reliance on physiognomy in judging character. We also wish to question Lucy's relativism and timidity. Why does she not confront Madame Beck when she discovers the mistress searching her personal effects? Lucy's justification, that she did not want to make trouble, is not satisfactory. Lucy therefore is a forerunner of the modern unreliable narrator found in works such as Sartre's *Nausea* and Moravia's *The Lie.* All of her judgments must be evaluated instead of being taken at face value.

Brontë had difficulty in making her heroine sympathetic and understandable, for Lucy Snowe has little of the fiery passion of Jane Eyre—at least for most of the novel. The reader may ask, with Ginevra, "Who *are* you, Miss Snowe?" and remain puzzled by Lucy's answer, "Perhaps a personage in disguise." Different characters see Lucy as possessing contradictory qualities: Madame Beck thinks her "learned and blue"; Ginevra regards her as "caustic, ironic, and cynical"; Mr. Home discovers a "sedate and discreet" person. Graham, says Lucy, misreads her character entirely, calling her his "inoffensive shadow"; Monsieur Paul alone persists in seeing her as "adventurous, indocile, and audacious." If in fact Monsieur Paul's estimation is correct, the reader cannot be faulted for agreeing with Graham's earlier view. For Lucy is so self-effacing at the beginning that we nearly forget it is *her* story and not little Polly's. Lucy Snowe's identity remains a theme of vital importance. Her birth and family situation are never made clear; though similar mysteries were solved in *Jane Eyre* and *Shirley,* in *Villette* Lucy is left alone to make her own destiny, to become the person she chooses.

One could say that *Villette* is less a story of Lucy Snowe's education than it is of her achieving an identity. Her inner conflict is always that of Reason and Imagination, Intellect and Passion. Her position, fortune, and upbringing most often favor Reason. She has trained herself to view her own prospects and emotions rationally, rejecting risks and avoiding disappointments, but her inner life is full of passion and turmoil. Imagination urges her to involve herself in life, but she reveals this side of herself only when illness, drugs, or an unreal situation suppress rationality. During a thunderstorm while the rest of the students offer frightened prayers, she creeps out on the roof to enjoy the spectacle; afterward she longs for a change in her existence. Instead of rebelling, however, Lucy figuratively "knocks her longing on the head." At a school play she is pressed into service as the foppish lover and is surprised and then frightened by the exhilaration of acting. Monsieur Paul is the only character who has correctly read the passionate part of her personality, and it is only as his affection for her grows that she gradually accepts and nourishes this part of her being. She expands her knowledge under his tutelage—he all the while mocking her in order to break down her reserve. She becomes less shy, more vocal, and harbors fewer feelings of inferiority.

The municipal fête visited by a drugged Lucy suggests how far she has come in her search for identity. The celebration commemorates an occasion in which the city successfully defended its freedom. Lucy's new free personality is at this time being threatened by Madame Beck. She sees various people she has depended on in the past, but now the active side of her being makes them unnecessary. Lucy is able to confront Madame Beck with honesty: "Oh, Madame! In *your* hand is both chill and poison." Finally, Lucy's new school, begun with Monsieur Paul's generosity, enables her to cultivate her precious new identity, conquering self-consciousness and timidity. That she does not submerge her personality into Monsieur Paul's is shown clearly in her maintenance of her Protestant faith. Her personality is disguised no more, and even Monsieur Paul's hinted death cannot change that.

A word about the fact that more than a little of the novel's conversation is carried on in French: without an annotated edition, a modern reader will have some difficulty if he cannot read French. The French conversation, though, helps to convey the sense of isolation Lucy feels until she is competent in the foreign tongue. Soon, however, she is making distinctions in the subtleties of the two languages, such as refusing to call Monsieur Paul "*mon ami*" while not quailing at "my friend."

Bibliography

Beer, Patricia. *Reader, I Married Him: A Study of the Women Characters of Jane Austen, Charlotte Brontë, Elizabeth Gaskell and George Eliot.* London: Macmillan, 1974, pp. 87–126.

Bentley, Phyllis. *The Brontës.* New York: Haskell House, 1975, pp. 75–81.

Blackall, Jean F. "Point of View in *Villette*," in *Journal of Narrative Technique.* VI (1976), pp. 14–28.

Burkhart, Charles. *Charlotte Brontë: A Psychosexual Study of Her Novels.* London: Gollancz, 1973, pp. 96–121.

_____. "The Names of *Villette*," in *Victorian Newsletter.* XLIV (1973), pp. 8–13.

Colby, Robert A. "*Villette* and the Life of the Mind," in *PMLA.* LXXV (1960), pp. 410–419.

Coursen, Herbert R., Jr. "Storm and Calm in *Villette*," in *Discourse.* V (Summer, 1962), pp. 318–333.

Craik, W.A. *The Brontë Novels.* London: Methuen, 1968, pp. 158–201.

Dunbar, Georgia S. "Proper Names in *Villette*," in *Nineteenth-Century Fiction.* XV (June, 1960), pp. 77–80.

Evans, Joan. *The Flowering of the Middle Ages.* New York: McGraw-Hill, 1966, pp. 11–40.

Goldfarb, Russell M. *Sexual Repression and ˙Victorian Literature.* Lewisburg, Pa.: Bucknell University Press, 1970, pp. 139–157.

Hook, Andrew D. "Charlotte Brontë, the Imagination, and *Villette*," in *The Brontës: A Collection of Critical Essays.* Edited by Ian Gregor. Englewood Cliffs, N.J.: Prentice-Hall, 1970, pp. 137–156.

Johnson, E.D.H. " 'Daring the Dread Glance': Charlotte Brontë's Treatment of the Supernatural in *Villette*," in *Nineteenth-Century Fiction.* XX (March, 1966), pp. 325–336.

Knies, Earl A. *The Art of Charlotte Brontë.* Athens: Ohio University Press, 1969, pp. 171–200.

Kroeber, Karl. *Styles in Fictional Structure: The Art of Jane Austen, Charlotte Brontë, George Eliot.* Princeton, N.J.: Princeton University Press, 1971, pp. 89–94, 109–112, 151–180.

Mews, Hazel. *Frail Vessels: Woman's Role in Women's Novels from Fanny Burney to George Eliot.* London: Athlone, 1969, pp. 77–80.

Oldfield, Jennifer. " 'The Homely Web of Truth': Dress as the Mirror of Personality in *Jane Eyre* and *Villette*," in *Brontë Society Transactions.* XVI (1973), pp. 181–193.

O'Neill, Judith.   *Critics on Charlotte and Emily Brontë: Readings in Literary Criticism.* Coral Gables, Fla.: University of Miami Press, 1968, pp. 38–47.

Pascal, Roy.   "The Autobiographical Novel and the Autobiography," in *Essays in Criticism.* IX (April, 1959), pp. 134–150.

Pinion, F.B.   *A Brontë Companion: Literary Assessment, Background, and Reference.* London: Macmillan, 1975.

Platt, Carolyn V.   "How Feminist Is *Villette*?," in *Women and Literature.* III (1975), pp. 16–27.

Sherry, Norman.   *Charlotte and Emily Brontë.* London: Evans, 1969, pp. 85–100.

Tillotson, Geoffrey.   *A View of Victorian Literature.* Oxford: Clarendon Press, 1978.

Williams, Raymond.   *The English Novel: From Dickens to Lawrence.* London: Chatto and Windus, 1970, pp. 70–74.

Wilson, F.A.C.   "The Primrose Wreath: The Heroes of the Brontë Novels," in *Nineteenth-Century Fiction.* XXIX (1974), pp. 48–49.

WUTHERING HEIGHTS

Type of work: Novel
Author: Emily Brontë (1818–1848)
Type of plot: Impressionistic romance
Time of plot: 1757–1803
Locale: The moors of northern England
First published: 1847

Published under the pseudonym Ellis Bell, this famous novel was once considered such a risk by its publishers that Emily Brontë had to defray the cost of publication until a sufficient number of copies had been sold. Despite some scenes of romantic exaggeration, Wuthering Heights *is an intriguing tale of revenge in which the main figures exist in the more than life-size vitality of their own consuming passions.*

Principal Characters

Heathcliff, a dark-visaged, violently passionate, black-natured man. A foundling brought to the Earnshaw home at an early age, he is subjected to cruel emotional sufferings during his formative years. His chief tormentor is Hindley Earnshaw, who is jealous of his father's obvious partiality toward Heathcliff. These he endures with the sullen patience of a hardened, ill-treated animal, but just as the years add age his suffering adds hatred in Heathcliff's nature and he becomes filled with an inhuman, almost demonic, desire for vengeance against Hindley. This ambition coupled with his strange, transcendent relationship with Catherine, Hindley's sister, encompasses his life until he becomes a devastatingly wasted human, in fact, hardly human at all. He evaluates himself as a truly superior person who, possessing great emotional energies and capabilities, is a creature set apart from the human. Some regard him as a fiend, full of horrible passions and powers. In the end he dies empty, his will gone, his fervor exhausted, survived by Cathy and Hareton, the conventionalists, the moralists, the victims of his vengeful wraths.

Catherine Earnshaw, the sister of Hindley, later the wife of Edgar Linton and mother of young Cathy Linton. Catherine is spirited as a girl, selfish, wild, saucy, provoking, and sometimes even wicked. But she can be sweet of eye and smile, and she is often contrite for causing pain with her insolence. In childhood she and Heathcliff form an unusually close relationship, but as her friendship with Edgar and Isabella Linton grows, she becomes haughty and arrogant. In spite of her devotion to Heathcliff she rejects him for fear marriage to him would degrade her. Instead, she accepts Edgar Linton's proposal. But her deep feeling for Heathcliff remains; he is her one unselfishness, and she insists that Edgar must at least tolerate him so that her marriage will not alter her friendship with Heathcliff. Her marriage is a tolerably happy one, possibly because Catherine becomes unspirited after Heathcliff's departure because of her rejection. Upon his return they become close friends again, despite his apparent vile character and foul treatment of her family. In their inhuman passion and fierce, tormented love they are lost to each other, each possessing the other's spirit as if it were his own. Her mind broken and anguished, Catherine finally dies in childbirth.

Hindley Earnshaw, the brother of Catherine Earnshaw, husband of Frances, and father of Hareton. As a child he is intensely jealous of Heathcliff and treats the boy cruelly. After the death of Frances, Hindley's character deteriorates rapidly; he drinks heavily and finally dies in disgrace, debt, and degradation as the result of Heathcliff's scheme of vengeance.

Edgar Linton, the husband of Catherine and father of Cathy. A polished, cultured man, he is truly in love with Catherine and makes her happy until Heathcliff returns to Wuthering Heights. He is a steady, unassuming person, patient and indulgent of both his wife and his daughter.

Cathy Linton, the daughter of Edgar and Catherine and wife of Linton Heathcliff. A bright, spirited affectionate girl, she pities Linton, becomes his friend, and through the trickery and bribery of Heathcliff is forced to marry the sickly young man. She becomes sullen and ill-tempered in Heathcliff's household, but she finds ultimate happiness with Hareton Earnshaw.

Hareton Earnshaw, the son of Hindley and Frances and the object of Heathcliff's revenge against Hindley. Under Heathcliff's instruction, or rather neglect, Hareton grows into a crude, gross, uneducated young man until Cathy, after Heathcliff's death, takes him under her charge and begins to improve his mind and manners. The two fall in love and marry.

Linton Heathcliff, the son of Heathcliff and Isabella and the husband of Cathy Linton. He is a selfish boy indulged and spoiled by his mother. After her death he returns to live with Heathcliff and at Wuthering Heights sinks into a weak-willed existence, a victim of his father's harsh treatment. Sickly since infancy, he dies at an early age, shortly after his marriage to Cathy Linton.

Isabella Linton, the sister of Edgar, Heathcliff's wife, and mother of Linton. A rather reserved, spoiled, often sulking girl, she becomes infatuated with Heathcliff, and in spite of her family's opposition and warnings she runs away with him. Later, regretting her foolish action, she leaves him and lives with her son Linton until her death.

Frances Earnshaw, the wife of Hindley; she dies of consumption.

Mr. Earnshaw, the father of Catherine and Hindley. He brings Heathcliff to Wuthering Heights after a business trip to Liverpool.

Mrs. Earnshaw, his wife.

Mrs. Ellen Dean, called **Nelly,** the housekeeper who relates Heathcliff's history to Mr. Lockwood and thereby serves as one of the book's narrators. A servant in the household at Wuthering Heights, she goes with Catherine to Thrushcross Grange when the latter marries Edgar Linton. Some years later she returns to live at Wuthering Heights as the housekeeper for Heathcliff. She is a humble, solid character, conventional, reserved, and patient. Although Hindley's disorderly home and Heathcliff's evil conduct distress her, often appall her, she does little to combat these unnatural personalities, perhaps through lack of imagination but certainly not from lack of will, for in the face of Heathcliff's merciless vengeance she is stanch and strong.

Mr. Lockwood, the first narrator, a foppish visitor from the city and Heathcliff's tenant. Interested in his landlord, he hears Mrs. Dean relate the story of the Earnshaw and Linton families.

Joseph, a servant at Wuthering Heights. He is forever making gloomy observations and predictions about other people and offering stern reprimands for their impious behavior.

Zillah, a servant at Wuthering Heights.

Mr. Green and   neighboring village.
Mr. Kenneth, lawyers in Gimmerton, a

The Story

In 1801 Mr. Lockwood became a tenant at Thrushcross Grange, an old farm owned by Mr. Heathcliff of Wuthering Heights. In the early days of his tenancy he made two calls on his landlord. On his first visit he met Heathcliff, an abrupt, unsocial man, surrounded by a pack of snarling, barking dogs. When he went to Wuthering Heights a second time, he met the other members of that strange household; a rude, unkempt but handsome young man named Hareton Earnshaw and a pretty young woman who was the widow of Heathcliff's son.

During his visit snow began to fall, covering the moor paths and making travel impossible for a stranger in that bleak countryside. Heathcliff refused to let one of the servants go with him as a guide, but said that if he stayed the night he could share Hareton's bed or that of Joseph, a sour, canting old servant. When Mr. Lockwood tried to borrow Joseph's lantern for the homeward journey, the old fellow set the dogs on him, to the amusement of Hareton and Heathcliff. The visitor was finally rescued by Zillah, the cook, who hid him in an unused chamber of the house.

That night Mr. Lockwood had a strange dream. Thinking that a branch was rattling against the window, he broke the glass in his attempt to unhook the casement. As he reached out to break off the fir branch outside, his fingers closed on a small ice-cold hand and a weeping voice begged to be let in. The unseen presence, who said that her name was Catherine Linton, tried to force a way through the broken casement, and Mr. Lockwood screamed.

Heathcliff appeared in a state of great excitement and savagely ordered Mr. Lockwood out of the room. Then he threw himself upon the bed by the shattered pane and begged the spirit to come in out of the dark and the storm. But the voice was heard no more—only the hiss of swirling snow and the wailing of a cold wind that blew out the smoking candle.

Ellen Dean satisfied part of Mr. Lockwood's curiosity about the happenings of that night and the strange household at Wuthering Heights. She was the housekeeper at Thrushcross Grange, but she had lived at Wuthering Heights during her childhood.

Her story of the Earnshaws, Lintons, and Heathcliffs began years before, when old Mr. Earnshaw was living at Wuthering Heights with his wife and two children, Hindley and Catherine. Once on a trip to Liverpool Mr. Earnshaw had found a starving and homeless orphan, a ragged, dirty, urchin, dark as a gypsy, whom he brought back with him to Wuthering Heights and christened Heathcliff—a name which was to serve the fourteen-year-old boy as both a given and a surname. Gradually the orphan began to usurp the affections of Mr. Earnshaw, whose health was failing. Wuthering Heights became a bedlam of petty jealousies; Hindley was jealous of both Heathcliff and Catherine; old Joseph, the servant, augmented the bickering; and Catherine was much too fond of Heathcliff. At last Hindley was sent away to school. A short time later Mr. Earnshaw died.

When Hindley Earnshaw returned home for his father's funeral, he brought a wife with him. As the new master of Wuthering Heights, he revenged himself on Heathcliff by treating him as a servant. Catherine became a wild and undisciplined hoyden who still continued her affection for Heathcliff.

One night Catherine and Heathcliff tramped over the moors to Thrushcross Grange, where they spied on their neighbors, the Lintons. Catherine, attacked by a watchdog, was taken into the house and stayed there as a guest for five weeks until she was able to walk again. Thus she became intimate with the pleasant family of Thrushcross Grange—Mr. and Mrs. Linton, and their two children, Edgar and Isabella. Afterward the Lintons visited frequently at Wuthering Heights. The combination of ill-treatment on the part of Hindley and arrogance on the part of Edgar and Isabella made Heathcliff jealous and ill-tempered. He vowed revenge on Hindley Earnshaw, whom he hated with all the sullen fury of his savage nature.

The next summer Hindley's consumptive wife, Frances, gave birth to a son, Hareton Earnshaw, and a short time later she died. In his grief Hindley became desperate, ferocious, and degenerate. In the meantime, Catherine Earnshaw and Edgar Linton had become sweethearts. The girl confided to Ellen Dean that she really loved Heathcliff, but she felt it would be degrading for her to marry the penniless orphan. Heathcliff, who overheard this conversation, disappeared the same night, not to return for many years. Edgar and Catherine soon married, taking up their abode at Thrushcross Grange with Ellen Dean as their housekeeper. There the pair lived happily until Heathcliff's return caused trouble between them. When he returned to the moors, Heathcliff, greatly improved in manners and appearance, accepted Hindley's invitation to live at Wuthering Heights—an invitation offered by Hindley because he found in Heathcliff a boon companion at cards and drink, and he hoped to recoup his own dwindling fortune from Heathcliff's pockets.

Isabella Linton began to show a sudden, irresistible attraction to Heathcliff, much to the dismay of Edgar and Catherine. One night Edgar and Heathcliff came to blows. Soon afterward Heathcliff eloped with Isabella, obviously marrying her only to avenge himself and provoke Edgar. Catherine, an expectant mother, underwent a serious attack of fever. When Isabella and her husband returned to Wuthering Heights, Edgar refused to recognize his sister and forbade Heathcliff to enter his house. Despite this restriction, Heathcliff managed a final tender interview with Catherine. Partly as a result of this meeting, her child, named Catherine Linton, was born prematurely. The mother died a few hours later.

Isabella, in the meantime, had found life with Heathcliff unbearable. Leaving him, she went to London, where a few months later her child, Linton, was born. With the death of Hindley, Heathcliff the guest became the master of Wuthering Heights, for Hindley had mortgaged everything to him. Hareton, the natural heir, was reduced to dependency on his father's enemy.

Twelve years after leaving Heathcliff, Isabella died and her brother took the sickly child to live at Thrushcross Grange. Heathcliff soon heard of the child's arrival and demanded that Linton be sent to Wuthering Heights to live with his father. Young Catherine once visited Wuthering Heights and met her cousin Linton. Her father had tried to keep her in ignorance about the tenants of the place, for Heathcliff had been at pains to let it be known that he wished the two children, Cathy and Linton, to be married. And Heathcliff had his way. About the time that Edgar Linton became seriously ill, Heathcliff persuaded Cathy to visit her little cousin, who was also in extremely bad health. Cathy, on her arrival, was imprisoned for five days at Wuthering Heights and forced to marry her sickly cousin Linton before she was allowed to go home to see her father. Although she was able to return to Thrushcross Grange before her father's death, there was not enough time for Edgar Linton to alter his will. Thus his land and fortune went indirectly to Heathcliff. Weak, sickly Linton Heathcliff died soon after, leaving Cathy a widow and dependent on Heathcliff.

Mr. Lockwood went back to London in the spring without seeing Wuthering Heights or its people again. Traveling in the region the next autumn, he had a fancy to revisit Wuthering Heights. He found Catherine and Hareton now in possession. From Ellen Dean he heard the story of Heathcliff's death three months before. He had died after four days of deliberate starvation, a broken man disturbed by memories of the beautiful young Catherine Earnshaw. His death freed Catherine Heathcliff and Hareton from his tyranny. Catherine was now teaching the ignorant boy to read and to improve his rude manners.

Mr. Lockwood went to see Heathcliff's grave. It was on the other side of Catherine Earnshaw from her husband. They lay under their three headstones; Catherine's in the middle weather-discolored and half-buried, Edgar's partly moss-grown, Heathcliff's still bare. In the surrounding countryside there was a legend that these people slept unquietly after their stormy, passionate lives. Shepherds and travelers at night claimed that they had seen Catherine and Heathcliff roaming the dark moors as they had done so many years before.

Critical Evaluation

F. R. Leavis, in his influential *The Great Tradition* (1948), calls *Wuthering Heights* a "sport." He cannot find a clear place for the book in his historical scheme of the English novel's development. The novel has eluded classification since its publication, and to this day its characters and ideas perplex and fascinate. The source of its energy lies in the powerful tension between its plot and its characters, between its organization and its themes. Dorothy

Van Ghent (*The English Novel,* 1953) observes that in plot and design the book has rigorous "limitation" although its characters are passionately immoderate; as a result the story is constantly explosive. Time and space force their restrictions on spirits straining to be free.

After an initial reading, the reader tends only to remember the most violent or emotional scenes and thinks back on the organization of the novel as a mere string for fiery gems: Lockwood's dream, Cathy and Heathcliff fighting off the dogs of Thrushcross Grange, Heathcliff at Cathy's deathbed, or countless moments of cruelty and ecstasy involving all the characters. On closer analysis, the reader discovers the intricate interweaving of the novel's four parts into the core-story of Catherine and Heathcliff. The scheme can be summarized as follows: the establishment of the violently passionate relationship betwen Catherine and Heathcliff; Catherine's rejection of marriage with Heathcliff, and her marriage to Edgar Linton and death in childbirth; Heathcliff's revenge; and Heathcliff's disintegration and death.

In addition to this four-part design, with its intricate changes in time and relationships among secondary characters, the novel is prescribed by the spatial and social polarity of Wuthering Heights and Thrushcross Grange. Without all these defining and prescriptive forms, the metaphysical revolt that underlies the relationship between Catherine and Heathcliff would not have a sufficient antagonist; to put it another way, the pressures designed to crush them help to make their haunting and demonic challenge to experience credible.

How do Catherine and Heathcliff do it? How does Emily Brontë empower her protagonists to overcome time, space and society? She makes their minds independent of empirical reality. Catherine confides to Ellen Dean that "dreams . . . have stayed with me . . . and changed my ideas; they've gone through and through me, like wine through water, and altered the colour of my mind." Unlike Lockwood, who is terribly frightened by his nightmare, Catherine connects her dreaming with self-definition. In Catherine's dream the angels in Heaven are so offended by her "weeping to come back to earth . . . that they flung" her out "into the middle of the heath on the top of Wuthering Heights," where she wakes "sobbing for joy." Long before she dies physically, Catherine resurrects herself in her imagination; the irony of this religious vision is that it reverses traditional priorities: earth becomes a paradise to Heaven's misery. A "vision" of Nature replaces the phenomenal world of time and space.

Gods are realized in the minds of their worshipers. Catherine has only one worshiper, Heathcliff, but he is powerful enough to substitute for the multitudes. Heathcliff is Catherine's Faith because their souls are interchangeable ("Nelly, I am Heathcliff"); powerless to resist her intensity, Heathcliff is sanctified by her identification with him. The terms are diabolical: " . . . you have treated me infernally," complains Heathcliff to Catherine after his return to Wuthering Heights. In response to Catherine's plea that he refrain from marrying Isabella Linton, Heathcliff lashes back: "The tyrant (and he means Catherine) grinds down his slaves and they don't turn against him, they crush those beneath them." The terms may be diabolical, but the actuality is seraphic. Emily Brontë is similar to William Blake in the way she reverses the values of Heaven and Hell in order to dramatize and release a spiritually revolutionary moral energy.

When Heathcliff learns of Catherine's illness, he tells Ellen Dean that "existence after losing her would be hell." Indeed, the love Heathcliff and Catherine share is a new kind of emotional paradise, despite its pain and destiny of frustration, so that when Catherine lies ill on what will be her death-bed, Heathcliff is literally witness to a crucifixion. Afraid that Heathcliff will be harmed by Linton once he discovers them together, Catherine's words ring with beatific self-denial: "Kiss me again; and don't let me see your eyes. I forgive what you have done to me. I love my murderer—but *yours!* How can I?" When Ellen tells him shortly afterward of Catherine's death, Heathcliff demands that she haunt him to his dying day since life without her is inconceivable. Just as Catherine preferred Nature with Heathcliff to Heaven without him in her dreams, Heathcliff spends the rest of his life rejecting earthly possibilities and directs the track of his spiritual and mental energies toward reunion with Catherine: "I cannot live without my soul!" And when the time comes, he prepares for his death as if it were salvation: "Last night, I was on the threshold of hell. Today, I am within sight of my heaven."

These two lovers literally inhabit a psychic and emotional world entirely their own. Ellen Dean seems an honest observer, but her conventional imagination makes her finally a spiritual stranger to all the facts she so carefully relates. Lockwood is awed by the lovers' story, but he "sees" it at a great distance because of limitations of feeling and perception. Three generations of Lintons and Earnshaws together with the conflicts of class and religious differences embodied in the juxtaposition of "Heights" and "Grange," seem merely an insignificant background to the classless, timeless, and eerily universal passion of these two children of the moor.

Bibliography

Blondel, Jacques. "Imagery in *Wuthering Heights*," in *Durham University Journal*. XXXVII (1976), pp. 1–7.

Brick, Allen R. "*Wuthering Heights*: Narrators, Audience and Message," in *College English*. XXI (November, 1959), pp. 80–86.

Burns, Wayne. "In Death They Were Not Divided: The Moral Magnificence of Unmoral Passion in *Wuthering Heights*," in *Hartford Studies in Literature*. V (1973), pp. 135–159.

Craik, W.A.   *The Brontë Novels*. London: Methuen, 1968, pp. 5–47.

Davies, Cecil W.   "A Reading of *Wuthering Heights*," in *Essays in Criticism*. XIX (July, 1969), pp. 254–272.

Drew, Elizabeth A.   *The Novel; A Modern Guide to Fifteen English Master-pieces*. New York: Norton, 1963, pp. 173–190.

Fraser, John.   "The Name of Action: Nelly Dean and *Wuthering Heights*," in *Nineteenth-Century Fiction*. XX (December, 1965), pp. 223–236.

Gose, Elliott B., Jr.   "*Wuthering Heights*: The Heath and the Hearth," in *Nineteenth-Century Fiction*. XXI (June, 1966), pp. 1–19.

Grove, Robin.   "*Wuthering Heights*," in *Critical Review*. VIII (1965), pp. 70–87.

Karl, Frederick R.   *An Age of Fiction; The Nineteenth-Century British Novel*. New York: Farrar, Straus and Giroux, 1964, pp. 77–103.

Kooiman-Van Middendorp, Gerarda M.   *The Hero in the Feminine Novel*. New York: Haskell House, 1966, pp. 78–81.

Langman, F.H.   "*Wuthering Heights*," in *Essays in Criticism*. XV (July, 1965), pp. 294–312.

Lettis, Richard and William E. Morris.   *A* Wuthering Heights *Handbook*. New York: Odyssey Press, 1961.

Madden, William A.   "*Wuthering Heights*: The Binding of Passion," in *Nineteenth-Century Fiction*. XXVII (1972), pp. 127–154.

Moser, Thomas.   "What Is the Matter with Emily Jane? Conflicting Impulses in *Wuthering Heights*," in *Nineteenth-Century Fiction*. XVII (June, 1962), pp. 1–19.

O'Neill, Judith.   *Critics on Charlotte and Emily Brontë; Readings in Literary Criticism*. Coral Gables, Fla.: University of Miami Press, 1968, pp. 50–101.

Roberts, Mark.   *The Tradition of Romantic Morality*. London: Macmillan, 1973, pp. 158–197.

Sagar, Keith.   "The Originality of *Wuthering Heights*," in *The Art of Emily Brontë*. Edited by Anne Smith. New York: Barnes & Noble, 1976, pp. 121–159.

Shapiro, Arnold.   "*Wuthering Heights* as a Victorian Novel," in *Studies in the Novel*. I (1969), pp. 284–296.

Shunami, Gideon.   "The Unreliable Narrator in *Wuthering Heights*," in *Nineteenth-Century Fiction*. XXVII (1973), pp. 449–468.

Sucksmith, H.P.   "The Theme of *Wuthering Heights* Reconsidered," in *Dalhousie Review*. LIV (1974), pp. 418–428.

Van de Laar, Elisabeth Th. M.   *The Inner Structure of* Wuthering Heights*: A Study of an Imaginative Field.* The Hague: Mouton, 1969.

Vargish, Thomas.   "Revenge and *Wuthering Heights*," in *Studies in the Novel.* III (1971), pp. 7–17.

Vogler, Thomas A.   *Twentieth-Century Interpretations of* Wuthering Heights. Englewood Cliffs, N.J.: Prentice-Hall, 1968.

Wilson, F.A.C.   "The Primrose Wreath: The Heroes of the Brontë Novels," in *Nineteenth-Century Fiction.* XXIX (1974), pp. 50–57.

SAMUEL BUTLER

Born: Langar, England (December 4, 1835)
Died: London, England (June 18, 1902)

Principal Works

NOVELS: *Erewhon*, 1872; *Erewhon Revisited*, 1901; *The Way of All Flesh*, 1903.

ESSAYS AND STUDIES: *Evolution, Old and New*, 1879; *Unconscious Memory*, 1880; *The Humor of Homer*, 1892; *The Authoress of Homer*, 1897; *Shakespeare's Sonnets Reconsidered*, 1899.

TRANSLATIONS: The *Iliad*, 1898; the *Odyssey*, 1900.

Samuel Butler, English novelist and essayist, was born at Langar, Nottinghamshire, December 4, 1835, the son of the Reverend Thomas Butler and the grandson of a Bishop of Lichfield. This clerical ancestry was to have its influence on his writings. He was educated at St. John's College, Cambridge, and was intended for the Church; but, because of religious doubts he declined to take orders, preferring to study painting. The resulting estrangement between his father and himself led him to emigrate to New Zealand in 1859, where he spent five years in sheep farming. He became interested in Darwin and wrote *Darwin Among the Machines* (1863), the germ of *Erewhon*. Returning to England in 1864, he continued his painting, exhibiting regularly, and also composed music. He became a friend of Darwin, but disagreed with the latter's theory of evolution and wrote several books to advance a theory of his own, which was not taken very seriously by scientists.

Butler's next phase was classical. He became interested in the Homeric question, maintaining that the *Iliad* and the *Odyssey* were by different authors and that the latter was written by a woman. Like his books on evolution, these writings now belong to the curiosities of literature.

Butler's importance lies in his contribution to the reaction against Victorianism. *Erewhon* ("nowhere") is a satire on the machine age and the forerunner of several modern novels. By depicting a society in which the possession of any mechanical device is illegal, he made fun of nineteenth century industrialism, and then proceeded to satirize much of Victorian morality. In *Erewhon* sickness is a crime, whereas crime is a sickness and is treated as such. Thus, society's attitude towards morals is the product of convention; it is as illogical to condemn a man for stealing as to condemn him for contracting influenza.

Butler's really important novel is *The Way of All Flesh*, written between 1873 and 1885 but not published until a year after his death. This book, which Shaw claimed had influenced him greatly, is a satiric portrait of Butler's own childhood. Theobald and Christina Pontifex are his parents, while Butler appears twice: as Overton, the narrator, and as Ernest, the repressed son. It is a terrible picture of the worst side of Victorian family life, with its excessive strictness, exaggerated piety, and hypocrisy. The book is hardly a novel; it is a series of essays in which Butler attacked the shams of the world of his childhood in a clergyman's family and at the same time expressed his philosophy of common sense. His hero is the prototype of the modern youth who revolts against his parents' *mores* and eventually builds a life of his own. It is the story of Butler's own struggle for freedom. Butler died in London, June 18, 1902.

Bibliography

The collected writings of Samuel Butler have been published in The Shrewsbury Edition, edited by H. F. Jones and A. T. Bartholomew, 20 vols., 1923–1926. The standard biography is H. F. Jones, *Samuel Butler: A Memoir*, 2 vols., 1919. For letters see Daniel F. Howard, ed., *The Correspondence of Samuel Butler with His Sister, May*, 1962; and Arnold Silver, ed., *The Family Letters of Samuel Butler, 1841–1886*, 1962. See also Clara G. Stillman, *Samuel Butler: A Mid-Victorian Modern*, 1932; Malcolm Muggeridge, *The Earnest Atheist*, 1937; George Bernard Shaw, Introduction to *The Way of All Flesh*, 1936 (Oxford University Press); Edmund Wilson, *The Triple Thinkers*, 1938; Lee E. Holt, *Samuel Butler*, 1964; and *ibidem*, "Samuel Butler's Rise to Fame," *Publications of the Modern Language Society*, LVII (1942), 867–878.

EREWHON

Type of work: Novel
Author: Samuel Butler (1835–1902)
Type of plot: Utopian satire
Time of plot: 1870's
Locale: Erewhon and England
First published: 1872

"Erewhon" is an anagram of "nowhere," but the institutions satirized in this novel are unmistakably British. Much of its satire growing out of the ideas of Charles Darwin and Thomas Huxley, Erewhon *begins as an adventure story but develops into an elaborate allegory. Some of the targets of satire are psychologists ("straighteners" in Butler's utopia) and the system of criminal justice.*

Principal Characters

Higgs, a blond young sheep farm worker who journeys into Erewhon; he discovers there a civilization partly the reverse of and partly similar to that of England. Somewhat like Swift's Gulliver, Higgs seems a thoughtful, observant, inquiring, and sometimes rather naïve traveler. He should not be identified with the author, since Butler used him only as a convenient mouthpiece to convey the satire in the novel.

Kahabuka (Chowbok), an old native, a sort of chief with a little knowledge of English and a great thirst for grog, with which Higgs bribes him for information about the land beyond the mountains. In England, upon his return, Higgs finds Chowbok posing as a missionary, the Reverend William Habakkuk.

Senoj Nosnibor (anagram for Jones Robinson), a citizen and leading merchant of Erewhon recovering, as if from sickness, from a serious case of embezzlement. He is assigned to instruct Higgs in Erewhonian customs.

Arowhena, his beautiful younger daughter, with whom Higgs falls in love. She helps him to escape from Erewhon, after which they marry and she is baptized into the Anglican Church, though she retains some of her former beliefs in Erewhonian deities who personify hope, fear, love, and the like.

Ydgrun (anagram of Grundy), Erewhon's main goddess, both an abstract concept and a silly, cruel woman. A law of Ydgrun enforces conformity to the point of intolerability. Her devotees, including priests, worship her in heart and deed rather than in words.

Zulora, the handsome older daughter of Nosnibor. She wishes to marry Higgs who develops a dislike for her.

Yram (anagram for Mary), the jailor's pretty daughter, who is attracted to Higgs. She teaches him the Erewhonian language and explains to him some of the customs of the land.

The Straighteners, specialists who treat Erewhonians suffering from ailments such as petty theft and embezzlement. They resemble twentieth century psychiatrists.

Mahaina, a homely woman, reputedly a drunkard, whose supposed drinking may perhaps be what would today be called a compensation for an inferiority complex.

Thims (anagram for Smith), a cashier at   Giovanni Gianni, captain of the ship
a musical bank; a friend of Higgs,   which rescues Higgs and Arowhena.

The Story

Higgs a young man of twenty-two, worked on a sheep farm. From the plains he
looked often at the seemingly impassable mountain range that formed the edge of
the sheep country and wondered about the land beyond those towering peaks.
From one old native named Chowbok he learned that the country was forbidden.
Chowbok assumed a strange pose when questioned further and uttered unearthly
cries. Curious, Higgs persuaded Chowbok to go on a trip with him into the
mountains.

They were unable to find a pass through the mountains. One day Higgs came
upon a small valley and went up it alone. He found that it led through the mountains. When he went back to get Chowbok, he saw the old native fleeing toward
the plains. He went on alone. After climbing down treacherous cliffs and crossing
a river on a reed raft, he finally came to beautiful rolling plain. He passed by
some strange manlike statues which made terrifying noises as the wind circled
about them. He recognized in them the reason for Chowbok's performance.

Higgs awoke next morning to see a flock of goats about him, two girls herding
them. When the girls saw him they ran and brought some men to look at him. All
of them were physically handsome. Convinced at last that Higgs was a human
being, they took him to a small town close by. There his clothing was searched
and a watch he had with him was confiscated. The men seemed to be especially
interested in his health, and he was allowed to leave only after a strict medical
examination. He wondered why there had been such confusion over his watch
until he was shown a museum in which was kept old pieces of machinery. Finally
he was put in jail.

In jail he learned the language and something of the strange customs of the
country, which was called Erewhon. The oddest custom was to consider disease a
crime; anyone who was sick was tried and put in jail. On the other hand, people
who committed robbery or murder were treated sympathetically and given hospital care. Shortly afterward the jailor informed Higgs that he had been summoned
to appear before the king and queen, and that he was to be the guest of a man
named Nosnibor. Nosnibor had embezzled a large sum of money from a poor
widow, but he was now recovering from his illness. The widow, Higgs learned,
would be tried and sentenced for allowing herself to be imposed upon.

In the capital Higgs stayed with Nosnibor and his family and paid several
visits to the court. He was well received because he had blond hair, a rarity
among the Erewhonians. He learned a great deal about the past history of the
country. Twenty-five hundred years before a prophet had preached that it was
unlawful to eat meat, as man should not kill his fellow creatures. For several
hundred years the Erewhonians were vegetarians. Then another sage showed that
animals were no more the fellow creatures of man than plants were and that if

man could not kill and eat animals he should not kill and eat plants. The logic of his arguments overthrew the old philosophy. Two hundred years before a great scientist had presented the idea that machines had minds and feelings and that if man were not careful the machine would finally become the ruling creature on earth. Consequently all machines had been scrapped.

The economy of the country was unusual. There were two monetary systems, one worthless except for spiritual meaning, one used in trade. The more respected system was the valueless one, and its work was carried on in Musical Banks where people exchanged coins for music. The state religion was a worship of various qualities of godhead, such as love, fear, and wisdom, and the main goddess, Ydgrun, was at the same time an abstract concept and a silly, cruel woman. Higgs learned much of the religion from Arowhena, one of Nosnibor's daughters. She was a beautiful girl, and the two fell in love.

Because Nosnibor insisted that his older daughter, Zulora, be married first, Higgs and his host had an argument, and Higgs found lodgings elsewhere. Arowhena met him often at the Musical Banks. Higgs visited the University of Unreason, where the young Erewhonian boys were taught to do anything except that which was practical. They studied obsolete languages and hypothetical sciences. He saw a relationship between these schools and the mass-mind which the educational system in England was producing. Higgs also learned that money was considered a symbol of duty, and that the more money a man had the better man he was.

Nosnibor learned that Higgs was meeting Arowhena secretly. Then the king began to worry over the fact that Higgs had entered the country with a watch, and he feared that Higgs might try to bring machinery back into use. Planning an escape, Higgs proposed to the queen that he make a balloon trip to talk with the god of the air. The queen was delighted with the idea. The king hoped that Higgs would fall and kill himself.

Higgs smuggled Arowhena aboard the balloon with him. The couple soon found themselves high in the air and moving over the mountain range. When the balloon settled on the sea, Higgs and Arowhena were picked up by a passing ship. In England, where they were married, Higgs tried to get up an expedition to go back to Erewhon. Only the missionaries listened to his story. Then Chowbok, Higgs' faithless native friend, showed up in England teaching religion, and his appearance convinced people that Erewhon actually did exist. Higgs hoped to return to the country soon to teach it Christianity.

Critical Evaluation

Erewhon is Butler's attempt to work into novel form four philosophic papers written between 1860 and 1870; these appear as the chapters in the novel entitled "The Book of the Machines," "The World of the Unborn," "The Musical Banks," and "Some Erewhonian Trials." While apparently dissimilar, these pivotal chapters all treat the theme of free will, thus unifying the book.

In adapting to his environment, man constructs machines which threaten his survival. With prophetic insight, Butler examines this irony. He argues that the laws governing organic evolution also apply to machines and their development. Challenging the distinction between "organic" and "inorganic," Butler reduces all processes to their mechanical basis and shows how machines are evolving independently of human control. Like Marx, he sees man's nature as changing under the impact of a mechanized environment. But unlike Marx, he predicts man's ultimate enslavement by this environment.

Both comic and serious elements mingle in the Erewhonian myth of pre-existence. Because the "unborn" *will* to become humans, they must bear the consequences of their choice. Thus the Erewhonians make babies sign "birth formulae" which absolve parents from responsibility for the deprivations and deficiencies which go with living. The unborn also elect to share man's essential fate: to be "fettered" to free will while knowing that its proper exercise requires such accidental advantages as innate talent and high social position.

In "The Musical Banks," Butler satirizes commercialism's corruption of religion; the Banks symbolize the existence of "a kingdom not of this world" whose laws measure and judge human laws. For Butler, there is a Divine Will which inhabits the subconscious and which all cultures tacitly acknowledge. In the trials of the unfortunate and sick, Butler uses absurdity to examine further the nature of freedom and responsibility. In Erewhon, crime is a disease and disease a crime; Butler accepts the first equation while mocking the second.

Bibliography

Bekker, Willem G.   *An Historical and Critical Review of Samuel Butler's Literary Works*. New York: Haskell House, 1966. Reprint of 1925 Edition.

Breuer, H.P.   "The Source of Morality in Butler's *Erewhon*," in *Victorian Studies*. XVI (March, 1973), pp. 317–328.

Cannan, Gilbert.   *Samuel Butler, a Critical Study*. New York: Haskell House, 1970. Reprint of 1915 Edition.

Furbank, Philip H.   *Samuel Butler, 1835–1902*. Hamden, Conn.: Archon Books, 1971. Reprint of 1948 Edition.

Garnett, Martha R.   *Samuel Butler and His Family Relations*. Folcroft, Pa.: Folcroft Library Editions, 1976. Reprint of 1926 Edition.

Harris, John F.   *Samuel Butler, Author of* Erewhon: *The Man and His Work*. Folcroft, Pa.: Folcroft Library Editions, 1973. Reprint of 1916 Edition.

Henderson, Philip.   *Samuel Butler, the Incarnate Bachelor*. New York: Barnes & Noble, 1968. Reprint of 1953 Edition.

Holt, Lee E. *Samuel Butler.* New York: Twayne, 1964.

_____. "Samuel Butler and His Victorian Critics," in *Journal of English Literary History.* VIII (June, 1941), pp. 146–159.

_____. "Samuel Butler's Revisions of *Erewhon*," in *Papers of Bibliographical Society of America.* XXXVIII (1944), pp. 22–38.

Jones, Henry F. *Samuel Butler, Author of* Erewhon *(1835–1902): A Memoir.* New York: Octagon, 1968. Reprint of 1920 Edition.

Jones, Joseph J. *The Cradle of* Erewhon: *Samuel Butler in New Zealand.* Austin: University of Texas Press, 1959.

Knoepflmacher, Ulrich C. *Religious Humanism and the Victorian Novel: Eliot, Pater, and Butler.* Princeton, N.J.: Princeton University Press, 1965.

Muggeridge, Malcolm. *The Earnest Atheist: A Study of Samuel Butler.* New York: Haskell House, 1971. Reprint of 1937 Edition.

Rattray, Robert F. *Samuel Butler: A Chronicle and an Introduction.* New York: Haskell House, 1974. Reprint of 1935 Edition.

Salter, William H. *Essays on Two Moderns: Euripides and Samuel Butler.* Port Washington, N.Y.: Kennikat, 1970. Reprint of 1911 Edition.

Stillman, Clara G. *Samuel Butler, a Mid-Victorian Modern.* Port Washington, N.Y.: Kennikat, 1972. Reprint of 1932 Edition.

Willey, Basil. *Darwin and Butler: Two Versions of Evolution.* London: Chatto, 1960.

THE WAY OF ALL FLESH

Type of work: Novel
Author: Samuel Butler (1835–1902)
Type of plot: Social criticism
Time of plot: Nineteenth century
Locale: England
First published: 1903

Aimed at a type of parent-children relationship during the Victorian era that bred maladjusted, introverted children, this influential "education" novel depicts one son who broke the parental ties, thereby freeing himself to make his own way in life. Butler's partly autobiographical work is witty and cruelly satiric.

Principal Characters

Edward Overton, the narrator. Born in the same year as Theobald Pontifex and in the village whence the Pontifexes sprang, he has known the family all his life. He has an intense dislike for Theobald but greatly admires Alethea Pontifex and takes an interest in Theobald's son Ernest. Alethea makes him the trustee of the money she leaves to Ernest, and it is to Overton that Ernest comes after his release from prison. Overton straightens out Ernest's affairs and helps him to reëstablish his life. Overton is also the spokesman for Butler's ideas.

Ernest Pontifex, the older son of Theobald Pontifex and the hero of the novel. Because of his repressed childhood under the savage domination of his father, Ernest is a tragic failure. He does poorly at school and emerges from Cambridge unable to face life. He is ordained in the Church of England, not from conviction but from lack of preparation for any other career; but he is a failure as a clergyman because he has no understanding of people. Through his extreme naïveté a friend is able to defraud him of his grandfather's legacy; through

his ignorance of the world he makes improper advances to a young woman and is sentenced to six months at hard labor. Upon his release, he meets Ellen, a former maid in his parents' house who has been discharged for immorality; he insists on marrying her, for he wants to drop from his position as a gentleman. They set up a second-hand clothes shop. Ellen proves to be a drunkard, and the marriage fails. Ernest is rescued only by the appearance of John, his father's old coachman, who confesses that he is the father of Ellen's child and had married her after her dismissal. Rid of Ellen, Ernest sends their two children to be reared in the country and devotes himself to writing. At the age of twenty-eight he comes into his aunt's legacy of seventy thousand pounds.

George Pontifex, the father of Theobald and the grandfather of Ernest. He is a wealthy publisher of religious books who browbeats his children. He forces Theobald into the clergy by threatening to disinherit him.

John Pontifex, his older son and successor in business.

Theobald Pontifex, his younger son, the father of Ernest. Forced into the clergy by his father, he obtains the living of Battersby. Thus he can marry Christina Allaby, by whom he has three children. He is savagely ill-tempered with them as the result of his own domination by his father. His ill-treatment of Ernest almost ruins the latter's life.

Christina Pontifex, Theobald's wife, one of five marriageable daughters of a clergyman. At their father's suggestion, they play cards to see who shall catch Theobald, and Christina wins. She is a submissive wife, given to piety and romantic daydreaming, with no understanding of her children.

Alethea Pontifex, Theobald's sister. She is more broad-minded and humane than he and, being independently wealthy, can help Ernest, whom she makes her heir without his knowledge.

Joey Pontifex, Ernest's younger brother, a clergyman.

Charlotte Pontifex, Ernest's unattractive sister.

Ellen, a pretty maid in the Pontifex home. She is dismissed for immorality and is given money by Ernest. Years later, he meets her by accident and marries her. But she is a confirmed drunkard and the marriage fails. He is able to get rid of her when he discovers that she was already married to John.

John, the Pontifex coachman, who defends Ernest against Theobald. He is the father of Ellen's illegitimate child.

Dr. Skinner, the tyrannical headmaster of Roughborough School where Ernest Pontifex was a pupil.

Pryer, a London curate and false friend. He absconds with the twenty-five hundred pounds which Ernest Pontifex had inherited from his grandfather and which had been entrusted to him for investment.

The Story

Mr. and Mrs. Pontifex were well up in years when their son George was born. When the time came for George to learn a trade, they accepted the offer of Mr. Pontifex's brother-in-law to take George with him to London as an apprentice in his printing shop. George learned his trade well, and when the uncle died he willed the shop to his nephew.

George had married, and five children were born to him and his wife; John, Theobald, Eliza, Maria, and Alethea, at whose birth Mrs. Pontifex died. George considered himself a parent motivated only by the desire to do the right thing by his children. When Theobald proved himself not as quick as John but more persistent, George picked the clergy as Theobald's profession. Shortly before his ordination, Theobald wrote to his father that he did not wish to become a minister. George, in reply, threatened to disinherit his son. Submitting, Theobald was ordained. His next step was to wait for some older member of the clergy to die so that he could be given a living.

The Allabys had three daughters, all of marriageable age. After having selected Theobald as a possible husband for one of the daughters, Mr. Allaby suggested to his offspring that they play a game of cards to decide who would become Theobald's wife. Christina won. Theobald unwittingly fell in with Mr. Allaby's plans and obligingly courted Christina until he won her promise to marry him. George wrote to Theobald that he objected to his son's marriage into the impoverished Allaby family, but Theobald was too deeply embroiled in his engagement to untangle himself. In five years he obtained a decent living in a community called Battersby, where he and Christina settled. Their first child was a son. Since this child was the first new male Pontifex, George was pleased, and Theobald felt that for the first time in his life he had done something to satisfy his father. After Ernest came Joseph and then Charlotte. Theobald and Christina reared their children with strict adherence to principles which they believed would mold fine character. The children were disciplined rigorously and beaten when their parents deemed it appropriate. When George Pontifex died, he left seventeen thousand, five hundred pounds to Theobald and twenty-five hundred pounds to Ernest.

From an oppressive existence under the almost obsessed rule of his parents, Ernest was sent to Roughborough to be educated under Dr. Skinner, who was as strict a disciplinarian as Theobald. Ernest was physically weak and mentally morose. He might have succumbed completely to his overpowering environment had he not been rescued by an understanding and loving relative. Alethea Pontifex, Theobald's sister, had retired to London, where she lived comfortably on an inheritance wisely invested. Looking about for someone to whom she could leave her money when she died, Alethea hit upon Ernest. Not wishing to bestow her fortune blindly, she determined to learn more about the boy. She moved to Roughborough so that she could spend a great deal of time with Ernest.

From the first, she endeared herself to the lonely youngster. She encouraged him to develop his own talents, and when she learned that he had a passion for music she suggested that he learn how to build an organ. Enthusiastically he set about to learn wood construction and harmony. Theobald disapproved, but he did not forbid Ernest's activities because he and Christina were eager to have Ernest inherit Alethea's money. Ernest's shrinking personality changed under the benevolent influence of his aunt. When Alethea died, she left her money in the hands of her best friend, Mr. Overton, whom she had appointed to administer the estate which would go to Ernest on his twenty-eighth birthday.

After Ernest had completed his course at Roughborough, Theobald sent him to Cambridge to study for the ministry. At Cambridge Ernest made a few friends and took part in athletics. He was ordained soon after he received his degree. Then he went to London. Still innocent and unworldly, he entrusted to a friend named Pryer the inheritance he had received from his grandfather. Pryer cheated him out of his legacy. Because he could not differentiate between good and evil in human character, Ernest also became entangled in a charge of assault and battery and was sentenced to a term in the workhouse. Theobald sent word that henceforth Ernest was to consider himself an orphan.

Ernest was twenty-three years old at the time. Mr. Overton, who held, unknown to Ernest, the estate Alethea had left for her nephew, began to take an interest in Ernest's affairs. When Ernest was released from prison, he went to Mr. Overton for advice concerning his future, since it was no longer possible for him to be a clergyman.

While Ernest was still at Roughborough, Christina had hired as a maid a young girl named Ellen. She and Ernest had become good friends simply because Ellen was kinder to him than anyone else at home. When Ellen became pregnant and Christina learned of her condition, she sent Ellen away. Ernest, fearing that the girl might starve, followed her and gave her all the money he had. Theobald learned what Ernest had done through John, the coachman, who had been present when Ernest had given Ellen the money. Theobald became angry and dismissed the coachman.

Soon after his release from prison, Ernest met Ellen in a London street. Because both were lonely, they married and set up a small second-hand clothing and book shop with the help of Mr. Overton, who deplored the idea of Ernest's marrying Ellen. Unknown to Ernest, Ellen was a habitual drunkard. Before long she had so impoverished him with her drinking and her foul ways that he disliked her intensely, but he could not leave her because of the two children she had borne him.

One day Ernest again met John, his father's former coachman, who revealed that he was the father of Ellen's illegitimate child and that he had married Ellen shortly after she had left Theobald's home in disgrace. Acting on this information, Mr. Overton arranged matters for Ernest. Ellen was promised an income of a pound a week if she would leave Ernest, a proposal she readily accepted. The children were sent to live in a family of happy, healthy children, for Ernest feared that his own upbringing would make him as bad a parent as Theobald had been.

When Ernest reached his twenty-eighth birthday, he inherited Alethea's trust fund of seventy thousand pounds. By that time Ernest had become a writer. With a part of his inheritance he traveled abroad for a few years and then returned to England with material for a book he planned to write.

Before he died he published many successful books, but he never told his own story. Mr. Overton, who had access to all the Pontifex papers and who knew Ernest so well, wrote the history of the Pontifex family.

Critical Evaluation

Samuel Butler wrote numerous essays and articles, and fifteen books, among them several travel books and five on science. Butler was frequently absorbed in theories of evolution for about twenty-five years after he read Darwin's *On the Origin of Species* in 1861-1862, an absorption strongly influencing the substance and style of *The Way of All Flesh*. That influence is not shown directly, however, and appears gradually in the philosophizing of Overton and Ernest. Butler began the novel in 1873, but interrupted its composition several times to do scientific writing and finally completed it in 1885. Butler used letters in the book actually written by his own mother and father to him (see Chapters VIII and XXV) as letters from Theobald and Christina to their son Ernest. The author refused to publish the novel so long as family members caustically satirized in it were living. His literary executor therefore arranged publication in 1903, although Butler's two sisters were still alive.

The letters mentioned above are among the countless bits of evidence in *The Way of All Flesh* which Butler wittily but relentlessly amasses through the narration of Edward Overton, friend of the Pontifex family, to persuade the reader that the "hero," Ernest, was indeed fortunate to survive, much less surmount his loving parents' Mid-Victorian Christian tutelage and his formal schooling. Ernest slowly and unevenly surmounts the narrow, stupid, and often cruel values imposed upon him. At last he dimly perceives what Butler thought man would instinctively remember had Victorianism not "educated" it out of him. Ernest learns mostly by hindsight in the wake of disastrous involvements such as those with Pryer and Ellen. But he also learns by a naïve and torturous sifting through the issues of fashionable intellectual controversy on religion and science. Butler gently satirizes Ernest's pursuit of "first causes" or other abstractions, and his fortunes take a decided change for the better when he gives up "abstractions" for the most part, sheds his alcoholic wife, and realizes that because he is a child of his own father and mother, he cannot be a good father himself. He therefore places his children with good, simple people who can love them and make them happy adults. Like Butler, Ernest then settles into bachelor quarters in London at about age thirty, where until his death he contentedly writes, paints, enjoys Handel's music, and reflects upon the folly of much that transpires in the world.

The circumstances of Ernest's life closely parallel those of Butler's life through the Cambridge period, and to a lesser extent following that period. Butler did not go to prison; instead he went to New Zealand where he raised sheep profitably from 1858-1864. Much critical discussion of the novel, however, centers on the author's personal life: Butler's fabled capacity for cruel parody of his well-meaning family, for instance. Walter Allen in *The English Novel* (1954) thinks Butler tips the scales unfairly against Theobald and Christina, thereby alienating the reader. Other critics have said of Butler, as Overton says of Ernest in contrasting him to Othello: "he hates not wisely but too well."

More productive critical comment might be made concerning the "coincidence" of Ernest's encountering John, the old family coachman, and learning that John and Ellen are legal man and wife, a fact which most happily frees Ernest from a dreadful marriage. Or, the wonderful ability of Overton to invest Ernest's inheritance from his Aunt Alethea and to increase it five times over so that Ernest may live his comfortable life.

Many critics interpret the autobiographical dimension in *The Way of All*

Flesh as a literary precedent for "parent-son" and self-discovery novels such as *Of Human Bondage, Sons and Lovers,* or *A Portrait of the Artist as a Young Man.* Other perspectives are possible, however, particularly for readers long familiar with Freudian and post-Freudian psychological approaches to the novel. Readers of Norman Mailer's autobiographical works or Roth's *Portnoy's Complaint* may view Butler's work as more than either personal diatribe or over-reaction to the excesses of Victorianism. Novelists now thread through mazes of neuroses, attempt to expose the origins of neurotic and self-destructive behavior such as that practiced by Ernest, and often they propose therapeutic solutions to the protagonists' problems. However imperfectly Butler integrated the autobiographical or personal and the theories which underlie his novel, he was doubtless trying to show the causes of Ernest's stunted personality and his path to relative self-respect and happiness.

The narrative of the novel, slow and tedious perhaps to a reader of the 1970's, moves as it does because only through thirty years of painful experience could Ernest achieve some intellectual objectivity and self-knowledge. He learned that he must totally reject his self-centered parents' pious domination to become his own person. He learns (expressed by Overton) that virtue springs from man's experience concerning his own well-being—this is the "least fallible thing we have." When meditating in prison Ernest decides that a true Christian is he who takes the "highest and most self-respecting view of his own welfare which is in his power to conceive, and adheres to it in spite of conventionality. . . . " But circumstances change, as Overton informs the reader, and the self is always changing: life is nothing but the "process of accommodation," and a life will be successful or not according to the individual's power of accommodation. As narrator, Overton is doubtless Butler's alter ego, and his detached view of Ernest reveals that "smug hedonism" is more accurately seen as less than a perfect resolution: Ernest is somewhat withdrawn, lonely, bearing ineradicable marks of his heredity and environment.

Butler explores the themes of heredity and environment plurally through telling the histories of four generations of Pontifexes: only Ernest's great-grandparents led happy, instinctive lives. The title of the novel gives a tag-summary of Butler's judgment: this is the way of all flesh—to learn if at all, by rejecting convention and dogma, and to live by self-direction.

Bibliography

Bekker, Willem G. *An Historical and Critical Review of Samuel Butler's Literary Works.* New York: Haskell House, 1966. Reprint of 1925 Edition.

Bissell, Clyde T. "A Study of *The Way of All Flesh,*" in *Nineteenth Century Studies.* Edited by Herbert Davis. Ithaca, N.Y.: Cornell University Press, pp. 277–303.

Cannan, Gilbert. *Samuel Butler, a Critical Study.* New York: Haskell House, 1970. Reprint of 1915 Edition.

Cole, George D. *Samuel Butler and* The Way of All Flesh. Norwood, Pa.: Norwood Editions, 1976. Reprint of 1947 Edition.

Furbank, Philip H. *Samuel Butler, 1835–1902.* Hamden, Conn.: Archon Books, 1971. Reprint of 1948 Edition.

Garnett, Martha R. *Samuel Butler and His Family Relations.* Folcroft, Pa.: Folcroft Library Editions, 1976. Reprint of 1926 Edition.

Henderson, Philip. *Samuel Butler, the Incarnate Bachelor.* New York: Barnes & Noble, 1968. Reprint of 1953 Edition.

Holt, Lee E. *Samuel Butler.* New York: Twayne, 1964.

————; "Samuel Butler and His Victorian Critics," in *Journal of English Literary History.* VIII (June, 1941), pp. 146–159.

————. Samuel Butler's Rise to Fame," in *PMLA.* LVII (September, 1942), pp. 867–878.

Howard, Daniel. "The Critical Significance of Autobiography in *The Way of All Flesh*," in *Victorian Newsletter.* XVII (Spring, 1960), pp. 12–18.

Jones, Henry F. *Samuel Butler, Author of* Erewhon *(1835–1902): A Memoir.* New York: Octagon, 1968. Reprint of 1920 Edition.

Knoepflmacher, Ulrich C. "Ishmael or Anti-Hero? The Division of Self in *The Way of All Flesh*," in *English Fiction in Transition.* IV (1961), pp. 28–35.

————. *Religious Humanism and the Victorian Novel: Eliot, Pater, and Butler.* Princeton, N.J.: Princeton University Press, 1965.

Linde, Ilse D. "*The Way of All Flesh* and *A Portrait of the Artist as a Young Man*: A Comparison," in *Victorian Newsletter.* IX (Spring, 1956), pp. 9–16.

Muggeridge, Malcolm. *The Earnest Atheist: A Study of Samuel Butler.* New York: Haskell House, 1971. Reprint of 1937 Edition.

Rattray, Robert F. *Samuel Butler: A Chronicle and an Introduction.* New York: Haskell House, 1974. Reprint of 1935 Edition.

Salter, William H. *Essays on Two Moderns: Euripides and Samuel Butler.* Port Washington, N.Y.: Kennikat, 1970. Reprint of 1911 Edition.

Stillman, Clara G. *Samuel Butler, a Mid-Victorian Modern.* Port Washington, N.Y.: Kennikat, 1972. Reprint of 1932 Edition.

Willey, Basil. *Darwin and Butler: Two Versions of Evolution.* London: Chatto, 1960.

LEWIS CARROLL
Charles Lutwidge Dodgson

Born: Daresbury, Cheshire, England (January 27, 1832)
Died: Guildford, Surrey, England (January 14, 1898)

Principal Works

FANTASIES AND CHILDREN'S STORIES: *Alice's Adventures in Wonderland,* 1865; *Through the Looking-Glass and What Alice Found There,* 1871; *A Tangled Tale,* 1885; *Sylvie and Bruno,* 1889; *Sylvie and Bruno Concluded,* 1893.

POEM: *The Hunting of the Snark,* 1876.

MATHEMATICAL STUDIES: *Euclid and His Modern Rivals,* 1879; *Curiosa Mathematica,* Part I, 1888; Part II, 1893; *Symbolic Logic, Specimens,* 1894.

Charles Lutwidge Dodgson, who under his pseudonym of Lewis Carroll came to be known to millions as the author of *Alice in Wonderland,* was born at Daresbury, England, January 27, 1832, the son of the rector of Daresbury, the Reverend Charles Dodgson and Frances Jane Lutwidge. He was the eldest of a family of eleven children, with seven sisters and three brothers. After a pleasant and for the most part solitary childhood he attended Richmond School and then Rugby for three extremely unhappy years. In 1851, the year he formally went into residence as a student at Christ Church College, Oxford, his mother died. He was probably deeply affected by her death; his later verses show the affection he felt for his gentle mother, and in his nonsense stories some critics have claimed to find signs of a childhood love for his mother that never matured.

Dodgson spent the rest of his life at Oxford. In 1856, two years after receiving the Bacholor of Arts degree, and after serving as a tutor in mathematics, he was made a regular member of the teaching faculty at Christ Church. Although the significance of the event was unrealized at the time, it was in the previous year, 1855, that he wrote the first lines of his famous "Jabberwocky" poem: "Twas bryllyg, and the slythy toves/Did gyre and gymble in the wabe...." This was a scholar's jest, an attempt to parody Anglo-Saxon poetry. He was twenty-three years old at the time.

As a teacher and mathematician, Charles Lutwidge Dodgson was conscientious, precise, sometimes inspired, but usually dull. His students reported finding his lectures very tiresome, even during the period when he was writing *Alice's Adventures in Wonderland.* Dodgson wrote many articles and several books in mathematics and logic, but he would not have been famous if he had relied on them or on his reputation as a teacher.

The pseudonym, Lewis Carroll, was devised in 1856 to accompany a poem which appeared in the magazine *The Train.* It appears to have been derived from the names Lutwidge and Charles by some fanciful logic of his own.

Dodgson had considerable skill as a humorous artist, but his drawings—which some have regarded as comparable to the nonsense drawings by Edward Lear—were rejected when he submitted them to the *Comic Times*. Discouraged, he turned to photography and became an excellent photographer of children and one of the notable amateurs in nineteenth century photography.

In 1856 he met the children of Dean Liddell of Christ Church, and was particularly interested in Alice Liddell, then four years old. A year after his ordination (for taking Holy Orders was a condition of his staying at Christ Church as a mathematics lecturer), on a picnic with another young clergyman and three of the Liddell girls—Alice, then ten years old, among them—Dodgson began in an extemporaneous way the story of *Alice's Adventures Underground*. He wrote the story, after expanding it considerably, and presented the manuscript to Alice. An even longer version was prepared for publication and was illustrated by John Tenniel, whose drawings have become as famous as the story. The book was published by Macmillan in 1865 with the title *Alice's Adventures in Wonderland*. This extremely popular story full of nonsense and logical fancy was followed by *Through the Looking-Glass and What Alice Found There*. *The Hunting of the Snark*, perhaps the most fascinating of his nonsense poems, became a great favorite with adults and, like the Alice books, continues to be popular. But the author's own favorite work was his long and involved *Sylvie and Bruno* which appeared in two parts, the first in 1889 and the second in 1893. Unfortunately, the public never fully shared the author's love, and compared to the other books it was a failure.

Dodgson's playful temperament, seldom in evidence in the classroom and often made wicked when he turned to criticism of his colleagues at the college, found an outlet in games of logic and mathematics, many of which he invented. He was always fascinated with girls; he liked to read to them, to make up stories for them, to draw them, and to photograph them—sometimes in the nude. But somehow he managed to stay out of trouble, if not free from all criticism. In all probability, his innocence was evident. He never married, but he probably had an unhappy love affair when he was young; the evidence is inconclusive. In any case, analysts have been amusing themselves by studying him; the maker of puzzles was something of a puzzle himself.

This solitary deacon, dull teacher, clever logician, and inspired teller of nonsense tales died of influenza and bronchial complications at Guildford on January 14, 1898. He was still ambitious, with several projects under way, but since he was more and more out of touch with "real life," living, although quite sanely, in the world of his imagination, it was not entirely inappropriate that after a long creative life he finally stopped dreaming.

Bibliography

The collected edition is *The Complete Works of Lewis Carroll*, edited by Alexander Woollcott, 1939 (reprinted 1947), with a critical introduction and illustrations by John Tenniel. The standard bibliography is *A Handbook of the*

Literature of the Rev. C. L. Dodgson, 1931, by S. H. Williams and Falconer Madan. Roger L. Green has edited *The Diaries of Lewis Carroll,* 2 vols., 1953, the most complete edition to date. Standard biographies are Langford Reed, *The Life of Lewis Carroll,* 1932; Florence B. Lennon, *Victoria Through the Looking Glass: The Life of Lewis Carroll,* 1945; and Derek Hudson, *Lewis Carroll,* 1954, the first critical biography to make use of the diaries. Other critical works are Walter de la Mare, *Lewis Carroll,* 1932; R. L. Green, *The Story of Lewis Carroll,* 1949; A. L. Taylor, *White Knight: A Study of C. L. Dodgson,* 1952; and Phyllis Greenacre, *Swift and Carroll,* 1955. An important short essay is Virginia Woolf, "Lewis Carroll," in *The Moment and Other Essays,* 1948. See also S. H. Williams and F. Madan, *The Lewis Carroll Handbook,* 1962.

THROUGH THE LOOKING-GLASS

Type of work: Imaginative tale
Author: Lewis Carroll (Charles Lutwidge Dodgson, 1832–1898)
Type of plot: Fantasy
Time of plot: Nineteenth century
Locale: The dream world of an imaginative child
First published: 1871

Its plot structured around moves in a chess game, the story of this fantasy, which continues Alice's Adventures in Wonderland, is set in a land peopled by live chessmen and talking insects, a land where everything happens backwards. Carroll's book may be read as a madcap children's fairy tale or interpreted as a complex, sophisticated adult fable laced with subtle ironies and inspired by inimitable humor.

Principal Characters

Alice, an imaginative English child who has fantastic adventures in Looking-Glass House.

The White Kitten, a good kitten who is not responsible for Alice's adventures.

The Black Kitten, told by Alice to pretend that they can go through the mirror to Looking-Glass House.

Dinah, the kittens' mother.

The White Queen, a live chess piece. In Alice's adventures she becomes a sheep, gives Alice some needles, and tells the little girl to knit. She reappears throughout the story in various guises.

The White King, a live chess piece. He has Alice serve a cake which cuts itself.

Tiger Lily,
Rose, and
Violet, flowers of whom Alice asks the path to take.

Gnat, a pleasant insect as big as a chicken. He melts away.

The Red Queen, a live chess piece. She tells Alice that one has to run to stay in the same place. Later she turns into the black kitten.

Tweedledum and
Tweedledee, two odd, fat, little men. They speak in ambiguities and recite poems to Alice. They fight over a rattle until frightened away by a crow.

The Red King, a live chess piece. He dreams about Alice, says Tweedledee, and thus gives her reality.

Humpty Dumpty, who has a conversation in riddles with Alice. He explains to her the Jabberwocky poem.

The Lion and
The Unicorn, who fight over the White King's crown.

The Red Knight, a live chess piece who claims Alice as his prisoner.

The White Knight, a live chess piece who also claims Alice as his prisoner. He leads Alice to a brook and tells her to jump into the next square in order to become a queen herself.

The Story

Alice was sure the whole thing was not the white kitten's fault. It must surely have been the fault of the black kitten. For Dinah, the mother cat, had been washing the white kitten's face when it happened; she certainly had had nothing to do with it. But the mischievous black kitten had been unwinding Alice's yarn and in all ways acting naughty enough to cause the whole strange affair.

While the black kitten curled up in Alice's lap to play with the yarn, Alice told it to pretend that the two of them could go right through the mirror and into Looking-Glass House. As she talked, the glass grew all misty and soft, and in a moment Alice was through the mirror and in the Looking-Glass room. The place was very strange, for although the room looked just the same as the real room she had seen in the mirror, the clock and the fire and the other things in the room seemed to be alive. Even the chessmen, for Alice loved to play chess, were alive.

When Alice picked up the White Queen and set her on the table, the White Queen screamed in terror, thinking that a volcano had shaken her about. The White King had the same fear, but he was too astonished to cry out. They seemed not to see or hear Alice, and even though she wanted to stay and watch them and read the king's rather funny poetry, she felt she must look at the garden before she had to go back through the Looking Glass. When she started down the stairs, she seemed to float, not even once touching the steps.

In the garden every path Alice took led her straight back to the house. She asked Tiger Lily and Rose and Violet whether there were any other people in the garden; she hoped they might help her find the right path. The flowers told her there was only one, and Alice found her to be the Red Queen—but a very strange chess figure, for the Red Queen was taller than Alice herself. As Alice walked toward the Red Queen, she once more found herself back at the door of the house. Then Alice figured out that in order to get to any place in this queer land one must walk in the *opposite* direction. Doing so, she came face to face with the Red Queen.

The queen took Alice to the top of a hill. There, spread out below them, was a countryside that looked like a large chessboard. Alice, delighted, said that she would love to play on this board. Then the Red Queen told her that they would play and that Alice could be the White Queen's Pawn. They would start on the Second Square and—but at that moment the Red Queen grabbed Alice's hand and they started to run. Alice had never run so fast in her life, but even though she was breathless from such fast running the things around them never changed a tiny bit. When they finally stopped running, the queen told Alice that in this land one had to run as fast as one could to stay in the same place and twice as fast as one could to get somewhere else. Then the queen showed Alice the pegs in the Second Square and told her how to move. At the last peg the Red Queen disappeared, leaving Alice alone to continue the game.

Alice started to run down the hill. The next thing she knew she was on a train filled with insects and having quite an unpleasant time because she did not have a ticket. All of the insects talked unkindly to her, and to add to her discomfort the train jumped over the brook and took them all straight up in the air. When she came down, she was sitting under a tree, talking to a Gnat. Gnat was as big as a chicken but very pleasant. He told her about the other insects that lived in the woods; then he too melted away and Alice had to go on alone.

Turning a corner, she bumped into two fat little men, called Tweedledum and Tweedledee, the funniest little creatures she had ever seen. Everything they said seemed to have two meanings. It was fun to listen to the merry little men as they recited a long poem about a Walrus and a Carpenter and some Oysters. While they were explaining the poem to Alice, she heard a puffing noise, like the sound of a steam engine. Tweedledee told her it was the Red King snoring. Sure enough, they found him asleep. Tweedledee told Alice that the Red King was dreaming about her and that if he stopped dreaming Alice would be gone for good. Alice cried when they told her she was not real but only a part of the Red King's dream.

As she brushed her tears away, she saw Tweedledum staring in terror at something on the ground. It was an old broken rattle, over which the two foolish men got into a terrible fight. That is, they *talked* a terrible fight, but neither seemed very anxious to have a real battle. The Crow flew over and frightened them so that the funny men ran away into the wood. Alice ran too, and as she ran she saw a shawl blowing about.

Alice, looking for the owner of the shawl, saw the White Queen running toward her. The White Queen was a very queer person; she lived backward and remembered things *before* they happened. For example, she hurt *before* she pricked her finger. While the queen was telling these strange things to Alice, the queen turned into a Sheep and was in a shop with Alice. It was a very curious shop, the shelves full of things that disappeared when Alice looked at them. Sometimes the boxes went right through the ceiling. Then Sheep gave Alice some needles and told her to knit.

As she started to knit, the needles became oars and she found herself and Sheep in a little boat rowing in a stream. The oars kept sticking in the water. Sheep explained that the crabs were catching them. Alice picked some beautiful, fragrant rushes that melted away as soon as she picked them. Soon, to her surprise, the river and boat vanished, and Alice and Sheep were back in the shop. She bought an egg, even though in this shop two were cheaper than one, but when she started to get the egg, as Sheep would not reach it for her, the egg began to grow larger and larger and more and more real, with eyes, a nose, and a mouth. Then Alice could tell as plain as day that the egg was Humpty Dumpty.

She had a queer conversation with Humpty Dumpty, a conversation all filled with riddles. They took turns at choosing the topic to talk about, but most of the subjects turned into arguments, even though Alice tried hard to be polite. Humpty Dumpty explained to Alice what the "Jabberwocky" poem meant, the one she had seen in the White King's book. Then, while reciting another poem, he stopped right in the middle, saying that was all. Alice thought it very queer but did not tell Humpty Dumpty so. She thought it time for her to leave, but as she walked away there was a terrible crash that shook the whole forest.

Thousands of soldiers and horses came rushing toward her, the riders constantly falling off their horses. Frightened, she escaped from the wood into the open. There she found the White King, who told her that he had sent the soldiers and horses and that the loud crash she had heard was the noise of the Lion and Unicorn fighting for the crown. She went with the king to watch the fight, which was indeed a terrible one. It was really silly of them to fight for the crown, since it belonged to the White King and he had no notion of giving it away. After the fight Alice met the Unicorn and the Lion. At the king's order she served them cake, a very strange cake which cut itself when she carried the dish around.

A great noise interrupted the party. When it stopped Alice thought she must have dreamed the whole thing until the Red Knight came along, followed soon by a White Knight. Each claimed her as a prisoner. Alice thought the whole business silly, since neither of them could do anything except fall off his horse and climb back on again, over and over and over. At last the Red Knight galloped off and the White Knight told her that she would be a queen as soon as she crossed the next brook. He was supposed to lead her to the end of the wood, but she spent the whole journey helping him back on his horse each time he fell off. The trip was filled with more queer conversation. By that time Alice was used to strange talk from her Looking-Glass friends. At last they reached the brook. The knight rode away and Alice jumped over the brook and into the last square of the chess board. To her delight, when she reached that square she felt something tight on her head—a crown! She was a queen.

Soon she found the Red Queen and the White Queen confronting her, very cross because she also thought she was a queen. They gave her a test for queens which she must have passed, for before long they were calling her "Your Majesty," and inviting people to a party which she was to give. The Red and the White Queens went to sleep after a time. Alice watched them until they disappeared. Then she found herself before a doorway marked "Queen Alice." All of her new friends were there, including the queens who had just vanished. The party was the most amazing experience of all. Puddings talked, guests poured wine over their heads, and the White Queen turned into a leg of mutton. Alice was exasperated, so much so that she seized the tablecloth and jerked it and everything on it to the floor. Then she grabbed the Red Queen and shook her as she would a kitten. But what was this? It *was* a kitten she was shaking, the black kitten.

Alice talked to Dinah and both the kittens about the adventure they had all had, but the silly kittens did nothing but purr.

Critical Evaluation

It is rare for the sequel to a highly creative literary work to surpass the original. Yet such is the case with *Through the Looking-Glass and What Alice Found There,* which in 1871 followed *Alice's Adventures in Wonderland,* published seven years earlier. For most readers the two books are so closely entwined that they are considered a unit, and many of Lewis Carroll's most famous Looking-Glass creations (Tweedledee, Tweedledum, and Humpty Dumpty, for example) are often mistakenly placed in *Alice's Adventures in Wonderland.* However, each, while joined by a common heroine and themes, is a distinct entity. And it is *Through the Looking-Glass* which most attracts adults, for it is in this second fantasy that Lewis Carroll (the pen name for Oxford mathematics lecturer and tutor the Rev. Charles Lutwidge Dodgson) presented an even more sophisticated puzzle about reality and logic than he did in the earlier story. It is in *Through the Looking-Glass* that one finds conscious suggestion of the cruel questions rather delicately presented in *Alice's Adventures in Wonderland.*

Sharing many characteristics, each book has twelve chapters, and both merge the fairy tale with science. Alice, seven years old in the first book, is seven and one-half on her second venture. A slight shift in scene turns the pleasant outdoor summer setting of *Alice's Adventures in Wonderland* into the more somber indoor winter stage of *Through the Looking-Glass.* Corresponding to the card game of the first book is chess in *Through the Looking-Glass,* another game which involves kings and queens. Within the chess-and-mirror framework of the Looking-Glass world, Carroll has, however, constructed an intricate symbolic plan unlike the seemingly spontaneous movement of Wonderland.

Although medieval and Renaissance sportsmen sometimes enjoyed chess which used human players on a giant field, Carroll is apparently the first to use the idea in literature. Science fiction has since, of course, often employed the technique. In the game plan, Alice is a white pawn on a giant chessboard of life in which the rows of the board are separated by brooks and the columns by hedges. Alice never speaks to any piece who is not in a square beside her, as appropriate for the pawn who never knows what is happening except at its spot on the board. Alice remains in the queen's field except for her last move by which time she has become a queen and captures the Red Queen (and shakes her into a kitten) and as a result checkmates the Red King who has slept throughout the game. Her behavior complements the personalities assigned to the other pieces, for each assumes the qualities of the figure it represents. As in chess, the queens are the most powerful and active beings and the kings are impotent. Erratic and stumbling, the White Knight recalls the movement of the chess knight which moves two squares in any direction, then again one square in a different direction, forming a sort of spastic "L."

Critics have noted inconsistencies in the chess game, charging that the White side makes nine consecutive moves; the White King is placed in an unnoticed check; the Queens castle; and the White Queen misses a chance to take the Red Knight. But Carroll, in a later explanatory note, said that the game is correct in relation to the moves even though the alternation of the sides is not strictly consistent, and that the "castling" of the Queens is merely his phrase to indicate that they have entered the palace. Not interested in the game as an example of chess strategy, Carroll conceived of it as a learning experience for a child who was to "be" a pawn warring against all the other pieces controlled by an adult, an idea apparently stimulated by the chess tales Carroll had fashioned for Alice Liddell, a young friend who was learning the game. Alice, daughter of the dean of Christ Church, Oxford, had also, of course, been the Alice whom he had placed in Wonderland.

Arising inevitably from Carroll's use of this structure has been the proposal that Alice is Everyman and that chess is Life. Like a human being who exists from birth to death only vaguely comprehending the forces directing his moves, Alice never understands her experience. Indeed none of the pieces really assimilates the total concept of the game. Even the mobile queens do not really grasp the idea that beyond the board there is a room and people who are determining the game. Our own reality thus becomes very unreal if we, like the chess pieces, have such a limited perception of the total environment.

Carroll pursues still another definition of reality when Alice confronts the Red King and is told that she exists merely as part of his dreams, not as an objective being. Upsetting to Alice is the sage advice of Tweedledum and Tweedledee to the effect that if the king were to wake, Alice would then vanish like the flame of a candle. The incident recalls Bishop Berkeley's empirical proposal that nothing exists except as it is perceived. Alice, like Samuel Johnson who refuted Berkeley by painfully kicking a stone, insists that she is "real" for she cries "real" tears. When she leaves the Looking-Glass world and supposedly awakens, Carroll mischievously permits her to ask herself: Which dreamed it? His final poem apparently provides the answer, for the last words in the book are: "Life, what is it but a dream?"

In examining the second structural device of the book, the mirror reversal theme (perfectly mated with chess since in that game the initial asymmetric arrangement of the pieces means that the opponents are mirror images of one another), we find that Carroll has achieved another *tour de force*. The left-right reversals—including, for example, the Tweedle brothers, Alice's attempt to reach the Red Queen by walking backwards, memory which occurs before the event, running to stay in the same place, and the like—are not merely mind-teasers. Scientists now seriously propose the existence of anti-matter which is, in effect, a mirror image of matter, just like Alice's Looking-Glass milk. And again we wonder: which is the real matter, the real milk?

Further developing this continuing paradox are Carroll's damaging attacks on our understanding of language. Humpty Dumpty (like the Tweedles, the Lion, the Unicorn, and Wonderland's Jack of Hearts, a nursery rhyme character) says a person's ideas are formulated in his mind and to express them he may use any word he pleases. Alice and the White Knight debate the difference between the name of the song and the song, between what the name is and what the name is called. The fawn becomes frightened of Alice only when it realizes she is a "child." In these and many more incidents, Carroll explores how our language works, directly and indirectly making fun of our misconceptions which, on the one hand, see language as part of a totally objective system of reality and, on the other, forget how language actually helps create that reality. His nonsense words and poems are his final jibe at our so-called logical language, for they are no more and no less disorderly than ordinary table talk.

A sparkling achievement, *Through the Looking-Glass* is, like *Alice's Adventures in Wonderland,* the incomparable vision of an alienated man who found in the world of fantasy all the delight and horror of the adult environment he was subconsciously attempting to escape.

Bibliography

Arnoldi, Richard. "Parallels Between *Our Mutual Friend* and the Alice Books," in *Children's Literature: The Great Excluded.* I (1972), pp. 54–57.

Auerbach, Nina. "Alice and Wonderland: A Curious Child," in *Victorian Studies.* XVII (1973), pp. 31–47.

Baum, Alwin L. "Carroll's *Alices*: The Semiotics of Paradox," in *American Imago.* XXXIV (1977), pp. 86–108.

Blake, Kathleen. *Play, Games and Sport: The Literary Works of Lewis Carroll.* Ithaca, N.Y.: Cornell University Press, 1974, pp. 132–148.

Boynton, Mary F. "An Oxford Don Quixote," in *Hispania.* XLIV (1964), pp. 738–750.

Ettleson, A. *Carroll's* Through the Looking-Glass *Decoded.* New York: Philosophical Library, 1966.

Gardner, Martin. "Introduction," in *The Wasp in a Wig, a "Suppressed" Episode of* Through the Looking-Glass and What Alice Found There. By Lewis Carroll. New York: Clarkson N. Potter, 1977, pp. 1–11.

Henkle, Roger B. "The Mad Hatter's World," in *Virginia Quarterly Review.* XLIX (1973), pp. 107–111.

Johnson, Paula. "Alice Among the Analysts," in *Hartford Studies in Literature.* IV (1972), pp. 114–122.

Jorgens, Jack J. "Alice Our Contemporary," in *Children's Literature: The Great Excluded.* I (1972), pp. 152–161.

Matthews, Charles.   "Satire in the Alice Books," in *Criticism*. XII (1971), pp. 105–119.

Otten, Terry.   "Steppenwolf and Alice—In and Out of Wonderland," in *Studies in the Humanities*. IV (1974), pp. 28–34.

Pattison, Robert.   *The Child Figure in English Literature*. Athens: University of Georgia Press, 1978, pp. 152–154.

Priestley, J.B.   "Walrus and Carpenter; Political Symbolism in *Through the Looking-Glass*," in *New Statesman*. LIV (August 10, 1957), p. 168.

WILKIE COLLINS

Born: London, England (January 8, 1824)
Died: London (September 23, 1889)

Principal Works

NOVELS: *Antonina*, 1850; *Basil*, 1852; *Hide and Seek*, 1854; *The Woman in White*, 1860; *No Name*, 1862; *Armadale*, 1866; *The Moonstone*, 1868; *Man and Wife*, 1870; *Poor Miss Finch*, 1872; *The New Magdalen*, 1873; *The Two Destinies*, 1875; *The Law and the Lady*, 1876; *The Fallen Leaves*, 1879; *Heart and Science*, 1883.

SHORT STORIES: *After Dark*, 1856; *"Miss or Mrs.?" and Other Stories*, 1873; *The Frozen Deep*, 1874; *Little Novels*, 1887; *The Lazy Tour of Two Idle Apprentices*, 1890 (with Charles Dickens).

PLAYS: *No Thoroughfare*, 1867 (with Charles Dickens); *The New Magdalen*, 1873; *Man and Wife*, 1873; *The Moonstone*, 1877.

ESSAYS AND SKETCHES: *My Miscellanies*, 1863.

TRAVEL SKETCHES AND IMPRESSIONS: *Rambles Beyond Railways*, 1851.

BIOGRAPHY: *Memoirs of the Life of William Collins, R.A.*, 1848.

In his own time (William) Wilkie Collins was regarded by many persons as the equal of Dickens and Thackeray and, in at least two novels, *The Woman in White* and *The Moonstone*, their superior in sheer popularity. In retrospect, his best work can be admired for the very elements that Collins himself esteemed: his emphasis on "the Actual" (his own term) and the element of suspense. Modern readers may qualify their admiration by finding "the Actual" strangely mixed with the melodramatic and the sentimental; and they may find that the suspenseful in Collins has suffered from the widespread imitation of his devices by generations of writers of mystery stories. But in justice to Collins it must be realized that precious gems that bear a curse, unjust confinement in lunatic asylums, and false marriages were more novel in his day than in ours. In his service to "the Actual" he gave expression to his own contempt for many of the Victorian taboos that Dickens and Thackeray submitted to. Collins was a pioneer in anticlericalism and other attacks on British complacency and insularity. He also took up, as in *Fallen Leaves*, such forbidden themes as prostitution and marital infidelity. At both these points he displays a boldness that is today thought to have its origin in Samuel Butler and George Bernard Shaw. It is not, however, strange that these historically important elements in Collins are overlooked; they cannot be detached from his coldly calculated sensationalism that kept his immediate public breathless.

The circumstances of his early life contributed to the coexistence in Collins of two opposing drives: a desire for material success and a desire to tell unpalatable truths about the society from which he wished to win this success. Collins' father was William Collins, R.A., who rose in the British art world by careful cultivation of important persons. (These included the well-known artist David Wilkie, the godfather of Wilkie Collins.) The elder Collins united with his search for success Tory political beliefs and a repressive kind of piety. Collins, born in London on January 8, 1824, was a small, weak child who soon learned to detect hypocrisy in his father and his other elders; he had, however, enough taste of comfort and foreign travel to determine to win his share of worldly goods.

Collins was, in his late teens, placed by his father in the office of a tea merchant in London, but he used his evenings and much of his employer's time in literary self-cultivation; he was particularly inspired by the financial success of Charles Dickens. His own first novel, *Antonina, or the Fall of Rome*, was inspired by the grandiose view of the past to be found in such works as Bulwer-Lytton's *The Last Days of Pompeii* (1834). His turn toward "the Actual," which he studied by riding in the London omnibuses, was encouraged by the beginning of his close association with Charles Dickens in 1851 in an amateur theatrical production. Dickens, as editor of *Household Words*, had need of talented assistance; he also found in a man much his junior a stimulating and admiring traveling companion. Throughout their lives the two men abetted each other's tastes in amusement and also left their marks on each other's novels. The growth of closely knit plot-structure in Dickens, e.g., the clues and false clues of *Great Expectations* (1861) shows Collins' influence on Dickens. Collins' increase in humor and the power of lively portraiture was due to Dickens' criticism of Collins' self-conscious and pompous gloom in his early novels.

Collins, like most writers who have a reputation for being "inventive," was always an industrious seeker for material; French police files, newspaper items, and encyclopedia articles aided him. He also exploited to the full, and quite explicitly, incidents in his own life. In 1854 he met his lifelong companion, Caroline Graves, whom he never married. The meeting was a romantic night encounter along a suburban road; with this incident *The Woman in White* begins. Caroline Graves had a child; the fate of such a child—its uncertain social position, the cruelty of the secure and righteous toward her—is the subject of *No Name*. Collins' and Caroline's own peculiar position suggested several themes of women suffering at the hands of society.

Collins' correspondence displays a keen concern over his literary profits; with a desire to extend these profits, he turned many of his novels into plays (usually with limited success), and he took a keen interest in the transatlantic publication of his novels and also in their translation into many languages. He displayed kindness toward Hall Caine and was, in his last years, on friendly terms with Oscar Wilde. He was concerned, after Dickens' death, with demonstrating the closeness of his relation to Dickens, especially after the appearance of Forster's *Life of Dickens* (1872–1874). But his last years were a time of acute suffering from the pain of the gout, which Collins could relieve only by draughts of laudanum and unremitting novel-writing (he had not only Mrs. Graves to support but another "morganatic household"). He died in London, his health wrecked by drugs and overwork, on September 23, 1889.

Much contemporary criticism regarded Collins as a wonderful entertainer but an unhealthy one. Actually Collins, unlike Samuel Butler and Shaw, did not give consistent and sustained expression of his views. The chief public battle he fought came early in his career and was in support of the Pre-Raphaelite Brotherhood, of which his brother Charles was a member. Perhaps his greatest legacy to oncoming generations of novelists, in contrast to most writers of sensational fiction, was his emphasis on careful planning and revision. In this respect he goes beyond Dickens and Trollope and looks toward James and many modern novelists.

Bibliography

There are two recent biographies of Collins: Kenneth Robinson, *Wilkie Collins: A Biography*, 1952, and Nuel Pharr Davis, *The Life of Wilkie Collins*, 1956. See also Samuel L. Ellis, *Wilkie Collins, Le Fanu, and Others*, 1931; Malcolm Elwin, *Victorian Wallflowers*, 1934; Michael Sadleir, *Nineteenth Century Fiction*, 1951; and Robert P. Ashley, *Wilkie Collins*, 1952. The most important foreign study is Ernst von Wolzogen, *Wilkie Collins, ein biographisch-kritischer*, 1885.

Reminiscences of Collins or related background material appear also in John Forster, *Life of Dickens*, 1872–1874; Harriet Martineau, *Autobiography*, 1877; William P. Frith, *John Leech: His Life and Work*, 1891; John G. Millais, *The Life and Letters of Sir Everett Millais*, 1899; R. C. Lehmann, *Memories of Half a Century*, 1908; Squire Bancroft, *Recollections of Sixty Years*, 1909; and Frank Archer, *An Actor's Notebooks*, 1912.

For criticism see Walter de la Mare, "The Early Novels of Wilkie Collins," in *The Eighteen-Sixties*, edited by John Drinkwater, 1932; T. S. Eliot, "Wilkie Collins and Charles Dickens," in *Selected Essays*, 1932; Clyde K. Hyder, "Wilkie Collins and *The Woman in White*," *Publications of the Modern Language Association*, LIV (1939), 297–303; and T. W. Hill, "The Engima of Wilkie Collins," *Dickensian*, XLVIII (1952), 57–57. Charles Rycroft in *Imagination and Reality: Psycho-analytical Essays 1951–1961*, has an essay on the psychological plot of *The Moonstone*, 1968.

THE MOONSTONE

Type of work: Novel
Author: Wilkie Collins (1824–1889)
Type of plot: Mystery romance
Time of plot: 1799–1849
Locale: India and England
First published: 1868

If not a true detective novel, The Moonstone *is, at the least, a classic mystery story. The theft of the cursed jewel is told in bits and pieces by several narrators who not only deepen the mystery, but also characterize themselves vividly and portray upper-middle-class life in Victorian England with fidelity.*

Principal Characters

Franklin Blake, a genial young man, Lady Verinder's nephew. According to the terms of John Herncastle's will he is given temporary charge of the Moonstone, a diamond which Herncastle had taken during the storming of Seringapatam and which is to be given to his niece, Rachel Verinder, on her birthday following her uncle's death. Of great religious significance in the worship of Brahma and Vishnu, the stone, which is worth about thirty thousand pounds, is supposed to bring ill fortune to any but worshipers of the Moon-God from whose forehead it had been stolen. After presenting the stone to Rachel, Blake, who has been suffering from insomnia, is given secretly a dose of laudanum. In his partly drugged state he goes to Rachel's sitting room during the night and takes the stone from a cabinet. Rachel witnesses the act but, being in love with Blake and thinking he is taking the stone because he needs money, she does not tell what she has seen. A year later, after the stone has been located and the details of its disappearance are cleared, Blake and Rachel are married.

Rachel Verinder, his cousin. In keeping the secret of the lost gem, she suffers the accusations of officials, servants, and friends. Thinking Blake does not love her, she vents her unhappiness on others. During Blake's absence from England she promises to marry Godfrey Ablewhite, but she suddenly breaks the engagement. She and Blake are married after the mystery has been solved.

Godfrey Ablewhite, a handsome young Londoner who, seeing that Blake is semiconscious when he takes the diamond, removes the gem from Blake's hand. Godfrey delivers the gem at once to a London moneylender for safe keeping. After a year he redeems the diamond with the intention of selling it in Amsterdam, in order to pay his debts. In the maneuver to get aboard ship, he disguises himself as a sailor. His dead body is found in a waterfront lodging house, but the stone is missing; it has been reclaimed by its Hindu owners.

Lady Julia Verinder, Rachel's mother and the sister of John Herncastle, who brought the diamond from India. A gentlewoman, she is unnerved by having the police in her home. She goes to London, where she dies of a heart ailment.

Gabriel Betteredge, the venerable house steward to Lady Julia Verinder; he narrates much of the story. His life is guided by philosophies he combs from "Robinson Crusoe," a book which he reads over and over and quotes constantly.

Sergeant Richard Cuff, a grizzled, elderly detective of the London police force, sent by Blake's father to investigate the loss of the diamond. Amiable and knowledgeable in human nature, he is loved by almost everyone who knows him. His keen interest is rose culture, which subject he argues ardently with the Verinder gardener during the investigation. Cuff tells the sixth narrative in the section titled "The Discovery of the Truth."

Mr. Bruff, the old lawyer who, as family counselor for three generations, executed John Herncastle's will. As the executor of Lady Julia Verinder's will, he becomes Rachel's guardian. Sensing the motive for the girl's silence and bitterness, he arranges to bring her and Franklin Blake together whenever possible. Bruff relates the second narrative in unraveling the mystery.

Rosanna Spearman, the second housemaid at Lady Julia Verinder's estate. The former inmate of a reformatory, she has been taken in by Lady Julia and given a fresh start in life. In love with Blake and suspecting him of the theft of the diamond because of paint (from the door to Rachel's sitting room) on his nightgown, Rosanna takes the garment, locks it in a box, and sinks the box in quicksand. She herself commits suicide. From a letter which she left with a friend, Blake and Betteredge learn, about a year later, the details of her love for Blake and her effort to help him.

Dr. Thomas Candy, the family physician, who administers laudanum for Franklin Blake's sleeplessness after Rachel Verinder's birthday party. Dr. Candy, pictured as a suspect, loses his memory after an illness contracted from exposure on the night of the party.

Ezra Jennings, Dr. Candy's assistant during the physician's long illness. Strange in appearance and of questionable background, Jennings is a likely suspect as an accomplice in the theft. Actually a congenial person, his behavior is due to a severe disease from which he dies. His explanation of the effects of laudanum leads to the solution of the mystery of the diamond's disappearance.

Mr. Murthwaite, an authority on Indian religions. At the end he writes to Bruff a letter describing a religious festival in India, a ceremony which revealed the Moon-God with the restored diamond gleaming in its forehead.

Septimus Lukier, the London moneylender with whom Godfrey leaves the Moonstone while he makes plans to get the gem out of England.

Superintendent Seegrave, the first police officer to investigate the disappearance of the Moonstone. His bungling tactics and manner emphasize Cuff's aptness.

Drusilla Clack, a poor relation of Lady Verinder and a religious fanatic. Her descriptions of tract-passing in her efforts to save people's souls are classics in literary humor.

Penelope, Betteredge's daughter and Lady Julia's servant, who reminds her father of events as he narrates his part of the story. Penelope tells of the actions of the servants during the investigation.

Lucy Yolland, Lady Julia's young clubfooted neighbor. Ugly, sullen, and distrustful, she becomes friendly with Rosanna. Lucy shows her loyalty by keeping Rosanna's suicide letter secret for a year.

Octavius Guy, Bruff's young employee, nicknamed "Gooseberry" because of his bulging eyes. Gooseberry follows Godfrey as he makes his way toward the boat with the diamond.

The Three Indians, whose actions are always related by another person. Never "seen" in the story, they are always in quest of the stolen diamond. Their presence at the scene of Godfrey Ablewhite's murder was proved, and they were re-

ported by Mr. Murthwaite as "disappear-
ing" in the throng gathered at the Hindu

ceremony where the Moonstone was last
seen.

The Story

In the storming of Seringapatam in India, in the year 1799, John Herncastle, a violent and cruel man, stole the sacred Hindu diamond called the Moonstone. The jewel had been taken years before from the forehead of the Moon-God in its Brahmin shrine, and Herncastle's theft was only one of a series. Since the stone had first been stolen three faithful Hindus had followed its trail, sworn to recover the gem and return it to the statue of the Moon-God. Herncastle took the gem to England and kept it in a bank vault. He saved himself from murder by letting the Hindus know that if he were killed the stone would be cut up into smaller gems, thus losing its sacred identity. Herncastle left the jewel to his niece, Rachel Verinder, at his death.

The stone was to be presented to Rachel on her birthday following her uncle's death, and young Franklin Blake, Lady Verinder's nephew, was asked by Herncastle's lawyer to take the gift to his cousin. Franklin took the stone to his cousin's estate and barely missed death at the hands of the Hindus before reaching his destination. On the advice of Gabriel Betteredge, the Verinders' old family servant, Franklin put the gem in the vault of a bank nearby until the birthday arrived, as the Hindus had been seen in the neighborhood about three weeks before. Franklin and Rachel fell in love, and even the appearance of Godfrey Ablewhite, a handsome and accomplished charity worker, failed to weaken Rachel's affection. Godfrey had been asked to attend the birthday celebration, together with a number of guests, including Dr. Candy, the town physician, and Mr. Bruff, the family lawyer.

While the guests at the birthday dinner were admiring the beauty of the jewel, they heard the beating of a drum on the terrace. Three Hindus had appeared, disguised as jugglers. One of the guests was Mr. Murthwaite, a famous traveler in the Orient, and at a sharply spoken word from him the Indians retreated. Watchdogs were released to protect the house that night. There was no disturbance to alarm the household, however, and everyone thought all had gone well until Rachel announced the jewel had disappeared from an unlocked cabinet in her dressing-room.

Over Rachel's protests, Franklin Blake insisted the police be called in. The Hindus were arrested and put in jail, but to the astonishment of everyone they were able to prove an alibi for the entire night.

Little about the crime was discovered until Sergeant Cuff of Scotland Yard arrived. He decided that some fresh paint from the door in Rachel's dressing-room must have come off on someone's clothes. Rachel, for some unknown reason, refused to allow a search for the stained clothing. Sergeant Cuff suspected that Rachel had staged the theft herself, and her actions seemed to substantiate his theory. He also thought that Rosanna Spearman, a maid with a criminal record, was a party to the plot, for he learned that Rosanna had made a new night-dress shortly after the theft. Sergeant Cuff guessed it was to take the place of another dress which was stained. Because the Verinders opposed his efforts, he dropped the case. The only other clue he had was that Rosanna might have hidden something in the rocks by the seashore. He suspect it was the stained dress. Rosanna committed suicide soon afterward by throwing herself into a pool of quicksand. Betteredge discovered she had left a letter for Franklin, who had departed from the country by the time it was found.

Rachel went to London with her mother, and in time became engaged to Godfrey Ablewhite. When Mr. Bruff told her Godfrey had secretly learned the terms of her mother's will before asking for her hand, Rachel broke the engagement. Franklin returned to England later in the year and went to visit Betteredge, who told him about Rosanna's letter. Franklin got the letter and learned from it that she had thought him guilty of the crime. The letter also gave him directions for recovering a box which, as Sergeant Cuff had thought, she had buried by the sea. The box proved to have the stained nightgown in it, but it was not Rosanna's nightgown. On the contrary, it was Franklin's!

Unable to account for this strange fact, Franklin returned to London, where he had a long talk with Mr. Bruff about the case. Mr. Bruff informed Franklin that the Moonstone must be in a certain bank in London, deposited there by a notorious pawnbroker named Luker. A mysterious attack upon the money-lender seemed to confirm this belief. Franklin told Mr. Bruff of the strange discovery of the nightgown. Mr. Bruff planned a surprise meeting between Franklin and Rachel, at which Franklin learned that Rachel had actually seen him come into the room and steal the stone. Because she loved him she had refused to let the investigation go on. Franklin tried to convince her he had no memory of the deed.

On Mr. Bruff's advice, Franklin returned to the country place and tried to discover what had happened to him that night. From Dr. Candy's assistant, Ezra Jennings, he learned that the doctor had secretly given him a dose of laudanum on the night of the theft, so that Franklin, suffering from insomnia, would get a good night's sleep. Jennings suggested administering a like dose to Franklin again, in the same setting, to see what he would do. Mr. Bruff and Rachel came down from London to watch the experiment.

With the help of Betteredge the scene was set and Franklin given the laudanum. Under its influence he repeated his actions on the night of the theft. Rachel watched him come to her room and take out a substitute stone. She was now convinced that his original act had been an attempt to protect her from the Hindus by removing the stone after he left Rachel's room, however, the drug took full effect and he fell sound asleep.

The experiment explained how the stone disappeared from Rachel's room, but not how it got into a London bank through the hands of Luker. Mr. Bruff suggested that the gem might shortly be redeemed from Luker. Sergeant Cuff was called back into the case, and a watch set on the bank. One day Luker came into the bank and claimed the stone. On his way out he could have passed it to any of three people. All three men were followed. Two proved to be innocent citizens. Bruff's office boy trailed the third, a bearded man who looked like a sailor, to an inn where the suspect took lodgings for the night.

When Franklin and Sergeant Cuff arrived at the inn, they found the sailor dead and the box from the bank empty. Sergeant Cuff examined the dead man closely and then tore away a false wig and beard to expose the features of Godfrey Ablewhite. From Luker they learned that Godfrey had seen Franklin go into Rachel's room the night of the robbery, and that Franklin had given Godfrey the stone with instructions to put it in the bank. Since Franklin had remembered nothing of this request the next day, Godfrey kept the jewel. The mystery solved, Rachel and Franklin were happily reunited.

Several years later Mr. Murthwaite, the explorer, told them of a great festival in honor of the Moon-God which he had witnessed in India. When the idol was unveiled, he saw gleaming in the forehead of the stone image the long-lost treasure of the god—the sacred Moonstone.

Critical Evaluation

T. S. Eliot's well-known statement that "*The Moonstone* is the first, longest, and best of English detective novels" is probably true in a general way, although it needs considerable qualification. Strictly speaking, *The Moonstone* is a novel with a detective, not a detective novel. A crime is committed and the detective, Sergeant Cuff, is brought in. While exhibiting impressive investigative skills, he does not solve the crime; in fact, he even falsely accuses the book's heroine of stealing her own jewel. Following this mistake, Cuff fades from the book and does not reappear until near the end, when he recoups somewhat by identifying the true villain. By this time, however, most of the questions have been answered and Cuff's final revelation is anticlimactic. The mystery is actually solved in bits and pieces over a considerable period of time by a large number of people, the most important of which, Franklin Blake, discovers himself to be the thief.

All of this is not to minimize the importance of *The Moonstone* to the development of the detective story, but only to point out that it is primarily a "sensation novel" in which the detective plays a prominent role. Actually, Collins does establish a number of conventions that are still requisite in the detective novel. Sergeant Cuff is the prototype for a host of fictional investigators. His physical appearance could be a description of Sherlock Holmes or a dozen other literary detectives. Cuff also possesses a humanizing "quirk" (he raises roses) which remains a must even for today's detective hero. His techniques, especially the scientific reconstruction of the crime and the summary explanation in front of the assembled suspects, are still integral to the genre. Other conventions that Collins either introduced or popularized include the incompetent local policeman versus the efficient big city detective, the withheld evidence, the skillful shifting of suspicion from character to character, the adroit amateur who catches clues the professionals miss, and the "fair play method." The reader in this novel is provided the same clues as the participants, and can, if perceptive enough, solve the puzzle for himself.

One difference between most "sensation novels" and "detective novels" is the setting, which is usually foreign or exotic in the former and contemporary in the latter. Collins was one of the first modern writers to combine the two elements in the same book and nowhere does he do it more expertly than in *The Moonstone*. The "myth" of the "Moonstone," with all of its supernatural overtones, the presence of three threatening Indian fakirs, and the general aura of Oriental intrigue which Collins introduces into the midst of everyday middle-class English domestic routine creates a powerful tension and infuses the book with sinister and mysterious overtones.

Another "exotic" touch that adds to the suspense and impact of the novel lies in the way the mystery is finally elucidated. After all the strictly logical procedures have failed, the crime is solved by a probing of the hero's subconscious mind. Thus, it could be said that *The Moonstone* not only established the model for that most rational of forms, the detective novel, but was also one of the first important fictional explorations of irrational behavior and psychological fragmentation—a subject that was to become central in twentieth century fiction.

Bibliography

Ashley, Robert P. "Wilkie Collins and the Detective Story," in *Nineteenth-Century Fiction*. VI (1951), pp. 47–60.

Hutter, Albert D. "Dreams, Transformations, and Literature: The Implications of Detective Fiction," in *Victorian Studies*. XIX (1975), pp. 181–209.

Laidlaw, R.P. " 'Awful Images and Associations': A Study of Wilkie Collins' *The Moonstone*," in *Southern Review*. IX (1976), pp. 211–227.

Lawson, Lewis A. "Wilkie Collins and *The Moonstone*," in *American Imago*. XX (1963), pp. 61–79.

McCleary, G.F. "A Victorian Classic," in *Fortnightly Review*. CLX (1946), pp. 137–141.

Marshall, William H. *Wilkie Collins*. New York: Twayne, 1970, pp. 77–85.

Milley, Henry James Wye. "*The Eustace Diamonds* and *The Moonstone*," in *Studies in Philology*. XXXVI (1939), pp. 651–663.

Murch, A.E. *The Development of the Detective Novel*. New York: Philosophical Library, 1958, pp. 108–113.

Ousby, Ian. *Bloodhounds of Heaven; The Detective in English Fiction from Godwin to Doyle*. Cambridge, Mass: Harvard University Press, 1976, pp. 117–128.

————. "Wilkie Collins's *The Moonstone* and the Constance Kent Case," in *Notes & Queries.* XXI (1974), p. 25.

Phillips, Walter Clarke. *Dickens, Reade, and Collins, Sensation Novelists: A Study in the Conditions and Theories of Novel Writing in Victorian England.* New York: Columbia University Press, 1919.

Reed, John R. "English Imperialism and the Unacknowledged Crime of *The Moonstone*," in *Clio.* II (1973), pp. 281–290.

Robinson, Kenneth. *Wilkie Collins, a Biography.* Westport, Conn.: Greenwood, 1972, pp. 212–224, 226–227.

Rycroft, Charles. "A Detective Story: Psychoanalytic Observations," in *Psychoanalytic Quarterly.* XXVI (1957), pp. 229–245.

Sayers, Dorothy L. *The Omnibus of Crime.* New York: Harcourt, Brace, 1929, pp. 22–25.

Symons, Julian. *Mortal Consequences; A History—From the Detective Story to the Crime Novel.* New York: Harper & Row, 1972, pp. 45–49.

Wolfe, Peter. "Point of View and Characterization in Wilkie Collins's *The Moonstone*," in *Forum* (Houston). IV (Summer, 1965), pp. 27–29.

THE WOMAN IN WHITE

Type of work: Novel
Author: Wilkie Collins (1824–1889)
Type of plot: Mystery romance
Time of plot: 1850's
Locale: England
First published: 1860

The story of The Woman in White. *a suspenseful romance based in part upon the case history of an actual crime, is told by a collection of papers by different hands. This method gives Collins a chance to show the versatility of his style and to lend variety to his narrative.*

Principal Characters

Walter Hartright, the chief narrator. Engaged as an art instructor to Laura Fairlie, he endears himself to his student, who is betrothed to an older man of rank. Laura decides to complete her wedding plans, and Hartright leaves to go to Central America. Returning, he learns of Laura's unhappy marriage. Hartright then gathers facts to incriminate the conspirators who have plotted to gain Laura's money. He marries Laura, who is now penniless, during the investigation.

Laura Fairlie, who becomes Lady Glyde. In her husband's conspiracy to secure her fortune, Laura is concealed for a time in her room. Meanwhile the woman in white is held incommunicado, dies, and is buried as Laura, Lady Glyde. Laura, committed by the conspirators to the asylum from which the woman in white has escaped, is abducted and hidden until Hartright completes his investigation.

Marian Halcombe, Laura's half sister, who works with Hartright as a protector of the frail Laura. Strong, courageous, she combats Laura's adversaries during Hartright's absence. Although in love with Hartright, Marian, absorbed in feminism, is willing to remain unmarried and to live with the Hartrights.

Sir Percival Glyde, Laura's husband, who resorts to conspiracy, involving his wife's incarceration, to get money for his debts. Knowing of Hartright's investigation of his parentage, Sir Percival sets fire to the vestry in order to destroy church records that would establish his illegitimacy; he dies in the fire.

Count Fosco, his Italian accomplice in the conspiracy. Identified as a foreign spy by Hartright, Fosco exposes his own and Sir Percival's villainy.

Countess Fosco, his wife, the former gay, socially prominent Eleanor Fairlie, dispossessed by her family when she married the Count. Cold and impenetrable because of the secrets sealed up during six years of marriage, she obeys her husband's orders in the conspiracy.

Anne Catherick, the woman in white, committed as a young girl to an asylum by Sir Percival because he feared she knew his secret. The illegitimate daughter of Philip Fairlie, Laura's father—hence, the marked resemblance to Laura—Anne is buried as Lady Glyde. Because of Mrs. Fairlie's attention to Anne as a child, Anne always dresses in white.

Mrs. Catherick, her mother, who lives on income from Sir Percival for her part in forging a marriage entry in the church records.

Professor Pesca, Hartright's long-time friend. Pesca's Italian background helps to identify Fosco as a spy.

Mrs. Elizabeth Clements, Anne's guardian, who reveals Sir Percival's past attentions to Mrs. Catherick, pointing to the supposition that Anne is Percival's child.

Frederick Fairlie, Laura's uncle. An artistic hypochondriac, he lives in seclusion on the family estate.

Mrs. Vesey, Laura's former governess.

Hester Pinkorn, Fosco's cook. She narrates the description of the mysterious young woman hidden in Fosco's house, her behavior during her illness, and the incidents of her death.

Alfred Goodricke, a doctor who tells of his attendance to the young woman;

he attributes her death to heart disease.

Mrs. Eliza Michelson, housekeeper at Sir Percival's estate. She acts as informant between Marian and Anne Catherick, when Anne calls secretly in her effort to save Laura from Sir Percival's wiles.

Margaret Porcher, a slatternly, obstinate housemaid, hired by Sir Percival to keep Marian away from Laura.

Fanny, Laura's maid, discharged by Sir Percival to rid the house of servants faithful to Laura and Marian.

Mrs. Rubelle, Fosco's friend, hired as nurse to Marian, to prevent her foiling the conspiracy.

Major Donthorne, the owner of a resort, who writes Hartright about Philip Fairlie's and Mrs. Catherick's early affair at his place. This information establishes Anne Catherick's parentage.

The Story

Through the help of his Italian friend, Professor Pesca, Walter Hartright was engaged as drawing master to the nieces of Frederick Fairlie, of Limmeridge House, in Cumberland, England. On the day before he left to take up his new position, he met a girl dressed in white wandering about the outskirts of London. Walter discovered that she knew Limmeridge and had once gone to school there with Laura Fairlie. Suddenly the strange girl left him. Shortly afterward a coach came by. Its passenger leaned from the window to ask a policeman if he had seen a girl in white. The policeman had not, and Walter hesitated to intrude. As the coach went off, he heard the man say the girl had escaped from an asylum.

On arriving at Limmeridge, Walter met the first of his two pupils, Marian Halcombe. Marian was homely, but intelligent and charming in manner. Her half-sister, Laura, was the beauty of the family and heiress of Limmeridge House. The two girls were living under the protection of Laura's uncle, Frederick Fairlie, a selfish and fastidious hypochondriac. Walter fell in love with Laura almost at once. Hearing his story about the strange woman in white, Marian searched her mother's letters and discovered that the woman must have been a girl named Anne Catherick, in whom Mrs. Fairlie had taken great interest because she looked so much like Laura.

After several months, Marian realized that Walter was deeply in love with Laura. She advised him to leave, as Laura's father had asked her on his deathbed to marry Sir Percival Glyde. Then Walter met the girl in white again. She was in the graveyard cleaning the stone which bore Mrs. Fairlie's name. She admitted that she hoped to thwart Laura's coming marriage to Sir Percival. Told of this incident, Marian promised she would request a full explanation from Sir Percival.

Walter left Limmeridge. When Sir Percival arrived he explained to Marian that Anne Catherick was the daughter of a woman in his family's service in the past, and that she was in need of hospital treatment. He said he had kept her in an asylum at her mother's request, and he proved the statement with a letter from Mrs. Catherick. His explanation was accepted, and his marriage to Laura took place. Walter, heartbroken, went to Central America as a painter for an archaeological expedition.

When Sir Percival and Laura came home from their wedding trip some months later, Marian found them much changed. Laura was extremely unhappy, and Sir Percival was not at all pleased to have Marian live with them in his house at Blackwater Park. Count Fosco, a huge and very self-assured Italian, arrrived with his wife, Laura's aunt, for a visit. Marian soon learned that the count was involved in money matters with Sir Percival. When Laura was asked to sign a document without looking at it, both she and Marian knew Sir Percival and Count Fosco were trying to get money from her by fraudulent means. Over Sir Percival's loud protests, Laura refused to sign the paper unless he would let her read it. The count interfered and made Sir Percival give up the matter for a time. Marian overheard a conversation between the count and Sir Percival in which they decided to get loans and wait three months before trying again to persuade Laura to sign away her money. The household became one of suspicion and fear.

By chance, one day, Laura met the woman in white and learned that there was some secret in Sir Percival's life, a secret involving both Anne Catherick and her mother. Before Anne could tell her the secret, Count Fosco appeared and frightened the girl away. As soon as Sir Percival learned Anne was in the neighborhood, he became alarmed. He tried to lock both Marian and Laura in their rooms. Marian spied on the two men by climbing to the roof during a pouring rain, where she overheard a plot to get Laura's money by killing her. Before she could act, however, Marian caught a fever from the chill of her rain-soaked clothing, and she was put to bed. Laura, too, became mysteriously ill.

When Laura was better, she was told that Marian had gone to London. She could not believe her sister had left her without saying goodbye and insisted on going to London herself. Actually, Marian had been moved to another room in the house. When Laura arrived in London, Count Fosco met her. She was given drugs, falsely declared insane, dressed in Anne Catherick's old clothes, and taken to the asylum from which Anne had escaped. In the meanwhile, Sir Percival had found Anne. Because of her resemblance to Laura, he planned to have her die and be buried under Laura's name. Anne was very ill anyway. When she died suddenly in London of natural causes, she was buried under the name of Laura, Lady Glyde.

After Marian recovered she was told that her sister was dead. She did not believe either the count or Sir Percival. She went to find Anne and discovered that the woman in the asylum was really Laura. Arranging Laura's escape, she took her back to Limmeridge. At Limmeridge, however, Frederick Fairlie refused to recognize the sickly Laura as anyone but Anne Catherick. Laura's memory had been so impaired by the experience that she could not prove who she was. Furious, Marian and Laura left, and went to look at the false tomb bearing the name of Lady Glyde. There they met Walter Hartright, recently returned from Central America. He had come to pay his respects at Laura's grave.

There was no possibility of returning Laura to her rightful estate as long as her mind was impaired by her terrible experience. Meanwhile Walter Hartright attempted to learn Sir Percival's secret. Finally he discovered that Sir Percival's father and mother had never been legally married. Hoping to destroy the evidence of his birth, Sir Percival attempted to burn an old church record that Walter needed. In the fire he set, Sir Percival burned up the church and himself as well. Mrs. Catherick, after his death, hinted that Laura's father had been the father of illegitimate Anne as well. After more searching, Walter found that this must be true.

Walter returned to London, and together the three planned to clear Laura by forcing the count to confess. Walter's old friend, Professor Pesca, revealed that Count Fosco was a traitor to the secret society to which both Pesca and the count had belonged. Through Pesca's help Walter was able to frighten the count into giving him a confession and written proof in Sir Percival's handwriting that Laura was still alive when Anne had been buried under the name of Lady Glyde. The count fled England, to be killed soon afterward by the secret society he had betrayed.

Walter, Marian, and Laura, who was now much improved, were happy to have proof of the substitution that had been made. Walter and Laura married and went to Limmeridge to confront Frederick Fairlie with the evidence. He was forced to admit Laura was really Laura and his heir. The friends then left, not to return until after Fairlie's death. After his death Laura's and Walter's son took over the estate. Marian lived with the happy family until she died.

Critical Evaluation

Throughout his career, Wilkie Collins, like many other modern writers, was torn between a need to satisfy the demands of the popular reading public and a personal desire to create works of lasting artistic merit. He achieved the desired synthesis only twice, initially with *The Woman in White* and, six years later, with *The Moonstone*. The first of the two was both his most popular work and his most important serious book.

As fantastic as the plot of *The Woman in White* is, it was based, as were many of Collins' crime stories, on an actual case history he discovered in Maurice Méjan's *Recueil des Causes Célèbres*. In 1787 one Mme. de Douhault was cheated out of a portion of her father's estate by a brother. En route to Paris to launch proceedings against her brother, she stopped at a relative's home where she was drugged, confined to a mental hospital, and declared dead, the unscrupulous relatives collecting all that remained of the father's estate. Like her fictional counterpart, Mme. de Douhault finally escaped—wearing a white dress—but, unlike Laura Fairlie, she was never able to legally reestablish her identity, in spite of positive identifications from friends and associates. She died a pauper in 1817.

The crime becomes more elaborate and complicated in Collins' hands. Not only is the heroine drugged and secreted in an asylum, but a deceased double is buried in her place. "The first part of the story," Collins commented in a newspaper interview, "will deal with the destruction of the victim's identity. The second with its recovery." To this basic plot movement Collins added a number of secondary lines: the question of Laura Fairlie's marriage to Percival Glyde, the identity and story of the mysterious "woman in white," Anne Catherick, the love affair between Laura and Walter Hartright, Laura's "death" and the events surrounding it, Percival Glyde's relationship with Anne's mother, Mrs. Catherick, and his mysterious "secret," and, finally, Count Fosco's background and his "secret."

But, complex as this outline may look, Collins handles the threads of the narrative in such a way that they support and complement one another without ever obscuring the central thrust of the book. As Collins answers one question for his reader, he uses that answer to introduce new, more provocative ones. As the puzzles are gradually unraveled, the pressures on the hero and heroines become more and more extreme. For most of the book the victims seem nearly helpless before the villains' power. The reversal does not come until late in the novel and, when it does occur, the shift is sudden. And even in the last important scene, Hartright's confrontation with Fosco, when the initiative is clearly the hero's, the sense of danger remains intense. Nowhere does Collins demonstrate his mastery of intricate plotting more effectively than in *The Woman in White* and it remains, with the possible exception of *The Moonstone,* the most perfectly structured example of the "sensation novel."

The gradual revelation of the intricate conspiracy is made doubly effective by Collins' narrative method. The story is told in bits and pieces by a number of characters who reveal only as much as they know. Some of the narrators are major participants, such as Walter Hartright, Marian Halcombe, and Count Fosco, who explain and interpret the events as they occur or after the fact. Others are minor personages, such as Laura's uncle, Frederick Fairlie, Glyde's housekeeper, Eliza Michelson, and Laura's "tombstone," who can only provide fragments of information that reflect their brief connection to the story. This technique gives Collins a maximum of flexibility, allows him to control the mystery and suspense by revealing only as much information at any one time as convenient, insures variety in the narrative style, mood, and tone, and sharpens the characterizations. As the speakers offer their information, they characterize themselves through their diction, prose style, habits, and attitudes. And, most importantly, Collins' multiple narrative method offers the reader a gigantic prose jigsaw puzzle and leaves it to him to sift through the conflicting versions for the truth. A few years later Collins was to use this same method in writing what many have called the first English detective novel, *The Moonstone*.

The object of the conspiracy, Laura Fairlie, is a passive creature with little color or character. The real conflict is between Marian Halcombe and Walter Hartright on the one one side and Percival Glyde and Count Fosco on the other. In the first half of the book, the events leading up to Laura's falsified "death," it is Marian who acts as a foil to the villains. After Laura's escape, Walter Hartright becomes the primary hero. On the other side, Glyde enters the novel before Fosco, but quickly retreats in the reader's mind to a subordinate position. Of all the characters, it is Fosco who dominates the novel and most impresses the reader.

As Walter Hartright describes her, Marian Halcombe is a physically unattractive woman: "the lady's complexion was almost swarthy, and the dark down on her upper lip was almost a mustache. She had a large, firm, masculine mouth and jaw; prominent piercing resolute brown eyes and thick coal-black hair, growing unusually low on her forehead." But morally and intellectually she is a very strong character. Her qualities, when summed up—loyalty, steadfastness, courage, propriety, intelligence, sensitivity—sound like a list of stock Victorian virtues, but, as Collins presents her, she is most real.

It is Marian who first senses a conspiracy, but it has gone too far to stop. She manages, however, to hamper the villains for a time. The irony of her situation is that when, having courageously risked her life and gained the information she needs to expose the plot, she catches pneumonia in the act— thus exposing herself and becoming helpless when most needed. In addition, her illness gives Fosco an opportunity to read her journal and learn everything about her counter-strategy. But one final irony remains. Having read Marian's comments, Fosco is so impressed by her character and resourcefulness that, for the first time, he allows sentiment to mitigate his treatment of an adversary. This modest moral hesitation is ultimately one of the primary factors in his downfall.

Fosco is one of the most memorable literary criminals of all time. By contrast, Glyde is, in Collins own words, "a weak shabby villain." Glyde is clearly dominated by Fosco and, when he operates alone, does very badly. He reacts emotionally and physically to situations with little planning and crude execution, the most obvious example being the vicarage fire that costs him his life. Because Collins thought "the crime too ingenious for an English villain," he felt it necessary to create Isidor Ottavio Baldassare Fosco.

Collins wisely never introduces or describes Fosco directly to the reader, but allows his presence to grow by means of the reactions and impressions experienced by the other characters. The Count's most obvious physical feature is his size; he is the first of the great fat criminals, a common type in later crime fiction, but unorthodox in Collins' time. "I had begun my story when it struck me that my villain would be commonplace, and I made him fat in opposition to the recognized type of villain." Fosco's physical size is matched by his appetites for food, culture, money, and intrigue: he is, in short, a daemonic Falstaff.

Fosco's intellectual powers are, likewise, impressive; his conspiracy has style as well as intelligence; he is quite witty, extremely articulate, and suavely ironical. And he is no ordinary criminal; he justifies his amoral actions philosophically: "Crime," he tells Marian, "is a good friend to man and to those about him as often as it is an enemy."

For all of his evil, Fosco is an attractive man. In addition to his intelligence, style, courage, and strong, if distorted, sense of honor, he also possesses a number of vivid humanizing traits: his fondness for animals, especially his birds and mice, his feelings for his wife, and his honest admiration, even devotion, toward Marian Halcombe. Perhaps Collins assigned Fosco's punishment to a mysterious Italian political group, rather than to Walter Hartright, because he realized that his readers' ambiguous feelings about Fosco would place some onus on the man who brought him to justice.

But, while critics have long lauded the characterizations of Marian and Fosco, they have tended to ignore Walter Hartright. But he is too important to the novel to be so easily dismissed. If he lacks some of the color and sympathy of Marian, he is, nevertheless, her equal in courage and intelligence. More importantly, looking at the novel from the standpoint of a nineteenth century reader, it is Hartright that one would most likely identify with and it is he who upholds the English national character and middle-class morality in the face of Fosco's threat.

Hartright is the hardworking son of a thrifty drawing master set up against a nobleman and baronet and frustrated by a decadent member of the gentry (Fairlie)—all vestiges of aristocracy. Walter takes his work seriously, is industrious, loyal, rational, courageous, and tenacious—in short, he possesses all of the Puritan middle-class virtues. In contrast to the amoral Fosco, Hartright believes that virtue, truth, and justice must ultimately triumph, and he is given the job of demonstrating that assumption in the action. Because he does it so efficiently, the novel answers the intellectual and moral expectations of the Victorian reading public. And, even to a twentieth century reader, despite Fosco's style and charm, Hartright's final victory seems inevitable and satisfying.

Bibliography

Caracciolo, Peter. "Wilkie Collins's 'Divine Comedy': The Use of Dante in *The Woman in White*," in *Nineteenth-Century Fiction.* XXV (1971), pp. 383–404.

Hyder, Clyde K. "Wilkie Collins and *The Woman in White*," in *PMLA*. LIV (1939), pp. 297–303.

Kendrick, Walter M. "The Sensationalism of *The Woman in White*," in *Nineteenth-Century Fiction.* XXXII (June, 1977), pp. 18–35.

Marshall, William H. *Wilkie Collins.* New York: Twayne, 1970, pp. 56–66.

Muller, C.H. "Incident and Characterization in *The Woman in White*," in *Unisa English Studies.* XI (1973), pp. 33–50.

Robinson, Kenneth. *Wilkie Collins, a Biography.* Westport, Conn.: Greenwood, 1972, pp. 137–154, 159–162.

Wright, Austin. *Victorian Literature; Modern Essays in Criticism.* London: Oxford University Press, 1961, pp. 128–135.

DANIEL DEFOE

Born: St. Giles, London, England (1660)
Died: Moorfields, London (April 26, 1731)

Principal Works

NOVELS: *The Life and Strange Surprizing Adventures of Robinson Crusoe, of York, Mariner,* 1719; *The Memoirs of a Cavalier,* 1720; *The Life, Adventures and Piracies of the Famous Captain Singleton,* 1720; *The Fortunes and Misfortunes of the Famous Moll Flanders,* 1722; *A Journal of the Plague Year,* 1722; *The History and Remarkable Life of Colonel Jacque,* 1722; *Roxana, or The Fortunate Mistress,* 1724; *The Memoirs of Captain Carleton,* 1728.

SHORT STORY: *A True Relation of the Apparition of One Mrs. Veal,* 1706.

POEM: *The True-Born Englishman,* 1701.

TRACTS: *An Essay Upon Projects,* 1697; *The Shortest Way with the Dissenters,* 1702.

MISCELLANEOUS: *A Tour Thro' the Whole Island of Great Britain,* 1724–1727; *A General History of the Pirates,* 1724–1728; *The Complete English Tradesman,* 1725–1727.

Daniel Defoe, best known as the author of *Robinson Crusoe,* is a writer whose journalistic writing still has an appeal because of its assertion of common sense principles and whose works of fiction are also convincing because of the same accent of common sense and esteem for fact.

Few writers have written more voluminously and continuously than Defoe. Though there is uncertainty about the authorship of some works attributed to him, three nineteenth century students compiled separately lists of Defoe's work; the number varies from 183 works of genuine authorship to 254. It was in the midst of such abundant and ceaseless journalism that Defoe produced his works that are remembered; but like the works that are now forgotten, his novels were designed to be in our phrase "newsworthy," to stimulate or satisfy public curiosity and, in some cases, to purify it.

His most famous work, *The Life and Strange Surprizing Adventures of Robinson Crusoe,* was founded on Dampier's *Voyage Round the World* (1697) and on Alexander Selkirk's adventures as actually told by Selkirk to Defoe. Thus, a work that commenced as "news" nevertheless took form as the classic story of civilized man alone with nature. Crusoe's shipwreck, his solitude, and his man Friday open wide vistas of adventure to every reader. Further, Defoe had amazing capacities for creating imaginative detail. His *Journal of the Plague Year* strikes the reader as an eye-witness account of hideous disaster; yet actually Defoe was writing at a distance of several decades. Similar perceptions about his talent can be supported by *Moll Flanders* and other works; whatever sort of adventure Defoe treats has the accent of truth. The events may be startling, but the tone in which they are told is sober, moralistic, even plodding. Such narrative one cannot doubt.

Defoe's life is like much of his work, a mixture of the utterly commonplace and the exciting. He was born in 1660 in the parish of St. Giles, London, to a Nonconformist family and was educated at Morton's Academy at Stoke Newington. He participated in Monmouth's rebellion (1685) but escaped punishment. He took up the business of hosier factor and married Mary Tuffley, by whom he had seven children. Later he became a merchant, dealing in Spanish and Portuguese goods; he even visited Spain. In 1692 his business failed, but he honorably paid off his creditors, a fact attested to by witnesses; he then became secretary and finally owner of a tile works at Tilbury. From this wealth of practical experience came, in 1698, an early and remarkable publication of Defoe's, *An Essay Upon Projects*, which contained far-sighted practical suggestions on road systems, insane asylums, schools for women, military colleges, and other subjects. Benjamin Franklin acknowledged his indebtedness to this study. But it was the vital question of religious conformity which produced the first of a long series of pamphlets in which Defoe argued the position of the Nonconformists; the most famous of these was *The Shortest Way with the Dissenters*, published anonymously in 1702. When the authorship was discovered, a price was put on his head in an advertisement describing Defoe as "a middle-sized spare man about forty years old, of a brown complexion and dark brown-colored hair, but wears a wig; a hooked nose, a sharp chin, grey eyes, and a large mole near his mouth"—a description, it may be remarked, in Defoe's own sober and factual vein. Finally apprehended, fined, put in the pillory three times, he was forced to find sureties for his behavior. Defoe spent only one year in prison, thanks to the aid of the influential Robert Harley.

After his release from prison Defoe began *The Review* (February, 1704). Published three times a week, this work extends to more than eight volumes. The publication contained news as well as essays on subjects of trade and national policy. There were also discussions of minor problems of morals and manners in the Scandal Club columns; these probably influenced the form soon taken by the *Tatler* and *Spectator* papers.

Defoe, like some of his heroes, united adventure and business. Involved in secret political missions for Robert Harley, Defoe wrote a *History of the Union* which appeared in 1709. In 1715 he was indicted for libel of Lord Annesley, whom he accused of using the army in Ireland to join a Jacobite rebellion. Before his trial he published *An Appeal to Honor and Justice*, an apologia that gives one some insight into Defoe's busy life. He was imprisoned and gained his freedom only by consenting to become a government agent. He was also a subeditor of *Mist's Journal*, a Jacobite publication which he agreed to chasten and tame.

In 1719 *Robinson Crusoe* had instant success. In 1724 came *A Tour Thro' the Whole Island of Great Britain*, followed soon after by *A New Voyage round the World*, apparently drawn only from the author's wide imagination, but apparently verified by his amazing zest for accurate detail.

All this journalistic activity must have built up a substantial income. However, Defoe did not die in his own home at Stoke Newington but in Moorfields, on April 26, 1731. It is known that at this time Defoe's journalistic employment came to an end, perhaps because Mist discovered he was a government agent and let it be known to other editors. Mist himself was imprisoned for attacking Defoe physically; perhaps he even planned further revenge. At any rate, in his last years Defoe wrote anonymously or under the name "Andrew Moreton"; in the summer previous to his death he was in hiding. For these reasons there is uncertainty about his final years, but all available facts show him to be like his Captain Singleton, a man of vigor, willing to shoulder the burden of his courageous convictions. His life casts a confirming light over his most famous books; the materials may be startling, but, written as they were by a man of affairs and simple moral perceptions, there is no nonsense in them.

Bibliography

There is no complete edition of Defoe. The best known of his works have been reprinted in *Novels and Selected Writings*, 14 vols., 1927. The standard biography in English is James R. Sutherland, *Defoe*, 1954. An important study in French is Paul Dottin, *Daniel Defoe et ses Romans*, 3 vols., 1924, rather poorly translated in part as *The Life and Surprising Adventures of Daniel Defoe*, 1929. See also William Minton, *Daniel Defoe*, 1879; John F. Ross, *Swift and Defoe: A Study in Relationship*, 1941; William Freeman, *The Incredible Defoe*, 1950; Brian Fitzgerald, *Daniel Defoe: A Study in Conflict*, 1954; John Robert Moore, *Daniel Defoe, Citizen of the Modern World*, 1958; M. E. Novak, *Defoe and the Nature of Man*, 1963; and Frank W. Ellis, ed., *Twentieth Century Interpretations of* Robinson Crusoe, 1969. A delightful book of non-scholarly pretentions is Walter de la Mare, *Desert Islands and Robinson Crusoe*, 1930.

A JOURNAL OF THE PLAGUE YEAR

Type of work: Novel
Author: Daniel Defoe (1660?–1731)
Time: 1665
Locale: London, England
First published: 1722

Essay-Review

Unlike Defoe's more obviously fictional books and novels, *A Journal of the Plague Year* is rarely read as a whole though a number of writers, such as Virginia Woolf, testify to its impact. The book shows on every page more clearly than *Moll Flanders* or the other episodic novels posing as "true accounts," the intricate and slow development of the English novel which attracted writers away from sermons and polemics in the early eighteenth century and established a formal tradition good for some two centuries. Thus when John Drinkwater called Defoe "the founder of the English novel," his justification may be found as much in the *Journal* as in *Robinson Crusoe* or *Roxana*.

The first problem in the development of the novel was to establish a working relationship between fact and fiction; the traditional novel still begins with a factual introduction to assist the "willing suspension of disbelief" so necessary to the novelist's manipulation of material and reader. Defoe's invention was to use a hard core of statistics, tabulated on the pages of the *Journal*, of the weekly death "bills" or returns from the ninety-seven parishes in the City of London and the sixteen or so in Southwark and outside the city limits; but the tables are disposed artistically throughout the work instead of being appendixed and are surrounded by further particulars which become more hedged with conditions as Defoe elaborates them. In a very short time the reader is in a region of rumor which Defoe first solemnly reports, then rationally dismisses or qualifies. Rumor is the middle ground between statistics and the imagination, and Defoe is careful to allow us to believe it or not as we wish. We accept such folklore at face value, perhaps, because gossip is more entertaining than truth. Thus the first sentence of the *Journal* does not begin "Once upon a time," but specifies September, 1664, as the date the narrator first heard that the plague had come to Holland for the second year running. The first paragraph then expands with rumors about its place of origin: "they say . . . some said . . . others . . . all agreed."

The subtitle of the *Journal*—"Being Observations or Memorials of the Most Remarkable Occurences, as well Publick as Private, which happened in London during the last Great Visitation in 1665. Written by a Citizen who continued all the while in London. Never made publick before"—is a bland lie, one which indicates the second way that Defoe encouraged the reader's imagination to work for him: "Observations or Memorials" sufficiently confuses the distinction between what was recorded at the time and what was remembered later. Defoe's sources, beyond the death bills, were not extensive and his memories second-hand, but his imagination was fertile. He carefully controlled and encouraged it by the threefold organization of his *Journal*. Contrary to its title, it is not a daily record, and the time references shift from September to August and over the whole summer of the plague. Instead of daily entries Defoe used time references, from September 1664 to December 1665, as ways of beginning and concluding his narrative, ending with the doggerel quatrain which celebrates the narrator's deliverance. Within the work he preserves a gradual movement of the plague from the west to the east parts of the city, ending with a central holocaust; and scattered throughout the work we find his tables of statistics. Neither the geographical, the chronological, nor the numerical progress of the plague is consistently followed. The jumps in geography and time make one want to restore logical order to the work and thereby turn it into a literal "journal," at the same time risking loss of its imaginative qualities.

Defoe's imagination proceeds mechanically but energetically by considering one general topic and its subheadings at a time. Thus we get several pages of increasingly horrific detail about the practices of nurses or a catalogue of various kinds of quacks, fortunetellers, prophets, and necromancers who flourished during that awful summer; the section on women in childbirth, for instance cooly divides their tragedies into those who died in childbirth with and without the plague, and the former are further subdivided into those who died before giving birth, or in the middle of giving birth, or before the cord was cut. Defoe's narrator could see little of these matters for himself, but "they say" and "I heard" fill up the paragraphs one after another until all possible contingencies have been covered.

Defoe's imagination works with three classes of corroborative detail: The quick summary, the brief anecdote, and the extended story, each of which could have supplied him with many more narratives, and did indeed in his *Due Preparations for the Plague* published about the same time in order to catch the same apprehensive market as his *Journal*. The summary paragraph often introduces a series of brief anecdotes but sometimes stands alone, as in his brief recital of the killing of forty thousand dogs and two hundred thousand housecats as a precaution against the spread of the plague. There are many brief anecdotes, such as the frequently anthologized account of purifying a purse, which exhibit at once the common-sense cautiousness Defoe admires, the honesty of the Londoner, and the current belief that the plague was spread by contaminated air. The longest of the stories, filling about one tenth of the *Journal*, is that of the three men and their company who spent the summer camping in Epping Forest. Defoe tells the story at length to show what happened to Londoners who left the city and retired to places where his narrator could not follow them.

Defoe's subject was epic in scope: a great metropolis in the midst of a boom following the Restoration is slowly strangled by a hidden enemy. The size of his subject gives ample scope for the inclusion of all sorts of material, but his handling of it is typically original. Instead of a heroic poem we get the sober account of an average Londoner, a superior type of the real heroes of his book—those from Lord Mayor to beggar who did not abandon their city. The narrator is simply identified by the subscription of "H. F." to the *Journal* (possibly an allusion to Defoe's uncle, Henry Foe) and is described as a saddler engaged in the American trade. This, like all trade and manufacturing, ended with the onslaught of the plague in June, 1665, and left his narrator free to observe the reactions of his townsfolk.

Defoe's choice of narrator serves to control his material by presenting it soberly and thus to press Defoe's own views on the prevention of the plague, as in his saddler's criticism of shutting up the living with the sick when one plague victim was found in the house. But the opinions of the narrator seem contradictory in two respects. The first is purely technical; the saddler recommends shutting up one's house at the beginning of the plague but acknowledges that supplies have to be brought in by servants and thus the plague spreads. He shuts up his house and servants but wanders through the streets even to the deathpits (he observes that one in his parish of Aldgate holds eleven hundred and fourteen corpses when full); he must wander in order to write his "journal." Except for a period of three weeks when he is conscripted as an "examiner" he remains an observer and thus uncharacteristic of the energetic and resourceful citizens, the details of whose organization seem practical and whose spirit Defoe lauds during the plague and bewails when it passes as the plague diminishes.

In a second respect the ambivalence of the narrator is more striking: he lauds common sense and courage where he finds it but ascribes to providence the salvation of the city in the despair most felt at the end of September, when deaths numbered over ten thousand weekly. Then, suddenly, the weekly bills showed a dramatic decrease. To whom should go the praise? Defoe has it both ways, as he had done when he solemnly introduced the scandalous history of Moll Flanders as a moral tract. It is this ambivalence which is the true foundation of the English novel, a recital of fictions which rings, and is, essentially true.

Bibliography

Bastian, F. "Defoe's *Journal of the Plague Year* Reconsidered," in *Review of English Studies.* XVI (1965), pp. 151–173.

Blair, Joel. "Defoe's Art in *A Journal of the Plague Year*," in *South Atlantic Quarterly.* LXXII (1973), pp. 243–254.

Flanders, W. Austin. "Defoe's *Journal of the Plague Year* and the Modern Urban Experience," in *Centennial Review.* XVI (1972), pp. 328–348.

Hahn, H.G. "An Approach to Character Development in Defoe's Narrative Prose," in *Philological Quarterly.* LI (1972), pp. 851–854.

James, E. Anthony. *Daniel Defoe's Many Voices: A Rhetorical Study of Prose Style and Literary Methods.* Amsterdam: Rodopi Nv, 1972, pp. 135–153, 156–158.

Johnson, Clifford. "Defoe's Reaction to Enlightened Secularism: *A Journal of the Plague Year,*" in *Enlightenment Essays.* III (1973), pp. 169–177.

Kay, Donald. "Defoe's Sense of History in *A Journal of the Plague Year,*" in *Xavier University Studies.* IX (1970), pp. 1–8.

Nicholson, Watson. *Historical Sources of Defoe's Journal of the Plague Year.* Port Washington, N.Y.: Kennikat, 1966.

Richetti, John J. *Defoe's Narratives: Situation and Structure.* Oxford: Clarendon Press, 1975, pp. 233–240.

Rynell, Alarik. "Defoe's *A Journal of the Plague Year,*" in *English Studies.* L (1969), pp. 452–464.

Schonhorn, Manuel. "Defoe's *Journal of the Plague Year*: Topography and Intention," in *Review of English Studies.* n.s., XIX (1968), pp. 387–402.

Sutherland, James. *Daniel Defoe.* Cambridge, Mass.: Harvard University Press, 1971, pp. 163–172.

Vickers, Brian. "Daniel Defoe's *Journal of the Plague Year*: Notes for a Critical Analysis," in *Filologia Moderna.* XIII (1973), pp. 161–170.

Walton, James. "The Romance of Gentility: Defoe's Heroes and Heroines," in *Literary Monographs.* IV (1971), pp. 110–122.

Zimmerman, Everett. "H.F.'s Meditations: *A Journal of the Plague Year,*" in *PMLA.* LXXXVII (1972), pp. 417–423.

MOLL FLANDERS

Type of work: Novel
Author: Daniel Defoe (1660–1731)
Type of plot: Picaresque romance
Time of plot: Seventeenth century
Locale: England and the American colonies
First published: 1722

The best introduction to Defoe's classic picaresque, an important forerunner of the modern novel, is to quote its full title: The Fortunes and Misfortunes of the famous Moll Flanders, who was born in Newgate, and during a life of continued variety, for threescore years, besides her childhood, was twelve years a Whore, five times a Wife (thereof once to her own brother), twelve years a Thief, eight years a transported Felon in Virginia, at last grew rich, lived honest, and died a penitent. Written from her own Memorandums.

Principal Characters

Moll Flanders, an English adventuress (known also as **Mistress Betty, May Flanders, Mrs. Flanders**), one of the most engaging female rogues in all literature. She relates her entire life story, from infancy to final years of repentance, with frankness and full detail. As the daughter of a woman convicted of a felony and transported to Virginia, Moll spends her early years in the company of some gipsies, then with several families who treat her well. By the age of fourteen, Moll is attractive, intelligent, resourceful, and womanly. Her first affair is with the elder son in a household where she has entered service. The younger son, Robin, falls in love with her and becomes her first husband. After five years of marriage and the birth of two children, he dies. Later Moll preys on mankind for many years. Using her beauty and wits to support herself in as much luxury and comfort as she can manage, she marries a succession of husbands, one of them her half brother, and eventually turns thief and pickpocket. She acquires a very sizable fortune before she is caught. At Newgate, where her life began, she receives the death sentence but succeeds in

getting transportation instead. A former husband, Jemmy E., is being sent to the colonies on the same ship. The two establish a plantation in Carolina, prosper greatly, and ultimately decide to go back to England to spend their remaining years in repentance. Moll maintains a moral tone in relating all her illegal, extra-marital, and exciting adventures, but her professed repentance never seems to keep her from enjoying the fruits of her actions.

Moll's Mother, a convicted felon transported to Virginia soon after Moll's birth. The mother does well in Virginia, builds up a large estate, lives to a satisfying old age, and leaves a farm to Moll.

Humphry, a sea captain. He marries Moll and takes her to Virginia, where he introduces her to his mother (and hers). He remains in Virginia when Moll returns to England after deciding that she can no longer live with her half brother as his wife.

Humphry, the son of Moll and the sea captain. When Moll returns home, he stays in Virginia, where he becomes a planter. He turns over to Moll the plantation willed her and proves a dutiful and loving son.

Jemmy E., an Irish adventurer and highway robber, Moll's former husband with whom she establishes a plantation in the Carolina Colony. He follows Moll back to England, where they spend their declining years in repentance and some luxury.

"Mother Midnight," a midwife who owns a nursing home for unwed mothers. She trains Moll as a thief. Later she takes care of Moll's money and is Moll's agent in sending valuable goods to Carolina.

A Gentleman of Bath, married to a woman mentally ill. Moll lives with him and bears him three children.

A Linen Draper, a spendthrift who marries Moll, runs through her money quickly, and abandons her.

Robin, Moll's first husband, the younger son in the family where she first takes service.

The Story

When her mother was transported to the colonies as a felon, eighteen-month-old Moll Flanders was left without family or friends to care for her. For a time she was befriended by a band of gipsies, who deserted her in Colchester. There the child was a charge of the parish. Becoming a favorite of the wife and daughters of the mayor, Moll received gentle treatment and no little attention and flattery.

At the age of fourteen Moll Flanders was again left without a home. When her indulgent instructress died, she was taken in service by a kindly woman of means, receiving instruction along with the daughters of the family. In all but wealth Moll was superior to these daughters. During her residence there she lost her virtue to the oldest son of the family and secretly became his mistress. Later when Robin, the youngest son, made her a proposal of marriage, she accepted him. At the end of five years Robin died. Soon afterward Moll married a spendthrift draper, who quickly went through her savings and was imprisoned. In the meantime Moll took lodgings at the Mint. Passing as a widow, she called herself Mrs. Flanders.

Her next venture in matrimony was with a sea captain with whom she sailed to the Virginia colony. There she discovered to her extreme embarrassment that she was married to her own half-brother. After eight years of residence in Virginia she returned to England to take up her residence at Bath. In due time she became acquainted with a gentleman whose wife was demented. Moll helpfully nursed him through a serious illness. Later she became his mistress. When she found herself with child, she made arrangements for her lying-in, sent the child to nurse, and rejoined her companion. During the six years in which they lived together, she gave birth to three children and saved enough money to support herself after the gentleman had regretted his indiscretions and left her.

Next the ambitious girl met a banker with whom she carried on a mild flirtation. However, she left him to marry an Irishman named Jemmy E., supposedly a very wealthy gentleman of Lancashire. Moll had allowed him to believe she had means. She soon learned that her new husband was penniless. He had played on her the same trick she had used on him. Both rogues, they were a congenial couple, but eventually they decided to separate; he to follow his unlawful profession of highway robbery, she to return to the city. After Jemmy had left her, Moll found that she was again to become a mother. Lying-in at the house of a midwife, Moll was delivered of a healthy boy who was boarded out.

In the meantime Moll Flanders had been receiving letters from her admirer, the bank clerk. They met at an inn and were married there. On the day after the ceremony she saw her Lancashire husband, the highwayman, in the courtyard of the inn, and she was able to save him from arrest. For five years, until his death, Moll lived with the banker in great happiness. After his death she sold her property and took lodgings. Forty-eight years old and with two children as dependents, she was prompted by the devil to steal a bundle from an apothecary shop. Next she stole a necklace from a pretty little girl on her way home from dancing school. Thus Moll Flanders embarked on a twelve-year period as a thief. Sometimes she disguised herself in men's clothing. A chance encounter with a gentleman at Bartholomew Fair resulted in an affair which the two carried on for some time. Moll became, after a period of apprenticeship, the richest thief in all England. Her favorite disguise was that of a beggar woman.

Finally she was seized while trying to steal two pieces of silk brocade and was imprisoned in Newgate prison. There she saw again her former husband, the highwayman, committed at Newgate for a robbery on Hounslow Heath. Before going up for trial and sentence, Moll repented of her sins; nevertheless she was sentenced to death by the court. But through the kind offices of a minister, Moll Flanders, now truly repentant, was given a reprieve. The next day she watched her fellow prisoners being carried away in carts for the fate which had been spared her. She was finally sentenced to transportation to America.

The highwayman, with whom she had become reconciled, was awarded a like sentence. The pair embarked for Virginia in the same ship, having made all arrangements for a comfortable journey, and stocked themselves with the tools and materials necessary for running a plantation in the new world. Forty-two days after leaving an Irish port they arrived in Virginia. Once ashore, Moll found that her mother had died. Her brother, whom she had once married, and her son were still living near the spot where she had disembarked.

Not yet wishing to meet her relatives, and not desiring to be known as a transported criminal in America, she arranged for transportation to the Carolina colony. After crossing Chesapeake Bay, she and the highwayman found the ship already overloaded. They decided to stay in Maryland and set up a plantation there. With two servants and fifty acres of land under cultivation, they soon prospered. Then Moll arranged an interview with her son in Virginia across the bay.

In due course she learned that her mother had willed her a plantation on the York River, a plantation complete with stock and servants. To her son she presented one of the stolen watches which she had brought from London. After five weeks she returned to Maryland, where she and her husband became wealthy and prosperous planters of good repute throughout all the colonies. This prosperity was augmented by the arrival of a second cargo of goods from England, for which Moll had arranged before she sailed. In the meantime the man who had been both brother and husband to Moll died and she was able to see her son without any embarrassment.

At the age of seventy years, Moll returned to England. Her husband soon joined her there, and they resolved to spend the rest of their lives in repentance for their numerous sins.

Critical Evaluation

Ever since it was first published in 1722, the reading public has enjoyed *Moll Flanders* as the lusty, energetic tale of a seventeenth century adventuress and manipulator. Many readers have assumed the story is true biography; Daniel Defoe himself rather coyly suggests as much, perhaps because he feared such a scandalous story could not be published or would not be popular if it were seen as the work of the imagination.

In this, as in his other great novels, such as *Robinson Crusoe* and *A Journal of the Plague Year,* Defoe achieves his realistic effect by incorporating a wealth of authentic detail. Having been a pamphleteer and journalist much of his life, Defoe knew how well the concrete fact, the specific example, build plausibility. He has Moll relate her remarkable story simply, thoroughly, and with candor. She is literal-minded and bothers little with description or metaphor. (In his preface, Defoe claims to have cleaned up the language and omitted some of the more "vicious part of her life"; thus Moll's sexual adventures are related in curious, sometimes amusing circumlocutions.) Moll sticks mainly to the stark realities of her life except for passages in which she moralizes about her misdeeds.

Despite the verisimilitude, however, there is a problem of tone which frequently puzzles the modern reader and has stirred a lively controversy among critics. The question may be stated thus: is the story full of conscious irony, or is it told in utter sincerity? If the former is the case, most scholars agree *Moll Flanders* is a masterwork both as social commentary and fictional art; if the latter, there are lapses in the author's moral scheme and his literal ability.

The problem centers more on Moll's attitudes than her actions. Given her situation, that of a woman of no status but with large ambitions, her behavior is entirely plausible. In her childhood, Moll is dependent for her very survival upon the whims and kindnesses of strangers. By the time she is eight years old, she is already determined to be a "gentlewoman"—an ambition very nearly impossible to fulfill in seventeenth century England when one has neither family nor, more importantly, money. She is quick to recognize the value of money in assuring not only one's physical security but one's place in the world—and she aims for a comfortable place indeed. Money thus becomes her goal and eventually her god. To attain it, she uses whatever means are at hand; as a beautiful woman, her sexuality is the handiest means available. When, after a number of marriages and other less legitimate alliances, sex is no longer a spendable coin, she turns to thieving, and rapidly becomes a master of the trade.

We know from other of Defoe's writings that the author sympathized with the plight of women in his society; education and most trades (except the oldest profession) were closed to them, and for the most part their welfare was entirely dependent upon that of their husbands or other men in their lives. As a hardheaded pragmatist who finds herself in straitened circumstances, Moll is much akin to Becky Sharp and Scarlett O'Hara; all three use their own ingenuity to survive in a hostile world, and although we do not entirely condone their behavior, we can understand it.

But after Moll has acted, she reflects; and it is this reflection that poses our problem. For convenience, she marries the younger brother of the man who first seduced her. After he dies, she remarks that "He had been really a very good husband to me, and we lived very agreeably together," but then she quickly complains that because he had not had time to acquire much wealth, she was "not much mended by the match." Another five-year marriage also ends in her widowhood; she wastes not a word in grieving the husband who has given her "an uninterrupted course of ease and content," but laments the loss of his money at excessive length. Soon afterwards, she steals a gold necklace from a child and admits that she was tempted to kill the child to prevent any outcry. She rationalizes that "I only thought I had given the parents a just reproof for their negligence in leaving the poor lamb to come home by itself, and it would teach them to take more care another time."

These recollections are told from the point of view of a woman seventy years old. She spends a good deal of time explaining that poverty and fear of poverty drove her to all her wickedness; yet she never admits that even when she is relatively secure, she keeps on scheming and thieving. Like many another entrepreneur, she has come to find excitement and fulfillment in the turning of the profit, the successful clinching of a "deal," the accumulation of wealth for its own sake. Although she repents her flagrant sins—deception, thieving, whoring—she apparently never recognizes the sin of her spirit in basing all human relationships upon their monetary worth. Furthermore, although she closes her account by declaring that she and her husband are "resolved to spend the remainder of our years in sincere penitence for the wicked lives we have lived," they are now free from want, partly because of an inheritance, but also because of the proceeds from her years as master thief. We see no indication that penitence goes any deeper than a rather gratified feeling that she has made peace with her Maker (a peace made, by the way, in Newgate prison while Moll was under sentence of death). There is no evidence that she intends to make restitution of stolen goods or apply herself in positive good works to offset some of her wicked deeds.

The question, then, is whether Defoe expects us to see the irony in what one critic has called Moll's moral "muddle"; or whether he is so outraged at what poverty and the lack of opportunity can do that he himself fails to see the lapses in her moral system. We get a few clues from Defoe's life, but they are contradictory. Like Moll, he was frequently haunted by poverty, like her he spent months in the "hell" of Newgate. His steadfast stand as a Dissenter (which made him a lifelong outsider in English society); his humane views of the treatment of the poor, of women, of the downtrodden; his dogged and successful efforts to pay every penny of a £17,000 bankruptcy—all give evidence of a man of high and stern principles. On the other hand, he worked for the Tories, then for the Whigs, writing, as Robert C. Elliott has pointed out, with passion and conviction on both sides of controversial issues; and in his numerous business ventures he was not above swindling (even his own mother-in-law). His own dreams of status are attested by his love for trade—"the whore I doated on"—and his addition of "De" to his name (his father was James Foe) to provide a touch of gentility.

Critics have not resolved the debate over morality and irony in the novel. But few will dispute that it is a fascinating account likely to hold the attention of readers for further centuries. Virginia Woolf went further: she named *Moll Flanders* as one of the "few English novels which we can call indisputably great."

Bibliography

Alter, Robert. "A Bourgeois Picaroon," in *Rogue's Progress: Studies in the Picaresque Novel*. Cambridge, Mass.: Harvard University Press, 1962, pp. 35–57.

Brooks, Douglas. "Defoe: *Moll Flanders* and *Roxana*," in *Number and Pattern in the Eighteenth-Century Novel*. London: Routledge, 1973, pp. 41–64.

————. "*Moll Flanders*: An Interpretation," in *Essays in Criticism*. XIX (January, 1969), pp. 46–59.

Columbus, Robert R. "Conscious Artistry in *Moll Flanders*," in *Studies in English Literature, 1500–1900*. III (Summer, 1963), pp. 415–432.

Donoghue, Denis. "The Values of *Moll Flanders*," in *Sewanee Review*. LXXI (Spring, 1963), pp. 287–303.

Donovan, Robert Alan. "The Two Heroines of *Moll Flanders*," in *The Shaping Vision: Imagination in the English Novel from Defoe to Dickens*. Ithaca, N.Y.: Cornell University Press, 1966, pp. 21–46.

Goldberg, M.A. "*Moll Flanders*: Christian Allegory in a Hobbesian Mode," in *University Review*. XXXIII (June, 1967), pp. 267–278.

Hahn, H.G. "An Approach to Character Development in Defoe's Narrative Prose," in *Philological Quarterly*. LI (1972), pp. 854–858.

Hartog, Curt. "Aggression, Fear and Irony in *Moll Flanders*," in *Literature and Psychology*. XXII (1972), pp. 121–138.

Karl, Frederick. "Moll's Many-Colored Coat: Veil and Disguise in the Fiction of Defoe," in *Studies in the Novel*. V (1973), pp. 89–95.

Koonce, Howard L. "Moll's Muddle: Defoe's Use of Irony in *Moll Flanders*," in *Journal of English Literary History*. XXX (1963), pp. 377–394.

Krier, William J. "A Courtesy Which Grants Integrity: A Literal Reading of *Moll Flanders*," in *Journal of English Literary History*. XXXVIII (1971), pp. 397–410.

McMaster, Juliet. "The Equation of Love and Money in *Moll Flanders*," in *Studies in the Novel*. II (1970), pp. 131–144.

Martin, Terence. "The Unity of *Moll Flanders*," in *Modern Language Quarterly*. XXII (July, 1961), pp. 115–124.

Novak, Maximillian E. "Conscious Irony in *Moll Flanders*: Facts and Problems," in *College English*. XXVI (1964), pp. 198–204.

————. "Defoe's 'Indifferent Monitor': The Complexity of *Moll Flanders*," in *Eighteenth Century Studies*. III (1970), pp. 351–365.

Piper, William B. "*Moll Flanders* as a Structure of Topics," in *Studies in English Literature, 1500–1900*. IX (Summer, 1969), pp. 489–502.

Rogal, Samuel J. "The Profit and Loss of *Moll Flanders*," in *Studies in the Novel*. V (1973), pp. 98–103.

Schorer, Mark. "A Study in Defoe: Moral Vision and Structural Form," in *Thought*. XXV (1950), pp. 275–287.

Shinagel, Michael. "The Maternal Theme in *Moll Flanders*: Craft and Character," in *Cornell Literary Journal*. VII (1969), pp. 3–23.

Smith, LeRoy W. "Daniel Defoe: Incipient Pornographer," in *Literature and Psychology*. XXII (1972), pp. 165–178.

Sutherland, James. *Daniel Defoe*. Cambridge, Mass.: Harvard University Press, 1971, pp. 175–194.

Watson, Tommy G. "Defoe's Attitude Toward Marriage and the Position of Women as Revealed in *Moll Flanders*," in *Southern Quarterly*. III (October, 1964), pp. 1–8.

ROBINSON CRUSOE

Type of work: Novel
Author: Daniel Defoe (1660–1731)
Type of plot: Adventure romance
Time of plot: 1651–1705
Locale: An island off the coast of South America, and the Several Seas
First published: 1719

Like many famous stories, Robinson Crusoe *is more known than read. The tale of the shipwrecked sailor who survives, rescues a servant (Friday), and eventually "civilizes" the island before being rescued, is universally familiar. Crusoe's adventures as a castaway actually occupy a modest portion of the book. The real story is that of a man who survives and prospers, whatever the environment, through hard work, intelligence, tenacity, and faith in his Protestant God.*

Principal Characters

Robinson Crusoe, a self-sufficient Englishman who, after several adventures at sea and on land, is cast away on a small uninhabited island. A practical, far-sighted man of talents, he sets about to make his island home comfortable, utilizing all his knowledge. His prudence and industry, aided by an imaginative insight, enable him to pass twenty-four years alone, providing for himself in every way from the resources of the island itself and what he is able to salvage from the shipwreck that puts him in his predicament. A God-fearing man, he reads his Bible and gives thanks each day for his delivery from death. Eventually he is rescued and returns to England after an absence of thirty-five years, only to go traveling again.

Mr. Crusoe, Robinson Crusoe's father, a middle-class Englishman. He wants his son to go into business and remain at home, rather than go to sea.

Friday, a savage rescued from cannibal captors by Robinson Crusoe. He proves an apt pupil and learns how to participate in his rescuer's life and labors. He learns to speak English and becomes a friend and companion, as well as a fellow laborer.

The Story

Robinson Crusoe was the son of a middle-class English family. Although his father desired that Robinson go into some business and live a quiet life, Robinson had such longing for the sea that he found it impossible to remain at home. Without his parents' knowledge he took his first voyage. The ship was caught in a great storm, and Robinson was so violently ill and so greatly afraid that he vowed never to leave the land again should he be fortunate enough to escape death.

But when he landed safely, he found his old longing still unsatisfied, and he engaged as a trader, shipping first for the coast of Africa. The ship on which he sailed was captured by a Turkish pirate vessel, and he was carried a prisoner into Sallee, a Moorish port. There he became a slave; because his life was unbearable, at the first opportunity he escaped in a small boat. He was rescued by a Portuguese freighter and carried safely to Brazil. There he bought a small plantation and began the life of a planter.

When another English planter suggested they make a voyage to Africa for a cargo of slaves, Robinson once more gave way to his longing and sailed again. This voyage was destined to be the most fateful of all, for it brought him his greatest adventure.

The ship broke apart on a reef near an island off the coast of South America, and of the crew and passengers only Robinson was saved. The waves washed him ashore, where he took stock of his unhappy plight. The island seemed to be completely uninhabited, and there was no sign of wild beasts. In an attempt to make his castaway life as comfortable as possible, he constructed a raft and brought away food, ammunition, water, wine, clothing, tools, sailcloth, and lumber from the broken ship.

He first set up a sailcloth tent on the side of a small hill. He encircled his refuge with tall, sharp stakes and entered his shelter by means of a ladder which he drew up after him. Into this area he carried all of the goods he had salvaged, being particularly careful of the gunpowder. His next concern was his food supply. Finding that there was little which had not been ruined by rats or by water, he ate sparingly during his first days on the island.

Before long, having found some ink and a quill among the things he had brought from the ship, he began to keep a journal. He also added the good and evil of his situation and found that he had much for which to thank God. He began to make his shelter permanent. Behind his tent he found a small cave which he enlarged and braced. With crude tools he made a table and a chair, some shelves, and a rack for his guns. He spent many months on the work, all the time able to find wild fowl or other small game which kept him well supplied with food. He also found several springs and so was never in want for water.

His life for the next twenty-four years was spent in much the same way as his first days upon the island. He explored the island and built what he was pleased to call his summer home on the other side of it. He was able to grow corn, barley, and rice. He carefully saved the new kernels each year until he had enough to plant a small field. With these grains he learned to grind meal and bake coarse bread. He caught and tamed wild goats to supply his larder and parrots for companionship. He made better furniture and improved his cave, making it even safer from intruders, whom he still feared, even though he had seen no sign of any living thing except small game and fowl and goats. From the ship he had brought also three Bibles, and he had time to read them carefully. At a devotional period each morning and night, he never failed to thank God for delivering him from the sea.

In the middle of Robinson's twenty-fourth year on the island, an incident occurred which altered his way of living. About a year and a half previously he had observed some savages who had apparently paddled over from another island. They had come in the night and gorged themselves on some other savages, obviously prisoners. Robinson had found the bones and torn flesh the next morning and had since been terrified that the cannibals might return and find him. Finally a band of savages did return. While they prepared for their gruesome feast, Robinson shot some of them and frightened the others away. Able to rescue one of the prisoners, he at last had human companionship. He named the man Friday after the day of his rescue, and Friday became his faithful servant and friend.

After a time Robinson was able to teach Friday some English. Friday told him that seventeen white men were prisoners on the island from which he came. Although Friday reported the men well-treated, Robinson had a great desire to go to them, thinking that together they might find some way to return to the civilized world. He and Friday built a canoe and prepared to sail to the other island, but before they were ready for their trip another group of savages came to their island with more prisoners. Discovering that one of the prisoners was a white man, Robinson managed to save him and another savage, whom Friday found to be his own father. There was great joy at the reunion of father and son. Robinson cared for the old man and the white man, who was a Spaniard, one of the seventeen of whom Friday had spoken. A hostile tribe had captured Friday's island, and thus it was that the white men were no longer safe.

Robinson dispatched the Spaniard and Friday's father to the neighboring island to try to rescue the white men. While waiting for their return, Robinson saw an English ship one day at anchor near shore. Soon he found the captain of the ship and two others, who had been set ashore by a mutinous crew. Robinson and Friday and the three seamen were able to retake the ship, and thus Robinson was at last delivered from the island. He disliked leaving before the Spaniard and Friday's father returned, and he determined to go back to the island some day and see how they had fared. Five of the mutinous crew chose to remain rather than be returned to England to hang. And so Robinson and Friday went to England, Robinson returning to his homeland after an absence of thirty-five years. He arrived there, a stranger and unknown, in June of 1687.

But he was not through with adventure. When he visited his old home, he found that his parents had died, as had all of his family but two sisters and the two children of one of his brothers. Having nothing to keep him in England, he went to Lisbon to inquire about his plantation. There he learned that friends had saved the income of his estate for him and that he was now worth about five thousand pounds sterling. Satisfied with the accounting, Robinson and Friday returned to England where Robinson married and had three children.

After his wife died, Robinson sailed again in 1695 as a private trader on a ship captained by his nephew and bound for the East Indies and China. The ship put in at his castaway island, where he found that the Spaniards and the English mutineers had taken native wives from an adjoining island, so that the population was greatly increased. Robinson was pleased with his little group and gave a feast for them. He also presented them with gifts from the ship.

After he had satisfied himself that the colony was well cared for, Robinson and Friday sailed away. On their way to Brazil some savages attacked the ship and Friday was killed. From Brazil, Robinson went around the Cape of Good Hope and on to the coast of China. At one port, after the sailors had taken part in a massacre, Robinson lectured them so severely that the crew forced their captain, Robinson's nephew, to set him ashore in China, as they would have no more of his preaching. There Robinson joined a caravan which took him into Siberia. At last he reached England. Having spent the greater part of fifty-four years away from his homeland, he was glad to live out his life in peace and in preparation for that longer journey from which he would never return.

Critical Evaluation

On the surface an exotic novel of travel and adventure, *Robinson Crusoe* functions primarily as Defoe's defense of his bourgeois Protestantism. Crusoe's adventures—the shipwrecks, his life as a planter in South America, and his years of isolation on the island—provide an apt context for his polemic. A political dissenter and pamphleteer, Defoe saw his enemies as the Tory aristocrats whose royalism in government and religion blocked the rise of the middle class. Further, like Swift in *Gulliver's Travels,* Defoe in his novel viewed England as religiously and politically corrupt. Each author was intent upon bringing about a moral revolution, using his hero as an exemplum. Gulliver, however, represents a moral failure, whereas Crusoe's adventures reveal his spiritual conversion, a return to the ethics and religion of his father. As one critic has said, "We read it [*Robinson Crusoe*] . . . in order to follow with meticulous interest and constant self-identification the hero's success in building up, step by step, out of whatever material came to hand, a physical and moral replica of the world he had left behind him. If *Robinson Crusoe* is an adventure story, it is also a moral tale, a commercial accounting and a puritan fable."

Significantly, Crusoe's origins are in northern England, in York, where he was born in the early part of the seventeenth century and where his father had made a fortune in trade. He is of the solid middle class, that class which was beginning to come to political power during the early eighteenth century, when Defoe published his book. Crusoe's father is an apologist for the mercantile, Puritan ethic, which he tries without success to instill in his son. As Crusoe says, "mine was the middle state," which his father "had found by long experience was the best state in the world, the most suited to human happiness, not exposed to the miseries and hardships, the labour and sufferings of the mechanick part of mankind, and not embarrassed with the pride, luxury, ambition and envy of the upper part of mankind." Its virtues and blessings were those of "temperance, moderation, quietness, health [and] society."

Yet his father's philosophy, which is designed to buy man happiness and pleasure in both this life and the next, fails to persuade the young Crusoe, who finds nothing but boredom amidst the comforts of the middle class. He longs to go to sea, to follow a way of life which represents the antithesis of his father's. He seeks the extremes of sensation and danger, preferring to live on the periphery rather than in the secure middle where all is mundane and sure. Crusoe's decision to become a sailor is an act of adolescent rebellion, yet it is also very much in the tradition of Puritan individualism. Not content with the wisdom of his class, the young man feels it is necessary to test himself, to discover himself and his own ethic.

Even after the first stage in his adventures, which culminates in Crusoe's amassing a modest fortune in South America, he refuses to follow his father's ethic and settle down. Intent on his own "inclination," as he says, he leaves his plantation and once again takes up the uncertain life of sea trade. It is at this point in the narrative that Crusoe is shipwrecked, abandoned alone on a tropical island without any hope of rescue.

Crusoe's first response to his isolation and the prospect of living the rest of his life alone is one of despair. Yet his instinct to survive remains dominant, and he sets to the task not only of staying alive but also of creating a humane, comfortable society. One of the first things he does is to mark time, to make a calendar. Despite all his efforts, however, to continue his own life and environment, he falls ill and it is at this point that he realizes his complete vulnerability, his absolute aloneness in the universe. Stripped of all his illusions, limited by necessity to one small place, Crusoe is thrown back upon himself, confronted by an immense emptiness. He asks desperately: "What is this earth and sea of which I have seen so much? Whence is it produced? And what am I and all the other creatures, wild and tame, human and brutal? Whence are we?"

All these questions predate Crusoe's religious conversion, the central and most significant act of the novel. His answer to the questions is that all creation comes from God and that the state of all creation, including his own, is an expression of the will of God. Upon this act of faith, he rebuilds not only his own life but also his own miniature society which reflects in its simplicity, moderation, and comfort the philosophy his father had taught. Further, his faith brings him to an acceptance of his own life and station, an acceptance that he was never able to make before: "I acquiesced in the dispositions of Providence, which I began now to own and to believe ordered everything for the best." And later, after two years on the island. he says, "It was now that I began sensibly to feel how much more happy this life I now led was, with all its miserable circumstances, than the wicked, cursed, abominable life I led all the past part of my days; and now I changed both my sorrows and my joys; my very desires altered, my affections changed their gusts, and my delights were perfectly new from what they were at my first coming."

Once the overwhelming question of the novel—"Whence are we?"—has been answered, the rest of the narrative and Crusoe's adventures justify, to his aristocrat readers, his religious faith and middle-class Puritan ethic. Besides this justification there remains the glorification of the self-reliant and self-directing man; he was a man unfamiliar to Defoe's readers, a new man who was beginning to appear on the fringes of the power structure and who was about to demand his place in a society that was evolving toward a new political structure that we now recognize as middle-class democracy.

Bibliography

Ayers, Robert W. "*Robinson Crusoe*: Allusive Allegorick History," in *PMLA*. LXXXII (1967), pp. 399–407.

Benjamin, Edwin R. "Symbolic Elements in *Robinson Crusoe*," in *Philological Quarterly*. XXX (1951), pp. 206–211.

Egan, James. "Crusoe's Monarchy and the Puritan Concept of the Self," in *Studies in English Literature, 1500–1900*. XIII (1973), pp. 451–461.

Gerber, Richard. "The English Island Myth: Remarks on the Englishness of Utopian Fiction," in *Critical Quarterly*. I (1959), pp. 36–43.

Grief, M.J. "The Conversion of Robinson Crusoe," in *Studies in English Literature, 1500–1900*. VI (Summer, 1966), pp. 551–574.

Halewood, William H. "Religion and Invention in *Robinson Crusoe*," in *Essays in Criticism*. XIV (October, 1964), pp. 339–351.

Hartog, Curt. "Authority and Autonomy in *Robinson Crusoe*," in *Enlightenment Essays*. V (1974), pp. 33–43.

Hearne, John. "Naked Footprint: An Enquiry into Crusoe's Island," in *Review of English Literature*. VIII (October, 1967), pp. 97–107.

James, E. Anthony. "Defoe's Narrative Artistry: Naming and Describing in *Robinson Crusoe*," in *Costerus*. V (1972), pp. 52–66.

MacDonald, Robert H. "The Creation of an Ordered World in *Robinson Crusoe*," in *Dalhousie Review*. LVI (1976), pp. 23–34.

Novak, Maximillian E. "Crusoe the King and the Political Evolution of His Island," in *Studies in English Literature, 1500–1900*. II (Summer, 1962), pp. 337–350.

————. "Imaginary Islands and Real Beasts: The Imaginative Genesis of *Robinson Crusoe*," in *Tennessee Studies in Literature*. XIX (1974), pp. 57–78.

————. "The Problem of Necessity in Defoe's Fiction," in *Philological Quarterly*. XL (1961), pp. 513–524.

————. "Robinson Crusoe's Fear and the Search for Natural Man," in *Modern Philology*. LVIII (1961), pp. 238–245.

Parker, George. "The Allegory of Robinson Crusoe," in *History*. X (1925), pp. 11–25.

Peck, Daniel H. "*Robinson Crusoe*: The Moral Geography of Limitation," in *Journal of Narrative Technique*. III (1973), pp. 20–31.

Robins, Harry. "How Smart Was Robinson Crusoe?," in *PMLA*. LXVII (1952), pp. 782–789.

Rogers, Pat. "Crusoe's Home," in *Essays in Criticism*. XXIV (1974), pp. 375–390.

Swados, Harvey. "Robinson Crusoe—The Man Alone," in *Antioch Review*. XVIII (1958), pp. 25–40.

Thornburg, Thomas R. "*Robinson Crusoe*," in *Ball State University Forum*. XV (1974), pp. 11–18.

Watson, Francis. "*Robinson Crusoe*: An Englishman of the Age," in *History Today*. IX (November, 1959), pp. 760–766.

————. "*Robinson Crusoe*: Fact and Fiction," in *Listener*. LXII (1959), pp. 617–619.

Watt, Ian. "*Robinson Crusoe* as a Myth," in *Essays in Criticism*. I (1951), pp. 95–119.

Zimmerman, Everett. "Defoe and Crusoe," in *Journal of English Literary History*. XXXVIII (1971), pp. 377–396.

ROXANA

Type of work: Novel
Author: Daniel Defoe (1660–1731)
Type of plot: Picaresque romance
Time of plot: Eighteenth century
Locale: England and Europe
First published: 1724

Roxana, *Defoe's last novel, resembles his earlier fiction, especially* Moll Flanders, *in its picaresque structure, its realistic picture of eighteenth century London low life, and its vigorous prose. Roxana, however, is much more complicated and ambiguous than her predecessors, and the novel concludes on a note of irresolution that is unusual for Defoe.*

Principal Characters

Roxana, a woman left penniless by her husband at the age of twenty-two. To support herself and her children she becomes her landlord's mistress and bears him a child. After his death she becomes the mistress of a prince, out of vanity rather than need. She bears the prince a child, too, during the eight years of their alliance. She then takes other lovers, receiving riches from them, until she is fifty. She finally leaves her role as a courtesan to marry and become a respectable wife.

Mr. ——, Roxana's landlord and first lover. He helps Roxana when her husband leaves her, becoming a boarder in her house and then her lover, treating her generously during their five years together. He wants children badly and, when Roxana does not at first bear him a child, Roxana's maid does so. Mr. —— is robbed and murdered. He leaves his wealth to Roxana.

The Prince de ——, Roxana's second lover. He protects her after her first lover's untimely death in Paris. He remains her lover for eight years and rewards her with rich gifts. Upon his wife's death, however, he repents his sinful life and leaves Roxana.

A Merchant, who takes care of Roxana's wealth for her during the years after she parts from the Prince de ——. Roxana bears the merchant a son, after a brief affair. Later he and Roxana are married, legitimize their son, and settle down to respectability in Holland.

Amy, Roxana's faithful maid. She serves her mistress without pay while Roxana is poor. She even bears a child for Mr. —— when it seems that Roxana cannot. Loyal to the end, she is finally dismissed by Roxana when she threatens to murder Roxana's legitimate daughter to quiet her tongue about Roxana's past.

The Story

Born in France, from which her parents fled because of religious persecution, Roxana grew to adolescence in England. At fifteen she married a handsome but conceited man. After seven years of marriage, during which time her husband went through all their money, Roxana was left penniless with five children.

She appealed for aid to her husband's relatives, all of whom refused her except one old aunt, who was in no position to help her materially. Amy, Roxana's maid, refused to leave her mistress, although she received no wages for her work. And a poor old woman, whom Roxana had aided during her former prosperity, added her efforts to those of the old aunt and Amy. These good people managed to extract money from the relatives of the children's father. All five of the little ones were given over to the care of the poor old woman.

Penniless, Roxana was at the point of despair when her landlord, after expressing his admiraion for her, praised her fortitude under all her difficulties and offered to set her up in housekeeping. He returned all the furniture he had confiscated, gave her food and money, and generally conducted himself with such kindness and candor that Amy urged Roxana to become the gentleman's mistress should he ask it. Roxana, however, clung to her virtuous independence. Fearing that the gentleman's kindness would go unrewarded, Amy, because she loved her mistress, offered to lie with the landlord in Roxana's place. This offer, however, Roxana refused to consider. The two women talked much about the merits of the landlord, his motive in befriending Roxana, and the moral implications of his attentions.

When he came to take residence as a boarder in Roxana's house, he proposed, since his wife had deserted him, that he and Roxana live as husband and wife. To show his good faith he offered to share his wealth with her, bequeathing her five hundred pounds in his will and promising seven thousand pounds should he leave her. There was a gay celebration that evening and a little joking about Amy's offer to lie with the gentleman. Finally Roxana, her conscience still bothering her, yielded to his protestations of love and bedded with him.

After a year and half had passed and Roxana had not conceived a child, Amy chided her mistress for her barrenness. Feeling that Mr. — was not her true husband, Roxana sent Amy to him to beget a child. Amy did bear a child, which Roxana took as her own to save the maid embarrassment. Two years later Roxana bore a daughter who died within six months. A year later she pleased her lover by bearing a son.

Mr. — took Roxana with him to Paris on business. There they lived in great style, until he was robbed and murdered for the jewels he carried on his person. Roxana managed to retain the gentleman's wealth and secured it against the possible claims of his wife, who was still living.

In France the Prince de —, hoping to make amends to Roxana for the murder of her protector, lavished gifts upon her and flattered her beauty until she consented to be his mistress, this time allowing her virtue to be sullied not because of poverty but through vanity. In order to suppress gossip, Roxana, pretending that she had gone back to England on business, confined herself to her quarters and instructed Amy to admit only Prince de —.

Roxana's new lover showered her bountifully with gifts. When she bore him a son, he promised to acknowledge the child as his own and never to let it want. After the birth of the child, Roxana thought that she recognized her husband, a member of the gendarmes. Amy visited the man and found him to be the same worthless scoundrel who, years before, had abandoned his wife and five children. When the prince had to go to Italy on an official assignment, he took Roxana with him. There they remained for two years. She bore another son who lived only two months. Then the prince's wife died, and he, repenting his sins, parted from Roxana, who had been his faithful mistress for eight years.

Roxana and her maid, after engaging a merchant to handle Roxana's wealth, sailed for England. Roxana had to go to Holland to receive her money from the merchant. The merchant, arriving in Holland from Paris, took lodgings in the same house, and he and Roxana became well acquainted. The merchant wanted to marry her, but she, too avaricious and calculating to risk her wealth for a mere caprice of love, suspected his motives. She did allow him to seduce her, however, for she felt that she owed him some token of gratitude for his assistance. She was already pregnant when they parted.

Returning to London, Roxana settled her financial affairs and bore her son. Bcause she established herself in a handsome apartment, she was courted by numerous fortune hunters, but her philosophy, as she chose to call it, would not permit her to marry anyone. As a wife she would have to share her wealth; as a mistress she received riches, and she was determined to amass a fortune.

Roxana gave lavish parties, attended by many fashionable people of London. Soon her name became famous. Her purpose was fulfilled when a rich lord offered her a substantial income if she would be his mistress. Retiring from society, she took a new apartment and saw only the lord. She passed several years in this fashion. By that time she was fifty years old. Tiring at last of her lover, she began to see her friends again.

With Amy's help she began to live a different kind of life so that eventually she could assist her children. She took rooms in another part of the city with a Quaker lady. Amy let people believe that her mistress had gone to Europe.

By chance Roxana met the merchant whom she had known in Holland and whose son she had borne. The merchant renewed his suit. Although Amy sent word from Europe that Prince de — was trying to find Roxana and wished to marry her, Roxana, having learned that her husband was dead, accepted the merchant's proposal. The pair planned to return to Holland and, taking residence there, declare themselves eleven years married in order to legitimize their son.

One of Roxana's legitimate daughters had by chance been her maid while Roxana lived in London. At first the mother had tried to help her daughter by giving her, through Amy, money and advantages above her station. When the girl began to suspect that her mistress was her mother, Roxana was distressed, for she would be undone should her past be known now. When Amy, infuriated with the prying girl, threatened to murder her, Roxana, after many years' friendship, dismissed her faithful maid. But at last the persistent daughter's inquiries were silenced and Roxana was able to go to Holland wih her husband.

Critical Evaluation

Roxana, Or, The Fortunate Mistress was the last novel in Daniel Defoe's
series of great fictional works written between 1719 and 1724, which included
Robinson Crusoe (1719), *Moll Flanders* (1722), and *A Journal of the
Plague Year* (1722). Like its predecessors, it reflected the author's pre-
occupation with economic individualism and middle-class values as well as his
dissenting Protestant orientation; like them, it was written in Defoe's characteristically robust style. At the same time, this last of the author's great prose
works is unique, as it departs from the earlier novels to some degree in its
point of view, its thematic variations, and its plot structure.

In *Roxana,* as in all his works of fiction, Defoe is preoccupied with his
characters' struggles for economic independence; Roxana, like Robinson
Crusoe and Moll Flanders, is faced with poverty and starvation, but through
her ambition, practicality, and shrewd business sense she overcomes tremendous obstacles, eventually to amass a fortune. Roxana and her predecessors
are fiercely individual entrepreneurs who succeed on their own terms and owe
their hard-won security to no one but themselves. In order to stress their
independence, Defoe typically isolates his heroes and heroines in some drastic
way—Crusoe by shipwrecking him on a deserted island; Moll and Roxana by
making them social outcasts as a result of their criminal careers. From these
dire circumstances he then shows how sheer necessity operates to make his
characters act as they do.

When he decided to create a heroine like Roxana, who is driven to a variety
of criminal activities when she and her five children are abandoned by a
worthless husband, Defoe had more than ample evidence upon which to draw;
it was during his age that modern urban civilization had first devised large
police forces, detective networks complete with organized informant systems,
and a complex court system for handling the huge newly evolved criminal
population. Not only in his fiction, but in countless journalistic pieces and
pamphlets, Defoe argued passionately for the repeal of inhumane debtor's
laws, which he recognized as the cause of so much crime and injustice. As he
argued in one eloquent plea, "Necessity will make us all Thieves."
At least partly connected with this intense social concern was Defoe's
Protestant background. While he did not believe in the religious tenets of
Puritanism, he inherited its conception of human existence as a continual
struggle, its habit of viewing everyday events as charged with potential moral
significance, and its tendency toward introspection.

In *Roxana,* Defoe's social conscience and ethical underpinnings combine
to produce a unique, and in many ways brilliant novel, which is difficult to
classify. The work resembles on the surface a picaresque tale, and does indeed share many features with other works of that category. In other essential
points, however, *Roxana* is radically different from a traditional picaresque

narrative, most significantly in the depth of its characterizations and in the implications of its plot. Whereas a *picaro* is primarily the tool through which his creator presents a series of comic episodes for the purpose of satirizing society and human folly, Defoe's heroine is a multi-dimensional individual. Roxana is revealed as a woman shaped by her environment and constantly striving to get the better of it. Also in contrast to the *picaro,* whose mis-adventures never pose a serious threat to his life, Roxana's danger is very real; she need only be apprehended to run the risk of hanging. Roxana's fears and pains, pleasures and ambitions, make her a very human and sympathetic heroine. This quality of realism is further heightened by Defoe's distinctive style, which shows all the influences of his journalist's profession. He has a reporter's eye for detail, and he crowds his scenes with particulars, all de-scribed in plain, straightforward prose; his objective, unadorned language creates a powerful effect of verisimilitude. Defoe always insisted that his fictions were not "romances." Although a romantic spirit breathes through many parts of this novel, Defoe's social and moral orientation, coupled with his wonderful capacity for "lying like the truth," place *Roxana* far beyond the realm of typical eighteenth century romances.

There is a strongly autobiographical flavor to all of Defoe's novels, which results largely from the author's close identification with his main characters; in its beginning sections, *Roxana* is no exception. But then a curious thing begins to happen. As Defoe develops Roxana's character—which he modeled closely on the actual careers of several real-life criminals—she begins to act in ways of which he cannot approve, and he loses his sympathy and close imaginative identification with her. This shifting sympathy, which occurs re-peatedly throughout the novel, results in a curious vacillation on the author's part between admiring and approving of his heroine, and being deeply shocked at her behavior. The basic reason for Defoe's ambivalence toward Roxana lies in the fact that in this novel, the same basic theme used in *Moll Flanders*—that of the innocent woman being corrupted by the pressures of poverty—is carried to much greater lengths. Moll is to be forgiven because she abandons her life of crime once she has gained sufficient wealth to be independent; but Roxana continues her illicit activities long after the demands of economic necessity are met.

Roxana also differs from its author's other works in the relative tightness of the plot, which is particularly unified by the threat of possible exposure and consequent ruin for the heroine. This threat is reinforced so often, and the daughter is so persistent a presence in the later narrative, that exposure seems, indeed, the only natural conclusion to which the plot can proceed—but it does not. Defoe is not willing to have his heroine hanged, any more than he can in right conscience allow her to live happily ever after; and it is from this conflict between sympathy and justice that much of the dramatic tension in the novel is generated. The solution to which Defoe resorts at the end of the novel solves not only the problem of plot, but that of the author's shifting attitude toward Roxana and of the difficult moral problem posed in the theme as well. In an insightful psychological twist, he imposes Roxana's punishment in the form of haunting guilt over her daughter's murder and consuming fear that her evil past will be revealed. Thus Roxana at the end of the novel suffers the fate of Tantalus; surrounded by wealth and friends, she can never enjoy them; her peace is poisoned, as she realizes that the simple pleasures of her friend the Quaker woman are forever unattainable for herself.

Bibliography

Bordner, Marsha. "Defoe's Androgynous Vision in *Moll Flanders* and *Roxana*," in *Gypsy Scholar*. II (1972), pp. 76–93.

Brooks, Douglas. *Number and Pattern in the Eighteenth-Century Novel.* London: Routledge, 1973, pp. 53–60.

Cather, Willa. "Defoe's *The Fortunate Mistress*," in *On Writing; Critical Studies on Writing as an Art.* New York: Knopf, 1949, pp. 75–88.

Hahn, H.G. "An Approach to Character Development in Defoe's Narrative Prose," in *Philological Quarterly*. LI (1972), pp. 854–858.

Higdon, David Leon. "The Critical Fortunes and Misfortune of Defoe's *Roxana*," in *Bucknell Review*. XX (1972), pp. 67–82.

Hume, Robert D. "The Conclusion of Defoe's *Roxana*: Fiasco or Tour de Force?," in *Eighteenth-Century Criticism*. III (1970), pp. 475–490.

Jackson, Wallace. "*Roxana* and the Development of Defoe's Fiction," in *Studies in the Novel*. VII (1975), pp. 181–194.

James, E. Anthony. *Daniel Defoe's Many Voices; A Rhetorical Study of Prose Style and Literary Method.* Amsterdam: Rodopi Nv., 1972, pp. 231–253.

Jenkins, Ralph E. "The Structure of *Roxana*," in *Studies in the Novel*. II (1970), pp. 145–158.

Kropf, C.R. "Theme and Structure in Defoe's *Roxana*," in *Studies in English Literature, 1500–1900*. XII (1972), pp. 467–480.

McKillop, Alan Dugald. *The Early Masters of English Fiction.* Lawrence: University of Kansas Press, 1956, pp. 35–38.

Novak, Maximillian E. "Crime and Punishment in Defoe's *Roxana*," in *Journal of English and Germanic Philology*. LXV (July, 1966), pp. 445–465.

Olshin, Toby A. " 'Thoughtful of the Main Chance': Defoe and the Cycle of Anxiety," in *Hartford Studies in Literature*. VI (1974), pp. 121–122.

Peterson, Spiro. "The Matrimonial Theme of Defoe's *Roxana*," in *PMLA*. LXX (1955), pp. 166–191.

Raleigh, John Henry. "Style and Structure and Their Import in Defoe's *Roxana*," in *University of Kansas City Review.* XX (Winter, 1953), pp. 128–135.

Richetti, John J. *Defoe's Narratives; Situations and Structures.* Oxford: Clarendon Press, 1975, pp. 192–232.

Smith, LeRoy W. "Daniel Defoe: Incipient Pornographer," in *Literature and Psychology.* XXII (1972), pp. 165–177.

Snow, Malinda. "Diabolic Intervention in Defoe's *Roxana*," in *Essays in Literature* (Western Illinois University). III (1976), pp. 52–60.

Starr, George A. "Sympathy vs. Judgment in Roxana's First Liaison," in *The Augustan Milieu: Essays Presented to Louis A. Landa.* Edited by Henry Knight Miller. Oxford: Clarendon Press, 1970, pp. 59–76.

Walton, James. "The Romance of Gentility: Defoe's Heroes and Heroines," in *Literary Monographs.* IV (1971), pp. 122–135.

Zimmerman, Everett. "Language and Character in Defoe's *Roxana*," in *Essays in Criticism.* XXI (1971), pp. 227–235.

THOMAS DELONEY

Born: London (?), England (c. 1543)
Died: Unknown (1600 ?)

Principal Works

PROSE ROMANCES: *The Pleasant History of John Winchcomb in His Younger Years Called Jack of Newberry,* c. 1597; *The Gentle Craft,* c. 1587–1598; *Thomas of Reading, or the Six Worthy Yeomen of the West,* c. 1600.

Thomas Deloney was a hack writer of Elizabethan London (where he was probably born in 1543), the author of innumerable occasional ballads and broadside sheets as well as a pioneer in English prose fiction. He had learned the trade of a weaver as a boy and he began writing ballads on contemporary events while working at his trade in Norwich. About 1585 he moved to London, where he seems to have devoted all his time to writing. He was the author of many ballads, which at the time were printed on single sheets of paper and hawked about the streets. Deloney, according to tradition, was the successor to William Elderton, the chief balladeer of the early 1580's. Although many of his ballads have long since been lost, there are two collections of his work: *The Garland of Goodwill* (c. 1604) and *Strange Histories* (c. 1607). These collections were apparently made after the author's death.

It is for his work as a writer of prose narratives that Deloney is usually remembered by students of literature. His best-known work is *The Pleasant History of John Winchcomb in His Younger Years Called Jack of Newberry*, usually referred to nowadays as *Jack of Newberry*. The earliest extant edition is one of 1619, which is labeled the eighth edition. The volume is a realistic prose narrative extolling the virtues of weavers, the author's fellow tradesmen. Another prose narrative by Deloney is *The Gentle Craft*, in two parts, in which he glorified shoemakers. This work probably influenced Thomas Dekker's *The Shoemaker's Holiday* (1599), a popular play. A third prose narrative by Deloney is *Thomas of Reading* (earliest extant edition, 1612), praising the clothiers of England. All three narratives combine romantic and realistic techniques in dealing with phases of the life of Elizabethan trades and crafts against semi-historic backgrounds.

The ultimate fate of Thomas Deloney is unknown. He simply disappeared from literary history about 1600.

Bibliography

The standard edition is *The Works of Thomas Deloney*, edited by F. O. Mann, 1912. There is also *The Novels of Thomas Deloney*, edited by Merritt E. Lawlis, 1961. See also A. Chevalley, *Thomas Deloney*, 1926; and Llewellyn Powys, "Thomas Deloney," *Virginia Quarterly Review*, IX (1933), 578–594.

JACK OF NEWBERRY

Type of work: Novel
Author: Thomas Deloney (1543?–1607?)
Type of plot: Picaresque adventure
Time of plot: Reign of Henry VIII
Locale: England
First published: 1597

Not truly a novel, this fictional work marks the first successful attempt by any writer to use the material found in the lives of ordinary people as material for prose fiction. For this reason, the book marks a great step toward the novel as we know it today. The pictures Deloney drew of bourgeois England were exaggerated, but highly entertaining.

Principal Characters

Jack Winchcomb, known as Jack of Newberry, a young weaver. Wild as a young man, he settles down, marries his master's widow, and becomes a solid businessman. He patriotically raises a company of men to fight for Henry VIII against the Scots. He is offered knighthood by that sovereign but declines, saying he knows his place in the world.

Jack's Master's Widow. She trusts the young man, putting her business and then herself in his hands. She dies, leaving Jack all her business and wealth.

Jack's Second Wife, a younger woman. She is a foolish gossip who makes difficulties for her husband.

Henry VIII, King of England. Pleased with Jack for being a witty and loyal subject, he offers the weaver knighthood.

Queen Catherine, Henry VIII's queen. She thanks Jack for bringing a company of men to help fight against the Scots.

Cardinal Wolsey, Henry VIII's chancellor. He has Jack and other weavers thrown into prison when they attempt to petition the King.

The Duke of Somerset, who intervenes on Jack's behalf when he is in prison and convinces Cardinal Wolsey that the weavers mean no harm.

Benedick, an Italian merchant. He has an amorous adventure in Newberry and is punished by being put to bed with a pig.

Joan, a pretty girl employed by Jack. She disdains Benedick when he makes advances to her.

Sir George Rigley, a knight who seduces one of Jack's women employees. He is tricked by Jack into marrying the girl. Angry at first, he comes to see the justice of Jack's action and becomes the weaver's friend.

The Story

In the days of King Henry VIII there lived in the English town of Newberry a young weaver named Jack Winchcomb. As a young man he was something of a prodigal, spending as much as he made and having a reputation as a gay young fellow, known in all the county of Berkshire as Jack of Newberry. But after his master died, Jack changed his ways, for his mistress, having acquired a fondness for the young man, entrusted to him the entirety of her husband's business. Jack became a careful man, both with his mistress' affairs and with his own, and soon lost his reputation for prodigality. In its place he acquired a reputation as an honest, hardworking, and intelligent businessman.

His mistress thought so highly of Jack that she even made him an adviser in affairs of the heart. His advice was of little value to her, however, for she had already made up her mind, despite the difference in their years, to marry Jack himself. She tricked him into agreeing to further her marriage with an unknown suitor. When they arrived at the church, Jack found that he was the man; thus Jack became her husband and the master of her house and business.

The marriage went none too smoothly at first, for despite her love for Jack the woman did not like to be ordered about by the man who had once been her servant. But at last they came to an understanding and lived happily for several years, at which interval the good woman died, leaving Jack master of the business and rich in the world's good.

Not long after his first wife died, Jack remarried, the second time to a young woman. The wife was a poor choice, even though he had the pick of the wealthy women of his class in the country. Not many months passed after the marriage, which had been a costly one, before James, King of Scotland, invaded England while King Henry was in France. The justices of the country called upon Jack to furnish six men-at-arms to join the army raised by Queen Catherine. Jack, however, raised a company of a hundred and fifty foot and horse, which he armed and dressed at his own expense in distinctive liveries. Jack himself rode at the head of his men. Queen Catherine was greatly pleased and thanked Jack Winchcomb personally for his efforts, although his men were not needed to achieve the English victory at Flodden Field. In reward for his services, Jack received a chain of gold from the hands of the queen herself.

In the tenth year of his reign King Henry made a trip through Berkshire. Jack Winchcomb introduced himself in a witty way to the king as the Prince of the Ants, who was at war with the Butterflies, a sally against Cardinal Wolsey. The king, vastly pleased, betook himself to Newberry, along with his train, where all were entertained by Jack at a fabulous banquet. After the banquet the king viewed the weaving rooms and warehouses Jack owned. Upon his departure the king wished to make Jack a knight, but the weaver refused the honor, saying he would rather be a common man and die, as he had lived, a clothier.

In his house Jack of Newberry had a series of fifteen paintings, all denoting great men whose fathers had been tradesmen of one kind and another, including a portrait of Marcus Aurelius, who had been a clothier's son. Jack kept the pictures and showed them to his friends and workmen in an effort to encourage one and all to seek fame and dignity in spite of their humble offices in life.

Because of the many wars in Europe during King Henry's reign, trade in general was depleted. The lot of the clothiers and weavers being particularly bad, they joined together and sent leaders to London to appeal to the government on their behalf. One of the envoys they sent was Jack Winchcomb of Newberry. The king remembered Jack and in private audience assured him that measures would be taken to alleviate the hardships of the clothiers. Another man who had not forgotten Jack was the Lord Chancellor, Cardinal Wolsey. In an attempt to circumvent the king's promise, he had Jack and the other envoys thrown into prison for a few days. Finally the Duke of Somerset intervened and convinced the cardinal that the clothiers meant no harm.

Some time later an Italian merchant named Benedick came to the house of Jack of Newberry to trade. While there, he fell in love with one of Jack's workers, a pretty girl named Joan. But she paid no attention whatever to Benedick and asked a kinsman to tell the Italian not to bother her. When the kinsman did as he was asked, he angered the Italian, who vowed to make a cuckold of the kinsman for his pains. With gifts and fair speech the Italian finally had his way with the weaver's wife, although the woman was immediately sorry. She told her husband, who had his revenge on the Italian by pretending that he would see to it that the Italian was permitted to go to bed with Joan. The Italian fell in with the scheme and found himself put to bed with a pig, whereupon all the Englishmen laughed at him so heartily that he left Newberry in shame.

Jack's second wife was a good young woman, but she sometimes erred in paying too much attention to her gossipy friends. At one time a friend told her that she was wasting money by feeding the workmen so well. She cut down on the quantity and the quality of the food she served the workers, but Jack, who remembered only too well the days when he had been an apprentice and journeyman forced to eat whatever was placed in front of him, became very angry and made her change her ways again. His workers were gratified when he said that his wife's friend was never to set foot in his house again.

At another time Jack of Newberry went to London, where he found a draper who owed him five hundred pounds working as a porter. Learning that the man, through no fault of his own, had become a bankrupt, Jack showed his confidence in the man by setting him up in business again. Friends warned him that he was sending good money after bad, but Jack's judgment proved correct. The man paid back every cent and later became an alderman of London.

Jack was always proud of his workers. One time a knight, Sir George Rigley, seduced a pretty and intelligent girl who worked for Jack. Jack vowed that he would make it right for her. He sent the woman, disguised as a rich widow, to London. There Sir George fell in love with her, not knowing who she was, and married her. The knight was angry at first, but he soon saw the justice of the case and was very well pleased with the hundred pounds Jack gave the girl as a dower. Still knowing their places in life, Jack and his wife gave precedence to Sir George and his new lady, even in their own house.

Critical Evaluation

Very little is known about the pamphleteer and balladeer who was Thomas Deloney, the English writer whose works were precursors of the English novel. By trade a silk weaver, probably of Norwich, Deloney wrote topical ballads and, through his pamphlets, took part in the religious controversies of the day. Even the date of his birth is not certain, some sources suggesting 1543, others the more likely date of 1560. But it seems certain that Deloney died early in 1600, after producing at least three "novels" (that is, episodic narratives) in a short but crowded life. He seems to have had more education than most weavers of the time would have had, and he translated from Latin into his uniquely vigorous English. The ballads of the day were the newspapers of the period, and Deloney's apprenticeship, like that of so many novelists, might be said to have been in journalism. Probably, that was how he learned how to write concisely and how to choose popular subjects. He wrote broadside ballads on such subjects as the defeat of the Spanish Armada, great fires, the execution of traitors, and domestic tragedies, but current events were not Deloney's only ballad subjects. Using Holinshed and other sources, he drew on English history for subject matter. A collection of Deloney's ballads titled *The Garland of Good Will* appeared in 1631, and earlier editions, like those of his prose fictions, were probably read out of existence. More than once, Deloney's pamphlets and more than fifty ballads put him in trouble with the authorities, even sending him to spend time in Newgate. One ballad in particular, showing disrespect for the queen, caused him serious difficulties.

Though widely read, Thomas Deloney's novels were scorned by the university educated writers of the day as mere plebian romances from the pen of a ballad-maker, and it was not until the twentieth century that his merits as a writer were recognized. The three novels, all approximately the same length, appeared between 1597 and 1600. Probably, *Jack of Newberry* was the first one written and published. Each novel was in praise of a trade: *Jack of Newberry* of weaving, *The Gentle Craft* of shoemaking, and *Thomas of Reading* of the clothiers' trade.

Deloney's stories contain excellent pictures of contemporary middle-class London life, introducing a variety of quaint characters. But the realism of the novels is only in matter of setting and dialogue; probability is disregarded and wish-fulfillment fantasy prevails as members of the hardworking trade class are rewarded for their diligence by large fortunes. The tales are rich with humor and told in a straightforward way, except for "ornamental" language used in some romantic passages.

Deloney may have been commissioned by the cloth-merchants to compose a life of one of their order, the result being *Jack of Newberry*. Jack was a real person who lived in Newberry under Henry VII, but his history is merely traditional. Deloney, however, knew the town and had a gift for elaborating a tale with circumstantial facts and humorous episodes.

Despite its popularity in its own day, Deloney's fiction probably had little real effect on the subsequent development of English prose fiction, which had to wait a hundred years and more for the geniuses of Defoe and Richardson to get it off the ground. On the other hand, *Jack of Newberry* may be considered the first really dramatic novel in English. The fictions of Nash and Greene are witty and satirical, but they do not have the dramatic plots of Deloney's work. Sidney's *Arcadia* and John Lyly's *Euphues* were only minor influences, if any, on Deloney, who seems to have been more impressed by the Elizabethan stage than anything else (the widow and the other characters display a sense of rhetoric in their dialogue reminiscent of the stage). Deloney's view of life was essentially dramatic, and the people he wrote about in *Jack of Newberry* and his other novels are people of action, people who set out to accomplish material things.

Deloney's focus is on the details of everyday life. Love and marriage and money and food are the main topics of conversation. Materialist to his heart, he is fascinated by business and household matters. Like Dickens, Deloney plunges into scenes that summarize dramatically an entire situation, painting a picture of an entire culture along the way. There are few irrelevant incidents in *Jack of Newberry*. The story of the middle-aged widow who falls in love with her young apprentice, and of his subsequent adventures (including that concerning the king) is told with great enthuiasm. The widow is portrayed as a lusty, self-sufficient female, a woman who knows what she wants and goes after it—in this case, Jack. Jack is apparently as virtuous and industrious an apprentice as Ben Franklin, but he is not as innocent as he pretends and soon moves up in the world.

The tradesmen heroes such as Jack are rather idealized characters. Jack rises less from his own efforts than from those of the people around him. It almost seems that he is above certain efforts, as the king, himself, is. The women in *Jack of Newberry* are the book's finest characterizations. In creating the gallery of female portraits, Deloney leaves behind him all of his rivals in the prose fiction of the time and approaches the best of Elizabethan stage comedy. Queen Catherine, the first Mistress Winchcomb, and other women in the story are colorful figures, alive with natural vitality. As the plots develop, the women are in the midst of the action. Perhaps it is a man's world, but the wife seems to be responsible for her husband's success. Deloney knew and understood middle-class women, and recorded their foibles and unique characteristics with a sharp eye and a precise pen. For the author, the good wife was one who was never idle, but knew her place and did not "gad about." Jack and his first wife made no headway at all until she decided to stay at home and manage the household.

The minor characters are well drawn, especially Randoll Pert. Recently out of debtor's prison, Pert becomes a porter to support his family. His description is delightful, and his antics add both comic and pathetic touches to the novel. The meeting of Jack and Pert at the Spread Eagle in London is superbly handled. The whole episode, including the part where Jack agrees not to collect five hundred pounds until Pert is sheriff of London, is excellent comedy.

Although the novel is episodic, it forms a coherent and often dramatic whole, and is filled with humorous scenes and witty dialogue. *Jack of Newberry* stands as a good "novel" in its own right, as well as the first example of its kind in English literature.

Bibliography

Cazanian, L.F. "Deloney," in *The Development of English Humor*. Durham, N.C.: Duke University Press, 1952, pp. 175–179.

Davis, Walter R. *Idea and Act in Elizabethan Fiction*. Princeton, N.J.: Princeton University Press, 1969, pp. 238–252.

Dorinsville, Max. "Design in Deloney's *Jack of Newby*," in *PMLA*.LXXXVIII (1973), pp. 233–239.

Kuehn, G.W. "Thomas Deloney: Two Notes," in *Modern Language Notes*. LII (February, 1937), pp. 103–105.

Lawlis, Merritt E. *Apology for the Middle Class: The Dramatic Novels of Thomas Deloney*. Bloomington: Indiana University Press, 1961.

Parker, David. "*Jack of Newby*: A New Source," in *English Language Notes*. X (1973), pp. 173–180.

Patzold, Kurt-Michael. "Thomas Deloney and the English Jest-Book Tradition," in *English Studies*. LIII (1972), pp. 313–328.

Pourys, Llewellyn. "Thomas Deloney," in *Virginia Quarterly Review*. IX (1933), pp. 578–594.

Roberts, Warren E. "Folklore in the Novels of Thomas Deloney," in *Studies in Folklore*. X (1958), pp. 119–129.

Rollins, H.E. "Deloney's Sources for Euphuistic Learning," in *PMLA*. LI (June, 1936), pp. 399–406.

————. "Thomas Deloney's Euphuistic Learning and the Forest," in *PMLA*. L (September, 1935), pp. 679–686.

CHARLES DICKENS

Born: Landport, England (February 7, 1812)
Died: Gadshill, England (June 9, 1870)

Principal Works

NOVELS: *The Pickwick Papers*, 1836–1837; *Oliver Twist*, 1837–1839; *Nicholas Nickleby*, 1838–1839; *The Old Curiosity Shop*, 1840–1841; *Barnaby Rudge*, 1841; *Martin Chuzzlewit*, 1843–1844; *Dombey and Son*, 1846–1848; *David Copperfield*, 1849–1850; *Bleak House*, 1852–1853; *Hard Times*, 1854; *Little Dorrit*, 1855–1857; *A Tale of Two Cities*, 1859; *Great Expectations*, 1860–1861; *Our Mutual Friend*, 1864–1866; *The Mystery of Edwin Drood*, 1870.

CHRISTMAS BOOKS: *A Christmas Carol*, 1843; *The Chimes*, 1844; *The Cricket on the Hearth*, 1845; *The Battle of Life*, 1846; *The Haunted Man*, 1848.

SKETCHES AND TALES: *Sketches by Boz*, 1836; *Sketches of Young Gentlemen*, 1838; *Sketches of Young Couples*, 1840; *The Uncommercial Traveller*, 1860; *George Silverman's Explanation*, 1868.

PLAYS: *The Strange Gentleman*, 1836; *The Village Coquettes*, 1836; *Mr. Nightingale's Diary*, 1851 (with Mark Lemon); *No Thoroughfare*, 1867 (with Wilkie Collins).

TRAVEL SKETCHES AND IMPRESSIONS: *American Notes*, 1842; *Pictures from Italy*, 1846.

MISCELLANEOUS: *A Child's History of England*, 1853; *The Life of Our Lord*, 1934.

Charles Dickens, British novelist, was born at Landport, near Portsmouth, England, February 7, 1812, the son of a minor government clerk. Owing to his parents' incompetence in money matters, at the age of ten, when the family moved to London, occurred the episode that many critics have found traumatic in its effect on the emotional and creative life of the novelist: that "deep sense of abandonment," symbolized for him by his parents' complacent relegation of him to the sordid drudgery of work in Warren's blacking warehouse. One side of its effect on him is almost certainly the way in which we find, at or near the center of so many of his novels, a suffering, neglected child; another, the almost hallucinatory intensity of his rendering of the externals of human beings. The episode was brief, and he returned to school, to leave at fifteen, his real education having been gained from the novels of Cervantes, Le Sage, Fielding, and Smollett, and his exposure to the London scene during his "abandonment." He became first a lawyer's clerk and then a shorthand reporter in the courts and the House of Commons.

His first book, *Sketches by Boz*, stemmed from his work as a journalist; it led to his being commissioned to write the text accompanying a collection of comic drawings about Cockney sportsmen which was to be published in monthly parts. "I thought," he wrote later, "of Mr. Pickwick"; and with the appearance of Sam Weller in Chapter X the success of *The Pickwick Papers* was not merely assured but unprecedentedly sensational. From then on, Dickens was the most popular of all English novelists in his lifetime and probably for posterity too.

Even while *The Pickwick Papers* was appearing, however, *Oliver Twist* was being published as a continued story in a magazine. The two novels show the two sides of Dickens' genius. *The Pickwick Papers* is a work of pure humor, in which the crudities and miseries of the real world are sterilized by laughter and the vicious are objects of comedy, good things in themselves, without reference to moral judgment, because they are seen as comic. The world of this novel is almost fairyland: in *Oliver Twist* fairyland has become the country of nightmare; the bad fairies have become ogres. There is still laughter, but it has become savage, satirical; the appeal is to derision. On the surface, *Oliver Twist* is an exposure novel, an attack on the working of the poor law of the day, but its real theme is the fate of innocence and weakness. The savage comedy, seen in a character like Bumble, is accompanied by equally savage melodrama, the melodrama of the Jew Fagin and the robber Bill Sikes.

From then on, fairyland and nightmare exist side by side in Dickens' novels. During the first part of his career, these novels are naïve in form, based on eighteenth century picaresque, in which we follow the fortunes of the hero who gives his name to the book, as in *Nicholas Nickleby* and *Martin Chuzzlewit*. The weaknesses of structure inherent in picaresque fiction were accentuated by Dickens' practice of writing for serialization and by his lack of what today would be called the artistic conscience: Martin Chuzzlewit was sent to America not because the pattern of the novel demanded it but because sales were falling off and an element of novelty seemed called for to revive interest. Today we read the earlier novels for their incidentals, not for their plots; for the scenes at Dotheboys Hall and the character of Mrs. Nickleby in *Nicholas Nickleby*; for the wonderful Pecksniff and the sublime Mrs. Gamp—as a comic creation second only to Falstaff in English literature—in *Martin Chuzzlewit*.

The masterpiece of this first part of Dickens' career is the semi-autobiographical *David Copperfield*, the most varied of the earlier works and the best proportioned, containing, too, some of his most delightful characters, among them Mr. Micawber, modeled on his father. The darkening of his genius is already apparent, however, in *Dombey and Son*; and henceforth his criticism of the age, which up to then had largely dealt with specific abuses, becomes general, focusing on the theme of money. The humor is no longer that of delighted appreciation of the absurd, but bitterly sardonic, as in the rendering of Mr. Podsnap in *Our Mutual Friend*. Plot becomes much more highly organized; and at the same time a rich symbolism enters his fiction, sometimes as an extraordinary intensification of atmosphere, as in the description of Dombey's house in *Dombey and Son*, sometimes as a feature of the London scene, like the dust-piles which dominate *Our*

Mutual Friend, sometimes even as an atmospheric condition, as in the fog that enshrouds the beginning of *Bleak House*. Symbolism of this kind was something almost entirely new in English fiction; and while his contemporaries preferred the earlier books, where he is "the unique portrayer of comical eccentrics" and the stress is on high spirits and the gospel of kindliness, critics in our time have tended more to admire the later novels, with their dark poetic sweep, the passionate intensity of their symbolism, and their affinity, in mood engendered, both with the later Elizabethan tragedy and with Dostoevski. Outstanding also among the later works are *Little Dorrit*, which is partly autobiographical in inspiration, and *Great Expectations*. His mystery story, *Edwin Drood*, was unfinished. He wrote two historical novels, *Barnaby Rudge*, based on the Gordon Riots of eighteenth century London, and *A Tale of Two Cities*, on the French Revolution. *A Christmas Carol in Prose* is the most famous of his shorter pieces.

Dickens married in 1836 and separated from his wife in 1858. His first visit to the United States, in 1841, resulted in *American Notes*, a work which, together with the American chapters in *Martin Chuzzlewit*, was extremely resented in America. A second visit, in 1867, was a triumphant success. He died at his home at Gadshill on June 9, 1870.

Bibliography

For Dickens' collected work, *The Nonesuch Dickens*, ed. by A. Waugh, W. Dexter, et al., 23 vols., 1937–1938, has been superseded by the *New Oxford Illustrated Dickens*, 1948–1958, and by the definitive Clarendon Dickens series, in progress. Dickens' collected letters, in the Pilgrim Edition under Madeline House and G. Storey, is also in progress, with Vol. 1, 1965, and Vol. 2, 1969. The authorized biography is John Forster's *The Life of Charles Dickens*, 1872–1874, revised by J. W. T. Ley, 1928; but this work should be supplemented by the major biography of Edgar Johnson, *Charles Dickens: His Tragedy and Triumph*, 2 vols., 1953, 1970. Among the still useful earlier studies of Dickens' life are G. K. Chesterton, *Charles Dickens*, 1906; J. W. T. Ley, *The Dickens Circle: The Novelist's Friendships*, 1919; Sir H. F. Dickens, *Memories of my Father*, 1928; and W. H. Bowen, *Charles Dickens and his Family*, 1936. More recent biographical studies include R. J. Cruikshank, *Charles Dickens and Early Victorian England*, 1949; Monroe Engel, *The Maturity of Dickens*, 1959; J. B. Priestly, *Charles Dickens*, 1961; I. Brown, *Dickens in his Time*, 1963; C. Hibbert, *The Making of Charles Dickens*, 1967; A. Wilson, *The World of Charles Dickens*, 1970; Ivor Brown, *Dickens and His World*, 1970; Ivor Brown, *Charles Dickens, 1812–1870*, 1970; Alexander Welsh, *The City of Dickens*, 1971; Joseph Gold, *Charles Dickens: Radical and Moralist*, 1972; John Greaves, *Dickens at Doughty Street*, 1975; and Duane DeVries, *Dickens' Apprentice Years: The Making of a Novelist*, 1976.

Modern Dickens criticism begins around 1940 with the publication of essays by George Orwell and Edmund Wilson, and with Humphrey House's *The*

Dickens World, 1941. See Edmund Wilson, *The Wound and the Bow*, 1941; George Orwell, *Dickens, Dali, and Others*, 1946; Sylvère Monod, *Dickens Romancier*, 1953; J. Hillis Miller, *Charles Dickens: The World of His Novels*, 1958; K. J. Fielding, *Charles Dickens: A Critical Introduction*, 1958, 1965; A. O. J. Cockshut, *The Imagination of Dickens*, 1961; John Gross and Gabriel Pearson, eds., *Dickens and the Twentieth Century*, 1962; Earle Davis, *The Flint and the Flame*, 1963; Mark Spilka, *Dickens and Kafka*, 1963; Robert Garis, *The Dickens Theatre*, 1965; T. Stoehr, *Dickens: The Dreamer's Stance*, 1966; G. H. Ford and L. Lane, eds., *Dickens Critics*, 1967; Harvey Sucksmith, *The Narrative Art of Charles Dickens: The Rhetoric of Sympathy and Irony in His Novels*, 1970; F. R. and Q. D. Leavis, *Dickens: The Novelist*, 1970; Anthony Dyson, *The Inimitable Dickens: A Reading of the Novels*, 1970; George L. Brook, *The Language of Dickens*, 1970, 1973; Herman M. Daleski, *Dickens and the Art of Analogy*, 1970; James R. Kincaid, *Dickens and the Rhetoric of Laughter*, 1971; Michael C. Kotzin, *Dickens and the Fairy Tale*, 1972; N. M. Lary, *Dostoevsky and Dickens: A Study of Literary Influence*, 1973; Garrett Stewart, *Dickens and the Trials of Imagination*, 1974; Fred Kaplan, *Dickens and Mesmerism: The Hidden Springs of Fiction*, 1975; A. L. Zambrano, *Dickens and Film*, 1976; John Romano, *Dickens and Reality*, 1978; and Robert L. Patten, *Charles Dickens and His Publishers*, 1978.

Specialized works include M. Price, ed., *Dickens: A Collection of Critical Essays*, 1967; A. E. Dyson, ed., *Dickens: A Selection of Critical Essays*, 1968; B. N. Schilling, ed., *The Comic World of Dickens*, 1969; Centenary number of *The Dickensian*, Vol. 66, No. 361, May 1960; E. W. F. Tomlin, ed. *Charles Dickens, 1812–1870: A Centenary Volume*, 1970; Robert B. Partlow, Jr., ed., *Dickens Studies Annual*, Vol. I, 1970; John Greaves, *Who's Who in Dickens*, 1972; and Philip Hobsbaum, *A Reader's Guide to Charles Dickens*, 1973. See also John Butt and Kathleen Tillotson, *Dickens at Work*, 1957, which investigates the novelist's methods of publication; and George H. Ford, *Dickens and His Readers*, 1955, 1965, a survey of his contemporary critics and audience.

BLEAK HOUSE

Type of work: Novel
Author: Charles Dickens (1812–1870)
Type of plot: Social criticism
Time of plot: Mid-nineteenth century
Locale: London, Lincolnshire, and Hertfordshire, England
First published: 1852–1853

Bleak House, *a satire on the methods of an English equity court, is based upon an actual case in Chancery, while several of the minor characters are caricatures of well-known literary figures of the day. Although the complicated Lady Dedlock plot which gave* Bleak House *its contemporary popularity is rather thin, the novel as a whole stands up remarkably well.*

Principal Characters

John Jarndyce, the unmarried, aging owner of Bleak House and a party in the famous and protracted Chancery suit of Jarndyce vs. Jarndyce. Generous to a fault, he makes two young cousins, Ada Clare and Richard Carstone, his wards, in the hope that they will fall in love and fill his ancestral home with renewed life. He also takes into his home an orphan, Esther Summerson, as a companion to Ada. He himself falls in love with Esther, but when he learns that she is in love with Allan Woodcourt, a young surgeon, he releases her from her promise to him and gives the couple a new Bleak House of their own. He is loyal to his old friend and is always scrupulously fair, even though he calls his library "The Growlery" and retreats there when the winds of adversity blow on him. Admirable in every way, the head of the Jarndyce family creates rather than preserves a family dignity.

Esther Summerson, the orphan whom John Jarndyce takes into his home and later into his heart. In reality she is the natural daughter of Lady Dedlock and a gallant named Captain Hawdon (who dies and is buried under the name of Nemo). Though part of the story is told by Esther, her ingenuousness makes of her less of a heroine and more of a companion and comforter who goes under various motherly terms of endearment. Although she respects and admires her benefactor, she truly loves the compassionate doctor, Allan Woodcourt, who woos her in spite of her disease-ravaged face, the result of a serious illness incurred while nursing Charley, her maid. Her immediate sympathies are aroused by any homeless beings and by those, as in the case of Caddy Jellyby, whose homes are friendless and loveless. She finally finds happiness with her husband and two daughters.

Ada Clare, John Jarndyce's cousin and ward. She secretly marries Richard Carstone, her cousin, to protect him from the grinding poverty that lawyers and the courts bring upon him. She manages to keep her loyalties and sympathies divided by remaining with her benefactor while extending her love to Carstone. Beautiful and tractable, she displays evenness of disposition and generous motives which make her a tearful heroine.

Richard Carstone, Ada's cousin and husband. Anything suits this young man who has already sold his soul to the case of Jarndyce vs. Jarndyce. He tries medicine, the law, and the army, only to die of disappointment after the suit in Chancery has been settled and he learns that legal costs have eaten up the whole of his inheritance. John Jarndyce provides for Ada and her infant son.

Lady Honoria Dedlock, secretly the mother of Esther Summerson by Captain Hawdon, a rake to whom she was once engaged. When Tulkinghorn, her husband's legal adviser, threatens to inform her husband of her past, she flees from her home and dies, a victim of shame and exposure, at the gate of the cemetery where her lover has been buried under the name of Nemo. Her body is discovered by Esther Summerson.

Sir Leicester Dedlock, an honorable gentleman of prejudice and pride of family, completely unaware of his wife's guilty secret.

Mr. Tulkinghorn, a conniving solicitor who threatens to expose the secret in Lady Dedlock's past. He is murdered by Lady Dedlock's French maid when he refuses to pay her blackmailing demands and threatens her with imprisonment.

Allan Woodcourt, the surgeon who attends Captain Hawdon at the time of his death and who extends his help to Esther Summerson and Richard Carstone as well. He marries Esther after John Jarndyce releases her from her promise to him.

Mrs. Woodcourt, his handsome mother, proud of her Welsh ancestry.

William Guppy, a lawyer's clerk in the firm of Kenge and Carboy, John Jarndyce's solicitors. Attracted to Esther Summerson, he "files a declaration" of his love. Later, discovering that she has lost her beauty as a result of illness, he regrets his proposal and asks her to make a statement, before a witness, that there was never any formal engagement between them. He also meddles, though in a cowardly and humorous fashion, in Tulkinghorn's intrigue to discover Lady Dedlock's connection with the dead Nemo.

Miss Flite, a Jarndyce relative, half-crazed by the frustrations and delays of the suit in Chancery. Bright, friendly, perceptive of the crushing power of the law, she raises birds for release when the case is settled, and she tries to keep others from her own sad fate.

Miss Barbary, Lady Dedlock's sister and Esther Summerson's aunt and godmother, a good, austere woman.

Mademoiselle Hortense, Lady Dedlock's French maid. She murders Tulkinghorn when he resists her attempt at blackmail.

Inspector Bucket, the police detective who solves the mystery of Tulkinghorn's murder.

Rosa, a village girl also employed as a maid by Lady Dedlock. She is engaged to marry Watt Rouncewell.

Mrs. Rouncewell, the Dedlock housekeeper.

Mr. Rouncewell, her son, the father of Watt Rouncewell.

George Rouncewell, another son, a soldier and later the owner of a shooting gallery in London. He is falsely arrested for the murder of Tulkinghorn.

Watt Rouncewell, the young man engaged to Rosa.

Mrs. Rachael, later **Mrs. Chadband,** a servant to Miss Barbary.

The Reverend Mr. Chadband, her husband, a self-conscious clergyman given to flowery speech.

Mrs. Snagsby, one of his parishioners, a

shrew.

Mr. Snagsby, a law-stationer, her mild, hen-pecked husband.

Captain Hawdon, now calling himself **Nemo,** a law writer, the former lover of Lady Dedlock. Dying in a garret over Krook's dingy shop, he is buried in the Potter's Field.

Jo, also called **Toughey,** a street sweeper, befriended by Nemo. Lady Dedlock pays him two half-crowns to point out Nemo's grave.

Krook, the owner of a rag-and-bottle shop and the landlord of Miss Flite and Nemo. He has in his possession a packet of papers belonging to the former Captain Hawdon. This fact has been ferreted out by Tony Jobling, who calls himself Weevle while lodging with Krook, and William Guppy has agreed to reclaim the papers for Lady Dedlock. On the night that the papers are to change hands, Krook, a habitual drunkard, perishes of spontaneous combustion. Apparently the papers are destroyed in the fire.

Mrs. Smallweed, Krook's sister.

Mr. Smallweed, her husband, a super-annuated man of unimpaired and irascible mind.

Bartholomew Smallweed, also called **Chickweed,** their grandson, a sponging friend of William Guppy.

Judy Smallweed, Bartholomew's twin sister.

Tony Jobling, a law writer for Mr. Snagsby and a friend of William Guppy. Calling himself **Weevle,** he takes lodgings in Krook's establishment and learns that Krook has in his possession a bundle of Captain Hawdon's papers.

Mrs. Jellyby, a plump, strong-minded woman who neglects her house and family while interesting herself in philan-thropic projects, one of which is to settle a colony of English poor in Borrioboola-Gha, on the Niger River in Africa.

Caroline Jellyby, also called **Caddy,** Mrs. Jellyby's oldest daughter. Tired of her mother's endless projects, she marries Prince Turveydrop. A close friend of Esther Summerson, Caddy names her first daughter Esther.

Mr. Jellyby, a mild, miserable man who goes bankrupt.

"Peepy" Jellyby, the Jellybys' weak and neglected son.

Prince Turveydrop, named in honor of the Prince Regent. He marries Caddy Jellyby.

Mr. Turveydrop, Prince Turveydrop's father, a model of deportment and a monster of selfishness.

Harold Skimpole, the sentimental, unworldly recipient of John Jarndyce's bounty, a character thought to have been modeled after Leigh Hunt.

Mrs. Skimpole, his sickly wife.

Arethusa, the "Beauty" daughter, **Laura,** the "Sentiment" daughter, and

Kitty, the "Comedy" daughter, the Skimpole children.

Lawrence Boythorn, John Jarndyce's friend. His character is modeled on that of Walter Savage Landor.

Mr. Gridley, also called **"The Man from Shropshire,"** a farmer's son ruined by a suit in Chancery, frequently jailed for contempt of court. While hiding from the law, he dies in a London shooting gallery.

Bayham Badger, a medical practitioner to whom Richard Carstone is articled for a time. He is proud of his wife's two former husbands.

Mrs. Badger, his wife, who brings glory to her present married state because she is the widow of Captain Swosser, an officer of the Royal Navy, and Professor Dingo, a scientist.

Charlotte Neckett, also called **Charley,** Esther Summerson's devoted maid.

Mr. Kenge, nicknamed "Conversation" **Kenge,** a member of the law firm of Kenge and Carboy. Through him John Jarndyce first meets Esther Summerson.

Mr. Vholes, Richard Carstone's solicitor. He helps to bring about the young man's ruin.

Mr. Quale, Mrs. Jellyby's partner in her impractical philanthropic schemes.

Miss Wisk, betrothed to Mr. Quale.

Mr. Tangle, a legal authority on the case of Jarndyce vs. Jarndyce.

The Story

The suit of Jarndyce vs. Jarndyce was a standing joke in the Court of Chancery. Beginning with a dispute as to how the trusts under a Jarndyce will were to be administered, the suit had dragged on, year after year, generation after generation, without settlement. The heirs, or would-be heirs, spent their lives waiting. Some, like Tom Jarndyce, blew out their brains. Others, like tiny Miss Flite, visited the Court in daily expectation of some judgment which would settle the disputed estate and bring her the wealth of which she dreamed.

Among those involved in the suit were John Jarndyce, great-nephew of the Tom Jarndyce who had shot himself in a coffee house, and his two cousins, Richard Carstone and Ada Clare. Jarndyce was the owner of Bleak House in Hertfordshire, a country place which was not as dreary as its name. His two young cousins lived with him. He had provided a companion for Ada in the person of Esther Summerson. Esther had suffered an unhappy childhood under the care of Miss Barbary, her stern godmother, and a servant, Mrs. Rachel. The two had told the girl that her mother was a wicked woman who had deserted her. Miss Barbary was now dead, and Mr. Jarndyce had become Esther's benefactor.

Two others who took a strange interest in the Jarndyce estate were Sir Leicester and Lady Dedlock of Chesney Wold, in Lincolnshire. Lord Dedlock had a solicitor named Tulkinghorn, who, like every other reputable lawyer in London, was involved in the Jarndyce suit. One day when Tulkinghorn was in the Dedlock's home, the lawyer presented Lady Dedlock with a document. At the sight of the handwriting on the paper she swooned. Immediately suspicious, Tulkinghorn resolved to trace the handwriting to its source. His search led him to Mr. Snagsby, a stationer, but the best that Snagsby could tell him was that the paper had been copied by a man named Nemo, a lodger in the house of Mr. Krook, a junk dealer. Mr. Tulkinghorn went to the house with Snagsby, only to find Nemo dead of an overdose of opium. Convinced that Nemo was not the dead man's real name, the lawyer could learn nothing of the man's identity or connections.

Esther Summerson soon found an ardent friend and admirer in William

Guppy, a clerk in the office of Kenge and Carboy, Jarndyce's solicitors. It was Guppy who first noticed Esther's resemblance to Lady Dedlock. Allan Woodcourt, a young surgeon who had been called to administer to the dead Nemo, requested an inquest. One of the witnesses called was Jo, a crossing sweeper whom Nemo had often befriended. A little later Jo was found with two half-crowns on his person. He explained that they had been given him by a lady he had guided to the gate of the churchyard where Nemo was buried. Jo was arrested, and in the cross-examination which followed, Mr. Guppy questioned the wife of an oily preacher named Chadband and found that the firm of Kenge and Carboy had once had charge of a young lady with whose aunt Mrs. Chadband had lived. Mrs. Chadband was, of course, the Mrs. Rachel of Esther Summerson's childhood. She revealed that Esther's real name was not Summerson, but Hawdon.

The mystery surrounding Esther Summerson began to clear. A French maid who had left Lady Dedlock's service identified her late mistress as the lady who had given two half-crowns to the crossing sweeper. The dead Nemo was promptly proved to have been Captain Hawdon. Years before he and the present Lady Dedlock had fallen in love; Esther was their child. But Miss Barbary, angry at her sister's disgrace, had taken the child and moved to another part of the country. The mother later married Lord Dedlock. She was now overjoyed that the child her unforgiving sister had led her to believe dead was still alive, and she resolved to reveal herself to her.

Mr. Guppy informed Lady Dedlock that a packet of Captain Hawdon's letters was in the possession of the junk dealer, Krook. Fearing that the revelation of these letters would ruin her position, Lady Dedlock asked Guppy to bring them to her, and the wily law clerk agreed. But on the night the letters were to be obtained the drunken Krook exploded of spontaneous combustion, and presumably the letters burned with him.

In the meantime, Richard Carstone, completely obsessed by the Jarndyce case, had abandoned all efforts to establish a career for himself. He lived in a false hope that the Chancery suit would soon be settled, spending the little money he had on an unscrupulous lawyer named Vholes. When Jarndyce remonstrated, Richard thought his cousin's advice prompted by selfish interests. Ada Clare, also worried over Richard's behavior, secretly married him so that her own small fortune might stand between Richard and his folly.

Esther Summerson fell desperately ill of a fever, and when Lady Dedlock heard of the girl's illness she went to her at once and revealed herself. So mother and daughter were finally reunited. As a result of her illness, Esther's beauty was completely destroyed. John Jarndyce, feeling free for the first time to declare his love for a woman so much younger than himself, asked her to marry him, and she accepted.

Tulkinghorn was murdered and several nights later when she knew her secret was about to be revealed to her husband, Lady Dedlock left home. It was discovered that Tulkinghorn had been murdered by the French maid through whom he had learned of Lady Dedlock's connection with the crossing sweeper. The maid had attempted to blackmail the lawyer, and when he threatened her with imprisonment she killed him. Inspector Bucket, who solved the mystery of the murder, also informed Lord Dedlock of his wife's past. The baronet told the detective to employ every means to bring about her return. It was Esther Summerson, however, who found her mother dead at the gate of the churchyard where Captain Hawdon was buried.

Among Krook's effects was a Jarndyce will made at a later date than the one which had been disputed in Chancery for so many years. It settled the question of the Jarndyce inheritance forever. Richard and Ada were declared the heirs, but unfortunately the entire fortune had been eaten up in court costs and the two young people were left to face a life of genteel poverty. Richard did not long survive this final blow. He died, leaving his wife and infant son in the care of John Jarndyce.

Esther became the mistress of her own Bleak House. John Jarndyce, discovering that her true love was young Doctor Woodcourt, released her from her promise to marry him and in his generosity brought the two lovers together. Before her wedding to Doctor Woodcourt, Jarndyce took her to see a country house he had bought at Yorkshire. He had named it Bleak House, and it was his wedding present to the bride and groom. There Esther lived, happy in the love of her husband and her two daughters and in the lasting affection of John Jarndyce, proprietor of that other Bleak House which would always be her second home.

Critical Evaluation

Bleak House, after publication as a serial, first appeared in book form in 1853 at the height of Dickens' career. Preceded by *Martin Chuzzlewit* and followed by *Hard Times,* it comes early in the group of Dickens' great novels of social analysis and protest. A major critical anatomy of mid-nineteenth century England, the novel nevertheless shows some unfortunate signs of serial publication and of the author's concessions to his audience. Pathos, melodrama, and a somewhat strident moralism all reflect weaknesses in the public taste, yet Dickens manages to weave out of these a controlled assessment of the corruption at the heart of his society.

At the center of its intricate plot is the lawsuit of Jarndyce and Jarndyce. To this meager frame Dickens piles sub-plot upon sub-plot, all ultimately interrelated. In one sense, the plot is a series of thin detective stories woven together in such a way as to involve all strata of society. As character after fascinating character appears, each episode is interesting in its own right and, in the masterly resolution, no action or detail remains extraneous.

The third-person narrator of most of *Bleak House* is a sharply ironic commentator on the political, social, and moral evils which abound in the book.

There is never any question of the narrator's attitude towards the selfishness and irresponsibility he recounts, but he is not quite so sardonic or homiletic as the narrator of *Hard Times*. The stern attitude of this narrator is both relieved and reinforced by the introduction of a second, first-person narrator, Esther Summerson. Many critics have seen the dual narration as an aesthetic flaw, but each narrator does contribute a different perspective. Although Esther is a bit simpering and saccharine, she does represent a sympathetic and morally responsible attitude which is rare in the world of *Bleak House*. She is a compassionate insider who adds both a perspective and a model which, if sometimes sentimental, are a corrective to her foul environment.

As the lawsuit of Jarndyce and Jarndyce lumbers to a close after years of litigation, a gallery of characters emerges and each reveals how the moral contagion has spread to his sector. With his talent for caricature, Dickens has created memorable minor characters to flesh out the corrupt world. There is Mr. Chadband, the preacher enamored of his own voice; Mrs. Pardiggle, who would feed the poor Puseyite tracts rather than bacon; Mr. Turveydrop, who is the Model of Deportment and little else; Mrs. Jellyby, who supports noble "causes" while neglecting her own children; Mr. Skimpole, the model of unproductivity. So many of these betray the varieties of egoism and irresponsibility which have left society stagnant and infected. Perhaps the most striking is Krook, the law stationer and small-scale surrogate of the Lord Chancellor, who dies of "spontaneous combustion." Krook is a microcosm of the self-destructive tendency of a diseased society.

However, despite Dickens' talent for plot and character, *Bleak House* is primarily a novel of image and symbol. The first chapter insistently sets the moral tone as it repeats its images of fog and mud which surround the court of Chancery and, by extension, all of English life. As the fog, which surrounds all in a miasma from which there seems no escape, is a symbol of Chancery, the court itself, with its inert, irresponsible, and self-destructive wranglings, is a symbol of the calcified social and economic system strangling English life. The case of Jarndyce and Jarndyce is the perfect model of the social canker. Characters sacrifice their lives to its endless wrangling and forfeit the opportunity to accept individual responsibility and make something of themselves because of the illusory hope of instant riches. When the suit is finally settled, the fortune has been eaten up in court costs—an ironic commentary on the futility of such vain hopes.

People and places, too, in *Bleak House* so consistently have symbolic value that the novel occasionally verges on allegory. The cloudiness and rain which surround Chesney Wold symbolize the hopelessness of the nobility. Even the name of its inhabitants, Dedlock, is a sign of the moral deadlock and immobility of the ruling class. At the other end of the social spectrum, Tom-all-alone's, dirty and disease-ridden, is a symbol of the vulnerability and victimhood of the lowest classes. In gloom of one sort or another, many characters act as detectives searching out the guilty secrets and hypocrisies which permeate this world.

On the more positive side is Bleak House itself where the kindly John Jarndyce, aloof from involvement in the lawsuit, presides over a more orderly and benevolent demesne. But the contagion cannot even be kept from there. Occasionally even the admirable John Jarndyce suffers when the East Wind, a symbol of the agony and frustration outside, blows across the estate. More strikingly, Ada and Richard Carstone bring into their uncle's house the effects of the lawsuit as Richard destroys himself and injures those around him in his obsession with the Chancery case. Richard is another victim of the anachronistic system which destroys those who participate in it, a system which is a symbol of the inertia, complacency, and hypocrisy of the whole society. Finally, that Esther, the housekeeper, contracts smallpox from Jo is a symbol of the interrelatedness of all levels of society. Jo is at the bottom, but his misfortune becomes the misfortune of many as his contagion spreads through the social organism. The implication is that an unfeeling society can create Jo and Tom-all-alone's but it cannot protect itself from its victims.

Dickens offers no programmatic, revolutionary solution. If there is a solution, it is to be found in people like John Jarndyce, Esther Summerson, and Allan Woodcourt. Jarndyce is a figure of the selflessness which is necessary if injustice is to be rectified. Esther Summerson, as her name implies, is a bright antidote to the fog and rain. Her keys, which she shakes regularly, are a sign of her commitment to her domestic duties, an acceptance of responsibility. Dr. Woodcourt is the kind of active man society needs. The marriage of Esther and Woodcourt is a vindication of what they have to offer, as is Jarndyce's generous acceptance of their love. The new Bleak House in which they live is ironically full of the joy and goodness which can reform society. The novel does not offer the easy optimism of radical political solutions, because it is only this revolution in the heart of man which Dickens believes can cure society.

Bibliography

Axton, William F.   "Religious and Scientific Imagery in *Bleak House*," in *Nineteenth-Century Fiction.* XXII (March, 1968), pp. 349–359.

————.   "The Trouble with Esther," in *Modern Language Quarterly.* XXVI (1965), pp. 545–557.

Barnard, Robert.   *Imagery and Theme in the Novels of Dickens.* New York: Humanities Press, 1974, pp. 62–76.

Blount, Trevor.   "Dickens' Slum Satire in *Bleak House*," in *Modern Language Review.* LX (July, 1965), pp. 340–351.

Burke, Alan R.   "The Strategy and Theme of Urban Observation in *Bleak*

House," in *Studies in English Literature, 1500–1900.* IX (Autumn, 1969), pp. 659–676.

Cohan, Steven. " 'They Are All Secret': The Fantasy Content of *Bleak House*," in *Literature and Psychology.* XXVI (1976), pp. 79–91.

Coolidge, Archibald. "Dickens' Complex Plots," in *The Dickensian.* LVII (Autumn, 1961), pp. 174–182.

Crompton, Louis. "Satire and Symbolism in *Bleak House*," in *Nineteenth-Century Fiction.* XII (March, 1958), pp. 284–303.

Daleski, Herman M. *Dickens and the Art of Analogy.* New York: Schocken, 1970, pp. 156–190.

Donovan, R.A. "Structure and Idea in *Bleak House*," in *Journal of English Literary History.* XXIX (June, 1962), pp. 175–201.

Dunn, Richard J. "Esther's Role in *Bleak House*," in *The Dickensian.* LXII (September, 1966), pp. 163–166.

Dyson, A.E. *The Inimitable Dickens; A Reading of the Novels.* London: Macmillan, 1970, pp. 154–182.

Johnson, Edgar. "*Bleak House*, The Anatomy of Society," in *Nineteenth-Century Fiction.* VII (September, 1952), pp. 73–89.

Korg, Jacob. *Twentieth Century Interpretations of* Bleak House. Englewood Cliffs, N.J.: Prentice-Hall, 1968.

Manning, Sylvia B. *Dickens as Satirist.* New Haven, Conn.: Yale University Press, 1971, pp. 101–131.

Moers, Ellen. "*Bleak House*: The Agitating Women," in *The Dickensian.* LXIX (1973), pp. 13–24.

Ousby, Ian. "The Broken Glass: Vision and Comprehension in *Bleak House*," in *Nineteenth-Century Fiction.* XXIX (1975), pp. 381–392.

Partlow, Robert B., Jr. *Dickens the Craftsman; Strategies of Presentation.* Carbondale: Southern Illinois University Press, 1970, pp. 115–139.

Pederson, Winifred J. "Jo in *Bleak House*," in *The Dickensian.* LX (Autumn, 1964), pp. 162–167.

Serlin, Ellen. "The Two Worlds of *Bleak House*," in *Journal of English Literary History.* XLIII (Winter, 1976), pp. 551–566.

Stoehr, Taylor. *Dickens: The Dreamer's Stance.* Ithaca, N.Y.: Cornell University Press, 1965, pp. 137–170.

Wilkinson, Ann Y. "*Bleak House*: From Faraday to Judgement Day," in *Journal of English Literary History.* XXXIV (1967), pp. 225–247.

Winslow, Joan D. "Esther Summerson: The Betrayal of the Imagination," in *Journal of Narrative Technique.* VI (1976), pp. 1–13.

Zabel, Morton D. *Craft and Character: Texts, Methods and Vocation in*

Modern Fiction. New York: Viking, 1957, pp. 15–49.

Zwerdling, Alex.   "Esther Summerson Rehabilitated," in *PMLA.* LXXXVIII (1973), pp. 429–439.

DAVID COPPERFIELD

Type of work: Novel
Author: Charles Dickens (1812–1870)
Type of plot: Sentimental romance
Time of plot: Early nineteenth century
Locale: England
First published: 1849–1850

One of the best-loved novels in the English language, David Copperfield *is a devastating exposé of the treatment of children in the nineteenth century. Admittedly autobiographical, it is a work of art which can be read and reread, chiefly for its gallery of immortalized characters. Though the novel has flaws, it enjoys a kind of freshness and spontaneity stemming from the first-person recounting of events and the sympathetic treatment of characters.*

Principal Characters

David Copperfield, the orphaned hero-narrator whose story of his early years and growing maturity comprises one of the best-known works of fiction in the English language. A posthumous child, extremely sensitive in retrospect, he first experiences cruelty and tyranny when his young widowed mother marries stern Mr. Murdstone, and he quickly forms emotional alliances with the underprivileged and the victimized. His loyalties are sometimes misplaced, as in the case of Steerforth, his school friend who seduces Little Em'ly, but his heart remains sound and generous toward even the erring. As he passes from childhood to disillusioned adolescence, his perceptions increase, though he often misses the truth because he misreads the evidence before him. His trust is all the more remarkable when one considers the recurrence of error which leads him from false friends to false love and on to near catastrophe. Finally, unlike his creator, David finds balance and completion in his literary career, his abiding friendships, and his happy second marriage.

Clara Copperfield, David's childlike but understanding and beautiful mother, destined to an early death because of her inability to cope with life. Strong in her own attachments, she attributes to everyone motives as good and generous as her own. Misled into a second marriage to an unloving husband, she is torn between son and husband and dies soon after giving birth to another child. Mother and child are buried in the same coffin.

Edward Murdstone, Clara Copperfield's second husband and David's irascible stepfather, who cruelly mistreats the sensitive young boy. Self-seeking to an extreme degree, Murdstone has become a synonym for the mean and low, the calculating and untrustworthy. His cruelty is touched with sadism, and his egoism borders on the messianic.

Jane Murdstone, Edward Murdstone's sister. Like her brother, she is harsh and unbending. Her severe nature is symbolized by the somber colors and metallic beads she wears. Her suspicious mind is shown by her belief that the maids have a man hidden somewhere in the house.

Clara Peggotty, Mrs. Copperfield's devoted servant and David's nurse and friend. Cheerful and plump, she always seems about to burst out of her clothing, and when she moves buttons pop and fly in all directions. Discharged after the death of her mistress, she marries Barkis, a carrier.

Daniel Peggotty, Clara Peggotty's brother, a Yarmouth fisherman whose home is a boat beached on the sands. A generous, kind-hearted man, he has made himself the protector of a niece and a nephew, Little Em'ly and Ham, and of Mrs. Gummidge, the forlorn widow of his former partner. His charity consists of thoughtful devotion as much as material support.

Ham Peggotty, Daniel Peggotty's stalwart nephew. He grows up to fall in love with his cousin, Little Em'ly, but on the eve of their wedding she elopes with James Steerforth, her seducer. Some years later, during a great storm, Ham is drowned while trying to rescue Steerforth from a ship in distress off Yarmouth beach.

Little Em'ly, Daniel Peggotty's niece and adopted daughter, a girl of great beauty and charm and David's first love. Though engaged to marry her cousin Ham, she runs away with James Steerforth. After he discards her, Daniel Peggotty saves her from a life of further shame, and she and her uncle join a party emigrating to Australia.

Barkis, the carrier between Blunderstone and Yarmouth. A bashful suitor, he woos Peggotty by having David tell her that "Barkis is willin'!" This tag-line, frequently repeated, reveals the carter's good and simple nature.

Mrs. Gummidge, the widow of Daniel Peggotty's fishing partner. After he takes her into his home she spends most of her time by the fire, meanwhile complaining sadly that she is a "lone, lorn creetur."

Miss Betsey Trotwood, David Copperfield's great-aunt, eccentric, sharp-spoken, but essentially kind-hearted. Present on the night of David's birth, she has already made up her mind as to his sex

and his name, her own. When she learns that the child is a boy, she leaves the house in great indignation. Eventually she becomes the benefactress of destitute and desolate David, educates him, and lives to see him happily married to Agnes Wickfield and established in his literary career.

Richard Babley, called **Mr. Dick,** a mildly mad and seemingly irresponsible man befriended by Miss Trotwood. He has great difficulty in keeping the subject of King Charles the First out of his conversation and the memorial he is writing. Miss Trotwood, who refuses to admit that he is mad, always defers to him as a shrewd judge of character and situation.

Dora Spenlow, the ornamental but helpless "child-wife" whom David loves protectively, marries, and loses when she dies young. Her helplessness in dealing with the ordinary situations of life is both amusing and touching.

Agnes Wickfield, the daughter of Miss Trotwood's solicitor and David's stanch friend for many years. Though David at first admires the father, his admiration is soon transferred to the sensible, generous daughter. She nurses Dora Copperfield at the time of her fatal illness, and Dora on her deathbed advises David to marry Agnes. The delicacy with which Agnes contains her love for many years makes her an appealing figure. Eventually she and David are married, to Miss Trotwood's great delight.

Uriah Heep, the hypocritical villain who, beginning as a clerk in Mr. Wickfield's law office, worms his way into the confidence of his employer, becomes a partner in the firm, ruins Mr. Wickfield, and embezzles Miss Trotwood's fortune. His insistence that he is a very humble person provides the clue to his sly, conniving nature. His villainy is finally uncovered by Wilkins Micawber, whom he has used as a tool, and he is forced to make restitution. After Mr. Wickfield and Miss Trotwood refuse to charge him with fraud, he continues his sharp practices in another section of the country until he is arrested for forgery and imprisoned.

Wilkins Micawber, an impecunious man who is "always waiting for something to turn up" while spending himself into debtors' prison, writing grandiloquent letters, indulging in flowery rhetoric, and eking out a shabbily genteel existence on the brink of disaster. David Copperfield lodges with the Micawbers for a time in London, and to him Mr. Micawber confides the sum of his worldly philosophy: "Annual income twenty pounds; annual expenditure nineteen, nineteen, six—result happiness. Annual income twenty pounds; annual expenditure twenty pounds nought six—result misery." He tries a variety of occupations in the course of the novel and is for a time employed by Uriah Heep, whose villainy he contemptuously unmasks. Miss Trotwood aids him and his family to emigrate to Australia, where he becomes a magistrate. A figure of improvidence, alternating between high spirits and low, well-meaning but without understanding of the ways of the worldly, Mr. Micawber is one of Dickens' great comic creations.

Mrs. Emma Micawber, a woman genteelly born (as she frequently insists) and as mercurial in temperament as her husband, capable of fainting over the prospect of financial ruin at three o'clock and of eating with relish breaded lamb chops and drinking ale, bought with money from two pawned teaspoons, at four. Loyal in nature, she says in every crisis that she will never desert Mr. Micawber.

**Master Wilkins and
Miss Emma,** the Micawber children.

James Steerforth, David Copperfield's fellow student at Salem House. The handsome, spoiled son of a wealthy widow, he hides his true nature behind pleasing manners and a seemingly engaging disposition. Introduced by David into the Peggotty household at Yarmouth, he succeeds in seducing Little Em'ly and persuading her to elope with him on the eve of her marriage to Ham. Later he tires of her and plans to marry her off to Littimer, the servant who aids him in his amorous conquests. He is drowned when his ship breaks up during a storm off Yarmouth.

Mrs. Steerforth, James Steerforth's mother, a proud, austere woman, at first devoted to her handsome, wayward son but eventually estranged from him.

Rosa Dartle, Mrs. Steerforth's companion. Older than Steerforth but deeply in love with him, she endures humiliation and many indignities because of her unreasoning passion. Her lip is scarred, the result of a wound suffered when Steerforth, in a childish fit of anger, threw a hammer at her.

Littimer, Steerforth's valet, a complete scoundrel. Tired of Little Em'ly, Steerforth plans to marry her to his servant, but the girl runs away in order to escape this degradation.

Miss Mowcher, a pursy dwarf. A hairdresser, she makes herself "useful" to a number of people in a variety of ways. Steerforth avails himself of her services.

**Markham and
Grainger,** Steerforth's lively, amusing friends.

Francis Spenlow, a partner in the London firm of Spenlow and Jorkins, proctors, in which David Copperfield becomes an articled clerk. During a visit at the Spenlow country place David meets Dora, Mr. Spenlow's lovely but childlike daughter and falls in love with her, but her father opposes David's suit after Miss Trotwood loses her fortune. Mr. Spenlow dies suddenly after a fall from his carriage and Dora is taken in charge by two maiden aunts. Following the discovery that Mr. Spenlow's business affairs were in great confusion and that he died almost penniless, David marries Dora.

Miss Clarissa and
Miss Lavinia Spenlow, Mr. Spenlow's sisters, who take Dora into their home after her father's death.

Mr. Jorkins, Mr. Spenlow's business partner.

Mary Anne Paragon, a servant to David and Dora during their brief married life.

Mr. Tiffey, an elderly, withered-looking clerk employed by Spenlow and Jorkins.

Mr. Wickfield, a solicitor of Canterbury and Miss Trotwood's man of business, brought to ruin by Uriah Heep's scheming and adroit mismanagement of the firm's accounts. He is saved from disaster when Wilkins Micawber exposes Heep's machinations. Mr. Wickfield is a weak, foolish, but high-principled man victimized by a scoundrel who exploits his weaknesses.

Mr. Creakle, the master of Salem House, the wretched school to which Mr. Murdstone sends David Copperfield. Lacking in scholarly qualities, he prides himself on his strict discipline. Years later he becomes interested in a model prison where Uriah Heep and Littimer are among the inmates.

Mrs. Creakle, his wife, the victim of her husband's tyranny.

Miss Creakle, their daughter, reported to be in love with Steerforth.

Charles Mell, a junior master at Salem House, discharged when Mr. Creakle learns that the teacher's mother lives in an almshouse. Emigrating to Australia, he eventually becomes the head of the Colonial Salem-House Grammar-School.

Mr. Sharp, the senior master at Salem House.

George Demple, one of David Copperfield's schoolmates at Salem House.

Thomas Traddles, another student at Salem House. As an unhappy schoolboy he consoles himself by drawing skeletons. He studies law, marries the daughter of a clergyman, and eventually becomes a judge. He, with David Copperfield, acts for Miss Trotwood after Uriah Heep's villainy has been revealed.

Miss Sophy Crewler, the fourth daughter of a clergyman's family, a pleasant, cheerful girl who marries Thomas Traddles. Her husband always refers to her as "the dearest girl in the world."

The Reverend Horace Crewler, a poor clergyman and the father of a large family of daughters.

Mrs. Crewler, his wife, a chronic invalid whose condition mends or grows worse according to the pleasing or displeasing circumstances of her life.

Caroline,
Sarah,
Louisa,
Lucy, and
Margaret, the other Crewler daughters. They and their husbands form part of the family circle surrounding happy, generous Traddles.

Dr. Strong, the master of the school at Canterbury where Miss Trotwood sends her great-nephew to be educated. After Miss Trotwood loses her money, Dr. Strong hires David to help in compiling a classical dictionary.

Mrs. Strong, a woman much younger than her husband.

Mrs. Markleham, the mother of Mrs. Strong. The boys at the Canterbury school call her the "Old Soldier."

Mr. Quinion, the manager of the warehouse of Murdstone and Grinby, where David Copperfield is sent to do menial work after his mother's death. Miserable in these surroundings, David finally resolves to run away and look for his only relative, Miss Betsey Trotwood, in Dover.

Tipp, a workman in the Murdstone and Grinby warehouse.

Mealy Potatoes and
Mick Walker, two rough slum boys who work with David at the warehouse of Murdstone and Grinby.

Miss Larkins, a dark-eyed, statuesque beauty with whom David Copperfield falls in love when he is seventeen. She disappoints him by marrying Mr. Chestle, a grower of hops.

Miss Shepherd, a student at Miss Nettingall's Establishment for Young Ladies and another of David Copperfield's youthful loves.

Mrs. Crupp, David Copperfield's landlady while he is an articled clerk in the firm of Spenlow and Jorkins. She suffers from "the spazzums" and takes quantities of peppermint for this strange disorder.

Martha Endell, the unfortunate young woman who helps to restore Little Em'ly to her uncle.

Janet, Miss Betsey Trotwood's servant.

Jack Maldon, Mrs. Strong's cousin, a libertine for whom her kind-hearted husband finds employment.

The Story

David Copperfield was born at Blunderstone, in Suffolk, six months after his father's death. Miss Betsey Trotwood, an eccentric great-aunt was present on the night of his birth, but she left the house abruptly and indignantly when she learned that the child was a boy who could never bear her name. David spent his early years with his pretty young mother, Clara Copperfield, and a devoted servant named Peggotty. Peggotty was plain and plump; when she bustled about the house her buttons popped off her dress.

The youthful widow was soon courted by Mr. Murdstone, who proved, after marriage, to be stingy and cruel. When his mother married a second time, David was packed off with Peggotty to visit her relatives at Yarmouth. There her brother had converted an old boat into a seaside cottage, where he lived with his niece, Little Em'ly, and his sturdy young nephew, Ham. Little Em'ly and Ham were David's first real playmates, and his visit to Yarmouth remained a happy memory of his lonely and unhappy childhood. After Miss Jane Murdstone arrived to take charge of her brother's household, David and his mother were never to feel free again from the dark atmosphere of suspicion and gloom the Murdstones brought with them.

One day in a fit of childish terror David bit his stepfather on the hand. He was immediately sent off to Salem House, a wretched school near London. There his life was more miserable than ever under a brutal headmaster named Creakle. But in spite of the harsh system of the school and the bullyings of Mr. Creakle, his life was endurable because of his friendship with two boys whom he was to meet again under much different circumstances in later life—lovable Tommy Traddles and handsome, lordly James Steerforth.

His school days ended suddenly with the death of his mother and her infant child. When he returned home, he discovered that Mr. Murdstone had dismissed Peggotty. Barkis, the stage driver, whose courtship had been meager but earnest, had taken Peggotty away to become Mrs. Barkis, and David was left friendless in the home of his cruel stepfather.

David was put to work in an export warehouse in which Murdstone had an interest. As a ten-year-old worker in the dilapidated establishment of Murdstone and Grinby, wine merchants, David was overworked and half-starved. He loathed his job and associates such as young Mick Walker and Mealy Potatoes. The youngster, however, met still another person with whom he was to associate in later life. That was Wilkins Micawber, a pompous ne'er-do-well in whose house David lodged. The impecunious Mr. Micawber found himself in debtor's prison shortly afterward. On his release he decided to move with his brood to Plymouth. Having lost these good friends, David decided to run away from the environment he detested.

When David decided to leave Murdstone and Grinby, he knew he could not return to his stepfather. The only other relative he could think of was his father's aunt, Miss Betsey Trotwood, who had flounced indignantly out of the house on the night of David's birth. Hopefully he set out for Dover, where Miss Betsey lived, but not before he had been robbed of all his possessions. Consequently, he arrived at Miss Betsey's home physically and mentally wretched.

David's reception was at first not cordial. Miss Betsey had never forgotten the injustice done her when David was born instead of a girl. However, upon the advice of Mr. Dick, a feeble-minded distant kinsman who was staying with her, she decided to take David in, at least until he had been washed thoroughly. While she was deliberating further about what to do with her bedraggled nephew, she wrote to Mr. Murdstone, who came with his sister to Dover to claim his stepson. Miss Betsey decided she disliked both Murdstones intensely. Mr. Dick solved her problem by suggesting that she keep David.

Much to David's joy and satisfaction, Miss Betsey planned to let the boy continue his education, and almost immediately sent him to a school in Canterbury, run by a Mr. Strong, a headmaster quite different from Mr. Creakle. During his stay at school David lodged with Miss Betsey's lawyer, Mr. Wickfield, who had a daughter, Agnes. David became very fond of her. At Wickfield's he also met Uriah Heep, Mr. Wickfield's cringing clerk, whose hypocritical humility and clammy handclasp filled David with disgust.

David finished school when he was seventeen. Miss Betsey suggested he travel for a time before deciding on a profession. On his way to visit his old nurse, Peggotty, David met James Steerforth and went home with his former schoolmate. There he met Steerforth's mother and Rosa Dartle, a girl passionately in love with Steerforth. Years before, the quick-tempered Steerforth had struck Rosa, who carried a scar as a reminder of Steerforth's brutality.

After a brief visit, David persuaded Steerforth to go with him to see Peggotty and her family. At Yarmouth, Steerforth met Little Em'ly. In spite of the fact that she was engaged to Ham, she and Steerforth were immediately attracted to each other.

At length David told his aunt he wished to study law. Accordingly, he was articled to the law firm of Spenlow and Jorkins. At this time David saw Agnes Wickfield, who told him she feared Steerforth and asked David to stay away from him. Agnes also expressed a fear of Uriah Heep, who was on the point of entering into partnership with her senile father. Shortly after these revelations, by Agnes, David encountered Uriah himself, who confessed he wanted to marry Agnes. David was properly disgusted.

On a visit to the Spenlow home, David met Dora Spenlow, his employer's pretty but childish daughter, with whom he fell instantly in love. Soon they became secretly engaged. Before this happy event, however, David heard some startling news—Steerforth had run away with Little Em'ly.

This elopement was not the only blow to David's happiness. Shortly after his engagement to Dora, David learned from his aunt that she had lost all her money, and from Agnes that Uriah Heep had become Mr. Wickfield's partner. David tried unsuccessfully to be released from his contract with Spenlow and Jorkins. Determined to show his aunt he could repay her, even in a small way, for her past sacrifices, he took a part-time job as secretary to Mr. Strong, his former headmaster.

But the job with Mr. Strong paid very little; therefore David undertook to study for a position as a reporter of parliamentary debates. Even poor simple Mr. Dick came to Miss Betsey's rescue, for Traddles, now a lawyer, gave him a job as a clerk.

The sudden death of Mr. Spenlow dissolved the partnership of Spenlow and Jorkins, and David learned to his dismay that his former employer had died almost penniless. With much study on his part, David became a reporter. At twenty-one he married Dora, who, however, never seemed capable of growing up. During these events, David had kept in touch with Mr. Micawber, now Uriah Heep's confidential secretary. Though something had finally turned up for Mr. Micawber, his relations with David, and even with his own family, were mysteriously strange, as though he were hiding something.

David soon learned what the trouble was, for Mr. Micawber's conscience got the better of him. At a meeting arranged by him at Mr. Wickfield's, he revealed in Uriah's presence and to an assembled company, including Agnes, Miss Betsey, David, and Traddles, the criminal perfidy of Uriah Heep, who for years had robbed and cheated Mr. Wickfield. Miss Betsey discovered that Uriah was also responsible for her own financial losses. With the exposure of the villainous Uriah, partial restitution both for her and for Mr. Wickfield was not long in coming.

His conscience cleared by his exposure of Uriah Heep's villainy, Mr. Micawber proposed to take his family to Australia. There, he was sure something would again turn up. To Australia, too, went Mr. Peggotty and Little Em'ly; she had turned to her uncle in sorrow and shame after Steerforth had deserted her. David watched as their ship put out to sea. It seemed to him the sunset was a bright promise for them as they sailed away to a new life in the new land. The darkness fell about him as he watched.

The great cloud now in David's life was his wife's delicate health. Day after day she failed, and in spite of his tenderest care he was forced to see her grow more feeble and wan. Agnes Wickfield, like the true friend she had always been, was with him on the night of Dora's death. As in his earlier troubles, he turned to Agnes in the days that followed and found comfort in her sympathy and understanding.

Upon her advice he decided to go abroad for a while. But first he went to Yarmouth to put into Ham's hands a last letter from Little Em'ly. There he witnessed the final act of her betrayal. During a storm the heavy seas battered a ship in distress off the coast. Ham went to his death in a stout-hearted attempt to rescue a survivor clinging to a broken mast. The bodies washed ashore by the rolling waves were those of loyal Ham and the false Steerforth.

David lived in Europe for three years. On his return he discovered again his need for Agnes Wickfield's quiet friendship. One day Miss Betsey Trotwood slyly suggested that Agnes might soon be married. Heavy in heart, David went off to offer her his good wishes. When she burst into tears, he realized that what he had hoped was true—her heart was already his. They were married, to match-making Miss Betsey's great delight, and David settled down to begin his career as a successful novelist.

Critical Evaluation

"But, like many fond parents, I have in my heart of hearts a favorite child. And his name is David Copperfield."

This is Charles Dickens' final, affectionate judgment of the work which stands exactly in the middle of his novelistic career, with seven novels before and seven after (excluding the unfinished *The Mystery of Edwin Drood*). When he began the novel, he was in his mid-thirties, secure in continuing success that had begun with *Sketches by Boz* (1836), and *Pickwick Papers* (1836-1837). It was a good time to take stock of his life, to make use of the autobiographical manuscript he had put by earlier. Nor did he try to conceal the personal element from his public, which eagerly awaited each of the nineteen numbers of *David Copperfield*. The novel was issued serially from May, 1849, through November, 1850. Charles Dickens, writer, is readily identified with David Copperfield, writer, viewing his life through the "long Copperfieldian perspective," as Dickens called it.

Although much in the life of the first-person narrator corresponds to Dickens' own life, details are significantly altered. Unlike David, Dickens was not a genteel orphan but the eldest son of living and improvident parents; his own father served as the model for Micawber. Dickens' childhood stint in a shoeblacking factory seems to have been somewhat shorter than David's drudgery in the warehouse of Murdstone and Grinby, wine distributors, but the shame and suffering were identical. Young Charles Dickens failed in his romance with a pretty young girl, but the author Dickens permits David to win his Dora. However, Dickens inflicts upon Dora as Mrs. Copperfield the faults of his own Kate, who, unlike Dora, lived on as his wife until their separation in 1858.

However fascinating the autobiographical details, *David Copperfield* stands primarily on its merits as a novel endowed with the bustling life of Dickens' earlier works but controlled by his maturing sense of design. The novel in its entirety answers affirmatively the question posed by David himself in the opening sentence: "Whether I shall turn out to be the hero of my own life. . . . "

In addition to the compelling characterization of the protagonist, the novel abounds with memorable portrayals. The square face and black beard of Mr. Murdstone, always viewed in conjunction with that "metallic lady" Miss Murdstone, evoke the horror of dehumanized humanity. Uriah Heep's writhing body, clammy skin, and peculiarly lidless eyes suggest a subhuman form more terrifying than the revolting nature of his "umbleness." Above all the figures that crowd the lonely world of the orphan rises the bald head of Wilkins Micawber, flourishing the English language and his quizzing glass with equal impressiveness, confidently prepared in case some opportunity turns up.

Nevertheless, David Copperfield is very definitely the hero of his own story. This is a novel of initiation, organized around the two major cycles of the hero's development, first in childhood, then in early manhood. It focuses steadily upon the testing which will qualify him for full manhood. He makes his own choices, but each important stage of his moral progress is marked by the intervention of Aunt Betsey Trotwood.

To begin with, David is weak simply because he is a child, the hapless victim of adult exploitation. But he is also heir to the moral weakness of his childish mother and his dead father, who was an inept, impractical man. David's birth is, portentously, the occasion of a conflict between his mother's Copperfieldian softness and Aunt Betsey's firmness, displayed in her rigidity of figure and countenance.

From a state of childish freedom, David falls into the Murdstone world. The clanking chains of Miss Murdstone's steel purse symbolize the metaphorical prison which replaces his innocently happy home. Indeed, for David, the world becomes a prison. After his five days of solitary confinement at Blunderstone, he enters the jail-like Salem House School. After his mother's death, he is placed in the grim warehouse, apparently for life. Nor is his involvement with the Micawbers any real escape, for he is burdened with their problems and retains his place in the family even after their incarceration in the King's Bench Prison.

Although David repudiates the tyrannical firmness of which he is a victim, he does not actively rebel, except for the one occasion when he bites Mr. Murdstone. Instead, like his mother, he indulges his weakness; he submits, fearfully to the Murdstones and Creakle, worshipfully to the arrogant Steerforth. In addition, he escapes into the illusory freedom of fantasy—through books and stories and through the lives of others, which he invests with an enchantment that conceals from him whatever is potentially tragic or sordid.

Nevertheless, David's pliant nature shares something of the resolute spirit of Aunt Betsey, despite her disappearance on the night of his birth. Looking back upon his wretched boyhood, David recalls that he kept his own counsel, and did his work. From having suffered in secret, he moves to the decision to escape by his own act. The heroic flight is rewarded when Aunt Betsey relents and takes him in. Appropriately, she trusses up the small boy in adult clothes and announces her own goal of making him a "fine fellow, with a will of your own," with a "strength of character that is not to be influenced, except on good reason, by anybody, or by anything." The first cycle of testing is complete.

The conventionally happy years in Dover and Canterbury mark an interlude before the second major cycle of the novel, which commences with David's reentry into the world as a young man. Significantly, he at first resumes the docile patterns of childhood. Reunited with Steerforth, he once again takes pride in his friend's overbearing attitude. He allows himself to be bullied by various inferiors. He evades the obligation to choose his own career by entering into a profession which affects him like an opiate. In Dora's childlike charms he recaptures the girlish image of his mother. However, at this point, the firm Aunt Betsey, having cut short his childhood trials, deliberately sets into motion his adult testing with her apparent bankruptcy.

In response to his new challenges, David is forced back upon his childhood resources. At first, he unconsciously imitates Murdstone in trying to mold Dora; but he again rejects tyranny, choosing instead resignation, understanding that she can be no more than his "child-wife." He responds with full sympathy to the tragedy of Little Em'ly's affair with Steerforth, but he is finally disenchanted with the splendid willfulness which had captivated his boyish heart. Most important, he recovers the saving virtue of his childhood, his ability to suffer in secrecy, to keep his own counsel, and to do his work. As his trials pile up—poverty, overwork, disappointment in marriage, his wife's death, and the tribulations of the friends to whom his tender heart is wholly committed—he conquers his own undisciplined heart.

The mature man who emerges from his trials profits from his experiences and heritage. His capacity for secret suffering is, for him as for Aunt Betsey, a source of strength; but his, unlike hers, is joined to the tenderheartedness inherited from his parents. Her distrust of mankind has made her an eccentric. His trusting disposition, though rendering him vulnerable, binds him to mankind.

Although Aunt Betsey sets a goal of maturity before David, Agnes Wickfield is the symbol of the hard-won self-discipline which he finally achieves. She is from the beginning his "better angel." Like him, she is tenderhearted and compliant. Yet, though a passive character, she is not submissive; and she is always in control of herself in even the most difficult human relationships. Moreover, her firmness of character is never distorted by fundamental distrust of mankind. Thus hers is the only influence which David should accept, "on good reason," in his pursuit of the moral goal which Aunt Betsey sets before him.

By the time David has recognized his love for Agnes, he has also attained a strength of character like hers. The appropriate conclusion to his quest for maturity is his union with Agnes—who is from the beginning a model of the self-disciplined person in whom gentleness and strength are perfectly balanced. Furthermore, the home he builds with her is the proper journey's end for the orphaned child who has grasped at many versions of father, mother, family, and home: "Long miles of road then opened out before my mind, and toiling on, I saw a ragged way-worn boy forsaken and neglected, who should come to call even the heart now beating against him, his own." He has outgrown the child-mother, the child-wife, the childhood idols, even the childhood terrors, and he is a mature man ready to accept love "founded on a rock."

In the context of a successful completed quest, the novel ends with a glimpse of the complete man, who writes far into the night to erase the shadows of his past, but whose control of the realities is sufficient in the presence of the woman who is always, symbolically, "near me, pointing upward!"

Bibliography

Bandelin, Carl. *"David Copperfield*: A Third Interesting Penitent," in *Studies in English Literature, 1500–1900.* XVI (1976), pp. 601–611.

Bell, Vereen M. "The Emotional Matrix of *David Copperfield*," in *Studies in English Literature, 1500–1900.* VIII (1968), pp. 633–649.

Brown, Janet H. "The Narrator's Role in *David Copperfield*," in *Dickens Studies Annual.* II (1972), pp. 197–207.

Davis, Earle. *The Flint and the Flame: The Artistry of Charles Dickens.* Columbia: University of Missouri Press, 1963, pp. 157–182.

Donovan, Frank. *Dickens and Youth.* New York: Dodd, Mead, 1968, pp. 24–60.

Dunn, Richard J. *"David Copperfield*: All Dickens Is There," in *English*

Journal. LIV (1965), pp. 789–794.

Dyson, A.E.   *The Inimitable Dickens; A Reading of the Novels.* London: Macmillan, 1970, pp. 119–153.

Gard, Roger.   *"David Copperfield,"* in *Essays in Criticism.* XV (July, 1965), pp. 313–325.

Hardy, Barbara.   *The Moral Art of Dickens.* New York: Oxford University Press, 1970, pp. 122–138.

Hornback, Bert G.   "Frustration and Resolution in *David Copperfield,"* in *Studies in English Literature, 1500–1900.* VIII (1969), pp. 651–667.

Hughes, Felicity.   "Narrative Complexity in *David Copperfield,"* in *Journal of English Literary History.* XLI (1974), pp. 89–105.

Kincaid, James R.   "Dickens' Subversive Humor: *David Copperfield,"* in *Nineteenth-Century Fiction.* XXII (March, 1968), pp. 313–329.

————. "The Structure of *David Copperfield,"* in *Dickens Studies.* II (1966), pp. 74–95.

————. "Symbol and Subversion in *David Copperfield,"* in *Studies in the Novel.* I (1969), pp. 196–206.

Kraus, W. Keith.   *Charles Dickens*: David Copperfield. New York: Barnes & Noble, 1966.

Lucas, John.   *The Melancholy Man: A Study of Dickens' Novels.* London: Methuen, 1970, pp. 166–201.

Manning, Sylvia B.   *Dickens as Satirist.* New Haven, Conn.: Yale University Press, 1971, pp. 96–98.

Maugham, William S.   *Art of Fiction; An Introduction to Ten Novels and Their Authors.* Garden City N.Y.: Doubleday, 1955, pp. 135–161.

Reed, John R.   "Confinement and Character in Dickens' Novels," in *Dickens Studies Annual.* I (1970), pp. 51–54.

Robison, Roselee.   "Time, Death and the River in Dickens' Novels," in *English Studies.* LIII (1972), pp. 436–454.

Schilling, Bernard N.   *The Comic Spirit; Boccaccio to Thomas Mann.* Detroit: Wayne State University Press, 1965, pp. 98–144.

Spilka, Mark.   *"David Copperfield* as Psychological Fiction," in *Critical Quarterly.* I (Winter, 1959), pp. 292–301.

Stone, Harry.   "Fairy Tales and Ogres; Dickens' Imagination and *David Copperfield,"* in *Criticism.* VI (1964), pp. 324–330.

Tick, Stanley.   "The Memorializing of Mr. Dick," in *Nineteenth-Century Fiction.* XXIV (September, 1969), pp. 142–153.

Worth, George J.   "The Control of Emotional Response in *David Copperfield,"* in his *The English Novel in the Nineteenth Century: Essays on the Literary*

Mediation of Human Values. Urbana: University of Illinois Press, 1972, pp. 97–108.

DOMBEY AND SON

Type of work: Novel
Author: Charles Dickens (1812–1870)
Type of plot: Sentimental romance
Time of plot: Early nineteenth century
Locale: England
First published: 1846–1848

Dombey and Son *was Dickens' effort to regain the popularity he had lost with the publication of* Martin Chuzzlewit, *which had heavily satirized America and Americans. The novel is noted for its complex structure and was a milestone in Dickens' work in that he placed the story at a higher social level than he had done in his previous novels. The novel is a very serious one, involving the downfall of a dignified, pompous merchant and his learning of the power of love over money. For the first time, Dickens indicates an interest in and a sympathy for the upper middle classes and the aristocracy, but continues to include a whole catalogue of characters to provide a humorous background.*

Principal Characters

Paul Dombey, a London merchant, referred to as Mr. Dombey throughout the novel. Twenty successful years in the firm of Dombey and Son have brought wealth to the stern and pompous Mr. Dombey. Ten years of marriage finally bring a son and happiness (despite his wife's death) to the unemotional, dignified, glossy businessman, for the son will occupy his rightful place in the firm. Jealous and possessive, Mr. Dombey resents his son's affection for Florence, the older Dombey daughter. Later he sends Walter Gay, a young clerk attentive to the daughter, on an extended trip to the West Indies, and he loses his second wife because he approaches personal relationships as if they were business transactions in his office. Through reversals in both personal and business affairs, Mr. Dombey senses that his shortcomings lie in what he has always considered his strength: a belief in his indomitability. This realization results in a modicum of happiness for him as he accepts his daughter's love after spurning her all her life.

Paul Dombey, his son and heir, who is the essence of Dombey's life. Before the child was born, Mr. Dombey had yearned for a son; during Paul's life, he is jealous of his attentions to others, over-solicitous for his health, and unrealistic in treating the child as his longed-for business partner; after Paul's death, at six years, Mr. Dombey in his disillusionment considers the death a personal injustice to himself. Paul, a weak, precocious child, is uncommonly preoccupied with death, an interest which seems, in the Dickensian manner, to portend his early demise.

Florence Dombey, six years older than Paul. Until she is grown, Florence is the brunt of her father's unreasonable animosity. Courageous and compassionate, she withstands her father's affronts and ill-temper. Of strong faith, she does not despair at failures or rebuffs. Devoted and appreciative of love, she is a good wife to Walter Gay. Ultimately, Florence's altruism comes full circle when she has a son, Paul, who aids in her father's realization of his daughter's long-standing love.

Walter Gay, her childhood friend and later her husband. The model of good upbringing and training, he is instrumental in her safety and well-being. The last instance of his protectorship is as her husband and father of their children, when the Gays return to London to save Dombey from self-destruction and to give him renewed interest in life when he sees his grandchildren in the light in which he should have viewed his own daughter and son.

Mrs. Fanny Dombey, Mr. Dombey's first wife, the mother of Florence and Paul.

Mrs. Edith Granger, Dombey's second wife and his female counterpart in stubbornness and pride. Thwarted in her role as wife, she strikes back by pretending to elope with James Carker, Dombey's head clerk. Her wounded pride continues through the years; she finally declares her innocence of an affair with Carker, but she refuses to see Dombey to ask his forgiveness.

James Carker, Dombey's trusted head clerk and manager, whose villainy brings about his employer's professional and personal ruin. Deserted by Mrs. Dombey in the hour of their elopement, he is killed by a train while trying to avoid a meeting with Dombey.

Solomon Gills, a maker of nautical instruments and Walter Gay's uncle. With his loyal friend and partner, Captain Cuttle, he produces instruments that make his name a byword in safe navigation.

Edward Cuttle, an old sailor generally known as **Captain Cuttle** or **Captain Ned.** Adding much to the story with his salty mariner jargon, he becomes Florence Dombey's protector when she is rejected by her father.

Miss Lucretia Tox, a friend of Dombey's sister, who finds the wet nurse for the infant Paul. In her attentions to the child, she obviously has designs on Dombey,

her devotion to him being sustained in a platonic manner throughout his life.

Major Joseph Bagstock, a retired army officer, a neighbor and an admirer of Miss Tox. The typically proud old officer is introduced to point up the transition in Miss Tox's affections. It is he who introduces Mr. Dombey to Edith Granger.

Mrs. Polly Toodle, the wet nurse, renamed Richards, a more respectable appellation for the atmosphere of the Dombey house. Summarily dismissed for negligence after Florence strays and suffers a traumatic experience with a derelict woman, Mrs. Toodle remains in the story in connection with Miss Tox and lesser characters.

Mr. Toodle, Polly Toodle's husband, a stoker and engine-driver.

Robin Toodle, their son, also called **Biler** and **Rob the Grinder.** Mr. Dombey secures him a place in the establishment of "The Honorable Grinders," but he meets with so much ridicule and abuse that he runs away. Later he acts as a spy for James Carker. Still later he enters the employ of Miss Tox in his attempt to regain respectability.

Dr. Blimber, the owner of a select private school attended by Paul Dombey.

Mrs. Blimber, his wife, a silly, stupid woman.

Cornelia Blimber, their daughter, a bluestocking and a lover of dead languages.

John Carker, James Carker's brother and an under-clerk in the employ of Dombey and Son. Years before he had stolen money from the firm, but, because he had been led astray by bad companions, he had not been discharged. He repays this trust by years of faithful service. Dismissed after his brother's elopement with Mrs. Dombey and death, he inherits his brother's fortune and is able to live quietly but comfortably. After Mr. Dombey goes bankrupt he turns the interest of his fortune over to his former employer and pretends that he is repaying an old, forgotten debt.

Harriet Carker, the sister of James and John Carker. She marries Mr. Morfin.

Mr. Morfin, the cheerful head clerk at Dombey and Son. He befriends John Carker and marries his sister Harriet.

Susan Nipper, Florence Dombey's maid and companion. Discharged after she reproves Mr. Dombey for his treatment of his daughter, she marries Mr. Toots.

Mr. P. Toots, a pupil at Doctor Blimber's school for young gentlemen. Rich and eccentric, he spends much of his time writing letters to himself and signing them with the names of famous personages, and his most commonplace remarks are filled with biblical and literary allusions. He falls in love with Florence Dombey, but when she discourages his attentions he marries Susan Nipper instead and fathers a large brood of children.

Captain Jack Bunsby, Captain Cuttle's close friend. Innocently unaware of the wiles of women, he marries Mrs. MacStinger, his landlady.

Mrs. MacStinger, a domineering, designing widow, as quick with her hand as with her tongue. She marries Captain Bunsby.

Alexander,
Charles (Chowley), and
Juliana, Mrs. MacStinger's children by her first marriage.

Mrs. Pipchin, an ill-favored widow with whom Paul and Florence Dombey are sent to board at Brighton, later Mr. Dombey's housekeeper.

Berinthia, also called **Berry,** Mrs. Pipchin's spinster niece and servant.

Alice Brown, also called **Alice Marwood,** James Carker's former mistress, transported for felony. She returns, filled with hate and defiance, to England.

Mrs. Brown, her mother.

Mrs. Louisa Chick, Mr. Dombey's sister, a good-natured but smug woman.

John Chick, her husband, who constantly hums or whistles tunes.

Mr. Feeder, B.A., an assistant at Doctor Blimber's school and later his son-in-law.

The Reverend Alfred Feeder, M.A., his brother.

The Hon. Mrs. Skewton, also called **Cleopatra,** an aged beauty and Edith Dombey's mother, who puts her daughter up for the highest bidder in the marriage market. She dies soon after her daughter's marriage to Mr. Dombey.

Lord Feenix, Mrs. Skewton's superannuated nephew, a man about town.

The Game Chicken, a professional prize fighter and Mr. Toot's boxing instructor.

The Reverend Melchisedech Howler, a ranting clergyman who predicts the end of the world.

Sir Barnet Skettles, a time-serving, self-seeking member of the House of Commons.

Lady Skettles, his wife.

Barnet Skettles, a pupil at Doctor Blimber's school.

Tozer and
Briggs, Paul Dombey's roommates at Doctor Blimber's school.

Anne, a housemaid,
Thomas Towlinson, a footman, and
Mary Daws, a kitchen maid, servants in the Dombey household.

Mr. Clark, a clerk, and
Mr. Perch, a messenger, employees of Dombey and Son.

Mrs. Perch, the messenger's wife, usually in an interesting condition.

Dr. Pilkins, Mr. Dombey's family doctor.

Dr. Parker Peps, the attending physician

at the birth of Paul Dombey because of his reputation as an obstetrician.

The Story

Mr. Dombey was a stiff and dignified man who rarely showed emotion. But the birth of an infant son, who was named Paul, was cause for rejoicing, as Mr. Dombey had longed many years for a child who would fill the second part of the mercantile firm of Dombey and Son. Even the fact that Mrs. Dombey died shortly after the boy's birth did not particularly concern him; he was centered entirely on the little infant who he hoped would someday take over the business. Mr. Dombey also had a daughter, Florence, but she meant almost nothing to him, for she could not take a place in the firm.

Little Paul was first given over to a wet nurse, but the woman proved to be unreliable and was dismissed. After her dismissal little Paul was cared for by Mr. Dombey's sister and a friend of hers. Despite their vigilant care, however, little Paul's health was poor. He was listless and never cared to play. At last Mr. Dombey made arrangements to have him sent to a home, together with his sister, at Brighton, there to gain the benefits of the sea air.

Paul, in spite of his father's dislike for little Florence, loved his sister very much, and they were constant companions. Paul's love for Florence only made Mr. Dombey dislike the girl more, for the father felt that his daughter was coming between himself and his son.

One weekend, while Mr. Dombey was visiting at Brighton, Walter Gay, a young clerk in the firm, came to the inn where Mr. Dombey and his children were having dinner. Some time before the clerk had rescued Florence from an old female thief. Now his uncle was about to become a bankrupt, and Walter had come to ask for a loan to save his uncle's shop. Mr. Dombey let little Paul, who was then six years old, make the decision. Paul asked Florence what he should do; she told him to lend the money, and he did.

Shortly afterward, little Paul was placed in a private school at Brighton, where he was to be educated as quickly as possible. The pace of his studies proved too much for him, and before the year was out his health broke down. He never seemed to grow any better, even after his father took him home to London. Before many months had elapsed, little Paul died, mourned by his father and his sister, though for different reasons.

Mr. Dombey took his son's death as a personal blow of fate at his plans. His sister and her friend became so concerned about him that they planned to have him take a trip with Major Bagstock, a retired officer, to Leamington. While they were there, they met Edith Granger, a young widow whose mother the major had known. Mr. Dombey, seeing in Mrs. Granger a beautiful, well-bred young woman who would grace his household, immediately began to court her. Mrs. Granger, coaxed by an aged mother who was concerned for her daughter's welfare, finally accepted Mr. Dombey, although she was not in love with him.

Florence Dombey had seen young Walter Gay several times since their meeting at Brighton, and after her brother's death she came to look upon young Walter as a substitute brother, despite his lowly station. Then their friendship was broken temporarily when Mr. Dombey sent Walter on a mission to the West Indies. Weeks passed, but no word was heard of the ship on which he had sailed. Everyone believed that it had sunk and that Walter had been drowned.

After Mrs. Granger had accepted Mr. Dombey's suit, they began to make plans for the wedding and for reopening the Dombey house in London. It was at the house that Edith Granger first met Florence. The two immediately became fast friends, even though Mr. Dombey disliked his daughter and made it plain that he did not want his wife to become too fond of the girl.

Mr. Dombey's second marriage was unsuccessful from the start. Edith Granger was too proud to give in to Mr. Dombey's attempts to dictate to her and to his claim upon her as a piece of merchandise, and she resisted him in every way. Dombey, who was too dignified to argue with her, sent his business manager, Mr. Carker, to tell his wife that he was dissatisfied with her conduct. Carker warned Mrs. Dombey that, unless she obeyed Mr. Dombey, Florence would be the one to suffer. Edith Dombey then became outwardly cool to her stepdaughter, but still she resisted her husband. Mr. Carker was once more dispatched to tell her that Mr. Dombey meant to be obeyed in everything.

The wife then openly revolted. She felt that she could get complete revenge by running off with Carker, her husband's most trusted employee, who was also so far below Mr. Dombey socially that the blow would hurt even more. After she and the employee disappeared, Florence was only rebuffed in her attempts to comfort her father. When he struck her, she ran away from the house and went to the shop owned by Walter Gay's uncle, Sol Gills. There she found that Gills had disappeared and that an old ship's captain named Cuddle was in charge. Captain Cuttle recognized Florence and took her in.

Mr. Dombey at last learned the whereabouts of his wife and Carker from a young woman whom Carker had seduced and deserted. Mr. Dombey followed the pair to France but failed to locate them. Carker, meanwhile, returned to England. Mrs. Dombey had refused to have anything to do with him. She had her revenge, she said, in ruining him and her husband. Carker, trying to escape into the English countryside, met Mr. Dombey at a railway station. An accident occurred, and Carker was killed by a train.

Florence, staying with Captain Cuttle, hoped that Walter would return, even though everyone had given him up for dead. Her faith was at last rewarded. Walter had been picked up by a China-bound vessel and so had not had the opportunity to send back word of his safety. Shortly after his return he revealed to Florence that he no longer felt as a brother toward her, since she had become a woman during his absence. Realizing that she, too, had fallen in love with him, she accepted his proposal. Walter had found work as clerk on a ship, and after their marriage they sailed on a ship bound for the Orient.

The failure of his marriage had broken Mr. Dombey's spirit, and he took little interest in his firm from that time on. His lack of interest was unfortunate, for the firm had been placed in a difficult position by certain dealings of Carker's while he had been Dombey's trusted agent. As a result of Carker's mismanagement and Dombey's lack of interest, the firm went bankrupt. After the bankruptcy Mr. Dombey stayed alone in his house, saw no one, and gradually drifted into despair.

On the very day that Mr. Dombey had decided to commit suicide, Florence returned to London from the Orient with her year-old son, who was named Paul, after his dead uncle. Florence and the baby cheered up Mr. Dombey, and he began to take a new interest in life. Reconciled to his daughter, he realized that she had always loved him, even though he had been exceedingly cruel to her. Walter Gay succeeded in business, and all of them lived together happily, for his misfortunes had made a changed man of the almost indomitable Mr. Dombey.

Critical Evaluation

In *Dombey and Son,* Dickens for the first time attempted to portray the full panorama of English society, from beggar to magnate, from baronet to housemaid. Although less successful than *Bleak House* in expressing the connection of each level of society to every other level, the novel is nonetheless prodigious in scope.

The theme of the work is the relationship between parents and children, chiefly Mr. Dombey's with Paul and Florence, and subordinately those of various parents and their offspring, ranging in social station from Mrs. Skewton and Edith down to Mrs. Brown and her Alice. Each family situation is thrown into relief by contrast with another, similar in social class yet utterly different in kind. Thus in opposition to Edith Granger, schooled almost from infancy to be "artful, designing, mercenary, laying snares for men," there is the son of Sir Barnet Skettles, whose parents willingly interrupt his studies at Dr. Blimber's academy in order to enjoy his company during their sojourn abroad. Mr. Dombey's crude attempt to mold his fragile son to a shape that does his father honor in the world's eyes contrasts with the honest and unpretentious course that Solomon Gills recommends to his nephew Walter: "Be diligent, try to like it, my dear boy, work for a steady independence, and be happy!" And the miserable devices of greed which Mrs. Brown urges on her daughter as the only recourse of the poor is given the lie by the love and warmth shown by Polly Toodle toward her erring son Rob.

The sad ends of Edith, little Paul, and Alice Marwood all result from two things, or perhaps two facets of one thing: the corruption of childhood by adult concerns, and that disregard of individuality in children which sees them as *things,* as counters in a game, or as a hedge against destitution or mortality. Mr. Dombey, for example, views Paul as an object, a little mirror of his own greatness. He expects his son to reflect himself, that is, to love him as he loves himself. When Paul in his stubborn individuality perceives the merit of Florence and turns to her, Mr. Dombey is amazed and outraged; because he sees Paul as an extension of himself, he cannot conceive of the little boy's having a private opinion. A mirror, after all, cannot have a point of view. Thus in Mr. Dombey's own mind, no blame accrues to himself; Florence, he decides, must be the cause of the "distortion" of Paul's feelings. In this way she too falls victim to her father's self-love, and becomes the object of his hatred, almost a scapegoat for his fiercely repressed feelings of guilt about Paul's death; for in his view she had spoiled Paul as a tool for advancing his father's self-approbation, the function for which his elaborate education was to prepare him.

In the same way, Edith Granger was formed in her youth to fulfill her mother's nasty ambitions. And the shining ideal that both Mrs. Skewton and Mr. Dombey urge on their children is a glossy standing in the eyes of the world, a value which is essentially an adult concern. In contrast, Walter's mentor in his own invincible childishness (he rebukes himself for being "old-fashioned") guides his charge in the path of honesty, the natural behavior of childhood. Young Paul is the chief exemplar of this virtue in the novel, and his resistance to corruption is likewise referrable to that curious quality of being "old-fashioned." Paul was "born old"; he possesses that wisdom of extreme age which constitutes a return to the innocence of childhood. He is fey and resists classification. His obdurate honesty shows itself in his concern for first principles. For example, he inquires of his father what money can do, and when his father proudly replies that money can do anything, suggests two things that it cannot do: bring back his mother or give him health. Then he asks the question again, still more pointedly: "What's money, *afterall?*" as if to direct his father's attention to the extreme paltriness of those things which money *can do,* to that vain show which nurtures his father's pride. But his father takes no notice; it is not for him to be lessoned by a child. Florence, despised and neglected, not thought fit to prepare for any great purpose, has her brother's memory for a master, and educates herself to his truth rather than to her father's ambition.

Dombey and Son is unique among Dickens' novels in its profusion of strongly drawn female characters. Indeed, the author seems intent on ringing the changes on female nature from best to worst. For the most part these figures though vivid have but one dimension, but two evidence a greater depth of understanding than the author had heretofore achieved in his representation of women. One is the character of Florence, whose states of mind illustrate a classic psychological progression. Rejected by a loved parent, she reasons thus: "I am unloved, therefore unlovable." Her early conviction of unworthiness dictates not only her subsequent actions, but indeed shapes the main plot of the novel.

Dickens marks Florence with the token of ideal womanhood, a little display of housewifery in Solomon Gills's parlor; where she learned it though is a mystery. Still, she is truly good without being saccharine, a major advance in Dickens' treatment of women characters. Miss Tox is even more an unusual creation; for heretofore Dickens had not produced a female character at once such an object of satire and so generally sympathetic. She comes in for her share of ridicule for her delusions about Mr. Dombey's intentions and for her genteel pretentions in general, but the author allows her the virtue of her consistency: " . . . poor excommunicated Miss Tox, who, if she were a fawner and a toad-eater, was at least an honest and a constant one. . . ." She is as unlikely a vessel of kindness and simple wisdom as the dandy Toots, or Cousin Feenix the exhausted aristocrat; yet Dickens puts wisdom into their mouths, as if to show that though corruption might seem to reign supreme everywhere, truth remains, and though hidden, can flourish and even prevail.

Bibliography

Adamowski, Thomas H. "Dombey and Son and Sutpan and Son," in *Studies in the Novel.* IV (1972), pp. 378–384.

Axton, William. "*Dombey and Son*: From Stereotype to Archetype," in *Journal of English Literary History.* XXXI (September, 1964), pp. 301–317.

Barnard, Robert. *Imagery and Theme in the Novels of Dickens.* New York: Humanities Press, 1974, pp. 49–61.

Chesterton, Gilbert K. *Criticisms and Interpretations of the Works of Charles Dickens.* London: Dent, 1933, pp. 114–128.

Davis, Earle. *The Flint and the Flame: The Artistry of Charles Dickens.* Columbia: University of Missouri Press, 1963, pp. 150–156.

Donoghue, Denis. "The English Dickens and *Dombey and Son*," in *Dickens Centennial Essays.* Edited by Ada Nisbet and Blake Nevius. Berkeley: University of California Press, 1971, pp. 1–21.

Donovan, Frank. *Dickens and Youth.* New York: Dodd, Mead, 1968, pp. 115–125.

Dyson, A.E. *The Inimitable Dickens; A Reading of the Novels.* London: Macmillan, 1970, pp. 96–118.

Halperin, John. *Egoism and Self-Discovery in the Victorian Novel: Studies in the Ordeal of Knowledge in the Nineteenth Century.* New York: Burt Franklin, 1974, pp. 81–103.

Howard, David, et al. *Tradition and Tolerance in Nineteenth Century Fiction; Critical Essays on Some English and American Novels.* New York: Barnes & Noble, 1967, pp. 99–140.

Kennedy, G.W. "The Two Worlds of *Dombey and Son*," in *English Studies*

Colloquium. IV (1976), pp. 1–11.

Leavis, F.R. *"Dombey and Son,"* in *Sewanee Review.* LXX (Spring, 1962), pp. 177–201.

Lucas, John. *The Melancholy Man: A Study of Dickens' Novels.* London: Methuen, 1970, pp. 141–165.

McDonald, Andrew. "The Preservation of Innocence in *Dombey and Son*: Florence's Identity and the Role of Walter Gay," in *Texas Studies in Literature and Language.* XVIII (1976), pp. 1–19.

Mack, Maynard and Ian Gregor. *Imagined Worlds; Essays on Some English Novels and Novelists in Honour of John Butt.* London: Methuen, 1968, pp. 173–182.

Manning, Sylvia B. *Dickens as Satirist.* New Haven, Conn.: Yale University Press, 1971, pp. 87–95.

Milner, Ian. "The Dickens Drama: Mr. Dombey," in *Dickens Centennial Essays.* Edited by Ada Nisbet and Blake Nevius. Berkeley: University of California Press, 1971, pp. 155–165.

Pattison, Robert. *The Child Figure in English Literature.* Athens: University of Georgia Press, 1978, pp. 76–80, 82–84, 86–87, 99.

Pearson, Gabriel. "Towards a Reading of *Dombey and Son,*" in his *The Modern English Novel: The Reader, the Writer, and the Work.* New York: Barnes & Noble, 1976, pp. 54–76.

Robison, Roselee. "Time, Death and the River in Dickens' Novels," in *English Studies.* LIII (1972), pp. 436–454.

Stone, Harry. "The Novel as Fairy Tale; Dickens' *Dombey and Son,*" in *English Studies.* XLVII (February, 1966), pp. 1–27.

Tillotson, Kathleen M. *Novels of the Eighteen-Forties.* London: Oxford University Press, 1961, pp. 157–199.

Williams, Raymond. *The English Novel; From Dickens to Lawrence.* London: Chatto and Windus, 1970, pp. 37–47.

Wright, Austin. *Victorian Literature; Modern Essays in Criticism.* London: Oxford University Press, 1961, pp. 136–153.

GREAT EXPECTATIONS

Type of work: Novel
Author: Charles Dickens (1812–1870)
Type of plot: Mystery romance
Time of plot: Nineteenth century
Locale: England
First published: 1860–1861

From two events, Miss Havisham's desertion by her fiancé on her wedding day, and the youngster Pip's aid to an escaped prisoner, Dickens weaves a story of vindictiveness on the one hand and gratitude on the other. The motives combine to affect the life of young Pip, for Miss Havisham has marked him as an object of her vindictiveness, while the prisoner has sworn to reward the boy. The novel, though resolved on a hopeful note, is primarily gloomy in tone, focusing on the constant pressures placed on the orphan boy, Pip.

Principal Characters

Philip Pirrip, called **Pip,** an orphan and the unwanted ward of his harsh sister, Mrs. Joe. Although seemingly destined for the blacksmith shop, he sees his fortunes improve after he meets a convict hiding in a graveyard. Afterward, through Miss Havisham, he meets Estella, the eccentric old woman's lovely young ward. Thinking Miss Havisham is his benefactor, he goes to London to become a gentleman. Unfortunately for his peace of mind, he forgets who his true friends are. Finally, after Magwitch dies and the Crown confiscates his fortune, Pip understands that good clothes, well-spoken English, and a generous allowance do not make one a gentleman.

Miss Havisham, a lonely, embittered old spinster. When her lover jilted her at the altar, she refused ever to leave her gloomy chambers. Instead, she has devoted her life to vengeance. With careful indoctrination she teaches Estella how to break men's hearts. Just before her death she begs Pip to forgive her cruelty.

Estella, Miss Havisham's ward. Cold, aloof, unfeeling, she tries to warn Pip not to love her, for she is incapable of loving anyone; Miss Havisham has taught her too well. But years later Pip meets her in the garden near the ruins of Satis House, Miss Havisham's former home. She has lost her cool aloofness and found maturity. Pip realizes that they will never part again.

Joe Gargery, Pip's brother-in-law. Even though he is married to the worst of shrews, Mrs. Joe, he manages to retain his gentle simplicity and his selfless love for Pip. After he marries Biddy, he finds the domestic bliss which he so richly deserves.

Mrs. Georgiana Maria Gargery, commonly called **Mrs. Joe,** Pip's vituperative sister, who berates and misuses him and Joe with impunity. When she verbally assails Joe's helper, Orlick, she makes a mortal enemy who causes her death with the blow of a hammer. Later he tries to do the same for Pip.

Abel Magwitch, alias **Mr. Provis,** Pip's benefactor. When Pip helps him, an escaped convict, Magwitch promises to repay the debt. Transported to New South Wales, he eventually makes a large fortune as a sheep farmer. When he returns illegally to England years later, the escaped felon reveals himself as Pip's real patron. Casting off his distaste, Pip finds a real affection for the rough old man and attempts to get him safely out of England before the law apprehends him once more. Recaptured, Magwitch dies in prison.

Mr. Jaggers, a criminal lawyer employed by Magwitch to provide for Pip's future. He is a shrewd man with the ability to size up a person at a glance. To him, personal feelings are unimportant; facts are the only trustworthy things. Although completely unemotional, he deals with Pip and Magwitch honestly throughout their long association.

Herbert Pocket, Miss Havisham's young relative and Pip's roommate in London. Almost always cheerful and uncomplaining, he is constantly looking for ways to improve his prospects. With Pip's aid he is able to establish himself in a profitable business.

John Wemmick, Mr. Jaggers' efficient law clerk. Dry and businesslike in the office, he keeps his social and business life completely separate. As a friend, he proves himself completely loyal to Pip.

Biddy, Joe Gargery's wife after the death of Mrs. Joe. A gentle, loving girl, she is a good wife to him.

Compeyson, a complete villain, the man who jilted Miss Havisham and betrayed Magwitch. He is killed by Magwitch as the two struggle desperately just before the ex-convict is recaptured.

The Aged, John Wemmick's deaf old father. In their neat little home, his chief pleasures are reading the newspaper aloud and listening to his son's nightly firing of a small cannon.

Dolge Orlick, Joe Gargery's surly helper in the blacksmith shop. After an alter-

cation with Mrs. Joe, he attacks her with a hammer. Later he plots to kill Pip, his hated enemy. Only the timely arrival of Herbert Pocket and Startop prevents the crime.

Molly, Mr. Jaggers' housekeeper, a woman of strange, silent habits, with extraordinarily strong hands. A murderess, she is also revealed as Magwitch's former mistress and Estella's mother.

Matthew Pocket, Miss Havisham's distant relative and Pip's tutor during his early years in London. He is also Herbert Pocket's father.

Mrs. Belinda Pocket, a fluttery, helpless woman, the daughter of a knight who had expected his daughter to marry a title.

Alick,
Joe,
Fanny, and
Jane, other children of the Pockets.

Sarah Pocket, another relative of Miss Havisham, a withered-appearing, sharp-tongued woman.

Uncle Pumblechook, a prosperous corn chandler and Joe Gargery's relative. During Pip's childhood he constantly discusses the boy's conduct and offers much platitudinous advice.

Clara Barley, a pretty, winning girl engaged to Herbert Pocket. Magwitch is hidden in the Barley house while Pip is trying to smuggle the former convict out of England.

Old Bill Barley, Clara's father. A former purser, he is afflicted by gout and bedridden.

Mr. Wopsle, a parish clerk who later becomes an actor under the name of Mr. Waldengarver. Pip and Herbert Pocket go to see his performance as Hamlet.

Bentley Drummle, called **The Spider,** a sulky, rich boy notable for his bad manners. He is Pip's rival for Estella's love.

After marrying her, he treats her cruelly. Pip meets him while Drummle is being tutored by Mr. Pocket.

Startop, a lively young man tutored by Mr. Pocket.

Mr. Trabb, a village tailor and undertaker.

Trabb's Boy, a young apprentice whose independence is a source of irritation to Pip.

Mr. John (Raymond) Camilla, a toady.

Mrs. Camilla, his wife, Mr. Pocket's sis-

ter. She and her husband hope to inherit a share of Miss Havisham's fortune.

Miss Skiffins, a woman of no certain age but the owner of "portable property," who marries John Wemmick.

Clarriker, a young shipping broker in whose firm, Clarriker & Company, Pip secretly buys Herbert Pocket a partnership.

Pepper, also called **The Avenger,** Pip's servant in the days of his great expectations.

The Story

Little Pip had been left an orphan when he was a small boy, and his sister, much older than he, had grudgingly reared him in her cottage. Pip's brother-in-law, Joe Gargery, on the other hand, was kind and loving to the boy. In the marsh country where he lived with his sister and Joe, Pip wandered alone. One day he was accosted by a wild-looking stranger who demanded that Pip secretly bring him some food, a request which Pip feared to deny. The stranger, an escaped prisoner, asked Pip to bring him a file to cut the iron chain that bound his leg. When Pip returned to the man with a pork pie and file, he saw another mysterious figure in the marsh. After a desperate struggle with the escaped prisoner, the stranger escaped into the fog. The man Pip had aided was later apprehended. He promised Pip he would somehow repay the boy for helping him.

Mrs. Joe sent Pip to the large mansion of the strange Miss Havisham upon that lady's request. Miss Havisham lived in a gloomy, locked house where all clocks had been stopped on the day her bridegroom failed to appear for the wedding ceremony. She often dressed in her bridal robes; a wedding breakfast moldered on the table in an unused room. There Pip went every day to entertain the old lady and a beautiful young girl, named Estella, who delighted in tormenting the shy boy. Miss Havisham enjoyed watching the two children together, and she encouraged Estella in her haughty teasing of Pip.

Living in the grim atmosphere of Joe's blacksmith shop and the uneducated poverty of his sister's home, Pip was eager to learn. One day a London solicitor named Jaggers presented him with the opportunity to go to London and become a gentleman. Pip imagined that his kind backer was Miss Havisham herself. Perhaps she wanted to make a gentleman out of him so he would be fit some day to marry Estella.

In London Pip found a small apartment set up for him, and for a living companion he had a young relative of Miss Havisham, Herbert Pocket. When Pip needed money, he was instructed to go to Mr. Jaggers. Although Pip pleaded with the lawyer to disclose the name of his benefactor, Jaggers advised the eager young man not to make inquiries, for when the proper time arrived Pip's benefactor would make himself known.

Soon Pip became one of a small group of London dandies, among them a disagreeable chap named Bentley Drummle. Joe Gargery came to visit Pip, much to Pip's disturbance, for by now he had outgrown his rural background and he was ashamed of Joe's manners. But Herbert Pocket cheerfully helped Pip to entertain the uncomfortable Joe in their apartment. Plainly Joe loved Pip very much, and after he had gone Pip felt ashamed of himself. Joe had brought word that Miss Havisham wanted to see the young man, and Pip returned with his brother-in-law. Miss Havisham and Estella marked the changes in Pip, and when Estella had left Pip alone with the old lady, she told him he must fall in love with the beautiful girl. She also said it was time for Estella to come to London, and she wished Pip to meet her adopted daughter when she arrived. This request made Pip feel more certain he had been sent to London by Miss Havisham to be groomed to marry Estella.

Estella had not been in London long before she had many suitors. Of all the men who courted her, she seemed to favor Bentley Drummle. Pip saw Estella frequently. Although she treated him kindly and with friendship, he knew she did not return his love.

On his twenty-first birthday Pip received a caller, the man whom Pip had helped in the marsh many years before. Ugly and coarse, he told Pip it was he who had been financing Pip ever since he had come to London. At first the boy was horrified to discover he owed so much to this crude ex-criminal, Abel Magwitch. He told Pip that he had been sent to the colonies where he had grown rich. Now he had wanted Pip to enjoy all the privileges he had been denied in life, and he had returned to England to see the boy to whom he had tried to be a second father. He warned Pip that he was in danger should his presence be discovered, for it was death for a prisoner to return to England once he had been sent to a convict colony. Pip detested his plight. Now he realized Miss Havisham had had nothing to do with his great expectations in life, but he was too conscious of his debt to consider abandoning the man whose person he disliked. He determined to do all in his power to please his benefactor. Magwitch was using the name Provis to hide his identity. Provis told Pip furthermore that the man with whom Pip had seen him struggling long ago in the marsh was his enemy, Compeyson, who had vowed to destroy him. Herbert Pocket, who was a distant cousin of Miss Havisham, told Pip that the lover who had betrayed her on the day of her wedding was named Compeyson.

Pip went to see Miss Havisham to denounce her for having allowed him to believe she was helping him. On his arrival he was informed that Estella was to marry Bentley Drummle. Since Miss Havisham had suffered at the hands of one faithless man, she had reared Estella to inflict as much hurt as possible upon the many men who loved her. Estella reminded Pip that she had warned him not to fall in love with her, for she had no compassion for any human being. Pip returned once more to visit Miss Havisham after Estella had married. An accident started a fire in the old, dust-filled mansion, and although Pip tried to save the old woman she died in the blaze that also badly damaged her gloomy house.

From Provis' story of his association with Compeyson and from other evidence, Pip had learned that Provis was Estella's father; but he did not reveal his discovery to anyone but Jaggers, whose housekeeper, evidently, was Estella's mother. Pip had learned also that Compeyson was in London and plotting to kill Provis. In order to protect the man who had become a foster father to him, Pip with the help of Herbert Pocket arranged to smuggle Provis across the channel to France. There Pip intended to join the old man. Elaborate and secretive as their plans were, Compeyson managed to overtake them as they were putting Provis on the boat. The two enemies fought one last battle in the water, and Provis killed his enemy. He was then taken to jail, where he died before he could be brought to trial.

When Pip fell ill shortly afterward, it was Joe Gargery who came to nurse him. Older and wiser from his many experiences, Pip realized that he need no longer be ashamed of the kind man who had given so much love to him when he was a boy. His sister, Mrs. Joe, had died and Joe had married again, this time very happily. Pip returned to the blacksmith's home to stay awhile, still desolate and unhappy because of his lost Estella. Later Herbert Pocket and Pip set up business together in London.

Eleven years passed before Pip went to see Joe Gargery again. Curiosity led Pip to the site of Miss Havisham's former mansion. There he found Estella, now a widow, wandering over the grounds. During the years she had lost her cool aloofness and had softened a great deal. She told Pip she had thought of him often. Pip was able to foresee that perhaps he and Estella would never have to part again. The childhood friends walked hand in hand from the place which had once played such an enormous part in both their lives.

Critical Evaluation

G. K. Chesterton once observed that all of Dickens' novels could be titled "Great Expectations," for they are full of an unsubstantial yet ardent expectation of everything. Yet, as Chesterton pointed out with irony, the only book to which Dickens gave the actual title was one in which most of the expectations were never realized. To the Victorians, the word *expectations* meant legacy as well as anticipations. In that closed society, one of the few means by which a person born of the lower or lower-middle class could rise dramatically to wealth and high status was through the inheritance of valuables. Consequently, a major theme of the Victorian social novel involved the hero's movement through the class structure. And often the vehicle for that movement was money, either bestowed before death or inherited. Unlike many nineteenth century novels that rely upon the stale plot device of a surprise legacy to enrich the fortunate protagonists, *Great Expectations* probes deeply into the ethical and psychological dangers of advancing through the class system by means of wealth acquired from the toil of others.

Although the story of Pip's expectations dominates the bulk of the novel, he is not the only person who waits to benefit from another's money. His beloved Estella, the ward of Miss Havisham, is wholly dependent upon the caprices of the unstable old woman. Moreover, other characters are the mysterious instrumentalities of legacies. The solicitor Jaggers, who acts as the legal agent for both Miss Havisham and Abel Magwitch, richly benefits from his services. Even his lackey Mr. Wemmick, a mild soul who changes his personality from lamb to wolf to please his employer, earns his living from the legal machinery of the courts. Just as the source of Pip's money is revealed at last to be socially corrupted, so the uses of tainted wealth inevitably bring about corruption.

In *Bleak House* (1852-1853) Dickens had already explored with great skill the ruthless precincts of the law courts. But his next three novels— *Hard Times* (1854), *Little Dorrit* (1855-1857), and *A Tale of Two Cities* (1859)—were not so well sustained and, in spite of memorable scenes, were less popular with the critics and public alike. *Great Expectations* (1860-1861, first published serially in *All the Year Round*) recovered for the author his supremacy with his vast reading audience. Serious, controlled, nearly as complex structurally as *Bleak House,* the novel also reminded Victorian readers of *David Copperfield* (1849-1850). Both are apprenticeship novels that treat the life-education of a hero. *Great Expectations* is somewhat less autobiographical than *David Copperfield,* but it repeats the basic formula of the genre, that of an honest, rather ingenuous but surely likeable young man who, through a series of often painful experiences, learns important lessons about life and himself. These lessons are always designed to reveal the hero's limitations. As he casts off his own weaknesses and better understands the dangers of the world, he succeeds—that is to say, he advances through the class system—and ends up less brash, a chastened but wiser man.

Great Expectations differs from *David Copperfield,* however, in the ways that the hero matures to self-knowledge. Both David and Pip are, in the beginning, young snobs (Pip more than David). Both suffer the traumas of a shattered childhood and troubled adolescence. But David's childhood suffering is fully motivated on the basis of his separation from loved ones. An innocent, he is the victim of evil which he does not cause. Pip, on the other hand, suffers from a childhood nightmare that forms a pattern of his later experience. An orphan like David, he lives with his brutal sister and her husband, the gentle blacksmith Joe Gargery. For whatever abuse he endures from Mrs. Joe, he more than compensates in the brotherly affection of this simple, generous man. Also he wins the loving sympathy of Biddy, another loyal friend. But he is not satisfied. And when he comes upon the convicts in the fog and is terrified, he feels a sense of guilt—misplaced but psychologically necessary—as much for his crimes against his protectors as for the theft of a pork pie. Thereafter, his motives, cloudy as the scene of his childhood terror, are weighted with secret apprehension and guilt. To regain his lost innocence, he must purge himself of the causes of this guilt.

Pip's life-apprenticeship, then, involves his fullest understanding of "crimes" against his loved ones and the ways to redeem himself. The causes of his guilt are, from lesser to greater, his snobbish pride, his betrayal of friends and protectors, and finally his participation in the machinery of corruption.

As a snob, he not only breaks the social mold into which he has been cast, but lords it over the underlings and unfortunates of the class system. Because of his presumed great expectations, he believes himself to be superior to the humbler Joe and Biddy. He makes such a pompous fool of himself that Trabb's boy—that brilliant comic invention, at once naughty boy and honest philosopher—parodies his absurd airs and pretensions. But his snobbery costs him a dearer price than humiliation by an urchin. He falls in love with Estella, like himself a pretender to high social class, only to be rejected in place of a worthless cad, Bentley Drummle. Finally, his fanciful dreams of social distinction are shattered forever when he learns the bitter truth about his benefactor, who is not the highborn Miss Havisham but the escaped convict Magwitch, the wretched stranger of his terror in the fog.

As Pip comes to understand the rotten foundations for his social position, he also learns terrible truths about his own weaknesses. Out of foolish pride he has betrayed his most loyal friends, Joe and Biddy. In a sense, he has even betrayed Miss Havisham. He has mistaken her insanity for mere eccentricity and allowed her to act out her fantasies of romantic revenge. When he tries to confront her with the reality of her life, he is too late. She expires in flames. He is almost too late, in fact, to come to the service of his real benefactor, Magwitch. So disturbed is he with the realization of the convict's sacrifice, that he nearly flees from the old man, now disguised as "Provis," when he is in danger. At best, he can return to Magwitch gratitude, not love. And his sense of guilt grows from his understanding that he cannot ever repay his debt to a man he secretly loathes.

Pip's final lesson is that, no matter how pure might be his motives, he has been one of the instruments of social corruption. In a sense, he is the counterpart to the malcontent Dolge Orlick. Like Orlick, as a youth he had been an apprentice at the forge. But whereas he was fortunate to move upward into society, Orlick, consumed by hatred, failed in every enterprise. In Chapter 53, a climactic scene of the novel, Orlick confronts his enemy and lays to Pip the blame for all of his failures. He even accuses Pip of responsibility for the death of Mrs. Joe. The charge, of course, is paranoiac and false: Orlick is the murderer. Yet, psychologically, Pip can—in his almost hallucinatory terror—accept Orlick's reasoning. As a child, Pip had hated his sister. If he had not been the active instrument of her death, nevertheless he profited from it. Similarly, Pip profited from the hard-earned toil of Magwitch. Indeed, most of the success he had enjoyed, thanks to the astute protection of Mr. Jaggers, had come not as his due but for a price, the payment of corrupted money. Since he had been the ignorant recipient of the fruits of corruption, his psychological guilt is all the greater.

Nevertheless, Pip, though chastened, is not overwhelmed by guilt. During the course of his apprenticeship to life he has learned something about himself, some valuable truths about his limitations. By the end of his career, when his apprenticeship is over and he is a responsible, mature being, he has cast off petty pride, snobbery, and the vexations of corrupted wealth. Although he has lost his innocence forever, he can truly appreciate Herbert Pocket, Joe, and Biddy, who have retained their integrity. When he turns to Estella, also chastened by her wretched marriage to the sadistic Drummle, he has at-least the hope of beginning a new life with her, one founded upon an accurate understanding of himself and the dangers of the world.

Bibliography

Barnard, Robert. "Imagery and Theme in *Great Expectations*," in *Dickens Studies Annual*. I (1970), pp. 238–251.

Bodelson, C.A. "Some Notes on Dickens' Symbolism," in *English Studies*. XL (December, 1959), pp. 420–431.

Crouch, W. George. *Critical Study Guide to Dickens'* Great Expectations. Totowa, N.J.: Littlefield, Adams, 1968.

Dessner, Lawrence J. "*Great Expectations*: 'the ghost of a man's own father,' " in *PMLA*. XCI (1976), pp. 436–449.

Donovan, Frank. *Dickens and Youth*. New York: Dodd, Mead, 1968, pp. 185–196.

Drew, Elizabeth A. *The Novel; A Modern Guide to Fifteen English Masterpieces*. New York: Norton, 1963, pp. 191–207.

Dyson, A.E. *The Inimitable Dickens; A Reading of the Novels*. London: Macmillan, 1970, pp. 228–247.

Hagan, John H., Jr. "The Poor Labyrinth: The Theme of Social Injustice in Dickens' *Great Expectations*," in *Nineteenth-Century Fiction*. IX (December, 1954), pp. 169–178.

Hynes, Joseph A. "Image and Symbol in *Great Expectations*," in *Journal of English Literary History*. XXX (1963), pp. 258–292.

Lelchuk, Alan. "Self, Family, and Society in *Great Expectations*," LXXVIII (1970), pp. 407–426.

Levine, George. "Communication in *Great Expectations*," in *Nineteenth-Century Fiction.* XVIII (September, 1963), pp. 175–181.

Lucas, John. *The Melancholy Man: A Study of Dickens' Novels.* London: Methuen, 1970, pp. 287–314.

Marcus, Phillip L. "Theme and Suspense in the Plot of *Great Expectations*," in *Dickens Studies.* II (Spring, 1966), pp. 57–73.

Marshall, William H. "The Conclusion of *Great Expectations* as the Fulfillment of Myth," in *Personalist.* XLIV (Summer, 1963), pp. 337–347.

Milhauser, Milton. "*Great Expectations*: The Three Endings," in *Dickens Studies Annual.* II (1972), pp. 267–277.

Moynahan, Julian. "The Hero's Guilt; The Case of *Great Expectations*," in *Essays in Criticism.* X (January, 1960), pp. 60–79.

New, William H. "The Four Elements in *Great Expectations*," in *Dickens Studies.* III (1967), pp. 111–121.

Pearce, Richard A. *Stages of the Clown; Perspectives on Modern Fiction from Dostoyevsky to Beckett.* Carbondale: Southern Illinois University Press, 1970, pp. 26–46.

Ricks, Christopher. "*Great Expectations*," in *Dickens and the Twentieth Century.* Edited by J. Gross and G. Pearson. London: Routledge and Kegan Paul, 1962, pp. 199–211.

Shapiro, Charles. *Twelve Original Essays on Great English Novels.* Detroit: Wayne State University Press, 1960, pp. 103–124.

Shores, Lucille P. "The Character of Estella in *Great Expectations*," in *Massachusetts Studies in English.* III (1972), pp. 91–99.

Stone, Harry. "Fire, Hand, and Gate: Dickens' *Great Expectations*," in *Kenyon Review.* XXIV (Autumn, 1962), pp. 662–691.

Tomlin, E.W.F. *Charles Dickens, 1812–1870; A Centennial Volume.* New York: Simon and Schuster, 1969, pp. 109–131, 237–263.

Van Ghent, Dorothy. *The English Novel.* New York: Rinehart, 1953, pp. 125–138.

Winner, Anthony. "Character and Knowledge in Dickens: The Enigma of Jaggers," in *Dickens Studies Annual.* III (1974), pp. 100–121.

OLIVER TWIST

Type of work: Novel
Author: Charles Dickens (1812–1870)
Type of plot: Sentimental romance
Time of plot: Early nineteenth century
Locale: English provinces and London
First published: 1837–1839

When the new 1834 Poor Law abolishing supplemental aid to the poor was passed, families were broken up and their members placed in separate workhouses; in protest of this situation, Dickens began publishing Oliver Twist *in serial form in 1837. The novel depicts the world of poverty and crime in London which forced men, women, and children into lives of theft and prostitution. Written when the author was in his twenties,* Oliver Twist *foreshadows his later works in its complicated plot, skillful change of pace, and control of dramatic tension and climax.*

Principal Characters

Oliver Twist, a workhouse foundling, the helpless, abused hero of the novel. Both innocent and morally sensible, he gives force and sharpness, as well as a full measure of sentimentality, to Dickens' vision of social injustice. Exploited from birth by the selfish managers of the poor farm and workhouse, he is apprenticed to a mortician. Treated cruelly, he runs off to London, where he is taken in by a gang of thieves. Falsely arrested as a pickpocket, he is rescued for a time by Mr. Brownlow and then recaptured by the thieves. He is wounded during a burglary attempt and saved from arrest by Mrs. Maylie and her adopted daughter, who care for him until the mystery of his birth is solved and the criminals are taken or killed. Mr. Brownlow offers him a permanent home.

Mr. Brownlow, the kind-hearted, benevolent man who delivers Oliver Twist from a vicious judge, gives him care and trust, solves the question of his parentage, and finally adopts him.

Mrs. Maylie, the gentle, good-hearted woman who takes Oliver in after he has been wounded and is being hunted as a burglar. She sees that he is happy and cared for until he finds a lasting home with Mr. Brownlow.

Rose Maylie, her adopted daughter, the tender, lovely girl who nurses Oliver and helps expose the treachery that surrounds him. Later it turns out that she is really Oliver's aunt.

Harry Maylie, Mrs. Maylie's wastrel son, who later becomes a clergyman and marries his foster sister Rose.

Fagin, a greasy, sinister old Jew who trains boys for stealing and receives stolen goods. Paid to bring Oliver up as a thief, he fails to retake the boy after a burglary attempt. He is finally executed by the law for complicity in a murder.

Bill Sikes, Fagin's accomplice, the leader of Fagin's band of trained thieves. A violent, brutal man, he deserts Oliver after the attempted burglary. Later he kills his mistress Nancy because he believes she has betrayed him. Haunted by guilt, he accidentally hangs himself while trying to escape the law.

Nancy, a female thief, a member of Fagin's gang. She befriends Oliver and informs on Fagin's activities in order to save the boy. Although she remains loyal to Bill Sikes, he murders her in a rage.

Monks, whose real name is **Edward Leeford,** Oliver Twist's stepbrother. A vengeful person, he plots with Fagin against Oliver to keep the boy from his inheritance. In the end he confesses his villainy, makes restitution, moves to America, and eventually dies in prison.

Mr. Bumble, the vain, bullying almshouse beadle who mistreats Oliver at every opportunity. He meets his match, however, when he marries Mrs. Corney, a workhouse matron. The two become paupers and end their days in the workhouse.

Mrs. Corney, his wife, formerly a vixenish workhouse matron.

Mr. Grimwig, Mr. Brownlow's gruff old friend, who speaks harshly against Oliver but wishes him well.

Mrs. Bedwin, Mr. Brownlow's warmhearted housekeeper, who comforts frightened, lonely Oliver.

Mr. Losberne, "The Doctor," a fat, goodhearted surgeon and the Maylies' family friend. He speaks roughly to Oliver Twist but cures his wound and saves him from the police.

Mrs. Mann, the alcoholic matron who keeps the poor farm where Oliver lives for a time.

Mr. Sowerberry, the mortician who takes Oliver as his apprentice and meekly befriends him. He makes thin, pale, sad-looking Oliver a mourner at children's funerals.

Mrs. Sowerberry, his wife, a shrew.

Noah Claypole, a lumpish bully charity boy who runs away from the mortician and becomes a member of Fagin's gang.

Charlotte, Mrs. Sowerberry's servant, who also misuses Oliver. She marries Noah Claypole.

Jack Dawkins, called the **Artful Dodger,** the clever young pickpocket who leads Oliver Twist to Fagin.

Charley Bates, the Artful Dodger's boisterous friend and assistant.

Mr. Fang, the cruel judge who tries Oliver Twist when he is charged with picking pockets. Mr. Brownlow, appearing as a witness, pities Oliver and, when his innocence is proved, takes the boy home with him.

Toby Crackit, the burglar who accompanies Oliver Twist and Bill Sikes on the attempted robbery of the Maylie house.

Old Sally, the beggar, present when Oliver Twist is born, who steals the tokens that eventually disclose his parentage.

[**Agnes Fleming,** Oliver's unwed mother. She dies in childbirth in a workhouse.]

[**Mr. Leeford,** Oliver Twist's father, unhappily married and separated from his wife when he falls in love with Agnes Fleming. After he dies suddenly in Rome, his wife and son destroy a will that provides for Agnes and her unborn child.]

[**Mrs. Leeford,** the jealous, vindictive wife who tries to deprive Agnes Fleming and her child of their inheritance.]

The Story

Oliver Twist was born in the lying-in room of a parochial workhouse about seventy-five miles north of London. His mother's name was not known. She had been found unconscious by the roadside, exhausted by a long journey on foot, and she died leaving as the only tokens of her child's identity a locket and a ring. These were stolen by old Sally, a pauper present at her death.

Oliver owed his name to Bumble, the parish beadle and a bullying official of the workhouse, who always named his unknown waifs in the order of an alphabetical system he had devised. Twist was the name between Swubble and Unwin on Bumble's list. Oliver Twist he was named.

An offered reward of ten pounds failing to discover his parentage, Oliver was sent to a nearby poor farm, where he passed his early childhood in neglect and near starvation. At the age of nine he was moved back to the workhouse. Always hungry, he asked one day for a second serving of porridge. The scandalized authorities put him in solitary confinement and posted a bill offering five pounds to some master who would take him off the parish.

Oliver was apprenticed to one Sowerberry, a casket maker, to learn a trade. Sowerberry employed little Oliver, dressed in miniature mourning clothing, as attendant at children's funerals. Another Sowerberry employee, Noah Claypole, teased Oliver about his parentage. Oliver, goaded beyond endurance, fiercely attacked Claypole and was subsequently locked in the cellar by Mrs. Sowerberry. Sowerberry released Oliver, who, that night, bundled up his meager belongings and started out for London.

In a London suburb Oliver, worn out from walking and weak from hunger, met Jack Dawkins, sharp-witted slum gamin. Dawkins, known as the Artful Dodger, offered Oliver lodgings in the city, and Oliver soon found himself in the midst of a gang of young thieves, led by a miserly old Jew, Fagin. Oliver was trained as a pickpocket. On his first mission he was caught and taken to the police station. There he was rescued by kindly Mr. Brownlow, the man whose pocket Oliver was accused of having picked. Mr. Brownlow, his gruff friend Grimwig, and the old housekeeper, Mrs. Bedwin, cared for the sickly Oliver. They marveled at the resemblance of the boy to a portrait of a young lady in Mr. Brownlow's possession. Recuperated, Oliver was one day given some books and money to take to a bookseller. Grimwig wagered that Oliver would not return. Meanwhile Fagin and his gang had been on constant lookout for the boy's appearance, and he was intercepted by Nancy, a young street girl associated with the gang.

Bumble, in London on parochial business, saw Mr. Brownlow's advertisement for word leading to Oliver's recovery. Hoping to profit, he hastened to Mr. Brownlow and reported that Oliver was incorrigible. After receiving this information, Mr. Brownlow refused to have Oliver's name mentioned in his presence.

Once more Oliver was in the hands of Fagin. During his absence the gang had been studying a house in Chertsey, west of London, preparatory to breaking into it at night. The time came for the adventure, and Oliver, much to his horror, was chosen to participate. He and Bill Sikes, brutal young co-leader of the gang, met Toby Crackit, another housebreaker, and the trio, in the dark of early morning, pried open a small window of the house. Oliver entered, determined to warn the occupants. The robbers were discovered, and the trio fled, Oliver wounded by gunshot.

In fleeing, Sikes threw the wounded Oliver into a ditch and covered him with a cape. Toby Crackit, the other housebreaker, returned and reported to Fagin. The old thief-trainer was more than ever interested in Oliver after an important conversation with one Monks. This discussion, overheard by Nancy, concerned Oliver's parentage and Monks' wish to have the boy made a youthful felon.

Oliver crawled feebly to the house into which he had gone the night before. He was taken in by the owner, Mrs. Maylie, and Rose, her adopted daughter. Oliver's story aroused their sympathy and he was saved from police investigation by Dr. Losberne, friend of the Maylies. Upon his recovery the boy went with the doctor to seek out Mr. Brownlow, but it was learned that the old gentleman, his friend Grimwig, and Mrs. Bedwin had gone to the West Indies.

Meanwhile Bumble courted the widow Corney. During one of their conversations, Mrs. Corney was called out to attend the death of old Sally, who had stood by at the death of Oliver's mother. After old Sally died, Mrs. Corney removed a pawn ticket from her hand. In Mrs. Corney's absence, Bumble appraised her property to his satisfaction. He proposed marriage.

The Maylies moved to the country, where Oliver studied gardening, read, and took long walks. During this holiday Rose Maylie fell sick and nearly died. After her recovery, Harry Maylie, wastrel son of Mrs. Maylie, joined the group. Harry, in love with Rose, asked for her hand in marriage. Rose refused on two grounds; she could not marry him before she discovered who she was, and she could not marry him unless he mended his ways. One night Oliver was frightened when he saw Fagin and Monks peering through the study window.

Bumble had discovered that married life with the former Mrs. Corney was not all happiness, for she dominated him completely. When Monks went to the workhouse seeking information about Oliver, he met with Mr. and Mrs. Bumble and learned that Mrs. Bumble had redeemed a locket and a wedding ring with the pawn ticket she had recovered from old Sally. Monks bought the trinkets from Mrs. Bumble and threw them in the river.

Monks told Fagin that he had disposed of the tokens of Oliver's parentage. Again Nancy overheard the two villains. After drugging Bill Sikes, whom she had been nursing to recovery from gunshot wounds received in the ill-fated venture at Chertsey, she went to see Rose Maylie, whose name and address she had overheard in the conversation between Fagin and Monks. Nancy told Rose everything she had heard concerning Oliver. Rose was unable to understand fully the various connections of the plot nor could she see Monks' connection with Oliver. She offered the miserable girl the protection of her own home, but Nancy refused, knowing that she could never leave Bill Sikes. The two young women agreed on a time and place for later meetings. Rose and Oliver went to call on Mr. Brownlow, whom Oliver had glimpsed in the street. The reunion of the boy, Mr. Brownlow, and Mrs. Bedwin was a joyous one. Even old Grimwig gruffly expressed his pleasure at seeing Oliver again. Rose told Mr. Brownlow Nancy's story.

Noah Claypole and Charlotte, maid-servant of the Sowerberrys, had in the meantime, run away from the casket maker and arrived in London, where they went to the public house which was the haunt of Fagin and his gang. Fagin flattered Noah into his employ, Noah's job being to steal small coins from children on household errands.

At the time agreed upon for her appointment with Rose Maylie, Nancy was unable to leave the demanding Bill Sikes. Noticing Nancy's impatience, Fagin decided that she had tired of Sikes and that she had another lover. Fagin hated Sikes because of the younger man's power over the gang, and he saw this situation as an opportunity to rid himself of Sikes. Fagin set Noah on Nancy's trail.

The following week Nancy got free with the aid of Fagin. She went to Rose and Mr. Brownlow and revealed to them the haunts of all the gang except Sikes. Noah, having overheard all this, secretly told Fagin, who in turn told Sikes. In his rage Sikes brutally murdered Nancy, never knowing that the girl had been faithful to him. He fled, pursued by the vision of murdered Nancy's staring eyes. Frantic from fear, he attempted to kill his dog, whose presence might betray him. The dog ran away.

Apprehended, Monks confessed to Mr. Brownlow the plot against Oliver. Oliver's father, Edward Leeford, had married a woman older than himself. Their son, Edward Leeford, was the man now known as Monks. After several years of unhappiness, the couple separated, Monks and his mother staying on the continent and Mr. Leeford returned to England. Later Leeford met a retired naval officer and fell in love with his seventeen-year-old daughter. There was another daughter aged three. Leeford contracted to marry the girl, but before the marriage could be performed he was called to Rome, where an old friend had died. On the way to Rome he stopped at the house of Mr. Brownlow, his best friend, and left a portrait of his betrothed. He himself fell sick in Rome and died. His former wife seized his papers. When Leeford's young wife-to-be, who was pregnant, heard of Leeford's death, she ran away to hide her condition. Her father died soon afterward and the younger sister was eventually adopted by Mrs. Maylie. She was Rose Maylie, Oliver's aunt. Monks lived a prodigal life. When his mother died, he went to the West Indies, where Mr. Brownlow had gone in search of him. But Monks had already returned to track down Oliver, whose part of his father's settlement he wished to keep from his young half-brother. It was Monks who had offered the reward at the workhouse for information about Oliver's parentage, and it was Monks who had paid Fagin to see that the boy remained with the gang as a common thief.

After Fagin and the Artful Dodger had been seized, Bill Sikes and the remainder of the gang met on Jacob's Island in the Thames River. They intended to stay there in a deserted house until the hunt had died down. But Sikes' dog led their pursuers to the hideout. Bill Sikes hanged himself accidentally with the rope he was using as a means of escape. The other robbers were captured. Fagin was hanged publicly at Newgate after he had revealed to Oliver the location of papers concerning the boy's heritage. Monks had entrusted these papers to the Jew for safekeeping.

Harry Maylie, who had become a minister, married Rose Maylie. Mr. Brownlow adopted Oliver and took up residence near the church of the Reverend Harry Maylie. Mr. and Mrs. Bumble lost their parochial positions and soon became inmates of the workhouse which once had been their domain. Monks, allowed to retain his share of his father's property, went to America and eventually died in prison. Oliver's years of hardship and unhappiness were at an end.

Critical Evaluation

When *Oliver Twist* was published in the late 1830's, it shocked quite a few people. Clergymen and magazine editors accused the young novelist (Dickens was then under thirty) of writing an immoral book. In later editions, Dickens defended his book, explaining that one of his purposes had been to take the romance out of crime, to show the underworld of London as the sordid, filthy place that he knew it to be. Few of his readers have ever doubted that he succeeded in this task.

When Dickens began writing, a popular form of fiction was the so-called "Newgate novel," or the novel dealing in part with prison life and the rogues and highwaymen who ended up in prison. These heroes were often cousins of Macheath of *The Beggar's Opera* fame. Dickens took this tradition and form and turned it around, making it serve the purposes of his new realism. The Bill Sikes-Nancy subplot still contains the melodramatic elements, but Sikes is no Macheath and Nancy no Polly Peachum.

From the beginning of the book, when the grim birth of the infant who was to become Oliver is revealed, the reader is in an uncomfortably unromantic world. If people are starving to death, if children are "accidentally" killed off by their charitable keepers, if the innocent suffer and the cruel and unscrupulous prosper, Dickens does not hesitate to lay the facts out for all to see. Nancy is a prostitute, Bill is a murderer, Fagin is a fence, and the boys are pickpockets; and the supporting cast includes all manner of Bumbles and Thingummys and Mrs. Manns, individuals who never hesitate to deprive someone else of anything that they, themselves, could use. Poverty is the great leveler, the universal corruptor, and in the pages of *Oliver Twist* the results of this widespread poverty are portrayed with a startling lack of sentimentality. Dickens becomes sentimental when dealing with virtue, but never when dealing with vice.

The petty villains, the small-time corrupt officials, such as Bumble, are treated humorously, but Bill Sikes is portrayed with complete realism. Although Dickens' contemporaries thought that Bill was too relentlessly evil,

Dickens challenged them to deny that such men existed in London, products of the foul life forced upon them from infancy. He holds up Bill Sikes for the reader to see in all of his blackness, without making any attempt to find "redeeming characteristics." Nancy is a more complicated character, both immoral and kindhearted. She is sentimental because she is basically good, while Bill is entirely practical, a man who will step on anybody who gets in his way—and feel no regrets.

With *Oliver Twist,* Dickens attempted a deliberate contrast to his previous work. While there is much humor in the novel, it is seldom like the humor of *The Pickwick Papers,* and is woven into a realistic and melodramatic narrative of a particularly grim and dark kind. The readers of Mr. Pickwick's exploits must have been startled when they picked up the magazines containing this new novel by Charles Dickens and discovered old Fagin teaching the innocent Oliver how to pick pockets, and read of children swigging gin like old drunkards. But Dickens was a man of many talents, and he introduced some new ones with this book. In *Oliver Twist,* Dickens exploited for the first time his abilities to invoke both pathos and horror, to combine these qualities to grip absolutely a reader's interest. United with the vitality which always infused Dickens' prose, these powers guaranteed this book a wide and faithful following as it was serialized.

Oliver Twist was the first of the young novelist's nightmare stories and the first of his social tracts. A certain amount of social protest could be read into Mr. Pickwick's time in prison, but it is a long distance from the prison of Mr. Pickwick to the almshouse in *Oliver Twist.* The leap from farce to melodrama and social reform was dramatically successful, and Dickens was to continue in the same vein for many years. Some critics called his work vulgar, but the masses loved it. He was accused of exaggeration, but as he made clear repeatedly, his readers had only to walk the streets of London to discover the characters and conditions of which he wrote so vividly. If his characterizations of some individuals suggested the "humours" theory of Ben Jonson rather than fully-rounded psychological portraits, the total effect of the characters in the book was that of an entire society, pulsing with life and energy.

In this book, Dickens displayed for the first time his amazing gift of entering into the psychology of a pathological individual. He follows closely Sikes and Fagin to their respective ends, and never flinches from revealing to the reader their true natures. The death of the unrepentant Sikes remains one of the most truly horrible scenes in English fiction. (When Dickens performed this passage to audiences in his public readings, it was common for ladies in the audience to scream or faint.) And when Fagin is sitting in court, awaiting the verdict of his trial, his thoughts roam from one triviality to another, although the fact of his approaching death by hanging is never far away. The combination of the irrelevant and the grimly pertinent suggests a kind of psychological realism that was completely new in 1838.

Dickens entertained a life-long fondness for the theater. His interest in the drama had a profound influence on his fiction. Dickens himself was an actor, and his readings from his books toward the end of his life became famous. In his novels, the actor in Dickens is also discernible. At times, the reader seems to feel that the author is impersonating a living individual, and often that is precisely the case. At other times, the plots bear the imprint of the popular stage fare of the day, including the heavy dose of melodrama, romance, and coincidence. All of these aspects are seen in *Oliver Twist,* particularly the violence of the melodrama and the coincidences which shuffle Oliver in and out of Mr. Brownlow's house. But over all, and ultimately much more important, stands the realism which Dickens used to unite the different elements of his story. Perhaps the greatest achievement of the author in this early novel was the giant stride forward he made in the realm of realism. He had not yet perfected his skills, but he knew the direction in which he was moving, and he was taking the novel with him.

Bibliography

Austen, Zelda. *"Oliver Twist*: A Divided View," in *Dickens Studies Newsletter.* VII (1976), pp. 8–12.

Bishop, Jonathan. "The Hero-Villain of *Oliver Twist*," in *Victorian Newsletter.* XV (Spring, 1959), pp. 14–16.

Cazamian, Louis. *The Social Novel in England, 1830–1850: Dickens, Disraeli, Mrs. Gaskell, Kingsley.* Translated by Martin Fido. London: Routledge and Kegan Paul, 1973, pp. 141–143.

Chesterton, Gilbert K. *Criticisms and Appreciations of the Works of Charles Dickens.* London: Dent, 1933, pp. 38–49.

Colby, Robert A. *Fiction with a Purpose; Major and Minor Nineteenth Century Novels.* Bloomington: Indiana University Press, 1967, pp. 105–137.

Daleski, Herman M. *Dickens and the Art of Analogy.* New York: Schocken, 1970, pp. 49–78.

Donovan, Frank. *Dickens and Youth.* New York: Dodd, Mead, 1968, pp. 61–87.

Duffy, Joseph M. "Another Version of Pastoral: *Oliver Twist*," in *Journal of English Literary History.* XXXV (1968), pp. 403–421.

Frederick, Kenneth C. "The Cold, Cold Hearth: Domestic Strife in *Oliver Twist*," in *College English.* XXVII (1966), pp. 465–470.

Gissing, George R. *Critical Studies of the Works of Charles Dickens.* New York: Greenberg, 1924, pp. 43–57.

Gold, Joseph. *Charles Dickens: Radical Moralist.* Minneapolis: University of Minnesota Press, 1972, pp. 25–65.

—————. "Dickens' Exemplary Aliens: Bumble the Beadle and Fagin the Fence," in *Mosaic.* II (1968), pp. 77–89.

Greaves, John. *Who's Who in Dickens.* New York: Taplinger, 1972.

Hollingsworth, Keith. *The Newgate Novel (1830–1847): Bulwer, Ainsworth, Dickens, and Thackeray.* Detroit: Wayne State University Press, 1963, pp. 111–131.

Johnson, Edgar, George Shuster and Lyman Bryson. *"Oliver Twist,"* in *Invitation to Learning: English and American Novels.* Edited by George D. Crothers. New York: Basic Books, 1966, pp. 99–107.

Kincaid, James R. *Dickens and the Rhetoric of Laughter.* Oxford: Clarendon Press, 1971, pp. 41–75.

Lucas, Alec. *"Oliver Twist* and the Newgate Novel," in *Dalhousie Review.* XXXIV (Spring, 1954), pp. 381–387.

Lucas, John. *The Melancholy Man: A Study of Dickens' Novels.* London: Methuen, 1970, pp. 21–54.

Manning, Sylvia B. *Dickens as Satirist.* New Haven, Conn.: Yale University Press, 1971, pp. 51–54.

Marcus, Steven. "Who Is Fagin?," in *Commentary.* XXXIII (June, 1962), pp. 48–59.

Patten, Robert L. "Capitalism and Compassion in *Oliver Twist,*" in *Studies in the Novel.* I (Summer, 1969), pp. 207–221.

Slater, Michael. "On Reading *Oliver Twist,*" in *The Dickensian.* LXX (1974), pp. 75–81.

Tillotson, Kathleen. *"Oliver Twist,"* in *Essays and Studies by Members of the English Society.* XII (1959), pp. 87–105.

Westburg, Barry. " 'His Allegorical Way of Expressing It': Civil War and Psychic Conflict in *Oliver Twist* and *A Child's History,*" in *Studies in the Novel.* VI (1974), pp. 27–37.

PICKWICK PAPERS

Type of work: Novel
Author: Charles Dickens (1812–1870)
Type of plot: Comic romance
Time of plot: 1827–1828
Locale: England
First published: 1836–1837

These sketches, originally published in serial form, were planned as prose accompaniments to caricatures by a popular artist. The title derives from the character of Mr. Pickwick, a naïve, generous, lovable old gentleman who reigns over the activities of the Pickwick Club. Many of the comic highlights in the work spring from the imperturbable presence of mind and ready wit of Sam Weller, whose cleverness and humor are indispensable to the Pickwickians.

Principal Characters

Mr. Samuel Pickwick, the stout, amiable founder and perpetual president of the Pickwick Club. An observer of human nature, a lover of good food and drink, and a boon companion, he spends his time traveling about the countryside with his friends, accepting invitations from local squires and dignitaries, pursuing Mr. Alfred Jingle in an effort to thwart that rascal's schemes, and promoting his friends' romances. The height of his development occurs at the Fleet Prison where, because of a breach of promise suit, he observes human suffering and learns to forgive his enemies. A rather pompously bustling and fatuous person at first, he grows in the course of events to be a truly monumental character.

Mr. Nathaniel Winkle, the sportsman of the group. Inept and humane, he finds himself involved in hunting misadventures, romances, and duels. In the end he wins Arabella Allen, his true love, over the objections of her brother, her suitor, and his own father.

Mr. Augustus Snodgrass, the poetic member of the Pickwick Club. Although he keeps extensive notes, he never writes verses. Eventually he gains his sweetheart, Emily Wardle, after several visits to Manor Farm.

Mr. Tracy Tupman, a rotund member of the Pickwick Club, so susceptible that he is constantly falling in and out of love. Longing for romance, he finds himself thwarted at every turn. His flirtation with Miss Rachel Wardle ends dismally when she elopes with Mr. Alfred Jingle.

Mr. Wardle, the owner of Manor Farm, Dingley Dell, the robust, genial, but sometimes hot-tempered host of the four Pickwickians. A patriarch, he rescues his sister from Mr. Jingle at the cost of one hundred and twenty pounds, and he objects at first to his daughter's romance with Mr. Snodgrass. Finally he gives the young couple his blessing.

Miss Rachel Wardle, a spinster of uncertain age. She flirts coyly with the susceptible Mr. Tupman but abandons him for the blandishments of Mr. Jingle, who has designs on her supposed wealth. Mr. Pickwick and Mr. Wardle pursue the elopers, Mr. Wardle buys off the rascal, and Miss Wardle returns husbandless to Manor Farm.

Mrs. Wardle, the aged, deaf mother of Mr. Wardle and Miss Rachel.

Emily Wardle, Mr. Wardle's vivacious daughter, in love with Mr. Snodgrass, whom she eventually marries.

Isabella Wardle, another daughter. She marries Mr. Trundle.

Mr. Trundle, Isabella Wardle's suitor. Though frequently on the scene, he remains a minor figure in the novel.

Joe, Mr. Wardle's fat, sleepy young servant. He is characterized by his ability to go to sleep at any time and under almost any circumstances, a trait which both amuses and irritates his master.

Mrs. Martha Bardell, Mr. Pickwick's landlady. When he consults her as to the advisability of taking a servant, she mistakes his remarks for a proposal of marriage and accepts him, much to Mr. Pickwick's dismay. The misunderstanding leads to the famous breach of promise suit of Bardell vs. Pickwick. Mr. Pickwick, refusing to pay damages, is sent to the Fleet Prison. After his refusal to pay, Mrs. Bardell's attorneys, unable to collect their fee, have her arrested and also sent to the Fleet Prison. Her plight finally arouses Mr. Pickwick's pity, and he pays the damages in order to release her and to free himself to aid his friend Mr. Winkle, who has eloped with Arabella Allen.

Tommy Bardell, Mrs. Bardell's young son.

Serjeant Buzfuz, Mrs. Bardell's counsel at the trial, a bombastic man noted for his bullying tactics with witnesses.

Mr. Skimpin, the assistant counsel to Serjeant Buzfuz.

Mr. Dodson and
Mr. Fogg, Mrs. Bardell's unscrupulous attorneys. Having taken the suit without fee, they have their client arrested and sent to prison when Mr. Pickwick refuses to pay damages after the suit has been decided against him.

Mr. Alfred Jingle, an amiable, impudent strolling player remarkable for his constant flow of disjointed sentences. He makes several attempts to marry women for their money, but Mr. Pickwick thwarts his plans in every case. He ends up in the Fleet Prison, from which he is rescued by Mr. Pickwick's generosity. He keeps his promise to reform.

Job Trotter, Mr. Jingle's cunning accomplice and servant. He is the only person whose wits prove sharper than those of Sam Weller.

Jem Huntley, a melancholy actor called **Dismal Jemmy,** Mr. Jingle's friend and Job Trotter's brother.

Sam Weller, Mr. Pickwick's jaunty, quick-witted, devoted Cockney servant. He and Mr. Pickwick meet at the inn to which Mr. Wardle has traced his sister and Mr. Jingle. Mr. Pickwick's decision to hire Sam as his valet leads to the famous breach of promise suit brought by Mrs. Bardell. Sam's aphorisms, anecdotes, and exploits make him one of Dickens' great comic creations, the embodiment of Cockney life and character.

Tony Weller, Sam Weller's hardy, affable father, a coachman who loves food, drink, and tobacco, and wants nothing from his shrewish wife except the opportunity to enjoy them.

Mrs. Susan Weller, formerly **Mrs. Clarke,** a shrew, a hypocrite, and a religious fanatic. At her death her husband inherits a small estate she has hoarded.

The Reverend Mr. Stiggins, called the **Shepherd,** a canting, hypocritical, alcoholic clergyman, greatly admired by Mrs. Weller, who gives him every opportunity to sponge off her husband.

Arabella Allen, a lovely girl whom Mr. Winkle first meets at Manor Farm. Her brother, Benjamin Allen, wants his sister to marry his friend Bob Sawyer, but Arabella rejects her brother's choice. After she marries Mr. Winkle in secret, Mr. Pickwick pays his friend's debts, effects a reconciliation between the young couple and Arabella's brother, and breaks the news of the marriage to Mr. Winkle's father.

Benjamin Allen, Arabella's coarse, roistering brother, a medical student. With no regard for his sister's feelings, he stubbornly insists upon her marriage to Bob Sawyer.

Mr. Winkle (Senior), a practical man of business, much opposed to his son's romance with Arabella Allen. He changes his mind when, through the services of Mr. Pickwick, he meets his daughter-in-law. He builds the couple a new house and makes his son an assistant in the family business.

Bob Sawyer, Benjamin Allen's friend and Arabella's unwelcome, oafish suitor. He hangs up his shingle in Bristol and practices medicine there. Eventually he and Benjamin Allen take service with the East India Company.

Bob Cripps, Bob Sawyer's servant.

Mrs. Mary Ann Raddle, Bob Sawyer's landlady, a shrew.

Mr. Raddle, her husband.

Mrs. Betsey Cluppins, Mrs. Raddle's sister and a friend of Mrs. Bardell.

Mr. Gunter, a friend of Bob Sawyer.

Jack Hopkins, a medical student, Bob Sawyer's friend. He tells Mr. Pickwick the story of a child who swallowed a necklace of large wooden beads that rattled and clacked whenever the child moved.

Peter Magnus, a traveler who journeys with Mr. Pickwick from London to Ipswich. He is on his way to make a proposal of marriage.

Miss Witherfield, his beloved, into whose room Mr. Pickwick, unable to find his own, accidentally blunders at the inn in Ipswich.

The Hon. Samuel Slumkey, a candidate for Parliament from the borough of Eatanswill. He is victorious over his opponent, Horatio Fizkin, Esq.

Mr. Slurk, the editor of "The Eatanswill Independent."

Mr. Pott, the editor of "The Eatanswill Gazette."

Mrs. Pott, his wife.

Mrs. Leo Hunter, a lady of literary pretensions, the author of "Ode to an Expiring Frog," whom Mr. Pickwick meets in Eatanswill.

Mr. Leo Hunter, who lives in his wife's reflected glory.

Count Smorltork, a traveling nobleman whom Mr. Pickwick meets at a breakfast given by Mrs. Leo Hunter.

Horatio Fizkin, Esq., defeated in the election at Eatanswill.

Mr. Perker, the agent for the Hon. Samuel Slumkey in the Eatanswill election, later Mr. Pickwick's attorney in the suit of Bardell vs. Pickwick. After his client has been sentenced to prison, Perker advises him to pay the damages in order to gain his freedom.

Serjeant Snubbin, Mr. Pickwick's lantern-faced, dull-eyed senior counsel in the breach of promise suit.

Mr. Justice Starleigh, the judge who presides at the trial of Bardell vs. Pickwick.

Mr. Phunky, the assistant counsel to Serjeant Snubbin; he is called an "infant barrister" because he has seen only eight years at the bar.

Thomas Groffin, a chemist, and
Richard Upwitch, a grocer, jurors at the trial of Bardell vs. Pickwick.

Mr. Jackson and
Mr. Wicks, clerks in the office of Dodson and Fogg.

Mr. Lowten, clerk to Mr. Perker.

Captain Boldwig, a peppery-tempered landowner on whose grounds the Pickwickians accidentally trespass while hunting.

Dr. Slammer, the surgeon of the 97th Regiment. At a charity ball in Rochester he challenges Mr. Jingle to a duel, but because the player is wearing a borrowed coat Mr. Winkle is the one actually called upon to meet the hot-tempered surgeon. Mr. Winkle, having been drunk, cannot remember what his conduct was or whom he might have insulted the night before. The situation is eventually resolved and Mr. Winkle and the doctor shake hands and part on friendly terms.

Lieutenant Tappleton, Dr. Slammer's second.

Colonel Bulder, the commanding officer of the military garrison at Rochester.

Mrs. Bulder, his wife.

Miss Bulder, their daughter.

Mrs. Budger, a widow, Mr. Tupman's partner at the charity ball in Rochester.

Mr. Dowler, a blustering, cowardly ex-army officer whom Mr. Pickwick meets at the White Horse Cellar. The Dowlers travel with Mr. Pickwick to Bath.

Mrs. Dowler, his wife.

Lord Mutanhed, a man of fashion and Mr. Dowling's friend, whom Mr. Pickwick meets in Bath.

The Hon. Mr. Crushton, another friend of Mr. Dowler.

Angelo Cyrus Bantam, Esq., a friend of Mr. and Mrs. Dowling and a master of ceremonies at Bath.

George Nupkins, Esq., the mayor of Ipswich, before whom Mr. Pickwick is brought on the charge, made by Miss

Witherfield, that he is planning to fight a duel. The mayor has recently entertained Mr. Jingle who, calling himself Captain Fitz-Marshall, was courting Miss Henrietta Nupkins.

Mrs. Nupkins, the mayor's wife.

Henrietta Nupkins, their daughter, the object of one of Mr. Jingle's matrimonial designs.

Mary, Mrs. Nupkins' pretty young servant. She eventually marries Sam Weller and both make their home with Mr. Pickwick in his happy, unadventurous old age.

Mr. Jinks, the clerk of the mayor's court at Ipswich.

Daniel Grummer, the constable of the mayor's court at Ipswich.

Frank Simmery, Esq., a young stock broker.

Solomon Pell, an attorney who, to his profit, assists in settling the deceased Mrs. Weller's modest estate.

Miss Tomkins, mistress of Westgate House, a boarding school for young ladies, at Bury St. Edmunds. Mr. Pickwick, tricked into believing that Mr. Jingle is planning to elope with one of the pupils, ventures into the school premises at night and finds himself in an embarrassing situation.

Tom Roker, a turnkey at the Fleet Prison.

Smangle,
Mivins, called The Zephyr,
Martin,
Simpson, and
The Chancery Prisoner, inmates of the Fleet Prison during Mr. Pickwick's detention.

Mrs. Budkin,
Susannah Sanders,
Mrs. Mudberry, and
Mrs. Rogers, Mrs. Bardell's friends and neighbors.

Anthony Humm, chairman of the Brick Lane Branch of the United Grand Junction Ebenezer Temperance Association.

Mr. Weller takes his son Sam to a lively meeting of the association.

The Story

Samuel Pickwick, Esquire, was the founder and perpetual president of the justly famous Pickwick Club. To extend his own researches into the quaint and curious phenomena of life, he suggested that he and three other Pickwickians should make journeys to places remote from London and report on their findings to the stay-at-home members of the club. The first destination decided upon was Rochester. As Mr. Pickwick, Mr. Tracy Tupman, Mr. Nathaniel Winkle, and Mr. Augustus Snodgrass went to their coach, they were waylaid by a rough gang of cab drivers. Fortunately the men were rescued by a stranger who was poorly dressed but of a magnificently friendly nature. The stranger, who introduced himself as Alfred Jingle, appeared to be going to Rochester also, and the party mounted the coach together.

After they had arrived at their destination, Mr. Tupman's curiosity was aroused when Mr. Jingle told him that there was to be a ball at the inn that very evening and that many lovely young ladies would be present. Because his luggage had gone astray, said Mr. Jingle, he had no evening clothes and so it would be impossible for him to attend the affair. This was a regrettable circumstance because he had hoped to introduce Mr. Tupman to the many young ladies of wealth and fashion who would be present. Eager to meet these young ladies, Mr. Tupman borrowed Mr. Winkle's suit for the stranger. At the ball Mr. Jingle observed a doctor in faithful attendnace upon a middle-aged lady. Attracting her attention, he danced with her, much to the anger of the doctor. Introducing himself as Dr. Slammer, the angry gentleman challenged Mr. Jingle to a duel.

The next morning a servant, identifying Mr. Winkle from the description given of the suit the stranger had worn, told Mr. Winkle that an insolent drunken man had insulted Dr. Slammer the previous evening and that the doctor was awaiting his appearance to fight a duel. Mr. Winkle had been drunk the night before, and he decided he was being called out because he had conducted himself in an unseemly manner which he could no longer remember. With Mr. Snodgrass as his second, Mr. Winkle tremblingly approached the battlefield. Much to his relief, Dr. Slammer roared that he was the wrong man. After much misunderstanding, the situation was satisfactorily explained and no blood was shed.

During the afternoon the travelers attended a parade, where they met Mr. Wardle in a coach with his two daughters and his sister, Miss Rachael Wardle, a plump old maid. Mr. Tupman, being quite taken with the elder Miss Wardle, accepted for his friends Mr. Wardle's invitation to visit his estate, Manor Farm. The next day the four Pickwickians departed for the farm, which was a distance of about ten miles from the inn where they were staying. Having difficulties with their horses, they arrived at Manor Farm in a disheveled state, but they were soon washed and mended under the kind assistance of Mr. Wardle's daughters. In the evening they played a hearty game of whist, and Mr. Tupman squeezed Miss Wardle's hand under the table.

The next day Mr. Wardle took his guests rook hunting. Mr. Winkle, who would not admit himself unable to cope with any situation, was given the gun to try his skill. He proved it by accidentally shooting Mr. Tupman in the arm. Miss Wardle offered her aid to the stricken man. Observing that their friend was in good hands, the others went off to a neighboring town to watch the cricket matches. There Mr. Pickwick unexpectedly encountered Mr. Jingle, and Mr. Wardle invited the fellow to return to Manor Farm with his party.

Convinced that Miss Wardle had a great deal of money, Mr. Jingle misrepresented Mr. Tupman's intentions to Miss Wardle and persuaded the spinster to elope with him. Mr. Wardle and Mr. Pickwick pursued the couple to London. There, with the assistance of Mr. Wardle's lawyer, Mr. Perker, they went from one inn to another in an attempt to find the elopers. Finally, through a sharp-featured young man cleaning boots in the yard of the White Hart Inn, they were able to identify Mr. Jingle. They indignantly confronted him as he was displaying a marriage license. After a heated argument, Mr. Jingle resigned his matrimonial designs for the sum of one hundred and twenty pounds. Miss Wardle went tearfully back to Manor Farm. The Pickwickians returned to London, where Mr. Pickwick engaged as his servant Sam Weller, the sharp, shrewd young bootblack of the White Hart Inn.

Mr. Pickwick was destined to meet the villainous Mr. Jingle soon again. A Mrs. Leo Hunter invited the learned man and his friends to a party. There Mr. Pickwick spied Mr. Jingle, who, upon seeing his former acquaintance, disappeared into the crowd. Mrs. Hunter told Mr. Pickwick that Mr. Jingle lived at Bury St. Edmonds. Mr. Pickwick set out in pursuit in company with his servant, Sam Weller, for the old gentleman was determined to deter the scoundrel from any fresh deceptions he might be planning. At the inn where Mr. Jingle was reported to be staying, Mr. Pickwick learned that the rascal was planning to elope with a rich young lady who stayed at a boarding-school nearby. Mr. Pickwick fell in with the suggestion that in order to rescue the young lady he should hide in the garden from which Mr. Jingle was planning to steal her. When Mr. Pickwick sneaked into the garden, he found nothing of a suspicious nature; in short, he had been deceived, and the blackguard had escaped.

Mr. Pickwick had for housekeeper Mrs. Bardell, a widow. When he was about to hire Sam Weller, Mr. Pickwick had spoken to her in such a manner that she had mistaken his words for a proposal of marriage. One day Mr. Pickwick was resting in his rooms when he received notice from the legal firm of Dodgson and Fogg that Mrs. Bardell was suing him for breach of promise. The summons was distressing, but first Mr. Pickwick had more important business to occupy his time. After securing the services of Mr. Perker to defend him, he went to Ipswich upon learning that Mr. Jingle had been seen in that vicinity. The trip to Ipswich was successful. The Pickwickians were able to catch Mr. Jingle in his latest scheme of deception and to expose him before he had carried out his plot.

At the trial for the breach of promise suit brought by Mrs. Bardell, lawyers Dodgson and Fogg argued so eloquently against Mr. Pickwick that the jury fined him seven hundred and fifty pounds. When the trail was over, Mr. Pickwick told Dodgson and Fogg that even if they put him in prison he would never pay one cent of the damages, since he knew as well as they that there had been no true grounds for suit.

The Pickwickians shortly afterward went to Bath, where fresh adventures awaited Mr. Pickwick and his friends. On that occasion Mr. Winkle's weakness for the fair sex involved them in difficulties. In Bath the Pickwickians met two young medical students, Mr. Allen and Mr. Bob Sawyer. Mr. Allen hoped to marry his sister, Arabella, to his friend, Mr. Sawyer, but Miss Allen professed extreme dislike for her brother's choice. When Mr. Winkle learned that Arabella had refused Mr. Sawyer because another had won her heart, he felt that he must be the fortunate man because she had displayed an interest in him when they had met earlier at Manor Farm. Kindly Mr. Pickwick arranged to have Mr. Winkle meet Arabella in a garden, where the distraught lover could plead his suit.

Mr. Pickwick's plans to further his friend's romance were interrupted, however, by a subpoena delivered because he had refused to pay money to Mrs. Bardell. Still stubbornly refusing to pay the damages, Mr. Pickwick found himself returned to London and lodged in Fleet Street prison. With the help of Sam Weller, Mr. Pickwick arranged his prison quarters as comfortably as possible and remained deaf to the entreaties of Sam Weller or Mr. Perker, who thought that he should pay his debt and regain his freedom. Dodgson and Fogg proved to be of lower caliber than even Mr. Pickwick had suspected. They had taken Mrs. Bardell's case without fee, gambling on Mr. Pickwick's payment to cover the costs of the case. When they saw no payment forthcoming, they had Mrs. Bardell arrested also and sent to the Fleet Street prison.

While Mr. Pickwick was trying to decide what to do, Mr. Winkle with his new wife, Arabella, came to the prison and asked Mr. Pickwick to pay his debts so that he could visit Mr. Allen with the news of Mr. Winkle's marriage to Arabella. Arabella herself felt that Mr. Pickwick was the only person who could arrange a proper reconciliation between her brother and her new husband. Kindness prevailed; Mr. Pickwick paid the damages to Mrs. Bardell so that he would be free to help his friends in distress.

Winning Mr. Allen's approval of the match was not difficult for Mr. Pickwick, but when he approached the elder Mr. Winkle, the bridegroom's father objected to the marriage and threatened to cut off his son without a cent. To add to Mr. Pickwick's problems, Mr. Wardle came to London to tell him that his daughter Emily was in love with Mr. Snodgrass and to ask Mr. Pickwick's advice. Mr. Wardle had brought Emily to London with him.

The entire party came together in Arabella's apartment. All misunderstandings happily ended for the two lovers, and a jolly party followed. The elder Mr. Winkle paid a call on his new daughter-in-law. Upon seeing what a charming and lovely girl she was, he relented his decision to disinherit his son, and the family was reconciled.

After Mr. Snodgrass had married Emily Wardle, Mr. Pickwick dissolved the Pickwick Club and retired to a home in the country, with his faithful servant, Sam Weller. Several times Mr. Pickwick was called upon to be a godfather to little Winkles and Snodgrasses, but for the most part he led a quiet life, respected by his neighbors and loved by all his friends.

Critical Evaluation

When in 1836 a publisher proposed that Charles Dickens write the text for a series of pictures by the sporting artist Robert Seymour, Dickens was experiencing the first thrill of fame as the author of *Sketches by Boz*. He was twenty-four, and had been for some years a court reporter and free-lance journalist; *Sketches by Boz* was his first literary effort of any length. The work that the publisher proposed was of a similar kind: short, usually humorous descriptions of cosmopolitan life, sometimes illustrated, and published monthly. Dickens, with the plan of a novel already in mind, but in need of cash, accepted the offer as a stopgap. He made one stipulation: that he and not Seymour have the choice of scenes to be treated. He did this because he himself was no sportsman and as a cockney had little knowledge of the country beyond what his journalistic travels had shown him. That he viewed the enterprise as an expedient is evident from the digressive character of the first few chapters.

Dickens was able to disguise his ignorance of country life by a canny selection of scenes and topics. Actual sporting scenes are kept to a minimum, and treated with broad humour and slight detail. Country elections, magistrates, and newspapers, on the other hand, he knew well, and the chapters describing the Eatanswill election and dealing with Mr. Nupkins, the mayor of Ipswich, and Mr. Pott, the editor of the Eatanswill *Gazette,* abound in atmosphere and choice observation. Most useful of all was his intimate knowledge of stagecoach travel, of life upon the road, and of the inhabitants and manners of inns great and small. The device of a journey by coach unifies the first part of the novel, and a large portion of the action, including several key scenes, takes place in inns and public houses; for example, Mr. Pickwick meets Sam Weller at the White Hart Inn, Mrs. Bardell is apprehended at the Spaniards, Sam is reunited with his father at the Marquis of Granby, and the Wellers plot Stiggins' discomfiture at the Blue Boar.

A theme that Dickens developed in later works appears in embryo here: the quicksand quality of litigation. We note that every figure connected with the law is portrayed as venal if not downright criminal, except Mr. Perker who is merely depicted as a remarkably cold fish. Another feature of later works is the awkward treatment of women. The author's attitude toward the fair sex is extremely ambiguous. Two of the women in the novel are unqualifiedly good. Sam's Mary is described perennially as "the pretty house-maid," and the fact that Sam loves her appear to complete the list of her virtues in Dickens' view. As a character she has neither depth nor ethical range; no more has Arabella Allen, the dark-eyed girl with the "very nice little pair of boots." She is distinguished at first by flirtatious archness and later by a rather servile docility. The daughters of old Wardle first come to our attention in the act of spiting their spinster aunt, and never redeem this impression. Other female characters are rather poorly developed. None has, as do some of the male figures such as Jingle and Trotter, a human dimension.

Curious too are the author's sentiments about the institution of marriage. Mr. Winkle makes a runaway match, Mr. Snodgrass is only forestalled from doing so by a lack of parental opposition, and Mr. Tupman escapes after a ludicrously close call. But Mr. Pickwick, the great advocate of heart over head, is not and never has been married, and in fact shows his greatest strength as a character in his struggle for justice in a breach-of-promise suit; while Mr. Weller, the other beneficent father-figure of the work, makes no bones about his aversion to the connubial state: " '. . . vether it's worth while goin' through so much, to learn so little . . . is a matter o' taste. *I* rayther think it isn't.' "

Angus Wilson, among others, contends that *Pickwick Papers* is, like most first novels, autobiographical, however well-disguised. There is evidence for this position in the fact that Dickens' estimation of the women in his life also tended to extremes of adulation and contempt. More pertinent to the main thrust of the novel, which is the development of Pickwick from buffoon to "angel in tights," and the concurrent development of Sam, is the author's relationship to his father, whom he adored. The elder Dickens' imprisonment for debt in 1824 was the great trauma of the author's childhood; it was made the more galling by the fact that he, the eldest son, was put out to work at a blacking factory and was able to join the family circle in the prison only on Sundays. Scarcely more than a child, he felt unable either to aid or to comfort his father in his distress; at the same time, he felt that his father had abandoned him to an ungentle world.

As a young man, Dickens wrote into his first novel an account of those times as he would have wished them to be. Mr. Pickwick is the epitome of those qualities of Dickens senior that so endeared him to his son, unsinkable good spirits and kindness that does not count the cost. To these, Pickwick adds financial sense, ethical size, and most important, a sensitivity to the best feelings of his spiritual son, Sam Weller. Sam, in turn, bends all his cockney keenness of eye and wit, all his courage and steadfastness, to the service not only of this ideal father unjustly imprisoned, but also of his immensely endearing shadow-father Tony Weller. Clearly, this material has its roots in Dickens' life. But it is just as clear that his genius tapped a universal longing of sons to see their fathers as heroes, and themselves as heroic helpers.

Bibliography

Axton, William. "Unity and Coherence in *The Pickwick Papers*," in *Studies in English Literature, 1500–1900.* V (1965), pp. 633–676.

Bevington, David M. "Seasonal Relevance in *The Pickwick Papers*," in *Nineteenth-Century Fiction.* XVI (1961), pp. 219–230.

Chesterton, Gilbert K. *Charles Dickens.* London: Methuen, 1936, pp. 51–71.

————. *Criticisms and Appreciations of the Works of Charles Dickens.* London: Dent, 1933, pp. 13–25.

Daleski, Herman M. *Dickens and the Art of Analogy.* New York: Schocken, 1970, pp. 17–48.

Easson, Angus. "Imprisonment for Debt in *Pickwick Papers*," in *The Dickensian.* LXIV (May, 1968), pp. 105–112.

Fadiman, Clifton. *Party of One; The Selected Writings of Clifton Fadiman.* New York: World, 1955, pp. 203–225.

Gold, Joseph. *Charles Dickens: Radical Moralist.* Minneapolis: University of Minnesota Press, 1972, pp. 12–24.

Greaves, John. *Who's Who in Dickens.* New York: Taplinger, 1972.

Hardy, Barbara. *The Moral Art of Dickens.* New York: Oxford University Press, 1970, pp. 81–99.

Herbert, Christopher. "Converging Worlds in *Pickwick Papers*," in *Nineteenth-Century Fiction.* XXVII (1972), pp. 1–20.

Killham, John. "*Pickwick*, Dickens and the Art of Fiction," in *Dickens and the Twentieth Century.* Edited by J. Gross and G. Pearson. London: Routledge and Kegan Paul, 1962, pp. 35–47.

Kincaid, James R. *Dickens and the Rhetoric of Laughter.* Oxford: Clarendon Press, 1971, pp. 20–40.

Lucas, John. *The Melancholy Man: A Study of Dickens' Novels.* London: Methuen, 1970, pp. 1–20.

Maclean, H.N. "Mr. Pickwick and the Seven Deadly Sins," in *Nineteenth-Century Fiction.* VIII (December, 1953), pp. 198–212.

Manheim, Leonard. "Dickens' Fools and Madmen," in *Dickens Studies Annual.* II (1972), pp. 74–77.

Manning, Sylvia B. *Dickens as Satirist.* New Haven, Conn.: Yale University Press, 1971, pp. 41–51.

Marcus, Steven. "Language into Structure: Pickwick Revisited," in *Daedalus.* CI (1972), pp. 183–202.

Patten, Robert L. "The Art of *Pickwick's* Interpolated Tales," in *Journal of English Literary History.* XXXIV (1967), pp. 349–366.

————. "Boz, Phiz, and Pickwick in the Pound," in *Journal of English Literary History*. XXXVI (1969), pp. 575–591.

Priestley, J.B. *The English Comic Characters*. London: J. Lane, 1928, pp. 198–223.

Rogers, Philip. "Mr. Pickwick's Innocence," in *Nineteenth-Century Fiction*. XXVII (1972), pp. 21–37.

Rubin, Stan S. "Spectator and Spectacle: Narrative Evasion and Narrative Voice in *Pickwick Papers*," in *Journal of Narrative Technique*. VI (1976), pp. 188–203.

A TALE OF TWO CITIES

Type of work: Novel
Author: Charles Dickens (1812–1870)
Type of plot: Historical romance
Time of plot: French Revolution
Locale: France and England
First published: 1859

Without attempting a rigorous analysis of the political, social, and economic causes or consequences of the French Revolution, Dickens uses this historical background as the panoramic setting for a complicated romantic novel culminating in Sidney Carton's famous personal drama of love and renunciation.

Principal Characters

Sydney Carton, the legal assistant to Mr. Stryver, a successful London barrister. A drunkard and a misanthrope, he has no aim or purpose in his life until he meets Lucie Manette and falls secretly in love with her. Because of his remarkable physical resemblance to Charles Darnay, who becomes Lucie's husband, he is able to sacrifice himself on the guillotine in Darnay's place, a deed which finally gives a real meaning to his life in his own eyes.

Charles Darnay, in reality **Charles St. Evrémonde,** an émigré and an anti-aristocrat who has renounced his title. In England, where he becomes a teacher of languages, he finds happiness and success as the husband of Lucie Manette. When he returns to France to aid an agent of the St. Evrémonde family who has been captured by the revolutionists, he himself is arrested and condemned to the guillotine. He escapes because Sydney Carton takes his place in the prison. Darnay returns to England with his wife and her father.

Lucie Manette, a beautiful young French girl, closely connected with political events in France. Her father, a physician, had been a prisoner in the Bastille for many years, where he is sent because he has gained knowledge of the hidden crimes of the St. Evrémonde family. Her husband, Charles Darnay, is a member of that family and is condemned to the guillotine during the Revolution. He escapes death through the efforts of his wife, her father, and Sydney Carton. Throughout these trials Lucie remains level-headed, practical, and devoted.

Dr. Alexander Manette, Lucie's father, a doctor imprisoned many years in the Bastille in France because he aided a poor servant girl who was forced to become the mistress of the Marquis St. Evrémonde, Charles Darnay's uncle. Dr. Manette loses his mind in the Bastille and becomes obsessed with making shoes. His mind mends after his release, but whenever he is reminded of the prison days he seeks out his shoe bench and begins work. He tries to free Charles Darnay from the French prison by appealing to the sympathies of the revolutionists, but he is unsuccessful. At Darnay's trial a document written by the doctor while in prison is presented as evidence to secure the young aristocrat's conviction and sentence of death.

Lucie, her mother's namesake, the small daughter of Charles Darnay and his wife.

Ernest Defarge, a wineshop keeper in St. Antoine, a suburb of Paris. A former houseservant of Dr. Manette, he cares for his former master after he is released from the Bastille and before he goes to England. He is also one of the most radical of the revolutionists and, with his wife, he tries to get Charles Darnay executed by producing the document Dr. Manette had written years before.

Madame Thérèse Defarge, the wife of the wineshop keeper, a ruthless, cold woman who hates all aristocrats. Madame Defarge attends every guillotining and knits a stitch for each head that drops. She dies while struggling with Miss Pross, Lucie Darnay's maid.

Mr. Stryver, a self-centered, proud lawyer employed as Charles Darnay's counsel when the young language teacher is accused of carrying treasonous papers between France and England. He is Sydney Carton's patron and employer, a shrewd, determined man who looks years older than his actual age.

Miss Pross, the devoted housekeeper who has looked after Lucie Manette from childhood. She is intelligent and physically strong. Left behind to cover their flight when the Manettes escape from Paris, she struggles with Madame Defarge, who tries to make her confess where the Manettes have gone. Madame Defarge is accidentally killed when her gun goes off. Miss Pross, deafened by the explosion, escapes with Jerry Cruncher and follows her master and mistress to freedom.

Monsieur the Marquis St. Evrémonde, a cruel French aristocrat and Charles Darnay's uncle. When he kills a child because his coachman drives his horses too fast, the child's father gains admittance to the château and kills the arrogant nobleman. The Marquis and his breed are responsible for the peasants' uprising, causing the French Revolution.

Gaspard, the father of the child who was killed by the Marquis' fast horses. He succeeds in murdering the Marquis by plunging a knife into the sleeping nobleman's heart.

Monsieur Théophile Gabelle, a village postmaster and keeper of rents. Arrested by the revolutionists, he appeals to Charles Darnay in England for aid. In response to his plea Darnay goes on his dangerous errand in France.

Solomon Pross, alias **John Barsad,** Miss Pross's brother. A complete scoundrel, he abandons his sister after obtaining all her money. Calling himself John Barsad, he becomes a spy for the English. He informs Madame Defarge of Charles Darnay's marriage to Lucie Manette. He is a turnkey at the Conciergerie in Paris while Darnay is imprisoned there. Sydney Carton recognizes him but does not reveal his identity.

Jerry Cruncher, an employee at the London banking house of Tellson and Company by day, a resurrection-man by night. Devoted to Lucie and her father, he aids in Charles Darnay's escape from France.

Mrs. Cruncher, his wife, whom he calls "Aggerawayter." A pious woman, she thinks her husband's night occupation sinful, and she prays for his reformation.

Young Jerry Cruncher, their son. Guessing shrewdly, he has a good idea of the grim trade his father follows at night.

Mr. Jarvis Lorry, the confidential clerk of Tellson and Company. He is instrumental in getting Dr. Manette out of France into England, and he goes with the Manettes to Paris during the dark days of the Revolution while Charles Darnay, in prison, is awaiting his execution.

Jacques One,
Jacques Two,
Jacques Three,

Jacques Four, the name taken by Defarge, and

Jacques Five, a roadmender, a group of
revolutionists in the suburb of St. Antoine.

The Vengeance, a woman revolutionist,

Madame Defarge's lieutenant.

Roger Cly, Solomon Pross's partner and
Charles Darnay's former servant, who
testifies falsely when Darnay is on trial at
the Old Bailey. He is supposed to be dead
and buried, but Jerry Cruncher knows
that his coffin had been empty.

The Story

The early rumbling of the French Revolution was echoing across the English
Channel. In Paris a lonely old man waited in an attic for his first meeting with a
daughter whom he had not seen since she was a baby. With the aid of Mr. Jarvis
Lorry, an agent for the Franco-British banking house of Tellson & Co., the lovely
Lucie Manette had been brought to Paris to find her father, imprisoned for eighteen years in the Bastille. Above the wine shop of Madame and M. Defarge, Dr.
Manette was kept secretly until his rescuers could take him safely back to England. Day after day Madame Defarge sat outside her wine shop, knitting into a
long scarf strange symbols which would later spell out a death list of hated
aristocrats.

Five years later Lucie Manette sat beside her father in the courtroom of the
Old Bailey, where Charles Darnay, a teacher of languages, was on trial for trea-
sonable activities which involved his passing between France and England on secret business. A man named John Barsad had brought charges against him.
Lucie and her father had testified they had met Darnay on the boat when they
had traveled from France five years earlier. But an unusual circumstance saved
the prisoner. Mr. Stryver, the prisoner's counsel, pointed across the courtroom to
another man who so resembled the prisoner that legal identification of Darnay
was shaken. The other man was Sydney Carton, and because of the likeness between the two Mr. Stryver secured an acquittal for the prisoner. Carton's relationship to Stryver was that of the jackal to the lion, for the alcoholic, aimless
Carton wrote the cases which Stryver pleaded in court.

Lucie and her father lived in a small tenement under the care of their maid,
Miss Pross, and their kindly friend, Mr. Lorry. Jerry Cruncher, porter at Tellson
& Co., and a secret resurrectionist, was often helpful. Darnay and Carton became frequent callers in the Manette household, after the trial which had
brought them together.

In France the fury of the people grew. Monseigneur the Marquis St. Evrémonde, was driving in his carriage through the countryside when he carelessly
killed a child of a peasant named Gaspard. The nobleman returned to his castle
to meet his nephew, who was visiting from England. Charles Darney's views dif-
fered from those of his uncle. Darnay knew that his family had committed grave
injustices, for which he begged his uncle to make amends. Monseigneur the marquis haughtily refused. That night the marquis was murdered in his bed.

Darnay returned to England to seek Dr. Manette's permission to court Lucie. In order to construct a bond of complete honesty, Darnay attempted to tell the doctor his true French name, but Manette fearfully asked him to wait until the morning of his marriage before revealing it. Carton also approached Lucie with a proposal of marriage. When Lucie refused, Carton asked her always to remember that there was a man who would give his own life to keep a life she loved beside her.

Meanwhile in France Madame Defarge knitted into her scarf the story of the hated St. Evrémondes. Gaspard had been hanged for the assassination of the marquis; monseigneur's house must be destroyed. John Barsad, the spy, brought news that Lucie Manette would marry Charles Darnay, nephew of the marquis. This news disturbed Defarge, for Dr. Manette, a former prisoner of the Bastille, held a special honor in the eyes of the Revolutionists.

Lucie and Darnay were married. Sydney Carton became a loyal friend of the family. Time passed, and tiny Lucie arrived. When the child was six years old, in the year 1789, the French people stormed the Bastille. At the Bastille Defarge went to the cell where Dr. Manette had been a prisoner and extracted some papers hidden behind a stone in the wall.

One day, while Darnay was talking to Mr. Lorry at Tellson & Co., a letter addressed to the Marquis St. Evrémonde was placed on Mr. Lorry's desk. Darnay offered to deliver it to the proper person. When he was alone, he read the letter. It was from an old family servant who had been imprisoned by the Revolutionists. He begged the Marquis St. Evrémonde to save his life. Darnay realized that he must go to Paris. Only Dr. Manette knew of Darnay's family name, and the doctor had been sworn to secrecy.

Darnay and Mr. Lorry went to Paris, the latter to look after the French branch of Tellson & Co. Shortly after his arrival Darnay was seized as an undesirable immigrant after Defarge had ordered his arrest. Mr. Lorry was considerably upset when Lucie and Dr. Manette suddenly arrived in Paris. Some of the doctor's friends had informed him of Darnay's arrest. The old man felt that his own imprisonment in the Bastille would win the sympathy of the Revolutionists and enable him to save his son-in-law.

After fifteen months of waiting, Darnay was brought to trial. Able to prove his innocence of harming the French people, he was freed, but forbidden to leave France. A short time later he was again arrested, denounced by Defarge and one other person whose name the officer refused to disclose.

While shopping one day in the Paris market, Miss Pross and Jerry Cruncher, who were in Paris with Lucie and Mr. Lorry, met a man who caused Miss Pross to scream in amazement and Jerry to stare in silent astonishment. The man was Solomon, Miss Pross' lost brother. Jerry remembered him as John Barsad, the man who had been a spy-witness at the Old Bailey. Carton arrived on the scene at that moment, and he was able to force Barsad to come with him to the office of Tellson & Co. for a private conference. Barsad feared detection of his duplicity for he was now an employee of the Republican French Government. Carton and Jerry threatened to expose him as a former spy for the English government, the enemy of France. Carton made a deal with Barsad.

When Darnay was once more brought before the tribunal, Defarge testified against him and named Dr. Manette as the other accuser. Defarge produced the papers which he had found in Dr. Manette's cell in the Bastille. Therein the doctor had written the story of his arrest and imprisonment because he had learned of a secret crime committed by a St. Evrémonde against a woman of humble birth and her young brother. His account was enough to convict Darnay. Sentenced for the crimes of his ancestors, Darnay, the young St. Evrémonde, was condemned by the tribunal to the guillotine.

Now Sydney Carton began to act. He visited the Defarge wine shop, where he learned that Madame Defarge was the sister of the woman ruined by St. Evrémonde years before. Then with the help of the false Barsad, he gained admittance to the prison where Darnay had been taken. There he drugged the prisoner and, still aided by the cowed Barsad, had him carried from the cell. Carton remained. The resemblance between the two would allow him to pass as Darnay and prevent discovery of the aristocrat's escape.

Madame Defarge went to the lodgings of Lucie and Dr. Manette to denounce them. Only Miss Pross was there; the others, including Darnay, were already on their way to safety. To keep Madame Defarge from learning of their escape, Miss Pross struggled with the furious woman demanding admittance to Lucie's apartment. Madame Defarge was killed when her pistol went off. Miss Pross was deaf for the rest of her life.

Lucy and Darnay returned safely to England. Sydney Carton died at the guillotine, giving his own life for the happiness of his dear friends.

Critical Evaluation

The central paradox of *A Tale of Two Cities* consists in the fact that its action involves the most important political event of modern European history—and perhaps of its entire history—the French Revolution, while the values of the novel are ultimately anti-political. Politics and history, neither of which Dickens renders with great faithfulness, loom as a necessity from which his characters must flee to save their souls. Throughout the novel Dickens reminds us that all of man's acts, whether magnanimous or petty, when viewed in a cosmic context, shrink to nil. Indeed, for him the goal of politics, the finding of a just community, is an absurd one in this world. To paraphrase Sydney Carton's famous last speech: it is a far better thing to die and join such a community in heaven—the existence of which Dickens cannot with certainty assert—than to engage with society. *A Tale of Two Cities* demonstrates that Dickens' political will, wan in his previous novels, has finally been exhausted.

In this regard and in one of the first substantial essays dealing with Dickens' art and thought, published a year before *A Tale of Two Cities* was completed, Walter Bagehot said: "Mr. Dickens has not unfrequently spoken, and what is worse, he has taught a great number of parrot-like imitators to speak, in what really is, if they knew it, a tone of objection to the necessary constitution of human society." Dickens' strength, Bagehot agreed, appeared in the quality of his moral cry, his protest against the injustices of society; yet, as he said, the novelist never indicated how these inequalities might be removed.

By the time of *A Tale of Two Cities,* distinguished by its outrage against both the tyranny of the governors and the governed, Dickens clearly indicates that society cannot be made to progress, or even be substantially ameliorated. For him the great grasp for freedom by the French people, for example, goes finally unsung, drowned out by the terrible cacaphony of the guillotine. To Dickens' unwillingness to accept the "necessary constitution of human society," then, must be added his refusal to understand and accept the necessarily slow and painful processes of history.

In his early comic and satiric novels, such as *Pickwick Papers, Nicholas Nickleby* and *Oliver Twist,* Dickens' simple stance of protest carried with it a zestful anger that was both invigorating and liberating. But as he grew more serious in his artistic intent, beginning with *Dombey and Son,* completed in 1848, and continuing through *David Copperfield, Bleak House, Hard Times* and *Little Dorrit,* for many readers his masterpiece, he lost his sense of the efficacy of the human will to deal with the complexities of a modern, industrial society. His gradual loss of faith was accompanied by a diminishing moral energy; his imagination seemed unable to create viable and pertinent responses to a civilization increasingly encroaching on individual freedom. Particularly in *Little Dorrit,* the novel published immediately before *A Tale of Two Cities,* we are stunned as well as enervated by the hopelessness of the conclusion.

There is a significant scene in *A Tale of Two Cities,* appearing at the conclusion of Book the First, relevant to Dickens' social despair. After Doctor Manette has been saved from the Bastille, and on the way from Paris to London, his rescuer, Mr. Jarvis Lorry, asks him, "I hope you care to be recalled to life?" Doctor Manette answers, "I can't say." In some ways, the question is never answered by the doctor, for at the novel's conclusion he is rendered an inarticulate vegetable by his sufferings during the Reign of Terror. But it does seem to be answered by the working out of the plot which culminates in Carton's self-sacrifice.

If to be "recalled to life" means to be called back into civilization and history, then the novel implies the answer: "No." For the quality of life in society is actually no better, Dickens tells us, than perpetual imprisonment in the Bastille: man is caught up in an undertow of events which leaves him helpless; his imagination, intelligence, and will are useless when pitted against politics.

Indeed the novelist goes further than this in his view of man's ineptitude: if he consents to join in the machinations of society, Dickens asserts, he must expect inevitable corruption. It is a tragic view unrelieved by any sense of man's dignity, a nobility obtained through a will to control time, even if that exertion is fated to be unrewarded. We are left with a vision of unmitigated pathos, unconsoled in our own existence, which is inextricably bound up with the demands of history and politics.

The consolation which Dickens offers—if indeed comfort can be forthcoming after the absoluteness of his negation—takes the form of a vague promise of supernatural communion and a picture of human fellowship and love. Composed of Doctor and Lucie Manette, Charles Darnay and Sydney Carton, together with the minor characters of Mr. Lorry, Miss Pross and Jerry Cruncher, the fellowship provides a sanctuary within the confines of history. There affection, trust, and sacrifice stand opposed to the hate, treachery, and tyranny of the world.

Yet even this consolation is finally unsatisfying. That sanctuary is populated by the good-hearted, naïve, sentimental, and feeble; it is a childlike fellowship in which passion and mind, those qualities we associate with a real, adult world, are absent. Not only does the merely innocent fail to attract us, but the refuge remains unconvincing and vulnerable when we realize the power that it is supposed to stand against. In short, one cannot imagine Charles and Lucie along with Doctor Manette and their faithful retainers surviving the *realpolitik* of civilization. Despite its great subject, *A Tale of Two Cities* is, at last, a simplistic novel; it is deficient in the complex human experience which we expect from great fiction.

Bibliography

Davis, Earle. *The Flint and the Flame: The Artistry of Charles Dickens.* Columbia: University of Missouri Press, 1963, pp. 238–254.

Dyson, A.E. *The Inimitable Dickens; A Reading of the Novels.* London: Macmillan, 1970, pp. 212–227.

Elliot, Ralph. *A Critical Commentary on Dickens'* A Tale of Two Cities. London: Macmillan, 1966.

Fleishman, Avrom. *The English Historical Novel; Walter Scott to Virginia Woolf.* Baltimore: Johns Hopkins University Press, 1971, pp. 114–126.

Gold, Joseph. *Charles Dickens: Radical Moralist.* Minneapolis: University of Minnesota Press, 1972, pp. 231–240.

Goldberg, Michael. *Carlyle and Dickens.* Athens: University of Georgia, 1972, pp. 100–128.

Greaves, John. *Who's Who in Dickens.* New York: Taplinger, 1972.

Gregory, Michael. "Old Bailey Speech in *A Tale of Two Cities*," in *Review of English Literature*. VI (April, 1965), pp. 42–55.

Gross, John. "*A Tale of Two Cities*," in *Dickens and the Twentieth Century*. Edited by J. Gross and G. Pearson. London: Routledge and Kegan Paul, 1962, pp. 187–197.

Halperin, John. *Egoism and Self-Discovery in the Victorian Novel: Studies in the Ordeal of Knowledge in the Nineteenth Century*. New York: Burt Franklin, 1974, pp. 103–109.

Lindsay, Jack. "*A Tale of Two Cities*," in *Life and Letters*. LXII (1949), pp. 191–204.

Manheim, Leonard. "A Tale of Two Characters: A Study in Multiple Projection," in *Dickens Studies Annual*. I (1970), pp. 229–237.

————. "*A Tale of Two Cities*: A Study in Psychoanalytic Criticism," in *English Review*. (Spring, 1959), pp. 13–28.

Manning, Sylvia B. *Dickens as Satirist*. New Haven, Conn.: Yale University Press, 1971, pp. 183–192.

Marcus, David D. "The Carlylean Vision of *A Tale of Two Cities*," in *Studies in the Novel*. VIII (1976), pp. 56–68.

Marshall, William H. "The Method of *A Tale of Two Cities*," in *The Dickensian*. LVII (Autumn, 1961), pp. 183–189.

Monod, Sylvère. "Dickens's Attitudes in *A Tale of Two Cities*," in *Dickens Centennial Essays*. Edited by Ada Nisbet and Blake Nevius. Berkeley: University of California Press, 1971, pp. 166–183.

Partlow, Robert B., Jr. *Dickens the Craftsman; Strategies of Presentation*. Carbondale: Southern Illinois University Press, 1970, pp. 165–186.

Rance, Nicholas. *The Historical Novel and Popular Politics in Nineteenth-Century England*. London: Vision, 1975, pp. 83–101.

Stange, G. Robert. "Dickens and the Fiery Past: *A Tale of Two Cities* Reconsidered," in *English Journal*. XLIV (1957), pp. 381–390.

Stoehr, Taylor. *Dickens: The Dreamer's Stance*. Ithaca, N.Y.: Cornell University Press, 1965, pp. 195–203.

Wagenknecht, Edward C. *Dickens and the Scandalmongers; Essays in Criticism*. Norman: University of Oklahoma Press, 1965, pp. 121–131.

Zabel, Morton D. *Craft and Character; Texts, Methods and Vocation in Modern Fiction*. New York: Viking, 1957, pp. 49–69.

Zambrano, Ana L. "The Styles of Dickens and Griffith: *A Tale of Two Cities* and *Orphans of the Storm*," in *Language and Style*. VII (1974), pp. 53–60.

BENJAMIN DISRAELI

Born: London, England (December 21, 1804)
Died: London (April 19, 1881)

Principal Works

NOVELS: *Vivian Grey*, 1826–1827; *The Young Duke*, 1831; *Contarini Fleming*, 1832; *The Wondrous Tale of Alroy*, 1833; *Henrietta Temple, A Love Story*, 1836; *Venetia*, 1837; *Coningsby*, 1844; *Sybil*, 1845; *Tancred*, 1847; *Lothair*, 1870; *Endymion*, 1880.

BURLESQUES: *The Voyage of Captain Popanilla*, 1828; *Ixion in Heaven*, 1833; *The Infernal Marriage*, 1833.

BIOGRAPHY: *The Political Biography of Lord George Bentinck*, 1852.

HISTORICAL STUDIES: *England and France*, 1832; *Vindication of the English Constitution,* 1835; *The Spirit of Whiggism*, 1836.

Benjamin Disraeli, born in London, December 21, 1804, was the son of Isaac D'Israeli, a well-known literary commentator and biographer. Like the title character of his sensational first novel, *Vivian Grey*, he was privately educated—chiefly in his father's library—and took the "grand tour." He chafed at his law studies and with a powerful self-assurance wrote a quick succession of shallowly brilliant novels: *The Young Duke, Contarini Fleming*, and *The Wondrous Tale of Alroy*, as well as a group of political pamphlets and a trio of burlesque extravaganzas, *The Voyage of Captain Popanilla, Ixion in Heaven*, and *The Infernal Marriage*. Then, despite the handicaps of his Jewish heritage and his foppish manners, he brazenly experimented with politics. Failing as a radical, he was elected to Parliament as a Tory. Out of this experience he wrote his three best-known novels, *Coningsby*, sometimes referred to as "the best novel of politics ever written"; *Sybil*; and *Tancred*. He gave up his writing temporarily, married in 1839 the widow of his colleague Wyndham Lewis, then gradually rose to be three times Chancellor of the Exchequer, and, finally, Prime Minister from 1867–1868 and again from 1874–1880.

During his second term of office, when he was knighted, he took a name from his first novel and became the first Earl of Beaconsfield. In his later years he resumed his writing and became an intimate friend of Queen Victoria. He died in London, April 19, 1881.

In *The Political Biography of Lord George Bentinck*, Disraeli summed up the basic message of all his social novels in the principle: "the few for the many; not the many for the few." Despite his many detractors, political and literary, he bluffed, schemed, fought, and insisted on his way to success—and achieved it.

Bibliography

The best edition is the Bradenham Edition of *The Novels and Tales of Benjamin Disraeli*, with an introduction by Philip Guedalla, 12 vols., 1926–1927. The fullest biography is William F. Monypenny and G. E. Buckle, *The Life of Benjamin Disraeli*, 1929. There are several other useful biographies: E. T. Raymond, *Disraeli: Alien Patriot*, 1925; Edward G. Clark, *Benjamin Disraeli*, 1926; D. L. Murray, *Disraeli*, 1927; and André Maurois, *Disraeli*, 1928. See also M. E. Speare, *The Political Novel*, 1924. More recent studies are Paul Bloomfield, *Disraeli*, 1961; Robert Blake, *Disraeli*, 1967; Richard A. Levine, *Benjamin Disraeli*, 1968; and Neil Grant, *Benjamin Disraeli: Prime Minister Extraordinary*, 1969.

CONINGSBY

Type of work: Novel
Author: Benjamin Disraeli (1804–1881)
Type of plot: Political romance
Time of plot: 1832–1840
Locale: England and Paris
First published: 1844

Besides being a fictional history of young Harry Coningsby's fortunes, Disraeli uses this novel to trace the decline of the Whig and Tory factions in the British Parliament and the events leading to the birth of the Conservative Party. Many of the characters are readily identifiable with real personages of the time.

Principal Characters

The Marquis of Monmouth, a British nobleman opposed to reform, especially the Reform Bill of 1832.

Harry Coningsby, a liberal-minded young English nobleman, grandson of the Marquis of Monmouth. Disinherited for defying his grandfather on political grounds, he is eventually elected to Parliament. He marries Edith Millbank and after the death of his grandfather he inherits the Marquis' fortune indirectly.

Edith Millbank, the beautiful but shy daughter of a wealthy industrialist. Harry Coningsby falls in love with her, but her father refuses at first to permit the marriage. Later he relents and she is married to Coningsby.

Oswald Millbank, Edith's father. A wealthy manufacturer, he thinks England should be governed by an aristocracy of talent, rather than a hereditary aristocracy. He was at one time the fiancé of Coningsby's mother.

Oswald Millbank, the son of the industrialist of the same name. He is one of Coningsby's close friends and Edith's brother.

Lucretia, a young Italian noblewoman. She tries to attract Coningsby and his friend Sidonia. Failing in these attempts, she settles for marriage with the Marquis of Monmouth for his wealth. Her husband sends her away when she proves to be unfaithful.

Princess Colonna, Lucretia's stepmother. She is a strong supporter of young Coningsby in his early relations with his grandfather.

Sidonia, a wealthy young Jew, a friend of Coningsby. He is also a friend of the Millbank family. He is suspected, wrongly, by Coningsby of being a rival for Edith's hand in marriage.

Flora, a young actress befriended by Coningsby. She turns out to be the natural daughter of the Marquis of Monmouth. The marquis leaves her his fortune, but she in turn wills it to Coningsby when she dies.

Mr. Rigby, a member of Parliament who is supported by the Marquis of Monmouth. He is young Coningsby's caretaker.

Lord and
Lady Wallinger, relatives of Edith who take her to Paris, where Coningsby renews his acquaintance with Edith and falls in love with her.

The Story

Harry Coningsby was fourteen when he met his grandfather, the Marquis of Monmouth, for the first time. He had been placed in his grandfather's charge when he was still very young with the understanding that his widowed mother, a commoner, was never to see him again. He had been turned over, sight unseen, to the care of Mr. Rigby, a member of Parliament who sat for one of Lord Monmouth's ten boroughs.

Lord Monmouth, who preferred to live abroad, had returned to his native land in 1832 in order to help fight the Reform Bill. Hearing favorable reports of his grandson, he had ordered Mr. Rigby to bring the boy from Eton to Monmouth House. Unfortunately, young Coningsby was unable to put out of his mind thoughts of his mother, who had died when he was nine, and he burst into tears at the sight of his grandfather. Lord Monmouth, disgusted by that sign of weakness, ordered him to be led away. He thought to himself that the sentimental boy's future probably lay with the church.

Fortunately, the boy became friendly with the marquis' guests, princess Colonna and her stepdaughter, Lucretia. The princess passed on such glowing descriptions of Coningsby to his grandfather that they were on excellent terms by the time he returned to school.

At Eton one of Coningsby's close friends was Oswald Millbank, a manufacturer's son. When Coningsby left Eton in 1835 he went to explore Manchester's factories before going to Coningsby Castle to join his grandfather. During his journey he visited the Millbank mills. Oswald was abroad, but he was hospitably greeted by his friend's father. At the Millbank mansion Coningsby met beautiful but shy young Edith Millbank and learned from her Whig father that he favored the rise of a new force in government—a natural aristocracy of able men, not one composed of hereditary peers.

Before departing for Coningsby Castle, young Coningsby was tempted to inquire about the striking portrait of a woman which graced the dining-room wall. His host, much upset by his question, made a brusque, evasive answer.

Lord Monmouth, backing Mr. Rigby for reëlection to Pariament, had returned to his borough and scheduled an elaborate program of dances, receptions, and plays, to gain a following for his Conservative candidate. Princess Colonna and Lucretia were again his grandfather's guests. Coningsby had no need, however, to confine his attentions to them, for as Lord Monmouth's kinsman and possible heir he found himself much sought after. He found time also to encourage Flora, a member of the troupe of actors entertaining the marquis' guests. The girl was shy and suffering from stage fright.

Here Coningsby met Sidonia, a fabulously wealthy young Jew. Coningsby found his new friend impartial in his political judgments, not only because his fortune allowed him to be just but also because his religion disqualified him as a voter. Sidonia taught him, during their lengthy discussions, to look to the national character for England's salvation. He believed that the country's weakness lay in developing class conflicts.

Lucretia made a brief effort to attract Coningsby when she observed the favor, in which his grandfather held him, but before long she found Sidonia, a polished man of the world, more intriguing. But Sidonia was not to be captured. He was attracted by others' intellects, and Lucretia could not meet him on his own level.

After his holiday Coningsby went to Cambridge for his last years of study. During his first year there King William IV died and the Conservative cause fell in defeat. Mr. Rigby was, as he had been for many years, the candidate from his borough, and with the marquis to back him his victory seemed certain until Mr. Millbank entered the field. The manufacturer and the marquis had been enemies for many years, and their feud reached a climax when Millbank not only bought Hellingsley, an adjoining estate which Lord Monmouth had long coveted, but also defeated his lordship's candidate.

Prepared for the worst, the defeated Mr. Rigby went to Monmouth House, where the marquis was in residence. He was pleasantly disappointed, however, for his employer's thoughts were not on him. Lord Monmouth was preparing to marry Lucretia, who, if she could not have the man she desired, was determined at least to obtain power and riches through marriage.

A year after the wedding, Coningsby was invited to join his grandfather and his bride in Paris at Christmas time. Stopping at his banker's on his way through London, he was given a package of his mother's correspondence. In the packet was a locket, with an exact copy of the portrait he had seen at Millbank. It was a picture of his mother.

While visiting an art gallery in Paris with Sidonia, Coningsby again met Edith Millbank, who was traveling with her relatives, Lord and Lady Wallinger. Coningsby, who fell in love with her immediately, was distressed to hear reports that Sidonia intended to marry her. Finding the couple conversing on familiar terms one evening, he regretfully decided to withdraw from the scene. He returned to England.

Disappointed in love, Coningsby devoted himself to his studies for the remainder of his stay at Cambridge. Then, learning that Edith had not married and that Sidonia was no more than an old family friend, he went to Coningsby Castle in order to be near the Millbanks.

Coningsby spent every possible moment with Edith and her family during the next few weeks. When her father discovered the lovers' feelings, he asked Coningsby to leave. He would not, he explained, submit his daughter to the same fate the young man's mother had suffered at Lord Monmouth's hands. In this manner Coningsby learned that his mother had once been Mr. Millbank's fiancée.

Leaving Hellingsley, Coningsby went on a sea voyage from which he was called home by the marquis. Parliament faced another crisis, and Lord Monmouth had decided that Coningsby should stand as his candidate. Coningsby refused, for he was of the opinion that men should cut across party lines to establish recognition of the bond between property and labor.

The same day Lord Monmouth faced his rebellious grandson he separated from Lucretia, who had proved unfaithful.

The marquis died at Christmas of that year. Most of his fortune he left to Flora, who was his natural daughter. Coningsby was cut off with the interest on ten thousand pounds.

Deeply disappointed in his expectations, Coningsby gave up his clubs and most of his friends and began to study law. He had resigned himself to the prospect of years of drudgery when Mr. Millbank repented his decision. The manufacturer withdrew his candidacy in the 1840 election to back Coningsby as the Tory candidate. Mr. Rigby was his rival candidate, but he was easily defeated.

Not many months later Edith became Coningsby's bride and went with him to live at Hellingsley, their wedding present from Mr. Millbank. As a final blessing, though not an unmixed one, Flora, who had always been weak, died, leaving the fortune she had inherited to the man who had befriended her many years before at Coningsby Castle.

Critical Evaluation

Reading *Coningsby,* one feels that one is in the company of a genuine Insider, who can describe from firsthand experience the workings of the government, the life at court, even the mode of existence at Eton. (Actually, Disraeli wrote with the obsessive fascination of an Outsider who had to struggle to get inside.) Life among the very rich and very powerful is meticulously detailed for the pleasure of the reader; and although this was not Disraeli's purpose in writing *Coningsby,* it made the novel popular and has contributed to its lasting interest. Disraeli's avowed intention was to give a picture of the growth of the Conservative Party and to illustrate the change facing the new generation in the 1840's. He also wanted to educate the public concerning the true history and influence of the Jews in Western Europe.

Throughout the novel, Disraeli stresses the importance of "character," that is, the moral and intellectual makeup of an individual. Some people possess weak characters, others strong, and the incidents of life reveal these characters for what they are. Some men rise to an occasion while others are incapable of coping with a situation; thus, Disraeli implies, history is made. Character reveals itself as early as in a youth's school days; Coningsby and his compatriots show at Eton the traits which cling to them throughout their lives.

The subtitle (*The New Generation*) is important because the novel immortalizes the group in the 1840's which was nicknamed "Young England." This group, which looked to Disraeli for their inspiration, was hostile to the traditional, humdrum middle-class Conservatism; they were romantic and aristocratic, and looked to a golden past where the people and the nobility were united in an alliance supporting throne and Church. In Coningsby,

Disraeli's distrust of the growing industrial class is strongly evident, and lends force and direction to much of the narrative.

GEORGE ELIOT
Marian or Mary Ann Evans

Born: Near Nuneaton, England (November 22, 1819)
Died: Chelsea, London, England (December 22, 1880)

Principal Works

NOVELS: *Scenes from Clerical Life*, 1858 *(The Sad Fortunes of the Reverend Amos Barton, Mr. Gilfil's Love Story,* and *Janet's Repentance); Adam Bede,* 1859; *The Mill on the Floss,* 1860; *Silas Marner,* 1861; *Romola,* 1863; *Felix Holt, Radical,* 1866; *Middlemarch,* 1871–1872; *Daniel Deronda,* 1876.

NOVELLA: *The Lifted Veil,* 1859.

POEMS: *How Lisa Loved the King,* 1867; *The Spanish Gypsy,* 1868; *The Legend of Jubal,* 1870.

ESSAYS: *The Impressions of Theophrastus Such,* 1879.

TRANSLATION: Strauss's *Life of Jesus,* 1846.

George Eliot was a pen name used by Marian or Mary Ann Evans. She was born on November 22, 1819, at Arbury Farm, Warwickshire, in the parish of Chivers Coton, and was baptized at what has since become the famous Shepperton Church. Her mother was Christina Pearson. Her father was Robert Evans, a carpenter, builder, and agent. Part of her early life was spent at Griff, an ancient red brick house of considerable charm. She attended numerous schools, at one of which she became an intimate friend of Miss Lewis, with whom she exchanged letters for years and who did much to deepen her strong sense of religion. Thus at the age of seventeen she already had an excellent background of education when her mother's death in 1836 and her sister's marriage made it necessary that she return home to look after the house for her father. Meanwhile, however, she continued her study with lessons in Greek, Latin, Italian, and German. She was also an accomplished musician, though shy of appearing in public. When her father gave up his duties on the estate, he re-moved in 1841 to Coventry. Here at twenty-two she came under a new and liberal influence. Among her new circle of friends were Mr. and Mrs. Charles Bray and Charles Hennell. Both men were writers, Bray having already published *The Philosophy of Necessity* in 1841. Hennell was the author of *An Inquiry Concerning the Origin of Christianity* (1838). Such influences caused the girl to question the evangelical beliefs which had always been such a strong and wholesome influence on her life. In fact, her liberal attitude and her refusal to attend church caused a temporary rift with her stern father. However, a reconciliation was effected and she returned to church, continuing to live with him until his death in 1849, upon which she inherited a small income for life.

Thus far she had spent two years translating David Friedrich Strauss's *Life of*

Jesus, which was published in 1846 with the author's preface. Printed anonymously, the volume is said to have brought its author only twenty pounds. After her father's death she traveled for a time on the Continent, spending about a year in Geneva. Upon her return to England she accepted a position as assistant editor of the *Westminster Review* (1850–1853). During this period her distinguished circle of friends included James A. Froude, John Stuart Mill, Thomas Carlyle, Harriet Martineau, Herbert Spencer, and George Henry Lewes. The last of this group was serving then as the editor of *The Leader*. Evans was strongly attracted to Lewes, who was not living with his mentally ill wife at the time. Flying in the face of public opinion, these two formed a union which they regarded as the same as a marriage, despite the lack of legal sanction—an arrangement which lasted until Lewes' death in 1878.

Meanwhile she continued her scholastic pursuits, working mostly on translations and on articles for *The Leader*, the *Westminster Review*, and the *Saturday Review*. Her first attempt at fiction was *The Sad Fortunes of The Reverend Amos Barton*, the first story in her *Scenes from Clerical Life*. First published in *Blackwood's Magazine* upon the insistence of Lewes, who recognized their merit, these short novels later appeared in two volumes in 1858. Once started on fiction, Marian Evans had at last found her proper métier. In 1859 she published *Adam Bede* under the pen name of George Eliot, which she continued to use in all her later writings. The next year marked the publication of the three-volume edition of *The Mill on the Floss*, which she had first named *Sister Maggie*. By this time George Eliot had joined the ranks of the successful and popular novelists: *Silas Marner*, *Romola*, and *Felix Holt, Radical* were avidly read by a large and eager public. Her works were admired by Dickens, Bulwer-Lytton, Trollope, Mrs. Gaskell, Reade, and Thackeray.

The Mill on the Floss, *Adam Bede*, and *Silas Marner* were skillfully written pictures of provincial life, in some instances drawn from the author's own observations, background, and family. During a trip to Italy she had collected the material for *Romola*, a historical novel of the period of Savonarola. Remarkable for its pictures of Florentine life, its outstanding character is Tito Melema. *Felix Holt*, her only novel concerned with politics, hardly ranks with the other famous titles. Published in 1868, *The Spanish Gypsy*, a blank-verse poem containing drama and narrative, was intended (said its author) to show doctrines of duty and heredity. Her next novel was *Middlemarch: A Study of Provincial Life*, which marked a return to her earlier locale. Probably based on her early life in Coventry, it draws a remarkable picture of middle-class life in an English town. Her last novel, *Daniel Deronda*, was published in 1876.

Having attained notable success as a writer, she and Lewes could now enjoy scholastic pursuits as they wished. They traveled on the Continent and visited the English universities; they even purchased a home in the country. But this life came to an end with the death of Lewes in 1878. Deeply grieved, she finally finished *The Impressions of Theophrastus Such*, a collection of essays which came out in 1879. She also edited Lewes' unpublished works.

Before Lewes' death, the couple had known J. W. Cross, a New York banker. He had also been of considerable service to the widow in settling her affairs. Mutual ties of sympathy brought the pair together, and they were married in the spring of 1880 at St. George's Hanover Square. After returning to London from a trip to the Continent, Mrs. Cross caught a cold at a concert. She died in London on December 22, 1880.

George Eliot, for under this famous name she is known the world over, has been called the most distinguished English woman novelist. Certainly her novels, and particularly those dealing intimately with English life, reach a high point of wisdom, wit, and human understanding.

Bibliography

The standard edition of George Eliot is The Warwickshire Edition, 25 vols., 1908; included is the authorized *Life, Letters and Journals* [1884–1885] by J. W. Cross. For the most important modern biography see Gordon S. Haight, *George Eliot*, 1968. Older biographical studies of some merit include Sir Leslie Stephen, *George Eliot*, English Men of Letters Series, 1902; J. I. May, *George Eliot*, 1930; Anna T. Kitchel, *George Lewes and George Eliot: A Review of the Records*, 1933; and Anne Freemantle, *George Eliot*, 1933. Modern critical biographies of George Eliot begin in the 1940's with Gordon S. Haight, *George Eliot and John Chapman*, 1940; Gerald Bullett, *George Eliot: Her Life and Books*, 1948; Lawrence and Elizabeth Hanson, *Marian Evans and George Eliot*, 1952; John Holloway, *The Victorian Sage*, 1953; Robert Speaight, *George Eliot*, 1954; Bernard J. Paris, *Experiments in Life: George Eliot's Quest for Values*, 1965; F. W. Kenyon, *The Consuming Flame: The Story of George Eliot*, 1970; Ruby Redinger, *George Eliot: The Emergent Self*, 1975; and Lou-Ann Gaeddert, *All-in-All: A Biography of George Eliot*, 1976.

Early but important criticism on George Eliot includes the essays by Virginia Woolf, *The Common Reader*, 1925; and Lord David Cecil, *Early Victorian Novelists*, 1935. Modern criticism begins with F. R. Leavis, *The Great Tradition*, 1948. See also Joan Bennett, *George Eliot, Her Mind and Art*, 1948; Reva Stump, *Movement and Vision in George Eliot's Novels*, 1959; Barbara Hardy, *The Novels of George Eliot*, 1959; Jerome Thale, *The Novels of George Eliot*, 1959; Richard Stang, ed., *Discussions of George Eliot*, 1960; W. J. Harvey, *The Art of George Eliot*, 1961; David Daiches, *George Eliot*, 1963; Walter Allen, *George Eliot*, 1965; Gordon S. Haight, ed., *A Century of George Eliot Criticism*, 1965; U. C. Knoepflmacher, *George Eliot's Early Novels: The Limits of Realism*, 1969; Barbara Hardy, ed., *Critical Essays on George Eliot*, 1970; George R. Creeger, ed., *George Eliot: A Collection of Critical Essays*, 1970; Calvin Bedient, *Architects of the Self: Eliot, D. H. Lawrence and E. M. Forster*, 1972; William Baker, ed., *Critics on George Eliot*, 1973; Marghanita Laski, *George Eliot and her World*, 1973; Barbara Smalley, *George Eliot and Flaubert: Pioneers of the Modern Novel*, 1974; and Neil Roberts, *George Eliot: Her Beliefs and Her Art*, 1975.

See also Gordon S. Haight, ed., *The George Eliot Letters*, 7 vols., 1954–1955; and Thomas Pinner, ed., *Essays of George Eliot*, 1963. Special studies of George Eliot include Jerome Beaty, *Middlemarch from Notebook to Novel*, 1960; Henry Auster, *Local Habitations: Regionalism in the Early Novels of George Eliot*, 1970; Isadore G. Mudge and M. E. Sears, comps., *A George Eliot Dictionary: The Characters and Scenes of the Novels, Stories, and Poems, Alphabetically Arranged*, 1972; Patrick Swinden, ed., *George Eliot, Middlemarch: A Casebook*, 1972; Ian Adam, ed., *This Particular Web: Essays on Middlemarch*, 1975; and Phyllis Hartnoll, *Who's Who in George Eliot*, 1977.

ADAM BEDE

Type of work: Novel
Author: George Eliot (Mary Ann Evans, 1819–1880)
Type of plot: Domestic romance
Time of plot: 1799
Locale: England
First published: 1859

This novel reflects powerfully Eliot's belief in the interrelatedness of all aspects of human life. Her conviction that there is a cause and effect relationship in human behavior led her to create in her fiction a moral universe inhabited by men and women who are responsible for the consequences of even their smallest actions, and Adam Bede *probes with particular power and insight the motivations and complex interdependencies of its characters.*

Principal Characters

Adam Bede, an intelligent young carpenter respected by everyone in the village of Hayslope. He is honored when Arthur Donnithorne, the young heir to Donnithorne Chase, has Adam put in charge of managing the woods on the estate. Three weeks later, however, he sees Arthur kissing Hetty Sorrel, the young woman Adam loves. Knowing that Arthur will never marry Hetty, Adam becomes angry and fights with Arthur. As a result, Arthur leaves to join his regiment and Hetty, deserted and pregnant, promises to marry Adam. When Hetty runs off, Adam is in despair. Later he stands by Hetty through her trial for the murder of her child. A man who has judged others—his drunken father, Arthur, and Hetty—harshly, Adam learns tolerance and forgiveness. Still later he falls in love with Dinah Morris, a Methodist preacher, and marries her.

Dinah Morris, a young Methodist preacher, niece of Mrs. Poyser, a farmer's wife in Hayslope. A compassionate young woman, she aids those ill or in trouble. When not needed by friends or her family in Hayslope, she preaches at Snowfield, a grimy industrial town twenty miles away. Seth Bede, Adam's younger brother, is in love with her and proposes several times, but she says that her religious dedication takes precedence over any private emotion. She sympathizes with Hetty Sorrel and gets Hetty to confess that she had abandoned her illegitimate baby. Dinah later falls in love with Adam Bede and recognizes the claim of private emotions by marrying him.

Captain Arthur Donnithorne, the pleasant and impulsive young heir to Donnithorne Chase who tries to forward Adam Bede's career. Attracted to Hetty Sorrel, he does not intend to marry her. After he learns that she has given birth to and abandoned his baby, he recognizes that his acts can have fateful consequences for other people. In disgrace, he leaves Hayslope, not to return for seven years.

Hester Sorrel (Hetty), niece of Mr. Poyser, a dairy farmer. Fond of jewels and petty finery, Hetty is an easy prey for young Donnithorne. When she realizes Donnithorne will not marry her, she becomes engaged to Adam Bede; however, in the later stages of her pregnancy, she goes to Windsor to find Donnithorne, only to learn that his regiment has been shipped to Ireland. She then tries to find Dinah Morris, but on the way her baby is born. In confusion, she abandons the child, who is discovered dead. She is tried, found guilty, and sentenced to death, but Donnithorne, just back from Ireland, manages to have her sentence changed to deportation. She dies, a few years later, while on her way back to Hayslope.

Mrs. Rachel Poyser, a bustling and efficient farmer's wife. Although meddling and talkative, Mrs. Poyser is generous and loyal. She also stands up for her rights and refuses to let old Squire Donnithorne impose a new farming arrangement on her and her husband. She is pleased when her niece Dinah marries Adam Bede.

Martin Poyser, her husband, the owner and manager of prosperous Hall Farm. A genial and understanding man, Poyser is regarded as the leader of the farmers and tradesmen in Hayslope. He is fond of Adam Bede and feels strongly about the deceit practiced by Hetty and Arthur Donnithorne.

Seth Bede, Adam's younger brother. Although more dreamy, less efficient, and less powerful than Adam, Seth is a fine and generous young man. A Methodist, he is in love with Dinah.

Jonathan Burge, Adam's employer, the owner of a firm of carpenters and builders. Burge makes Adam his partner.

Mrs. Lisbeth Bede, the cantankerous yet devoted mother of Adam and Seth. She is strongly partial to Adam and encourages him to marry Dinah Morris.

The Reverend Adolphus Irwine, the rector of Broxton and vicar of Hayslope. He is a genial Anglican clergyman, little interested in doctrine or conversion, who is friendly with both Arthur Donnithorne and Adam Bede. Shocked by Arthur's desertion of Hetty, he does all he can for her at the trial.

Bartle Massey, the intelligent, misogynous local schoolmaster. He values Adam as his prize pupil and teaches him mathematics in night school.

Matthias Bede, the father of Adam and Seth. Once a skillful carpenter, he has become an indolent drunkard. While drunk, he falls into a creek and drowns.

Squire Donnithorne, Arthur's aged and parsimonious grandfather, the owner of Donnithorne Chase. He dies just before Hetty's trial.

Joshua Rann, a shoemaker of Hayslope who also serves as parish clerk and strongly supports the Anglican Church.

Ben Cranage (Wiry Ben), a carpenter who works in Burge's firm. An iconoclastic man and a spirited dancer, he is the only villager who prefers Seth to Adam.

Jim Salt, another carpenter who works for Burge.

Mum Taft, a silent carpenter who works for Burge.

Chad Cranage, Ben's cousin, a blacksmith who is strongly opposed to Methodism.

Bess Cranage (Chad's Bess), his daughter, a young woman fond of wearing finery. She is intermittently converted to Methodism.

Bess Salt (Timothy's Bess), her cousin, the wife of Jim Salt.

Will Maskery, the Hayslope wheelwright and one of the few local Methodists.

Mr. Casson, the rubicund landlord of the Donnithorne Arms.

Mary Burge, the daughter of Jonathan Burge. The townspeople expect her to marry Adam Bede.

Mrs. Irwine, Mr. Irwine's attractive and sophisticated mother.

Miss Lydia Donnithorne, Arthur's aunt and the daughter of old Squire Donnithorne. Adam's insistence on just payment for a screen he made for her causes the old Squire to become antagonistic to him.

Sarah Stone, a widow of Stoniton who takes in Hetty Sorrel and helps her when the baby is born.

John Olding, the farm laborer who discovers Hetty's dead child.

Marty Poyser, the Poysers' oldest, literal-minded son.

Tommy Poyser, the Poysers' second son, dependent and fond of his mother.

Charlotte Poyser (Totty), the Poysers' spoiled young daughter.

Martin Poyser Sr., the old father of Martin Poyser.

Alick, a shepherd on the Poyser farm.

Pym, Arthur Donnithorne's trusted servant.

Satchell, the Donnithorne steward; he suffers a stroke.

Mrs. Pomfret, a lady's maid at Donnithorne Chase who teaches Hetty to mend lace.

Mrs. Best, the housekeeper at Donnithorne Chase.

Mr. Craig, a gardener at Donnithorne Chase who is in love with Hetty.

Dolly, the Burge housekeeper.

Miss Kate Irwine, the older daughter of Mrs. Irwine.

Miss Anne Irwine, her younger sister, frequently subject to headaches.

Lisbeth Bede, the daughter of Dinah and Adam Bede.

Adam Bede, Jr., the son of Dinah and Adam Bede.

The Story

In the village of Hayslope at the close of the eighteenth century, there lived a young carpenter named Adam Bede. Tall and muscular, Adam was respected by everyone as a good workman and an honest and upright man. Even the young squire, Captain Arthur Donnithorne, knew Adam and liked him, and Adam in turn regarded the squire as his best friend.

Adam was, in fact, so good a workman that his employer, Mr. Jonathan Burge, the builder, would have welcomed him as his son-in-law and partner. But Adam had no eyes for Mary Burge; his only thoughts were of distractingly pretty Hetty Sorrel, niece of Mrs. Poyser, whose husband, Martin, ran the Hall Farm. Hetty, however, cared nothing for Adam. She was interested only in Captain Donnithorne, whom she had met one day in her aunt's dairy.

No one in Hayslope thought Hetty would make Adam a good wife, least of all Adam's mother, Lisbeth, who would have disapproved of any girl who threatened to take her favorite son from her. Her feelings of dependence upon Adam were intensified after her husband, Matthias Bede, drowned in Willow Brook while on his way home from the village inn.

In the meantime, Adam's brother Seth had fallen in love with the young Methodist preacher, Dinah Morris. Dinah was another niece of Mrs. Poyser, as unlike her cousin Hetty as Adam was unlike Seth. Hetty resembled nothing so much as a soft, helpless kitten, but Dinah was firm and serious in all things. One evening while she and Seth were walking home together from the village green, he had proposed marriage. Dinah sadly declined, saying she had dedicated her life to preaching the gospel.

When funeral services for Matthias Bede were held in Hayslope Church on the following Sunday, the thoughts of the congregation were on many things other than the solemn occasion they were attending. Adam's thoughts of Hetty blended with memories of his father. Hetty's thoughts were all of Captain Donnithorne, who had promised to make his appearance. She was disappointed, however, for Donnithorne had already departed with his regiment. When he returned on leave, the young squire celebrated his twenty-first birthday with a great feast to which nearly all of Hayslope was invited. Adam was singled out as a special guest to sit at Donnithorne's table. Adam's mother was both proud and jealous lest her son be getting more and more out of her reach.

One August night, exactly three weeks after the Donnithorne party, Adam was returning home from his work on the Donnithorne estate when he saw two figures in close embrace. They were Donnithorne and Hetty Sorrel. When Adam's dog barked, Hetty hurried away. Donnithorne, embarrassed, tried to explain that he had met the girl by chance and had stolen a kiss. Adam called his friend a scoundrel and a coward. They came to blows, and Donnithorne was knocked senseless. Adam, frightened that he might have killed the young squire in his rage, revived him and helped him to a nearby summerhouse. There he demanded that Donnithorne write a letter to Hetty telling her that he would not see her again.

The next day Donnithorne sent the letter to Hetty in Adam's care, thus placing the responsibility for its possible effect upon Adam himself. Adam gave her the letter while they were walking the following Sunday. When, in the privacy of her bedchamber, she read the letter, Hetty was in despair. Her dreams shattered, she thought only of finding some way out of her misery. Then in November Adam was offered a partnership in Mr. Burge's business, and he proposed to Hetty. Mr. and Mrs. Poyser were delighted to find that their niece was to marry the man they so much admired.

But the wedding had to be delayed until two new rooms could be added to the Bede house. In February, Hetty told her aunt she was going to visit Dinah Morris at Snowfield. Actually, however, she was determined to find Donnithorne. When she arrived at Windsor, where he was supposed to be stationed, she found that his regiment had been transferred to Ireland. Now in complete despair Hetty roamed about until in a strange village, and in the house of a widow named Sarah Stone, her child by Donnithorne was born. Frightened, Hetty wandered on, leaving her baby to die in a wood. Later, tortured by her conscience, she returned to find the child gone.

When his grandfather died, Donnithorne returned to Hayslope to discover that Hetty was in prison, charged with the murder of her child. He did everything in his power to free her, and Dinah Morris came to her prison cell and prayed with her to open up her heart and tell the truth. Finally poor Hetty broke down and confessed everything that had happened since she left Hayslope. She had not intended to kill her baby; in fact, she had not actually killed the child. She had considered taking her own life. Two days later, Donnithorne, filled with shame and remorse, brought a reprieve. Hetty's sentence was committed to deportation. A few years later she died on her way home. Donnithorne went to Spain.

Dinah Morris stayed with the Poysers often now, and gradually she and Adam were drawn to each other. But Dinah's heart was still set on her preaching. She left Hall Farm and went back to Snowfield. Adam Bede found his only satisfaction toiling at his workbench. Then one day his mother spoke again of Dinah and her gentle ways. Adam could wait no longer. He went to find her.

Critical Evaluation

In *Adam Bede,* George Eliot makes three important contributions to the development of the modern novel in her use of narrative technique and in her handling of both physical realism and psychological realism.

In her overall narrative, Eliot uses the third-person, omniscient-author voice; but she frequently sets aside this basic form to address the reader directly. Eliot uses these first-person comments to establish an intimacy with the reader —such as in the first paragraph of the novel—or to heighten the verisimilitude of the plot. In addition, she experiments quite successfully with stream-of-consciousness narration in chapters fifteen and sixteen. A few critics have faulted Eliot for what they see is inconsistency and choppiness resulting from shifts in narrative voice, but the only genuine disruption of narrative continuity occurs in chapter seventeen, where Eliot digresses from the story to explain her theory of art. Aside from this digression, most critics praise her ingenuity and her willingness to experiment with what were then avant-garde narrative techniques.

Physical realism deals with outward appearance; it attempts to represent scene, atmosphere, and characters exactly as they are observed in real life. Eliot is more successful with scene and atmosphere than with characters. Certainly she presents some vivid portraits, such as her description of the physical contrast between Adam and Seth, or her memorable introduction of Dinah Morris. Other character descriptions, however, are not as effective. Hetty, for example, is repeatedly compared to a kitten, and is so frequently described with words such as "dimpled," "round," "soft," "pink," and "white," that the effect is monotonous. By contrast, Eliot's treatment of scene and atmosphere is guided by a landscapist's eye for detail and a peasant's intuitive understanding of the relationship between weather and crops, producing what has been called the most natural setting in any English novel.

Psychological realism, focusing on the inner being of a character, derives from details about the thoughts and the emotions of characters: their personalities, their motives, their feelings about themselves, each other, and their surroundings. In this regard, Eliot's work is superb. She carefully plots the actions and motivations of her characters, never over-simplifying. Her forte is the "soul struggle" to which both Adam and Arthur Donnithorne fall victim —in which a character is torn in conscience between something he knows is morally and ethically right, and something that is tempting and attractive. Eliot's penetrating insights into Hetty's motives are another example of her grasp of psychological realism. In fact, Eliot has been hailed as one of the first psychological novelists, while *Adam Bede* is recognized as one of the earliest novels in the psychological tradition.

Bibliography

Adam, Ian. *George Eliot.* New York: Humanities, 1969, pp. 10–12, 34–37, 57–63, 85–88.

————. "The Structure of Realisms in *Adam Bede*," in *Nineteenth-Century Fiction.* XXX (September, 1975), pp. 127–149.

Colby, Robert A. "Miss Evans, Miss Mulock, and Hetty Sorrel," in *English Language Notes.* II (1965), pp. 206–211.

Creeger, George R. "An Interpretation of *Adam Bede*," in *Journal of English Literary History.* XXIII (September, 1956), pp. 218–238. Reprinted in *George Eliot: A Collection of Critical Essays.* Edited by George R. Creeger. Englewood Cliffs, N.J.: Prentice-Hall, 1970, pp. 86–106.

Diekhoff, J.S. "The Happy Ending of *Adam Bede*," in *Journal of English Literary History.* III (1936), pp. 221–227.

Edwards, Michael. "A Reading of *Adam Bede*," in *Critical Quarterly.* XIV (1972), pp. 205–218.

Fyfe, A.J. "The Interpretation of *Adam Bede*," in *Nineteenth-Century Fiction.* IX (1954), pp. 134–139.

Goode, John. "*Adam Bede*," in *Critical Essays on George Eliot.* Edited by Barbara Hardy. New York: Barnes & Noble, 1970, pp. 19–41.

Halperin, John. *Egoism and Self-Discovery in the Victorian Novel: Studies in the Ordeal of Knowledge in the Nineteenth Century.* New York: Burt Franklin, 1974, pp. 126–143.

Harvey, W.J. "The Treatment of Time in *Adam Bede*," in *Anglia.* LXXV (1957), pp. 429–440.

Herbert, Christopher. "Preachers and the Schemes of Nature in *Adam Bede*," in *Nineteenth-Century Fiction.* XXIX (1975), pp. 412–427.

Hussey, M. "Structure and Imagery in *Adam Bede*," in *Nineteenth-Century Fiction.* X (1955), pp. 115–129.

Jones, R.J.   *George Eliot*. Cambridge: Cambridge University Press, 1970, pp. 6–18.

Knoepflmacher, Ulrich Camillus.   *George Eliot's Early Novels: The Limits of Realism*. Berkeley: University of California Press, 1968, pp. 89–127.

————.   "The Post-Romantic Imagination: *Adam Bede*, Wordsworth and Milton," in *Journal of English Literary History*. XXXIV (December, 1967), pp. 518–540.

Kooiman-Van Middendorp, Gerarda M.   *The Hero in the Feminine Novel*. New York: Haskell House, 1966, pp. 96–123.

Krieger, Murray.   "*Adam Bede* and the Cushioned Fall: The Extenuation of Extremity," in *The Classic Vision: The Retreat from Extremity in Modern Literature*. Baltimore: Johns Hopkins Press, 1971, pp. 197–220.

Lerner, Laurence.   *The Truthtellers: Jane Austen, George Eliot, D.H. Lawrence*. New York: Schocken, 1967, pp. 33–40, 89–92, 141–143.

Liddell, Robert.   *The Novels of George Eliot*. New York: St. Martin's, 1977, pp. 33–50.

Martin, Bruce K.   "Rescue and Marriage in *Adam Bede*," in *Studies in English Literature, 1500–1900*. XII (1972), pp. 745–763.

Paterson, John.   "Introduction," in *Adam Bede* (Riverside Edition). Boston: Houghton Mifflin, 1968.

Roberts, Neil.   *George Eliot: Her Beliefs and Her Art*. Pittsburgh: University of Pittsburgh Press, 1975, pp. 63–83.

Thale, Jerome.   *The Novels of George Eliot*. New York: Columbia University Press, 1959, pp. 14–35.

Van Ghent, Dorothy.   "On *Adam Bede*," in *The English Novel: Form and Function*. New York: Holt, Rinehart and Winston, 1953, pp. 172–181. Reprinted in *A Century of George Eliot Criticism*. Edited by Gordon S. Haight. Boston: Houghton Mifflin, 1965, pp. 281–285.

Wiesenfarth, Joseph.   "*Adam Bede* and Myth," in *Papers on Language and Literature*. VIII (1972), pp. 39–52.

MIDDLEMARCH

Type of work: Novel
Author: George Eliot (Mary Ann Evans, 1819–1880)
Type of plot: Psychological realism
Time of plot: Nineteenth century
Locale: England
First published: 1871–1872

Middlemarch *is the most comprehensive and sweeping of George Eliot's novels and is usually considered her masterpiece. Structuring the book around four major plotlines—the story of Dorothea Brooke, the story of Lydgate's marriage, the history of Mary Garth, and the fall ofe banker Bulstrode—the author creates a dynamic pattern that encompasses an entire spectrum of life, attitudes, and events in early nineteenth century England.*

Principal Characters

Dorothea Brooke (Dodo), the sensitive and well-bred heroine who, in her desire to devote herself to something meaningful, marries an arid clerical scholar, Edward Casaubon. After Casaubon's death Dorothea, against the advice of friends and family, marries Will Ladislaw, an impulsive artist anad political thinker. Dorothea also befriends the progressive young doctor of Middlemarch, Tertius Lydgate.

The Rev. Edward Casaubon, the clergyman at Lowick, near Middlemarch. Casaubon is a gloomy, severe, unimaginative, and unsuccessful scholar who soon destroys Dorothea's enthusiasm. He is so jealous of Dorothea's friendship with his cousin, Will Ladislaw, that he adds a codicil to his will depriving Dorothea of his property should she marry his younger relative.

Will Ladislaw, Casaubon's young cousin, whose English heritage is mixed with alien Polish blood. Ladislaw is forceful, imaginative, energetic, and unconventional. An artist and a liberal, he represents an appropriate object of devotion for Dorothea, although many in Middlemarch are shocked by his views. After marrying Dorothea, he becomes a member of Parliament.

Celia Brooke, called **Kitty,** Dorothea's younger sister, a calm and placid young lady. She has none of Dorothea's aspirations, but a great deal of affection. She marries Sir James Chettam, a staid landowner.

Sir James Chettam, the owner of Freshitt Hall. A conservative gentleman, Sir James loves, first, Dorothea, then Celia, whom he happily weds.

Dr. Tertius Lydgate, a young doctor who comes to Middlemarch to establish a new hospital along progressive lines and to pursue scientific research. His noble career is destroyed by his improvident marriage and consequent debts.

Rosamond Vincy Lydgate, the beautiful, spoiled, and selfish daugher of the mayor of Middlemarch. Once married, she insists on living in a style that her husband, Dr. Lydgate, cannot afford.

Mr. Arthur Brooke, of Tipton Grange, the genial, rambling, and ineffectual uncle of Dorothea and Celia. His vague benevolence leads him to run for Parliament and he is soundly beaten.

Fred Vincy, Rosamond's brother, equally spoiled but less selfish. Although Fred gets into debt as a student and rebels against his family's plans to establish him as a respectable vicar, he later reforms, becomes an industrious farmer, and marries Mary Garth.

Mary Garth, the level-headed, competent daughter of a large, old-fashioned family securely tied to the land. She takes care of her aged, ailing relative, Peter Featherstone, before she marries Fred Vincy, her childhood sweetheart.

Mr. Walter Vincy, the mayor of Middlemarch and a prosperous manufacturer. Mr. Vincy, who loves comfort and genial company, is neither wise nor sympathetic in dealing with the problems his children face.

Mrs. Lucy Vincy, his wife, a warm, sentimental woman who spoils her children and has vast pretentions to social gentility. She objects to Fred's relationship with the simple, commonplace Garths.

Mr. Nicholas Bulstrode, the enormously pious, evangelical, wealthy banker of Middlemarch. Bulstrode uses his public morality and his money to control events in Middlemarch; however, the questionable connections and the shady early marriage that built up his fortune are eventually revealed.

Mrs. Harriet Vincy Bulstrode, his wife and the sister of Mayor Vincy. Although she seems to care only for social prestige, she loyally supports her husband after his disgrace.

Peter Featherstone, the wealthy aged owner of Stone Court. He tries to give his fortune to Mary Garth while she is nursing him during his final illness, but she refuses. His capricious will, cutting off all his grasping relatives, brings to Middlemarch strangers who precipitate Bulstrode's disgrace.

The Rev. Camden Farebrother, the vicar of St. Botolph's, a genial and casual clergyman. An expert whist-player and a friend of Lydgate, he is also, unsuccessfully, in love with Mary Garth.

The Rev. Humphrey Cadwallader, of Freshitt and Tipton, another genial clergyman who is particularly fond of fishing.

Mrs. Elinor Cadwallader, his wife, a talkative woman always acquainted with the latest scandal.

Caleb Garth, Mary's father, a stalwart and honest surveyor, land agent, and unsuccessful builder. He pays Fred Vincy's debts.

Susan Garth, his loyal, devoted wife, who educates her children with scholarly care and insight.

Mrs. Selina Plymdale, a Middlemarch gossip, friendly with the Vincys and the Bulstrodes.

Ned Plymdale, her son, a disappointed suitor of Rosamond Vincy.

Borthrop Trumbull, a florid auctioneer and cousin to old Featherstone.

John Raffles, an old reprobate and blackmailer who enters Middlemarch because he has married the mother of Featherstone's unexpected heir and periodically appears to get money. Just before he dies he reveals Bulstrode's sordid past.

Joshua Rigg, an enigmatic man who inherits Featherstone's house and money. He must adopt Featherstone's name as well.

Mr. Tyke, an evangelical clergyman, supported by Bulstrode and Lydgate for the post of chaplain at the new hospital.

Naumann, a German artist and a friend of Will Ladislaw.

Mrs. Jane Waule, the widowed, avaricious sister of Peter Featherstone.

Solomon Featherstone, her wealthy and equally avaricious brother.

Jonah Featherstone, another of Peter's disappointed brothers.

Mrs. Martha Cranch, a poor sister of

Peter Featherstone, also neglected in his will.

Tom Cranch, her unintelligent and unenterprising son.

Ben Garth, the active, athletic son of the Garths.

Letty Garth, the Garths' very bright younger daughter.

Alfred Garth, the son for whose engineering career the Garths are saving the money they use to pay Fred Vincy's debts.

Christy Garth, the Garths' oldest son, who becomes a scholar and tutor.

Mrs. Farebrother, the mother of the Reverend Mr. Camden.

Miss Henrietta Noble, her pious, understanding sister.

Miss Winifred Farebrother, Camden's sister, who idolizes him.

The Dowager Lady Chettam, Sir James's stiff and formal mother.

Arthur Chettam, the child of Sir James and Celia.

Sir Godwin Lydgate, of Quallingham in the north of England, Lydgate's distant and distinguished cousin. Rosamond appeals to him for money, but is denied.

Tantripp, Dorothea's faithful and understanding maid.

Mme. Laure, a French actress whom Lydgate once loved.

Dr. Sprague and
Dr. Minchin, conservative Middlemarch physicians.

Mr. Wrench, at first physician to the Vincys, replaced by the more competent and progressive Lydgate.

Mr. Standish, the local lawyer who represents Peter Featherstone.

Mr. Mawmsey, a Middlemarch grocer.

Mrs. Mawmsey, his wife, a Middlemarch gossip.

Harry Toller, a local brewer.

Miss Sophy Toller, his daughter, who finally marries Ned Plymdale.

Edwin Larcher, a local businessman.

Mrs. Larcher, his wife, a local gossip.

Mr. Bambridge, a horse dealer who swindles Fred Vincy.

Mr. Horrock, his friend.

Mr. Hawley, a local citizen who frequently comments on people and events.

Mr. Chichely, another local citizen.

Dagley, an insolent farmer on Arthur Brooke's land.

Pinkerton, Mr. Brooke's political opponent in the election for Parliament.

The Story

Dorothea Brooke and her younger sister, Celia, were young women of good birth, who lived with their bachelor uncle at Tipton Grange near the town of Middlemarch. So serious was Dorothea's cast of mind that she was reluctant to keep jewelry she had inherited from her dead mother, and she gave all of it to her sister. Upon reconsideration, however, she did keep a ring and bracelet.

At a dinner party where Edward Casaubon, a middle-aged scholar, and Sir James Chettam both vied for her attention, she was much more attracted to the serious-minded Casaubon. Casaubon must have had an inkling that his chances with Dorothea were good, for the next morning he sought her out. Celia, who did not like his complexion or his moles, escaped to other interests.

That afternoon Dorothea, contemplating the wisdom of the scholar, was walking and by chance encountered Sir James; he, in love with her, mistook her silence for agreement and supposed she might love him in return.

When Casaubon made his proposal of marriage by letter, Dorothea accepted him at once. Mr. Brooke, her uncle, thought Sir James a much better match; Dorothea's acceptance merely confirmed his bachelor views that women were difficult to understand. He decided not to interfere in her plans, but Celia felt that the event would be more like a funeral than a marriage, and frankly said so.

Casaubon took Dorothea, Celia, and Mr. Brooke to see his home so that Dorothea might order any necessary changes. Dorothea, intending in all things to defer to Casaubon's tastes, said she would make no changes in the house. During the visit Dorothea met Will Ladislaw, Casaubon's second cousin, who seemed to be hardly in sympathy with his elderly cousin's marriage plans.

While Dorothea and her new husband were traveling in Italy, Tertius Lydgate, an ambitious and poor young doctor, was meeting pretty Rosamond Vincy, to whom he was much attracted. Fred Vincy, Rosamond's brother, had indicated that he expected to come into a fine inheritance when his uncle, Mr. Featherstone, should die. Vincy, meanwhile, was pressed by a debt he was unable to pay.

Lydgate became involved in petty local politics. When the time came to choose a chaplain for the new hospital of which Lydgate was the head, the young doctor realized that it was to his best interest to vote in accordance with the wishes of Nicholas Bulstrode, an influential banker and founder of the hospital. A clergyman named Tyke received the office.

In Rome, Ladislaw encountered Dorothea and her middle-aged husband. Dorothea had begun to realize too late how pompous and incompatible she found Casaubon. Seeing her unhappiness, Ladislaw first pitied and then fell in love with his cousin's wife. Unwilling to live any longer on Casaubon's charity, Ladislaw announced his intention of returning to England and finding some kind of gainful occupation.

When Fred Vincy's note came due, he tried to sell a horse at a profit but the animal turned out to be vicious. Caleb Garth, who had signed his note, now stood to lose a hundred and ten pounds because of Fred's inability to raise the money. Fred fell ill, and Lydgate was summoned to attend him. Lydgate used his professional calls to further his suit with Rosamond.

Dorothea and her husband returned from Rome in time to hear of Celia's engagement to Sir James Chettam. Will Ladislaw included a note to Dorothea in a letter he wrote to Casaubon. This attention precipitated a quarrel which was followed by Casaubon's serious illness. Lydgate, who attended him, urged him to give up his studies for the time being. To Dorothea, Lydgate confided that Casaubon had a weak heart and must be guarded from all excitement.

Meanwhile all the relatives of old Mr. Featherstone were waiting impatiently for his death, but he hoped to circumvent their desires by giving his fortune to Mary Garth, daughter of the man who had signed Fred Vincy's note. When she refused it, he fell into a rage and died soon afterward. When his will was read, it was learned he had left nothing to his relatives; most of his money was to go to a Joshua Riggs, who was to take the name of Featherstone, and a part of his fortune was to endow the Featherstone Almshouses for old men.

Plans were made for Rosamond's marriage with Lydgate. Fred Vincy was ordered to prepare himself finally for the ministry, since he was to have no inheritance from his uncle. Mr. Brooke, having gone into politics, enlisted the help of Ladislaw in publishing a liberal paper. Mr. Casaubon had come to dislike Ladislaw intensely after his cousin had rejected further financial assistance, and he had forbidden Ladislaw to enter his house.

Casaubon died suddenly. A codicil to his will gave Dorothea all of his property as long as she did not marry Ladislaw. This strange provision caused Dorothea's friends and relatives some concern because if publicly given out, it would appear that Dorothea and Ladislaw had been indiscreet.

Mr. Brooke, on the advice of his Tory friends, gave up his liberal newspaper and thus cut off his connection with Ladislaw. The latter realized that Dorothea's family was in some way trying to separate him from Dorothea but he refused to be disconcerted about the matter. He resolved to stay on in Middlemarch until he was ready to leave. When he heard of the codicil to Casaubon's will, he was more than ever determined to remain so that he could eventually disprove the suspicions of the village concerning him and Dorothea.

Meanwhile Lydgate and Rosamond had married, and the doctor had gone deeply in debt to furnish his house. When he found that his income did not meet his wife's spendthrift habits, he asked her to help him economize. He and his wife began to quarrel. His practice and popularity decreased.

A disreputable man named Raffles appeared in Middlemarch. Raffles knew that Ladislaw's grandfather had amassed a fortune as a receiver of stolen goods and that Nicholas Bulstrode, the highly respected banker, had once been the confidential clerk of Ladislaw's ancestor. More than that, Bulstrode's first wife had been his employer's widow. Upon money inherited from her, money which should have gone to Ladislaw's mother, Bulstrode had built his own fortune.

Already blackmailed by Raffles, Bulstrode reasoned that the scoundrel would tell Ladislaw the whole story. To forestall trouble, he sent for Ladislaw and offered him an annuity of five hundred pounds and liberal provision in his will. Ladislaw, feeling that his relatives had already tainted his honor, refused, unwilling to be associated in any way with the unsavory business. Deciding to leave Middlemarch, Ladislaw went to London without the assurance that Dorothea loved him.

Lydgate drifted deeper into debt. When he wished to sell what he could and take cheaper lodgings, Rosamond managed to make him hold on, to keep up the pretense of prosperity a little longer. At the same time Bulstrode gave up his interest in the new hospital and withdrew his financial support.

Faced at last with the seizure of his goods, Lydgate went to Bulstrode and asked for a loan. The banker advised him to seek aid from Dorothea and abruptly ended the conversation. But when Raffles, in the last stages of alcoholism, returned to Middlemarch and Lydgate was called in to attend him, Bulstrode, afraid the doctor would learn the banker's secret from Raffles' drunken ravings, changed his mind and gave Lydgate a check for a thousand pounds. The loan came in time to save Lydgate's goods and reputation. When Raffles died, Bulstrode felt at peace at last. But it soon became common gossip that Bulstrode had given money to Lydgate and that Lydgate had attended Raffles in his final illness. Bulstrode and Lydgate were publicly accused of malpractice in Raffles' death. Only Dorothea took up Lydgate's defense. The rest of the town was busy with gossip over the affair. Rosamond was anxious to leave Middlemarch to avoid public disgrace. Bulstrode also was anxious to leave town after his secret, which Raffles had told while drunk in a neighboring village, became known. But he became ill and his doctors would not permit him to leave his bed.

Dorothea, sympathetic with Lydgate, determined to give her support to the hospital and to try to convince Rosamond that the only way Lydgate could recover his honor was by remaining in Middlemarch. Unfortunately, she came upon Will Ladislaw, to whom poor Rosamond was pouring out her grief. Afraid Rosamond was involved with Ladislaw, Dorothea left abruptly. Angered at the false position Rosamond had put him in, Ladislaw explained that he had always loved Dorothea, but from a distance. When Dorothea forced herself to return to Lydgate's house on the following morning, Rosamond told her of Ladislaw's declaration. Dorothea realized she was willing to give up Casaubon's fortune for Ladislaw's affection.

In spite of the protests of her family and friends, they were married several weeks later and went to London to live. Lydgate and Rosamond lived together with better understanding and prospects of a happier future. Fred Vincy became engaged to Mary Garth, with whom he had long been in love. For a time Dorothea's family disregarded her, but they were finally reconciled after Dorothea's son was born and Ladislaw was elected to Parliament.

Critical Evaluation

Modestly subtitled "A Study in Provincial Life," George Eliot's *Middlemarch* has long been recognized as a work of great psychological and moral penetration. Indeed, the novel has been compared with Tolstoy's *War and Peace* and Thackeray's *Vanity Fair* for its nearly epic sweep and its perspective of early nineteenth century history. Yet these comparisons are partly faulty. Unlike *War and Peace, Middlemarch* lacks a philosophical bias, a grand *Weltanschauung* that oversees the destinies of nations and generations. And unlike *Vanity Fair,* Eliot's novel is not neatly moralistic. In fact, much of *Middlemarch* is morally ambiguous, in the modern sense of the term. Eliot's concept of plot and character derives from psychological rather than philosophical or social necessity. This is another way of saying that *Middlemarch*, despite its Victorian trappings of complicated plot and subplot, its slow development of character, accumulated detail concerning time and place, its social density is—in many other respects—a "modern" novel that disturbs as well as comforts the reader.

At the height of her powers, George Eliot published *Middlemarch* in eight books, from December 1871 to December 1872, eight years before her death. She had already achieved a major reputation with *Adam Bede* (1859), *The Mill on the Floss* (1860), and *Silas Marner* (1861). But her most recent fiction, *Felix Holt, Radical* (1866), and *The Spanish Gypsy* (1868), both inferior to her best writing, had disappointed her public. *Middlemarch*, however, was received with considerable excitement and critical acclaim. Eliot's publisher, Blackwood, was so caught up with the action, as he received chapters of her novel by mail, that he wrote back to her asking questions about the fates of the characters, as though they were real people with real histories. As a matter of fact, Eliot researched the material for her novel scrupulously. Her discussion of the social climate in rural England directly before the passage of the Reform Bill of 1832 is convincingly detailed; she accurately describes the state of medical knowledge during Lydgate's time; and she treats the dress, habits, and speech of Middlemarch impeccably, creating the metaphor of a complete world, a piece of provincial England that is a microcosm of the greater world beyond.

Yet the theme of the novel itself revolves around the slenderest of threads: the mating of "unimportant" people. This theme, which engages the talents of other great writers as well—Jane Austen, Thomas Hardy, Henry James, D. H. Lawrence—allows George Eliot scope to examine the whole range of human nature. She is concerned with the mating of lovers, because they are most vulnerable in love, most nearly the victims of their romantic illusions. Each of the three sets of lovers in *Middlemarch*—Dorothea Brooke/Edward Casaubon/Will Ladislaw; Rosamond Vincy/Tertius Lydgate; and Mary Garth/Fred Vincy—mistake illusion for reality. Eventually all come to understand themselves better, whether or not they are completely reconciled with their mates. Each undergoes a sentimental education, a discipline of the spirit that teaches the heart its limitations.

Paradoxically, the greater capacity Eliot's characters have for romantic self-deception, the greater is their suffering and subsequent tempering of spirit. Mary Garth, plain, witty, honest, is too sensible to arouse our psychological curiosity to the same degree that we are interested in the proud Dorothea, rash Ladislaw, pathetic Casaubon, ambitious Lydgate, or pampered Rosamond. Mary loves simply, directly. Fred, her childhood sweetheart, is basically a good lad who must learn from his own misfortunes the lessons of thrift and perseverance. He "falls" in class, from that of an idle landowner to one of a decent but socially inferior manager of property. In truth, what he seems to lose in social prominence he more than recovers in the development of his moral character. Moreover, he wins as a mate the industrious Mary, who will strengthen his resolve and make of him an admirable provider like her father Caleb.

Dorothea, on the other hand, more idealistic and noble-hearted than Mary, chooses the worst possible mate as her first husband. Edward Casaubon, thirty years her senior, is a dull pedant, cold, hopelessly ineffectual as a scholar, absurd as a lover. Despite his intellectual pretentions, he is too timid, fussy, and dispirited ever to complete his masterwork, "A Key to All Mythologies." Even the title of his project is an absurdity. He conceals as long as possible his "key" from Dorothea, fearing that she will expose him as a sham. Yet it is possible that she might have endured the disgrace of her misplaced affection were Casaubon only more tender, reciprocating her own tenderness and self-sacrifice. But Casaubon, despotic to the last, tries to blight her spirit when he is alive and, through his will, to restrict her freedom when he is dead.

Dorothea's second choice of a mate, Will Ladislaw is very nearly the opposite of Casaubon. A rash, sometimes hypersensitive lover, he is capable of intense affection, above all of self-sacrifice. He is a worthy suitor for Dorothea, who finds greatness in his ardor, if not his accomplishments. Yet Will, allowing for his greater vitality, is after all a logical successor to Casaubon. Dorothea had favored the elderly scholar because he was unworldly, despised by the common herd. In her imagination he seemed a saint of intellect. In time she comes to favor Will because he is also despised by most of the petty-minded bigots of Middlemarch, because he has suffered from injustice; and because he seems to her a saint of integrity. A Victorian St. Theresa, Dorothea is passive, great in aspiration rather than deed. Psychologically she requires a great object for her own self-sacrifice, and therefore chooses a destiny that will allow her the fullest measure of heroism.

Tertius Lydgate, quite the opposite, is a calculating, vigorous, ambitious young physician who attempts to move others to his own iron will. His aggressive energy contrasts with Dorothea's passiveness. However, like her, he is a victim of romantic illusion. He believes that he can master, through his intelligence and determination, those who possess power. Nevertheless, his choice of a mate, Rosamond Vincy, is a disastrous miscalculation. Rosamond's fragile beauty conceals a petulant, selfish will equal to his own. She dominates him through her own weakness rather than strength of character. Insensitive except to her own needs, she offers no scope for Lydgate's sensitive intelligence. In his frustration, he can only battle with himself. He comes to realize that he is defeated not only in his dreams of domestic happiness but in his essential judgment of the uses of power.

For George Eliot, moral choice does not exist in a sanctified vacuum; it requires an encounter with power. To even the least sophisticated dwellers in Middlemarch, power is represented by wealth and status. As the widow Mrs. Casaubon, Dorothea's social prestige rests upon her personal and inherited fortune. When she casts aside her estate under Casaubon's will to marry Ladislaw, she loses also a great measure of status. At the same time, she acquires moral integrity, a superior virtue for Eliot. Similarly, when Mary Garth rejects Mr. Featherstone's dying proposition to seize his wealth before his relatives make a shambles of his will, she chooses morally, justly, and comes to deserve the happiness that she eventually wins. As for Lydgate, whose moral choices are most nearly ambiguous, he returns Bulstrode's bribe to save himself from a social embarrassment, but his guilt runs deeper than mere miscalculation. He has associated himself, first through his choice of Tyke instead of the worthier Farebrother as vicar, with Bulstrode's manipulation of power. Lydgate's moral defeat is partial, for at least he understands the extent of his compromise with integrity. Bulstrode's defeat is total, for he loses both wealth and social standing. As for Middlemarch, that community of souls is a small world, populated with people of good will and bad, mean spirits and fine, and is the collective agent of moral will. After all, it is the town that endures, the final arbiter of moral judgment in a less than perfect world.

Bibliography

Adam, Ian. *George Eliot.* New York: Humanities, 1969, pp. 21–28, 45–52, 71–77, 97–104.

Anderson, Quentin. "George Eliot in *Middlemarch*," in *The Pelican Guide to English Literature*, Volume VI. Edited by Boris Ford. New York: Penguin Books, 1958, pp. 274–293. Reprinted in *George Eliot: A Collection of Critical Essays.* Edited by George R. Creeger. Englewood Cliffs, N.J.: Prentice-Hall, 1970, pp. 141–160. Also reprinted in *A Century of George Eliot Criticism.* Edited by Gordon S. Haight. Boston: Houghton Mifflin, 1965, pp. 313–324.

Armstrong, Isobel. "*Middlemarch*: A Note on George Eliot's 'Wisdom,' " in *Critical Essays on George Eliot.* Edited by Barbara Hardy. New York: Barnes & Noble, 1970, pp. 116–132.

Beaty, J. Middlemarch *from Notebook to Novel: A Study of George Eliot's Creative Method.* Urbana: University of Illinois Press, 1960.

Blake, Kathleen. "*Middlemarch* and the Woman Question," in *Nineteenth-Century Fiction.* XXXI (December, 1976), pp. 285–312.

Carroll, David R. "Unity Through Analogy: An Interpretation of *Middlemarch*," in *Victorian Studies.* II (1959), pp. 305–316.

Coles, Robert. *Irony in the Mind's Life: Essays on Novels by James Agee,*

Elizabeth Bowen, and George Eliot. Charlottesville: University Press of Virginia, 1974, pp. 154–204.

Daiches, David. *George Eliot:* Middlemarch. Great Neck, N.Y.: Barron's, 1963.

Ferris, Sumner J. *"Middlemarch*: George Eliot's Masterpiece," in *From Jane Austen to Joseph Conrad: Essays Collected in Memory of James T. Hillhouse.* Edited by Robert C. Rathburn and Martin Steinman. Minneapolis: University of Minnesota Press, 1958, pp. 194–207.

Hagan, John. *"Middlemarch*: Narrative Unity in the Story of Dorothea Brooke," in *Nineteenth-Century Fiction.* XVI (June, 1961), pp. 17–31.

Hardy, Barbara. *"Middlemarch* and the Passions," in *This Particular Web: Essays on* Middlemarch. Edited by Ian Adam. Toronto: University of Toronto Press, 1975, pp. 3–21.

Harvey, W.J. "The Intellectual Background of the Novel: Casaubon and Lydgate," in Middlemarch: *Critical Approaches to the Novel.* Edited by Barbara Hardy. New York: Oxford University Press, 1967, pp. 25–37. Reprinted in *The Victorian Novel: Modern Essays in Criticism.* Edited by Ian Watt. New York: Oxford University Press, 1971, pp. 311–323.

Jones, R.T. *George Eliot.* Cambridge: Cambridge University Press, 1970, pp. 57–96.

Kettle, Arnold. *An Introduction to the English Novel,* Volume I. London: Hutchinson, 1951, pp. 171–190.

Kitchel, Anna Theresa. *Quarry for* Middlemarch. Berkeley: University of California Press, 1950.

Knoepflmacher, Ulrich Camillus. *Laughter and Despair: Readings in Ten Novels of the Victorian Era.* Berkeley: University of California Press, 1971, pp. 168–201.

Liddell, Robert. *The Novels of George Eliot.* New York: St. Martin's, 1977, pp. 123–161.

Lyons, Richard S. "The Method of *Middlemarch,*" in *Nineteenth-Century Fiction.* XXI (June, 1966), pp. 35–47.

Roberts, Neil. *George Eliot: Her Beliefs and Her Art.* Pittsburgh: University of Pittsburgh Press, 1975, pp. 145–182.

Schorer, Mark. "Fiction and the 'Matrix of Analogy,' " in *Kenyon Review.* XI (Autumn, 1949), pp. 539–559. Reprinted in *A Century of George Eliot Criticism.* Edited by Gordon S. Haight. Boston: Houghton Mifflin, 1965, pp. 270–278.

————. "The Structure of the Novel: Method, Metaphor and Mind," in Middlemarch: *Critical Approaches to the Novel.* Edited by Barbara Hardy. New York: Oxford University Press, 1967, pp. 12–24.

Stallknecht, Newton P.   "Resolution and Independence: A Reading of *Middlemarch*," in *Twelve Original Essays on Great English Novels*. Edited by Charles Shapiro. Detroit: Wayne State University Press, 1960, pp. 125–152.

Thale, Jerome,   *The Novels of George Eliot*. New York: Columbia University Press, 1959, pp. 106–120.

Willey, Frederick.   "Appearance and Reality in *Middlemarch*," in *Southern Review*. V (1969), pp. 419–435.

Williams, Raymond.   *The English Novel: From Dickens to Lawrence*. London: Chatto and Windus, 1970, pp. 87–94.

THE MILL ON THE FLOSS

Type of work: Novel
Author: George Eliot (Mary Ann Evans, 1819–1880)
Type of plot: Domestic realism
Time of plot: Nineteenth century
Locale: England
First published: 1860

George Eliot probably identified with Maggie Tulliver, the heroine of The Mill on the Floss, *and that gives the novel much of its immediacy and charm, especially in the early chapters. Like Eliot, Maggie is a girl of deep sensitivity, intellectual capacity, and spiritual longings. But, unlike her creator, Maggie can never realize those inclinations and talents in the provincial, male-dominated environment that surrounds and finally destroys her.*

Principal Characters

Mrs. Jane Glegg, the sister of Mrs. Tulliver. She is wealthy, parsimonious, and the proudest of the Dodson sisters. Although she dislikes Maggie, she defends her after the episode with Stephen Guest.

Mrs. Sophy Pullet, another of the Dodson sisters. She is wealthy and sentimental, crying copiously at every misfortune.

Mrs. Susan Deane, another Dodson sister, the pale and ailing mother of Lucy. She and Tulliver die about the same time.

Mr. Deane, her husband, who has worked his way up in the prosperous firm of Guest and Co., bankers, ship owners, and tradesmen. Although rather pompous about his achievements, he helps Tom get established in his firm.

Mrs. Gritty Moss, Mr. Tulliver's sister, a kind, poor woman with eight children. She has Maggie's ardent nature, although she lacks her niece's intelligence.

Mr. Moss, her husband, an unsuccessful farmer.

Mr. Glegg, husband of Jane Glegg, a wealthy, retired, prudent gentleman who had made a fortune in the wool business.

Mr. Pullet, husband of Sophy Pullet, a tiny, wealthy gentleman farmer who sucks lozenges throughout all family discussions.

Bob Jakin, Tom Tulliver's boyhood friend. He becomes Tom's partner in numerous investments.

John Wakem, the father of Philip and a lawyer in St. Ogg's. Although he does not hate Mr. Tulliver initially, Tulliver's frequent insults cause him to enjoy the family's downfall. His love for his son, however, later leads him to approve of the possibility of Philip's marrying Maggie.

The Rev. Walter Stelling, the owner of King's Lorton, the school attended by Tom Tulliver and Philip Wakem. He regards Tom as hopelessly stupid.

Luke Moggs, the head miller at Dorlcote Mill, fond of Maggie and entirely loyal to the Tullivers.

Mr. Riley, a local auctioneer, surveyor, and engineer who dies, leaving Mr. Tulliver with his debts.

The Rev. Dr. Kenn, rector of St. Ogg's, a clergyman sympathetic toward Maggie.

Mrs. Kenn, his wife, who runs a charity bazaar in St. Ogg's.

Mr. Poulter, the village schoolmaster.

Mr. Pivart, the owner of land near Dorlcote Mill who wishes to irrigate his land and is sued unsuccessfully by Mr. Tulliver.

Mr. Dix, another gentleman unsuccessfully sued by Mr. Tulliver.

Mr. Furley, the gentleman who owns the mortgage on Mr. Tulliver's land and transfers it to lawyer Wakem.

Mr. Gore, a scheming lawyer.

Mr. Jetsome, the young manager of the mill under Wakem after Tulliver dies. While drunk, he is pitched off his horse and severely injured.

Prissy Jakin, Bob Jakin's tiny "Dutch doll" wife.

Mrs. Jakin, Bob's massive mother.

Maggie Tulliver, the impetuous and generous young heroine. Regarded as wild and gipsy-like by most of her respectable relatives, the sensitive and imaginative Maggie does not fit into the provincial society in and near St. Ogg's on the River Floss. She worships her brother Tom, who judges her harshly and thinks her unreliable. She loves Philip Wakem, the crippled son of her father's worst enemy, but must promise never to see him. Despite her feeling for Philip and her love for her cousin, Lucy Deane, Maggie is strongly attracted to her cousin's fiancé, Stephen Guest. Stephen persuades her to go boating, but they neglect their destination and are forced to spend the night on a freighter that rescues them. Almost everyone in St. Ogg's, her brother included, thinks Maggie responsible and regards her as an evil and designing woman. In the final scene, during a flood, Maggie takes a boat to rescue Tom, who is at the family mill. The two are reconciled before the raging river drowns them.

Tom Tulliver, Maggie's brother. Although never quick at school, Tom assumes financial responsibility for the family when he is only sixteen, after the father has lost his mill and home through a series of lawsuits. Tom pledges to follow his father in having nothing to do with the Wakem family. He works hard and, through his industry and careful investments in partnership with Bob Jakin, pays off his father's debts and eventually gets the mill back. Somewhat priggish, Tom judges others severely, but he is also generous to his mother and sister.

Edward Tulliver, the father of Maggie and Tom and the owner of Dorlcote Mill, near St. Ogg's on the River Floss. An emotional and hot-tempered man, Tulliver engages in several lawsuits which, in addition to other financial reverses, cause him to lose his mill. Tulliver must swallow his pride and work in the mill as the hated Wakem's manager. When Tom finally earns the money to pay off his father's debts, Tulliver meets Wakem and thrashes him. The exertion produces Tulliver's second stroke and he dies. He is always partial to his clever and imaginative daughter Maggie.

Mrs. Elizabeth Tulliver (Bessy), Edward's wife, proud of her birth as a Dodson and grieved that her husband's temper and improvidence cause her to lose her home and furnishings. She is dependent on the advice and opinions of her more prosperous sisters. Her pleading visit to Wakem inadvertently causes him to plan to buy the mill when Tulliver is bankrupt. Regarding Maggie as wild and unladylike, she is partial to her son Tom.

Philip Wakem, a lawyer's son, humpbacked as the result of a childhood accident. An excellent scholar and a talented artist, he loves Maggie from the time he first meets her, for she does not judge him by his infirmity. He hopes to marry Maggie despite family objections and her temporary attraction to Stephen Guest.

Lucy Deane, Maggie's blonde and pretty cousin. She and Maggie go to boarding school together and become great friends. Maggie confesses her feeling for Philip Wakem to Lucy. At the end, Lucy understands that Maggie was essentially blameless in the boating escapade with Stephen Guest and she forgives Maggie. She marries Stephen after Maggie is dead.

Stephen Guest, the handsome son of the wealthiest and most socially prominent family in St. Ogg's. Although engaged to Lucy, he is so attracted to Maggie that he pleads with her to marry him. After the boating trip, when Maggie is in disgrace, he goes off to Holland.

The Story

Dorlcote Mill stood on the banks of the River Floss near the village of St. Ogg's. Owned by the ambitious Mr. Tulliver, it provided a good living for him and his family, but he dreamed of the day when his son Tom would climb to a higher station in life.

Mrs. Tulliver's sisters, who had married well, criticized Mr. Tulliver's unseemly ambition and openly predicted the day when his air castles would bring himself and his family to ruin. Aunt Glegg, richest of the sisters, held a note on his property, and when he quarreled with her over his plans for Tom's education, Mr. Tulliver determined to borrow the money and repay her.

For Tom, who had inherited the placid arrogance of his mother's people, life was not difficult. He was resolved to be just in all his dealings and to deliver punishment to whomever it was due. His sister Maggie grew up with an imagination beyond her years of understanding. Her aunts predicted she would come to a bad end, because she was tomboyish, dark-skinned, dreamy, and indifferent to their wills. Frightened by ill luck in her attempts to please her brother Tom, her cousin Lucy, and her mother and aunts, Maggie ran away, determined to live with the gypsies. But she was glad enough to return. Her father scolded her mother and Tom for abusing her. Her mother was sure Maggie would come to a bad end because of the way Mr. Tulliver humored her.

Tom's troubles began when his father sent him to study at Mr. Stelling's school. Having little interest in spelling, grammar, or Latin, Tom found himself wishing he were back at the mill, where he might dream of someday riding a horse like his father's and giving orders to people around him. Mr. Stelling was convinced that Tom was not only obstinate but also stupid. Returning home for the Christmas holidays, Tom learned that Philip Wakem, son of a lawyer who was his father's enemy, would also enter Mr. Stelling's school.

Philip Wakem was a cripple, and so Tom was not able to beat him up as he should have liked at first. Philip could draw, and he knew Latin and Greek. After they overcame their initial reserve, the two boys became useful to one another. Philip admired Tom's arrogance and self-possession, and Tom needed Philip's knowledge to help him in his studies. But their fathers' quarrel kept a breach between them. Tom felt that Philip needed to be watched, that he was the son of a rascal.

When Maggie came to visit Tom, she met Philip, and the two became close friends. Then, after Maggie had been sent away to school with her cousin Lucy, Mr. Tulliver became involved in a lawsuit. Because Mr. Wakem defended the opposition, Mr. Tulliver said his children should have as little as possible to do with Philip.

Mr. Tulliver lost his suit and stood to lose all his property as well. In order to pay off Aunt Glegg, he had borrowed money on his household furnishings. Now he hoped Aunt Pullet would lend him the money to pay the debt against which his household goods stood forfeit. He could no longer afford to keep Maggie and Tom in school. Then Mr. Tulliver learned that Mr. Wakem had bought up his debts, and the discovery brought on a stroke. Tom made Maggie promise never to speak to Philip Wakem again. Mrs. Tulliver wept because her household things were to be put up at auction. In the ruin which followed, Tom and Maggie rejected the scornful offers of help from their aunts.

Bob Jakin, a country lout with whom Tom had fought as a boy, turned up to offer Tom partnership with him in a venture where Tom's education would help Bob's native business shrewdness. But both were without capital. For the time being Tom took a job in a warehouse and studied bookkeeping each night.

Mr. Wakem bought the mill but permitted Mr. Tulliver to act as its manager for wages. It was Wakem's plan eventually to turn the mill over to his son. Tulliver, not knowing what else to do, stayed on as an employee of his enemy, but he asked Tom to sign a statement in the Bible that he would wish the Wakems evil as long as he lived. Against Maggie's entreaties, Tom signed his name. Finally Aunt Glegg gave Tom some money which he invested with Bob Jakin. Slowly Tom began to accumulate funds to pay off his father's debts.

Meanwhile Maggie and Philip had been meeting secretly in the glades near the mill. One day he asked Maggie if she loved him. She put him off. Later, at a family gathering, she betrayed her feeling for Philip in a manner which aroused Tom's suspicions. He made her swear on the Bible not to have anything more to do with Philip, and then he sought out Philip and ordered him to stay away from his sister.

Shortly afterward Tom showed his father his profits. The next day Mr. Tulliver thrashed Mr. Wakem and then suffered another stroke, from which he never recovered.

Two years later Maggie, now a teacher, went to visit her cousin, Lucy Deane, who was also entertaining young Stephen Guest in her home. One difficulty Lucy foresaw was that Philip, who was friendly with both her and Stephen, might absent himself during Maggie's visit. Stephen had already decided that Lucy was to be his choice for a wife, but at first sight he and Maggie were attracted to one another. Lucy, blind to what was happening, was pleased that her cousin Maggie and Stephen were becoming good friends.

Maggie asked Tom's permission to see Philip Wakem at a party Lucy was giving. Tom replied that if Maggie should ever consider Philip as a lover, she must expect never to see her brother again. Tom stood by his oath to his father. He felt his dignity as a Tulliver, and he believed Maggie was apt to follow the inclination of the moment without giving consideration to the outcome. He was right. Lacking the iron will which marked so many of her relatives, Maggie loved easily and without restraint.

Meanwhile Lucy's father had promised to try to buy back the mill for Tom. Learning of this plan, Philip hoped to persuade his father to sell the mill. For this service Philip felt sure Tom would forget his old hatred.

At a dance Stephen Guest tried to kiss Maggie. She evaded him and the next day avoided Philip Wakem as well. She felt she owed it to Lucy not to allow Stephen to fall in love with her, and she felt that she owed it to her brother not to marry Philip.

She was carried along by the tide. Her relatives would not let her go back into teaching, for Tom's good luck continued and he repossessed his father's mill. Both Stephen and Philip urged her to marry them without the knowledge of each other's aims. Certainly, Lucy did not suspect Stephen's growing indifference to her.

One day Stephen took Maggie boating and tried to convince her to run away with him and be married. She refused his offer. Then the tide carried them beyond the reach of shore and they were forced to spend the night in the boat.

Maggie dared the wrath and judgment of her relatives when she returned and attempted to explain to Lucy and the others what had happened. They refused to listen to her. Tom turned her away from the mill house, with the word that he would send her money but that he never wished to see her again. Mrs. Tulliver resolved to go with Maggie, and Bob Jakin took them in.

Maggie slowly began to realize what ostracism meant, for one by one people deserted her. Only Aunt Glegg and Lucy offered any sympathy. Stephen wrote to her in agony of spirit, as did Philip. Maggie wanted to be by herself. She wondered if there could be love for her without pain for others.

That autumn a terrible flood ravaged St. Ogg's. Knowing that Tom was at the mill, Maggie attempted to reach him in a boat. The two were reunited and Tom took over the rowing of the boat. But the full force of the flood overwhelmed them and they drowned, together at the end as they had been when they were children.

Critical Evaluation

Shortly after George Eliot published *Adam Bede* in 1858, she began to work on a new novel under the tentative title "Sister Maggie." As the book was taking shape, she considered other possible titles—"The House of Tulliver," "The Tulliver Family," "The Tullivers"—before her editor, Blackwood, suggested *The Mill on the Floss,* a title she approved with some reservations. She objected at first that the "mill is not strictly on the Floss, being on its small tributary" and that the title "is of rather laborious utterance." Having voiced her usual nice concern for precise details and delicacy of style, she allowed that Blackwood's title was "the only alternate so far as we can see." On March 21, 1860, she completed the book, vacationed in Rome with her husband George Henry Lewes, and awaited the news of the critics' reception, which proved to be almost wholly favorable. With satisfaction Eliot wrote: "From all we can gather, the votes are rather on the side of 'The Mill' as a better book than 'Adam.' "

It is certainly the more poignant novel. Although both fictions have as their setting the Warwickshire background that George Eliot remembered from her youth, *The Mill on the Floss* is less genially picturesque, more concerned with psychological truth. *Adam Bede* concludes, probably contrary to the author's best artistic judgment, with a happy marriage for Adam and Dinah. But Tom and Maggie Tulliver die in the flood, their fate unmitigated by sentimentality. Indeed, much of the novel's power derives from the consistent play of tragic forces that appear early and unify the whole work.

As a boy, Tom entrusts his pet rabbits to his sister Maggie's care. Preoccupied, she allows the creatures to die. Tom upbraids her bitterly, in spite of her tearful protestations, but finally forgives her. This childhood pattern of close sibling affection, followed by deep hurt and estrangement, then by reconciliation, becomes the structural pattern of the novel. Although Henry James admired the design of *The Mill on the Floss,* he criticized the conclusion for its melodrama. As a matter of fact, the conclusion is implicit in the story from the beginning. The flood that carries to their doom the beloved brother and sister is not so much an accidental catastrophe. Rather, it is symbolic of the tide that sweeps away two passionate souls divided in conflict yet united by the closest bonds of affection.

Tom Tulliver, like his father, has a tenacious will that is not always under control of his reason. Even as a child, he is fiercely although honorably competitive. He is slow to forgive injury. Robust and vigorous, he despises weakness in others. As a youth, he insults Philip Wakem by drawing attention to the hunchback's physical deformity. And when Maggie demeans, as Tom mistakenly believes, the good name of the Tulliver family through her foreshortened "elopement" with Stephen Guest, he scorns her as a pariah. Yet Tom's tempestuous nature is also capable of generosity. To redeem his father's good name and restore Dorlcote Mill to the family, he disciplines himself to work purposefully. To this end, he sacrifices his high spirits, his love of strenuous excitement, indeed any opportunities for courtship and marriage. He dies as he had lived and labored, the provider of the Tulliver family.

His sister Maggie, many of whose sprightly qualities are drawn from George Eliot's memories of her own childhood, is psychologically the more complex character. Whereas Tom is sturdily masculine, Maggie is sensitive, introspective, tenderly feminine. Quick to tears—to the modern reader perhaps too effusive in her emotions—she cannot control her sensibilities, just as her brother cannot hold his temper. As a youngster, she has much of the tomboy in her. She is energetic and, unlike the typical Victorian girl, fights for her place in the world. Intelligent, diligent, earnest, she would make better use of Mr. Stelling's classical schooling than her brother; but girls of her time rarely had the opportunity to advance in education. So she must content herself, although secretively restive, with the narrow place Victorian society allows for girls of her class. Like Dorothea Brooke in *Middlemarch,* she is attracted to a scholarly but fragile lover, Philip. Her sympathetic nature completes what is lacking in the young man's disposition—courage and self-esteem. And in turn he offers her a sense of artistic dedication for which she yearns.

Some astute critics of *The Mill on the Floss* have objected to Maggie's other suitor, Stephen Guest, who is Lucy Deane's fiancé. For Lucy, a more typical Victorian heroine, sweet but passive, the impetuous Stephen would be a satisfactory mate. According to Sir Leslie Stephen, Maggie, in her passion for Lucy's betrothed, throws herself away upon a "low creature." His daughter, Virginia Woolf, repeated Sir Leslie's judgment in describing Stephen's "courseness." But a modern view of the character does not support such hostile interpretations. Stephen is neither low nor coarse. Instead he is an ardent lover who rouses in Maggie a sexual response that she does not feel, in spite of her tender empathy, for Philip. Maggie's torment is to be torn between her promises to Philip (who certainly loves and needs her) and her deeper feelings for Stephen. On one hand, she senses the call of duty and propriety; on the other, she feels the sweep of wild emotion. She masters her feelings, betrays her needs as a woman, and returns to Philip.

For the same reason that some critics refuse to accept Maggie as a mature woman with normal sexual responses, some readers are troubled by the apparent change in her character as she grows from child to adult. So vital, charming, and convincing is the portrait of Maggie the girl, that readers may wish to cherish her youthful image. But Maggie the woman does not really change. Within the prudish conventions of the Victorian novel, George Eliot can only suggest her heroine's psychological and moral development. Nevertheless, she conveys a sense of Maggie's greater sexual vulnerability because of her "highly strung, hungry nature." When she renounces Stephen, she renounces her own happiness. From that point, her tragedy is inevitable. The provincial gossips of St. Ogg's cast her off. Her beloved brother rejects her. To be sure, her mother, Lucy, and Philip have faith in her to the last. But Maggie, characteristically, determines: "I must not, cannot seek my own happiness by sacrificing others." Thus, the flood waters that carry Maggie and her brother downstream cleanse their guilts, unite them as when they were children, innocent with hope. Finally in their death as in their life, Eliot tells us, they are "not divided."

Bibliography

Adam, Ian.   *George Eliot.* New York: Humanities, 1969, pp. 12–18, 37–41, 63–68, 88–94.

Auerbach, Nina.   "The Power of Hunger: Demonism and Maggie Tulliver," in *Nineteenth-Century Fiction.* XXX (September, 1975), pp. 150–171.

Buckler, William E.   "Memory, Morality, and the Tragic Vision in the Early Novels of George Eliot," in *The English Novel in the Nineteenth Century: Essays on the Literary Mediation of Human Values.* Edited by George Goodin. Urbana: University of Illinois Press, 1972, pp. 149–159.

Buckley, Jerome Hamilton.   *Season of Youth: The Bildungs-roman from Dickens to Golding.* Cambridge, Mass.: Harvard University Press, 1974, pp. 95–115.

Carroll, David R.   "An Image of Disenchantment in the Novels of George Eliot," in *Review of English Studies.* XI (1960), pp. 29–41.

Colby, Robert Alan.   *Fiction with a Purpose: Major and Minor Nineteenth Century Novels.* Bloomington: Indiana University Press, 1967, pp. 213–255.

Drew, Elizabeth A.   *The Novel: A Modern Guide to Fifteen English Masterpieces.* New York: Norton, 1963, pp. 127–140.

Ermarth, Elizabeth.   "Maggie Tulliver's Long Suicide," in *Studies in English Literature, 1500–1900.* XIV (1974), pp. 587–601.

Goldfarb, Russell M.   "Robert P. Warren's Tollivers and George Eliot's Tullivers," in *University Review.* XXXVI (1970), pp. 209–213.

————.   "Warren's Tollivers and Eliot's Tullivers, II," in *University Review.* XXXVI (1970), pp. 275–279.

Hagan, John.   "A Reinterpretation of *The Mill on the Floss*," in *PMLA.* LXXXVII (1972), pp. 53–63.

Haight, Gordon S.   "Introduction," in *The Mill on the Floss* (Riverside edition). Boston: Houghton Mifflin, 1961, pp. v-xix. Reprinted in *A Century of George Eliot Criticism.* Edited by Gordon S. Haight. Boston: Houghton Mifflin, 1965, pp. 339–348.

Hardy, Barbara.   "*The Mill on the Floss*," in *Critical Essays on George Eliot.* Edited by Barbara Hardy. New York: Barnes & Noble, 1970, pp. 42–58.

Higdon, David Leon.   "Failure of Design in *The Mill on the Floss*," in *Journal of Narrative Technique.* III (1973), pp. 183–192.

Jones, R.T.   *George Eliot.* Cambridge: Cambridge University Press, 1970, pp. 19–30.

Knoepflmacher, Ulrich Camillus.   *George Eliot's Early Novels.* Berkeley: University of California Press, 1968, pp. 162–220.

————.   *Laughter and Despair: Readings in Ten Novels of the Victorian Age.* Berkeley: University of California Press, 1971, pp. 109–136.

Levine, George.   "Intelligence as Deception: *The Mill on the Floss*," in *PMLA*. LXXX (September, 1965), pp. 402–409. Reprinted in *George Eliot: A Collection of Critical Essays*. Edited by George R. Creeger. Englewood Cliffs, N.J.: Prentice-Hall, 1970, pp. 107–123.

Liddell, Robert.   *The Novels of George Eliot*. New York: St. Martin's, 1977, pp. 51–71.

Molstad, David.   "*The Mill on the Floss* and *Antigone*," in *PMLA*. LXXXV (1970), pp. 527–531.

Paris, Bernard J.   *A Psychological Approach to Fiction: Studies in Thackeray, Stendhal, George Eliot, Dostoevsky, and Conrad*. Bloomington: Indiana University Press, 1974, pp. 165–189.

_____.   "Toward a Revaluation of George Eliot's *The Mill on the Floss*," in *Nineteenth-Century Fiction*. XI (June, 1956), pp. 18–31.

Roberts, Neil.   *George Eliot: Her Beliefs and Her Art*. Pittsburgh: University of Pittsburgh Press, 1975, pp. 85–106.

Thale, Jerome.   *The Novels of George Eliot*. New York: Columbia University Press, 1959, pp. 36–57.

Williams, Ioan.   *The Realist Novel in England: A Study in Development*. London: Macmillan, 1974, pp. 178–182.

SILAS MARNER

Type of work: Novel
Author: George Eliot (Mary Ann Evans, 1819-1880)
Type of plot: Domestic realism
Time of plot: Early nineteenth century
Locale: England
First published: 1861

This charming tale of a poor dissenting weaver who, betrayed and unjustly accused, becomes bitter and miserly until redeemed and transformed by a foundling, is virtually perfect in structure, tone, and execution. As several critics have pointed out, the novel combines the emotional and moral satisfactions of the fairy tale with the solid intellectual appeal of the realistic narrative.

Principal Characters

Silas Marner, a weaver of Raveloe. As a resident of Lantern Yard, he had been simple, trusting, and religious until falsely accused of theft. He then loses his faith in religion and people. Turning away from humanity, he directs his stunted affections towards his steadily increasing pile of coins. However, when Eppie enters his life, he regains his belief in the fundamental goodness of man. In his bewildered fashion he accepts help from his Raveloe neighbors and decides to rear the motherless child who has captured his heart; under her influence he no longer despairs because of the stolen money.

Eppie (Hephzibah), Marner's adopted daughter. Fair-haired and blue-eyed, she captivates everyone who meets her, including young Aaron Winthrop, her future husband. After years of loneliness, Silas is sustained and his spirit nurtured by having her constantly near him. Even after she marries Aaron, she is determined to care for Marner, now frail and bent from years of unremitting toil at the loom.

Godfrey Cass, Eppie's real father and the weak son of Squire Cass, a prominent Raveloe landowner. Blackmailed by his brother Dunstan, he lacks the moral courage to acknowledge to the public that Eppie is his daughter. Instead, fearing disinheritance. he keeps silent for many years with his guilt gnawing at his soul. Later, however, when Dunstan's skeleton is found in the Stone Pits, he finally confesses to Nancy his previous marriage to Molly, dead for sixteen years. Belatedly, he wants, with Nancy's consent, to accept Eppie as his daughter. Thinking she will be overcome by his generosity, he is shocked by her determination to remain with Silas.

Dunstan Cass (Dunsey), Godfrey's dull-minded, spendthrift brother. Drunken and dissolute, he forces Godfrey to give him money by threatening to reveal the secret of Godfrey's marriage to Molly, a low-bred, common woman. After stealing Silas' gold, he falls into the Stone Pit. Years later his skeleton, the gold still beside it, is found wedged between two huge stones.

Nancy Lammeter, Godfrey's second wife, a lovely, decorous, and prim young woman. Although living by a narrow moral code, she surprises her husband, who has underestimated her, by courageously accepting the knowledge of his marriage to Molly.

Squire Cass, a prominent Raveloe landowner. Often lax in his discipline, he can be unyielding when aroused. At times this inflexibility of character makes both his sons and tenants fear his anger.

William Dane, Silas Marner's treacherous friend in Lantern Yard. While mouthing religious platitudes, he steals money from the church and implicates Marner, thus forcing the latter's exile from the village. By planting Silas' pocketknife at the scene of the crime, Dane can steal the money with impunity, knowing that his friend will receive the blame.

Aaron Winthrop, a sturdy young Raveloe citizen. For many years he has wor-

shiped Eppie; when she promises to marry him, he is overjoyed. He promises Silas security and love in the old man's increasing feebleness.

Molly Cass, Godfrey's first wife. A drug addict who marries him when he is drunk, she is walking to Raveloe to expose him as her husband. Fortunately for Godfrey, she takes an overdose of laudanum and freezes to death in the snow, leaving her baby to toddle into the warmth and security of Silas' cottage.

Dolly Winthrop, Aaron's mother, the wife of Raveloe's wheelwright. She and her little son often visit Silas and it is she who defends his right to keep Eppie when the villagers question Silas' suitability as a parent.

The Story

In the small community of Raveloe lived the linen-weaver, Silas Marner. Long years at his spinning-wheel had left Silas extremely near-sighted so that his vision was limited to only those objects which were very bright or very close to him. Because of an unjust accusation of theft, Silas had left his former home at Lantern Yard and had become a recluse. For fifteen years the lonely, shriveled man had lived for no purpose but to hoard the money he received in payment for his weaving. Night after night he took his golden hoard from its hiding place in the floor of his cottage and let the shining pieces run through his fingers.

The leading man in Raveloe was Squire Cass, who had one fine son, Godfrey, and one wastrel son, Dunstan. It was said that Godfrey would marry Nancy Lammeter. But Godfrey had become involved in Dunstan's gambling debts. He had lent his spendthrift brother some of the squire's rent money, which Dunstan had lost in gambling. Since neither brother could raise the money, they decided that Dunstan must sell Godfrey's favorite horse, Wildfire, at a nearby fair. Godfrey's one fear was that this affair would harm his reputation in the neighborhood and his chance with Nancy. Another thing that weighed on Godfrey's conscience and prevented his declaration to Nancy was the fact that he was already married. Once he had been drunk in a tavern in a distant hamlet, and in that condition he had married a low-bred, common woman. Sober, he had fled back to Raveloe and kept his marriage a secret.

Dunstan rode Wildfire across the fog-dimmed fields and crippled the animal on a high jump. With no means of raising the money, half-drunk and fear-driven,

Dunstan came to Silas Marner's cottage. He knew the neighborhood gossip that the weaver had a hoard of gold hidden away. The cottage was empty, and instinct soon led the drunken boy to the hiding place of the gold. Stealing out of the cabin with his prize and stumbling through the night, Dunstan fell into an abandoned quarry pit and was killed.

The robbery of Silas' cottage furnished gossip for the entire community. Another mystery was the disappearance of Dunstan Cass. Godfrey was forced now to tell his father about the rent money he had given Dunstan and about the loss of the valuable horse, which had been found dead. Silas began to receive visitors from the neighborhood. One of his most frequent callers was Dolly Winthrop and her son Aaron, a charming little boy. Yet Silas could not be persuaded to come out of his hermitage; he secretly mourned the loss of his gold.

On New Year's Eve a destitute woman died in the snow near Silas' cottage. She had with her a little yellow-haired girl who made her way toward the light shining through the cottage window and entered the house. Returning from an errand, Silas saw a golden gleam in front of his fireplace, a gleam which he mistook for his lost gold. On closer examination, he discovered a sleeping baby. Following the child's tracks through the snow, he came upon the body of the dead woman.

Godfrey was dancing happily with Nancy when Silas appeared to say that he had found a body. Godfrey went with the others to the scene and saw to his horror that the dead woman was his estranged wife. He told no one of her identity, and had not the courage to claim the baby for his own. Silas, with a confused association between the golden-haired child and his lost hoard, tenaciously clung to the child. After Dolly Winthrop spoke up in favor of his proper attitude toward children, the villagers decided to leave the baby with the old weaver.

Years passed. Under the spell of the child who in her baby language called herself Eppie instead of the Biblical Hephzibah that Silas had bestowed upon her, the cottage of the weaver of Raveloe took on a new appearance. Lacy curtains decorated the once drab windows, and Silas himself outgrew his shell of reticence. Dolly brought her son to play with Eppie. Silas was happy. After many years he even returned to Lantern Yard, taking Eppie. He searched his old neighborhood hopefully but could find no one who could clear his blighted past.

Godfrey Cass married Nancy, but it was a childless union. For sixteen years Godfrey secretly carried with him the thought of his child growing up under the care of Silas. At last the old stone quarry was drained and workmen found a skeleton identified by Dunstan's watch and seals. Beside the skeleton was Silas' lost bag of gold, stolen on the night of Dunstan's disappearance. With this discovery, Godfrey's past reopened its sealed doors. He felt that the time had come to tell Nancy the truth. When he confessed the story of Eppie's birth, Nancy agreed with him that they should go to Silas and Eppie with their tale. Hearing this strange story of Eppie's parentage, the unselfish weaver opened the way for Eppie to take advantage of her wealthy heritage; but Eppie fled to the arms of the man who had been a father and a mother to her when no one else would claim her.

There was one thing remaining to complete the weaver's happiness. Eppie married Aaron Winthrop, her childhood playmate, while Silas beamed happily on the scene of her wedding.

Critical Evaluation

In four remarkable years George Eliot published in succession *Scenes from Clerical Life* (1858), *Adam Bede* (1859), *The Mill on the Floss* (1860), and *Silas Marner* (1861). The last, a short novel or novella, is unlike the other works, for its narrative combines elements of myth—some critics have called it a fairy tale—with the otherwise realistic details of English country life centering around the rustic village of Raveloe. Certainly the novel can be understood as a moral tale. Its message, however sentimental to a modern reader, is unambiguous: true wealth is love, not gold. As a myth of loss and redemption, the novel concerns the miser Silas Marner, who loses his material riches only to reclaim a greater treasure of contentment. Silas comes to learn that happiness is possible only for the pure and self-sacrificing. Because of his love for Eppie, he is transformed, as if by magic, from a narrow, selfish, bitter recluse into a truly human, spiritually fulfilled man.

The novel, however, has a dimension other than the moralistic. George Eliot skillfully counterpoints the experiences of Silas with those of Godfrey Cass. Whereas Godfrey appears, when the reader first meets him, to be a fortunate man entirely the opposite of the sullen miser, his fortunes fail just as Silas' improve. The wealthy, genial Godfrey has a secret guilt—an unacknowledged marriage to a woman beneath him in social class and refinement. Silas, on the other hand, carries with him the smoldering resentment for a wrong which he had suffered (and suffered innocently) from his friend William Dane. Godfrey's sense of guilt festers, especially after he learns about the terrible circumstances of the woman's death. Nevertheless, he remains silent, fearful of exposing his past. Eppie, the child of his brief union with the woman, thus becomes the miser's treasure, to replace the sterile gold stolen by Dunstan. Thereafter for Godfrey, the happiness of the old man is his doom. His second wife, Nancy, is barren; and when he offers, too late, to adopt Eppie as his own child, she clings to her foster father. Silas' love has earned what Godfrey's power had failed to command.

By contrasting Silas' good fortune with Godfrey's disappointment, the author expands the mythic scope of her fiction. If some men—the pure and deserving—discover almost by accident the truths of happiness, others, maybe no less deserving, pass by their chances and endure misery. Silas is reformed not only spiritually but also psychologically. Once blasphemous, he returns to the Christian faith of his childhood. But his religious reaffirmation is not so important as the improvement of his psychological health. Freed of his neurotic resentment for past injustices, he becomes a friend to all, beloved of the village. For Godfrey, whose history is realistic rather than marvelous, quite the opposite fate happens. Without an heir, he shrinks within himself. He may endure his disgrace, even eventually make up to Eppie and her husband Aaron some of the material things he owes her; yet he cannot shake his sense of wrongdoing, appease his sorrow for betrayal, nor make restitution for the evils of the past. George Eliot, who once described her novel as "rather somber," thus balances her miraculous fable of rebirth for the favored Silas with another more common human story, that of the defeated Godfrey Cass.

Bibliography

Adam, Ian. *George Eliot.* New York: Humanities, 1969, pp. 18–21, 94–97.

Allen, Walter. *George Eliot.* New York: Macmillan, 1964, pp. 118–127.

Buckler, William E. "Memory, Morality, and the Tragic Vision in the Early Novels of George Eliot," in *The English Novel in the Nineteenth Century: Essays on the Literary Mediation of Human Values.* Edited by George Goodin. Urbana: University of Illinois Press, 1972, pp. 159–163.

Carroll, David R. "*Silas Marner*: Reversing the Oracles of Religion," in *Literary Monographs.* I (1967), pp. 165–200.

Dunham, Robert H. "*Silas Marner* and the Wordsworthian Child," in *Studies in English Literature, 1500–1900.* XVI (1976), pp. 645–659.

Fairlay, E. "The Art of George Eliot in *Silas Marner*," in *English Journal.* II (1913), pp. 221–230.

H., J. "The Schoolteacher's Novel: *Silas Marner*," in *Saturday Review of Literature.* XV (March 20, 1937), p. 13.

Haddakin, Lilian. "*Silas Marner*," in *Critical Essays on George Eliot.* Edited by Barbara Hardy. New York: Barnes & Noble, 1970, pp. 59–77.

Heilman, Robert B. "Return to Raveloe: Thirty-Five Years After," in *English Journal.* XLVI (1957), pp. 1–10.

Jones, R.T. *George Eliot.* Cambridge: Cambridge University Press, 1970, pp. 31–42.

Knoepflmacher, Ulrich Camillus. *George Eliot's Early Novels.* Berkeley: University of California Press, 1968, pp. 221–259.

Law, Frederick Houk. "*Main Street* and *Silas Marner*," in *Independent.* CVIII (1922), pp. 263–265.

Liddell, Robert. *The Novels of George Eliot.* New York: St. Martin's, 1977, pp. 72–84.

Martin, Bruce K. "Similarity Within Dissimilarity: The Dual Structure of *Silas Marner*," in *Texas Studies in Literature and Language*. XIV (1972), pp. 479–489.

Milner, Ian. "Structure and Quality in *Silas Marner*," in *Studies in English Literature, 1500–1900*. VI (1966), pp. 717–729.

Parson, Coleman O. "Background Material Illustrative of *Silas Marner*," in *Notes and Queries*. CXCI (1946), pp. 266–270.

Pauncz, Arpad. "The Lear Complex in World Literature," in *American Imago*. XI (1954), pp. 50–83.

Quick, Jonathan R. "*Silas Marner* as Romance: The Example of Hawthorne," in *Nineteenth-Century Fiction*. XXIX (1974), pp. 287–298.

Roberts, Neil. *George Eliot: Her Beliefs and Her Art*. Pittsburgh: University of Pittsburgh Press, 1975, pp. 107–118.

Squires, Michael. *The Pastoral Novel: Studies in George Eliot, Thomas Hardy, and D.H. Lawrence*. Charlottesville: University Press of Virginia, 1974, pp. 86–105.

Swann, Brian. "*Silas Marner* and the New Mythus," in *Criticism*. XVIII (1976), pp. 101–121.

Thale, Jerome. *The Novels of George Eliot*. New York: Columbia University Press, 1959, pp. 58–69.

Thomson, Fred C. "The Theme of Alienation in *Silas Marner*," in *Nineteenth-Century Fiction*. XX (June, 1965), pp. 69–84.

Wisenfarth, Joseph. "Demythologizing *Silas Marner*," in *Journal of English Literary History*. XXXVII (1970), pp. 226–244.

HENRY FIELDING

Born: Near Glastonbury, England (April 22, 1707)
Died: Lisbon, Portugal (October 8, 1754)

Principal Works

NOVELS: *The History of the Adventures of Joseph Andrews, and his Friend Mr. Abraham Adams*, 1742; *The History of the Life of the Late Mr. Jonathan Wild the Great*, 1743; *Tom Jones, the History of a Foundling*, 1749; *Amelia*, 1751.

PLAYS: *Love in Several Masques*, 1728; *The Temple Beau*, 1730; *The Life and Death of Tom Thumb the Great*, 1730; *The Covent Garden Tragedy*, 1731; *Pasquin*, 1736; *The Historical Register*, 1737.

JOURNAL OF TRAVEL: *The Journal of a Voyage to Lisbon*, 1755.

Henry Fielding was born in Somersetshire on April 22, 1707, probably at Sharpham Park near Glastonbury, the home of his grandfather, Sir Henry Gould. When he was two and a half years of age his parents moved to a home of their own at the village of East Stour in the adjoining county of Dorset. The remarriage of his father, after his mother's death in 1718, brought on a bitter family quarrel, partly concerned with money, and a lawsuit which resulted in Fielding and his sisters and brother being made wards of Chancery, with their grandmother, Lady Gould, as their principal guardian. The old lady allowed her grandson far more freedom than was advisable for so boisterous and high-spirited a boy. He was sent to school at Eton between the ages of thirteen and eighteen and there received a thorough and valuable education, especially in the Greek and Latin classics. There followed three more years of complete freedom in the country, spent mainly in hunting, fishing, visiting various country estates, and courting half a dozen or more young girls. Early in 1728 he was in London, where his first play was produced at Drury Lane just before his twenty-first birthday. It was based in part on his unsuccessful attempt, at the age of eighteen, to abduct a beautiful young heiress, aged sixteen. Although the play was moderately successful, it was decided that he should go to Holland for further study at the University of Leyden, where he remained for most of the next two years.

On his return to England in 1730, he found himself without any regular means of support, even though his improvident father had promised him an income of £200. He began writing plays for a living and was launched on his career with the assistance of his cousin, Lady Mary Wortley Montagu, and the American, James Ralph, a friend of Benjamin Franklin then living in London. At the end of seven years he was the author of twenty-one plays, the majority of which had been successfully produced. Although he was then unquestionably England's most popular living dramatist, his career was brought to an end by the Licensing Act of 1737. This provided for government censorship of all plays before they could be produced and was aimed directly at Fielding, who had offended the powerful Prime Minister, Sir Robert Walpole, by his sharp political satires.

He then turned to the study of law and was called to the bar in less than three years, although the average time required was six or seven. He never developed a lucrative practice, however, and was obliged to supplement his income with his pen. During the next fourteen years he edited and chiefly wrote four periodicals, wrote and published four novels and a very large number of tracts and pamphlets, mostly political. As a reward for his political services, he was in 1748 appointed Justice of the Peace for Westminster and a few months later for Middlesex as well. Although the position had brought his predecessor an income of about £1000, Fielding received only about a third of that amount because, unlike the other corrupt "trading justices" of the time, he declined to accept bribes. He labored so ardently and so successfully that he practically cleared of crime one of the worst districts of London and in so doing established England's first efficient detective force, which has since developed into the famous Criminal Investigation Department of Scotland Yard. Largely through his influence, Parliament passed Acts greatly improving criminal laws and through his efforts the scandalous practice of holding public executions was abolished for a time. However, his attempts to abolish debtors' prisons and to establish institutions for the proper care of minor criminals and the poor failed and his suggestions were not put into effect until a century after his death.

In the summer of 1754 the ill health which had plagued his existence for more than a decade caused him to journey to Lisbon for the benefit of the warm climate. He died there the following October at the age of forty-seven and was buried in the Protestant Cemetery on a hill outside the city.

Fielding's outspoken honesty and his gift for witty, biting satire made him many enemies, who abused him roundly in print without much regard for the truth. Until recently, much of the mud that was slung at him has stuck to his reputation. Careful investigation by modern scholars, especially Wilbur L. Cross, has shown that he was by no means the dissipated rake his earlier biographers were led to believe him. A principal cause of criticism and merciless abuse was that after the death of his first wife—the beautiful Charlotte Cradock whom he adored and made the model for Sophia Western in *Tom Jones*—he married her maid. His motive for this action was that she was about to bear his child and he wanted to save her from disgrace. Few if any other men of his generation would have behaved as decently.

In physique he was tall, handsome, and well made. His high spirits, convivial nature, and great wit as a conversationalist made him one of the most sought-after of companions. Those who knew him well knew him to be scrupulously honest, generous to a fault, and wise in the ways of the world. The most democratic of men, he chose his friends for what they were rather than for who they were.

Although Fielding was immensely popular as a dramatist in his own day and although several of his plays held the boards until the end of the eighteenth century, there is only one, *Tom Thumb the Great*, which is at all widely read today. Nearly all of them are topical and require a knowledge of contemporary events to be fully understood. He edited and largely wrote four periodicals of which two *The Champion* and *The Covent-garden Journal* are among the best of their time. All four of his novels, *Jonathan Wild*, *Amelia*, *Joseph Andrews*, and *Tom Jones*, are rewarding reading today, especially the latter two, which are read and studied in most American schools and colleges.

To his masterpiece *Tom Jones*, Fielding devoted all the art of which he was master and all the wisdom he had gained from a life lived to the hilt. Its greatness lies not so much in its wealth of characters and incidents, abundant and splendid as they are, nor in its plot, which Coleridge over-enthusiastically declared to be one of the three most perfect ever devised. It is rather in the open-minded acceptance of human nature as it is and in the enlightened view of life, at the same time panoramic and profound. In this book we see life as clearly as the light of comedy can show it. We breathe and move in the sparkling, invigorating air which pervades also the *Odyssey* and *Don Quixote* and the comedies of Shakespeare and Molière.

Bibliography

The most recent edition of the complete works is that edited by W. E. Henley and others, 16 vols., 1903. A new edition under the general editorship of William B. Coley is in progress, 1967—. The novels are available in the Shakespeare Head Press Edition, 10 vols., 1926. The standard biography is Wilbur L. Cross, *The History of Henry Fielding*, 3 vols., 1918, a basic work which has not been superseded by the more recent scholarship and detailed study presented in Frederick H. Dudden, *Henry Fielding: His Life, Works, and Times*, 2 vols., 1952. There are a number of shorter but reliable biographical and critical studies: Austin Dobson, *Fielding*, 1883; Frederick T. Blanchard, *Fielding the Novelist*, 1926; H. K. Benerji, *Henry Fielding: His Life and Works*, 1929; Ethel M. Thornbury, *Henry Fielding's Theory of the Comic Prose Epic*, University of Wisconsin Studies in Language and Literature, No. 30, 1931; F. O. Bissell, Jr., *Fielding's Theory of the Novel*, 1933; B. M. Jones, *Henry Fielding, Novelist and Magistrate*, 1933; W. R. Irwin, *The Making of Jonathan Wild*, 1941; Elizabeth Jenkins, *Henry Fielding*, 1947; Michael Irwin, *Henry Fielding: The Tentative Realist*, 1967; Robert Alter, *Fielding and the Nature of the Novel*, 1968; and Claude J. Rawson, *Henry Fielding*, 1968. See also Ronald Paulson, ed., *Fielding: A Collection of Critical Essays*, 1962.

For general studies of the novel and Fielding's influence on its development see Ernest A. Baker, *The History of the English Novel*, Vol. IV, 1930, 1950; Robert M. Lovett and H. S. Hughes, *The History of the Novel in England*, 1932; and Edward Wagenknecht, *Cavalcade of the English Novel*, 1943. See also Kenneth Chester Slagle, *The English Country Squire as Depicted in English Prose Fiction from 1740 to 1800*, 1938.

Additional references will be found in F. Cordasco, *Henry Fielding: A List of Critical Studies from 1895 to 1946*, 1946.

AMELIA

Type of work: Novel
Author: Henry Fielding (1707–1754)
Type of plot: Domestic realism
Time of plot: 1740's
Locale: England
First published: 1751

Although Amelia *lacks the extravagant humor of Fielding's earlier novels, it develops several memorably true-to-life characterizations. Also noteworthy are the realistic pictures of English courts and prison life, worked into the narrative by the author, for many years a magistrate, for the purpose of interesting readers in penal and legal reform.*

Principal Characters

Amelia Harris Booth, a beautiful and virtuous young Englishwoman whose troubles begin when she marries William Booth, a young army officer, against her mother's wishes. After the Gibraltar campaign, when her husband is on half-pay in an inactive status, Amelia's life becomes a constant struggle against genteel poverty. Her beauty complicates matters, for several high-ranking men who might help her husband acquire a new command pursue her, in hopes that she will capitulate her charms in return for the help they can give. Amelia also faces the problem of her husband's gambling and philandering. She bears all her tribulations with patience and humility; finally her virtue is rewarded by the inheritance of her mother's estate.

William Booth, a British captain and Amelia's husband. Although he is a meritorious junior officer who served well at Gibraltar, incurring two wounds in the King's service, he has extreme difficulty in securing a new command because he is too poor to buy a commission and without sufficient political influence to gain one. He loves his wife deeply and fears their poverty for her sake. Captain Booth has other problems as well, his weaknesses for gambling and women.

Dr. Harrison, a benevolent Anglican clergyman who regards Amelia almost as a daughter. His kindness and help save Amelia and her family from disaster several times, for the good man lends them his house, advances them money, and is the person whose discoveries eventually place Amelia in possession of her inheritance.

Colonel Robert James, a fellow officer of William Booth during his active military duty. He, unlike Booth, remains in the military service, having the money and influence to rise in the military hierachy and become a member of Parliament. He extends help many times to the Booths through the years, but only because he is secretly desirous of having Amelia as his mistress.

Colonel Bath, another fellow officer. Always conscious of his honor and ready to fight a duel or encourage someone else to fight one, he forces a quarrel on Booth, who wounds the colonel.

Mrs. James, Colonel James's wife and Colonel Bath's sister. She is a great friend to Amelia until the latter's poverty causes that friendship to cool.

Betty Harris, Amelia's sister, a selfish, malicious woman who spreads lies about Amelia and enters into a complicated plot of forgery to deprive Amelia of her rightful inheritance.

Mr. Robinson, a shady character who is in and out of prison. On his deathbed his confession to Dr. Harrison reveals the plot to keep Amelia from her inheritance.

Mr. Murphy, a dishonest lawyer. He plots with Betty Harris to deprive Amelia of her fortune. Eventually apprehended by Dr. Harrison, he is tried, found guilty, and hanged at Tyburn.

Mrs. Ellison, the Booths' landlady in London. Although she seems an honest and well-meaning woman, she serves as bawd to an unnamed nobleman, procuring for him a whole series of women. Amelia's friends prevent her from being so victimized.

Mrs. Bennet, an unfortunate young widow who becomes Amelia's friend. Having been an earlier victim of Mrs. Ellison and the unnamed nobleman, she is able to help Amelia save herself from the plot against her virtue. Mrs. Bennet is loved by Sergeant Atkinson and becomes his wife.

Joseph Atkinson, the son of Amelia's nurse and, in a sense, her foster brother. He enlists in the army in order to be with William Booth and afterward remains in the service. Loyal to Amelia and her husband, he helps in every way he can to keep disaster from overtaking the Booths. He falls in love with Mrs. Bennet, marries her, and buys a commission with their pooled resources.

Fanny Matthews, a handsome, amoral woman who loves William Booth and tries to become his mistress. She is also Colonel James's mistress at the time. She and Booth renew their acquaintance while both are in prison.

The Story

One night the watchmen of Westminster arrested Captain William Booth, seizing him during his attempt to rescue a stranger who was being attacked by two ruffians. The footpads secured their own liberty by bribing the constables, but Booth, in spite of his protests, was hailed before an unjust magistrate. The story he told was a straightforward one, but because he was penniless and shabbily dressed the judge dismissed his tale and sentenced him to prison. Booth was desperate, for there was no one he knew in London to whom he could turn for aid. His plight was made worse by his reception at the prison. His fellow prisoners stripped him of his coat, and a pickpocket made off with his snuffbox.

While he was smarting from these indignities, a fashionably dressed young woman was brought through the gates. Flourishing a bag of gold in the face of her keepers, she demanded a private room in the prison. Her appearance and manner reminded Booth of an old friend of questionable background, a Miss Matthews whom he had not seen for several years. But when the woman passed him without a sign of recognition, he believed himself mistaken.

Shortly afterward a guard brought him a guinea in a small parcel, and with the money Booth was able to redeem his coat and snuffbox. The rest of the windfall he lost in a card game. Booth was penniless once more when a keeper came to conduct him to Miss Matthews, for the woman was indeed she. Seeing his wretched condition as he stood by the prison gate, she had sent him the mysterious guinea.

Reunited under these distressing circumstances, they proceeded to relate the stories of their experiences. Miss Matthews told how she had been committed to await sentence for a penknife attack on a soldier who had seduced her under false promises of marriage.

Booth, in turn, told this story. He had met a Miss Amelia Harris, a beautiful girl whose mother at first opposed her daughter's marriage to a penniless soldier. The young couple eloped but were later, through the efforts of Dr. Harrison, a wise and kindly curate, reconciled with Amelia's mother. Booth's regiment was ordered to Gibraltar, shortly before a child was to be born to Amelia. He left reluctantly, leaving Amelia in the care of her mother and her older sister, Elizabeth. At Gibraltar Booth earned the good opinion of his officers by his bravery. Wounded in one of the battles of the campaign, he was very ill, and Amelia, learning of his condition, left her child with her mother and sister and went to Gibraltar to nurse her sick husband. Then Amelia, in her turn, fell sick. Wishing to take her to a milder climate, Booth wrote to Mrs. Harris for money, but in reply received only a rude note from Elizabeth. He hoped to get the money from his army friend, Major James, but that gentleman was away at the time. Finally he borrowed the money from Sergeant Atkinson, his friend and Amelia's foster brother, and went with his wife to Montpelier. There the couple made friends with an amusing English officer named Colonel Bath and his sister.

Joy at the birth of a second child, a girl, was dampened by a letter from Dr. Harrison, who wrote to tell them that old Mrs. Harris was dead, and that she had left her property to Amelia's sister. The Booths returned home, to be greeted so rudely by Elizabeth that they withdrew from the house. But for the help of Dr. Harrison, they would have been destitute. Harrison set Booth up as a gentleman farmer and tried to help him make the best of his half-pay from the Army. But because of several small mistakes, Booth made enemies among the surrounding farmers. Dr. Harrison was traveling on the continent at the time and in his absence Booth was reduced almost to bankruptcy. He came to London to try his fortunes anew. He preceded Amelia, found modest lodgings, and wrote her where they were. It was at this point that another misfortune landed him in prison. At the end of Booth's story, Miss Matthews sympathized with his unfortunate situation, congratulated him on his wife and children, and paid the jailer to let Booth spend the next few nights with her in her cell.

Booth and Miss Matthews were shortly released from prison. The soldier wounded by Miss Matthews having completely recovered, charges against her were dropped. Miss Matthews also secured the release of Booth, and the two were preparing to leave prison when Amelia arrived. She had come up from the country to save him, and his release was a welcome surprise for the distressed wife. The Booths set themselves up in London. Shortly afterward, Booth met his former officer, now Colonel James, who in the meanwhile had married Miss Bath and grown quickly tired of her. Mrs. James and Amelia resumed their old friendship. Booth, afraid that Miss Matthews would inform Amelia of their affair in prison, told Colonel James of his difficulties and fears. The colonel gave him a loan and told him not to worry. Colonel James was himself interested in Miss Matthews, but he was unable to help Booth by his intercession. Miss Matthews continued to send Booth reproachful and revealing letters which might at any time have been intercepted by Amelia.

While walking in the park one day, the Booths met Sergeant Atkinson. He joined their household to help care for the children, and soon he started a half flirtation with a Mrs. Ellison, Booth's landlady.

Mrs. Ellison proved useful to the Booths, for a lord who came also to visit her advanced money to pay some of Booth's debts. Meanwhile Miss Matthews had spitefully turned Colonel James against Booth. Colonel Bath, hearing his brother-in-law's poor opinion of Booth, decided that Booth was neither an officer nor a gentleman, and challenged him to a duel. Colonel Bath believed in nothing so much as a code of honor, and when, in the duel, Booth had run him through, without serious injury, the colonel was so much impressed by Booth's gallantry that he forgave him and brought about a reconciliation between James and Booth.

During this time Mrs. Ellison had been trying to arrange an assignation between Amelia and the nobleman who had given Booth money to pay his gambling debts. Amelia was innocently misled by her false friends. But the nobleman's plan to meet Amelia secretly at a masquerade was thwarted by another neighbor, Mrs. Bennet. This woman, who had been a boarder in Mrs. Ellison's house, had also met the noble lord, had encountered him at a masquerade, and had drunk the drugged wine he provided. To prevent Amelia's ruin in the same manner, Mrs. Bennet came to warn her friend. Then she informed Amelia that she had recently married Sergeant Atkinson, whom Amelia had thought in love with Mrs. Ellison. But Amelia's joy at learning of both the plot, which she now planned to escape, and of the marriage, was marred by the news that Booth had again been put into prison for debt, this time on a warrant of their old friend Dr. Harrison.

Amelia soon discovered that Dr. Harrison had been misled by false rumors of Booth's extravagance, and had put him in jail in order to stop his rash spending of money. Learning the truth, Dr. Harrison had Booth released from prison.

On the night of the masquerade Amelia remained at home but sent Mrs. Atkinson dressed in her costume. At the dance Mrs. Atkinson was able to fool not only the lord but also Colonel James. The complications of the affair were many, almost every relationship being misunderstood. Booth fell in with an old friend and lost a large sum of money to him. Again he became worried about being put in jail. Then he became involved in a duel with Colonel James over Miss Matthews, whom Booth had visited only at her insistence. Before the duel could take place, Booth was again imprisoned for debt, and Dr. Harrison was forced to clear his name with Colonel James. Finally James forgave Booth, and Miss Matthews promised never to bother him again.

Called by chance into a strange house to hear the deathbed confession of a man named Robinson, Dr. Harrison learned that Robinson had at one time been a clerk to a lawyer named Murphy who had made Mrs. Harris' will. He learned also that the will which had left Amelia penniless was a false one prepared by Elizabeth and Murphy. Dr. Harrison had Robinson write a confession so that Amelia could get the money that was rightfully hers. The lawyer Murphy was quickly brought to trial and convicted of forgery.

Booth's troubles were now almost at an end. With Dr. Harrison he and Amelia returned home to confront Elizabeth with their knowledge of her scheme. Elizabeth fled to France, where Amelia, relenting, sent her an annual allowance. Booth's adventures had finally taught him not to gamble, and with his faithful Amelia he settled down to a quiet and prosperous life blessed with many children and the invaluable friendship of Dr. Harrison and the Atkinsons.

Critical Evaluation

Amelia was intended to appeal to a psychological and social awareness, rather than to an intellectual consciousness. Between the publication of *Tom Jones* and *Amelia,* the nature of Fielding's moral feelings deepened and with it the means and techniques by which he expressed his thoughts concerning his intensified ethical purposes. Impressed by the social problems he daily encountered in the world around him, he adopted a reformist spirit and felt an immediate necessity to promote virtue and to expose the evils which infected England. He abandoned his satirical comic mode and all of its traits such as impartiality, restraint, mockery, irony, and aesthetic distance. He adopted a serious and sentimental tone that is almost consciously middle class.

The characters in *Amelia* give strong indications of Fielding's intensified moral purposes. They are more fiery, vehement, and immediate embodiments of his beliefs and concern than the figures of his earlier works. Abandoning the aesthetic distance between himself and his characters, he seems, in *Amelia,* to live and act directly in them. This results in a new kind of immediacy and closeness between the novel's characters and the writer's psychological concerns. The cost of this immediacy is the rejection of almost all formal conventions of characterization. The description of the heroine is typical. On a number of occasions she is described by the emotions which are reflected in her face or by her physical reactions to situations which bring pain or joy; but in contrast to Fielding's elaborate descriptions of the beauty of the heroines of his earlier works, the beauty of Amelia is never delineated. Amelia's beauty in Fielding's eyes and in those of the reader is embodied in the qualities she represents. The same might be said for the other characters in the novel. Fielding is more concerned with the moral make-up of each one than in their physical appearance.

In *Amelia,* the author does not segregate the reader and the characters. Each character reveals himself to the reader through his own words and deeds. This technique causes the characters to appear as individuals rather than types.

The central theme of Fielding's portrait of a marriage concerns not so much the issue of adultery as it does the tragic irony of the marital distrust that accompanies it. Although Booth's infidelity with Miss Matthews strains the marriage and seems disgusting when contrasted with Amelia's steadfast loyalty, that is not what almost wrecks the marriage. Amelia, of course, knew about it before Booth made his confession and had forgiven him for it. The marriage is almost undone because Booth, throughout most of the novel, cannot bring himself, because of fear and pride, to confess his adultery. He does not trust in his wife's understanding and love for him. Amelia, who is beset, almost from the beginning of her marriage, by amorous advances, fails to confide to her husband the real motive behind James's pretense of friendship because she fears Booth will lose his temper and attack James. Thus man and wife, because they will not trust in each other totally, work unconsciously to the detriment of their marriage.

In *Amelia,* the reader cares more about the heroine but the action turns on Booth. It is on the adequacy or inadequacy of Booth that the novel succeeds or fails for the reader. Amelia is the stable character. Booth constantly poses the problems of marriage while she endures and solves them.

Booth's ordeal reflects Fielding's own increasing despair with social conditions. The grim social picture of this novel is Fielding's solemn warning that society may destroy itself on the larger plane, as it very nearly destroys the Booths on the smaller plane. The placement of a woman of Amelia's moral character within a society which preys upon her, effectively points up the evils of that society in relation to the constant moral Christianity of the heroine. It is Fielding's most emphatic statement of Christian morality through the treatment of the subject within marriage. The loss of faith in individual morality portrayed in this novel through the assaults on Amelia's virtue and the setbacks suffered by Booth are easily transferred from the plane of individuals to reflect criticism of society as a whole.

Amelia was published to much rancor and ridicule on the part of the majority of the critics. This book unfortunately lent itself to ridicule more readily than any other Fielding wrote. The characters were reviled as being low and the situations as being too sordid. Enemies gleefully pounced on Fielding's oversight in failing to mend his heroine's broken nose. Earlier victims of Fielding's satire, notably Samuel Richardson, author of *Pamela,* were gleeful over the adverse reception of this novel and joined in denouncing it.

In spite of the early critical reaction, the success of the novel with the modern reader depends on a willingness to take it for what it is, a serious denunciation, as Fielding himself said, "of glaring evils of the age."

Bibliography

Baker, Sheridan. "Fielding's *Amelia* and the Materials of Romance," in *Philological Quarterly*. XLI (April, 1962), pp. 437–449.

Battestin, Martin C. "The Problem of *Amelia*: Hume, Barrow, and the Conversion of Captain Booth," in *ELH Essays for Earl R. Wasserman*. Edited by Ronald Paulson and Arnold Stein. Baltimore: Johns Hopkins University Press, 1976, pp. 320–355.

Bevan, C.H.K. "The Unity of Fielding's *Amelia*," in *Renaissance and Modern Studies*. XIV (1970), pp. 90–110.

Cross, Wilbur L. *The History of Henry Fielding*, Volume 2. New Haven, Conn.: Yale University Press, 1918, pp. 301–356.

Dudden, Frederick Homes. *Henry Fielding: His Life, Works and Times*, Volume 2. Oxford: Clarendon Press, 1952, pp. 797–885.

Hassall, Anthony J. "Fielding's *Amelia*: Dramatic and Authorial Narration," in *Novel*. V (1972), pp. 225–233.

Hunter, J. Paul. "The Lesson of *Amelia*," in *Quick Springs of Sense: Studies in the Eighteenth Century*. Athens: University of Georgia Press, 1974, pp. 157–182.

Jenkins, Elizabeth. *Henry Fielding.* London: Home and Van Thal, 1947, pp. 82–90.

Johnson, Maurice. *Fielding's Art of Fiction: Eleven Essays on* Shamela, Joseph Andrews, Tom Jones, *and* Amelia. Philadelphia: University of Pennsylvania Press, 1961, pp. 139–172.

Lane, William G. "Relationship Between Some of Fielding's Major and Minor Works," in *Boston University Studies in English*. V (Winter, 1961), pp. 219–231.

Longmire, Samuel E. "*Amelia* as a Comic Action," in *Tennessee Studies in Literature*. XVII (1972), pp. 69–79.

McKillop, Alan D. *The Early Masters of English Fiction.* Lawrence: University of Kansas Press, 1956, pp. 136–145.

Oakman, R.L. "Character of the Hero: A Key to Fielding's *Amelia*," in *Studies in English Literature, 1500–1900*. XVI (Summer, 1976), pp. 473–489.

Palmer, Eustace. "*Amelia*—The Decline of Fielding's Art," in *Essays in Criticism*. XXI (1971), pp. 135–151.

Price, Martin. *To the Palace of Wisdom: Studies in Order and Energy from Dryden to Blake.* New York: Doubleday, 1964, pp. 285–311.

Rawson, Claude J. "Fielding's *Amelia*," in *Eighteenth-Century Studies: A Journal of Literature and the Arts*. III (1970), pp. 491–522.

Rothstein, Eric. *Systems of Order and Inquiry in Later Eighteenth-Century Fiction*. Berkeley: University of California Press, 1975, pp. 154–207.

Sherburn, George. "Fielding's *Amelia*: An Interpretation," in *Journal of English Literary History*. III (March, 1936), pp. 1–14. Reprinted in *Studies in the Literature of the Augustan Age*. Edited by Richard C. Boys. Ann Arbor, Mich.: George Wahr, 1952, pp. 267–280.

Spacks, Patricia Meyer. *Imagining a Self: Autobiography and Novel in Eighteenth-Century England*. Cambridge, Mass.: Harvard University Press, 1976, pp. 264–299.

Thomas, D.S. "Fortune and the Passions in Fielding's *Amelia*," in *Modern Language Review*. LX (April, 1965), pp. 176–187.

Tichý, Aleš. "Remarks on the Flow of Time in the Novels of Henry Fielding," in *BRNO Studies in English*. II (1959), pp. 55–75.

Towers, A.R. "*Amelia* and the State of Matrimony," in *Review of English Studies*. V (1954), pp. 144–157.

Wolff, Cynthia M. "Fielding's *Amelia*: Private Virtue and Public Good," in *Texas Studies in Language and Literature*. X (1968), pp. 37–55.

JONATHAN WILD

Type of work: Novel
Author: Henry Fielding (1707–1754)
Type of plot: Social criticism
Time of plot: Late seventeenth century
Locale: England
First published: 1743

The characters of this satirical novel are vivid, the plot sure and swift, and Fielding's barbs at society both delightful and accurate. The book presents the story of a "great" man, but not a good one, for, says Fielding, a great man must necessarily be a villain.

Principal Characters

Jonathan Wild, a descendant of many men hanged for thievery and treason. He becomes a notorious criminal, beginning as a pickpocket while still a schoolboy. He becomes a criminal leader and gathers about him a gang of thieves who do his bidding. He shows his "greatness" as a criminal by being dishonest even to his friends and companions. His highest aim is to send his honest friend, Heartfree, to the gallows. Instead, he himself dies on the gallows, cursing mankind.

Count La Ruse, a fellow criminal with Jonathan Wild. He is a pickpocket befriended by Jonathan while in debtors' prison. He has a long career in crime which ends when he is executed by being broken on the wheel in France.

Laetitia Snap, who becomes Jonathan's wife. She keeps him at a distance for a time in order to keep her lover a secret. She is a fitting wife for Jonathan, being herself a pickpocket and a cheat at cards. She ends up on the gallows.

Mr. Heartfree, a good man who loves his family and is honest in his dealings. He is a former schoolmate of Jonathan. He is a jeweler by trade and is ruined by Jonathan and his gang, who steal his stock, beat him terribly, and say at the same time they are his friends.

Mrs. Heartfree, an honest woman. Jonathan convinces her that her husband wants her to go with Jonathan to Holland. Jonathan mistreats her, but she returns from her extensive travels in time to save her husband from hanging, after he has been framed by Jonathan. When she returns she has a fabulous jewel, the gift of a savage chief, which restores the family's prosperity.

The Story

Jonathan Wild was prepared by nature to be a "great man." His ancestors were all men of greatness, many of them hanged for thievery or treason. Those who escaped were simply shrewder and more fortunate than the others. But Jonathan was to be so "great" as to put his forefathers to shame.

As a boy he read about the great villains of history. At school he learned little, his best study being to pick the pockets of his tutors and fellow students. When he was seventeen, his father moved to town, where Jonathan was to put his talents to even better use. There he met the Count La Ruse, a knave destined to be one of the lesser "greats." La Ruse was in prison for debt, but Jonathan's skill soon secured his friend's freedom. Together they had many profitable ventures, picking the pockets of their friends and of each other. Neither became angry when the other stole from him, for each respected the other's abilities.

Jonathan, for unknown reasons, traveled in America for seven or eight years. Returning to England he continued his life of villainy. Since he was to be a truly "great" man, he could not soil his own hands with too much thievery because there was always the danger of the gallows if he should be apprehended. He gathered about him a handful of lesser thieves who took the risks while he collected most of the booty. La Ruse joined him in many of his schemes, and the two friends continued to steal from each other. This ability to cheat friends showed true "greatness."

Jonathan admired Laetitia Snap, a woman with qualities of "greatness" similar to his own. She was the daughter of his father's friend, and she too was skilled in picking pockets and cheating at cards. In addition, she was a lady of wonderfully loose morals. But try as he would, Jonathan could not get Laetitia to respond to his passion. The poor fellow did not at first know that each time he approached her she was hiding another lover in the closet. Had he known, his admiration would have been even greater.

Jonathan's true "greatness" did not appear until he renewed his acquaintance with Mr. Heartfree, a former schoolmate. Heartfree would never be a "great" man because he was a good man. He cheated no one, held no grudges, and loved his wife and children. These qualities made him the sort of person Jonathan liked to cheat. Heartfree was a jeweler who by hard work and honest practices had become moderately prosperous. With the help of La Ruse, Jonathan was able to bring Heartfree to ruin. They stole his jewels and his money and hired thugs to beat him unmercifully, all the time convincing the good man that they were his friends.

La Ruse approached the greatness of Jonathan by leaving the country after stealing most of their booty. Poor Heartfree was locked up for debt after the two scoundrels had ruined him. Then Jonathan performed his greatest act. He had also a strong passion for Mrs. Heartfree, a good and virtuous woman, and he persuaded her that her husband had asked him to take her and some remaining jewels to Holland until her husband could obtain his release. So cleverly did he talk that the woman did not even tell her husband goodbye, though she loved him dearly. Instead, she put her children in the hands of a faithful servant and accompanied the rogue on a ship leaving England immediately.

When a severe storm arose, Jonathan was sure that death was near. Throwing caution aside, he attacked Mrs. Heartfree. Her screams brought help from the captain. After the storm subsided, the captain put Jonathan adrift in a small boat. The captain did not know that Jonathan was a "great" man, not destined to die in ignoble fashion. After a while he was rescued. He returned to England with tall tales of his adventure, none of which were the least bit true.

In the meantime Heartfree had begun to suspect his friend of duplicity. When Jonathan returned, he was for a time able to persuade Heartfree that he had done everything possible to help the jeweler. He told just enough of the truth to make his story acceptable, for in "greatness" the lie must always contain some truth. But Jonathan went too far. He urged Heartfree to attempt an escape from prison by murdering a few guards. Heartfree saw his supposed friend as the rogue he was and denounced Jonathan in ringing tones. From that time on Jonathan lived only to bring Heartfree to complete destruction.

While Jonathan was plotting Heartfree's trip to the gallows, Laetitia's father finally gave his consent to his daughter's marriage to the rogue. It took only two weeks, however, for his passion to be satisfied; then the couple began to fight and cheat each other constantly.

After his marriage Jonathan continued in all kinds of knavery, but his most earnest efforts were directed toward sending Heartfree to the gallows. At last he hit upon a perfect plan. He convinced the authorities that Heartfree himself had plotted to have his wife take the jewels out of the country in order to cheat his creditors. Mrs. Heartfree had not returned to England. Although Jonathan hoped she was dead, he thought it better to have her husband hanged at once in case she should somehow return. Before Heartfree's sentence was carried out, however, Jonathan was arrested and put in jail. He was surprised by a visit from Laetitia. She came only to revile him. She, having been caught picking pockets, was also a prisoner. Her only wish was that she could have the pleasure of seeing Jonathan hanged before her turn came to die on the gallows.

On the day that Heartfree was to be hanged his wife returned. After many adventures and travel in many lands, she came back in time to tell her story and to save her husband from hanging. She had brought with her a precious jewel which had been given to her by a savage chief she met on her travels. Heartfree was released and his family was restored to prosperity. It was otherwise with Jonathan whose former friends hastened to hurry him to the gallows. On the appointed day he was hanged, leaving this world with a curse for all mankind. His wife and all his friends were hanged, save one. La Ruse was captured in France and broken on the wheel. Jonathan Wild was a "great" man because he was a complete villain.

Critical Evaluation

Jonathan Wild is an exceptionally brilliant novel. It reflects and comments upon the life of London and, at the same time, offers a profound moral analysis of human behavior.

The London in which Henry Fielding lived was characterized by wildness, extravagances and corruption. London was a "wide-open" city, a sort of American frontier town on a huge scale. During the years when Fielding was beginning his career, Sir Robert Walpole dominated the Parliament, the King, and the Courts. He stifled opposition and succeeded in amassing enormous power and wealth; he also attracted the brilliant and biting satire of some of England's most talented writers, including Swift, Gay, Pope, and Fielding. Jonathan Wild, a "great man," is intended as a satire of Walpole as well as of the moral position he occupied. Viewing this "great man" as a gangster and an opportunist, Fielding combined him with another personage, an actual small time criminal named Jonathan Wild, who was hanged at Tyburn before a large, interested crowd.

Henry Fielding offers an alternative to the blind respect that those in authority often demand. By stressing throughout the novel the distinction between "greatness" and "goodness," Fielding makes moral judgments independent of social standing. He implies not only that we must distinguish between greatness and goodness, but that the two are mutually exclusive.

But there is a further point that Fielding makes about "greatness": it amounts to nothing but the untrammeled selfish instincts of men. For Jonathan Wild, it means stealing from friend and foe alike, taking advantage of women whenever possible, and, above all, thinking and acting in behalf of no one but himself. This unrestricted and uncivilized behavior accounts for his name: he is wild indeed. But although he is as wild as an animal, he is basically not free. At every step, he is entirely possessed by his own desires and driven by his own selfish instincts. The more he looks after "number one," and the more he lets himself go, the fewer choices he has left open to him. Thus it is philosophically appropriate, as well as morally necessary, for Jonathan Wild to be jailed and hanged at the conclusion of the novel.

Fielding intends Wild to be contrasted with his enemy, Heartfree, who, because he thinks of others and lacks ambition, is basically free as well as morally acceptable. Freedom for Henry Fielding, then, lies not in the possession of power or wealth or license, but in the practice of a simple morality and a consideration for others. Thus, in *Jonathan Wild*, freedom arises from social responsibility and not from individual prerogative.

Bibliography

Benerji, Hiran Kumar. *Henry Fielding: Playwright, Journalist and Master of the Art of Fiction.* Oxford: Blackwell, 1929, pp. 151–166.

Bispham, G.T. "Fielding's *Jonathan Wild*," in *Eighteenth Century Literature: An Oxford Miscellany.* Oxford: Clarendon Press, 1909, pp. 56–75.

Braudy, Leo. *Narrative Form in History and Fiction: Hume, Fielding, and Gibbon.* Princeton, N.J.: Princeton University Press, 1970, pp. 121–143.

Cross, Wilbur L. *The History of Henry Fielding*, Volume I. New Haven, Conn.: Yale University Press, 1918, pp. 403–425.

Digeon, Aurélien. *The Novels of Fielding.* London: Routledge and Kegan Paul, 1925, pp. 96–128. Reprinted in *Fielding: A Collection of Critical Essays.* Edited by Ronald Paulson. Englewood Cliffs, N.J.: Prentice-Hall, 1962, pp. 69–80.

Dircks, Richard J. "The Perils of Heartfree: A Sociological Review of Fielding's Adaptation of Dramatic Convention," in *Texas Studies in Literature and Language.* VIII (1966), pp. 5–13.

Dudden, Frederick Homes. *Henry Fielding: His Life, Works, and Times*, Volume I. Oxford: Clarendon Press, 1952, pp. 449–501.

Evans, David L. "The Theme of Liberty in *Jonathan Wild*," in *Papers on Language and Literature.* III (1967), pp. 302–313.

Farrell, William J. "The Mock-Heroic Form of *Jonathan Wild*," in *Modern Philology.* LXIII (1966), pp. 216–226.

Hopkins, Robert H. "Language and Comic Play in Fielding's *Jonathan Wild*," in *Criticism.* VIII (Summer, 1966), pp. 213–228.

Irwin, William Robert. *The Making of* Jonathan Wild: *A Study in the Literary Method of Henry Fielding.* New York: Columbia University Press, 1941.

Kettle, Arnold. *An Introduction to the English Novel*, Volume I. London: Hutchinson's, 1951, pp. 45–51.

Kronenberger, Louis. *The Republic of Letters: Essays on Various Writers.* New York: Knopf, 1955, pp. 81–88.

McKillop, Alan D. *The Early Masters of English Fiction.* Lawrence: University of Kansas Press, 1956, pp. 114–118.

Pinkus, Philip. "Satire and St. George," in *Queen's Quarterly.* LXX (Spring, 1963), pp. 30–49.

Preston, John. "The Ironic Mode: A Comparison of *Jonathan Wild* and *The Beggar's Opera*," in *Essays in Criticism.* XVI (July, 1966), pp. 268–280.

Rawson, Claude J. *Henry Fielding and the Augustan Ideal Under Stress.* London: Routledge and Kegan Paul, 1972, pp. 101–259.

————. "The Hero as Clown: Jonathan Wild, Felix Krull, and Others," in *Studies in the Eighteenth Century.* Toronto: University of Toronto Press, 1973, pp. 17–52.

Robbins, Alfred F. "*Jonathan Wild the Great*: Its Germ," in *Notes and Queries.* Series XI. II (October, 1910), pp. 261–263.

Shea, Bernard. "Machiavelli and Fielding's *Jonathan Wild*," in *PMLA.* LXXII (1957), pp. 55–73.

Shesgreen, Sean.   *Literary Portraits in the Novels of Henry Fielding.* De Kalb: Northern Illinois University Press, 1972, pp. 45–71.

Smith, Raymond.   "The Ironic Structure of Fielding's *Jonathan Wild*," in *Ball State University Forum.* VI (Autumn, 1965), pp. 3–9.

Wells, J.E.   "Fielding's Political Purpose in *Jonathan Wild*," in *PMLA.* XXVIII (1913), pp. 1–55.

Wendt, Allan E.   "The Moral Allegory of *Jonathan Wild*," in *Journal of English Literary History.* XXIV (December, 1957), pp. 306–320.

Williams, Muriel Brittain.   *Marriage: Fielding's Mirror of Morality.* University: University of Alabama Press, 1973, pp. 62–69.

JOSEPH ANDREWS

Type of work: Novel
Author: Henry Fielding (1707–1754)
Type of plot: Comic epic
Time of plot: Early eighteenth century
Locale: England
First published: 1742

Originally begun as a satiric rebuttal of what Fielding felt was the distasteful, maudlin sentimentality of Richardson's Pamela, Joseph Andrews *takes its title from the hero, who is Pamela Andrews' brother. However, the work soon grew into something much more serious than a mere takeoff. Often called the first realistic novel of English literature, the work brilliantly satirizes affectation and the vanities of human nature. The structure of the novel is loose, but its realistic settings and vivid portrayal of eighteenth century English life more than compensate for this weakness.*

Principal Characters

Joseph Andrews, a simple, handsome young man of great virtue who, because of his looks and purity, becomes the erotic prey of various women. Discharged from his post as Lady Booby's footman when he fails to respond to her advances, he leaves London to return to his native Somersetshire and his true love, Fanny Goodwill. On the way he is robbed, beaten, made fun of, and nearly raped. At an inn he meets his old tutor, Parson Adams, and together they travel home. On the way Parson Adams rescues Fanny from a brutal ruffian. At home, however, Joseph's marriage to Fanny is thwarted by a jail term on charges brought by revengeful Lady Booby, the objections of his relatives, and the discovery that Fanny is supposedly his sister. When it turns out that he is really a son of a family named Wilson—the children had been exchanged by gipsies—the marriage takes place.

Fanny Goodwill, Joseph Andrews' attractive, virtuous sweetheart. Traveling to meet Joseph in London, after hearing that Lady Booby has dismissed him, she accompanies her lover and Parson Adams back to Somersetshire. Her adventures consist mainly of hairbreadth escapes from attackers until she is married.

Parson Abraham Adams, an earthy man who loves food, drink, and tobacco. At the same time he is idealistic and charitable. An absent-minded tutor and the friend of Joseph and Fanny, he accompanies them home, protecting them with his fists and sharing their troubles, and at last marries them.

Lady Booby, a noblewoman torn between her pride of class and her love for her handsome young footman. After dismissing him, she returns to her Somersetshire estate and uses all her influence to prevent his marriage to Fanny.

Mrs. Slipslop, Lady Booby's housekeeper, an aggressive, misshapen woman who almost rapes Joseph and tries continually to win him over.

Pamela Booby, Joseph's sister, who tries to prevent his marriage to Fanny.

Adapted from Richardson's novel "Pamela," she exemplifies virtue based on vanity rather than, as in Fanny's case, on natural goodness.

Squire Booby, Pamela's husband, a good man who frees Joseph from jail and accepts him as an equal, but because of class pride he objects to Joseph's marriage to Fanny.

Peter Pounce, Lady Booby's steward, a stingy, uncharitable man who, on one occasion, saves Fanny from rape but plans to enjoy her himself.

Mr. Wilson, a kindly, intelligent man who serves as host to the penniless Joseph, Fanny, and Parson Adams. He later turns out to be Joseph's true father.

Mrs. Wilson, his wife.

The Pedlar, a good-hearted person who pays a debt for Parson Adams, saves his son from drowning, and explains the mystery of Fanny's parentage.

Mrs. Adams, the Parson's good but practical wife. She objects to Joseph's marriage because she thinks it will interfere with her children's advancement.

Beau Didapper, a London fop who visits Lady Booby and tries to seduce Fanny.

Gammer and
Gaffer Andrews, Joseph and Pamela's rather fatuous parents.

A Lecherous Squire. He sets his hounds on Parson Adams, humiliates him at dinner, and tries to gain Fanny first by cunning and then by force.

A Captain, his agent, who captures Fanny at the inn, takes her off to the Squire, but is stopped in time by Peter Pounce.

A Gentleman. He promises food and lodging to Joseph, Fanny, and Parson Adams, but fails to make good.

A Generous Innkeeper. He promises nothing but lets the group stay at his inn without payment.

Parson Trulliber, a gluttonous, bad-tempered minister who refuses charity to Parson Adams.

Mr. Tow-Wouse, an innkeeper who is meek and stingy.

Mrs. Tow-Wouse, his vixenish wife.

Betty, their servant, who nearly ravishes Joseph while nursing him.

Mr. Scout, Lady Booby's lawyer, who throws Joseph and Fanny into jail on trumped up charges.

The Story

Joseph Andrews was ten or eleven years in the service of Sir Thomas Booby, uncle of the Squire Booby who married the virtuous Pamela, Joseph's sister. When Lord Booby died, Joseph remained in the employ of Lady Booby as her footman. This lady, much older than her twenty-one-year-old servant, and apparently little disturbed by her husband's death, paid entirely too much attention to pleasant-mannered and handsome Joseph. But Joseph was as virtuous as his famous sister, and when Lady Booby's advances became such that even his innocence could no longer deny their true nature, he was as firm in resisting her as Pamela had been in restraining Squire Booby. Insulted, the lady discharged Joseph on the spot, in spite of the protests of Mrs. Slipslop, her maid, who found herself also attracted to the young man.

With very little money and fewer prospects, Joseph set out from London to Somersetshire to see his sweetheart, Fanny, for whose sake he had withstood Lady

Booby's advances. The very first night of his journey, Joseph was attacked by robbers, who stole his money, beat him soundly, and left him lying naked and half dead in a ditch. A passing coach stopped when the passengers heard his cries, and he was taken to a nearby inn.

Joseph was well cared for until the innkeeper's wife discovered that he was penniless. He was recognized, however, by another visitor at the inn, his old tutor and preceptor, Parson Adams, who was on his way to London to sell a collection of his sermons. He paid Joseph's bill with his own meager savings; then, discovering that in his absentmindedness he had forgotten to bring the sermons with him, he decided to accompany Joseph back to Somersetshire.

They started out, alternately on foot and on the parson's horse. Fortunately, Mrs. Slipslop overtook them in a coach on her way to Lady Booby's country place. She accommodated the parson in the coach while Joseph rode the horse. The inn at which they stopped next had an innkeeper who gauged his courtesy according to the appearance of his guests. There Joseph was insulted by the host. In spite of the clerical cassock he was wearing, Parson Adams stepped in to challenge the host, and a fist fight followed, the ranks being swelled by the hostess and Mrs. Slipslop. When the battle finally ended, Parson Adams was the bloodiest looking, since the hostess in the excitement had doused him with a pail of hog's blood.

The journey continued, this time with Joseph in the coach and the parson on foot, for with typical forgetfulness the good man had left his horse behind. However, he walked so rapidly and the coach moved so slowly that he easily outdistanced his friends. While he was resting on his journey, he heard the shrieks of a woman. Running to her rescue, he discovered a young woman being cruelly attacked by a burly fellow, whom the parson belabored with such violence that he laid the attacker at his feet. As some fox hunters rode up, the ruffian rose from the ground and accused Parson Adams and the woman of being conspirators in an attempt to rob him. The parson and the woman were quickly taken prisoners and led off to the sheriff. On the way the parson discovered that the young woman whom he had aided was Fanny. Having heard of Joseph's unhappy dismissal from Lady Booby's service, she had been on her way to London to help him when she had been so cruelly molested.

After some uncomfortable moments before the judge, the parson was recognized by an onlooker, and both he and Fanny were released. They went to the inn where Mrs. Slipslop and Joseph were staying.

Joseph and Fanny were overjoyed to be together once more. Mrs. Slipslop, displeased to see Joseph's display of affection for another woman, drove off in the coach, leaving Parson Adams and the young lovers behind.

None of the three had any money to pay their bill at the inn. Parson Adams, with indomitable optimism, went to visit the clergyman of the parish in order to borrow the money, but with no success. Finally a poor peddler at the inn gave them every penny he had, just enough to cover the bill.

They continued their trip on foot, stopping at another inn where the host was more courteous than any they had met, and more understanding about their financial difficulties. Still farther on their journey, they came across a secluded house at which they were asked to stop and rest. Mr. and Mrs. Wilson were a charming couple who gave their guests a warm welcome. Mr. Wilson entertained the parson with the story of his life. It seemed that in his youth he had been attracted by the vanity of London life, had squandered his money on foppish clothes, gambling, and drinking, and had eventually been imprisoned for debt. From this situation he was rescued by a kindly cousin whom he later married. The two had retired from London to this quiet country home. They had two lovely children and their only sorrow, but that a deep one, was that a third child, a boy with a strawberry mark on his shoulder, had been stolen by gypsies and had never been heard of since.

After a pleasant visit with the kindly family, the travelers set out again. Their adventures were far from ended. Parson Adams suddenly found himself caught in the middle of a hare hunt, with the hounds inclined to mistake him for the hare. Their master goaded on the dogs, but Joseph and the parson were victorious in the battle. They found themselves face to face with an angry squire and his followers. But when the squire caught sight of the lovely Fanny, his anger softened, and he invited the three to dine.

Supper was a trying affair for the parson, who was made the butt of many practical jokes. Finally the three travelers left the house in great anger and went to an inn. In the middle of the night, some of the squire's men arrived, overcame Joseph and the parson, and abducted Fanny. On the way, however, an old acquaintance of Fanny, Peter Pounce, met the party of kidnapers, recognized Fanny, and rescued her.

The rest of the journey was relatively uneventful. When they arrived home, however, further difficulties arose. Joseph and Fanny stayed at the parsonage and waited eagerly for the publishing of their wedding banns. Lady Booby had also arrived in the parish, the seat of her summer home. Still in love with Joseph, she exerted every pressure of position and wealth to prevent the marriage. She even had Fanny and Joseph arrested. At this point, however, Squire Booby and his wife Pamela arrived. That gentleman insisted on accepting his wife's relatives as his own, even though they were of a lower station, and Joseph and Fanny were quickly released from custody.

All manner of arguments were presented by Pamela, her husband, and Lady Booby in their attempts to turn Joseph aside from his intention of marrying Fanny. Her lowly birth made a difference to their minds, now that Pamela had made a good match and Joseph had been received by the Boobys.

Further complications arose when a traveling peddler revealed that Fanny, whose parentage until then had been unknown, was the sister of Pamela. Mrs. and Mr. Andrews were summoned at this disclosure, and Mrs. Andrews described how, while Fanny was still a baby, gypsies had stolen the child and left behind them a sickly little boy she had brought up as her own. Now it appeared that Joseph was the foundling. However, a strawberry mark on Joseph's chest soon established his identity. He was the son of the kindly Wilsons.

Both lovers were now secure in their social positions, and nothing further could prevent their marriage, which took place, to the happiness of all concerned, soon afterward.

Critical Evaluation

Joseph Andrews is many things: a parody of Richardson's *Pamela,* a sentimental tale of virtue rewarded; a realistic portrayal of the English road in the eighteenth century; a resetting of the values of comic epic poetry in prose, resulting in what Fielding calls a "comic epic romance" and by which he has in mind the model of Cervantes' *Don Quixote*; an experiment in social satire which brands affectation as ridiculous. All these characteristics blend in a master function. It is an oversimplification merely to conceive of this function in generic terms, to formulate an all-encompassing descriptive label like "comic epic in prose" or "comic novel" and consider the book defined.

Fielding, along with Richardson, is sometimes called the father of the English novel because he ventilated the concept of narrative itself; his brilliant plotting in *Tom Jones* and the desultory Odyssean travels of *Joseph Andrews* are contrasting patterns for realizing a broadly imagined action rich in human nature. *Joseph Andrews,* then, is one of the earliest examples of modern literature's successful extension of mimetic possibilities beyond the models of classical antiquity and the folk tradition. The novel is a mixed genre; it is composed of tale, parable, ballad, and, of course, epic. But the mixture becomes a whole greater than its parts with true innovators such as Fielding.

What holds Fielding's book together is its cosmic exposure of appearance. Wherever Joseph and Parson Adams go, their naïveté and innocence make them inadvert exposers of affectation. Affectation is the most ridiculous form of "appearance" among men. It invites derision and must be exposed: the effect is morally healthy, but even more to the point, mimetically revealing. Behind appearance lies the "true springs of human action." The essence of a man is often better than his appearance, even though his vanity may commit him to affectation. Parson Adams is a loveable character mainly because under his pedantries and vanities beats a heart of gold. His naïve trust in human goodness, and his unshakeable belief in practiced Christianity define the true man: the "real" Adam is better than his affectations. Similarly, when Joseph is robbed, beaten, and stripped of his clothes, Fielding takes the opportunity to demonstrate the fact that true human charity may emanate from a person whose appearance and life history would seem to mark him incapable of any kindness: "the postillion (a lad who has since been transported for

robbing a hen-roost) . . . voluntarily stripped off a great-coat, his only garment; at the same time swearing a great oath, for which he was rebuked by
the passengers, that he would rather ride in his shirt all his life, than suffer a
fellow passenger to lie in so miserable a condition."

Fielding trusts in his satiric method—the exposure of affectation and the
questioning of appearance—because he senses that it will not ground his
comic vision in despair or cynicism. He avoids the satiric fate of Swift, whose
contempt for human imperfections of character and principle drove him to
contempt for men in general. Fielding maintains a love of life itself, an essential state of mind for an artist who presumes to epic achievements in the
imaginative grasp of social reality. Swift could never have written *Tom Jones*
(1749), Fielding's great comic novel with its tolerant but firmly objective
picture of human nature. *Joseph Andrews* is a preface, in theme and style,
to the more carefully plotted masterpiece.

As tolerant as Fielding is of human nature, he is also capable of biting
judgment. Not a misanthrope like Swift, as Walter Allen reminds us in *The
English Novel* (1954), Fielding is nevertheless a tough-minded moralist who
delights in passing harsh comic judgment when it is called for. He was, after
all, a court judge in real life. Parson Trulliber is a case in point. Fielding
has Parson Adams fall into the mud with Trulliber's pigs, but this embarrassment is typical of the many other physical beatings and discomforts that the
good Parson suffers throughout the novel. They are emblematic of Fielding's
mild judgment of Adams' clerical vanity. Once the mud is washed off, the
naïve but true Christian in Parson Adams is all the more shiningly revealed.
Things are exactly the opposite with Trulliber. His Christianity is completely
superficial; Parson Adams' innocent request for fourteen shillings of charity is
met by cries of thief. Once Trulliber's fake Christianity is exposed, he is all
hog's mud underneath. This is established from the beginning of his encounter with Parson Adams, whom he mistakes for a hog merchant. Trulliber
sees and feels with the eyes and temperament of a hog. He is stingy with food
as well as money and like his angry pigs is quick to belligerence. The only
way he can defend himself against Parson Adams' accusation that he is not
a good Christian is by clenching his fist. The most telling irony is Trulliber's
contempt for Parson Adams' appearance. How can this horseless man with a
torn "cassock" call himself a man of the cloth? Because Trulliber's Christianity is all surface, it is he who is dripping in hog's mud from first to last,
not Parson Adams.

Fielding's pursuit of essential humanity in his characters, through the strip-
ping away of affectation and appearance, is so successful that by the end of
the novel he can indulge in burlesque without dehumanizing. Two chapters
from the end, Parson Adams, thinking he is about to rescue Fanny from rape,
finds himself wrestling with Slipslop, whom he mistakes for the rapist.
Aroused to his mistake by Slipslop's huge bosom and Lady Booby's entrance,

he staggers back to what he mistakenly thinks is his own room and lies down beside Fanny. In the morning Joseph discovers them lying together. Everything is explained and everyone is appeased. Even Slipslop seems to have enjoyed the "attention" of both the rapist (Beau Didapper) and her attacker, the Parson. All this is pure farce, a broad joke to usher in the warmly comic conclusion of the novel. It is a measure of Fielding's fictive power that he can people a story with characters rich enough to shift from burlesque to comedy without compromising their credibility. In fact, both plot and character seem to benefit mutually from the author's comic exuberance.

Bibliography

Alter, Robert. *Fielding and the Nature of the Novel.* Cambridge, Mass.: Harvard University Press, 1968, pp. 123–130.

Battestin, Martin C. *The Moral Basis of Fielding's Art: A Study of* Joseph Andrews. Middletown, Conn.: Wesleyan University Press, 1959.

Benerji, Hiran Kumar. *Henry Fielding: Playwright, Journalist and Master of the Art of Fiction.* Oxford: Blackwell, 1929, pp. 110–133.

Bissell, Frederick O. *Fielding's Theory of the Novel.* Ithaca, N.Y.: Cornell University Press, 1933, pp. 24–37, 67–74.

Cross, Wilbur L. *The History of Henry Fielding,* Volume I. New Haven, Conn.: Yale University Press, 1918, pp. 314–359.

Digeon, Aurélien. *The Novels of Fielding.* London: Routledge and Kegan Paul, 1925, pp. 39–90.

Dudden, Frederick Homes. *Henry Fielding: His Life, Works, and Times,* Volume I. Oxford: Clarendon Press, 1952, pp. 327–392.

Ehrenpreis, Irvin. "Fielding's Use of Fiction: The Autonomy of *Joseph Andrews,*" in *Twelve Original Essays on Great English Novels.* Edited by Charles Shapiro. Detroit: Wayne State University Press, 1960, pp. 23–41.

Goldberg, Homer. *The Art of* Joseph Andrews. Chicago: University of Chicago Press, 1969.

Jenkins, Elizabeth. *Henry Fielding.* London: Home and Van Thal, 1947, pp. 31–42.

Johnson, Maurice. *Fielding's Art of Fiction: Eleven Essays on* Shamela, Joseph Andrews, Tom Jones, *and* Amelia. Philadelphia: University of Pennsylvania Press, 1961, pp. 47–82.

Kaul, A.N. *The Action of English Comedy: Studies in the Encounters of Abstraction and Experience from Shakespeare to Shaw.* New Haven, Conn.: Yale University Press, 1970, pp. 166–174.

Kettle, Arnold. *An Introduction to the English Novel*, Volume I. London: Hutchinson's, 1951, pp. 72–77.

Levine, George R. *Henry Fielding and the Dry Mock: A Study of the Techniques of Irony in His Early Works*. The Hague: Mouton, 1967, pp. 91–125.

Mack, Maynard. "Introduction," in *Joseph Andrews*. New York: Holt, Rinehart and Winston, 1948. Reprinted in *Fielding: A Collection of Critical Essays*. Edited by Ronald Paulson. Englewood Cliffs, N.J.: Prentice-Hall, 1962, pp. 52–58.

McKillop, Alan D. *The Early Masters of English Fiction*. Lawrence: University of Kansas Press, 1956, pp. 100–114.

Palmer, Eustace. "Fielding's *Joseph Andrews*: A Comic Epic in Prose," in *English Studies*. LII (1971), pp. 331–339.

Priestley, J.B. *The English Comic Characters*. London: J. Lane, 1928, pp. 106–127.

Schilling, Bernard Nicholas. *The Comic Spirit: Boccaccio to Thomas Mann*. Detroit: Wayne State University Press, 1965, pp. 43–97.

Spilka, Mark. "Comic Resolution in Fielding's *Joseph Andrews*," in *College English*. XV (October, 1953), pp. 11–19. Reprinted in *Fielding: A Collection of Critical Essays*. Edited by Ronald Paulson. Englewood Cliffs, N.J.: Prentice-Hall, 1962, pp. 59–68. Also reprinted in *Essays on the Eighteenth Century Novel*. Edited by Robert Donald Spector. Bloomington: Indiana University Press, 1965, pp. 78–91.

Taylor, Dick, Jr. "Joseph as Hero in *Joseph Andrews*," in *Tulane Studies in English*. VII (1957), pp. 91–109.

Thornbury, Ethel Margaret. *Henry Fielding's Theory of the Comic Prose Epic*. Madison: University of Wisconsin Press, 1931, pp. 95–111.

Tichý, Aleš. "Remarks on the Flow of Time in the Novels of Henry Fielding," in *BRNO Studies in English*. II (1959), pp. 55–75.

Watt, Ian. *The Rise of the Novel: Studies in Defoe, Richardson, and Fielding*. Berkeley: University of California Press, 1957, pp. 239–259.

Wright, Andrew. "*Joseph Andrews*: Mask and Feast," in *Essays in Criticism*. XIII (July, 1963), pp. 209–221.

TOM JONES

Type of work: Novel
Author: Henry Fielding (1707–1754)
Type of plot: Comic epic
Time of plot: Early eighteenth century
Locale: England
First published: 1749

Tom Jones. *a major contribution to the history of the English novel, has been admired by many readers as the most meticulously crafted book of its type. With neoclassic objectivity, humor, and fine psychological delicacy, Fielding dissects the motives of his characters to reveal universal truths about human nature.*

Principal Characters

Tom Jones, a foundling. Although befriended by his foster father, Squire Allworthy, Tom encounters many vicissitudes, some of them of his own making, for he is a somewhat wild and foolish, though good-hearted young man. His wild ways, exaggerated by enemies, including Master Blifil, cause Tom to be cast off by Squire Allworthy. After Tom's goodness and virtue eventually triumph over disastrous circumstances, the young man is reconciled with the Squire and, even more important, with Sophia Western, the beautiful and virtuous woman he loves. He is acknowledged as the Squire's nephew when the secret of his real parentage becomes known.

Squire Allworthy, an extremely just and virtuous country gentleman who becomes Tom's foster father after the infant is discovered in the Squire's bed. Tom's enemies play upon the Squire's gullibility, for Allworthy, like many another honest man, finds it difficult to believe that there is dishonesty in other people. Eventually he sees Tom's essential goodness, receives him as his nephew, and makes the young man his heir.

Sophia Western, the virtuous daughter of a domineering country squire. She loves Tom Jones, even to facing down her father and aunt when they try to marry her off to Master Blifil and Lord Fellamar. Though she loves Tom, she is disappointed by his escapades, particularly those of an amorous nature, and until she is convinced he can be a faithful husband she refuses to accept his suit.

Squire Western, Sophia's domineering, profane father, who loves his hounds, his horses, and his bottle almost as much as his only child. When he insists upon forcing her to marry Master Blifil, the husband of his choice, Sophia is forced into running away from home, placing herself and her virtue in the path of adventure and danger. The Squire, though uncouth, is a good man at heart. Both he and Squire Allworthy are exceptionally well-drawn characters.

Master Blifil, the villainous son of the Squire's sister Bridget. A great hypocrite, he hides his villainy under a cloak of seeming honesty and virtue. He plays false witness against Tom Jones many times. He becomes Sophia Western's suitor only because he wants her money and hates Tom, the man she loves. His villainy is done, too, in the face of his knowing that Tom is really an older half brother, not a foundling.

Bridget Blifil, Squire Allworthy's seemingly virtuous spinster sister. She bears Tom out of wedlock and lets him become a foundling. Later she marries and has another son, Master Blifil. On her deathbed she sends to her brother a letter telling the story of Tom's parentage. The letter is stolen and concealed by her legitimate son.

Captain Blifil, Bridget's husband, who marries her for her money. He dies of apoplexy, however, before he can enjoy any of it.

Mr. Partridge, a schoolteacher and barber-surgeon. Long Tom's loyal, if loquacious, companion, he is for many years suspected of being Tom's father.

Jenny Jones, later **Mrs. Waters.** A maid in Mr. Partridge's house, she is accused of being Tom's mother, and her surname is given to him. As Mrs. Waters she has a brief love affair with Tom, much to the horror of some of his acquaintances, who believe the supposed mother and son have committed incest. Through her testimony the identity of Tom's real mother becomes known.

Mr. Dowling, a not-so-honest lawyer. Through his testimony Tom's identity is proved, as he corroborates Jenny Jones' statements. He keeps the secret many years, thinking that he is following Mr. Allworthy's wishes.

Black George Seagrim, so-called because of his extremely black beard, a rustic and poacher. Though befriended by Tom, he steals from the young man and plays him ill turns.

Molly Seagrim, a young woman of easy virtue, Black George's daughter. Tom's escapades with her cause him grave trouble until her affairs with other men take some of the blame from him.

The Rev. Roger Thwackum, an Anglican clergyman retained by Mr. Allworthy to tutor Tom Jones and Master

Blifil during their boyhood. A self-righteous, bigoted man, he voices his prejudices at all times. He beats Tom often and severely, living up to his name.

Mr. Thomas Square, a deistically inclined philosopher who is a pensioner in Mr. Allworthy's household and Mr. Thwackum's opponent in endless debates over the efficacy of reason and religious insight. Though he dislikes Tom Jones, he makes a deathbed confession that clears Tom of some of his supposed misdeeds.

Lady Bellaston, a sensual noblewoman of loose morals who takes a fancy to Tom Jones and, when she is spurned, tries to do him a great deal of evil.

Mrs. Western, Lady Bellaston's cousin and Sophia's aunt. To satisfy her own social pretensions she tries to marry off Sophia to Lord Fellamar against the girl's will.

Mrs. Fitzpatrick, Sophia's cousin. They travel to London together.

Mr. Fitzpatrick, her jealous husband. Tom is jailed for wounding him in a duel.

Lord Fellamar, a licentious nobleman who makes love to Sophia and, with Mrs. Western's approval, even attempts to ravish the girl in order to force her to marry him. Misled by Lady Bellaston's advice, he tries to have Tom Jones impressed into the naval service.

Mrs. Arabella Hunt, a pretty and wealthy widow who offers formally by letter to marry Tom Jones. His refusal of this handsome offer helps reëstablish Tom with Sophia.

Honour Blackmore, Sophia's loyal, if somewhat selfish, maid, who shares in most of her mistress' adventures.

Mrs. Miller, Tom's landlady in London. Convinced of his virtue by his many good deeds she pleads on his behalf with Squire Allworthy and is instrumental in helping restore Tom to his foster father's good graces.

Nancy and
Betty Miller, the landlady's daughters.

Mr. Nightingale, Tom's fellow lodger at the Miller house. Tom persuades the elder Nightingale to permit the son to marry Nancy.

Mr. Summer, a handsome young cleric befriended as a student by Mr. Allworthy. It was he who seduced Bridget Allworthy and fathered Tom Jones.

The Story

Squire Allworthy lived in retirement in the country with his sister Bridget. Returning from a visit to London, he was considerably surprised upon entering his room to find an infant lying on his bed. His discovery caused much astonishment and consternation in the household, for the squire himself was a childless widower. The next day Miss Bridget and the squire inquired in the community to discover the baby's mother, and their suspicions were shortly fixed upon Jenny Jones, who had spent many hours in the squire's home while nursing Miss Bridget through a long illness. The worthy squire sent for the girl and in his gentle manner reprimanded her for her wicked behavior, assuring her, however, that the baby would remain in his home under the best of care. Fearing malicious gossip of the neighborhood, Squire Allworthy sent Jenny away.

Jenny Jones had been a servant in the house of a schoolmaster named Mr. Partridge, who had educated the young woman during her four years in his house. Mrs. Partridge, because of Jenny's comely face, was jealous of her. Neighborhood gossip soon convinced Mrs. Partridge that her husband was the father of Jenny's son, whereupon Squire Allworthy called the schoolmaster before him and talked to him at great length concerning morality. Mr. Partridge, deprived of his school, his income, and his wife, also left the country.

Not long afterward Captain Blifil won the heart of Bridget Allworthy. Eight months after their nuptials Bridget bore a son. The squire thought it would be well to rear the foundling and his sister's child together. The foundling had been named Jones, after his mother.

Squire Allworthy became exceedingly fond of the foundling. Captain Blifil died during his son's infancy, and Master Blifil grew up as Squire Allworthy's acknowledged heir. Otherwise, he remained on even terms with the foundling so far as opportunities for advancement were concerned. But Tom was such a mischievous lad that he had but one friend among the servants, the gamekeeper, Black George, an indolent man with a large family. Hired to instruct the lads were Mr. Thwackum and Mr. Square, who considered Tom a wicked soul. Tom's many deceptions were always discovered through the combined efforts of Mr. Thwackum, Mr. Square, and Master Blifil, who as he grew older disliked Tom more and more. It had been assumed by all that Mrs. Blifil would dislike Tom, but at times she seemed to show greater affection for him than for her own son. In turn, the compassionate squire took Master Blifil to his heart and became censorious of Tom.

Mr. Western, who lived on a neighboring estate, had a daughter whom he loved more than anyone else in the world. Sophia had a tender fondness for Tom because of a deed of kindness he had performed for her when they were still children. At the age of twenty, Master Blifil had become a favorite with the young ladies, while Tom was considered a ruffian by all but Mr. Western, who admired his ability to hunt. Tom spent many evenings at the Western home, with every opportunity to see Sophia, for whom his affections were increasing daily. One afternoon Tom had the good fortune to be nearby when Sophia's horse ran away. Tom, in rescuing her, broke his arm. He was removed to Mr. Western's house, where he received medical care and remained to recover from his hurt. One day he and Sophia had occasion to be alone in the garden, where they exchanged confessions of love.

Squire Allworthy became mortally ill. Assuming that he was dying, the doctor sent for the squire's relatives. With his servants and family gathered around him, the squire announced the disposal of his wealth, giving generously to Tom. Tom was the only one satisfied with his portion; his only concern was the impending death of his foster father and benefactor. On the way home from London to see the squire, Mrs. Blifil died suddenly. When the squire was pronounced out of danger, Tom's joy was so great that he became drunk through toasting the squire's health, and quarreled with young Blifil.

Sophia's aunt, Mrs. Western, perceived the interest her niece showed in Blifil, for Sophia, wishing to conceal her affection for Tom, gave Blifil the greater part of her attention when she was with the two young men. Informed by his sister of Sophia's conduct, Mr. Western suggested to Squire Allworthy that a match be arranged between Blifil and Sophia. When Mrs. Western told the young girl of the proposed match, Sophia thought that she meant Tom, and she immediately disclosed her passion for the foundling. But it was unthinkable that Mr. Western, much as he liked Tom, would ever allow his daughter to marry a man without a family and a fortune, and Mrs. Western forced Sophia to receive Blifil under the threat of exposing the girl's real affection for Tom. Sophia met Tom secretly in the garden and the two lovers vowed constancy. Discovering them, Mr. Western went immediately to Squire Allworthy with his knowledge.

Blifil, aware of his advantage, told the squire that on the day he lay near death Tom was out drinking and singing. The squire felt that he had forgiven Tom any wrongs, but his show of unconcern for the squire's health infuriated the good man. He sent for Tom, reproached him, and banished him from his house.

With the help of Black George, the gamekeeper, and Mrs. Honour, Sophia's maid, Tom and Sophia were able to exchange love letters. When Sophia was confined to her room because she refused to marry Blifil, she bribed her maid to flee with her from her father's house. Tom, setting out to seek his fortune, went to an inn with a small company of soldiers. A fight followed in which he was severely injured, and a barber was summoned to treat his wound. When Tom had told the barber his story, the man surprisingly revealed himself to be Partridge, the schoolmaster, banished years before because he was suspected of being Tom's father. When Tom was well enough to travel, the two men set out together on foot.

Before they had gone far they heard screams of a woman in distress and came upon a woman struggling with a soldier who had beguiled her to that lonely spot. Promising to take her to a place of safety, Tom accompanied the unfortunate creature to the nearby village of Upton, where the landlady of the inn refused to receive them because of the woman's torn and disheveled clothing. But when she heard the true story of the woman's misfortune and had been assured that the woman was the lady of Captain Waters, a well-known officer, she relented. Mrs. Waters invited Tom to dine with her so that she could thank him properly for her rescue.

Meanwhile a lady and her maid arrived at the inn and proceeded to their rooms. They were followed, several hours later, by an angry gentleman in pursuit of his wife. Learning from the chambermaid that there was a woman resembling his wife in the inn, he burst into Mrs. Waters' chambers, only to confront Tom Jones. At his intrusion, Mrs. Waters began to scream. The gentleman, abashed, identified himself as Mr. Fitzpatrick and retreated with apologies. Shortly after this disturbance had subsided, Sophia and Mrs. Honour arrived at the inn. When Partridge unknowingly revealed Tom's relation with Mrs. Waters and the embarrassing situation which Mr. Fitzpatrick had disclosed, Sophia, grieved by Tom's fickleness, decided to continue on her way. Before leaving the inn, however, she had Mrs. Honour place on Tom's empty bed a muff which she knew he would recognize as hers.

Soon after setting out, Sophia overtook Mrs. Fitzpatrick, who had arrived at the inn early the previous evening and who had fled during the disturbance caused by her huband. Mrs. Fitzpatrick was Sophia's cousin, and they decided to go on to London together. In London Sophia proceeded to the home of Lady Bellaston, who was known to her through Mrs. Western. Lady Bellaston was sympathetic with Sophia's reasons for running away.

Unable to overtake Sophia, Tom and Partridge followed her to London, where Tom took lodgings in the home of Mrs. Miller, whom Squire Allworthy patronized on his visits to the city. The landlady had two daughters, Nancy and Betty, and a lodger, Mr. Nightingale, who was obviously in love with Nancy. Tom found congenial residence with Mrs. Miller, and he became friends with Mr. Nightingale. Partridge was still with Tom in the hope of future advancement for himself. Repeated visits to Lady Bellaston and Mrs. Fitzpatrick finally gave Tom the opportunity to meet Sophia during an intermission at a play. There Tom was able to allay Sophia's doubts as to his love for her. During his stay with the Millers, Tom learned that Mr. Nightingale's father objected to his marrying Nancy. Through the kindness of his heart Tom persuaded the elder Nightingale to permit the marriage, to Mrs. Miller's great delight.

Having learned Sophia's whereabouts from Mrs. Fitzpatrick, Mr. Western came to London and took Sophia from Lady Bellaston's house to his own lodgings. When Mrs. Honour brought the news to Tom, he was in despair. Penniless, he could not hope to marry Sophia, and now his beloved was in the hands of her father once more. Then Partridge brought news that Squire Allworthy was coming to London, bringing with him Master Blifil to marry Sophia. In his distress Tom went to see Mrs. Fitzpatrick, but encountered her jealous husband on her doorstep. In the duel which followed, Tom wounded Fitzpatrick and was carried off to jail.

There he was visited by Partridge, the friends he had made in London, and Mrs. Waters, who had been traveling with Mr. Fitzpatrick ever since their meeting in Upton. When Partridge and Mrs. Waters met in Tom's cell, Partridge recognized her as Jenny Jones, Tom's reputed mother. Horrified, he revealed his knowledge to everyone, including Squire Allworthy, who by that time had arrived in London with Blifil.

In Mrs. Miller's lodgings so many people had praised Tom's goodness and kindness that Squire Allworthy had almost made up his mind to relent in his attitude toward the foundling when news of his conduct with Mrs. Waters reached his ears. But fortunately the cloud was soon dispelled by Mrs. Waters herself, who assured the squire that Tom was no son of hers but the child of his sister Bridget and a student the squire had befriended. Tom's true father having died before his son's birth, Bridget had concealed her shame by putting the baby on her brother's bed upon his return from a long visit to London. Later she had paid Jenny liberally to let suspicion fall upon her former maid.

Squire Allworthy also learned that Bridget had claimed Tom as her son in a letter written before her death, a letter Blifil probably had destroyed. There was further proof that Blifil had plotted to have Tom hanged for murder, although Fitzpatrick had not died. That gentleman recovered sufficiently to acknowledge himself the aggressor in the duel, and Tom was released from prison.

Upon these disclosures of Blifil's villainy, Squire Allworthy dismissed Blifil and made Tom his true heir. Tom's proper station having been revealed, Mr. Western withdrew all objections to his suit. Reunited, Tom and Sophia were married and retired to Mr. Western's estate in the country.

Critical Evaluation

In a relatively short life span, Henry Fielding was a poet and a playwright, a journalist and a jurist, as well as a pioneer in the formal development of the modern novel. The early poetry may be disregarded, but his dramatic works gave Fielding the training which later enabled him to handle adeptly the complex plots of his novels. Although he wrote perhaps half-a-dozen novels (some attributions are disputed) Fielding is best remembered for *The History of Tom Jones, a Foundling*. This novel contains a strong infusion of autobiographical elements. The character Sophia, for example, was based on Fielding's wife Charlotte, who was his one great love. They eloped in 1734 and had ten years together before she died in 1744. Squire Allworthy combined traits of a former schoolmate from Eton named George Lyttelton (to whom the novel is dedicated), and a generous benefactor of the Fielding family named James Ralph. Moreover, Fielding's origins in a career army family and his rejection of that background shaped his portrayal of various incidental military personnel in this and his other novels; he had an anti-army bias. Fielding's own feelings of revulsion against urban living are reflected in the conclusion of *Tom Jones* (and in his other novels): the "happy ending" consists of a retreat to the country. Published a scant five years before Fielding's death, *Tom Jones* was a runaway bestseller, going through four editions within a twelve-month period.

The structure of the novel is carefully divided into eighteen books in a fashion similar to the epic form which Fielding explicitly praised. Of those eighteen books, the first six are set on the Somersetshire estate of Squire Allworthy. Books VII-XII deal with events on the road to London. And the culmination of the six books is laid in London. The very midpoint of the novel, Books IX and X, covers the hilarious hiatus at the inn in Upton. Apparent diversions and digressions are actually intentional exercises in character exposition. And all episodes are deliberately choreographed to advance the plot —sometimes in ways not evident until later. Everything contributes to the overall organic development of the novel.

This kind of coherence was intimately connected with Fielding's concern about the craft of fiction. It is no accident that *Tom Jones* is one of the most carefully and meticulously written novels in the history of English literature. It is, in fact, remarkably free of inconsistencies and casual errors. Fielding saw his task as a novelist to be a "historian" of human nature and human events. And he felt obligated to emphasize the moral aspect of his work. But more importantly, Fielding introduced each of his eighteen books with a chapter about the craft of prose fiction. Indeed, the entire novel is dotted with intercalary chapters on the craft of the novel and on literary criticism. And the remainder of the novel applies the principles enunciated in the chapters on proper construction of prose fiction—an amazing *tour de force*. The detailed analyses in themselves constitute a substantial work of literary criticism; however, Fielding amplified these theories with his own demonstration of their application by writing a novel, *Tom Jones,* according to his own principles. So compelling a union of theory and practice rendered Fielding's hypotheses virtually unassailable.

As Fielding made practical application of his theories of craftsmanship, their validity became readily apparent in his handling of characterization. He viewed human nature ambivalently, as a combination of good and bad. But whereas the bad person had almost no hope of redemption, the fundamentally good person could be (and would and should be) somewhat tinged with bad but nonetheless worthy for all that, according to Fielding. Thus the good person could occasionally be unwise (as Allworthy was) or indiscreet (as Jones often was) but still be an estimable human being, for such a person was more credible as a "good" person, Fielding thought, than one who was without defect. Consequently, the villain Blifil is unreconstructibly wicked, but the hero Tom Jones is essentially good, although morally flawed. In order to succeed, Jones had to improve morally—to cultivate "prudence" and "religion," as Squire Allworthy recommended. In this dichotomy between evil and good, villain and hero, a species of determinism—possibly not a factor consciously recognized by Fielding—creeps in. Both Blifil and Jones are born and reared in the same environment, but one is wicked and one is good. Only innate qualities could logically explain the difference. Of course, some minor characters are not so fully psychologized; they are essentially allegorical, representing ideas (Thwackum and Square, for example). Yet overall, Fielding's command of characterization in general comprised a series of excellent portraits. But these portraits are never allowed to dominate the novel, for all of them are designed to contribute to the development of the story. Such a system of priorities provides insight into Fielding's aesthetic and epistemological predispositions.

Fielding subscribed to a fundamentally Classical-Neo-Classical set of values, ethically and aesthetically. He saw the novel as a *mirror* of life, not an *illumination* of life. He valued literary craftsmanship; he assumed a position of detached objectivity; he esteemed wit; and he followed the Neo-Classical Unity of Action: his plot brought Tom Jones full circle from a favored position to disgrace back to the good graces of Squire Allworthy and Sophia. In the course of the novel, Fielding demonstrated his objectivity by commenting critically on the form of the novel. He further revealed his Classical commitments by embellishing his novel with historical detail, creating a high degree of verisimilitude. His sense of humor and his sharp wit also testified to his reliance on Classical ratiocination. The easygoing development of the plot additionally reveals Fielding's detachment and objectivity. And the great variety in types of characters whom he presents is another indication of his Classical inclinations toward universality. But above all, Fielding's moral stance and his insistence on ethical principles unequivocally mark him as a Neo-Classicist.

Bibliography

Alter, Robert. "Fielding and the Uses of Style," in *Novel: A Forum on Fiction.* I (Fall, 1967), pp. 53–63. Reprinted in *Twentieth Century Interpretations of Tom Jones: A Collection of Critical Essays.* Edited by Martin C. Battestin. Englewood Cliffs, N.J.: Prentice-Hall, 1968, pp. 97–109.

————. "The Picaroon Domesticated," in *Rogue's Progress: Studies in the Picaresque Novel.* Cambridge, Mass.: Harvard University Press, 1964, pp. 80–105.

Baker, Sheridan. "Bridget Allworthy: The Creative Pressures of Fielding's Plot," in *Papers of the Michigan Academy of Science, Arts, and Letters.* LII (1966), pp. 345–356.

Battestin, Martin C. "Fielding's Definition of Wisdom: Some Functions of Ambiguity and Emblem in *Tom Jones*," in *Journal of English Literary History.* XXXV (June, 1968), pp. 188–217.

Booth, Wayne C. *The Rhetoric of Fiction.* Chicago: University of Chicago Press, 1961, pp. 215–218. Reprinted in *Twentieth Century Interpretations of* Tom Jones: *A Collection of Critical Essays.* Edited by Martin C. Battestin. Englewood Cliffs, N.J.: Prentice-Hall, 1968, pp. 94–96.

Combs, William W. The Return to Paradise Hall: An Essay on *Tom Jones*," in *South Atlantic Quarterly.* LXVII (1967), pp. 419–436.

Crane, Ronald S. "The Plot of *Tom Jones*," in *Journal of General Education.* IV (January, 1950), pp. 112–130. Reprinted in *Critics and Criticism: Ancient and Modern.* Edited by Ronald S. Crane. Chicago: University of Chicago Press, 1952, pp. 616–647. Also reprinted in *Essays on the Eighteenth Century Novel.* Edited by Robert Donald Spector. Bloomington: Indiana University Press, 1965, pp. 92–130. Also reprinted in *Twentieth Century Interpretations of* Tom Jones: *A Collection of Critical Essays.* Edited by Martin C. Battestin. Englewood Cliffs, N.J.: Prentice-Hall, 1968, pp. 68–93.

Drew, Elizabeth A. *The Novel: A Modern Guide to Fifteen English Masterpieces.* New York: Norton, 1963, pp. 59–74.

Ehrenpreis, Irvin. *Fielding:* Tom Jones. London: Edward Arnold, 1964.

Empson, William. "*Tom Jones*," in *The Kenyon Review.* XX (Spring, 1958), pp. 217–249. Reprinted in *Fielding: A Collection of Critical Essays.* Edited by Ronald Paulson. Englewood Cliffs, N.J.: Prentice-Hall, 1962, pp. 123–145. Also reprinted in *Twentieth Century Interpretations of* Tom Jones: *A Collection of Critical Essays.* Edited by Martin C. Battestin. Englewood Cliffs, N.J.: Prentice-Hall, 1968, pp. 33–55.

Goldknopf, David. "The Failure of Plot in *Tom Jones*," in *Criticism.* XI (1969), pp. 262–274.

Hatfield, Glenn W. "The Serpent and the Dove: Fielding's Irony and the Prudence Theme of *Tom Jones*," in *Modern Philology.* LXV (1967), pp. 17–32.

Hutchens, Eleanor Newman. *Irony in* Tom Jones. University: University of Alabama Press, 1965.

Johnson, Maurice. *Fielding's Art of Fiction: Eleven Essays on* Shamela, Joseph Andrews, Tom Jones, *and* Amelia. Philadelphia: University of Pennsylvania Press, 1961, pp. 83–138.

Kettle, Arnold. "*Tom Jones*," in *An Introduction to the English Novel*, Volume I. London: Hutchinson's University Library, 1951, pp. 76–81. Reprinted in *Fielding: A Collection of Critical Essays.* Edited by Ronald Paulson. Englewood Cliffs, N.J.: Prentice-Hall, 1962, pp. 84–88.

McKillop, Alan D. "Some Recent Views of *Tom Jones*," in *College English.* XXI (October, 1959), pp. 17–22.

Mandel, Jerome. "The Man of the Hill and Mrs. Fitzpatrick: Character and Narrative Technique in *Tom Jones*," in *Papers on Language and Literature.* V (1969), pp. 26–38.

Maugham, William Somerset. *Art of Fiction: An Introduction to Ten Novels and Their Authors.* Garden City, N.Y.: Doubleday, 1955, pp. 33–54.

Milburn, Daniel Judson. *The Age of Wit, 1650–1750.* New York: Macmillan, 1966, pp. 77–119.

Murry, John Middleton. "In Defence of Fielding," in *Unprofessional Essays.* London: Jonathan Cape, 1956, pp. 25–39. Reprinted in *Fielding: A Collection of Critical Essays.* Edited by Ronald Paulson. Englewood Cliffs, N.J.: Prentice-Hall, 1962, pp. 89–97.

Preston, John. "Plot as Irony: The Reader's Role in *Tom Jones*," in *Journal of English Literary History.* XXXV (September, 1968), pp. 365–380.

Price, Martin. *To the Palace of Wisdom: Studies in Order and Energy from Dryden to Blake.* New York: Doubleday, 1964, pp. 285–311.

Spacks, Patricia Meyer. "Young Men's Fancies: James Boswell, Henry Fielding," in *Imagining a Self: Autobiography and Novel in Eighteenth-Century England.* Cambridge, Mass.: Harvard University Press, 1976, pp. 227–263.

Van Ghent, Dorothy. "On *Tom Jones*," in *The English Novel: Form and Function.* New York: Holt, Rinehart, and Winston, 1953, pp. 65–81.

Watt, Ian. *The Rise of the Novel: Studies in Defoe, Richardson, and Fielding.* Berkeley: University of California Press, 1957, pp. 260–289. Reprinted in *Fielding: A Collection of Critical Essays.* Edited by Ronald Paulson. Englewood Cliffs, N.J.: Prentice-Hall, 1962, pp. 98–122. Also reprinted in *Twentieth Century Interpretations of* Tom Jones: *A Collection of Critical Essays.* Edited by Martin C. Battestin. Englewood Cliffs, N.J.: Prentice-Hall, 1968, pp. 19–32.

Wright, Andrew. *Henry Fielding: Mask and Feast.* Berkeley: University of California Press, 1965, pp. 31–44. Reprinted in *Twentieth Century Interpretations of* Tom Jones: *A Collection of Critical Essays.* Edited by Martin C. Battestin. Englewood Cliffs, N.J.: Prentice-Hall, 1968, pp. 56–67.

WILLIAM GODWIN

Born: Wisbeach, England (March 3, 1756)
Died: London, England (April 7, 1836)

Principal Works

NOVELS: *The Adventures of Caleb Williams, or Things as They Are*, 1794; *St. Leon: A Tale of the Sixteenth Century*, 1799.

POLITICAL PHILOSOPHY: *The Inquiry concerning Political Justice and its Influence on General Virtue and Happiness*, 1793; *Of Population*, 1820.

HISTORY: *History of the Commonwealth*, 1820–1824.

William Godwin, born at Wisbeach, England, on March 3, 1756, made dissent the theme of his life. In a sense he was born to this theme, being the seventh of thirteen children in the family of a dissenting minister. Because of the father's religious views, the children were reared in a strict, Puritanic tradition. As a boy Godwin was educated at various academies run by and for nonconformists. Trained for the ministry, he entered church work in 1771. But he continued to study philosophy and by 1782 so completely disagreed with his sect that he left the ministry to earn a living by writing. Taking up residence in London, he became a hack writer, an atheist, and a radical.

Godwin's first book, the key to his thinking, was *Political Justice*, published in 1793. The volume received wide attention, and according to report the author narrowly escaped being prosecuted for his unorthodox views. In the book Godwin announced his principle of dispassionate advocation of extremes; the work is a compendium criticizing society, advocating a new ethics, and prophesying a Utopian future. People, thought Godwin, could exercise reason in all activities and through education could learn to apply the basic motivation of pleasure and pain to all their activities, thus producing a new ethics and a better society.

In 1792 Godwin met Mary Wollstonecraft, notorious at the time for her *Vindication of the Rights of Women.* In 1796 they began to live together without marriage, such conduct being basic to their principles, but they bowed to convention and married when Mary became pregnant. In 1797 Mary Godwin died a few days after giving birth to a daughter, leaving Godwin with two small children. One was their infant daughter, who became the wife of the poet Shelley, and the other was Mary Godwin's illegitimate child by Gilbert Imlay, an American novelist. Soon after becoming a widower, needing help in his household, Godwin married Mary Jane Clairmont, a widow with two children, one of whom, Clara ("Claire"), was to obtain notoriety as Lord Byron's mistress. To this marriage was born Godwin's own son William, who had a brief literary career of his own.

During the 1790's Godwin published two novels. His first, *Caleb Williams*, published in 1794, is his best known. It portrays what Godwin saw as the power

of the privileged few opposed to the helplessness of the many poor people, and it
was intended as an indictment of society, a fictional presentation of the same
principles Godwin had presented in *Political Justice* just a year before. In addition to being a novel with a social purpose, *Caleb Williams* is an interesting study
in suspense and fear, even terror. In his second novel, *St. Leon*, Godwin wrote a
historical romance, heavy with Gothicism, about sixteenth century England. His
later novels are less important simply because they are less interesting and tend to
be dull. In this category are *Fleetwood* (1805), *Mandeville* (1817), *Cloudsley*
(1830), and *Deloraine* (1833). He also wrote several biographies, including one of
Geoffrey Chaucer, several volumes of history, two plays, and volumes in philosophy. Only *Political Justice* and *Caleb Williams* have received long-term popular
or scholarly attention.

Godwin's life after his second marriage was dismal. His wife operated a publishing house and embittered her own and her husband's life by a combination of
shrewishness and bankruptcy. Money troubles dogged Godwin constantly; Percy
Bysshe Shelley, his son-in-law, contributed for a time to his support. Godwin suf-.
fered a stroke in 1818, but he continued writing to earn a living. Only in 1833,
just three years prior to his death, did he have any financial relief. At that time
the British government gave him a sinecure as a yeoman usher of the exchequer,
a post which gave him financial security. He died in London on April 7, 1836. But
even then he was not left in peace, for when a railroad was put through St. Pan-
cras' cemetery in London his body had to be disinterred and moved to another
grave.

Bibliography

There is no collected edition of Godwin, but his two chief works are available
in good editions: *Political Justice*, edited by R. A. Preston, 1926, and *Caleb
Williams*, edited by Van Wyck Brooks, 1926. There are several reliable studies of
Godwin's career and influence: C. K. Paul, *William Godwin, his Friends and Contemporaries*, 2 vols., 1876; H. N. Brailsford, *Shelley, Godwin and Their Circle*,
1913; F. K. Brown, *William Godwin*, 1926; and George Woodcock, *William Godwin*, 1946. See also Sir Leslie Stephen, *English Thought in the Eighteenth Century*, Vol. II, 1902; Ernest A. Baker, *The History of the English Novel*, Vol. V,
1929; and E. E. and Esther G. Smith, *William Godwin*, 1965. See also Ralph M.
Wardle, ed., *Godwin and Mary: Letters of William Godwin and Mary
Wollstonecraft*, 1966.

CALEB WILLIAMS

Type of work: Novel
Author: William Godwin (1756–1836)
Type of plot: Mystery romance
Time of plot: Eighteenth century
Locale: England
First published: 1794

The unity of Caleb Williams *suffers somewhat from the divided interest of being both social criticism and adventure story. Godwin, a social reformer, arranged his plot so that all of Caleb's miseries are caused by unjust English laws, which permitted wealthy landowners to hold power over the poor, who comprised a majority of the citizens.*

Principal Characters

Caleb Williams, a naïve, bookish, courageous, and incurably inquisitive secretary puzzled by his employer's black moods and determined to trace them to their source. Having received Falkland's confession, Caleb becomes Falkland's prisoner until he escapes. Accused on a false charge of theft and jailed, he escapes, joins a thieves' gang, leaves it, is rearrested on a theft charge, but is released when Falkland drops the charge. Relentlessly followed by Gines, Caleb finally makes a public charge of murder against Falkland who, touched by Caleb's recital of his own miseries, confesses. The remorseful Caleb, feeling that he has saved his own good name only through contributing to Falkland's death, resolves to live a better life.

Ferdinando Falkland, Caleb's employer, a wealthy and highly respected squire intensely desirous of keeping his reputation. He is a considerate employer but is subject to uncharacteristic fits of distemper. Formerly a man of graceful manners and warm intelligence, he is secretly embittered by his difficulties with Tyrrel and troubled by his guilt over Tyrrel's murder. Caleb's nemesis until his better nature triumphs, Falkland confesses publicly and dies shortly afterward from his

long inward torture.

Barnabas Tyrrel, Falkland's enemy, a proud, jealous, combative man finally murdered by Falkland out of resentment for his cruelties.

Gines, a member of a thieves' gang and Caleb's enemy, responsible for his second arrest and the repeated exposure of his imprisonment.

Captain Raymond, the philosophical leader of the thieves' gang.

Emily Melvile, Tyrrel's cousin, saved by Falkland from death by fire and later from a forced marriage to Grimes. She finally dies as a result of Tyrrel's continued cruelties.

Thomas, a servant of Falkland and a former neighbor of Caleb's father. He helps Caleb escape from prison.

Collins, another of Falkland's servants. He tells Caleb the story of Falkland's early life.

Grimes, a clumsy, loutish tenant whom Tyrrel intends as Emily's husband. When Grimes attempts to seduce Emily, Falkland saves her.

The Story

Caleb Williams was engaged as secretary by Mr. Fernando Falkland, the wealthiest and most respected squire in the country. Falkland, although a considerate employer, was subject to fits of distemper which bewildered Caleb. Because these black moods were so contrary to his employer's usual gentle nature, Caleb soon questioned Collins, a trusted servant of the household, and learned from him the story of Falkland's early life.

Studious and romantic in his youth, Falkland lived many years abroad before he returned to England to live on his ancestral estate. One of his neighbors was Barnabas Tyrrel, a man of proud, combative nature. When Falkland returned to his family estate, Tyrrel was the leading gentleman in the neighborhood. Soon Falkland, because of his graceful manners and warm intelligence, began to win the admiration of his neighbors. Tyrrel, jealous, showed his feelings by speech and actions. Falkland tried to make peace, but the ill-tempered Tyrrel refused his proffered friendship.

Miss Emily Melvile, Tyrrel's cousin, occupied somewhat the position of a servant in his household. One night she was trapped in a burning building, and Falkland saved her from burning. Afterward Emily could do nothing but praise her benefactor. Her gratitude annoyed her cousin, who planned to revenge himself on Emily for her admiration of Falkland. He found one of his tenants, Grimes, a clumsy ill-bred lout, who consented to marry Emily. When Emily refused to marry a man whom she could never love, Tyrrel confined her to her room. As part of the plot Grimes helped Emily to escape and then attempted to seduce her. She was rescued from her plight by Falkland, who for the second time proved to be her savior. Further cruelties inflicted on her by Tyrrel finally killed her, and Tyrrel became an object of disgrace in the community.

One evening Tyrrel attacked Falkland in a public meeting and Falkland was deeply humiliated. That night Tyrrel was found dead in the streets. Since the quarrel had been witnessed by so many people just before the murder of Tyrrel, Falkland was called before a jury to explain his whereabouts during that fatal night. No one really believed Falkland guilty, but he was hurt by what he considered the disgrace of his inquisition. Although an ex-tenant was afterward arrested and hanged for the crime, Falkland never recovered his injured pride. He retired to his estate where he became a recluse, moody and disconsolate.

For a long time after learning these details Caleb pondered over the apparent unhappiness of his employer. Attempting to understand his morose personality, he began to wonder whether Falkland suffered from the unearned infamy that accompanied suspicion of murder or from a guilty conscience. Determined to solve the mystery, Caleb proceeded to talk to his master in an insinuating tone, to draw him out in matters concerning murder and justice. Caleb also began to look for evidence which would prove Falkland guilty or innocent. Finally the morose man became aware of his secretary's intent. Swearing Caleb to secrecy, Falkland confessed to the murder of Barnabas Tyrrel and threatened Caleb with irreparable harm if he should ever betray his employer.

Falkland's mansion became a prison for Caleb, and he resolved to run away no matter what the consequences might be. When he had escaped to an inn, he received a letter ordering him to return to defend himself against a charge of theft. When Falkland produced from Caleb's baggage some missing jewels and bank notes, Caleb was sent to prison in disgrace. His only chance to prove his innocence was to disclose Falkland's motive, a thing no one would believe.

Caleb spent many months in jail, confined in a dreary, filthy dungeon and bound with chains. Thomas, a servant of Falkland and a former neighbor of Caleb's father, visited Caleb in his cell. Perceiving Caleb in his miserable condition, Thomas could only wonder at English law which kept a man so imprisoned while he waited many months for trial. Compassion forced Thomas to bring Caleb tools with which he could escape from his dungeon. At liberty once more, Caleb found himself in a hostile world with no resources.

At first he became an associate of thieves, but he left the gang after he had made an enemy of a man named Gines. When he went to London, hoping to hide there, Gines followed him and soon Caleb was again caught and arrested. Falkland visited him and explained that he knew every move Caleb had made since he had escaped from prison. Falkland told Caleb that although he would no longer prosecute him for theft, he would continue to make Caleb's life intolerable. Wherever Caleb went, Gines followed and exposed Caleb's story to the community. Caleb tried to escape to Holland, but as he was to land in that free country, Gines appeared and stopped him.

Caleb returned to England and charged Falkland with murder, asking the magistrate to call Falkland before the court. At first the magistrate refused to summon Falkland to reply to this charge. But Caleb insisted upon his rights and Falkland appeared. The squire now had grown terrible to behold; his haggard and ghostlike appearance showed that he had not long to live.

Caleb pressed his charges, in an attempt to save himself from a life of persecution and misery. So well did Caleb describe his miserable state and his desperate situation that the dying man was deeply touched. Demonstrating the kindness of character and the honesty for which Caleb had first admired him, Falkland admitted his wrong doings and cleared Caleb's reputation.

In a few days the sick man died, leaving Caleb remorseful but determined to make a fresh start in life.

Critical Evaluation

Historians of the novel have always encountered great difficulty in categorizing William Godwin's *Caleb Williams*. It has been called a great "tragic" novel, the first "pursuit" novel, a "crime" or "mystery" novel, a "chase-and-capture" adventure, a political thesis fiction, a Gothic Romance, a "terror" or "sensation" novel, even a "sentimental" tale. To some extent it is all of these —and none of them. The novel has, like most enduring works of art, taken on many shapes and meanings as new readers interpret the narrative in terms of their own personal, cultural, and historical experiences.

Godwin himself had no doubts about the book's meaning or about the effect he hoped to achieve with it: "I will write a tale that shall constitute an epoch in the mind of the reader, that no one, after he has read it, shall ever be exactly the same man that he was before." Having achieved fame in 1793 with his powerful, influential, and controversial political treatise *Enquiry Concerning the Principles of Political Justice,* he sought a form in which to dramatize his ideas. Thus, *Caleb Williams* can be seen at the most obvious level as a fictional gloss on Godwin's previous political masterpiece.

But *Caleb Williams* is no simple political tract. Godwin knew that he must first of all develop a narrative, in his words, "distinguished by a very powerful interest," if he expected readers to absorb and seriously consider his philosophical and social ideas. So he took the most exciting situation he could conceive, creating, as he said, "a series of adventures of flight and pursuit; the fugitive in perpetual apprehension of being overwhelmed with the worst calamities, and the pursuer, by his ingenuity and resources, keeping his victim in a state of the most fearful alarm." And thus, having first decided on the outcome of his adventure, Godwin worked backwards, like a modern mystery story writer, to develop a sequence of events leading up to his climax. The result is a well-constructed narrative in which each of the three volumes are tightly connected, both structurally and thematically, the action developing logically and directly with ever-mounting tension to a powerful, even tragic, dénouement.

Ferdinando Falkland has the ability to, in Godwin's words, "alarm and harass his victim with an inextinguishable resolution never to allow him the least interval of peace and security," because of an unjust and fundamentally corrupt society. The worst villain is a legal system that gives absolute power to the rich and victimizes the poor, all in the name of "justice." Falkland fears Caleb's knowledge because Falkland has committed the only crime that an aristocrat can commit in eighteenth century England—a crime against a social equal. Had Tyrrel been poor, the issue would never have been raised. Caleb's alleged crime—stealing from his master and accusing the master of conspiracy against him—arouses such extreme repugnance because it challenges the social hierarchy and the assumptions that support it.

But the problem is not one of simple, conscious tyranny. Both rich and poor are unaware of the injustice and cruelty that their social institutions foster. They have been conditioned by their environment to accept the system as necessary, proper, and even benevolent. It js not the willful malevolence of a few, but "society" itself that distorts and dissipates the best qualities in men, regardless of their social class, although the poor suffer the most obvious physical oppressions. Falkland is not an example of deliberate evil; he is a good man who has, because of his social role, accepted a body of attitudes and moral values which are destructive. His passion to conceal his crime and his persecution of Caleb are the result not of any fear of legal punishment, but of his obsessive concern for his aristocratic "honor." "Though I be the blackest of villains," he tells Caleb, "I will leave behind me a spotless and illustrious name. There is no crime so malignant, no scene of blood so horrible in which that object cannot engage me."

Thus, there are no human villains in this novel; social institutions are Godwin's targets. This explains the novel's strange ending which seems to reverse all of the book's previous assumptions. Having finally succeeded in turning the law against his tormentor, Caleb realizes, as he faces a broken Falkland, that he, Caleb, is the real enemy. Falkland, for his part, admits his guilt and embraces Caleb. But, to Godwin, neither man is guilty. Both have been caught up in a series of causal circumstances created by their environment and resulting in their inevitable mutual destruction. Only when the environment can be altered to allow men's natural capacities to emerge, undistorted and unfettered by artificial, malevolent environmental conditioning, can such self-destruction be avoided and human potential realized.

THOMAS HARDY

Born: Higher Bockhampton, England (June 2, 1840)
Died: Dorchester, England (January 11, 1928)

Principal Works

NOVELS: *Desperate Remedies*, 1871; *Under the Greenwood Tree*, 1872; *A Pair of Blue Eyes*, 1873; *Far from the Madding Crowd*, 1874; *The Hand of Ethelberta*, 1876; *The Return of the Native*, 1878; *The Trumpet-Major*, 1880; *A Laodicean*, 1881; *Two on a Tower*, 1882; *The Mayor of Casterbridge*, 1886; *The Woodlanders*, 1887; *Tess of the d'Urbervilles*, 1891; *Jude the Obscure*, 1895; *The Well-Beloved*, 1897.

SHORT STORIES: *Wessex Tales*, 1888; *A Group of Noble Dames*, 1891; *Life's Little Ironies*, 1894; *A Changed Man*, 1913.

POEMS: *Wessex Poems*, 1898; *Poems of the Past and the Present*, 1901; *Time's Laughingstocks*, 1909; *Satires of Circumstance*, 1914; *Moments of Vision*, 1917; *Late Lyrics and Earlier*, 1922; *Human Shows, Far Phantasies, Songs and Trifles*, 1925; *Winter Words*, 1928; *Collected Poems*, 1931.

PLAYS: *The Dynasts: A Drama in Three Parts*, 1903, 1906, 1908; *The Famous Tragedy of the Queen of Cornwall*, 1923.

MISCELLANEOUS: *Life and Art*, 1925; *Letters: Transcribed from the Original Autograpns in the Colby College Library*, 1954.

About three miles east of Dorchester, in Dorset, England, there is a hamlet known as Higher Bockhampton. In a thatched-roof cottage which still stands at one end of this hamlet, Thomas Hardy was born on June 2, 1840. The place of his birth is important, for it is the center of a region he learned to know and love—a region he called "Wessex" and wrote about in all his books.

The first of these books was published in 1871 when Hardy was nearly thirty-one years old and was still lacking in literary training and experience. His entire schooling had been confined to eight years between the ages of eight and sixteen. For five years he had worked as an apprentice in the drafting office of a Dorchester architect, John Hicks. When Hardy was twenty-one he went to London and found employment with Arthur Blomfield, a successful metropolitan architect, and remained with him for five years. But Gothic churchs and old manor houses never succeeded in crowding books out of the central place in Hardy's affections. During his years in London, he tried his hand at composing verses, and when he discovered that editors showed no readiness to publish his poems, he turned at the age of twenty-seven to novel-writing.

Hardy called his first attempt at fiction *The Poor Man and the Lady*. He sent his manuscript to Alexander Macmillan, the London publisher, who replied encouragingly but found too many faults in the work to be willing to print it. Hardy thereupon tried a second publisher, Chapman & Hall, and was fortunate enough to have his manuscript placed in the hands of their reader, George Meredith, the novelist. Meredith had an interview with Hardy and advised him to suppress *The Poor Man* (because of the vehemence of its social satire) and to write another novel "with more plot." Hardy took Meredith's advice and wrote *Desperate Remedies*, which was published anonymously and at his own expense in 1871. This was the beginning of a quarter-century's activity as one of the most successful and influential novelists that England has produced.

Like *Desperate Remedies*, Hardy's next novel, *Under the Greenwood Tree*, was published anonymously. In 1872 he was invited to contribute a story for serialization in *Tinsleys' Magazine* and this novel, *A Pair of Blue Eyes* (1873), was the first to carry his name. When *Far from the Madding Crowd* was serialized in the *Cornhill Magazine* in 1874, the acclaim from critics as well as from the general public was cordial enough to encourage Hardy to do three things: he discarded further use of anonymity, he gave up all further practice as an architect, and in September, 1874, he married.

In the twenty years that followed, Hardy turned out ten more full-length novels, besides numerous short stories and articles. His fourteenth and last novel, *Jude the Obscure*, resulted in such an outcry that Hardy, always oversensitive to criticism, shrank from further attempt to find expression in fiction and returned to his first love, poetry. In 1898 he surprised the world by publishing *Wessex Poems*, and throughout the next thirty years he produced volume after volume of verse until, by the time of his death, he had composed nearly a thousand poems. In addition to this achievement in metrical composition, Hardy wrote a gigantic dramatic epic on the Napoleonic wars which he called *The Dynasts* (published in three parts, 1904, 1906, 1908).

As stated above, Hardy's success with *Far from the Madding Crowd* enabled him to marry. He had met Emma L. Gifford, the young lady who became his wife, when he had gone to Cornwall in 1870 to supervise the restoration of a dilapidated church. Ten years after this marriage, he built a house near Dorchester, and from 1885 on, his address remained "Max Gate." He had no children. Mrs. Hardy died in 1912 and was buried in the country churchyard beside the Stinsford parish church which Hardy had attended as a boy. He had these words carved on her tombstone: "This for remembrance." The reader interested in the significance of this inscription should examine Hardy's poignant "Poems of 1912–1913" in his volume, *Satires of Circumstance, Lyrics and Reveries*.

In 1914 Hardy married again. Florence Emily Dugdale, who had helped him with research on *The Dynasts*, became the second Mrs. Hardy. When Hardy died, on January 11, 1928, burial in the Poets' Corner in Westminster Abbey was offered, but there were many people who felt that an author whose heart had always been with Wessex folk among Wessex scenes ought not to have that heart carried off to alien soil. Hardy's heart was accordingly buried in the grave of his first wife at Stinsford, while his ashes were deposited next to those of Charles Dickens in Westminster Abbey.

In the course of the three decades that followed Hardy's death, there came to be general critical agreement that his literary output was of very uneven quality. Some of his novels are excellent, others are mediocre, or worse; and many of his poems have seemed harsh and unmusical, even to modern ears attuned to the discordant. But a reading of Hardy's best novels and a study of his best poems will show the same gifted author at work in both. There is the same attentive eye for nature in all seasons and in her moods, the same tender, sympathetic heart, and the same sorrowing mind. In studying this record of Hardy's earlier years, the reader should avoid making the all-too-common mistake of thinking that his novels were all written from a single, unchanging point of view. Hardy grew and developed, his philosophy of life matured, and the novels show this development. *Far from the Madding Crowd*, and *The Return of the Native* are the most "fatalistic" (to use an overworked word that needs strict definition); *The Mayor of Casterbridge*, in which Hardy quotes "Character is Fate," marks a distinct shift in his viewpoint; and *The Woodlanders, Tess of the d'Urbervilles*, and *Jude the Obscure* are all three written by an older author with a riper social outlook and a clearer understanding of the causes of human unhappiness. The reader who grasps this immense advance on Hardy's part over the fragile charm of *Under the Greenwood Tree* will have no difficulty in understanding why, when John Dewey was asked to name, among books published in the last fifty years, the twenty-five which he regarded as the most influential, he put *Tess of the d'Urbervilles* first among English novels, or why Henry C. Duffin, when appraising the entire literary career of the Wessex author, called *Jude the Obscure* "the greatest of Hardy's novels."

Bibliography

For balanced judgment Carl J. Weber's *Hardy of Wessex: His Life and Literary Career*, 1940, is still the outstanding critical biography among the great quantity of Hardy studies. Other important biographies include Florence Hardy, *The Early Life of Thomas Hardy, 1840–1891*, 1928; Florence Hardy, *The Later Years of Thomas Hardy, 1892–1928*, 1930; Evelyn Hardy, *Thomas Hardy: A Critical Biography*, 1954; Irving Howe, *Thomas Hardy*, 1968; J. I. M. Stewart, *Thomas Hardy: A Critical Biography*, 1971; J. Hollis Miller, *Thomas Hardy: His Career as a Novelist*, 1971; F. E. Halliday, *Thomas Hardy: His Life and Work*, 1972; Robert Gittings, *Young Thomas Hardy*1975; Desmond Hawkins, *Thomas Hardy*, 1976; Norman Page, *Thomas Hardy*, 1977; and Lance St. John Butler, *Thomas Hardy*, 1978.

Among the earlier but still useful critical studies see Lascelles Abercrombie, *Thomas Hardy: A Critical Study*, 1912; J. W. Beach, *The Technique of Thomas Hardy*, 1922; Ernest Brennecke, *Thomas Hardy's Universe*, 1924; H. B. Grimsditch, *Character and Environment in the Novels of Thomas Hardy*, 1925; Mary Ellen Chase, *Thomas Hardy: From Serial to Novel*, 1927; Samuel C.

Chew, *Thomas Hardy: Poet and Novelist*, 1928; A. S. McDowell, *Thomas Hardy: A Critical Study*, 1931; and Lord David Cecil, *Hardy the Novelist*, 1946. Modern Hardy studies began in the late 1940's with H. C. Webster, *On a Darkling Plain*, 1947; and Albert J. Guerard, *Thomas Hardy: The Novels and Stories*, 1949. See also Carl J. Weber, *Hardy in America*, 1952; J. Hollis Miller, *Thomas Hardy, Distance and Desire*, 1970; Perry Meisel, *Thomas Hardy: The Return of the Repressed—A Study of the Major Fiction*, 1972; Dale Kramer, *Thomas Hardy: The Forms of Tragedy*, 1974; F. B. Pinion, *Thomas Hardy and the Modern World*, 1974; Margaret Drabble, ed., *The Genius of Thomas Hardy* (a collection of essays), 1976; and F. B. Pinion, *Budmouth Essays on Thomas Hardy*, 1976.

For poetry studies see Sameul L. Hynes, *The Pattern of Hardy's Poetry*, 1961; Kenneth Marsden, *The Poems of Thomas Hardy: A Critical Interpretation*, 1969; J. O. Bailey, *The Poetry of Thomas Hardy: A Handbook and Commentary*, 1971; Chester A. Garrison, *The Vast Venture: Hardy's Epic-Drama The Dynasts*, 1972; Donald Davie, *Thomas Hardy and English Poetry*, 1972; Tom Paulin, *Thomas Hardy: The Poetry of Perception*, 1975; and James Richardson, *Thomas Hardy: The Poetry of Necessity*, 1977.

Among the useful specialized studies see Herman Lea, *Thomas Hardy's Wessex*, 1913; the Thomas Hardy Centennial Issue of *The Southern Review*, V (1940), which contains articles on Hardy by Allen Tate, Jacques Barzun, and other critics; Carl J. Weber, *The First Hundred Years of Thomas Hardy, 1840–1940: A Centenary Bibliography of Hardiana*, 1942; Carl J. Weber, *Hardy Letters*, 1954; Reginald G. Cox, ed., *Thomas Hardy: The Critical Heritage*, 1970; Frank R. Southerington, *Hardy's Vision of Man*, 1971; Merryn Williams, *Thomas Hardy and Rural England*, 1972; Glenda Leeming, *Who's Who in Thomas Hardy*, 1975; J. T. Laird, *The Shaping of Tess of the d'Urbervilles*, 1975; R. P. Draper, ed., *Hardy, The Tragic Novels: A Casebook*, 1975; and Lance St. John Butler, ed., *Thomas Hardy after Fifty Years* (collection of articles), 1978.

JUDE THE OBSCURE

Type of work: Novel
Author: Thomas Hardy (1840–1928)
Type of plot: Philosophical realism
Time of plot: Nineteenth century
Locale: Wessex
First published: 1894

Hardy's sexual frankness and unconventional treatment of the theme of marriage in this novel outraged readers when the book was first published; now Jude the Obscure *is seen as one of the author's most powerful achievements. A somber, at times grim novel, it is rich in its portrayal of suffering, powerful in its evocation of nature, and tragic in its vision of a universe where men are powerless to avert the fates inflicted by impersonal external forces.*

Principal Characters

Jude Fawley, a village stonemason who is thwarted in every attempt to find success and happiness. His chief desire from the time of his youth is to become a religious scholar, but because of his sensuous temperament he is forced into an early marriage. After his first wife leaves him he falls in love with his cousin and lives with her illegally for several years. The weight of social disapproval forces them downhill. After the tragic death of their children his cousin leaves him also, and Jude, having turned to drink, dies a miserable death.

Arabella Donn, a country girl who tricks Jude into his first marriage. She has nothing in common with Jude and soon leaves him to go to Australia. She later returns but makes no immediate demands on him, preferring to marry another and advance her station in life. After the death of her second husband and the separation of Jude and his cousin, she tricks him into marrying her a second time. But instead of helping to brighten the last of his life she increases his misery

and is planning her next marriage even before his death.

Sue Bridehead, Jude's cousin. Although priding herself on being a free-thinker, she marries a much older man out of a sense of obligation and leaves him shortly afterward because of her revulsion toward him. She lives with Jude for several years and bears him three children. She is a strong influence on him and through her unorthodox thought becomes the primary reason for his giving up his attempts to enter the ministry. After the tragic death of her children, she undergoes a complete change in personality; now wanting to conform, she returns to her first husband.

Richard Phillotson, a village schoolmaster who instills in Jude his first desires to learn. He falls in love with Sue after she becomes his assistant and marries her in spite of obvious differences in age, thought, and belief. When she expresses her desire to live with Jude, he allows her a divorce, although it causes his own

The Story

In the nineteenth century eleven-year-old Jude Fawley said goodbye to his
schoolmaster, Richard Phillotson, who was leaving the small English village of
Marygreen for Christminster, to study for a degree. Young Jude, hungry for learning, yearned to go to Christminster too, but he had to help his great-grand-aunt,
Drusilla Fawley, in her bakery. At Christminster, Phillotson did not forget his
former pupil. He sent Jude some classical grammars which the boy studied
eagerly.

Anticipating a career as a religious scholar, Jude apprenticed himself, at nineteen, to a stonemason engaged in the restoration of medieval churches in a nearby
town. Returning to Marygreen one evening, he met three young girls who were
washing pigs' chitterlings by a stream bank. One of the girls, Arabella Donn,
caught Jude's fancy and he arranged to meet her later. The young man was swept
off his feet and tricked into marriage, but he soon realized that he had married a
vulgar country girl with whom he had nothing in common. Embittered, he tried
unsuccessfully to commit suicide; when he began to drink, Arabella left him.

Jude, now free, decided to carry out his original purpose. With this idea in
mind, he went to Christminster, where he took work as a stonemason. He had
heard that his cousin, Sue Bridehead, lived in Christminster, but he did not seek
her out because his aunt had warned him against her and because he was already
a married man. Eventually he met her and was charmed. She was an artist employed in an ecclesiastical warehouse. Jude met Phillotson, again a simple schoolteacher. Sue, at Jude's suggestion, became Phillotson's assistant. The teacher

soon lost his heart to his bright and intellectually independent young helper. Jude was hurt by evidence of intimacy between the two. Disappointed in love and ambition, he turned to drink and was dismissed by his employer. He went back to Marygreen.

At Marygreen Jude was persuaded by a minister to enter the church as a licentiate. Sue, meanwhile, had won a scholarship to a teacher's college at Melchester; she wrote Jude asking him to come to see her. Jude worked at stonemasonry in Melchester in order to be near Sue, even though she told him she had promised to marry Phillotson after her schooling. Dismissed from the college after an innocent escapade with Jude, Sue influenced him away from the church with her unorthodox beliefs. Shortly afterward she married Phillotson. Jude, despondent, returned to Christminster, where he came upon Arabella working in a bar. Jude heard that Sue's married life was unbearable. He continued his studies for the ministry and thought a great deal about Sue.

Succumbing completely to his passion for Sue, Jude at last forsook the ministry. His Aunt Drusilla died, and at the funeral Jude and Sue realized that they could not remain separated. Phillotson, sympathizing with the lovers, released Sue, who now lived apart from her husband. The lovers went to Aldbrickham, a large city where they would not be recognized. Phillotson gave Sue a divorce and subsequently lost his teaching position. Jude gave Arabella a divorce so that she might marry again.

Sue and Jude now contemplated marriage, but they were unwilling to be joined by a church ceremony because of Sue's dislike for any binding contract. The pair lived together happily, Jude doing simple stonework. One day Arabella appeared and told Jude that her marriage had not materialized. Sue, jealous, promised Jude that she would marry him. Arabella's problem was solved by eventual marriage, but out of fear of her husband she sent her young child by Jude to live with him and Sue. This pathetic boy, nicknamed Little Father Time, joined the unconventional Fawley household.

Jude's business began to decline, and he lost a contract to restore a rural church when the vestry discovered that he and Sue were unmarried. Forced to move on, they traveled from place to place and from job to job. At the end of two and a half years of this itinerant life, the pair had two children of their own and a third on the way. They were five, including Little Father Time. Jude, in failing health, became a baker and Sue sold cakes in the shape of Gothic ornaments at a fair in a village near Christminster. At the fair Sue met Arabella, now a widow. Arabella reported Sue's poverty to Phillotson, who was once more the village teacher in Marygreen.

Jude took his family to Christminster, where the celebration of Remembrance Week was under way. Utterly defeated by failure, Jude still had a love for the atmosphere of learning which pervaded the city.

The family had difficulty finding lodgings and they were forced to separate. Sue's landlady, learning that Sue was an unmarried mother and fearful lest she should have the trouble of childbirth in her rooming-house, told Sue to find other lodgings. Bitter, Sue told Little Father Time that children should not be brought into the world. When she returned from a meal with Jude, she found that the boy had hanged the two babies and himself. She collapsed and gave premature birth to a dead baby.

Her experience brought about a change in Sue's point of view. Believing she had sinned and wishing now to conform, she asked Jude to live apart from her. She also expressed the desire to return to Phillotson, whom she believed, in her misery, to be still her husband. She returned to Phillotson and the two remarried. Jude, utterly lost, began drinking heavily. In a drunken stupor, he was again tricked by Arabella into marriage. His lungs failed; it was evident that his end was near. Arabella would not communicate with Sue, whom Jude desired to see once more, and so Jude traveled in the rain to see her. The lovers had a last meeting. She then made complete atonement for her past mistakes by becoming Phillotson's wife completely. This development was reported to Jude, who died in desperate misery of mind and body. Fate had grown tired of its sport with a luckless man.

Critical Evaluation

A unique transitional figure between the literary worlds of the Victorian and the modern, Thomas Hardy was an undistinguished architect whose novels and poems were to become his chief profession. Although his rustic characters and some of his poems exhibit a humorous hand at work, invading most of his creations are a brooding irony reflecting life's disappointments and a pessimistic belief that man is a victim of a neutral force which darkly rules the universe. Hardy himself divided his novels into three groups: Novels of Ingenuity (such as *Desperate Remedies*); Romances and Fantasies (for example, *A Pair of Blue Eyes*); and Novels of Character and Environment. This last class includes his best and most famous works, *Tess of the D'Urbervilles, The Return of the Native, Far from the Madding Crowd, The Mayor of Casterbridge,* and *Jude the Obscure.*

First published in a modified form as an 1894 serial in *Harper's, Jude the Obscure* is considered by many to be Hardy's top-ranking novel. Yet today it is read less often than many of his works, and it was the outraged reception of *Jude the Obscure* which turned Hardy from the novel to a concentration on his poetry. His disgust at the reactions, which ranged from moral outrage to an incident where an American gentleman furiously flung the book across the room when he found it was not as harmful as touted, was bitter and enduring.

The best explanation of the book's basic framework was stated by Hardy himself in his preface: the novel, meant for adults, was intended "to tell, without a mincing of words, of a deadly war waged between flesh and spirit;

and to point the tragedy of unfulfilled aims." To these, we may add two other important themes: an attack on convention and society, and an examination of man's essential loneliness.

Exhibiting the flesh-spirit division is, of course, Jude's conflicting nature. His relationship with Arabella represents his strong sexual propensities, while his attraction to intellectual pursuits and his high principles reveal his spiritual side. His obsession with Sue is a reflection of both sides of his personality, for while he is compelled by her mind and emotion, he is also drawn to her physically. At the crucial moments of his life, Jude's fleshly desires are strong enough to temporarily devour his other hopes. His two major goals are checked by this flaw, for his initial attempt at a university career is halted when he succumbs to Arabella, and his plans for the ministry end when he kisses Sue and decides that as long as he loves another man's wife he cannot be a soldier and servant of a religion which is so suspicious of sexual love.

"The tragedy of unfilled aims" is forcefully present in both Jude and Sue. For years Jude, in a truly dedicated and scholarly fashion, devotes himself to preparing to enter Christminster (Hardy's name for Oxford). Even when he frees himself from the sexual entanglement with Arabella, his hopes for an education are dashed, for the master of the college who bothers to reply advises him to "remain in your own sphere." Through no fault of his own, despite his seeming ability, he is again denied what he so desperately seeks. The fact of his birth as a poor person is unchangeable, and Jude must accept its results. His second great desire, a spiritual (as well as sexual) union with Sue, is also doomed. When Jude first sees Sue's picture, he thinks of her as a saint, and he eventually derives many of his maturing intellectual concepts from her. His passion for Sue is true and full, yet as the deeply flawed character she is, she must destroy Jude as well as herself. She drains Jude while simultaneously serving as a source of his growth, for she is irresponsible, cold, and cruel. She is an imperfect being, afraid not only of her physical side but of her very ideas. She tells Jude that she does not have the courage of her convictions, and when he adopts her iconoclastic stance, she abandons it and demonstrates how conventional she really is. Her pagan shouts, her free thought, her brave spirit prove as much a sham as Christminster's promises. Her tragedy, the gap between what she is and what she might have been, is not hers alone, but is shared by Jude and becomes his.

As an attack on convention and society, *Jude the Obscure* focuses on three major areas: the British university system, marriage, and religion. Jude's exclusion from Christminster is an indictment of the structure of an institution which allegedly symbolizes the noble part of man's mind yet actually stands only for a closed, tightly-knit social club. In its criticism of marriage, a union which Hardy said should be dissolvable by either side if it became a burden, the novel reveals how false is the view of marriage as a sacred contract. Marriage, as in Jude's merger with Arabella, is often the fruit of a temporary urge, but its harvest can be lifelong and ruinous. Sue's fear of marriage also suggests that the bond can be one of suffocation. Perhaps most important are the novel's charges against Christianity. The fundamental hollowness and hypocrisy of Christianity, Hardy asserts, damn it dreadfully. A farmer thrashes Jude for lovingly letting the birds feed, and the sounds of the beating echo from the church tower which the same farmer had helped finance. Hardy's scorn for such inconsistencies rebounds throughout the book, and he proposes that the only valuable part of Christianity is its idea that love makes life more bearable.

Mirroring the development of these themes is the final impression that the book is also a cry of loneliness. Jude's hopelessness is in the final analysis a result of his alienation not only from Arabella and Sue but from his environment. Used in connection with Jude, the word "obscure," in addition to conveying his association with darkness, his lack of distinction in the eyes of the world, and his humble station, suggests also that he is not understood, that he is hidden from others and is only faintly perceptible. In Hardy's world, the happiest people are those who are most in touch with their environment, a condition which usually occurs, of course, in the least reflective characters. But Jude, ever grasping for the ideal, ignores the unpleasantness about him as much as he possibly can and inevitably places himself on the path to isolation. Such, Hardy hints, is the price man must pay for the refusal to accept unquestionably his status.

All the ills which Hardy ascribes to this world are, he feels, merely a reflection of the ills of the universe. Man ruins society because he is imperfect and caught in the grip of a fatal and deterministic movement of the stars. Defending his dark outlook, Hardy tells us: "If a way to the better there be, it demands a full look at the worst." In a philosophy which he terms evolutionary meliorism, Hardy further amplifies this concept in both a brighter and a more disastrous vein. That philosophy proposes that not only may he improve, but that man *must* find the way to that better condition if he is to survive.

Bibliography

Abercrombie, Lascelles. *Thomas Hardy: A Critical Study.* London: Martin Secker, 1912, pp. 152–169.

Beach, Joseph Warren. *The Technique of Thomas Hardy.* Chicago: University of Chicago Press, 1922, pp. 218–244.

Bragg, M. "Thomas Hardy and *Jude the Obscure*," in *Essays by Divers Hands; Being the Transactions of the Royal Society of Literature*, Volume XXXIX. Edited by John Press. New York: Oxford University Press, 1977, pp. 24–46.

Butler, Lance St. John. *Thomas Hardy.* New York: Cambridge University Press, 1978, pp. 120–141.

Carpenter, Richard C. *Thomas Hardy.* New York: Twayne, 1964, pp. 138–152.

Clifford, Emma. "The Child, the Circus, and *Jude the Obscure*," in Cambridge Journal. VII (June, 1954), pp. 531–546. Reprinted in *Jude the Obscure.* Edited by Norman Page. New York: Norton, 1978, pp. 459–467.

Duffin, Henry C. *Thomas Hardy: A Study of the Wessex Novels.* Manchester, England: Manchester University Press, 1921, pp. 159–188.

Friedman, Alan. *The Turn of the Novel.* New York: Oxford University Press, 1966, pp. 38–74.

Gregor, Ian. *The Great Web: The Form of Hardy's Major Fiction.* Totowa, N.J.: Rowman and Littlefield, pp. 208–288. Reprinted in *Hardy: The Tragic Novels.* Edited by R.P. Draper. London: Macmillan, 1975, pp. 227–247.

Heilman, Robert B. "Hardy's Sue Bridehead," in *Nineteenth-Century Fiction.* XX (March, 1966), pp. 307–323. Reprinted in *Hardy: The Tragic Novels.* Edited by R.P. Draper. London: Macmillan, 1975, pp. 209–226.

Howe, Irving. *Thomas Hardy.* New York: Macmillan, 1967, pp. 132–146. Reprinted in *The Victorian Novel: Modern Essays in Criticism.* Edited by Ian Watt. New York: Oxford University Press, 1971, pp. 432–445.

Knoepflmacher, Ulrich Camillus. *Laughter and Despair: Readings in Ten Novels of the Victorian Age.* Berkeley: University of California Press, 1971, pp. 202–239.

Lea, Hermann. *Thomas Hardy's Wessex.* London: Macmillan, 1913, pp. 45–66.

Meisel, Perry. *Thomas Hardy: The Return of the Repressed.* New Haven, Conn.: Yale University Press, 1972, pp. 136–158.

Millgate, Michael. *Thomas Hardy: His Career as a Novelist.* New York: Random House, 1971, pp. 317–335.

Mizener, Arthur. "*Jude the Obscure* as a Tragedy," in *Southern Review.* VI (Summer, 1940), pp. 193–213. Reprinted in *Jude the Obscure.* Edited by Norman Page. New York: Norton, 1978, pp. 406–413. Also reprinted in *Modern British Fiction.* Edited by Mark Schorer. New York: Oxford University Press, 1961, 45–64.

Rachman, Shalom. "Character and Theme in Hardy's *Jude the Obscure*," in *English.* XXII (1973), pp. 45–53.

Rutland, W.R. *Thomas Hardy: A Study of His Writings and Their Background.* Oxford: Blackwell, 1938, pp. 239–257.

Southerington, F.R. *Hardy's Vision of Man.* London: Chatto and Windus, 1971, pp. 136–147.

Stewart, John I.M.   *Thomas Hardy, A Critical Biography.* New York: Dodd, Mead, 1971, pp. 184–203.

Tomlinson, Mary.   "*Jude the Obscure,*" in *South Atlantic Quarterly.* XXIII (October, 1924), pp. 235–246.

Vigar, Penelope.   *The Novels of Thomas Hardy: Illusion and Reality.* London: Athlone, 1974, pp. 189–212.

Weber, Carl J.   *Hardy of Wessex: His Life and Literary Career.* New York: Columbia University Press, 1940, pp. 141–153.

Webster, Harvey C.   *On a Darking Plain: The Art and Thought of Thomas Hardy.* Chicago: University of Chicago Press, 1947, pp. 183–190.

Williams, Merryn.   *Thomas Hardy and Rural England.* New York: Columbia University Press, 1972, pp. 180–190.

THE MAYOR OF CASTERBRIDGE

Type of work: Novel
Author: Thomas Hardy (1840–1928)
Type of plot: Psychological realism
Time of plot: Nineteenth century
Locale: Wessex
First published: 1886

Many critics consider Michael Henchard, the mayor of Casterbridge, to be Hardy's finest tragic hero. As in all Hardy novels, the forces of nature dwarf and manipulate human beings. But Henchard is a man who contains the violence of nature within himself, and it is this fact that both guarantees his defeat and gives that defeat the force of classical tragedy.

Principal Characters

Michael Henchard, the mayor of Casterbridge and a prosperous corn merchant. In his youth, while drunk, he had sold his wife and child to a seaman. Years later this information becomes known in Casterbridge; as a result Henchard is ruined. Too stern and unyielding to resume his friendship with Donald Farfrae, his former manager, the headstrong ex-mayor faces declining fortune. Finally he is forced to declare bankruptcy and is publicly humiliated during the visit of royalty. At last, broken in spirit, he takes refuge in a shack and dies practically friendless.

Susan Henchard-Newson, Henchard's wife. A plain simple woman, she finally tires of her husband's repeated threats to sell her to the highest bidder. When he offers her for sale, she throws her wedding ring at him and leaves with the sailor Newson, her baby in her arms. Years later, thinking Newson drowned, she returns and remarries Henchard.

Elizabeth-Jane Newson, Henchard's attractive stepdaughter. A proper young woman, she is attracted to the personable young Farfrae. After the death of Lucetta, she marries the young corn merchant.

Donald Farfrae, a corn merchant in Casterbridge and Henchard's thriving business competitor. At first Henchard's good friend and manager, he gradually drifts apart from the mayor when the latter becomes jealous of the young man's capability and popularity. The estrangement, however, helps to bring Farfrae increasing prosperity, Efficiently, he captures much of the grain market and, against his will, gradually takes away much of his former employer's business. When Farfrae marries Lucetta, the break between the two men is complete.

Lucetta Templeman, a woman Henchard had known as Lucetta Le Sueur, later Farfrae's wife. An attractive, but imperceptibly aging coquette, she intended to marry Henchard until she encountered the handsome Farfrae. After meeting him, she decides that she does not care to see Henchard again, even though the latter was once her lover. Her marriage to Farfrae goes smoothly until Jopp reads some love letters, which Lucetta had sent to Henchard, aloud to the denizens of Mixen Lane. Learning she is exposed as a loose woman, she has a miscarriage and dies.

Richard Newson, a bluff, hearty sailor. In

his youth he had bought Henchard's wife and child. The ex-mayor's destruction is complete when the sailor comes to Casterbridge to claim his daughter, Elizabeth-Jane.

Jopp, a surly former employee of Henchard. Snubbed by Lucetta, he gets his revenge when he has the chance to read her love letters aloud in the Three Mariners Inn and takes part in the parade which exposes her to the people.

Abel Whittle, Henchard's simple-minded employee. Although abused by his former employer, Abel, remembering how good the sick man had been to Abel's mother, takes care of him in his final illness.

The Story

One late summer afternoon, early in the nineteenth century, a young farm couple with their baby arrived on foot at the village of Weydon-Priors. A fair was in progress. The couple, tired and dusty, entered a refreshment tent where the husband proceeded to get so drunk that he offered his wife and child for sale. A sailor strange to the village bought the wife, Susan, and the child, Elizabeth-Jane, for five guineas. The young woman tore off her wedding ring and threw it in her drunken husband's face; then, carrying her child, she followed the sailor out of the tent.

When he awoke sober the next morning, Michael Henchard, the young farmer, realized what he had done. After taking an oath not to touch liquor for twenty years, he searched many months for his wife and child. In a western seaport he was told that three persons answering the description he gave had emigrated a short time before. He gave up his search and wandered on until he came to the town of Casterbridge. There he stayed to seek his fortune.

Richard Newson, the sailor, convinced Susan Henchard that she had no moral obligations to the husband who had sold her and her child. He married her and moved with his new family to Canada. Later they returned to England. Susan, meanwhile, had learned of the illegality of her marriage to Newson, but before she could make a positive move Newson was lost at sea. Susan and Elizabeth-Jane, now eighteen and attractive, returned to Weydon-Priors. There they heard that Henchard had gone to Casterbridge.

Henchard, in the intervening period, had become a prosperous grain merchant and the mayor of Casterbridge. When the women arrived in the town they heard that Henchard had sold some bad grain to bakers and restitution was expected. Donald Farfrae, a young Scots corn expert who was passing through Casterbridge, heard of Henchard's predicament and told him a method for partially restoring the grain. Farfrae so impressed Henchard and the people of the town that they prevailed on him to remain. Farfrae became Henchard's manager.

At the meeting of Susan and Henchard, it was decided Susan and her daughter would take lodgings and Henchard would pay court to Susan. Henchard, trusting young Farfrae, told the Scot of his philandering with a young woman named Lucetta Le Sueur, from Jersey. He asked Farfrae to meet Lucetta and keep her from coming to Casterbridge.

Henchard and Susan were married. Elizabeth-Jane developed into a beautiful young woman for whom Donald Farfrae had a growing attraction. Henchard wanted Elizabeth-Jane to take his name, but Susan refused his request, much to his mystification. He noticed that Elizabeth-Jane did not possess any of his personal traits.

Bad feeling came between Henchard and Farfrae over Henchard's harsh treatment of a simple-minded employee. Farfrae had succeeded Henchard in popularity in Casterbridge. The complete break came when a country dance sponsored by Farfrae drew all the populace, leaving Henchard's dance unattended. Farfrae, anticipating his dismissal, set up his own establishment but refused to take any of Henchard's business away from him. Henchard, antagonized, would not allow Elizabeth-Jane and Farfrae to see each other.

Henchard received a letter from Lucetta saying she would pass through Casterbridge to pick up her love letters. When Lucetta failed to keep the appointment, Henchard put the letters in his safe. Susan fell sick and wrote a letter for Henchard to open on the day Elizabeth-Jane was married. Soon afterward she died and Henchard told the girl that he was her real father. Looking for some documents to corroborate his story, he found the letter his wife had left in his keeping for Elizabeth-Jane. Henchard, unable to resist, read Susan's letter and learned that Elizabeth-Jane was really the daughter of Newson and Susan, his own daughter having died in infancy. His wife's reluctance to have the girl take his name was now clear, and Henchard's attitude toward Elizabeth-Jane became distant and cold.

One day Elizabeth-Jane met a strange woman at the village graveyard. The woman was Lucetta Templeman, formerly Lucetta Le Sueur, who had inherited property in Casterbridge from a rich aunt named Templeman. She took Elizabeth-Jane into her employ to make it convenient for Henchard, her old lover, to call on her.

Young Farfrae came to see Elizabeth-Jane, who was away at the time. He and Miss Templeman were immediately attracted to each other, and Lucetta refused to see Henchard after meeting Farfrae. Elizabeth-Jane overheard Henchard berate Lucetta under his breath for refusing to admit him to her house; she was made further uncomfortable when she saw that Farfrae had succumbed to Lucetta's charms. Henchard was now determined to ruin Farfrae. Advised by a weather prophet that the weather would be bad during the harvest, he bought grain heavily. When the weather stayed fair, Henchard was almost ruined by low grain prices. Farfrae bought cheap. The weather turned bad late in the harvest, and prices went up. Farfrae became wealthy.

In the meantime, Farfrae continued his courtship of Lucetta. Henchard, jealous, threatened to expose Lucetta's past unless she married him. Lucetta agreed. But an old woman disclosed to the village that Henchard was the man who had sold his wife and child years before. Lucetta, ashamed, left town. On the day of her return, Henchard rescued her and Elizabeth-Jane from an enraged bull. He asked Lucetta to give evidence to a creditor of their engagement. Lucetta confessed that in her absence she and Farfrae had been married. Henchard, utterly frustrated, again threatened to expose her. Elizabeth-Jane, upon learning of the marriage, left Lucetta's service.

The news that Henchard had sold his wife and child spread through the village. His creditors closed in, and he became a recluse. He and Elizabeth-Jane were reconciled during his illness. Upon his recovery he hired out to Farfrae as a common laborer.

Henchard's oath having expired, he began to drink heavily. Farfrae planned to set up Henchard and Elizabeth-Jane in a small seed shop, but the project did not materialize because of a misunderstanding. Farfrae became mayor of Casterbridge despite the desire of Lucetta to leave the village.

Jopp, a former employee of Henchard, blackmailed his way into the employ of Farfrae through Lucetta, whose past he knew, because he had lived in Jersey before he came to Casterbridge. Henchard, finally taking pity on Lucetta, gave Jopp the love letters to return to her. Before delivering them, Jopp read the letters aloud in an inn.

Royalty visited Casterbridge. Henchard, wishing to retain his old stature in the village, forced himself among the receiving dignitaries, but Farfrae pushed him aside. Later, Henchard got Farfrae at his mercy, during a fight in a warehouse loft, but the younger man shamed Henchard by telling him to go ahead and kill him.

The townspeople, excited over the letters they had heard read, devised a mummery employing effigies of Henchard and Lucetta riding back to back on a donkey. Farfrae's friends arranged to have him absent from the village during the mummers' parade, but Lucetta saw it and was prostrated. She died of a miscarriage that night.

Richard Newson, not lost after all, came to Casterbridge in search of Susan and Elizabeth-Jane. He met Henchard, who sent him away with the information that both Susan and Elizabeth-Jane were dead.

Elizabeth-Jane went to live with Henchard in his poverty. They opened a seed shop and began to prosper in a modest way. Farfrae, to the misery of the lonely Henchard, began to pay court to Elizabeth-Jane, and they planned to marry soon. Newson returned, obviously knowing he had been duped. Henchard left town but returned for the marriage festivities, bringing with him a goldfinch as a wedding present. When he saw that Newson had completely replaced him as Elizabeth-Jane's father, he went sadly away. Newson, restless, departed for the sea again, after Farfrae and his daughter were settled. Henchard pined away and died, ironically enough, in the secret care of the simple-minded old man whom he had once tyrannized.

Critical Evaluation

This is the first novel in which Thomas Hardy focuses his primary attention upon one individual; all other characters are drawn without depth so that in contrast Michael Henchard stands out in great animal strength and weakness. The story is *his* tragedy, although the two women with whom he is intimately involved die: his wife Susan, whom he sold with their child when a young man in a state of drunken recklessness; and Lucetta, with whom he has a secret affair, and who subsequently marries his rival, Farfrae. But death is not the main disaster of this narrative; rather, it is the slow downfall and disintegration of a "man of character."

The Mayor of Casterbridge marks a great development in Hardy as artist. He masterfully delineates Henchard's character and the complex social and economic life of Casterbridge. Both Michael Henchard and his town are governed by the grain market; the mayor's rise and fall are dependent not so much on his personal relations with Susan, Farfrae, Lucetta, and Elizabeth-Jane, as upon fluctuations of the harvest. The power struggle between Henchard and Farfrae is engendered and governed not by their abilities and popularity with the townsfolk, but more basically by the supply and demand of grain. Even sexual interests, which figure largely in the story, are dominated by the shifting economics of Casterbridge fortunes.

Also notable are the new dimensions Hardy has given both individuals and events; these have greater symbolism than those in his earlier works. For example, primitive ritual is suggested by the marriage transaction that begins Henchard's tragedy, and some critics suggest that the mayor himself has attributes or implicit qualities of a vegetation god or corn king.

Henchard also has affinities with Melville's Ahab in a relentless pursuit of revenge in the face of adverse circumstances and nature's power, though both men recognize that such pursuit must lead to their destruction. The story's course also demonstrates supernatural revenge for the hero's violation of moral order—a revenge which relentlessly demands the violator's atonement and death. This is crime and punishment beyond human control, though ironically Henchard's own character is the instrument for the retribution.

The past, whose sinister force Hardy constantly invokes, is best symbolized by the Roman earthworks of Casterbridge, particularly the amphitheater where gladiatorial combats were once held. For Casterbridge citizens it is a place of furtive assignations, even murders because of its obscure location and "dismal privacy." This spot Henchard chooses for a meeting with his long-lost wife, Susan. He also selects another area surrounded by an ancient Roman earthwork for his ill-advised Casterbridge entertainment, which, in contrast to Farfrae's dance in town, turns out to be a failure.

Henchard seems a pawn of the goddess Fortune, who throws him from a position of assured success down to the bottom of her wheel; in this respect

The Mayor of Casterbridge is a tragedy in a long *de casibus* tradition, one which shows, because of Fortune's fickle nature, the downfall of a man with incipient greatness and strength. Henchard also resembles the Greek tragic hero who through destructive acts arising from his own character destroys himself. But it attests to Hardy's artistry that in his ruin, Henchard is to the reader stronger and elicits more admiration than does the clever Farfrae, who, in turn, has risen to the position of fortune and happiness Henchard once had.

Bibliography

Abercrombie, Lascelles. *Thomas Hardy: A Critical Study.* London: Martin Secker, 1912, pp. 97–128.

Beach, Joseph W. *The Technique of Thomas Hardy.* Chicago: University of Chicago Press, 1922, pp. 134–157.

Braybrooke, Patrick. *Thomas Hardy and His Philosophy.* London: C.W. Daniel, 1928, pp. 36–45.

Brown, Douglas. *Thomas Hardy.* London: Longmans, 1954, pp. 63–70.

Butler, Lance St. John. *Thomas Hardy.* New York: Cambridge University Press, 1978, pp. 55–74.

Carpenter, Richard C. *Thomas Hardy.* New York: Twayne, 1964, pp. 102–114.

Duffin, Henry. *Thomas Hardy: A Study of the Wessex Novels.* Manchester, England: Manchester University Press, 1921, pp. 99–106.

Gardner, W.H. *Some Thoughts on* The Mayor of Casterbridge. Oxford: Oxford University Press, 1930.

Guerard, Albert J. *Thomas Hardy: The Novels and the Stories.* Cambridge, Mass.: Harvard University Press, 1949, pp. 146–152. Reprinted in *The Victorian Novel: Essays in Criticism.* Edited by Ian Watt. New York: Oxford University Press, 1971, pp. 401–406.

Heilman, Robert B. "Introduction," in *The Mayor of Casterbridge.* Boston: Houghton Mifflin, 1962.

Karl, Frederick R. "Thomas Hardy's *Mayor* and the Changing Novel," in *An Age of Fiction: The Nineteenth Century British Novel.* New York: Farrar, Straus and Giroux, 1964, pp. 295–322.

Kramer, D. "Character and the Cycle of Change in *The Mayor of Casterbridge,*" in *Tennessee Studies in Literature.* XVI (1971), pp. 111–120.

Lea, Hermann. *Thomas Hardy's Wessex.* London: Macmillan, 1913, pp. 83–106.

Maxwell, J.C. "The 'Sociological' Approach to *The Mayor of Casterbridge,*" in *Imagined Worlds: Essays on Some English Novels and Novelists in Honour of John Butt*. Edited by Maynard Mack and Ian Gregor. London: Methuen, 1968, pp. 225–236.

Meisel, Perry. *Thomas Hardy: The Return of the Repressed*. New Haven, Conn.: Yale University Press, 1972, pp. 90–108.

Millgate, Michael. *Thomas Hardy: His Career as a Novelist*. New York: Random House, 1971, pp. 221–234.

Page, Norman. *Thomas Hardy*. London: Routledge and Kegan Paul, 1977, pp. 77–82.

Paterson, John. "*The Mayor of Casterbridge* as Tragedy," in *Victorian Studies*. III (December, 1959), pp. 151–172.

Rutland, W.R. *Thomas Hardy: A Study of His Writings and Their Background*. Oxford: Blackwell, 1938, pp. 197–211.

Schweik, Robert C. "Character and Fate in *The Mayor of Casterbridge*," in *Nineteenth-Century Fiction*. XXI (December, 1966), pp. 249–262. Reprinted in *Hardy: The Tragic Novels*. Edited by R.P. Draper. London: Macmillan, 1975, pp. 133–147.

Stewart, John I.M. *Thomas Hardy, A Critical Biography*. New York: Dodd, Mead, 1971, pp. 108–126.

Vigar, Penelope. *The Novels of Thomas Hardy: Illusion and Reality*. London: Athlone, 1974, pp. 146–168.

Weber, Carl J. *Hardy of Wessex: His Life and Literary Career*. New York: Columbia University Press, 1940, pp. 99–107.

Webster, Harvey C. *On a Darkling Plain: The Art and Thought of Thomas Hardy*. Chicago: University of Chicago Press, 1947, pp. 147–152.

Williams, Merryn. *Thomas Hardy and Rural England*. New York: Columbia University Press, 1972, pp. 146–156.

THE RETURN OF THE NATIVE

Type of work: Novel
Author: Thomas Hardy (1840–1928)
Type of plot: Romantic tragedy
Time of plot: Mid-nineteenth century
Locale: Egdon Heath, in southern England
First published: 1878

In this novel Thomas Hardy creates two strong opposing forces: Egdon Heath, a somber tract of wasteland symbolic of an impersonal fate, and Eustacia Vye, a beautiful, romantic young woman representing the opposing human element. Her marriage to the idealistic Clym Yeobright is doomed both by the external forces of nature and the intense, differing needs of the two characters. Eustacia's death by drowning in the company of Wildeve, her lover, is the fitting symbolic end to her life.

Principal Characters

Clement Yeobright, called **Clym,** a native of Egdon Heath who returns to visit with his mother and cousin after having made a career for himself as a successful diamond merchant in Paris. His success and his education make him an outstanding figure among the humble people who live scattered about the wild heath, and his return for a visit is a great occasion for them. During his stay he decides to remain, finding that the heath and its people mean far more to him than worldly success in Paris; his intention is to become a teacher and open a school to educate the people among whom he grew up, a superstitious and ignorant, if lovable and kindly, set. A sensitive and somewhat rash young man, he falls in love with Eustacia Vye, a beautiful and passionate woman. In her Clym sees a perfect helpmeet for a schoolmaster, but she sees in him only a chance to escape the heath and to live abroad. Clym and Eustacia Vye are married, over the protests of his mother. These protests arouse the anger of Clym, who after his marriage does not communicate with her. Disaster, in the form of partial blindness, strikes Clym, but he accepts his plight philosophically and turns to the homely task of furze-cutting to earn a living. Unhappy in her lot, Eustacia turns against him. On one occasion she refuses to let his mother into the house, an inhospitable act that indirectly causes the death of the older woman. Stricken by his mother's death and, a short time later, by his wife's suicide, Clym becomes a lay preacher to the people of the heath.

Eustacia Vye, the self-seeking and sensuous young woman who marries Clym Yeobright. Unhappy on the heath, bored by life with her grandfather, she tries to escape. First she seeks an opportunity to do so by marrying Clym. When he cannot and will not leave the heath, she turns to a former fiancé, now a married man. At the last, however, she cannot demean herself by unfaithfulness to her husband; instead of running away with her lover she commits suicide by plunging into a millpond.

Damon Wildeve, a former engineer, still a young man, who settles unhappily upon the heath as keeper of the Quiet Woman Inn. Selfish and uninspired, when he loses Eustacia Vye to Clym Yeobright he marries Thomasin Yeobright, Clym's cousin, out of spite. The marriage is an unhappy one, for Wildeve still pursues Eustacia, also unhappy because her husband cannot give her the life she wishes. Wildeve's pursuit of illicit love ends in his own death, for he drowns while trying to save Eustacia's life after she throws herself into a pond rather than elope to Paris as his mistress.

Thomasin Yeobright, called **Tamsin,** Clym's cousin, reared with Clym by his mother. A simple and faithful girl who loves Damon Wildeve despite his treatment of her, she is also faithful to the conventions and clings to her marriage even after it turns out badly. At her husband's death she inherits a small fortune left by his uncle shortly before Wildeve's end. She finds happiness eventually in a second marriage and in her little daughter.

Diggory Venn, an itinerant young reddleman in love with Thomasin Yeobright. Once of good family and some little fortune, he has fallen upon evil days. His lonely existence gives him opportunity to act in his love's behalf, and he tries to circumvent Wildeve's pursuit of Eustacia Vye. Having saved up a little money, he becomes a dairyman and presents himself, after a decent time, as Thomasin's suitor, following her husband's death. His patience, love, and understanding are rewarded when she accepts him.

Mrs. Yeobright, Clym Yeobright's mother and Thomasin Yeobright's aunt. In her good sense she opposes both their marriages, although the young people misinterpret her motives as selfish. Being of a forgiving nature, she tries to be reconciled with her son and his

wife, as she became with Thomasin and her husband. But Eustacia refuses her overtures and is indirectly the cause of the older woman's death; Mrs. Yeobright dies of exposure and snakebite after having been refused admittance to her son's home.

Captain Vye, Eustacia Vye's grandfather, a retired seaman who brings his granddaughter to live on the heath with no thought of how such a place will affect her. He is a self-contained old man with little knowledge of the intense personality of his charge; therefore he makes no effort to prevent her tragedy.

Johnny Nunsuch, a little boy who plays upon the heath and unwittingly becomes involved as a witness to the fate of the Yeobrights, Eustacia Vye, and Damon Wildeve. His testimony concerning Mrs. Yeobright's last words brings about the separation of Clym Yeobright and his wife.

Mrs. Nunsuch, Johnny's mother. Convinced that Eustacia Vye is a witch who has cast a spell upon the child, Mrs. Nunsuch, an uneducated, superstitious woman, resorts to black arts to exorcise the spell. On the night of Eustacia Vye's death she forms a doll in the girl's image and destroys it in a fire.

Granfer Cantle, an ancient,
Christian Cantle, his elderly youngest son,
Olly Dowden,
Sam, a turf-cutter,
Humphrey, a furze-cutter, and
Timothy Fairway, residents of Egdon Heath. They voice much of the rural wisdom and observe the folk customs of the region.

The Story

Egdon Heath was a gloomy wasteland in southern England. Against this majestic but solemn, brooding background a small group of people were to work out their tragic drama in the impersonal presence of nature.

Fifth of November bonfires were glowing in the twilight as Diggory Venn, the reddleman, drove his van across the Heath. Tired and ill, Thomasin Yeobright lay in the rear of his van. She was a young girl whom Diggory loved, but she had rejected his proposal in order to marry Damon Wildeve, proprietor of the Quiet Woman Inn. Now Diggory was carrying the girl to her home at Blooms-End. The girl had gone to marry Wildeve in a nearby town, but the ceremony had not taken place because of an irregularity in the license. Shocked and shamed, Thomasin had asked her old sweetheart, Diggory, to take her home.

Mrs. Yeobright, Thomasin's aunt and guardian, heard the story from the reddleman. Concerned for the girl's welfare, she decided that the wedding should take place as soon as possible. Mrs. Yeobright had good cause to worry, for Wildeve's intentions were not wholly honorable. Later in the evening, after Wildeve had assured the Yeobrights, rather casually, that he intended to go through with his promise, his attention was turned to a bonfire blazing on Mistover Knap. There old Cap'n Vye lived with his beautiful granddaughter, Eustacia. At dusk the girl had started a fire on the Heath as a signal to her lover, Wildeve, to come to her. Though he had intended to break with Eustacia, he decided to obey her summons.

Eustacia, meanwhile, was waiting for Wildeve in the company of young Johnny Nunsuch. When Wildeve threw a pebble in the pond to announce his arrival, Eustacia told Johnny to go home. The meeting between Wildeve and Eustacia was unsatisfactory for both. He complained that she gave him no peace. She, in turn, resented his desertion. Meanwhile Johnny Nunsuch, frightened by strange lights he saw on the Heath, went back to Mistover Knap to ask Eustacia to let her servant accompany him home, but he kept silent when he came upon Eustacia and Wildeve. Retracing his steps, he stumbled into a sand pit where stood the reddleman's van. From the boy, Diggory learned of the meeting between Eustacia and Wildeve. Later, he overheard Eustacia declare her hatred of the Heath to Wildeve, who asked her to run away with him to America. Her reply was vague, but the reddleman decided to see Eustacia without delay to beg her to let Thomasin have Wildeve.

Diggory's visit to Eustacia was fruitless. He then approached Mrs. Yeobright, declared again his love for her niece, and offered to marry Thomasin. Mrs. Yeobright refused the reddleman's offer because she felt that the girl should marry Wildeve. She confronted the innkeeper with vague references to another suitor, with the result that Wildeve's interest in Thomasin awakened once more.

Shortly afterward Mrs. Yeobright's son, Clym, returned from Paris, and a welcome-home party gave Eustacia the chance to view this stranger about whom she had heard so much. Uninvited, she went to the party disguised as one of the mummers. Clym was fascinated by this interesting and mysterious young woman disguised as a man. Eustacia dreamed of marrying Clym and going with him to Paris. She even broke off with Wildeve, who, stung by her rejection, promptly married Thomasin to spite Eustacia.

Clym Yeobright decided not to go back to France. Instead he planned to open a school. Mrs. Yeobright strongly opposed her son's decision. When Clym learned that Eustacia had been stabbed in church by a woman who thought that Eustacia was bewitching her children, his decision to educate these ignorant people was strengthened. Much against his mother's wishes, Clym visited Eustacia's home to ask her to teach in his school. Eustacia refused because she hated the Heath and the country peasants, but as the result of his visit Clym fell completely in love with the beautiful but heartless Eustacia.

Mrs. Yeobright blamed Eustacia for Clym's wish to stay on the Heath. When bitter feeling grew between mother and son, he decided to leave home. His marriage to Eustacia made the break complete. Later Mrs. Yeobright relented somewhat and gave a neighbor, Christian Cantle, a sum of money to be delivered in equal portions to Clym and Thomasin. Christian foolishly lost the money to Wildeve in a game of dice. Fortunately, Diggory won the money from Wildeve, but, thinking that all of it belonged to Thomasin, he gave it to her. Mrs. Yeobright knew that Wildeve had duped Christian. She did not know that the reddleman had won the money away from the innkeeper, and she mistakenly supposed that Wildeve had given the money to Eustacia. Meeting Eustacia, she asked the girl if she had received any money from Wildeve. Eustacia was enraged by the question and in the course of her reply to Mrs. Yeobright's charge she said that she would never have condescended to marry Clym had she known that she would have to remain on the Heath. The two women parted angrily.

Eustacia's unhappiness was increased by Clym's near-blindness, a condition brought on by too much reading, for she feared that this meant she would never get to Paris. When Clym became a woodcutter, Eustacia's feeling of degradation was complete. Bored with her life, she went by herself one evening to a gypsying. There she accidentally met Wildeve and again felt an attachment for him. Seeing Eustacia and Wildeve together, the reddleman told Mrs. Yeobright of the meeting and begged her to make peace with Eustacia for Clym's sake. She agreed to try.

But Mrs. Yeobright's walk at noon across the hot, dry Heath to see her son and daughter-in-law proved fatal. When she arrived in sight of Clym's house, she saw her son from a distance as he entered the front door. Then, while she rested on a knoll near the house, she saw another man entering, but she was too far away to recognize Wildeve. After resting for twenty minutes, Mrs. Yeobright went on to Clym's cottage and knocked. No one came to the door. Heartbroken by what she considered a rebuff by her own son, Mrs. Yeobright started home across the Heath. Overcome by exhaustion and grief, she sat down to rest and a poisonous adder bit her. She died without knowing that inside her son's house Clym had been asleep, worn out by his morning's work. Eustacia did not go to the door because, as she later explained to her husband, she had thought he would answer the knock. The real reason for Eustacia's failure to go to the door was fear of the consequences, should Mrs. Yeobright find Eustacia and Wildeve together.

Clym awoke with the decision to visit his mother. Starting out across the Heath toward her house, he stumbled over her body. His grief was tempered by bewilderment over the reason for her being on the Heath at that time. When Clym discovered that Eustacia had failed to let his mother in and that Wildeve had been in the cottage, he ordered Eustacia out of his house. She went quietly because she felt in part responsible for Mrs. Yeobright's death.

Eustacia took refuge in her grandfather's house, where a faithful servant thwarted her in an attempt to commit suicide. In utter despair over her own wretched life and over the misery she had caused others, Eustacia turned to Wildeve, who had unexpectedly inherited eleven thousand pounds and who still wanted her to run away with him. One night she left her grandfather's house in order to keep a prearranged meeting with the innkeeper, but in her departure she failed to receive a letter of reconciliation which Thomasin had persuaded Clym to send to her. On her way to keep her rendezvous with Wildeve she lost her way in the inky blackness of the Heath and either fell accidentally or jumped into a small lake and was drowned. Wildeve, who happened to be near the lake when she fell in, jumped in to save her and was drowned also.

(Originally *The Return of the Native* ended with the death of Eustacia and of Wildeve; but in order to satisfy his romantic readers, in a later edition Hardy made additions to the story. The faithful Diggory married Thomasin. Clym, unable to abolish ignorance and superstition on the Heath by teaching, became in the end an itinerant preacher.)

Critical Evaluation

Thomas Hardy was born in Dorset, England, on June 2, 1840. Although he attended several grammar schools and studied French at King's College, Hardy had little formal education. Later, however, he read extensively in the Bible, the classics, and recent scientific publications. From 1856 to 1874 he was an architect's apprentice and later an ecclesiastical architect. During this time he wrote poetry, which was not published until after he was a well-known novelist. His first novel, *Desperate Remedies,* was published in 1871. In 1872 he married Emma Gifford; after her death in 1912 he married Florence Dugdale. When storms of protest arose over the pessimism and the violation of strict Victorian sexual mores in *Tess of the D'Urbervilles* and *Jude the Obscure,* Hardy gave up the novel but continued to write poetry. He died on January 11, 1928, and his ashes were placed in the poets' corner at Westminster Abbey. Among his best works are *Far from the Madding Crowd* and *The Return of the Native.*

In *The Return of the Native,* there is a strong conflict between nature or fate, represented by Egdon Heath, and human nature, represented by the characters in the novel, especially Eustacia. The title of the first chapter, "A Face on Which Time Makes But Little Impression," establishes the heath's role as much more significant than merely a setting for the action. The word "face" suggests that the heath assumes anthropomorphic proportions and becomes, in essence, a major character in the novel; somber and dark, "The storm was its lover, and the wind its friend." And, while the characters struggle and become tired and disillusioned—or die—the heath remains indifferent and unchanged. The heath is a formidable foe; in fact, those who struggle against it—Eustacia, Wildeve, and Mrs. Yeobright—eventually die.

The heath, then, becomes a symbol of permanence. Other aspects of the setting become symbolic, and they also intensify the somber tone of the novel. Light and dark imagery is significant in that the dominance of dark imagery adds to the novel's pessimism. The bonfires on the heath provide small areas of light in the blackness of the night, yet the furze burns quickly and is soon extinguished, like the momentary happiness of Eustacia and Clym and the wild passion of Eustacia and Wildeve. The moon's eclipse on the night Clym proposes to Eustacia foreshadows the eclipse of their love. On the night of Eustacia's death, the violent storm echoes her violent emotions as she cries out against her fate.

Like his character Eustacia, Hardy often seems to blame fate for many of the catastrophes of life. Many critics believe that in this novel fate is completely dominant and that the characters are helpless victims of its malevolence. Such a view, however, seems inadequate. Admittedly, fate does play a significant role; for example, Eustacia accidentally meets Wildeve at the maypole dance. Mrs. Yeobright just happens to choose an extremely hot day to visit Clym, just happens to arrive when Wildeve is there, and just happens to be bitten by the adder when she collapses from fatigue. Eustacia does not receive Clym's letter because her grandfather believes she is asleep. However, much of the novel's tragedy can be traced to the characters' motivations, decisions, and actions.

Mrs. Yeobright may seem victimized by Eustacia's failure to open the door to her, but one must remember that Mrs. Yeobright never accepts Eustacia and attempts to turn Clym against her. She feels socially superior to Eustacia, distrusts her because she is a free spirit, calls her lazy and irresponsible, hints that she is behaving indiscreetly with Wildeve, and, in general, is jealous of her because she wants to keep Clym to herself. She refuses to attend Clym's wedding and treats Eustacia in a condescending manner as they speak together near the pool. Then, she harbors her grudge and keeps away from her son and his wife long enough for the gulf between them to widen greatly.

Clym, too, brings much of his trouble upon himself. He is flattered by Eustacia's attention and passion for him but never really sees her as an individual totally different from himself. Without regard for her hatred of the heath and her longing for the excitement of Paris, he assumes that she will be a vital part of his teaching mission. After their marriage, he ignores her and devotes his time to his studies, which, perhaps, helps to bring about the physical blindness that becomes symbolic of his blindness to reality. Martyr-

ing himself as a furze cutter, he intensifies Eustacia's hatred for the heath and
fails to see that his physical fatigue and his degrading work deal a crushing
blow to his marriage. Even his desire to teach is selfish and unrealistic; he
tries to escape from life's conflicts into an abstraction of truth, and he desires
to impose his views on others. The view of Clym at the end of the novel is
ironic; as an itinerant preacher "less than thirty-three," he may suggest a
Christ figure; yet in his self-righteousness he fails to find the meaning of love.

Eustacia, who blames fate for her tragedy, is the novel's most ambiguous
character; even the author seems to have ambivalent feelings toward her.
She is an exciting, passionate "queen of the night" whose romanticism makes
her long to "be loved to madness" by a man great enough to embody her
dreams. Allowing her imagination to convince her that Clym can master this
role, she marries him, hoping to manipulate him, as she had manipulated
Wildeve, and thus get to Paris. After her marriage, however, her liaison with
Wildeve is at first innocent; only after Clym banishes her from his house
does she agree to accept Wildeve's offer to help her leave the heath. Yet in
spite of her desperation, Eustacia refuses to be humbled. Realizing that a lack
of money will cause her to lose her honor for a man who is "not great
enough" to meet her desires, she drowns herself to avoid humiliation. It is
more believable that she dies willingly rather than accidentally, because only
in death does she seem to find peace.

Though Eustacia has lost in her battle with the heath, her struggle proves
that she is a strong, defiant character who is defeated partly by forces beyond
her control and partly by her own refusal to give up her dream. And, in
spite of her selfishness and hauteur, her lively spirit gives life to the novel
and makes her, in the end, its tragic but unforgettable heroine.

Bibliography

Abercrombie, Lascelles.   *Thomas Hardy: A Critical Study.* London: Martin
Secker, 1912, pp. 97–128.

Beach, Joseph W.   *The Technique of Thomas Hardy.* Chicago: University of
Chicago Press, 1922, pp. 80–105.

Braybrooke, Patrick.   *Thomas Hardy and His Philosophy.* London: C.W.
Daniel, 1928, pp. 24–35.

Brown, Douglas.   *Thomas Hardy.* London: Longmans, 1954, pp. 55–63.

Butler, Lance St. John.   *Thomas Hardy.* New York: Cambridge University
Press, 1978, pp. 32–54.

Carpenter, Richard C.   *Thomas Hardy.* New York: Twayne, 1964, pp. 91–102.

Deen, Leonard W.   "Heroism and Pathos in Hardy's *Return of the Native*," in
Nineteenth-Century Fiction. XV (December, 1960), pp. 207–219. Reprinted

in *Hardy: The Tragic Novels.* Edited by R.P. Draper. London: Macmillan, 1975, pp. 109–118.

Duffin, Henry C. *Thomas Hardy: A Study of the Wessex Novels.* Manchester, England: Manchester University Press, 1921, pp. 106–113.

Goldberg, M.A. "Hardy's Double-Visioned Universe," in *Essays in Criticism.* VII (1957), pp. 374–382.

Grabo, Carl H. *The Technique of the Novel.* New York: Scribner's, 1928, pp. 113–133.

Grimsditch, Herbert B. *Character and Environment in the Novels of Thomas Hardy.* London: Witherby, 1925, pp. 53–62.

Hagan, John. "A Note on the Significance of Diggory Venn," in *Nineteenth-Century Fiction.* XVI (September, 1961), pp. 147–155.

Hornback, Bert G. *The Metaphor of Chance: Vision and Technique in the Works of Thomas Hardy.* Athens: Ohio University Press, 1971, pp. 15–40.

McCullough, Bruce W. *Representative English Novelists: Defoe to Conrad.* New York: Harper, 1946, pp. 237–249.

Meisel, Perry. *Thomas Hardy: The Return of the Repressed.* New Haven, Conn.: Yale University Press, 1972, pp. 68–89.

Millgate, Michael. *Thomas Hardy: His Career as a Novelist.* New York: Random House, 1971, pp. 130–144.

Paterson, John. "Introduction," in *The Return of the Native.* New York: Harper & Row, 1966. Reprinted in *Hardy: The Tragic Novels.* Edited by R.P. Draper. London: Macmillan, 1975, pp. 109–118.

Rutland, W.R. *Thomas Hardy: A Study of His Writings and Their Background.* Oxford: Blackwell, 1938, pp. 177–188.

Schweik, Robert C. "Theme, Character, and Perspective in Hardy's *The Return of the Native*," in *Philological Quarterly.* XLI (October, 1962), pp. 757–767.

Southerington, F.R. *Hardy's Vision of Man.* London: Chatto and Windus, 1971, pp. 80–95.

Stewart, John I.M. *Thomas Hardy, A Critical Biography.* New York: Dodd, Mead, 1971, pp. 91–107.

Walcutt, Charles C. "Character and Coincidence in *The Return of the Native*," in *Twelve Original Essays on Great English Novels.* Edited by Charles Shapiro. Detroit: Wayne State University Press, 1960, pp. 153–173.

Weber, Carl J. *Hardy of Wessex: His Life and Literary Career.* New York: Columbia University Press, 1940, pp. 70–77.

Webster, Harvey C. *On a Darkling Plain: The Art and Thought of Thomas Hardy.* Chicago: University of Chicago Press, 1947, pp. 118–125.

Williams, Merryn. *Thomas Hardy and Rural England.* New York: Columbia University Press, 1972, pp. 136–145.

TESS OF THE D'URBERVILLES

Type of work: Novel
Author: Thomas Hardy (1840–1928)
Type of plot: Philosophical realism
Time of plot: Late nineteenth century
Locale: England
First published: 1891

A powerful tragic novel that shows how crass circumstances influence the destinies of people, Tess of the D'Urbervilles *is also a moral indictment of the smug Victorian attitude toward sexual purity.*

Principal Characters

Tess Durbeyfield, a naïve country girl. When her father learns that his family is descended from an ancient landed house, the mother, hoping to better her struggling family financially, sends Tess to work for the Stoke-d'Urbervilles, who have recently moved to the locality. In this household the innocent girl, attractive and mature beyond her years, meets Alec d'Urberville, a dissolute young man. From this time on she is the rather stoical victim of personal disasters. Seduced by Alec, she gives birth to his child. Later she works on a dairy farm, where she meets Angel Clare and reluctantly agrees to marry him, even though she is afraid of his reaction if he learns about her past. As she fears, he is disillusioned by her loss of innocence and virtue. Although deserted by her husband, she never loses her unselfish love for him. Eventually, pursued by the relentless Alec, she capitulates to his blandishments and goes to live with him at a prosperous resort. When Angel Clare returns to her, she stabs Alec and spends a few happy days with Clare before she is captured and hanged for her crime.

Angel Clare, Tess's husband. Professing a dislike for effete, worn-out families and outdated traditions, he is determined not to follow family tradition and become a clergyman or a scholar. Instead, he wishes to learn what he can about farming, in hopes of having a farm of his own. When he meets Tess at a dairy farm, he teaches her various philosophical theories which he has gleaned from his reading. He learns that she is descended from the d'Urbervilles and is pleased by the information. After urging reluctant Tess to marry him, at the same time refusing to let her tell him about her past life, he persuades her to accept him; later he learns to his great mortification about her relations with Alec. Although he himself has confessed to an episode with a woman in London, he is not so forgiving as Tess. After several days he deserts her and goes to Brazil. Finally, no longer so provincial in his moral views, he remorsefully comes back to Tess, but he returns too late to make amends for his selfish actions toward her.

Alec d'Urberville, Tess's seducer. Lusting after the beautiful girl and making brazen propositions, he boldly pursues her. At first she resists his advancements, but she is unable to stop him from having his way in a lonely wood where he has taken her. For a time he reforms and assumes the unlikely role of an evangelist. Meeting Tess again, he lusts after her more than ever and hounds her at every turn until she accepts him as her protector. Desperate when Angel Clare returns, she kills her hated lover.

Jack Durbeyfield, a carter of Marlott, Tess's indolent father. After learning of his distinguished forebears, he gives up work almost entirely and spends much time drinking beer in the Rolliver Tavern. He thinks that a man who has grand and noble "skillentons" in a family vault at Kingsbere-sub-Greenhill should not have to work.

Joan Durbeyfield, Tess's mother. After her hard labor at her modest home, she likes to sit at Rolliver's Tavern while her husband drinks a few pints and brags about his ancestors. A practical woman in a harsh world, she is probably right when she tells Tess not to reveal her past to Angel Clare.

Sorrow, Tess's child by Alec d'Urberville. The infant lives only a few days. Tess herself performs the rite of baptism before the baby dies.

Eliza-Louisa, called **Liza-Lu,** Tess's younger sister. It is Tess's hope, before her death, that Angel Clare will marry her sister. Liza-Lu waits with Angel during the hour of Tess's execution for the murder of Alec d'Urberville.

Abraham,
Hope, and
Modesty, the son and young daughters of the Durbeyfields.

The Reverend James Clare, Angel Clare's father, a devout man of simple faith but limited vision.

Mrs. Clare, a woman of good works and restricted interests. She shows little understanding of her son Angel.

Felix and
Cuthbert Clare, Angel Clare's conventional, rather snobbish brothers. They are patronizing in their attitude toward him and disapprove of his marriage to Tess Durbeyfield.

Mercy Chant, a young woman interested in church work and charity, whom Angel Clare's parents thought a proper wife for him. Later she marries his brother Cuthbert.

Mrs. Stoke-d'Urberville, the blind widow of a man who grew rich in trade and added the name of the extinct d'Urberville barony to his own. Her chief interests in life are her wayward son Alec and her poultry.

Car Darch, also called **Dark Car,** a vulgar village woman. Because of her previous relations with Alec d'Urberville she is jealous of Tess Durbeyfield. Her nickname is the Queen of Spades.

Nancy, her sister, nicknamed the Queen of Diamonds.

Mr. Tringham, the elderly parson and antiquarian who half-jokingly tells Jack Durbeyfield that he is descended from the noble d'Urberville family.

Richard Crick, the owner of Talbothays Farm, where Angel Clare is learning dairy farming. Farmer Crick also hires Tess Durbeyfield as a dairymaid after the death of her child. Tess and Angel are married at Talbothays.

Christiana Crick, Farmer Crick's kind, hearty wife.

Marian, a stout, red-faced dairymaid at Talbothays Farm. Later she takes to drink and becomes a field worker at Flintcomb-Ash Farm. She and Izz Huett write Angel Clare an anonymous letter in which they tell him that his wife is being pursued by Alec d'Urberville.

Izz Huett, a dairymaid at Talbothays Farm. In love with Angel Clare, she openly declares her feelings after he has deserted Tess. He is tempted to take Izz with him to Brazil, but he soon changes his mind. She and Marian write Angel a letter warning him to look after his wife.

Retty Priddle, the youngest of the dairymaids at Talbothays Farm. Also in love with Angel Clare, she tries to drown herself after his marriage.

Farmy Groby, the tight-fisted, harsh owner of Flintcomb-Ash Farm, where Tess works in the fields after Angel Clare has deserted her.

The Story

It was a proud day when Jack Durbeyfield learned that he was descended from the famous D'Urberville family. Durbeyfield had never done more work than was necessary to keep his family supplied with meager food and himself with beer, but from that day on he ceased doing even that small amount of work. His wife joined him in thinking that such a high family should live better with less effort, and she persuaded their oldest daughter, Tess, to visit the Stoke-D'Urbervilles, a wealthy family who had assumed the D'Urberville name because no one else claimed it. It was her mother's hope that Tess would make a good impression on the rich D'Urbervilles and perhaps a good marriage with one of the sons.

When Tess met her supposed relatives, however, she found only a blind mother and a dapper son who made Tess uncomfortable by his improper remarks to her. The son, Alec, tricked the innocent young Tess into working as a poultry maid, not letting her know that his mother was unaware of Tess's identity. After a short time Tess decided to look for work elsewhere to support her parents and her numerous brothers and sisters. She was innocent, but she knew that Alec meant her no good. Alec, more clever than she, at last managed to get her alone and then possessed her.

When Tess returned to her home and told her mother of her terrible experience, her mother's only worry was that Alec was not going to marry Tess. The poor girl worked in the fields, facing the slander of her associates bravely. Her trouble was made worse by the fact that Alec followed her from place to place, trying to possess her again. By going about to different farms during the harvest season, Tess managed to elude Alec long enough to give birth to her baby without his knowledge. The baby did not live long, however, and a few months after its death, Tess went to a dairy farm far to the south to be dairymaid.

At the dairy farm Tess was liked and well treated. Also at the farm was Angel Clare, a pastor's son who had rejected the ministry to study farming. It was his wish to own a farm some day, and he was working on different kinds of farms, so that he could learn something of the many kinds of work required of a general farmer. Although all the dairymaids were attracted to Angel, Tess interested him the most. He thought her a beautiful and innocent young maiden, as she was, for it was her innocence which had caused her trouble with Alec.

Tess felt that she was wicked, however, and rejected the attentions Angel paid to her. She urged him to turn to one of the other girls for companionship. It was unthinkable that the son of a minister would marry a dairymaid, but Angel did not care much about family tradition. In spite of her pleas, he continued to pay court to Tess. At last, against the wishes of his parents, Angel asked Tess to be his wife. Not only did he love her, but also he realized that a farm girl would be a help to him on his own land. Although Tess was in love with Angel by this time, the memory of her night with Alec caused her to refuse Angel again and again. At last his insistence, coupled with the written pleas of her parents to marry someone who could help the family financially, won her over, and she agreed to marry him.

On the night before the wedding, which Tess had postponed many times because she felt unworthy, she wrote Angel a letter, telling everything about herself and Alec. She slipped the letter under his door, sure that when he read it he would renounce her forever. But in the morning Angel acted as tenderly as before and Tess loved him more than ever for his forgiving nature. When she realized that Angel had not found the letter, she attempted to tell him about her past. Angel only teased her about wanting to confess, thinking that such a pure girl could have no black sins in her history. They were married without Angel's learning about Alec and her dead baby.

On their wedding night Angel told Tess about an evening of debauchery in his own past. Tess forgave him and then told about her affair with Alec, thinking that he would forgive her as she had him. But such was not the case. Angel was at first stunned, and then so hurt that he could not even speak to Tess. Finally he told her that she was not the woman he loved, the one he had married, but a stranger with whom he could not live, at least for the present. He took her to her home and left her there. Then he went to his home and on to Brazil, where he planned to buy a farm. At first neither Tess nor Angel told their parents the reason for their separation. When Tess finally told her mother, that ignorant woman blamed Tess for losing her husband by confessing something he need never have known.

Angel had left Tess some money and some jewels which had been given to him by his godmother. The jewels Tess put in a bank; the money she spent on her parents. When it was gone, her family went hungry once more, for her father still thought himself too high-born to work for a living. Tess again went from farm to farm, doing hard labor in the fields in order to get enough food to keep herself and her family alive.

While she was working in the fields, she met Alec again. He had met Angel's minister father and, repenting his evil ways, had become an itinerant preacher. The sight of Tess, for whom he had always lusted, caused a lapse in his new religious fervor, and he began to pursue her once more. Frightened, Tess wrote to Angel, sending the letter to his parents to forward to him. She told Angel that she loved him and needed him, that an enemy was pursuing her. She begged him to forgive her and to return to her.

The letter took several months to reach Angel. Meanwhile Alec was so kind to Tess and so generous to her family that she began to relent in her feelings toward him. At last, when she did not receive an answer from Angel, she wrote him a note saying that he was cruel not to forgive her and that now she would not forgive his treatment of her. Then she went to Alec again, living with him as his wife.

It was thus that Angel found her. He had come to tell her that he had forgiven her and that he still loved her. But when he found her with Alec, he turned away, more hurt than before.

Tess, too, was bitterly unhappy. She now hated Alec because once again he had been the cause of her husband's repudiation of her. Feeling that she could find happiness only if Alec were dead, she stabbed him as he slept. Then she ran out of the house and followed Angel, who was aimlessly walking down a road leading out of the town. When they met and Tess told him what she had done, Angel forgave her everything, even the murder of Alec, and they went on together. They were happy with one another for a few days, even though Angel knew that the authorities would soon find Tess.

When the officers finally found them, Tess was asleep. Angel asked the officers to wait until she awoke. As soon as she opened her eyes, Tess saw the strangers and knew that they had come for her and that she would be hanged, but she was not unhappy. She had had a few days with the husband she truly loved, and now she was ready for her punishment. She stood up bravely and faced her captors. She was not afraid.

Critical Evaluation

English fiction assumed a new dimension in the hands of Thomas Hardy. From its beginnings it had been a middle-class genre; it was written for and about the bourgeois, with the working class and the aristocracy taking only minor roles. The British novelist explored the workings of society in the space between the upper-reaches of the gentry and the new urban shopkeepers. In the eighteenth century Daniel Defoe treated the rogue on his or her way to wealth; Henry Fielding was concerned with the manners of the gentry; and Samuel Richardson dramatized romantic, middle-class sentimentality. In the nineteenth century, Jane Austen's subject matter was the comedy of manners among a very closely knit segment of the rural gentry; the farm laboring classes were conspicuous by their absence. After Walter Scott and his historical romances, the great Victorian novelists—the Brontës, Thackeray, Dickens, Trollope, and George Eliot—were all concerned with the nuances of middle class feelings and morality, treating their themes either romantically or comically.

Although he certainly drew on the work and experience of his predecessors, Hardy opened and explored fresh areas: indeed, he was constantly hounded by critics and censors for his realistic treatment of sexuality and the problems of faith. After his last novel, *Jude the Obscure,* was attacked for its immorality, he was driven from the field. The final thirty years or so of his life were devoted entirely to poetry. Even more important than this new honesty and openness toward sex and religion, however, was Hardy's development of the tragic possibilities of the novel and his opening of it to the experience of the rural laborer and artisan. His rendering of nature, moreover, influenced by Greek thought and Darwin's *On the Origin of the Species,* radically departed from the nineteenth century view of nature as benevolent and purposeful. In retrospect, Hardy's novels, written between 1868 and 1895, have a unity of thought and feeling that challenges all the accepted truths of his time. He is part of and perhaps the most formidable spokesman for that group of artists—including the Rossettis, Swinburne, Wilde, Yeats, and Housman—which reacted against the materialism, pieties, and unexamined faith of the Victorian Age. As he said of the age in his poem, "The Darkling Thrush": "The land's sharp features seemed to be / The Century's corpse outleant. . . ." And, finally, he can be viewed as not only the last Victorian, but also as the first modern who defined the themes which were to occupy such great successors as Joseph Conrad and D. H. Lawrence.

Tess of the D'Urbervilles ranks as one of Hardy's finest achievements, along with *Far from the Madding Crowd, The Return of the Native, The Mayor of Casterbridge,* and *Jude the Obscure.* Together with the last novel mentioned, it forms his most powerful indictment of Victorian notions of virtue and social justice. Its subtitle, "A Pure Woman Faithfully Presented," is itself a mockery of a moral sense that works in rigid categories. Mesmerized and seduced by Alec D'Urberville, the mother of a bastard child, the married mistress of Alec, a murderess who is eventually hanged, Tess is yet revealed as an innocent victim of nature, chance, and a social and religious system which denies human feeling. Her purity is not only a matter of ethics—for Hardy finds her without sin—but also one of soul. Tess maintains a kind of gentle attitude toward everyone, and even when she is treated with the grossest injustice, she responds with forgiveness. It is not until the conclusion of the novel, when she has been deprived once again of her beloved, Angel Clare (a love which the reader has great difficulty in accepting, since he lacks any recognizable human passion), that she is ultimately overcome by forces beyond her control and murders Alec. Like her sister in tragedy, Sophocles' Antigone, she is driven by a higher justice to assert herself. That she must make reparation according to a law that she cannot accept does not disturb her, and like Antigone's, her death is a triumph rather than a defeat.

It is precisely at this point that Hardy most effectively challenges Victorian metaphysics. In Tess we witness a woman disposed of by irrational and accidental forces. Such impulses which the Victorians tried to deny—not always easily to be sure—through a devotion to reason in matters of law, science, and religion, were anomalies that could not be admitted if their world view were to stand. To insist, moreover, as Tess does, that she is not to be judged by human law is a radical attack on a culture that rested uncertainly on a fragile social contract. To compound the enigma, Tess acquiesces in the judgment and gives her life—for society does not really take it—with a sense of peace and fulfillment.

Thus, Hardy exposed the primitive passions and laws of nature to his readers. He threw them back into a state which they believed, in their smugness over social and material progress, was safely behind them and their culture. Breaking past the manners of the drawing room and ignoring the conventions of the novel, he called up to the Victorian memory scenes of the most fundamental kind of human behavior. Not only did he call into question their idea of law but also their notion of human nature. Indeed, Hardy seems to suggest that no matter the success of politics in removing social abuses, there remains an element in man that cannot be legislated; that is of course his instinctual nature that drives him to demand justice for his being, no matter the consequences. For Victorian civilization to accept Tess, therefore, would be to admit its own myopia—which it was not yet prepared to do.

Bibliography

Abercrombie, Lascelles. *Thomas Hardy, A Critical Study.* London: Martin Secker, 1912, pp. 129–152.

Beach, Joseph W. *The Technique of Thomas Hardy.* Chicago: University of Chicago Press, 1922, pp. 180–217.

Brown, Douglas. "A Novel of Character and Environment," in *Thomas Hardy.* London: Longmans, 1954, pp. 90–98. Reprinted in *Hardy: The Tragic Novels.* Edited by R.P. Draper. London: Macmillan, 1975, pp. 158–164.

Butler, Lance St. John. *Thomas Hardy.* New York: Cambridge University Press, 1978, pp. 96–119.

Carpenter, Richard C. *Thomas Hardy.* New York: Twayne, 1964, pp. 124–138.

Duffin, Henry C. *Thomas Hardy: A Study of the Wessex Novel.* Manchester, England: Manchester University Press, 1921, pp. 145–158.

Friedman, Alan. *The Turn of the Novel.* New York: Oxford University Press, 1966, pp. 38–74.

Guerard, Albert J. "Introduction," in *Tess of the d'Urbervilles.* New York: Washington Square Press, 1955, pp. v–vi. Reprinted in *Twentieth Century Interpretations of* Tess of the d'Urbervilles*: A Collection of Critical Essays.* Edited by Albert J. LaValley. Englewood Cliffs, N.J.: Prentice-Hall, 1969, pp. 101–102.

Hamilton, Horace E. "A Reading of *Tess of the D'Urbervilles*," in *Essays in Literary History.* Edited by Rudolph Kirk and C.F. Main. New Brunswick, N.J.: Rutgers University Press, 1960, pp. 197–216.

Howe, Irving. "Let the Day Perish," in *Thomas Hardy.* New York: Macmillan, 1967, pp. 108–113, 130, 132. Reprinted in *Twentieth Century Interpreta-*

tions of Tess of the d'Urbervilles: *A Collection of Critical Essays.* Edited by Albert J. LaValley. Englewood Cliffs, N.J.: Prentice-Hall, 1969, pp. 62–68.

Kettle, Arnold. "Introduction," in *Tess of the d'Urbervilles.* New York: Harper & Row, 1966, pp. vii–xxiii. Reprinted in *Twentieth Century Interpretations of* Tess of the d'Urbervilles: *A Collection of Critical Essays.* Edited by Albert J. LaValley. Englewood Cliffs, N.J.: Prentice-Hall, 1969, pp. 14–29.

Lea, Hermann. *Thomas Hardy's Wessex.* London: Macmillan, 1913, pp. 3–31.

Lodge, David. "Tess, Nature, and the Voices of Hardy," in *Language of Fiction: Essays in Criticism and Verbal Analysis of the English Novel.* New York: Columbia University Press, 1966, pp. 164–188. Reprinted in *Twentieth Century Interpretations of* Tess of the d'Urbervilles: *A Collection of Critical Essays.* Edited by Albert J. LaValley. Englewood Cliffs, N.J.: Prentice-Hall, 1969, pp. 74–84.

Meisel, Perry. *Thomas Hardy: The Return of the Repressed.* New Haven, Conn.: Yale University Press, 1972, pp. 118–135.

Miller, Joseph H. "Fiction and Repetition: *Tess of the d'Urbervilles*," in *Forms of Modern British Fiction.* Edited by Alan Warren Friedman. Austin: University of Texas Press, 1975, pp. 43–71.

Millgate, Michael. *Thomas Hardy: His Career as a Novelist.* New York: Random House, 1971, pp. 263–280, 399–405.

Rutland, W.R. *Thomas Hardy: A Study of His Writings and Their Background.* Oxford: Blackwell, 1938, pp. 221–239.

Southerington, F.R. *Hardy's Vision of Man.* London: Chatto and Windus, 1971, pp. 123–135.

Stewart, John I.M. *Thomas Hardy, A Critical Biography.* New York: Dodd, Mead, 1971, pp. 165–183.

Tanner, Tony. "Colour and Movement in *Tess of the d'Urbervilles*," in *Critical Quarterly.* X (Autumn, 1968), pp. 219–239. Reprinted in *Hardy: The Tragic Novels.* Edited by R.P. Draper. London: Macmillan, 1975, pp. 182–208. Also reprinted in *The Victorian Novel: Modern Essays in Criticism.* Edited by Ian Watt. New York: Oxford University Press, 1971, pp. 407–431.

Tomlinson, Thomas Brian. "Hardy's Universe: *Tess of the d'Urbervilles*," in his *The English Middle-Class Novel.* New York: Barnes & Noble, 1976, pp. 131–147.

Van Ghent, Dorothy. "On *Tess of the d'Urbervilles*," in *The English Novel: Form and Function.* New York: Holt, Rinehart and Winston, 1953, pp. 195–209. Reprinted in *Twentieth Century Interpretations of* Tess of the d'Urbervilles: *A Collection of Critical Essays.* Edited by Albert J. LaValley.

Englewood Cliffs, N.J.: Prentice-Hall, 1969, pp. 48–61.

Weber, Carl J.   *Hardy of Wessex: His Life and Literary Career.* New York: Columbia University Press, 1940, pp. 116–133, 263–265.

Webster, Harvey C.   *On a Darkling Plain: The Art and Thought of Thomas Hardy.* Chicago: University of Chicago Press, 1947, pp. 173–180.

Williams, Merryn.   *Thomas Hardy and Rural England.* New York: Columbia University Press, 1972, pp. 90–99, 169–179.

THE WOODLANDERS

Type of work: Novel
Author: Thomas Hardy (1840–1928)
Type of plot: Tragic romance
Time of plot: Nineteenth century
Locale: Rural England
First published: 1887

The Woodlanders, *a romance that includes both scenes of rustic humor and of tragedy, is memorable for its mythic quality—in which characters are related symbolically to plants—and for the touching figure of Marty South, one of Hardy's noblest women.*

Principal Characters

Grace Melbury, a young Englishwoman whose expensive education sets her apart from her family and neighbors in the village of Little Hintock. She returns to find that she is intended by her father to be the bride of Giles Winterborne, until that young man loses his little fortune. Later she is courted by a young physician, Edgar Fitzpiers, whom she marries without love at her father's urging. As she begins to mature, Grace realizes that she has been mistaken in her marriage. When her husband turns to a rich, young widow, Grace is surprised at her lack of feeling until she realizes that as she has outgrown an external view of life she has come for the first time to appreciate her rural neighbors. Though her pride is hurt by her husband's philandering, she takes joy in discovering what love can be, for she truly falls in love with Giles Winterborne, but only later, as Winterborne lies dying, having sacrificed himself for her, does she really mature as a woman. Some months later she and her husband become reconciled and prepare to start life anew in another part of England.

Edgar Fitzpiers, a young physician of good family. Though an excellent doctor, he is a vain and shallow young man who wastes his skill and his time in all sorts of romantic studies. Living alone in Little Hinton village, he is attracted to Grace Melbury and marries her, although he feels he is marrying beneath his station. Soon afterward he drifts into an affair with Felice Charmond, a wealthy widow of the neighborhood. Through this unhappy passion he loses his wife, his practice, and almost his life. After the scandalous death of his mistress abroad he realizes his selfishness and courts his wife anew, winning a new start in marriage and in his profession.

George Melbury, a timber merchant. Conscience-stricken because he had stolen a friend's fiancée years before, he proposes to make amends by marrying his daughter Grace to the friend's son, Giles Winterborne; but he finds that he cannot bring himself to enforce the marriage after the young man has lost his lands. He then marries Grace to the local doctor, who he believes is the only man in the community suitable for her. Throughout the story, until Grace matures enough to take her life into her own hands, George Melbury dominates his daughter and several times plunges her into grief by his decisions, even though he means well by her.

Giles Winterborne, a young timberman and landowner, a natural gentleman. He loves Grace Melbury devotedly during his lifetime and sacrifices his health and life for her happiness and good name. He endures many embarrassments at the hands of the Melburys, even to being jilted when, through no fault of his own, he loses his lands and is forced to become an itinerant worker. His noble nature is a great factor in helping Grace Melbury achieve emotional maturity.

Felice Charmond, a rich young widow and a former actress who has inherited a great estate, including the local manor house, from her deceased husband. A creature of sensual passion, she readily begins an affair with Dr. Fitzpiers. The affair, the last of a long series for her, is no mere flirtation, for she learns truly to love the young physician and follows him to the Continent after he and his wife separate. There her death at the hands of an earlier lover, an American from South Carolina, frees the doctor from his passion and eventually he and his wife are reunited.

Marty South, a poor young woman in love with Giles Winterborne. Her letter to Dr. Fitzpiers causes an argument between the physician and Felice Charmond. The argument takes Fitzpiers away from the widow shortly before her death and saves him from being involved in scandal when she is shot and killed by a former lover.

Suke Damson, a pretty, amoral young village girl who has an affair with Dr. Fitzpiers before his marriage. Though it is a passing relationship for him, Suke falls deeply in love. After her marriage she reveals unwittingly to her husband that her affections lie elsewhere.

Tim Tang, Suke Damson's husband, a sawyer employed by Mr. Melbury. Bitter because his wife still loves Dr. Fitzpiers rather than himself, he sets a mantrap, such as is used to catch poachers, for the physician. The jealous husband's plan goes wrong and the trap almost gives serious injury to innocent Grace Melbury. The incident turns out to be the unintended catalyst that brings Grace and her husband together once more. Tang and his wife emigrate to New Zealand.

Robert Creedle, an old servant loyal to Giles Winterborne in both prosperity and adversity.

John South, Marty South's father. His death influences the careers of Giles Winterborne and the others because Giles' leases to his lands are written to expire at the death of the old man.

The Story

Mr. George Melbury, timber merchant, had spared no expense in educating Grace, his only daughter. She had been gone from home a year, and he was eagerly awaiting her return. Another man also waited for Grace's homecoming. He was Giles Winterborne, an itinerant farmer and apple grower. Mr. Melbury had wronged Giles' father many years before, and in order to atone for this wrong he had half promised Giles that he should have Grace for his wife.

When Grace returned, it was soon evident that she was now much too cultured and refined for the ways of a simple farmer. But Grace knew that her father had promised her to Giles, and she meant to go through with the plans even though she shrank a little from his plainness. It was Mr. Melbury who was the most concerned. He was an honorable man and liked Giles, but he also loved his only child above everything else. He could not bear to see her throw herself away when she could no doubt marry better.

Giles agreed that he was not worthy of Grace, and so the three vacillated, no one wanting to make a decision. Then through a series of unfortunate and unforeseen circumstances Giles lost the houses that meant his living. His loss decided the issue. Although Mr. Melbury could easily have supported them both, it was unthinkable that such a lady as Grace should be tied to a man without a steady income. But when her father told her that she must forget Giles, Grace found herself for the first time thinking of her would-be lover with real affection.

Another person was destined to change the lives of all three. In the area was a doctor, Edgar Fitzpiers, descendant of a former fine family and in his own right a brilliant and charming man. The local folk thought he consorted with the devil, for he performed many weird experiments. From the first time Edgar saw Grace, he was enchanted with her beauty and her bearing. At first he thought she must be the lady of the manor, Mrs. Charmond, for he could not believe that the daughter of a merchant could be so well educated and charming. Before long the two young people met and Edgar asked Grace's father for her hand. Mr. Melbury gladly gave his permission, for Edgar was far above Grace in position. In spite of his sorrow at disappointing Giles and at failing to keep his pledge to the faithful fellow, Mr. Melbury encouraged Grace to accept Edgar. Since she had always obeyed her father in all things, she accepted Edgar even as she realized that she grew fonder of Giles each day.

When the young couple returned from a long honeymoon, they settled in a newly decorated wing of her father's house. Edgar continued his practice. It grew alarmingly smaller, however, for the country folk who had once looked up to him now felt him one of their own. He decided that perhaps he should accept a practice in a neighboring town.

Before he could make a final decision on this question, Mrs. Felice Charmond entered the picture. The lady of the manor was well known for her many love affairs and her questionable reputation. When she had a slight accident and sent for Edgar, he was attracted to her immediately. The few scratches she had suffered were enough to take him to her house day after day, until even the servants and farmers were talking about them. At last Mr. Melbury could no longer stand by idly and see his daughter suffer, and so he appealed in person to Mrs. Charmond to leave Edgar alone. Grace herself was rather immune to the whole affair, not caring enough for her husband to suffer any great jealousy.

The climax to the affair occurred when Mr. Melbury found Edgar near Mrs. Charmond's home after Edgar had been thrown from a horse. Mr. Melbury picked him up and placed him on his own mount. Edgar was drunk and not aware that he was riding with his father-in-law. He berated Mr. Melbury and Grace as ignorant peasants and cursed his ill luck in having married beneath himself. His drunken ravings were too much for the kind-hearted merchant, who threw Edgar off the horse and rode away. Edgar, who was injured in the first fall, made his way to Mrs. Charmond and begged her to hide him until he could travel. He must now leave the district; there could be no forgiveness for his many sins.

Mrs. Charmond left her home to travel on the continent and before long rumors came back that Edgar was with her. Grace was stoic through it all. Unknown to her husband, she was also aware that he had had an affair with a peasant girl of the neighborhood before his marriage. She would have let things stand as they were, but an unscrupulous lawyer persuaded her father that a new law would permit her to divorce Edgar. While he was making arrangements for the divorce, Mr. Melbury encouraged both Giles and Grace to renew their old plans to marry. By that time they both felt sure they loved each other, but they were more cautious than Grace's father. Thus when the word came that she could not be free of her husband, they were resigned to their unhappiness.

Grace and Giles did resume the friendship they had known since childhood, but decorously in all respects, for neither wished a hint of scandal to touch the other. Then, after many months, Grace heard from her husband that he wanted her to live with him again. Mrs. Charmond was dead, killed by a thwarted lover who afterward committed suicide. Edgar did not mention this fact, but a newspaper told the whole story. Grace and her father decided she should not meet Edgar as he had asked. When she failed to do so, he threatened to come to their home.

Hearing Edgar approaching, Grace slipped out of the house and ran into the woods. Stumbling and afraid, she came at last to the hut occupied by Giles. On learning that she did not wish to see her husband, Giles installed her in his hut and went out into the rain to sleep. What Grace did not know was that Giles had been very ill of a fever, and a few days and nights in the cold rain made him desperately ill. When she found her faithful friend so ill, she ran for Edgar, forgetting her desire not to see him in her anxiety for Giles. Edgar returned with her but there was nothing to be done. Grace held her one real love in her arms as he died, seeming not aware that her husband was present.

For a long time Grace would not listen to her husband's pleas to return to him. Wanting to hurt him as she had been hurt, she told him that she and Giles had lived together those last few days. Before he learned that her self-accusation was not true, Edgar realized that he truly loved her. When a man trap, set for Edgar by the husband of the peasant girl he had once wronged, almost caught Grace in its steel jaws, Edgar found his wife and helped her to safety. After he told her that he had bought a practice at a great distance from her old home and that he would be a faithful husband, devoting himself to her happiness, she went away with him. She intended to be a good wife, but part of her remained with Giles in the country churchyard grave.

Critical Evaluation

The oppressively enclosed society of Hintock, where the "woodlanders" dwell, is one of contrasting sets of individuals, rural and urban. Giles Winterborne, Marty South, George Melbury and the workers are opposed to exotic Felice Charmond of Hintock Manor and Edgar Fitzpiers, the new doctor. Grace Melbury vacillates between the two groups, finally committing herself, after the death of Giles, presumably to life with Fitzpiers in another area; Hardy leaves the end of the novel rather ambiguous.

The story revolves not only upon Grace's decisions and indecisions, but also upon those of Fitzpiers, who is simultaneously trapped in marriage with Grace and in an affair with Felice; of Mr. Melbury, who cannot make up his mind to marry his daughter to the apple grower or the doctor; and of Felice, who cannot settle on one lover.

Most events in the novel take place in dense woods, on forest paths, or in remote huts almost hidden by foliage. Trees and undergrowth are so omnipresent as to be stifling. Hintock dwellers plant trees, trim or tend them, fell them at maturity, and strip the bark to sell. The woods have utilitarian as well as symbolic significance. They are real and so are Giles and Marty, accepting with stolid, earth-like quality, their fate of endless hard work. The woodland here lacks the gentleness and beauty of that in *Under the Greenwood Tree*; it demands its price from those who make it their living.

The characters are even compared implicitly to trees and plants: Giles and Marty are the indigenous trees, Felice and Fitzpiers the imported plants that finally uproot themselves and seek climates more favorable to their growth.

After an almost unbelievable network of promises made and broken, infidelities, romantic seductions, and accidental deaths, Grace and the repentant Fitzpiers are left to repair their ill-starred marriage. But the last chapter points to no satisfactory or simple solution. Hardy does not extol their renewed love; instead, he focuses on Marty South's devoted soliloquy as she places flowers on Giles' grave. She, too, loved him but faithfully. In contrast to other women in the novel, she is the epitome of self-sacrifice, and it is Marty whom Hardy leaves with the reader, perhaps embodying in her the residual human values when he comments, "she touched sublimity at points, and looked almost like a being who had rejected . . . the attribute of sex for the loftier quality of abstract humanism." Marty is more a figure of stoic resignation, however, than of sublimity; and even Giles, for all his loyalty and sacrifice for Grace, does not attain, like the Mayor of Casterbridge or the later Jude, tragic stature.

Bibliography

Abercrombie, Lascelles. *Thomas Hardy: A Critical Study.* London: Martin Secker, 1912, pp. 97–128.

Beach, Joseph Warren. *The Technique of Thomas Hardy.* Chicago: University of Chicago Press, 1922, pp. 158–176.

Brown, Douglas. *Thomas Hardy.* London: Longmans, 1954, pp. 70–89.

Butler, Lance St. John. *Thomas Hardy.* New York: Cambridge University Press, 1978, pp. 75–95.

Carpenter, Richard C. *Thomas Hardy.* New York: Twayne, 1964, pp. 114–124.

Drake, Robert Y., Jr. "*The Woodlanders* as Traditional Pastoral," in *Modern Fiction Studies.* VI (Autumn, 1960), pp. 251–257.

Edgar, Pelham. *The Art of the Novel from 1700 to the Present.* New York: Macmillan, 1933, pp. 164–171.

Fayen, George. "*The Woodlanders*: Inwardness and Memory," in *Studies in English Literature, 1500–1900.* I (Autumn, 1961), pp. 81–100.

Gittings, Robert. *Thomas Hardy's Later Years.* Boston: Little, Brown, 1978, pp. 44–48.

Grimsditch, Herbert B. *Character and Environment in the Novels of Thomas Hardy.* London: Witherby, 1925, pp. 63–68, 124–128.

Hornback, Bert G. *The Metaphor of Chance: Vision and Technique in the Works of Thomas Hardy.* Athens: Ohio University Press, 1971, pp. 69–72.

Howe, Irving. *Thomas Hardy.* London: Macmillan, 1967, pp. 102–107.

Lea, Hermann. *Thomas Hardy's Wessex.* London: Macmillan, 1913, pp. 107–117.

McDowall, Arthur. *Thomas Hardy: A Critical Study.* London: Faber and Faber, 1931, pp. 75–79.

Matchett, William H. "*The Woodlanders*, or, Realism in Sheep's Clothing," in *Nineteenth-Century Fiction.* IX (March, 1955), pp. 241–261.

Meisel, Perry. *Thomas Hardy: The Return of the Repressed.* New Haven, Conn.: Yale University Press, 1972, pp. 109–117.

Page, Norman. *Thomas Hardy.* London: Routledge and Kegan Paul, 1977, pp. 40–41, 52–53, 54–55, 75–77.

Sherman, G.W. *The Pessimism of Thomas Hardy.* Cranbury, N.J.: Fairleigh Dickinson University Press, 1976, pp. 141–150.

Southerington, F.R. *Hardy's Vision of Man.* London: Chatto and Windus, 1971, pp. 119–123.

Squires, Michael. *"The Woodlanders,"* in his *The Pastoral Novel: Studies in George Eliot, Thomas Hardy, and D.H. Lawrence.* Charlottesville: University Press of Virginia, 1974, pp. 150–173.

Stewart, John I.M. *Thomas Hardy, A Critical Biography.* New York: Dodd, Mead, 1971, pp. 127–146.

Toliver, Harold E. *Pastoral Forms and Attitudes.* Berkeley: University of California Press, 1971, pp. 279–285.

Weber, Carl J. *Hardy of Wessex: His Life and Literary Career.* New York: Columbia University Press, 1940, pp. 108–114.

Webster, Harvey C. *On a Darkling Plain: The Art and Thought of Thomas Hardy.* Chicago: University of Chicago Press, 1947, pp. 166–173.

Williams, Merryn. *Thomas Hardy and Rural England.* New York: Columbia University Press, 1972, pp. 157–168.

GEORGE MEREDITH

Born: Portsmouth, England (February 12, 1828)
Died: Box Hill, Surrey, England (May 18, 1909)

Principal Works

NOVELS: *The Shaving of Shagpat,* 1856; *Farina,* 1857; *The Ordeal of Richard Feverel,* 1859; *Evan Harrington,* 1861; *Sandra Belloni, or Emilia in England,* 1864; *Rhoda Fleming,* 1865; *Vittoria,* 1867; *The Adventures of Harry Richmond,* 1871; *Beauchamp's Career,* 1876; *The Egoist,* 1879; *The Tragic Comedians,* 1880; *Diana of the Crossways,* 1885; *Lord Ormont and His Aminta,* 1894; *One of Our Conquerors,* 1891; *The Amazing Marriage,* 1895; *Celt and Saxon,* 1910 (unfinished).

SHORT STORIES: *The Tale of Chloe,* 1879; *The Case of General Ople and Lady Camper,* 1890.

POEMS: *Poems,* 1851; *Modern Love,* 1862; *Poems and Lyrics of the Joy of Earth,* 1883; *Ballads and Poems of Tragic Life,* 1887; *A Reading of Earth,* 1888; *A Reading of Life,* 1901; *Last Poems,* 1909.

ESSAY: *On the Idea of Comedy and the Uses of the Comic Spirit,* 1897 (first separate publication).

A highly original writer, perhaps too original and idiosyncratic ever to be very popular, George Meredith has always been one of those unfortunate writers whose work is more praised than read. He did not receive much popular attention until he was past fifty, and after that, though he received most of the honors his fellow writers could award, he never attracted the general reader as Dickens, Thackeray, or Trollope did. An age in which the ability to invent a lively plot was highly valued was not likely to be much pleased by a novelist who, like his equally neglected contemporary Henry James, was almost exclusively interested in the subtle depiction of human motivation. Meredith's style also gave the common reader trouble: it was epigrammatic and involved, totally unlike the swift narrative flow of the prose of Dickens or Thackeray. In his poetry Meredith again refused to conform to popular taste; his diction was often rough, his syntax obscure, in contrast to the melodic sweetness of the popular Tennysonian tradition.

His style, however, is admirably suited to his purposes. He considered it the purpose of art to correct the excesses of men in society and to bring them closer to the ideal of the golden mean. His novels usually expose the flaws in human beings so that the reader may eliminate them in himself. His celebrated lecture, *On the Idea of Comedy and the Uses of the Comic Spirit,* delivered in 1877 but not published separately until 1897, is one of the great expressions of the moral value of literature. To this end he developed a style that is leisurely yet challenging, designed to penetrate to the hidden motivations of character by pithy thrusts and subtle implications. His poetry, too, is highly metaphoric; Meredith's nimble mind is too impatient always to make the transitions from image to image clear, and the result is a colorful, affecting style that sometimes cannot fully bear the thought of the poem. His observations of nature are fresh and vivid, and his poetry generally tries to reconcile the forces of passion and intellect.

The son of a naval outfitter, Meredith was born at Portsmouth, England, on February 12, 1828. He received a good early education but was forced to support himself rather than go to college, and he took to journalism in order to secure a reasonably steady income. In 1849 he married Mrs. Mary Ellen Nicholls, a widow almost seven years his senior. The daughter of Thomas Love Peacock, she was a talented and witty woman who was quite unsuited to the even more talented and witty Meredith. The marriage was unhappy; after 1858, when Mrs. Meredith went to Capri with another man, unreconcilable. After her death in 1861 Meredith told the psychological history of their estrangement in the brilliant lyric sequence, *Modern Love*. In 1864 he married Marie Vulliamy, and two years later he served as a war correspondent in the Austro-Italian War of 1866. On his return to England he edited the *Fort-nightly Review* and worked as a publisher's reader. A careful and sensitive critic, he gave needed encouragement to Thomas Hardy and George Gissing.

Meanwhile Meredith was slowly gaining a reputation as a novelist. His first important novel, *The Ordeal of Richard Feverel*, had little success, though it is a fine study of the emotional growth of a young man. The complex characterization and the delicately shaded style of *Evan Harrington* and *Beauchamp's Career* attracted a small but growing group of readers, but it was not until his comic masterpiece, *The Egoist*, appeared in 1879 that he received much popular attention. *Diana of the Crossways*, published in 1885, was his first novel to have a great popular success.

In the same year his second wife died. Meredith's own health was poor. Although a spinal ailment confined him to a wheelchair, he became in his last years the intellectual leader of his time. To his home at Box Hill, just outside of London, came aspiring young men, and Meredith, grown dogmatic and certain, was free with his literary advice. Following the death of Tennyson in 1892, Meredith was made president of the Society of Authors, thereby becoming the titular head of English letters. In 1905 he was awarded the Order of Merit and the medal of the Royal Society of Literature. At his death, on May 18, 1909, at Box Hill, he was England's most honored author and the last of the great Victorians.

Meredith's technique as a novelist is to use the point of view not of an onlooker, but of a particular character. In this way, he can describe the peculiar emotion of the character and, with his powerfully figurative style, catch the interest of the reader. As a result, his characters are extremely complex and varied. His heroines are particularly well drawn and are perhaps the finest since Shakespeare.

Bibliography

The fiction, poetry, and letters of George Meredith have been collected in the Memorial Edition edited by G. M. Trevelyan, 29 vols., 1909–1912. There are several separate collections of letters: *Letters*, edited by W. M. Meredith, 2 vols., 1912; *Letters to Edward Clodd and C. K. Shorter*, edited by T. J. Wise, 1913; and *Letters to Alice Meynell*, 1923. For a modern edition see *Letters*, edited by C. L. Cline, 3 vols., 1970.

The major modern biography of Meredith is Lionel Stevenson, *The Ordeal of George Meredith*, 1953. Among the earlier biographical studies are Richard Curle, *Aspects of George Meredith*, 1908; Constantin Photiades, *George Meredith: sa vie, son imagination, son art, sa doctrine*, 1911 (translated 1913); J. H. E. Crees, *George Meredith: A study of His Works and Personality*, 1918; S. M. Ellis, *George Meredith: His Life and Friends in Relation to His Work*, 1920; René Galland, *George Meredith: les cinquante premières années*, 1923; J. B. Priestley, *George Meredith*, 1926; Mary Sturge Gretton, *The Writings and Life of George Meredith*, 1926; R. E. Sencourt, *The Life of George Meredith*, 1929; and A. H. Able, *George Meredith and Thomas Love Peacock*, 1933. More recent critical biographies include Siegfried Sassoon, *Meredith*, 1948; Gillian Beer, *Meredith: A Change of Masks*, 1970; and Diane Johnson, *The True History of the First Mrs. Meredith and Other Lives*, 1973.

Early but still useful critical studies of George Meredith include G. M. Trevelyan, *The Poetry and Philosophy of George Meredith*, 1906; E. J. Bailey, *The Novels of George Meredith*, 1907; James Moffatt, *George Meredith: A Primer to the Novels*, 1909; and Joseph Warren Beach, *The Comic Spirit in George Meredith*, 1911. More recent criticism is by Sir Osbert Sitwell, *The Novels of George Meredith and Some Notes on the English Novel*, 1947; W. F. Wright, *Art and Substance in George Meredith*, 1953; V. S. Prichett, *George Meredith and English Comedy*, 1970; I. M. Williams, comp., *Meredith: The Critical Heritage*, 1971; Ian Fletcher, ed., *Meredith Now: Some Critical Essays*, 1971; Judith Wilt, *The Readable People of George Meredith*, 1975; and Maurice McCullen and Lewis Sawin, *A Dictionary of the Characters in George Meredith's Fiction*, 1977.

DIANA OF THE CROSSWAYS

Type of work: Novel
Author: George Meredith (1828–1909)
Type of plot: Psychological realism
Time of plot: Nineteenth century
Locale: England
First published: 1885

Diana, beautiful, witty, and skeptical of social convention and moral expediency, is the embodiment of George Meredith's philosophy and art. As such, she is a character far above most heroines of nineteenth century English novels. She offers the charm of femininity, perplexed by convention and yet aware of its force. Her career compels a belief that life will not let go its harvest of errors until they are thoroughly winnowed in a human drama of deepest interest, for life extracts the wisdom experience can offer.

Principal Characters

Diana Merion Warwick, a witty, charming, and beautiful woman. She is a person who makes mistakes because she does not believe that the conventional thing is always the right thing. She learns from her experiences, however, and becomes a wiser woman. She marries Augustus Warwick primarily as a matter of convenience. When she becomes friendly with the elderly Lord Dannisburgh, her husband accuses her of infidelity. She is found not guilty of this charge by a court, but she refuses to return to her husband. She becomes a novelist, but her initial success does not last and she finds herself reduced to poverty. In these circumstances, she sells some information told to her by Sir Percy Dacier, who is in love with her, thus betraying his confidence. She finally consents to become the wife of a man who has loved her for many years. Diana makes many enemies, but she is also the sort of woman who is loved and admired by many men.

Augustus Warwick, the politician whom Diana marries when she is a young woman. He is calculating and ambitious and is completely incapable of understanding his wife's innocence of the demands of conventionality. He tries to force Diana to return to him, but she will not. He is finally struck down and killed by a cab in the street.

Sir Percy Dacier, a young politician who falls in love with Diana after she has refused to return to her husband. He spends a great deal of time following her about and, in a moment of indiscretion, tells her a very important political secret. Diana sends him away. Needing money desperately, she sells his information to a newspaper. Feeling betrayed, he turns from her and marries an heiress.

Thomas Redworth, a brilliant member of Parliament who falls in love with Diana. He announces his love too late, after she is engaged to Warwick. He is steadfast, however, and, when Diana is forced to sell her family home and all of her belongings, he buys them, expecting that some day she will consent to become his wife. His loyalty is rewarded when Diana marries him.

Lady Emma Dunstane, a friend of Diana who introduces her to Redworth. She remains faithful to Diana through all of her troubles and unpopularity.

Lord Dannisburgh, the older man with whom Diana is friendly and with whom she appears, rather indiscreetly, while her husband is away on a government mission. He is Sir Percy Dacier's uncle.

When he dies, he leaves Diana a sum of money in his will.

Sullivan Smith, a hot-tempered Irishman who challenges Redworth to a duel because he objects to Redworth's attentions to Diana. He proposes to Diana, but she refuses him.

The Story

All of fashionable London was amazed and shocked when Diana Warwick suddenly left her husband's house. Society should not have been surprised at her action, however; the marriage had been ill-fated from the start. For Augustus Warwick, a calculating, ambitious politician, his marriage to the beautiful and charming Diana Merion had been largely one of convenience. Diana, in her turn, accepted his proposal as a refuge from unwelcome attentions to which her own position as an orphan had exposed her.

Diana Merion had first appeared in society at a state ball in Dublin, where her unspoiled charm and beauty attracted many admirers. Lady Emma Dunstane introduced Diana to Thomas Redworth, a friend of her husband, Sir Lukin Dunstane, and Redworth's attentions so enraged Mr. Sullivan Smith, a hot-tempered Irishman, that he attempted to provoke the Englishman to a duel. Redworth pacified the Irishman, however, to avoid compromising Diana by a duel fought on her account.

Later, while visiting Lady Emma at Copsley, the Dunstane country home in England, Diana was forced to rebuff Sir Lukin when he attempted to make love to her. Leaving Copsley, she went to visit the Warwicks. Meanwhile, Thomas Redworth announced to Lady Emma that he loved Diana. His announcement came too late. Diana was already engaged to Augustus Warwick.

In London the Warwicks took a large house and entertained lavishly. Among their intimates was Lord Dannisburgh, an elderly peer who became Diana's friend and adviser. While Warwick was away on a government mission, the two were often seen together, and Diana was so indiscreet as to let Lord Dannisburgh accompany her when she went to visit Lady Emma. Gossip began to circulate. On his return Warwick, who was incapable of understanding his wife's innocence and charm, served Diana with a process in suit. Accusing her of infidelity, he named Lord Dannisburgh as corespondent. Diana disappeared from Warwick's house and from London. In a letter to Lady Emma she had said that she intended to leave England. Her friend, realizing that flight would be tantamount to confession, felt sure that Diana would go to Crossways, her father's old home, before she left the country. Determined that Diana should remain and boldly defend the suit, Lady Emma sent Redworth to Crossways with instructions to detain Diana and persuade her to go to stay with the Dunstanes at Copsley.

Lady Emma had guessed correctly; Diana was at Crossways with her maid. At first Diana was unwilling to see Lady Emma's point of view, for she thought of her flight as a disdainful stepping aside from Warwick's sordid accusations; but at last she gave in to Redworth's arguments and returned with him to Copsley.

Although the court returned a verdict of not guilty to the charge Warwick had brought against her, Diana felt that her honor had been ruined and that in the eyes of the world she was still guilty. For a time she was able to forget her own distress by nursing her friend, Lady Emma, who was seriously ill. Later she left England to go on a Mediterranean cruise. Before her departure she had written a book, *The Princess Egeria.*

In Egypt she met Redworth, now a brilliant member of Parliament. He was accompanied by Sir Percy Dacier, Lord Dannisburgh's nephew and a rising young politician. Falling in love with Diana, Sir Percy followed her to the continent. He was recalled to London by the illness of his uncle. Diana followed him a short time later, to learn on her arrival in London that Redworth had been active in making her book a literary triumph. He had stirred up interest among the critics because he knew that Diana was in need of money.

Lord Dannisburgh died, with Diana at his bedside during his last illness. He had been her friend, and she paid him that last tribute of friendship and respect regardless of the storm of criticism it created. When Lord Dannisburgh's will was read, it was learned that he had left a sum of money to Diana.

In the meantime Diana had made an enemy of the socially ambitious Mrs. Wathin, who thought it her social duty to tear Diana's reputation to shreds. Part of her dislike was motivated by jealousy that Diana should be accepted by people who would not tolerate Mrs. Wathin. Some of her actions were inspired by Warwick, Mrs. Wathin's friend, who, having lost his suit against Diana, was trying to force his wife to return to him.

Sir Percy's attentions were also distressing to Diana. Half in love with him, she was not free to marry again. She faced a crisis in her affairs when Mrs. Wathin called to announce that Warwick, now ill, wanted Diana to return and to act as his nurse. Diana refused. Warwick then threatened to exercise his legal rights as her husband. Sir Percy, who informed her of Warwick's intention, asked her to elope with him to Paris. She agreed. She was saved from that folly by the appearance of Redworth, who arrived to tell her that Lady Emma was ill and about to undergo a serious operation at Copsley. Diana went with him to be at her friend's side.

Lady Emma nearly died, and the gravity of her condition restored Diana's own sense of responsibility. She ordered Sir Percy to forget her, but in spite of her protests he continued to follow her about. One day he confided a tremendous political secret to her—the prime minister was about to call upon Parliament to pass some revolutionary reform measures. Having told her his secret, he attempted to resume his former courtship. Diana refused to listen to his pleadings. After he had gone, she felt broken and cheated. If she would not have Sir Percy as a lover, she felt, she could not keep him as a friend. Diana was desperately in need of money. She had been forced to sell Crossways to pay her debts and her later novels had been failures. Feeling herself a complete adventuress, she went to the editor of a paper which opposed the government party and sold him the information Sir Percy had given her.

When the paper appeared with a full disclosure of the prime minister's plan, Sir Percy accused her of betraying him and broke with her. A short time later he proposed to a young lady of fortune. About the same time Warwick was struck down by a cab in the street and killed. Diana had her freedom at last, but she was downcast in spirit. She knew that she was in public disgrace. Although she had burned the check in payment for the information she had disclosed, it was common knowledge that she had betrayed Sir Percy and that he had retaliated by his marriage to Constance Asper, an heiress. When Sullivan Smith proposed for her hand, Diana refused him and sought refuge in the company of her old friend, Lady Emma. Her stay at Copsley freed her from her memories of Sir Percy, so much so that on her return to London she was able to greet him and his bride with dignity and charm. Her wit was as sharp as ever, and she took pleasure in revenging herself upon those who had attempted to destroy her reputation with their gossip and slander.

On another visit to Copsley she again encountered Redworth, now a railroad promoter and still a distinguished member of Parliament. When he invited her and Lady Emma to visit Crossways, Diana learned that it was Redworth who had bought her old home and furnished it with her own London possessions, which she had been forced to sell in order to pay her debts. He bluntly told Diana that he had bought the house and furnished it for her because he expected her to become his wife. Not wishing to involve him in the scandals which had circulated about her, she at first pretended indifference to his abrupt wooing. Lady Emma, on the other hand, urged her to marry Redworth, who had loved her for many years, so that he could protect her from social malice. At last, knowing that she brought no real disgrace to Redworth's name, she consented to become his wife.

Critical Evaluation

Diana of the Crossways is the most emphatically "feminist" of Meredith's novels, but the woman too intelligent and spirited to accept willingly her "place," as defined by Victorian society, figures prominently in virtually all of his fiction. Some, such as Diana's friend Emma Dunstane or Lady Blandish of *The Ordeal of Richard Feverel,* manage to confine their protest to witty commentary while playing their assigned roles; others, like Diana, are forced by circumstances into active rebellion.

It is generally agreed that Meredith's chief model for his beautiful, brilliant, and hard-beset heroines was his own first wife. In the fine poem sequence *Modern Love,* he traces in thin disguise the course of their marriage, from its happy and passionate beginnings, through the conflicts that led to his wife's running off with an artist, to her early death. Although bitter at first, Meredith learned much from the failure of his first love and came to accept major responsibility for it. His novels repeatedly depict a loving and loyal woman virtually driven into the arms of another man by the blind egotism of her husband or lover. Asked by Robert Louis Stevenson whether the protagonist of *The Egoist* was not a portrait of him, Meredith replied that his fatuous hero was drawn "from all of us but principally from myself."

Meredith saw his society as dominated by egotism, chiefly male, and both fearful and suspicious of the bright and beautiful because of the threat they posed to complacency. He shared the Victorian belief in progress, but he defined progress in terms of intelligence and sensibility. Choosing the comedy of wit as his preferred mode, he attacked the dull and smug, and called for "brain, more brain." He recognized the tragedy of life but ascribed it to human failure. As he wrote in *Modern Love,* "no villain need be. We are betrayed by what is false within." The falseness may spring from self-deception or from unquestioning acceptance of what "the world" proclaims. What can save us is the ability to be honest with ourselves and see the world as it is, and the courage to act on our perceptions even in defiance of social norms.

Many of Meredith's contemporaries shared his belief in a continuing evolution of man's spiritual and intellectual capacities, but few besides Browning were as ardent in affirming also "the value and significance of flesh." For Meredith, the goal of life was to realize one's full potentialities in a vital balance: "The spirit must brand the flesh that it may live."

Meredith's Diana fully exemplifies his philosophy of life. The central metaphor of the novel is the "dog-world" in hot pursuit of its quarry, a beautiful woman too intelligent and sensitive to play the roles society demands of her, either "parasite" or "chalice." Yet Diana is no spotless, perfect victim of malign persecutors. In precept and practice, Meredith scorned sentimental melodrama. Young and inexperienced, Diana brings much of her trouble on herself. She marries for protection and position, a prudent move by worldly standards, but disastrous in its consequences. Achieving a measure of independence, she soon endangers it by her extravagance, and she is finally almost destroyed by an impulsive act of desperation. Although elements of the "dog-world" are moved by envy and malice, most of Diana's adversaries act "honorably" in their own eyes; it is the conventions of honor, respectability, and— most importantly—of woman's place in Victorian society that nearly overpowers her.

The resolution of the plot would seem a compromise if the novel were the feminist tract it has been called: Diana does not finally triumph as a fully independent person, accepted by society on her own terms and admired for her wit and nerve. Only rescued from despair by her friend Emma, she does prove herself capable of standing alone but chooses instead to marry again. As Meredith presents her choice, however, it is not compromise but fulfillment. Her marriage to Redworth, who truly understands and values her, represents the ideal wedding of flesh and spirit, achieved not by good luck but by striving, blundering, learning from mistakes, and finally seeing and accepting life as it is.

Diana of the Crossways was an immediate success upon publication, probably because its theme had been taken from a recent scandal involving a brilliant and beautiful Irishwoman, Mrs. Caroline Norton, who had been accused (as it proved, falsely) of selling an important government secret. However, the novel has not maintained its popularity, despite its wit, its vitality, and its vivid characterizations. Critics generally rate it high among Meredith's works, often second only to his masterpiece *The Egoist,* and its themes are of perhaps even broader interest today than they were in 1885, yet it is apparently little read. The difficulty is probably with Meredith's famous style, the joy and the despair of his admirers.

From his first work of fiction, *The Shaving of Shagpat,* to his last, the prose of this admirable poet became progressively more poetic in its richness, its precision, its compactness, and its indirection. In the earlier novels, it is a beautiful addition to plot and characterization; in the later, it may detract from or even obscure them. Oscar Wilde may not have been entirely right in saying that as a novelist Meredith could do everything but tell a story; but in *Diana of the Crossways* and other later novels, he often seems fastidiously averse to saying anything directly. The texture of his prose places demands upon his readers that not all are willing to meet. The attentive reader is richly rewarded in beauty, wit, and subtlety of thought and expression. Let his attention waver, though, and he may find that he has missed a significant turn in the plot.

The very dazzle and density of Meredith's style, embodying as it does his vigorous and invigorating vision of life, will certainly continue to delight those willing to submit to it; among less strenuous readers, however, he may continue to be as he has been for decades, more honored than read.

Bibliography

Bailey, Elmer James. *The Novels of George Meredith: A Study.* New York: Haskell House, 1971, pp. 149–158.

Baker, Ernest A. *The History of the English Novel,* Volume VIII. New York: Barnes & Noble, 1950, pp. 374–376.

Baker, Robert S. "Sanctuary and Dungeon: The Imagery of Sentimentalism in Meredith's *Diana of the Crossways,*" in *Texas Studies in Literature and Language.* XVIII (1976), pp. 63–81.

Beach, Joseph Warren. *The Comic Spirit in George Meredith: An Interpretation.* New York: Longmans, Green, 1911, pp. 169–175.

Beer, Gillian. *Meredith: A Change of Masks, A Study of the Novels.* London: Athlone, 1970, pp. 140–167.

Booth, Thornton Y. *Mastering the Event: Commitment to Fact in George Meredith's Fiction.* Logan: Utah State University Press, 1967, pp. 42–46.

Conrow, Margaret. "Coming to Terms with George Meredith's Fiction," in her *The English Novel in the Nineteenth Century: Essays on the Literary Mediation of Human Values.* Urbana: University of Illinois Press, 1972, pp. 191–193.

Eaker, J. Gordon. "Meredith's Human Comedy," in *Nineteenth-Century Fiction.* V (March, 1951), pp. 265–266.

Edgar, Pelham. *The Art of the Novel From 1700 to the Present Time.* New York: Macmillan, 1933, pp. 158–161.

Fowler, Lois Josephs. "*Diana of the Crossways*: A Prophecy for Feminism," in *In Honor of Austin Wright.* Edited by Joseph Baim. Pittsburgh: Carnegie-Mellon University, 1972, pp. 32–36.

Gindin, James. *Harvest of a Quiet Eye: The Novel of Compassion.* Bloomington: Indiana University Press, 1971, pp. 63–76.

Gordon, Jan B. "*Diana of the Crossways*: Internal History and the Brainstuff of Fiction," in *Meredith Now: Some Critical Essays.* Edited by Ian Fletcher. New York: Barnes & Noble, 1971, pp. 246–264.

Gretton, Mary Sturge. *The Writings and Life of George Meredith, A Centenary Study.* London: Oxford University Press, 1926, pp. 161–173.

Kelvin, Norman. *A Troubled Eden: Nature and Society in the Works of George Meredith.* Stanford, Calif.: Stanford University Press, 1961, pp. 58–61.

Kerpneck, Harvey. "George Meredith, Sunworshipper and Diana's Redworth," in *Nineteenth-Century Fiction.* XVIII (June, 1963), pp. 77–82.

Lindsay, Jack. *George Meredith: His Life and Work.* London: Bodley Head, 1956, pp. 262–268.

Marcus, Jane. " 'Clio in Calliope': History and Myth in Meredith's *Diana of the Crossways*," in *Bulletin of the New York Public Library.* LXXIX (1976), pp. 167–192.

Moffatt, James. *George Meredith: A Primer to the Novels.* Port Washington, N.Y.: Kennikat, 1969, pp. 291–308.

Sassoon, Siegfried. *Meredith.* New York: Viking, 1948, pp. 183–190.

Skilton, David. "New Approaches: Meredith, Hardy and Butler," in his *The English Novel: Defoe to the Victorians.* New York: Barnes & Noble, 1977, pp. 167–168.

Stevenson, Lionel. *The Ordeal of George Meredith, A Biography.* New York: Scribner's, 1953, pp. 253–261.

Weygandt, Cornelius. "George Meredith and His Reading of Life," in his *A Century of the English Novel.* New York: Century, 1925, pp. 207–208.

Wilt, Judith. "Meredith's Diana: Freedom, Fiction, and the Female," in *Texas Studies in Literature and Language.* XVIII (1976), pp. 42–62.

Wright, Walter F. *Art and Substance in George Meredith, A Study in Narrative.* Lincoln: University of Nebraska Press, 1953, pp. 140–146.

THE EGOIST

Type of work: Novel
Author: George Meredith (1828–1909)
Type of plot: Social satire
Time of plot: Nineteenth century
Locale: England
First published: 1879

In this unique comedy, Meredith satirizes with droll, intellectual humor the various virtues and vices of his characters. The focal point of the satire and the basis for numerous digressions on the author's theory of comedy is the egoist, Sir Willoughby, a wealthy, handsome, self-satisfied country gentleman whose lack of humility and any sense of humor leads to his desertion by two successive fiancées.

Principal Characters

Sir Willoughby Patterne, a nobleman whose pattern of egocentricities includes duplicity, austerity, snobbery, and sententiousness. Though he has played on the heartstrings of his most devoted Laetitia Dale, he learns through two broken engagements that all his barren heart can hope for is the solace of the good woman whom he has converted to egoism. Finally, Sir Willoughby is forced to abandon double dealing, to come down from the pedestal where he has viewed himself only in a favorable light, to bend his pride for the sake of a young cousin and a former servant whom he has wronged, and to accommodate himself to the understanding that his wife sees through him and cannot therefore love him. He will, of course, continue to be an egoist, though a more enlightened and flexible one.

Laetitia Dale, his silent admirer for many years and finally his public scourger. A long-time tenant of Sir Willoughby's in a cottage where she nursed her invalid father and wrote for a living, she finally sickens of Patterne's self-centered ways, particularly toward his kinsman and her student, young Crossjay Patterne, whose life is being forced into the wrong mold. Always gentle, amenable, trustworthy,

Laetitia finally tires of being a confidante and becomes defiant in her refusal of the nobleman's hand after all others have failed him. Her warmth of admiration has been chilled by observation; her youth has gone in yearning; her health has suffered from literary drudgery. She makes her own terms for becoming Lady Patterne, to which Sir Willoughby agrees.

Clara Middleton, the betrothed of Sir Willoughby and his severest critic. At first attracted by the force of his personality, she soon discovers in him the tendency to manipulate lives and to order life. Feeling stifled and caged, she begs for her release, which the egoist cannot grant since he has only recently been jilted by Constantia Durham. Despairing of gaining her father's permission to break the engagement, she tries to escape to the home of her best friend and maid of honor. In this desperate but abortive effort she is aided by the sensitive scholar-cousin of Sir Willoughby, Vernon Whitford, whom she will later marry. She, too, defends young Crossjay against the benevolent tyranny of the egotistical nobleman.

The Rev. Dr. Middleton, Clara's father,

a retired clergyman, learned scholar, and warm-hearted wit. Dr. Middleton becomes more enamored of Sir Willoughby's fine wine and library than his daughter feels necessary, but he humorously involves himself in the plot to remake the egoist after he learns that the two-faced lover wishes to abandon his spirited daughter for the more complacent Laetitia.

Vernon Whitford, a poor relation of the Patternes and a writer who has taken in young Crossjay Patterne out of sympathy when his wealthy cousin refuses to aid the boy. Almost morbidly shy with women, and the more pitied by his benefactor, Vernon finally asserts himself in league with Clara and Laetitia to save his young charge from education as a "gentleman" when it is service with the Marines that the boy wants.

Colonel Horace De Craye, the Irish

cousin and best man at a wedding which does not come off, partly because of his machinations. The best friend of Sir Willoughby, Colonel De Craye has long been suspicious of the nobleman's lack of nobility. He finds it easy to side with Clara, with whom he is in love, and all the others who wish to thwart the egoist.

Crossjay Patterne, the penniless son of a Marine hero who is not welcomed at Patterne Place. Though not scholarly by nature, the youth is irrepressibly happy and loving, strangely in contrast to his distant, rich relative. He loves most his guardian, Vernon Whitford, and Clara Middleton, his benefactress.

Constantia Durham, Sir Willoughby's betrothed, who jilts him ten days before their wedding date.

Harry Oxford, a military man with whom Constantia elopes.

The Story

On the day of his majority Sir Willoughby Patterne announced his engagement to Miss Constantia Durham. Laetitia Dale, who lived with her old father in a cottage on Willoughby's estate, bore her love for him—she thought—secretly, but everyone, including Willoughby himself, knew about it. Ten days before the wedding day Constantia astonished her betrothed by eloping with Harry Oxford, a military man. For a few weeks after that, the proud Willoughby courted Laetitia while the neighborhood gossiped about the poor girl's chances to become his wife. There was great disappointment when he suddenly decided to go abroad for three years. On his return to his estate he brought with him his cousin, Vernon Whitford, as an adviser in the management of his properties, and a young distant kinsman named Crossjay Patterne.

At first Laetitia, the faithful, was overjoyed at Willoughby's return, but soon she saw that again she was to lose him, for he became engaged to Clara Middleton, the daughter of a learned doctor. Middleton and his daughter came to Willoughby's estate to visit for a few weeks. It might have been the controversy over Crossjay or even the existence of Laetitia that caused Clara to see Willoughby for what he really was. In spite of Willoughby's objections, Vernon wanted Crossjay to enter the Marines and the young man was sent to Laetitia to be tutored for his examination. Vernon, a literary man, wanted to go to London, but Willoughby overruled him. Noting Willoughby's self-centered attitude toward Crossjay, his complete and selfish concern with matters affecting himself and his attempt to dominate her own mind, Clara began to feel trapped by her betrothal. She reflected that Constantia had escaped by finding a gallant Harry Oxford to take her away, but she sorrowfully realized that she had no one to rescue her.

When Clara attempted to break her engagement, she found Willoughby intractable and her father too engrossed in his studies to be disturbed. Meanwhile, Willoughby had picked Laetitia Dale as Vernon's wife. This was Willoughby's plan to keep near him both his cousin and the woman who fed his ego with her devotion. Vernon could retire to one of the cottages on the estate and write and study. Asked by Willoughby to aid him in his plan, Clara took the opportunity to ask Vernon's advice on her own problem. He assured her that she must move subtly and slowly.

In desperation, she persuaded Doctor Middleton to agree to take a trip to France with her for a few weeks. From such a trip she hoped never to return to Willoughby. But this wary lover introduced Dr. Middleton to his favorite brand of claret. Two bottles of the wine put the doctor in such an amiable mood that when Clara asked him if he were ready to go to London with her, he told her that the thought was preposterous. Willoughby had won the first round.

Colonel De Craye arrived to be best man at the wedding. Little by little he sensed that Clara was not happy at the prospect of her approaching marriage. In desperation Clara resorted to other means of escape. She wrote to her friend Lucy Darleton in town and received from that young lady an invitation to visit her in London.

Clara gave Crossjay the privilege of accompanying her to the train station. A hue and cry was raised at her absence from the estate, and Vernon, accidentally discovering her destination, followed her to the station and urged her to come back. Only because she believed that her behavior might cause an injury to Crossjay's future did Clara return to her prison. If she were to leave now, Willoughby would have full control of the young boy, for Vernon was soon to go to London to follow his writing career.

Complications resulted from Clara's attempted escape. At the station Vernon had had her drink some brandy to overcome the effects of the rainy weather. The neighborhood began to gossip. Willoughby confronted Crossjay, who told him the truth about Clara's escape. Clara hoped that Willoughby would release her because of the gossip, but he refused. Doctor Middleton seemed ignorant of what was happening. He was determined that his daughter should fulfill her pledge to marry Sir Willoughby. Furthermore, he liked Willoughby's vintage wines and Willoughby's estate.

By this time the Egoist knew that his marriage to Clara would not take place. He decided upon the one move that would soothe his wounded vanity—he asked Laetitia to become his wife. She refused, declaring she no longer loved him.

Colonel De Craye shrewdly surmised what had happened. He told Clara the hopeful news. Clara felt that her only remaining obstacle was her father's insistence that she must not break her promise to Willoughby. Now she could show that Willoughby had broken his promise first by proposing to Laetitia while he was still pledged to Clara.

Willoughby's world blew up in his face. Dr. Middleton announced firmly that Clara need not marry Willoughby. He had decided that he admired Vernon's scholarship more than he liked Willoughby's wines. But the twice-jilted lover had other plans for his own protection. He must even the score. If he could get Clara to consent to marry Vernon, he felt there would be some measure of recompense for himself, for such a marriage would have the ironic touch to satisfy Willoughby. But Clara told him it was already her intention to wed Vernon as soon as her engagement to Willoughby could be broken. The Egoist's selfishness and arrogance had brought them together.

The Egoist was defeated. He went straight to Laetitia, offering her his hand without love. He was willing for her to marry him only for money. Laetitia accepted on the condition that Crossjay be permitted to enter the Marines. Clara and the doctor planned to leave for Europe. Vernon arranged to meet them in the Swiss Alps, where he and Clara would marry.

Critical Evaluation

Two years after Meredith delivered at the London Institution his famous lecture "On the Idea of Comedy and the Uses of the Comic Spirit," he published *The Egoist* (1879), a novel which in many ways exemplifies his concept of high comedy. In his lecture he had distinguished comedy from satire, through which one ridicules folly; from irony, through which one is anguished and "rendered dubious" because of folly; and from humor, through which one laughs at folly. Instead, the comic "is the perceptive, is the governing spirit, awakening and giving aim to these powers of laughter." It is the spirit of refined good sense, of lively intelligence, and of social tolerance. In his Prelude to *The Egoist*, Meredith directs this perceptive, inquiring spirit upon his subject, the Book of Earth, "whose title is the Book of Egoism." To Meredith, *egoism* means more than vanity, more than self-love (*narcissism* as a psychological concept first appears in the writings of Havelock Ellis in the late 1890's); egoism is a recidivistic force, going backward in evolutionary history to uncivilized men and women, to the primitive consciousness. Its opposite force is enlightened, tolerant society, my which men and women shake free their destructive self-involved habits of gratification.

As a pattern of egoism, Meredith's Sir Willoughby Patterne is not intended to be a monster, but merely an exaggerated example of the ordinary person. Sir Willoughby, like Sir Austin Feverel of *The Ordeal of Richard Feverel* (1859), has become a grotesque because of his single-minded devotion to an impossible objective: to make another person perfect. Both mistakenly believe that they are faultless; Sir Austin tries to create a perfect pattern for his son, Sir Willoughby for his mate. Although each character may be seen from the vantage of the Comic Sense as an eccentric deviation from the normal, he can also be viewed as a pathetic, even tragic type. Sir Willoughby's impossible demands for perfection drive from his arms Clara Middleton; and his second choice for a mate, Laetitia Dale, jilts, then publicly humiliates, and at last turns upon him as his most severe critic, to take lifelong vengeance upon a husband she despises. Yet Meredith does not encourage his readers to sympathize with Sir Willoughby. The egoist brings his fate upon himself. In other respects intelligent, he is hopelessly dense in comprehending his limitations. "There you have the Egoist," he smugly tells Clara (Chapter 10), narrating an anecdote about a man who pleads with a doctor to save the life of his dying wife—not for her sake but for his own. "Beware of marrying an Egoist, my dear!" he advises. Quite ignorant that he has described himself, he offers Clara a remedy for her troubles.

From a Victorian point of view, Sir Willoughby superficially seems to be a paragon of virtues, an ideal mate for any nubile maiden. Wealthy, physically attractive, athletic, aristocratic, honorable: he is in a position to offer Clara a secure position in society. As a husband he would be, from what we know about his character, faithful, decent, and protective. More than protective, he would be suffocating in his attentions to her; he would keep her closely confined, an acquisition like a valued piece of property or art. Soon after her engagement to Sir Willoughby, Clara comes to understand that he "enfolded her," that she had been "caged" by him, that "she deemed herself a person entrapped." From such an overprotective mate, her lot would be a "lifelong imprisonment." So Sir Willoughby's ostensible virtues count for naught. His fatal flaw, egoism, would make life miserable for any free-born, sensitive woman.

Such a person is Clara Middleton, opposite in most respects from Sir Willoughby. He is an aristocrat, she is lower-middle class genteel; he is wealthy, she is relatively poor; he is sentimental, she is prudent; he is an egoist, she is a realist. In a few matters, their characters are similar. Both are intelligent, sensitive, scrupulous. Indeed, Willoughby is scrupulous to a fault in refusing, as a man conventionally honorable, to release Clara from her engagement. And Clara is scrupulous to her sense of integrity. Neither will yield. Should Willoughby allow Clara the freedom to break their engagement, his egoism—which he calls honor—would suffer embarrassment. Should Clara acquiesce and allow Patterne to marry her, she would surrender more than her happiness: she would surrender her stubborn pride in her freedom.

So the battle is joined. With nearly classical unity of action, Meredith simplifies his plot so that no side issues or entangling subplots interfere with the central conflict. On the one side, Sir Willoughby in pride and desperate egoism demands that Clara stick to her promised betrothal. On the other, Clara struggles to maintain her freedom. For modern readers, Clara's plight seems difficult to understand. Why does she not simply break off her engagement, with or without her fianceé's consent? To Victorians—or at least to Victorians of Clara's genteel class—such an action would not be understood to be simple. A betrothal publicly announced had nearly the same binding force upon lovers as wedlock. Sir Willoughby assures Clara (Chapter 15): "Bride is bride, and wife is wife, and *affianced* is, in honor, *wedded*. . . . We are united. Recognize it—united." Even though Clara rejects her tormentor's appeal based upon the engagement vows, she is intimidated by Willoughby because she lacks an honorable means to escape from his entrapment. In Chapter 21, "Clara's Meditation," Meredith shows clearly the causes of her moral dilemma. A victim not only of her particular situation with Sir Willoughby, she is also a victim of society's injustice to women who play at the game of courtship.

Victorian readers could not help but sympathize with Clara's rebellion; surely they were amused to read how the plucky maiden resolved to free herself from Patterne before it was too late. They could understand Meredith's address to his audience (Chapter 12): "What of wives miserably wedded? What aims in view have these most woeful captives?" For modern readers, Clara appears to be less a rebel than a sensible young woman, and certainly not the "rogue in porcelain" by which phrase she is called several times in the novel. The epithet "rogue" would seem to apply more justifiably to Laetitia, who changes from a demure maiden to a waspish egoist. But in a special sense Clara is an appropriate rogue, for she rebels against Sir Willoughby's porcelain-fine world of perfection. In Chapter 34 especially, Meredith plays upon his symbol of the rogue in porcelain, relating Laetitia, Clara, and Sir Willoughby to the pattern of Willow china.

This pattern, as Professor Robert D. Mayo has convincingly argued, is a key to understanding the symbolism of the novel. The scene depicted in the familiar Willow design corresponds to the old story about a wealthy mandarin who had a lovely daughter named Koong-see. He wished to marry his daughter to a wealthy suitor, but she had chosen for her lover a poor but honorable man, her father's secretary, with whom she had exchanged vows under the blossoming trees in the Willow pattern. Suspicious of his daughter, the mandarin imprisoned her in a pavillion in his garden, commanding her to marry the wealthy suitor of his choice when the peach tree blossoms. But Koong-see's lover found her, released her from her prison, and carried her off—over the Willow bridge. Now the story, obviously, relates to Meredith's plot in a number of ways. Sir Willoughby is like the tyrannous mandarin who would cage his captive, Clara; but she, like Koong-see, escapes with her lover—Sir Willoughby's secretary, Vernon Whitford. Thus Clara smashes the porcelain image of perfect, obedient womanhood, to escape roguishly from the Willow pattern and create her own destiny.

What sort of destiny will that be? As the counterpart to Sir Willoughby, Clara would seem to deserve a mate who will permit her greater freedom. In Vernon Whitford, she will have a respectable but poor scholar (modeled after the young Sir Leslie Stephen), an intellectual freethinker like herself, a man sensitive to her needs as an independent person. He had been previously disappointed by a rash early marriage to a drunken woman. Now he has matured and can fully appreciate a fine-spirited wife like Clara. Yet Meredith draws a curtain of reticence over the passions of his lovers; and the marriage scene that resolves Clara's courtship problems (Chapter 48) seems curiously rushed. Although Vernon "was practiced in self-mastery," he will have to prove the effects of his discipline; for he offers Clara little in the way of wealth and social distinction that Sir Willoughby could offer.

Ironically, it is Laetitia, formerly rejected by Patterne in favor of Clara, who turns the tables on the egoist. After refusing his lengthy and humiliating proposal of marriage (Chapter 40—a scene of particularly brilliant comedy), she finally accepts his far more abject proposal (Chapter 49)—after disgracing him. So Sir Willoughby wins for his bride a termagant with "a hard detective eye," and Laetitia captures a husband who promises to be servile, persecuted, fit for a cage. Worse, he marries a self-proclaimed egoist, a woman "hard, materialistic" who has "lost faith in romance." Sir Willoughby's purge is almost more terrible than his offense. For the modern reader, Laetitia's scornful, vindictive actions place her on the same level as her enemy. But from a larger viewpoint, other characters in *The Egoist* are similarly self-indulgent. Dr. Middleton (whose character is based upon a satirical portrait of Thomas Love Peacock) is less concerned about the happiness of his daughter than about drinking a bottle of excellent port; De Craye is a philanderer, Dale a self-centered valetudinarian, Vernon Whitford a dusty scholar, and the aristocratic ladies surrounding Sir Willoughby crass gossip-mongers. Against these partly egoistic types, Patterne seems merely the worst offender among a generally unwholesome group. Only Crossjay is perfectly free from self-love: but then, he is a youth.

Isolated from the companionship of friends and the love of any woman's heart because of his egoism, Sir Willoughby may be seen ultimately as a pathetic figure. Indeed, Meredith is severe to Patterne precisely because he recognizes in the character many offensive qualities in his own nature: querulousness, intolerance of imperfection in others, arrogance, dyspepsia. And in her intellectual pride Clara resembles Mary Ellen Nicolls, Meredith's first wife, who left him for another man. Yet the general tone of the novel is sophisticated comedy, not pathos. Witty, urbane, aphoristic, the language of *The Egoist* is polished to a jeweled brilliance: hard, clear, lustrous. Many chapters resemble scenes of miniature comedies, with sparkling dialogue or fragments of dialogue that ring like real (although finely lucid) conversation. Other scenes are elaborately artificial, staged like comic burlesques. Still others are static, mannered like a design in porcelain.

With characteristic pessimism, Meredith predicted that the novel would fail. But most critics praised the high polish of the prose, one reviewer for *The Daily News* describing the novel as a "highly seasoned dish." W. E. Henley acclaimed the book in four different reviews, and James Thomson joined the chorus of admirers. But Meredith was not cheered. In deep, pathological despondency, he refused to acknowledge the favorable reception of the book. Later, Henley confided to a friend: "It is curious that Meredith should have winced under my articles as he seems to have done. I go and worry my guts out and try to teach the blasted public something of the author's meaning and games, and the author repudiates me on all hands, and says that he 'should have preferred to have been criticised'!" But Henley missed the point: the author of *The Egoist* had not entirely driven Sir Willoughby Patterne from his nature.

Bibliography

Bailey, Elmer James. *The Novels of George Meredith: A Study.* New York: Haskell House, 1971, pp. 133–142.

Baker, Robert S. "Faun and Satyr: Meredith's Theory of Comedy and *The Egoist,*" in *Mosaic.* IX (1976), pp. 173–193.

Beach, Joseph Warren. *The Comic Spirit in George Meredith: An Interpretation.* New York: Longmans, Green, 1911, pp. 123–141.

Beer, Gillian. *Meredith: A Change of Masks, A Study of the Novels.* London: Athlone, 1970, pp. 122–137.

Buchen, Irving H. "The Egoists in *The Egoist*: The Sensualists and the Ascetics," in *Nineteenth-Century Fiction.* XIX (1964), pp. 255–269.

―――――. "Science, Society and Individuality," in *University Review.* XXX (1964), pp. 185–192.

Gindin, James. *Harvest of a Quiet Eye: The Novel of Compassion.* Bloomington: Indiana University Press, 1971, pp. 58–61, 63–70, 74–76.

Goode, John. "*The Egoist*: Anatomy or Striptease?," in *Meredith Now: Some Critical Essays.* Edited by Ian Fletcher. New York: Barnes & Noble, 1971, pp. 205–230.

Gretton, Mary Sturge. *The Writings and Life of George Meredith, A Centenary Study.* London: Oxford University Press, 1926, pp. 131–141.

Halperin, John. *The Language of Meditation: Four Studies in Nineteenth Century Fiction.* Elms Court, England: Stockwell, 1973, pp. 98–114.

Hill, Charles J. "Theme and Image in *The Egoist,*" in *University of Kansas City Review.* XX (Summer, 1954), pp. 281–285.

Hudson, Richard B. "The Meaning of Egoism in George Meredith's *The Egoist,*" in *Trollopian.* III (December, 1948), pp. 163–176.

Kelvin, Norman. *A Troubled Eden: Nature and Society in the Works of George Meredith.* Stanford, Calif.: Stanford University Press, 1961, pp. 104–113.

Lindsay, Jack. *George Meredith: His Life and Work.* London: Bodley Head, 1956, pp. 238–244.

McCullough, Bruce W. *Representative English Novelists: Defoe to Conrad.* New York: Harper, 1946, pp. 221–230.

Mannheimer, Monica. *The Generations in Meredith's Novels.* Stockholm: Almquist and Wiksell, 1972, pp. 155–164.

Sassoon, Siegfried. *Meredith.* New York: Viking, 1948, pp. 143–154.

Stevenson, Lionel. *The Ordeal of George Meredith, A Biography.* New York: Scribner's, 1953, pp. 224–233.

Stevenson, Richard C.   "Laetitia Dale and the Comic Spirit in *The Egoist*," in *Nineteenth-Century Fiction*. XXVI (1972), pp. 406–418.

Stone, Donald David.   *Novelists in a Changing World: Meredith, James and the Transformation of English Fiction in the 1880's*. Cambridge, Mass.: Harvard University Press, 1972, pp. 116–137.

Van Ghent, Dorothy.   "On *The Egoist*," in *The English Novel: Form and Function*. New York: Rinehart, 1953, pp. 183–194.

Wilkenfeld, R.B.   "Hands Around: Image and Theme in *The Egoist*," in *Journal of English Literary History*. XXXIV (September, 1967), pp. 367–379.

Williams, David.   *George Meredith: His Life and Lost Love*. London: Hamish Hamilton, 1977, pp. 149–159.

Williams, Orlo.   "*The Egoist*," in his *Some Great English Novels: Studies in the Art of Fiction*. London: Macmillan, 1926, pp. 84–119.

Wright, Walter F.   *Art and Substance in George Meredith, A Study in Narrative*. Lincoln: University of Nebraska Press, 1953, pp. 60–78.

THE ORDEAL OF RICHARD FEVEREL

Type of work: Novel
Author: George Meredith (1828–1909)
Type of plot: Tragi-comedy
Time of plot: Mid-nineteenth century
Locale: England
First published: 1859

In this story of an idyllic romance between two sincere and idealistic young people, Meredith examines the results of a disillusioned, misogynistic father's attempt to rear his son according to a scientific system of education that all but excludes women. The sometimes artificial dialogue and the intellectual styles are characteristic of Meredith's works, but the details of the love story itself are told with captivating simplicity.

Principal Characters

Richard Feverel, the only son and sole heir of Sir Austin Feverel. Richard is the subject of his father's plan to produce a young man, reared according to a System, in which women are to be excluded from the life of the boy until he is twenty-five. Richard becomes the obvious proof that the System will not work. He manages, simply by being human, to foil all plans to keep him from physical danger and from women.

Sir Austin Feverel, master of Raynham Abbey and Richard's woman-hating father, who devises the System for rearing his son. Although he is unrealistic in his approach, his belief in the basic soundness of his System is complete.

Adrian Harley, Sir Austin's nephew, who is designated as Richard's mentor. He is responsible for carrying out the System. Always dubious, Adrian finally is convinced, when Richard marries, that the System has failed utterly.

Lucy Desborough, the niece of a neighboring farmer. Richard falls in love with her and marries her. She bears him a child and finally dies of brain fever and shock when she learns that Richard has been wounded in a duel.

Ripton Thompson, the son of Sir Austin's lawyer, brought to Raynham Abbey as Richard's youthful playmate and companion.

Giles Blaize, Lucy's uncle. He horsewhips Richard and Ripton when he finds that they have shot a pheasant on his property. Richard is responsible for setting fire to Blaize's hayricks.

Clare Forey, Richard's cousin, who falls in love with him. She marries a man much older than she. When she dies, a ring that Richard had lost is found on her finger.

Tom Bakewell, the man Richard bribes to set fire to Blaize's hayricks. Richard insists that he is responsible for the fire and so confuses Blaize's witness that Tom is released, although the witness saw Tom set the fire. He becomes Richard's devoted servant.

The Story

Richard Feverel was the only son of Sir Austin Feverel, of Raynham Abbey. After Sir Austin's wife left him, the baronet became a woman-hater who was determined to rear his son according to a System, which, among other things, virtually excluded females from the boy's life until he was twenty-five. Then, Sir Austin thought, his son might marry, providing a girl good enough for the youth could be found.

Because of the System, Richard's early life was carefully controlled. The boy was kept from lakes and rivers so that he would not drown; from firecrackers so that he would not be burned; from cricket fields so that he would not be bruised. Adrian Harley, Sir Austin's nephew, was entrusted with Richard's education.

When he was fourteen, the Hope of Raynham, as Adrian called his charge, became restless. It was decided that he needed a companion—masculine, of course—near his own age. The candidate for this position was young Ripton Thompson, the none-too-brilliant son of Sir Austin's lawyer. In their escapades around Raynham Abbey together, Richard led and Ripton followed.

In spite of Ripton's subordinate position, he apparently had much to do with corrupting his companion and weakening Sir Austin's System. Soon after Ripton arrived at Raynham, the two boys decided to go shooting. A quarrel arose between them when Ripton, not a sportsman by nature, cried out as Richard was aiming his piece at a bird. Richard called his companion a fool, and a fight ensued. Richard won because he was a scientific boxer. The two boys soon made up their differences but their state of harmony was short-lived. The same afternoon they trespassed on the farm of a neighbor named Blaize, who came upon them after they had shot a pheasant on his property.

Blaize ordered the boys off his land, and when they refused to go he horsewhipped them. Richard and Ripton were compelled to retreat. Ripton suggested that he stone the farmer, but Richard refused to let his companion use such ungentlemanly tactics. The two boys did, however, speculate on ways to get even with farmer Blaize.

Richard was in disgrace when he returned to Raynham because his father knew of his fight with Ripton. Sir Austin ordered his son to go to bed immediately after supper; but he later discovered that Richard had gone, not to bed, but to meet Ripton, and the boys were overheard talking mysteriously about setting something on fire. Shortly afterward, when Sir Austin discovered that farmer Blaize's hayricks were on fire, he suspected Richard. Sir Austin was chagrined, but he did not try to make his son confess. Adrian Harley suspected both Richard and Ripton, who was soon sent home to his father.

The next day a laborer named Tom Bakewell was arrested on suspicion of committing arson. Tom really had set fire to Blaize's property, Richard having bribed him to do so, but he refused to implicate Richard. Conscience-stricken and aware of the fact that a commoner was shielding him, Richard was persuaded to go to Blaize and confess that he was responsible for Tom's action.

Blaize was not surprised by Richard's visit, for Sir Austin had already called and paid damages. Richard was humiliated by the necessity of apologizing to a farmer. He told Blaize that he had set fire to the farmer's grain stacks; and Blaize implied that Richard was a liar because the farmer had a witness, a dull-witted fellow, who said that Tom Bakewell had done the deed. Richard insisted that he himself was responsible, and he succeeded in confusing Blaize's star witness. Richard, however, left the farmer's place in a most irritated frame of mind, not even noticing the farmer's pretty little thirteen-year-old niece, Lucy Desborough, who had let the young man in and out of Blaize's house.

At Tom's trial, Blaize's witness was so uncertain about the identity of the arsonist that the accused was released. Thereafter Tom became Richard's devoted servant.

When Richard reached the age of eighteen, Sir Austin set about finding a prospective wife for the Hope of Raynham, a girl who could be trained for seven years to be a fit mate for Sir Austin's perfect son. Richard, however, could not wait seven years before he at least showed an interest in women, partly because they had no place in the System. He was attracted first to his cousin Clare, who adored him and dreamed of marrying the handsome young man, but in a single afternoon Richard completely forgot Clare. Boating on the weir, he came upon a young lady in distress and saved her boat from capsizing. In that instant the System collapsed completely. She introduced herself as farmer Blaize's niece, Lucy Desborough. Richard was immediately smitten with her, and she with him. Every day they met in the meadow by the weir.

Sir Austin, meanwhile, thought that he had found in London the perfect mate for his son, a young girl named Carola Grandison. Informed by Adrian and his butler that Richard was secretly meeting Lucy, Sir Austin ordered his son to come to London immediately in order to meet Carola. Richard at first refused to obey his father, but Adrian tricked Richard into going to London by saying that Sir Austin had apoplexy.

Richard found his father physically well, but mentally disturbed by the young man's interest in Lucy. He told Richard that women were the ordeal of all men, and though he hoped for a confession of Richard's affair with Lucy, he got none. Sir Austin, however, refused to let the young man return to Raynham as soon as Richard would have liked. Richard met the Grandisons, listened to his father's lectures on the folly of young men who imagined themselves in love, and moped when, after two weeks, Lucy mysteriously stopped writing.

When Sir Austin and his son finally returned to the abbey, Richard found that Lucy had been sent away to school against her will by her uncle so that she would not interfere with Sir Austin's System. Although the farmer did not object to Richard, he refused to have his niece brought back because of his promise to Sir Austin.

After his unsuccessful attempt to have his sweetheart returned to him, Richard decided upon drastic measures. Sir Austin unwittingly aided his son's designs, when he sent Richard to London to see the Grandisons. Tom Blaize, destined by Sir Austin and her uncle to be Lucy's husband, went to London by the same train. Richard got in touch with his old friend, Ripton Thompson, and asked him to get lodgings for a lady. While in London, Richard came upon Adrian Harley, Clare's mother, and Clare, who had picked up a wedding ring which Richard had dropped. Tom Blaize was tricked into going to the wrong station to find Lucy, and Richard met her instead. He installed her with Mrs. Berry in lodgings in Kensington and married her soon afterward, good-hearted Mrs. Berry giving them her own wedding ring to replace the one Richard had lost.

When Adrian learned of Richard's marriage, he admitted that the System had failed. Ripton himself broke the news to Sir Austin, who remarked bitterly that he was mistaken to believe that any System could be based on a human being. Actually Sir Austin objected not so much to the marriage of his son as to the deception involved.

Efforts were made to reconcile Richard and his father, but to no avail. Richard was uneasy because he had not heard from his father, and Sir Austin was too proud to take the first step. While Richard and Lucy were honeymooning in the Isle of Wight, he was introduced to a fast yachting crowd, including Lord Mountfalcon, a man of doubtful reputation, whom Richard naïvely asked to watch over Lucy while Richard himself went to London to see his father and ask his forgiveness.

In London he met a woman Lord Mountfalcon had bribed to bring about Richard's downfall, for his plan was to win Lucy for himself by convincing her of Richard's infidelity. Richard did not know that Mrs. Mount, as she was called, was being bribed to detain him and that while she kept him in London Lord Mountfalcon was attempting to seduce Lucy.

Because he could not bear separation from his son any longer, Sir Austin consented to see Richard. Relations between Richard and his father were still strained, however, for Sir Austin had not yet accepted Lucy. Since she could not have Richard, Clare, meanwhile, had married a man much older than she. Shortly after her marriage, she died and was buried with her own wedding ring and Richard's lost one on her finger.

The death of Clare and the realization that she had loved him deeply shocked Richard. Moreover, his past indiscretions with Mrs. Mount made him ashamed of himself; unworthy, he thought to touch Lucy's hand. He did not know that Mrs. Berry had gone to the Isle of Wight and had brought Lucy back to live with her in Kensington. Richard himself had gone to the continent, where he traveled aimlessly, unaware that Lucy had borne him a son. Then an uncle who disbelieved in all systems returned to London. Learning of Lucy and her child, he bundled them off to Raynham Abbey, and prevailed on Sir Austin to receive them. Then he went to the continent, found Richard, and broke the news that he was a father. Richard rushed back to Raynham to be with Lucy and to become completely reconciled with his father.

The reunion between Lucy and Richard was brief. Richard saw his son and received from his wife complete forgiveness for his past misdeeds. A letter from Mrs. Mount to Richard had revealed how Lord Mountfalcon had schemed so that his lordship could see Lucy and separate her from Richard. Knowing Lucy's innocence and Mountfalcon's villainy, Richard went immediately to France, where he was slightly wounded in a duel with Lord Mountfalcon. The news of the duel was, however, fatal for Lucy. She became ill of brain fever and died of shock, crying for her husband. Richard was heartbroken. Sir Austin was grieved too, but his closest friend often wondered whether he had ever perceived any flaws in his System.

Critical Evaluation

The Ordeal of Richard Feverel was Meredith's first novel, although he had already published poetry, journalism, and two entertaining prose fantasies; and it was not well received critically. George Eliot praised it, but other critics found it unconvincing and excessively intellectualized. Later critics have generally agreed that it is somewhat thesis-ridden, but they find its flaws counterbalanced by wit and emotional force, and it has remained probably the most popular if not the most admired of Meredith's novels.

There is no denying that at times Meredith's concern for his thesis acts to the detriment of the novel; in this, the novel serves as a kind of unintentional exemplification of the thesis, that life is too various, too rich, too spontaneous to conform to even the most admirable system. Few readers can quite believe that Richard would remain separated from Lucy for as long as the plot requires, and the deaths of both Lucy and Clare seem less from natural than from authorial causes. These events are necessary to Meredith's design, but he is unable to give them the quality of inevitability that other elements of the plot have.

Even so, the novel works remarkably well. Meredith may have intended to keep Sir Austin Feverel in center stage, demonstrating the fatuity of high intelligence and lofty ideals without the precious leaven of humor and common sense. The message is effectively conveyed, and Meredith's comic purpose is served by our last sight of Sir Austin still blindly clinging to his theories in the shipwreck of his beloved son's life. Yet it is the romantic pathos of the love of Richard and Lucy which most fully engages the reader and is most vivid at the conclusion. Meredith's later revisions, for a new edition, suggest that he recognized what had happened to his original intention and concluded that the gain in emotional power was worth preserving. To value intense feeling about strict adherence to a preconceived system was thoroughly Meredithian.

Bibliography

Bailey, Elmer James. *The Novels of George Meredith: A Study.* New York: Haskell House, 1971, pp. 49–63.

Baker, Robert S. "*The Ordeal of Richard Feverel*: A Psychological Approach to Structure," in *Studies in the Novel.* VI (1974), pp. 200–217.

Bartlett, Phyllis. "The Novels of George Meredith," in *Review of English Literature.* III (1962), pp. 31–46.

Beach, Joseph Warren. *The Comic Spirit in George Meredith: An Interpretation.* New York: Longmans, Green, 1911, pp. 34–55.

Beer, Gillian. *Meredith: A Change of Masks, A Study of the Novels.* London: Athlone, 1970, pp. 6–34.

Buchen, Irving H. "The Importance of the Minor Characters in *The Ordeal of Richard Feverel*," in *Boston University Studies in English.* V (Autumn, 1961), pp. 154–166.

Buckley, Jerome Hamilton. *Season of Youth: The Bildungsroman from Dickens to Golding.* Cambridge, Mass.: Harvard University Press, 1974, pp. 68–82.

Curtin, Frank D. "Adrian Harley: The Limits of Meredith's Comedy," in *Nineteenth-Century Fiction.* VII (March, 1953), pp. 272–282.

Ekeberg, Gladys W. "*The Ordeal of Richard Feverel* as Tragedy," in *College English.* VII (April, 1946), pp. 387–393.

Erskine, John. "*The Ordeal of Richard Feverel*," in *The Delight of Great Books.* Indianapolis, Ind.: Bobbs-Merrill, 1928, pp. 243–259.

Fisher, Benjamin Franklin, IV. "Sensational Fiction in a Minor Key: *The Ordeal of Richard Feverel*," in *Nineteenth-Century Literary Perspectives: Essays in Honor of Lionel Stevenson.* Edited by Clyde de L. Ryals. Durham, N.C.: Duke University Press, 1974, pp. 283–294.

Gindin, James. *Harvest of a Quiet Eye: The Novel of Compassion.* Bloomington: Indiana University Press, 1971, pp. 64–75.

Goldfarb, Russell M. *Sexual Repression and Victorian Literature.* Lewisburg, Pa.: Bucknell University Press, 1970, pp. 158–177.

Gretton, Mary Sturge. *The Writings and Life of George Meredith, A Centenary Study.* London: Oxford University Press, 1926, pp. 29–43.

Halperin, John. *Egoism and Self-Discovery in the Victorian Novel: Studies in the Ordeal of Knowledge in the Nineteenth Century.* New York: Burt Franklin, 1974, pp. 202–214.

Kelvin, Norman. *A Troubled Eden: Nature and Society in the Works of George Meredith.* Stanford, Calif.: Stanford University Press, 1961, pp. 5–14.

Knoepflmacher, Ulrich Camillus. *Laughter and Despair: Readings in Ten Novels of the Victorian Age.* Berkeley: University of California Press, 1971, pp. 109–136.

Korg, Jacob. "Expressive Styles in *The Ordeal of Richard Feverel*," in *Nineteenth-Century Fiction.* XXVII (1972), pp. 253–267.

Lawrence, F.B. "Lyric and Romance: Meredith's Poetic Fiction," in *Victorian Essays: A Symposium.* Edited by Warren D. Anderson and Thomas D. Clareson. Kent, Oh.: Kent State University Press, 1967, pp. 87–106.

Mitchell, Juliet. "*The Ordeal of Richard Feverel*: A Sentimental Education," in *Meredith Now: Some Critical Essays.* Edited by Ian Fletcher. New York: Barnes & Noble, 1971, pp. 69–94.

Poston, Lawrence, III. "Dramatic Reference and Structure in *The Ordeal of Richard Feverel*," in *Studies in English Literature, 1500–1900.* VI (1966), pp. 743–752.

Stevenson, Lionel. "Meredith and the Art of Implication," in *The Victorian Experience: The Novelists.* Edited by Richard A. Levine. Athens: Ohio University Press, 1976, pp. 177–201.

Stevenson, R.C. "Comedy, Tragedy, and the Spirit of Critical Intelligence in *Richard Feverel*," in *The Worlds of Victorian Fiction.* Edited by Jerome H. Buckley. Cambridge, Mass.: Harvard University Press, 1975, pp. 205–222.

Williams, David. *George Meredith: His Life and Lost Love.* London: Hamish Hamilton, 1977, pp. 109–114.

Wright, Walter F. *Art and Substances in George Meredith, A Study in Narrative.* Lincoln: University of Nebraska Press, 1953, pp. 147–161.

THOMAS NASH

Born: Lowestoft, Surrey, England (1567)
Died: Yarmouth (?), England (1601)

Principal Works

NOVEL: *The Unfortunate Traveller*, 1594.

PLAY: *Summer's Last Will and Testament*, 1592.

PAMPHLETS: *Strange News of the Intercepting of Certain Letters*, 1592; *Christ's Tears over Jerusalem*, 1593; *Have with You to Saffron Walden, or Gabriel Harvey's Hunt Is Up*, 1596.

Thomas Nash (or Nashe), dramatist, novelist, and pamphleteer, was born in 1567 in Lowestoft, England, the son of William Nash, a minister, and his second wife Margaret. He spent several years at St. John's College, Cambridge, and received his B.A. degree in 1585. By 1588 he was living in London, trying to make a living with his pen as one of the University Wits. *A Countercuff to Martin Junior, Martin's Month's Mind*, and *Pasquil's Apology* are sometimes attributed to him. Among his friends were Greene, Daniel, Lodge, and Marlowe. At this time the Puritan writers, under the pseudonym of Martin Marprelate, were attacking the bishops and the government of the Church. Using the name Pasquil, Nash joined the controversy against the Puritans, especially against Gabriel Harvey. His contributions to the "paper war" include *Strange News of the Intercepting of Certain Letters*, *Christ's Tears over Jerusalem*, and *Have with You to Saffron Walden, or Gabriel Harvey's Hunt Is Up*.

The most notable of his works was a picaresque novel of romantic adventure entitled *The Unfortunate Traveller, or The Life of Jack Wilton*, the story of a page who attended the Earl of Surrey on his Grand Tour and who married a Venetian lady. The realistic use of detail in this work set the pattern for the novels of Defoe. Nash also wrote several plays, and the title page of Marlowe's *Dido, Queen of Carthage* credits him with the joint authorship, or possibly the completion, of that work. *Summer's Last Will and Testament*, originally a masque presented at the house of Sir George Carey, was produced in 1592. A lost play, *The Isle of Dogs* (1597), a slanderous work of which he wrote at least a part, led to his being sentenced to the Fleet prison, a sentence he seems to have avoided somehow. He died in 1601, probably at Yarmouth.

Bibliography

The standard edition of Nash's *Works* was edited by R. B. McKerrow, 1904–1910. This is in part supplanted by *Selected Writings*, edited by Stanley Wells, 1965. See also J. J. Jusserand, *The English Novel in the Time of Shakespeare*,

1890; F. G. Harman, *Gabriel Harvey and Thomas Nashe*, 1923; Fredson T. Bowers, "Thomas Nashe and the Picaresque Novel," in *Studies in Honor of John Calvin Metcalf*, 1941; G. R. Hibbard, *Thomas Nash: A Critical Introduction*, 1962; and *Dictionary of National Biography*, Vol. XIV.

THE UNFORTUNATE TRAVELLER

Type of work: Novel
Author: Thomas Nash (1567–1601)
Type of plot: Picaresque romance
Time of plot: Reign of King Henry VIII
Locale: England and Europe
First published: 1594

The Unfortunate Traveller. Or. The Life of Jack Wilton. *an episodic tale, is an important forerunner of the English novel as it was to develop in the eighteenth century. Nash's work abounds in realistic details, but the author catered also to the Elizabethan taste for the romantic and far-fetched, especially in the Italian scenes.*

Principal Characters

Jack Wilton, a page to Henry VIII of England. Bored with his life, he leaves King Henry's service to become a soldier of fortune. Since he is a bright and merry lad, he has all sorts of adventures and scrapes. He travels with the Earl of Surrey as a companion throughout Europe. Finally he returns to England and the service of Henry VIII.

The Earl of Surrey. Jack's friend, benefactor, and traveling companion. He is a gallant courtier.

Tabitha, a Venetian prostitute who meets Jack and the Earl of Surrey. She and her pander try to kill the Earl but are caught and executed.

Geraldine, a beautiful woman of Florence loved by the Earl of Surrey. The Earl fights all comers in a tourney to prove his love for her.

Diamante, a goldsmith's wife suspected of infidelity by her husband. She takes Jack as a lover to punish her husband for his suspicions. After the goldsmith's death Diamante travels with Jack, and the two share many adventures, including being bondservants in the household of one of the Pope's mistresses.

Johannes de Imola, a citizen of Rome with whom Jack and Diamante live for a time. He is unfortunate enough to die of the plague during an epidemic.

Heraclide de Imola, wife of Johannes. She commits suicide after being raped by a band of cutthroats, and her death is blamed on Jack, putting him for a time in danger of hanging.

Cutwolfe, a famous brigand whose execution Jack witnesses. Cutwolfe confesses to murdering the bandit who led the assault on Heraclide and Diamante.

The Story

Jack Wilton was a page serving in the army of King Henry VIII of England when his adventures began. While the English troops were encamped near Turwin, in France, Jack, pretending that he had overheard the king and his council planning to do away with a certain sutler, convinced the sutler that he ought to give away all his supplies to the soldiers and then throw himself on the king's mercy. The sutler, completely fooled, did just that. The king, enjoying the prank, gave him a pension and forgave Jack.

Shortly after that escapade Jack fell in with a captain who forced the page to help him get rich by throwing dice. Jack, tiring of his subservience to the captain, persuaded the officer that the best means of getting ahead in the army was to turn spy and seek out information valuable to the king. The gullible captain, entering the French lines, was discovered by the French and almost killed before he was sent hustling back to the English camp.

The campaign over, Jack found himself back in England once again. When the peacetime duties of a page began to pall, he left the king's household and turned soldier of fortune. After crossing the English Channel to find some means of making a livelihood, he reached the French king too late to enter that monarch's service against the Swiss, and so he traveled on to Münster, Germany. There he found John Leiden leading the Baptists against the Duke of Saxony. He observed a notorious massacre, in which the Baptists were annihilated because they refused to carry the weapons of war into battle. After the battle Jack met the Earl of Surrey, who was on the continent at the time.

Surrey, having been acquainted with Jack at court, was glad to see the page and confided to him his love for Geraldine, a lovely Florentine. Surrey proposed that Jack travel with him to Italy in search of the woman. Jack, having no future in sight, readily consented to accompany the earl.

Jack and Surrey then proceeded southward out of Germany into Italy. As they traveled Surrey proposed to Jack that they exchange identities for a time, so that the nobleman could behave in a less seemly fashion. Jack, pleased at the prospect of being an earl, even temporarily, agreed.

Upon their arrival in Venice, on the way to Florence, they were taken up by a courtesan named Tabitha, who tried to kill the man that she thought was the Earl of Surrey, with the true earl as her accomplice. Surrey and Jack, turning the tables on her, caused her and her pander to be executed for attempting to conspire against a life. In turning the tables, however, Jack came into possession of some counterfeit money. When they used the coins, Jack and the earl were seized as counterfeiters and sentenced to death.

While languishing in prison, Jack met Diamante, the wife of a goldsmith who had imprisoned her because he suspected her of infidelity. The page made her his mistress after assuring her that thereby she revenged herself on the husband who thought little of her chastity.

After a few weeks Jack and the earl were released through an English gentleman who had heard of their plight and had secured the efforts of the poet Aretine to prove to the court that Tabitha and her procurer had been the real counterfeiters. Aretine also saw to it that Diamante was released from prison to become the mistress of Jack once again. Within a few weeks Diamante's husband died of the plague. Jack married Diamante and, in view of his new fortune, decided to travel.

He left the Earl of Surrey in Venice, but the pleasure of bearing the nobleman's title was so great that Jack kept it. After some time Surrey heard that there was another earl by the same name and went to investigate. Learning that the double was Jack, Surrey forgave him, and they started once again on their interrupted trip to Florence. Upon their arrival the earl, wishing to do battle to prove his love for Geraldine, issued a challenge to all the knights and gentlemen of the city. The tourney was a great success, with Surrey carrying off all the honors of the day. After that event Surrey and Jack parted company. Jack, still accompanied by Diamante, went on to Rome.

There they lived with Johannes and Heraclide de Imola. During the summer Signor de Imola died of the plague. Shortly after his death and before his corpse could be removed from the house, bandits broke in and raped Heraclide de Imola and Diamante. Jack, overpowered by the bandits, was unable to help the women. Heraclide killed herself after the attack. After police broke into the house they blamed Jack for what had happened. He was unable to clear himself because the only other witness was Diamante, whom the bandits had kidnaped.

A banished English earl, appearing in time to save Jack from the hangman's noose, produced witnesses to show that one of the bandits had made a deathbed confession clearing the page of any part in the crimes. Released, Jack went in search of Diamante. While searching for her he fell through an unbarred cellar door into the house of a Jew, and there he found Diamante making love to an apprentice. The Jew, roused by the noise of the fall and Jack's anger at Diamante, came into the cellar and accused them both of breaking into his house and corrupting his apprentice. Under the law, they became the Jew's bond servants. Jack was turned over to another Jew, the pope's physician, to be used in a vivisection.

He was saved from that horrid death when one of the pope's mistresses fell in love with him and used her influence to secure his person for herself. Diamante also fell into the woman's hands. Jack and Diamante, keeping their previous relations a secret, hoped in that way to be able to escape from the house. One day, when the woman went to a religious festival, they escaped, taking with them as much loot as they could carry.

Traveling northward, Jack went to Bologna, where he saw a famous criminal executed. The assassin, Cutwolfe, had confessed to murdering the bandit who had led the assault on Heraclide de Imola and Diamante months before. Moving on into France, Jack found the English armies once again in the field and returned to King Henry's service.

Critical Evaluation

Following the example of Robert Greene, one of his predecessors at St. John's College, Cambridge, Nash overcame whatever religious scruples might have been bred into him as a preacher's son and set out with profane determination to become one of the first "professional writers" in England, and one of the most controversial. As a member of the University Wits, he distinguished himself by the diversity of his authorial talents, unashamedly plying the writer's trade as polemical pamphleteer, poet, dramatist, and reporter. He said of himself, "I have written in all sorts of humours more than any young man of my age in England." And when he died, still a young man in his thirties, Nash left behind a veritable explosion of miscellaneous literary pieces. Picking up the pieces since then, critics have often concluded that Nash's explosive productivity was more comparable to that of a scatter-gun than to the big cannons of his contemporaries Shakespeare, Jonson, and Marlowe. Nash has been accused of superficiality, both of thought and style; and he richly merits the accusation. Nonetheless all would agree that at least two of his works deserve the continued attention of all those interested in the development of English literary style—*The Unfortunate Traveller, Or, The Life of Jack Wilton* and *Pierce Penniless His Supplication to the Devil* (the latter receiving three editions in the year of its first publication alone, 1592). *Pierce Penniless,* Nash's most popular and widest-ranging satirical pamphlet, is a graphic indictment of the follies and vices of contemporary England seen from the harshly realistic perspective of one of the first indisputable forerunners of yellow journalism. Nash's ready talent for immediately distilling the fruits of his observation and experience into gripping first-hand reports served him as well in his perplexing narrative of Jack Wilton.

Rambling narrative, travelogue, earthy memoirs, diary, tavern yarn, picaresque adventure, political, nationalistic, and religious diatribe, *The Unfortunate Traveller,* though impossible to classify generically, is nonetheless clearly one seminal starting-point in the development of the English novel. The critics are in general agreement with Wells, who declares that the work "has no organic principle; it is not a unified work of art." Though Nash's narrative is certainly not "a unified work of art" by the severest standards of unity, it definitely has an organic wholeness. But that wholeness is as much external as internal, provided more by the pen of Nash than by the ephemeral character of Jack. Therefore the lack of unity is still a true *imitation* because it reflects accurately the mind of the author—a mind as chaotically diverse as the narrative it has produced. The structure of the book is absolutely arbitrary, simply a loosely organized recounting of Jack's travels through Great Britain, the Low Countries, Germany, France, and Italy—a structure comfortably suited to Nash's always changeable purpose and varying (not alternating) interests. The reader will look in vain for a balance between one part of Jack's travels and another; there is none, since Nash sees contemporary life as completely unbalanced. Like Jack, the author stays where he likes as long as he likes, and especially as long as he senses the reader can still be interested. Nash's sense of his audience is one of his most charming assets, and it is highly appropriate that this tale is set up in the guise of a barroom brag on the part of Jack, lately returned from Bologna. Nash's structural nonchalance almost certainly influenced Sterne's

Tristram Shandy.

Sterne must also have been intrigued by the ambiguity of viewpoint found in *The Unfortunate Traveller.* There are times when it is almost certain that the author forgets about Jack entirely, setting off on his own to denounce, castigate, ridicule, expound on one thing or another. At other times Nash can be most subtle in his handling of the complicated relationship between narrator and fictive reader—as when Jack constantly quotes a Latin phrase to justify his actions, mistranslating it for his ignorant victims while we are left to wonder whether the mistranslation is also intended to poke fun at us (for example, *Tendit ad sydera virtus,* which Jack renders as, "there's great virtue belongs, I can tell you, to a cup of cider"). If *Tristram Shandy* overlooks the neat narrative distinctions, drawn by Dante between his naïve pilgrim and his narrator-pilgrim or by Chaucer in *The Booke of the Duchesse,* it does so with the comfortable knowledge that Nash did it first and succeeded brilliantly.

Nash's style reaches its finest and most characteristic expression in this book: the vivacity of an undiminishing *sprezzatura*—brilliantly uneven, uncontrolled and disorganized. *The Unfortunate Traveller* walks a precarious line between realistic and romantic perspective and frequently, as Nash did in his own mind and life, gains its appeal from its inability to prevent one side of the line from flowing over into the other. The journalistic nature of Nash's prose is marked both positively and negatively; positively, for its unprecedented precision of detail, proving the author's considerable powers of observation (equalled only by his lack of discipline); negatively, for his inability to separate objective narration from personal viewpoint—indeed, his unwillingness to see the value of such a separation. The result is a work as prodigious for its literary "faults" as it is for its "virtues," a work that constantly raises the question of why it is still being read and taught.

The beginning of the answer lies in the character of Jack Wilton, the semi-fictional counterpart of Nash's own personality. In his ambivalence between ambition and cowardice, the desire for adventure and the need for security, aggressiveness and passivity; in his switch from awestruck observer to cantankerous prankster, innocent victim to devious culprit; in his love of acting and enjoyment of performance, passionate enthusiasms and vicious hatred; in all these things Jack is an earthy, everyday kind of Everyman with whom every new reader may associate. But he is just as truly typical of the Renaissance English spirit as he is universal. In him Nash has depicted brilliantly that rare mixture of the devout and the debauched, the sacred and the profane, the scholarly and the vulgar, the delicate and the hideously brutal, the aristocratic and the common (a mixture emphasized when Jack and Surrey exchange identities, like the beasts in Spenser's *Mother Hubberd's Tale,* and discover that each delights in living in the other's shoes), the explorer and the patriot that made Elizabethan and Tudor England an era quite different from any other before or after. The singularity of an age, after all, can be found only in its tensions, in the peculiar coupling of opposing forces; all forces can be found at all times and only special magnetic attraction that brings them into new configurations at one period or another really makes uniqueness possible. *The Unfortunate Traveller*, in the unforgettable crudity and refinement of its humor, in its instantaneous leaps from highly serious didacticism to profoundly trivial farce, is a kind of templet shaped by and reproducing the shape of its times.

Bibliography

Broron, L. "The Unfortunate Traveller," in *Journal of Jewish Lore and Philosophy*. I (January, 1919), pp. 244–254.

Chandler, F.W. "*The Unfortunate Traveller*," in his *The Literature of Roguery*. Boston: Franklin, 1907, pp. 192–198.

Croston, A.K. "The Use of Imagery in Nashe's *The Unfortunate Traveller*," in *Review of English Studies*. XXIV (April, 1948), pp. 90–101.

De Beer, E.S. "Thomas Nashe: The Notices of Rome in *The Unfortunate Traveller*," in *Notes and Queries*. CLXXXV (July, 1943), pp. 67–70.

Gibbon, Marina. "Polemic, the Rhetorical Tradition and *The Unfortunate Traveller*," in *Journal of English and Germanic Philology*. LXIII (1964), pp. 408–421.

Gohlke, Madelon S. "Wits Wantonness: *The Unfortunate Traveller* as Picaresque," in *Studies in Philology*. LXXIII (1976), pp. 397–413.

Hibbard, G.R. *Thomas Nashe: A Critical Introduction*. London: Routledge and Kegan Paul, 1962, pp. 145–179.

Jusserand, J.J. "Account of Jack Wilton," in his *The English Novel in the Time of Shakespeare*. London: 1890, pp. 308–321.

Kettle, Arnold. *An Introduction to the English Novel*, Volume I. London: Hutchinson's, 1951, p. 25.

Latham, Agnes C. "Satire on Literary Themes and Modes in Nashe's *Unfortunate Traveller*," in *English Studies*. XXIX (1948), pp. 85–100.

MRS. ANN RADCLIFFE

Born: London, England (July 9, 1764)
Died: London (February 7, 1823)

Principal Works

NOVELS: *A Sicilian Romance*, 1790; *The Romance of the Forest*, 1791; *The Mysteries of Udolpho*, 1794; *The Italian, or, The Confessional of the Black Penitents*, 1797; *Gaston de Blondeville*, 1826.

Mrs. Ann (Ward) Radcliffe, although little known today, was considered the greatest romanticist of her age, both for her imaginative plotting and for her poetic prose. Her novels have become a minor landmark in English literary history because their author formulated a Gothic school of writing that owed more to her invention than to the influence of her contemporaries in the same genre, and her tales of terror are unblurred by the awkward supernaturalism of Walpole, the sentimentality of Clara Reeves, or the turgid horrors of Matthew Gregory Lewis.

Born in London on July 9, 1764, Ann Ward included among her ancestors the celebrated classical scholar, Dr. S. Jebb. Stimulated by her wide reading, she delighted as a child in daydreams of things supernatural; however, a shy, asthmatic girl isolated in a society of her elders, she was not encouraged to exercise her abilities or to express herself. At twenty-three, pretty and demure, she married William Radcliffe, the future editor of the *English Chronicle*. Living in London, intimate with literary people, and childless, she began to write. Her first book, *The Castles of Athlin and Dunbayne* (1789), went almost unnoticed, but her second, *A Sicilian Romance*, established her reputation as a master of suspense and description. With *The Romance of the Forest*, published in 1791, she attracted the attention of a wide reading public. For her fourth novel, *The Mysteries of Udolpho*, she received £500 before it was published.

This novel typifies the two strongest elements in Mrs. Radcliffe's fiction: the suggestion of imminent evil and the atmosphere of refinement and beauty. Juxtaposed, each element intensifies the other. Mrs. Radcliffe carries the reader into a beautiful Eden, and by contrasting excellent description with vague references to impending doom an effect of mystery and terror results. That some terrible mystery suggested by a low groan from a distant tomb or an uncertain light on a castle stairs turns out to be wind or moonlight does not alter the effect of the story. Mrs. Radcliffe discriminated carefully between terror and horror, and her ability to evoke the former while avoiding the latter points to her skillful handling of atmosphere and dramatic situation.

Mrs. Radcliffe's novels are built on the same plot: a chaste, helpless young woman achieves a good marriage after a series of attempts on her life by sinister villains in an exotic setting. Although the plots are improbable and the characters are two-dimensional to the modern reader, the novels had great influence on other writers of the time, notably Scott and Byron; early in Scott's career he was hailed as Mrs. Radcliffe's successor, and certainly Schedoni, the villain of *The Italian*, is the forerunner of the Byronic hero.

Although she was in literature a mistress of the strange and picturesque, her own biography is commonplace because of the regularity of her life, and modern scholarship now discounts the contemporary belief that madness, induced by the terrors she created, accounts for the long interval of time between the publication of *The Italian* and her posthumous *Gaston de Blondeville*. A figure deserving more attention in literary history than she has received, Mrs. Radcliffe died in London on February 7, 1823.

Bibliography

The edition of 1824 was reprinted in 1971. A modern edition of *The Italian* was issued as *The Confessional of the Black Penitents* by the Folio Society of London in 1956. For biography and criticism see Clara F. McIntyre, *Ann Radcliffe in Relation to Her Time, Yale Studies in English*, LXII, 1920; and A. A. S. Wieten, *Mrs. Radcliffe: Her Relation to Romanticism*, 1926. For more general studies of the Gothic Revival and its writers see also Dorothy Scarborough, *The Supernatural in Modern English Fiction*, 1917; Edith Birkhead, *The Tale of Terror*, 1921; Eino Railo, *The Haunted Castle*, 1927; the Rev. Montague Summers, *The Gothic Quest*, 1938, and *A Gothic Bibliography*, 1941. See further Donald Thomas, "The First Poetess of Romantic Fiction: Ann Radcliffe," *English*, XV (1964), 91–95; and Harrison Ross Steeves, "The Gothic Romance," *Before Jane Austen*, 1965, 243–271.

THE MYSTERIES OF UDOLPHO

Type of work: Novel
Author: Mrs. Ann Radcliffe (1764–1823)
Type of plot: Gothic romance
Time of plot: Late sixteenth century
Locale: France and Italy
First published: 1794

In her own age Ann Radcliffe was justly annointed "Queen of the Gothic Novel," a title that still remains valid. Emily St. Aubert, the main character in The Mysteries of Udolpho, *is the prototype of the threatened heroine of the gothic romance, and her adventures assume the pattern that is characteristic of the genre.*

Principal Characters

M. St. Aubert (săn·tō·bĕr′), a French aristocrat and widower. He takes his daughter on a trip into the Pyrenees Mountains. While on the trip he falls ill and dies, leaving his daughter with some letters he has asked her to destroy. With the letters is a mysterious miniature portrait.

Emily St. Aubert (ā·mē·lē′ săn·tō·bĕr′), daughter of M. St. Aubert. She wants to marry Valancourt, but her villainous uncle, who wants her property, prevents the marriage and forces the girl to sign over her property to him. Her property is returned, however, when her uncle is captured as a brigand. She is reunited with her beloved Valancourt, marries him, and settles down to a tranquil life.

Valancourt (vȧ·län·kōōr′), a young French nobleman who falls in love with Emily St. Aubert and prepares to marry her, until her uncle interferes. Rumors have him a wild young man, but he proves he is worthy of Emily and finally marries her.

Mme. Montoni, Emily's aunt, who marries Signor Montoni. Her husband locks her in a castle tower to make her sign over her property to him. She dies of harsh treatment.

Signor Montoni, a villainous Italian nobleman who marries Emily's aunt and forbids the girl's marriage to Valancourt. He tries to wrest his wife's and his niece's property from them. He takes them to a castle high in the Apennines, where he is a brigand. He is captured and forced to return his ill-gotten gains.

Count Morano, a Venetian nobleman. Signor Montoni tries to marry Emily off to him.

Lady Laurentini, previous owner of the Castle of Udolpho. She disappears to become a nun. She confesses her true identity as she lies dying. She says she plotted at one time to have Emily's aunt killed by her first husband, who was also Lady Laurentini's lover.

Ludovico, a servant at Udolpho who befriends Emily and helps her escape from the castle.

M. Du Pont (dü pōṅ′), a friend of Emily's father. He proves that Valancourt, Emily's beloved, actually gambled only to help some friends.

M. Villefort (vēl·fôr′), a French aristocrat whose family gives Emily refuge after a shipwreck.

The Marquis de Villeroi (dǝ vēl·rwȧ′), Lady Laurentini's lover, the first husband of Emily's aunt.

The Story

After the death of his wife, Monsieur St. Aubert, a French aristocrat, took his daughter on a trip in the Pyrenees Mountains. High on a mountain road the St. Auberts met a young nobleman dressed in hunting clothes. He was Valancourt, the younger son of a family with which M. St. Aubert was acquainted. Joining the St. Auberts on their journey, the young man soon fell in love with eighteen-year-old Emily St. Aubert, and the girl felt that she, too, might lose her heart to him.

St. Aubert became desperately ill and died in a cottage near the Chateau-le-Blanc, ancestral seat of the noble Villeroi family. After her father's burial at the nearby convent of St. Clair, Emily returned to her home at La Vallée and promptly burned some mysterious letters which her father had requested her to destroy. With the letters she found a miniature portrait of a beautiful unknown woman. Since she had not been told to destroy the portrait, she took it with her when she left La Vallée to stay with her aunt in Toulouse.

Valancourt followed Emily to Toulouse to press his suit. After some re-monstrance, the aunt gave her permission for the young couple to marry. Then, a few days before the ceremony, the aunt married Signor Montoni, a sinister Italian, who immediately forbade his new niece's nuptials. To make his refusal doubly positive, he took Emily and her aunt to his mansion in Venice.

There Emily and Madame Montoni found themselves in unhappy circum-stances, for it soon became apparent that Montoni had married in order to secure for himself the estates of his new wife and her niece. When he tried to force Emily to marry a Venetian nobleman, Count Morano, Emily was in despair. Sud-denly, on the night before the wedding, Montoni ordered his household to pack and leave for his castle at Udolpho, high in the Apennines.

When the party arrived at Udolpho, Montoni immediately began to repair the fortifications of the castle. Emily did not like the dark, cold, mysterious castle from which the previous owner, Lady Laurentini, had disappeared under myste-rious circumstances. Superstitious servants claimed that apparitions flitted about the halls and galleries of the ancient fortress.

Soon after Montoni and his household had settled themselves, Count Morano attempted to kidnap Emily. Foiled by Montoni, who wounded him severely in a sword fight, Morano threatened revenge.

A few days later Montoni tried to force his wife to sign over her estates to him. When she refused, he caused her to be locked up in a tower of the castle. Emily tried to visit her aunt that night. Terrified at finding fresh blood on the tower stairs, she believed her aunt murdered.

Ghostly sounds and shadows about Udolpho began to make everyone uneasy. Even Montoni, who had organized a band of marauders to terrorize and pillage the neighborhood, began to believe the castle was haunted. Emily heard that several hostages had been taken. She was sure that Valancourt was a prisoner because she had heard someone singing a song he had taught her and because one night a mysterious shadow had called her by name. Her life was made one long torment by Montoni's insistence that she sign away her estates to him, lest she suffer the same fate as her aunt.

The aunt had not been murdered, as Emily found out through her maid, but had become so ill because of harsh treatment that she had died and had been buried in the chapel of the castle.

Morano made another attempt to steal Emily away from the castle, this time with her assistance, as she was now afraid for her life. But Montoni and his men discovered the attempt in time to seize the abductors outside the castle walls. Shortly afterward Montoni sent Emily away, after forcing her to sign the papers which gave him control of her estates in France. At first she thought she was being sent to her death, but Montoni sent her to a cottage in Tuscany because he had heard that Venetian authorities were sending a small army to attack Udolpho and seize him and his bandits. His depredations had caused alarm after the villas of several rich Venetians had been robbed.

When Emily returned to the castle, she saw evidence that there had been a terrible battle. Emily's maid and Ludovico, another servant, disclosed to Emily on her return that a prisoner who knew her was in the dungeons below. Emily immediately guessed that the prisoner was Valancourt and made arrangements to escape with him. But the prisoner turned out to be Monsieur Du Pont, an old friend of her father. Emily, Monsieur Du Pont, the girl's maid, and Ludovico made their escape and reached Leghorn safely. There they took a ship for France. Then a great storm drove the ship ashore close to the Chateau-le-Blanc, near which Emily's father had been buried.

Emily and her friends were rescued by Monsieur Villefort and his family. The Villeforts had inherited the chateau and were attempting to live in it, although it was in disrepair and said to be haunted. While at the chateau Emily decided to spend several days at the convent where her father was buried. There she found a nun who closely resembled the mysteriously missing Lady Laurentini, whose portrait Emily had seen at the castle of Udolpho.

When Emily returned to the chateau she found it in a state of turmoil because of weird noises that seemed to come from the apartments of the former mistress of the chateau. Lucovico volunteered to spend a night in the apartment. Although all the windows and doors were locked, he was not in the rooms the next morning. When the old caretaker came to tell Emily this news, she noticed the miniature Emily had found at La Vallée. The miniature, said the servant, was a portrait of her former mistress, the Marquise de Villeroi. More than that, Emily closely resembled the portrait.

Meanwhile Valancourt reappeared and once again made plans to marry Emily, but Monsieur Villefort told her of gambling debts the young man had incurred and of the wild life he had led in Paris while she had been a prisoner in Italy. Because of that report Emily refused to marry him. She returned in distress to her home at La Vallée to learn that Montoni had been captured by the Venetian authorities. Since he had criminally secured the deeds to her lands, the court now restored them to her, and she was once again a young woman of wealth and position.

While Emily was at La Vallée, the Villefort family made a trip high into the Pyrenees to hunt. Almost captured by bandits, they were rescued by Ludovico, who had so inexplicably disappeared from the chateau. He had been kidnaped by smugglers who had used the vaults of the chateau to store their treasure, and he disclosed that the noises in the chateau had been caused by the outlaws in an effort to frighten away the rightful owners.

Informed of what had happened, Emily returned to the chateau to see her friends. While there, she again visited the convent of St. Clair. The nun whom she had seen before, and who resembled the former mistress of Udolpho, was taken mortally ill while Emily was at the convent. On her deathbed the nun confessed that she was Lady Laurentini, who had left Udolpho to go to her former lover, the Marquis de Villeroi. Finding him married to M. St. Aubert's sister, she ensnared him once more and made him an accomplice in her plot to poison his wife. When the marquis, overcome by remorse, fled to a distant country and died there, she had retired to the convent to expiate her sins.

Emily's happiness was complete when Monsieur Du Pont, who had escaped with her from Udolpho, proved that Valancourt had gambled only to secure money to aid some friends who were on the brink of misfortune. Reunited, they were married and went to La Vallée, where they lived a happy, tranquil life in contrast to the many strange adventures which had parted them for so long.

Critical Evaluation

Christmas Eve of 1764 saw the issuance of Horace Walpole's *The Castle of Otranto,* a story of supernatural terror set in a vaguely medieval past, complete with a gloomy castle, knights both chivalrous and wicked, and virtuous fair maidens in distress—the first English Gothic novel. During the previous summer, while Walpole at Strawberry Hill was transforming a nightmarish dream into a Gothic novel, Ann Ward was born in London. Twenty-three years later when she married law student William Radcliffe, the era of the Gothic novel was finally under way, having begún to flourish with Clara Reeve's professed imitation of *The Castle of Otranto* in *The Old English Baron* (1777). And Ann Radcliffe, born in the same year as the genre itself, was to be supreme among the Gothic novelists whose works were so popular in the last decades of the eighteenth century.

Her total output as a novelist, except for one posthumously published novel, comprises five Gothic novels, all immensely successful, published between 1789 and 1797. *The Mysteries of Udolpho* was her fourth and most popular. Mrs. Anna Laetitia Barbauld in her Preface to this novel for *British Novelists* (1810), noting that a "greater distinction is due to those which stand at the head of a class," asserts that "such are undoubtedly the novels of Mrs. Radcliffe." This estimate is still valid.

Nevertheless, Ann Radcliffe might have been relegated entirely to the pages of literary history had it not been for Jane Austen's delightful burlesque of Gothic novels, *Northanger Abbey,* in which a sentimental heroine under the inspiration of *The Mysteries of Udolpho* fancies herself involved in Gothic adventures. Through the exaggerated sentiment of her heroine, Jane Austen ridicules a major element in Gothic novels in general—in *The Mysteries of Udolpho* specifically—sensibility. A reliance upon feeling, in contradiction of the dominant rationalism of the eighteenth century, the cult of sensibility was nonetheless a vital part of the age. The man of sensibility was peculiarly receptive to the simple joys of country life, to the "sublime" as well as to the "beautiful" aspects of nature, and, above all, inclined to benevolence, his own depth of feeling compelling sympathy. And it was considered proper to manifest sensibility through such traits as a readiness to weep or faint and a taste of melancholia.

In *The Mysteries of Udolpho,* the "good" characters are endowed with sensibility; the "bad" are not. Emily St. Aubert, her father, and her lover Valancourt are exemplars of this highly refined capacity for feeling. St. Aubert, scorning worldly ambition, is retired from the world, represented by the city of Paris, to his rural estate, La Vallée, where his days are spent in literary, musical, and botanical pursuits, his pleasures heightened by his pensive melancholy. The villainous Montoni loves power and the wielding of it, responding to the idea of any daring exploit with eyes that appeared to gleam instantaneously with fire. At home in cities with their atmosphere of fashionable dissipation and political intrigue, he thrives in the solitary Castle of Udolpho only when he has made it a bustling military fortress. Cold, haughty, and brooding, he is—unlike the ingenuous St. Aubert—adept at dissimulation.

Much of Emily's anguish is caused by the lack of sensibility in Montoni's world, her own ingenuousness and benevolence misinterpreted as mere policy, spurring her enemies to further mischief. However, Emily's sensibility functions sometimes as an effective defense, her profuse tears and spells of fainting postponing immediate confrontations. Sometimes, too, sensibility assisted discovery, as Emily, shutting herself away to read, play her lute and sing, sketch, or simply meditate and gaze rapturously upon the landscape at hand, became vulnerable to mystery.

The conventionally spurious medieval setting, in this novel set in the year 1584, serves well the solitude of sensibility and gives scope for a range of feelings as the heroine is forced to travel about France and Italy, inhabiting gloomy, ruined castles from the Alps and the Apennines to the Adriatic and the Mediterranean, encountering chevaliers, noble ladies, courtesans, mercenary soldiers, bandits, peasants, monks, nuns, war, and murder—deaths by poisoning, by stiletto, by sword, by torture, by pistol, and by cannon fire. Emily's wide-ranging adventures in a remote, dark age are the fit trials of her sensibility, foreshadowed in her dying father's lecture on the danger of uncontrolled sensibility. And if the modern reader is overwhelmed by evidence of her frequent trembling, weeping, and fainting, Emily herself is more conscious of her constant endeavor to be resolute, her ultimate survival with honor unscathed sufficient proof of her strength of sensibility.

Although Jane Austen ridicules this excessive sensibility, she also allows Henry Tilney, her spokesman for reason, to praise Mrs. Radcliffe's novel, however facetiously, by claiming that he could hardly put down *The Mysteries of Udolpho* once he had begun reading it and, in fact, had finished the novel, hair standing on end, in two days. Henry's count of two entire days accurately indicates average reading time, but, more importantly, his appreciation of the suspense maintained throughout does justice to Mrs. Radcliffe's novelistic powers.

The essential quality which sustains Gothic suspense is a pervasive sense of the irrational elements in life. Emily herself provides the appropriate image in the description about her life appearing like the dream of a distempered imagination. Although basically a straightforward, chronological narrative, *The Mysteries of Udolpho* seems timeless and dreamlike, the sweeping length of the story suggesting the cinematic technique of slow-motion. The novel accomplishes shifts in scenery with the rapidity peculiar to dreams: now Emily is in Leghorn; now she is in a ship tossed amid white foam in a dark and stormy sea, incredibly, upon the very shores where lies the mysterious Château-le-Blanc. The vast amount of scenic description, written in the generalizing poetic diction of the eighteenth century, contributes to the unreal atmosphere suggestive of a dream world where forms are vague, where time and space ignore ordinary delimitations. Thus the Castle of Udolpho seems limitless in size; its actual shape and substance, typically viewed in the solemn evening dusk, seems indefinite, gloomy and sublime with clustered towers. Other scenes call up boundless space, for example, in recurrent images of blue-tinged views of distant mountain tops.

The repetitive pattern of Emily's adventures is also dreamlike: she is repeatedly trapped in a room with no light; again and again she flees down dark, labyrinthine passages or seemingly endless staircases. People who are rationally assumed to be far away suddenly materialize, often in shadowy forms, their features obscure, known to Emily only intuitively. Disembodied voices, music from unseen instruments, are commonplace. Continually beset with a dread of undefined evil, she experiences recurrently a paralysis of body and will before a danger imminent, yet concealed.

In these post-Freudian days, readers detect the realm of the subconscious emerging in Emily's nightmare world, not only in the repetitious, dreamlike patterns, but also in the very nature of her predicament—that of the pure, innocent "orphan child" whose physical attractions precipitate sword fights, subject her to would-be rapists who pursue her down the dark corridors, and render her helpless before the cold, cruel Montoni, whose so-called preposterous depravity holds for her the fascination of the abomination.

However, Mrs. Radcliffe is too much a part of the Age of Reason to permit irrationality to rule. Emily is preserved by her innate strength of sensibility from assaults on her person and her mind. In all her melancholy meditations, once her ordeal has ended, she is never required to wonder why Montoni appealed to her as he did when he was triumphant, bold, spirited, and commanding. Instead, her mind dismissing him as one who was insignificant, she settles down to a secure life with Valancourt, a candid and open-handed man. In her retirement to La Vallée, Emily may never be able to avoid counterparts of Madame Montoni, whose fashionable repartee recalls the comedy of manners in which Jane Austen was to excel, but she will be safe from such men as Montoni.

In the spirit of reason, the author also banishes the mystery of the supernatural happenings which provide so much suspense. Every inexplicable occurrence finally has its rational explanation. Mrs. Barbauld, herself a rationalist, complains with some justice about the protracted suspense and the high expectations which defuse Radcliffe's increment of horrors and nebulous challenges to the imagination. Nonetheless, when one has, like Henry Tilney, kept pace with this lengthy novel, the impression of Emily St. Aubert's nightmare world is more vivid than the skepticism of reason which explains away all the dark secrets. Ultimately, the vague shapings of the imagination triumph.

Bibliography

Allen, M.L. "The Black Veil: Three Versions of a Symbol," in *English Studies*. XLVII (1966), pp. 286–289.

Beaty, Frederick L. "Mrs. Radcliffe's Fading Gleam," in *Philological Quarterly*. XLII (January, 1963), pp. 126–129.

Christensen, Merton A. "Udolpho, Horrid Mysteries, and Coleridge's Machinery of the Imagination," in *Wordsworth Circle*. II (1971), pp. 153–159.

Grant, Aline. *Ann Radcliffe*. Denver: Swallow, 1951.

Kiely, Robert. *The Romantic Novel in England*. Cambridge, Mass.: Harvard University Press, 1972, pp. 65–80.

Kooiman-Van Middendorp, Gerarda. *The Hero in the Feminine Novel*. New York: Haskell, 1966, pp. 35–38.

McIntyre, Clara F. *Ann Radcliffe in Relation to Her Time*. New Haven, Conn.: Yale University Press, 1920.

Murray, E.B. *Ann Radcliffe*. New York: Twayne, 1972, pp. 112–134.

Scott, Sir Walter. "Ann Radcliffe," in *Sir Walter Scott on Novelists and Fiction*. Edited by Ioan Williams. New York: Barnes & Noble, 1968.

Shackford, Martha H. "*The Eve of St. Agnes* and *The Mysteries of Udolpho*," in *PMLA*. XXXVI (1921), pp. 104–118.

Smith, Nelson C.   "Sense, Sensibility and Ann Radcliffe," in *Studies in English Literature, 1500–1900.* XIII (1973), pp. 577–590.

Swigert, Ford H., Jr.   "Ann Radcliffe's Veil Imagery," in *Studies in the Humanities.* I (1969), pp. 55–59.

Sypher, Wylie.   "Social Ambiguity in a Gothic Novel," in *Partisan Review.* XII (1945), pp. 50–60.

CHARLES READE

Born: Oxfordshire, England (June 8, 1814)
Died: London, England (April 11, 1884)

Principal Works

NOVELS: *Peg Woffington*, 1853; *Christie Johnstone*, 1853; *It Is Never Too Late to Mend*, 1856; *The Cloister and the Hearth*, 1861; *Hard Cash*, 1863; *Griffith Gaunt*, 1866; *Foul Play*, 1868; *Put Yourself in His Place*, 1870; *A Terrible Temptation*, 1871; *A Woman Hater*, 1877.

PLAYS: *The Ladies' Battle*, 1851; *Angelo*, 1851; *A Village Tale*, 1852; *Masks and Faces*, 1852 (with Tom Taylor); *The Lost Husband*, 1852; *Gold*, 1853; *The Courier of Lyons*, 1854 (*The Lyons Mail*); *Peregrine Pickle*, 1854; *Drink*, 1879.

Charles Reade, born at Ipsden House, June 8, 1814, was the youngest in a family of eleven children born to a wealthy family of the landed gentry in Oxfordshire. Unlike his brothers, who were given the usual "public school" education, Charles Reade was educated at home by tutors. As a result of the private education he was faced with difficulties, personal and academic, when he entered Oxford. He had not learned to get along with people, nor had he acquired the academic knowledge he should have had. During his four years at Oxford, from 1832 to 1835, he received honors, apparently more by luck than ability and, in the case of a Vinerian Scholarship, by absolute chicanery. After leaving Oxford he went to London, studied law, and in 1843 was admitted to the bar, although he never actively practiced law. From 1837 to 1848 Reade, who was independently wealthy, spent his time in relative idleness. He traveled a great deal in Europe, adding to his collection of Cremona violins. Returning to London in 1849, he began to write plays. His first successful production was a comedy, *The Ladies' Battle*. Within two years five other plays were produced, and Reade made many friends among theatrical people, among them Laura Seymour, the famous actress, who was his friend and adviser until her death in 1879.

It was at the suggestion of Mrs. Seymour that Reade first turned to fiction. She suggested that he turn a play into a novel, and so *Masks and Faces* became the novel *Peg Woffington*. In 1856 Reade's first long novel was published, *It Is Never Too Late to Mend*. Following the publication of this novel, Reade turned his efforts almost exclusively to writing fiction rather than drama. His *White Lies* appeared in serial form in the *London Journal*, in 1856–1857. Serial publication was common at the time. His greatest novel, *The Cloister and the Hearth*, appeared in 1861. Part of that novel had been published earlier under the title "A Good Fight" in a periodical, *Once a Week*. The story had proved so popular that Reade decided to expand it into its eventual four-volume length.

Probably under the influence of Charles Dickens, who was Reade's friend, the author turned from writing historical romances to writing problem novels. Just how much influence Dickens had on this change is impossible to assess, but as the editor of *All the Year Round*, in which much of Reade's fiction appeared, the influence was probably great. After his change to problem novels, Reade wrote such volumes as *Hard Cash, Griffith Gaunt*, and *Foul Play*. During his career as a writer, Reade wrote more than twenty novels, and he wrote, too, almost as many plays. Of all his works, only *The Cloister and the Hearth* draws any wide group of readers today. His problem novels deal with problems that have long since been solved or alleviated, and so are uninteresting to modern-day readers. The plays are deemed by most scholars to be too stagy and melodramatic. None has found any acceptance on the stage for years, although Reade himself thought that his dramatic work was more important than his fiction, even to requesting that the title of dramatist be put first upon his tombstone. He never lost interest in the novel, however, and when he died in London, April 11, 1884, he left a completed novel, *A Perilous Secret* (1884), ready for publication.

Bibliography

The authorized biography is C. L. and Compton Reade, *Charles Reade, A Memoir*, 2 vols., 1887. A more recent study is Malcolm Elwin, *Charles Reade, A Biography*, 1934. See also A. C. Swinburne, *Miscellanies*, 1886; Walter C. Philips, *Dickens, Reade and Collins, Sensation Novelists*, 1919; A. M. Turner, *The Making of the Cloister and the Hearth*, 1938; and Wayne Burns, *Charles Reade: A Study in Victorian Authorship*, 1961.

THE CLOISTER AND THE HEARTH

Type of work: Novel
Author: Charles Reade (1814–1884)
Type of plot: Historical romance
Time of plot: Fifteenth century
Locale: Holland, Germany, France, and Italy
First published: 1861

Utilizing a variety of literary forms, including dramatic dialogue, the tale within a tale, poetry, extended letters, and picaresque romance, Reade produced a remarkably vivid, minutely detailed picture of fifteenth century life. His characterizations ring true in their vitality and humanness.

Principal Characters

Gerard Eliason, an artist. He goes to Rome, where he becomes a Dominican monk named Brother Clement. Believing his fiancée is dead, he returns to his homeland to find she is alive and has borne him a son. After becoming a parson at Gouda, he lives apart from Margaret, his beloved, but allows her to help him in his religious work.

Elias, Gerard's father, a Dutch cloth and leather merchant. He does not want his artist son to marry Margaret Brandt and has him imprisoned to prevent the suit. However, he is finally reconciled to her.

Katherine, Elias' wife. Like her husband, she does not want her son to marry Margaret.

Margaret Van Eyck, sister of the famous painter Jan. She is Gerard's teacher.

Reicht Heynes, Margaret Van Eyck's servant, who encourages Gerard as an artist.

Peter Brandt, an old man befriended by Gerard.

Margaret Brandt, Peter's daughter. She is betrothed to Gerard and bears him a son. When he returns to Holland as a monk she helps him in his religious work.

Gerard, son of Gerard and Margaret Brandt, who grows up to be Erasmus, the famous scholar.

Ghysbrecht Van Swieten, burgomaster of Gerard's village. He is an evil man who cheats his people and makes life difficult for Gerard and Margaret.

Giles, Gerard's dwarf brother, who helps Gerard escape from prison.

Kate, Gerard's crippled sister, who helps Gerard escape from prison.

Denys, a Burgundian soldier who befriends Gerard on his way to Italy. Denys is a worldly but loyal man. He finds Margaret Brandt and befriends her for Gerard's sake.

Martin, an old retired soldier who procures a pardon for Gerard after the young man's escape from prison.

Hans Memling, a messenger who takes false word to Gerard that Margaret has died.

Pietro, a young artist in Rome with whom Gerard works for a time.

Fra Colonna, a classical scholar for whom Gerard works in decorating manuscripts.

Luke Peterson, a suitor for Margaret Brandt's hand in marriage.

The Story

Gerard, the son of Elias, a Dutch cloth and leather merchant, and Katherine, his wife, developed at an early age his talent for penmanship and illuminating. At first he was aided by the monks of the local convent for which he was destined. When the monks could teach the young artist no more, he became the pupil of Margaret Van Eyck, sister of the famous painter, Jan Van Eyck. She and her servant, Reicht Heynes, encouraged the lad to enter a prize art competition sponsored by Philip the Good, Duke of Burgundy and Earl of Holland.

On his way to Rotterdam to an exhibit of the entries, Gerard met an old man, Peter Brandt, and his daughter, Margaret, who sat exhausted by the wayside. He went with them into the town. There he took to the Princess Marie, daughter of Prince Philip, a letter of introduction from Dame Van Eyck. Impressed by the lad's talent, the princess promised him a benefice near his village of Tergou as soon as he had taken holy orders. He won a prize in the contest and returned to Tergou wondering whether he would ever again see Margaret Brandt, with whom he had fallen in love.

Gerard, learning accidentally from Ghysbrecht Van Swieten, Tergou's burgomaster, that the old man and his daughter lived in Sevenbergen, a nearby village, began to frequent their cottage. Ghysbrecht disclosed to Katherine, Gerard's mother, that the young man was interested in Margaret Brandt. A quarrel ensued in the family, Elias threatening to have Gerard imprisoned to prevent his marrying. Margaret Van Eyck gave Gerard money and valuable advice on art and recommended that he and the girl go to Italy, where Gerard's talents were sure to be appreciated. Gerard and Margaret Brandt became betrothed, but before they could be married the burgomaster had Gerard seized and put in jail. He was rescued at night from the prison by Margaret, his sweetheart, Giles, his dwarf brother, and Kate, his crippled sister. In the rescue, Giles removed from a chest in the cell some parchments which the villainous Ghysbrecht had hidden there. At Sevenbergen, Gerard buried all of the parchments except a deed which concerned Margaret's father.

After an exciting pursuit, Gerard and Margaret escaped the vicinity of Tergou. They separated, Margaret to return to Sevenbergen, Gerard to proceed to Rome. On the way, he was befriended by a Burgundian soldier named Denys, and the pair traveled toward the Rhine. They went through a variety of adventures together.

In Sevenbergen, meanwhile, Margaret Brandt fell sick and was befriended by Margaret Van Eyck. Martin, an old soldier friend of the young lovers, went to Rotterdam where he procured a pardon for Gerard from Prince Philip. Dame Van Eyck gave a letter to Hans Memling to deliver to Gerard in Italy, but Memling was waylaid by agents of the burgomaster and the letter was taken from him.

Gerard and Denys came upon a company of Burgundian soldiers on their way to the wars and Denys was ordered to ride with them to Flanders. Gerard was left to make his solitary way to Rome. Later Denys, released because of wounds received in the duke's service, set out for Holland, where he hoped to find Gerard. Elias and Katherine welcomed him in Tergou when he told them that he had been Gerard's comrade. Meanwhile old Brandt and Margaret disappeared from Sevenbergen, and Denys searched all Holland for the girl. They had gone to Rotterdam, but only the burgomaster knew their whereabouts. When Margaret practiced medicine illegally, she was arrested and sentenced to pay a large fine. In order to stay alive she took in laundry. Denys discovered Margaret in Rotterdam and the pair returned to Tergou, where Gerard's family had become reconciled to Gerard's attachment to the girl.

Gerard made his dangerous way through France and Germany to Venice. From there he took a coastal vessel and continued to Rome. When the ship was wrecked in a storm, Gerard displayed bravery in saving the lives of a Roman matron and her child. He went on to Rome and took lodgings, but he found work all but impossible to obtain. He and another young artist, Pietro, decorated playing cards for a living. Finally through the good graces of the woman whose life he had saved in the shipwreck, Gerard was hired to decorate manuscripts for Fra Colonna, a leading classical scholar.

Hans Memling brought to Rome a letter, sent by Ghysbrecht, which gave Gerard the false news that Margaret had died. Gerard forsook the Church and in despair threw himself into the Tiber. But he was saved and carried to a monastery, where he recovered and eventually took monastic vows. He became Brother Clement of the Dominican Order. After a period of training he was sent to teach at the University of Basle, in Switzerland. Meanwhile, in Holland, Margaret gave birth to Gerard's son.

Brother Clement received orders to proceed to England. Preaching as he went, he began the journey down the Rhine.

In Rotterdam, Luke Peterson became Margaret's suitor. She told him he could prove his love for her by seeking out Gerard, but Luke's and Brother Clement's paths were fated not to cross. The priest went to Sevenbergen, where he was unable to find the grave of Margaret. He proceeded to Rotterdam, and there Margaret heard him preach without recognizing him as Gerard. He next went to Tergou to see Ghysbrecht. The burgomaster was dying; he confessed to Brother Clement that he had defrauded Margaret of wealth rightfully hers. On his deathbed Ghysbrecht made full restitution.

When Brother Clement left the burgomaster, he returned to Rotterdam and took refuge in a hermit's cave outside the city. There he mortified himself out of hatred for mankind.

Margaret, having learned his whereabouts through court gossip, went to him, but he repulsed her in the belief that she was a spirit sent by Satan. Margaret took her son to the cave in an attempt to win back his reason. Brother Clement's acquaintance with his son, also named Gerard, brought him to his senses. Margaret by shrewd argument persuaded him to come with her to Gouda, where he would be parson by arrangement with church authorities. They lived in Gouda, but apart, Gerard tending his flock and Margaret assisting him in his many charitable works.

After ten years at Gouda, Margaret died of the plague. Gerard, no longer anxious to live after her death, died two weeks later. Their son, Gerard, grew up to be Erasmus, the world-famous sixteenth century Biblical scholar and man of letters.

Critical Evaluation

The Cloister and the Hearth is essentially a picaresque novel, rich with incident and vividly drawn characters, if not always profound or thoughtful. The accurate detail is never boring and a good-natured humor pervades the narrative. Despite its great length, the novel moves briskly, maintaining the reader's interest constantly. The scenes at the Burgundian Inn, for example, describing the gory battle between Gerard and Denys and the gang of thieves, are among the most thrilling in English fiction, and are worthy of the senior Dumas or Balzac.

Denys, the Burgundian bowman and "Pilgrim of Friendship," bursts with vitality and every page on which he strides and boasts is filled with life. Katherine, Gerard's mother, is another excellent characterization: lively, witty, and sensible. She begins as a type, but soon transcends type to become a sympathetic, clever, and delightfully amusing individual. One suspects that Reade was, himself, fond of her. The spinster Margaret Van Eyck emerges as a vivid personality, an intelligent, liberated female in an age when women were required to be both married and docile.

Reade kept voluminous files of clippings and notebooks in which were recorded all manner of information which interested him; in writing his novels, he made use of this material. A novel, he believed, must be based on "facts." His method brought to his books artistic truth in the handling of detail, setting, and episodes. He saturated himself in medieval history, art, and social customs and manners to write *The Cloister and the Hearth*. By absorbing himself in the literature and history of the period, Reade produced in this novel a picture of a remote era so faithfully and so finely etched, and so vividly realistic, that it never has been surpassed and rarely approached.

Charles Reade caught in *The Cloister and the Hearth* much of the tone of light and dark that dominated the end of the Middle Ages and the beginnings of the Renaissance; it was a brutal and turbulent time, stiff and heavy with death. The Dukes of Burgundy, with their ostentation, violence, and half-mad pride, were perhaps its representative rulers. At times the novel, crowded with wandering, lost individuals, becomes a *danse macabre,* a picture of rapidly growing cities, violence, wild superstition, crumbling religion, cynical realism, and ever-lusty humor. Reade's style is sometimes nervous and irritating, but it is always vigorous and compelling, and never fake or gushing like that of so many of his contemporaries. His perspective on the period of the novel is acute and perceptive, and his panorama crowded and colorful, yet never confusing.

Born in 1814 in Oxfordshire, the son of a country squire, Reade took his B.A. at Magdalen College, Oxford, and became a fellow of the college. He kept his fellowship at Magdalen all of his life, but spent the greater part of his time in London where he began his career as a dramatist. On the advice of the actress Laura Seymour, who later became his housekeeper and mistress, he transformed one of his plays into a novel. Several other novels followed in quick succession. The flaws of his fiction, a certain theatricality and occasional falseness of tone, can be attributed to the sensational theater pieces of the day and their influence upon him.

The Cloister and the Hearth was originally published serially as a long story titled "A Good Fight" in the magazine *Once a Week,* but was expanded to more than five times its length before it was published in four volumes. The novel, published (at the author's expense) on commission, provided Reade with his first real financial success. He was forty-eight.

Returning from the fifteenth century to modern English life, Reade produced another well-received novel, *Hard Cash,* in which he directed attention to the abuses of private lunatic asylums. Three other novels "with a purpose" followed, in which he grappled with trade unions, the degrading conditions of village life, and other problems. The Reade of later years, who had earned the admiration of such different artists as Dickens and Swinburne, was accused of wasting his talents in pursuit of social reforms.

Reade's greatest success as a dramatist was his last, *Drink,* an adaptation of Zola's *L'Assommoir,* produced in 1879. In that year, Laura Seymour died, and soon Reade's health failed. He died in 1884, leaving behind him a completed novel, *A Perilous Secret,* which showed no falling off in his abilities to weave a complicated plot and devise thrilling situations.

The epic theme of *The Cloister and the Hearth* is the misery caused by the vow of celibacy demanded of its priests by the Roman Church. The situation of Margaret, who loves and is beloved by Gerard, is the mother of his child, and yet is denied the privilege of being his wife because he is a priest, is described with excruciating pathos. Reade's own study of medicine led to the minor theme and indictment of the practice of bleeding patients that is so vividly presented in the novel. The growth of the arts during the first days of the Renaissance provides a continuing theme which reaches its peak of interest in the chapters in Italy.

The imaginative power of the narration is shown in many vivid scenes (for example, the frail wooden ship battling the storm off the Italian coast), yet the author's imagination seems to fail with the minor characters, who tend to be reduced to clichés of good and evil. This over-simplification of character is the one serious flaw in the novel, but it does not detract from the power and sweep of the story and the impact of the conclusion, when the reader learns that from these two troubled lives (Gerard and Margaret) will come the greatest humanist and writer of the period.

Bibliography

Baker, Ernest. *The History of the English Novel*, Volume VIII. New York: Barnes & Noble, 1950, pp. 206–207.

Burns, Wayne. *Charles Reade: A Study in Victorian Authorship.* New York: Bookman Associates, 1961, pp. 309–321.

Dawson, W.J. "Charles Reade," in his *Makers of English Fiction*. New York: Fleming H. Revell, 1905, pp. 164–178.

Elwin, Malcolm. *Charles Reade*. London: Jonathan Cape, 1931, pp. 150–159.

Fleishman, Avrom. *The English Historical Novel: Walter Scott to Virginia Woolf.* Baltimore: Johns Hopkins University Press, 1971, pp. 152–155.

Hornung, E.W. "Charles Reade," in *London Mercury*. VI (1921), p. 150.

Lord, Walter Frewen. "Charles Reade," in his *The Mirror of the Century*. London: John Lane, 1906, pp. 252–268.

Quiller-Couch, Arthur T. "Charles Reade," in his *Studies in Literature*. Cambridge: Cambridge University Press, 1918, pp. 274–289.

Smith, Elton E. *Charles Reade*. New York: Twayne, 1976, pp. 135–151.

Sutcliffe, Emerson Grant. "Plotting in Reade's Novels," in *PMLA*. XLVII (September, 1932), pp. 834–863.

Swinburne, Algernon Charles. "Charles Reade," in *Miscellanies*. New York: Worthington, 1886, pp. 271–302.

Turner, Albert Morton. *The Making of* The Cloister and the Hearth. Chicago: University of Chicago Press, 1938.

Wagenknecht, Edward C. "The Disciples of Dickens," in his *Cavalcade of the English Novel, from Elizabeth to George VI*. New York: Holt, 1954, pp. 243–251.

SAMUEL RICHARDSON

Born: Derbyshire, England (1689)
Died: London, England (July 4, 1761)

Principal Works

NOVELS: *Pamela, or Virtue Rewarded*, 1740; *Clarissa, or The History of a Young Lady*, 1747–1748; *Sir Charles Grandison*, 1753–1754.
LETTERS: *The Correspondence of Samuel Richardson*, 1804.

About Samuel Richardson's life and personality there seems to be a great deal of information, most of it uninteresting. He was born in 1689, the son of a Derbyshire joiner and a pious but nowise unusual mother. As a boy, his thoughtful and serious nature would have recommended him for the Church, but his parents could not afford the requisite education. Instead, after moderate schooling, he was apprenticed to a London printer, John Wilde. He proved a conscientious worker for a demanding master, and in due time reaped his reward by marrying his employer's daughter and succeeding to the business. By dint of hard work and honesty his became one of the most prosperous and sought-after publishing concerns in London.

There is no evidence that Richardson had any youthful ambitions to be a writer; he was over fifty, and a successful businessman, when he stumbled, quite by accident, into his role as "father" of the English novel. From youth to old age, Richardson was unusually fond of what he characteristically called "epistolary correspondence." As a boy in Derbyshire he had been commissioned by various young ladies to compose or embellish their love letters, and in the process he had gained considerable insight into feminine emotional life and had developed an imagination that took pleasure in creating in detail fantasies concerned with the distresses of love. Later, as an apprentice, he carried on a long correspondence, often on moral subjects, with a man he describes as being a "master of the epistolary style." With this background in letter-writing, it was not unusual that two bookseller friends should suggest that he turn his talents to account by publishing a volume of model letters of various sorts. Richardson took up the idea, but characteristically amended it by proposing that the letters should teach not only how to write but also "how to think and act justly and prudently in the common concerns of human life."

The book, entitled *Familiar Letters*, appeared in 1741, but in the meantime Richardson, while writing a connected group of letters "to instruct handsome young girls, who were obliged to go out to service, . . . how to avoid the snares that might be laid against their virtue," remembered an appropriate story told him some twenty-five years before, and *Pamela*, published in 1740, was born. Perhaps the best concise description of this milestone in the development of the novel is given by Richardson himself on the title page: *Pamela: or Virtue Rewarded. In a Series of Familiar Letters from a beautiful Young Damsel, to her Parents. Now first published in order to cultivate the Principles of Virtue and Religion in the Minds of the Youth of both Sexes. A Narrative which has its Foundation in Truth and Nature; and at the same time that it agreeably entertains, by a Variety of curious and affecting Incidents, is entirely divested of all those Images, which, in too many Pieces calculated for Amusement only, tend to inflame the Minds they should instruct.* The book was not only an immediate and unparalleled success—with the average reader for its detailed descriptions of situations and emotions that at times approach the salacious, with the pious for its moral rectitude—but by adding to the realism of Defoe a power of minute mental analysis which Defoe did not possess, it set a new fashion in fiction, the novel of sensibility.

For all its success, and its importance as both one of the first epistolary novels and the prototype of the novel of sentimental analysis, *Pamela* is not without its faults. Although Richardson makes dramatic use of the letter-writing technique, the device demands an annoying degree of almost priggish self-righteousness on the part of the heroine. Further, the morality of the "lesson" taught is not above suspicion. Pamela defends her virtue valiantly, but not without an eye to the main chance, and in the end is rewarded handsomely by an offer of marriage from her master and would-be seducer.

Richardson's next novel, *Clarissa, or The History of a Young Lady*, avoids both these weaknesses. The story, which tells of the "Distresses that may attend the Misconduct both of Parents and Children in Relation to Marriage," is a truly tragic one. Not only is the characterization in this novel superbly handled, and always believable, but the central dilemma is more genuinely a moral one than in *Pamela*; the problem is not whether Clarissa will be seduced, but whether she can forgive her seducer. But the heroine is no pale, self-righteous prude. Indeed, in this novel Richardson rises to the heighth of his powers as a novelist, both in his ability to present moving and convincing situations and in his power to describe minutely human emotions at times of extreme stress.

Richardson's last novel, *Sir Charles Grandison*, is an attempt to depict a model good man and fine gentleman combined. Like the others, it is in epistolary form; and although the characterization and analysis of emotions are still excellent, it lacks the intense central dilemma that holds the attention in the first two books, and tends to make tedious reading.

After *Sir Charles Grandison* Richardson wrote little more of any importance. He continued to prosper in business, grew rich, was elected Master of the Stationers' Company, was employed to print the journals of the House of Commons, and was eventually appointed Law Printer to the king. Full of years and honors, he died in Parson's Green, London, on July 4, 1761.

Colorless as Richardson was personally, and pedestrian and prolix as his style often became, his importance in the history of the novel should not be underestimated. His books have an extraordinary power which at first attracts and in time holds the reader, and his ability to describe and his insight into the workings of the female heart are unusual. Although English fiction which came after him followed slightly different lines, it is impossible to deny Richardson the credit for inaugurating the novel of sensibility, which for a time became the fashion even more on the Continent than in England.

Bibliography

There are two modern editions of Richardson's novels, that edited by Ethel M. M. McKenna, 20 vols., 1902, and the Blackwell Edition, 19 vols., 1930. The basic source for all biographical studies is *The Correspondence of Samuel Richardson*, edited by Anna L. Barbauld, 6 vols., 1804. The definitive biography is now T. C. D. Eaves and B. I. Kimpel, *Samuel Richardson*, 1971. See also Alan D. McKillop, *Samuel Richardson, Printer and Novelist*, 1936; Clara L. Thomson, *Samuel Richardson*, 1900; Austin Dobson, *Samuel Richardson*, 1902; Brian W. Downs, *Richardson*, 1928; Paul Dottin, *Samuel Richardson, imprimeur de Londres*, 1931; and William M. Sale, Jr., *Samuel Richardson, Master Printer*, 1950. Two companion books to Richardson studies are W. M. Sale, *Samuel Richardson: A Bibliographical Record of His Literary Career*, 1936; and Francesco Cordasco, *Samuel Richardson: A List of Critical Studies Published from 1896 to 1946*, 1948. Recent studies are Ira Konigsberg, *Samuel Richardson and the Dramatic Novel*, 1968; and John Carroll, ed., *Samuel Richardson: A Collection of Critical Essays*, 1969.

CLARISSA

Type of work: Novel
Author: Samuel Richardson (1689–1761)
Type of plot: Sentimental romance
Time of plot: Early eighteenth century
Locale: England
First published: 1747–1748

This epistolary novel, Richardson's masterpiece, is the longest novel in the language. The story of Clarissa Harlowe is told with subtlety and psychological depth, as we watch Robert Lovelace become obsessed with breaking down the heroine's virtue, simply because she is apparently incorruptible. He finally drugs and rapes her, causing her to flee to a secret dwelling, where she dies of shame.

Principal Characters

Mr. Harlowe, a domineering man who cannot understand how his children can disobey him. He arranges a loveless marriage for his daughter Clarissa. When she refuses to obey his commands, he locks her in her room with only an insolent servant allowed to see her. After her elopement with Robert Lovelace, another suitor, her father disowns her and will not let her have clothes or money. Not until she is dying does he lift his ban and seek a reconciliation.

Clarissa Harlowe, his young and beautiful daughter, who accepts Lovelace's attentions as a way of escaping from her father's demands. Thinking that he is taking her to the home of Lord M—, his kinsman, she flees with Lovelace, only to be put into a house of ill repute where, for fear of being tracked down by her father, she claims to be Lovelace's wife. Once she escapes, only to be dragged back, drugged, and raped. Escaping again, she is caught and jailed for debt. She is freed but goes into a physical decline and buys her casket, inscribed with her death date, the day she left the Harlowe home. Though the repentant Lovelace now wants to marry her, she refuses him. Despite letters from her contrite family—for the whole novel is told in letters—she dies, to the grief and remorse of all.

Arabella, the older Harlowe daughter. She hates Clarissa for attracting her own suitor, Robert Lovelace.

James Harlowe, Clarissa's older brother, selfish and domineering, like his father. Having known and disliked Lovelace at Oxford University, he starts rumors that Lovelace is a profligate. He is also jealous of Clarissa because she is the heiress of their wealthy grandfather.

Robert Lovelace, a young Englishman of noble family. Brought by an uncle to the Harlowe home as suitor of Arabella, he falls in love with Clarissa. Because of his choice he is spurned by the whole family. In revenge for their insults, he determines to seduce Clarissa and gets her to run away with him under promises of marriage, only to break his word. Finally, when he discovers he really loves her, he vainly offers her marriage. After her death he goes to France, where he fights a duel by Clarissa's cousin, Colonel Morden, and is killed. He dies repentant of his crimes.

John Belford, a friend of Lovelace, who frees Clarissa from jail by proving that the charges of debt against her are false. He receives from Lovelace letters that narrate the course of his courtship and his perfidy.

Roger Solmes, a rich, elderly, but uncouth man chosen as Clarissa's husband by her father. When Clarissa writes him, begging him to end their relationship, he refuses.

Mrs. Sinclair, the keeper of the London bawdy house where Clarissa is kept prisoner.

Colonel William Morden, Clarissa's cousin, who tries first to reconcile Clarissa and her family and then to persuade her to marry Lovelace. He finally avenges her death when he kills Lovelace in a duel fought in France.

Miss Anna Howe, the friend and confidante of Clarissa; through their interchange of letters most of the story is told.

Aunt Hervey, who wants Lovelace to marry Arabella.

Uncle Harlowe, who brings Lovelace to the house.

Mr. Mennell, who manages the affairs of Mrs. Fretchville and wants to rent her apartment to Clarissa.

Hannah, Clarissa's faithful servant.

Mr. Diggs, the surgeon who looks after James Harlowe's wound after he and Lovelace duel.

Elizabeth Lawrence, Lovelace's aunt, who wants to meet his "wife."

Charlotte Montague, a cousin of Lovelace.

Dorcas Martindale, who tries to help Clarissa escape.

F. J. de la Tour, who writes the final letter describing the duel and death of the Chevalier Lovelace.

The Story

Robert Lovelace, a young Englishman of a noble family, was introduced into the Harlowe household by Clarissa's uncle, who wished Lovelace to marry Clarissa's older sister, Arabella. The young man, finding nothing admirable in the older girl, fell deeply in love with Clarissa, but he quickly learned that his suit was balked by Clarissa's brother and sister. James Harlowe had disliked Lovelace since they had been together at Oxford, and Arabella was offended because he had spurned her in favor of Clarissa. Both were jealous of Clarissa because she had been left a fortune by their grandfather and they had not.

James Harlowe, having convinced his mother and father that Lovelace was a profligate, proposed that Clarissa be married to Mr. Solmes, a rich, elderly man of little taste and no sensibility. When Solmes found no favor in the eyes of Clarissa, her family assumed she was in love with Lovelace, despite her protestations to the contrary.

Clarissa refused to allow Solmes to visit with her in her parlor or to sit next to her when the family was together. Her father, outraged by her conduct, ordered her to be more civil to the man he had chosen as her husband. When she refused, saying she would never marry a man against her will, not even Lovelace, her father confined her to her room.

Lovelace, smitten with the girl's beauty and character, resolved to seduce her away from her family, partly out of love for her and partly in vengeance for the insults heaped upon him by the Harlowe family.

He was greatly aided in his scheme by the domineering personalities of Mr. Harlowe and his son. They took away Clarissa's trusted maid and replaced her with a girl who was impertinent and insolent to the young woman. They refused to let her see any member of the family, even her mother. Clarissa's only adviser whom she could trust was Miss Howe, a friend and correspondent who advised her to escape the house if she could, even if it meant accepting Lovelace's aid and his proposal of marriage.

One evening Lovelace slipped into the garden where Clarissa was walking and entreated her to elope with him. Thinking only to escape her domineering father, she went with him after some protest. Lovelace told her she would be taken to the home of Lord M—, a kinsman of Lovelace, who would protect her until her cousin, Colonel Morden, could return to England and arrange for a reconciliation between Clarissa and her family. Lovelace was not as good as his word, however, for he took her to a house of ill repute, where he introduced her to a woman he called Mrs. Sinclair. Inventing reasons why he could not take her to Lord M—'s house, he persuaded the bewildered girl to pass as his wife, for the time being, and he told Mrs. Sinclair that Clarissa was his wife with whom he could not live until certain marriage settlements had been arranged. Clarissa permitted him to tell the lie, in the belief that it would prevent her father and her brother from discovering her whereabouts.

In Mrs. Sinclair's house she was almost as much a prisoner as she had been in her father's home. Meanwhile her family had disowned her and refused to send her either money or clothes. Indeed, her father declared she was no longer his daughter and he hoped she would have a miserable existence in both this world and the next.

This state of affairs was distressing to Clarissa, who was now dependent upon Lovelace for her very existence. He took adventage of the circumstances to press his love upon her without mentioning his earlier promises of marriage. Clarissa tried to escape and got as far as Hampstead before Lovelace overtook her. There he had two women impersonate his cousins to convince Clarissa that she should return to her lodgings with them. Upon her return to Mrs. Sinclair's house, they filled her with drugs and later Lovelace raped her. A few days later Clarissa received from Miss Howe a letter in which she learned that she was in a house in which no woman of her station would be seen. Again Clarissa tried to escape, this time by calling for aid from a window. Lovelace finally promised to leave her unmolested until she could get aid from her cousin or from Miss Howe.

Lovelace left London for a few days to visit Lord M—, who was ill. While he was gone, Clarissa contrived to steal the clothes of a serving-girl and escape from the house, but within a day or two Mrs. Sinclair discovered Clarissa's where-abouts and had her arrested and imprisoned for debt. When John Belford, a friend of Lovelace, heard of the girl's plight, he rescued her by proving the debt a fraud. He found shelter for Clarissa with a kindly glove-maker and his wife. Tired of her miserable existence, Clarissa began to go into physical decline, in spite of all that the apothecary and doctor secured by John Belford could do for her.

She spent her time writing letters in an effort to secure a reconciliation with her family and to acquaint her friends with the true story of her plight. She refused to have anything to do with Lovelace, who was by that time convinced that he loved her dearly. He wished to marry her, to make amends for the treatment she had suffered at his hands, but she refused his offer with gentle firmness.

As she declined in health, Clarissa's friends did what they could to have her family forgive her. When her father and brother refused to receive her, she went to an undertaking establishment and bought a coffin which she had fitted as she wished, including a plaque which gave the date of her death as the day on which she left her father's house.

On his return to England Colonel Morden tried to raise her spirits, but his efforts failed because he, too, was unable to effect any change in the attitude of the Harlowe family. He also had an interview with Lovelace and Lord M—. The nobleman and Lovelace assured him that their family thought very highly of Clarissa and wished her to marry Lovelace and that Lovelace wanted to marry her. But even her cousin was unable to persuade Clarissa to accept Lovelace as a husband.

Everyone, including the Harlowe family, saw that Clarissa was determined to die. Her father and brother lifted their ban upon her ever entering the Hawlowe house; her sister was sorry she had been cruel to Clarissa; and the mother was convinced that she had failed in her duty toward her daughter. They all wrote to Clarissa, begging the girl's forgiveness and expressing their hope she would recover quickly and be reunited with her family. Their letters, however, arrived too late, for Clarissa had breathed her last.

Clarissa was returned to her father's house for her funeral. She was interred in the family vault at the feet of the grandfather whose fortune had been one of the sources of her troubles. Lovelace, who was quite broken up at her death, was persuaded by Lord M— to go to the continent.

There Clarissa was avenged. Lovelace met Colonel Morden in France, and early one winter morning Clarissa's cousin fought a duel with her betrayer. Lovelace was mortally wounded by a thrust through his body. As he lay dying, he expressed the hope that his death would expiate his crimes.

Critical Evaluation

Few men would have seemed less likely than Samuel Richardson to be influential in the history of the novel. A successful printer, he did not publish his first work until after he was fifty. Because of a reputation as an accomplished letter writer, he was encouraged to write a book of sample letters. Even before the publication of this volume, *Familiar Letters* (1741), he turned his epistolary talent to didactic purposes in fiction with the publication of *Pamela* (1740). Predictably, *Pamela* was greeted with popular approval and critical disdain. By 1744, he had prepared a summary of his epistolary masterpiece, *Clarissa*. The massive novel was published in three installments between December, 1747, and December, 1748, and was subsequently printed in eight volumes. Richardson was aware of length (about one million words) as a serious failing in his narrative and, indeed, *Clarissa* is now rarely read except in George Sherburn's abridgement. The length was probably less an impediment for the more leisurely reading class of the mid-eighteenth century.

Richardson's main literary contribution is his mastery of the epistolary style. The use of letters as a means of narration has obvious drawbacks. Certainly the flow of the narrative is repeatedly interrupted and it takes all of the strength of one's will to suspend disbelief concerning the writing of thoughtful and informative letters by characters during periods of extra-ordinary stress. Conventions aside, it is difficult in this form, to sustain a continuous and progressive narrative. The method frustrated Samuel Johnson, a friend of Richardson, who concluded that one should read the work for its sentiment. Richardson himself worried that his narrative technique had let his characters do too much in too short a period of time.

Richardson did, however, capitalize on the correlative advantages of the epistolary method. The immediacy of "writing to the moment" is a prime means of developing concerned attention in the reader. In addition, Richardson's talent for dialogue transforms many of the lengthier letters into poignant scenes and the text of each letter is most decorously cast in a style appropriate to the correspondent. Moreover, there is the advantage, especially for a didactic novel, of the multiple points of view which add complexity and sympathy to the interpretation of the action. As Alan McKillop says, letters are not simply presented but "copied, sent, received, shown about, discussed, answered, even perhaps hidden, intercepted, stolen, altered or forged." The whole process of correspondence comes alive as Richardson blends theater, moral discourse, courtesy book, and romance into a compellingly tense analysis of contemporary morals and manners.

As the use of the epistolary style would suggest, action is less important to Richardson's fiction than reflection on the moral significance of actions. It may be that the author was familiar with the life of the gentry only through the theater. Nevertheless, despite an apparent ignorance of the frequent occupations of a rich country family, the focus is so much on the tenseness of the situations and the meaning of actions that little is lost by the absence of sociological verisimilitude. Although Richardson occasionally presents drama-tically vivid details, he usually is less interested in setting than in what Sher-burn calls, in the contemporary eighteenth century terminology, a "distress."

The main theme of the novel, as described by Richardson on the title page, is "the distresses that may attend the misconduct both of parents and children in relation to marriage." There is no doubt that the motives of the Harlowes are crassly materialistic—to improve the already comfortable family fortune by forcing Clarissa to marry the suitable, but elderly, Solmes. There is a lack of tenderness and family feeling towards Clarissa, which softens only after it is too late and she is well along in her final decline. Clarissa, for her part, is also strong-willed. As Richardson explains about his fiction, "The principal of the two young Ladies is proposed as an exemplar of her Sex. Nor is it any objection to her being so, that she is not in all respects a perfect character." This from an author especially fond of the companionship and adulation of ladies.

At first Clarissa is attracted by the roguish but fascinating Lovelace. In fact, he occasionally seems not all a bad fellow. At least he is the most vivid character in the novel. Yet his egocentrism and his attraction to intrigue, however appealing, are inconsiderate of others and are not recanted until his sentimental dying breaths. His assaults on Clarissa seem almost an agression on her sex. Still, after the deed is done, practicality seems to demand that Clarissa turn virtue into its own reward, as Pamela had done, by marrying her seducer. However, *Clarissa* is a more complex novel than *Pamela* and Clarissa and Lovelace have already shown a moral incompatibility which makes acquiescence by Clarissa impossible (despite the impassioned pleadings of Richardson's sentimental readers before the last third of the novel appeared.)

At the heart of the incompatibility is Clarissa's admirable, but rigid, idealism. Although a gentle person, she is unreserved in her commitment to virtue and, as Sherburn puts it, to decorous behavior. She is not so much a puritan as a devotee of what is morally fit, and she carries her commitment to the grave. When her friend Miss Howe suggests that she take the expedient way out by marrying the ostensibly repentant Lovelace, Clarissa cannot give in. First, she would prefer reconciliation with her intransigent family, but second, and more important, her sense of propriety would not allow such moral and personal compromise. Nevertheless, it must be admitted that she is less interesting for her idealism than for the distressing situations and dilemmas her idealism occasions.

Despite its narrative improbabilities and the moral obstinacy of its main character, *Clarissa* became a revered example not only of the epistolary novel but also of the refined novel of sentiment and, by the end of the century, it had been imitated and acclaimed both in England and on the Continent.

Bibliography

Baker, Gerard A. "The Complacent Paragon; Exemplary Characterization in Richardson," in *Studies in English Literature, 1500–1900.* IX (Summer, 1969), pp. 503–519.

Brissenden, R.F. *Virtue in Distress: Studies in the Novel of Sentiment from*

Richardson to Sade. New York: Barnes & Noble, 1974, pp. 159–186.

Browstein, Rachel M. " 'An Exemplar to Her Sex': Richardson's *Clarissa,*" in *Yale Review.* LXVII (Autumn, 1977), pp. 30–47.

Carroll, John. "Lovelace as Tragic Hero," in *University of Toronto Quarterly.* XLII (1972), pp. 14–25.

Cohan, Steven M. "*Clarissa* and the Individuation of Character," in *Journal of English Literary History.* XLIII (1976), pp. 163–183.

Copeland, Edward W. "Allegory and Analogy in *Clarissa*: The 'Plan' and 'No-Plan,' " in *Journal of English Literary History.* XXXIX (1972), pp. 254–265.

Drew, E.A. "Samuel Richardson: *Clarissa,*" in *The Novel: A Modern Guide to Fifteen English Masterpieces.* New York: Dell, 1963, pp. 39–58.

Dussinger, John A. "Conscience and the Pattern of Christian Perfection in *Clarissa,*" in *PMLA.* LXXXI (1966), pp. 236–245.

Farrell, William J. "The Style and the Action in *Clarissa,*" in *Studies in English Literature, 1500–1900.* III (1963), pp. 365–375.

Golden, Morris. *Richardson's Characters.* Ann Arbor: University of Michigan Press, 1963.

Harvey, A.D. "*Clarissa* and the Puritan Tradition," in *Essays in Criticism.* XXVIII (January, 1978), pp. 38–51.

Kaplan, F. "Our Short Story; the Narrative Devices of *Clarissa,*" in *Studies in English Literature, 1500–1900.* XI (Summer, 1971), pp. 549–562.

Kinkead-Weekes, Mark. *Samuel Richardson: Dramatic Novelist.* Ithaca, N.Y.: Cornell University Press, 1973, pp. 123–276, 404–411, 433–447.

Konigsberg, Ira. *Samuel Richardson and the Dramatic Novel.* Lexington: University of Kentucky Press, 1968, pp. 28–29, 33–34, 64–65, 74–94.

————. "The Tragedy of *Clarissa,*" in *Modern Language Quarterly.* XXVII (1966), pp. 285–298.

McCullough, Bruce. "The Novel of Sentiment; Samuel Richardson: *Clarissa,*" in *Representative English Novelists: Defoe to Conrad.* New York: Harper, 1946, pp. 23–41.

Napier, Elizabeth R. " 'Tremble and Reform': The Inversion of Power in Richardson's *Clarissa,*" in *Journal of English Literary History.* XLII (1975), pp. 214–223.

Palmer, William J. "Two Dramatists: Lovelace and Richardson in *Clarissa,*" in *Studies in the Novel.* V (1973), pp. 7–21.

Park, William. "*Clarissa* as Tragedy," in *Studies in English Literature, 1500–1900.* XVI (1976), pp. 461–471.

Price, Martin. "Clarissa and Lovelace," in *To the Palace of Wisdom.* Garden

City, N.Y.: Doubleday, 1964.

Sacks, Sheldon. "*Clarissa* and the Tragic Traditions," in *Studies in Eighteenth-Century Culture: Proceedings of the American Society for Eighteenth-Century Studies*. Volume II. Edited by Harold E. Pagliaro. Cleveland, Oh.: Case Western Reserve University Press, 1972, pp. 195–221.

Schmitz, Robert M. "Death and Colonel Morden in *Clarissa*," in *South Atlantic Quarterly*. LXIX (1970), pp. 346–353.

Sherbo, Arthur. "Time and Place in Richardson's *Clarissa*," in *Boston University Studies in English*. III (1957), pp. 139–146.

Smidt, Kristian. "Character and Plot in the Novels of Samuel Richardson," in *Critical Quarterly*. XVII (1975), pp. 155–166.

Winner, Anthony. "Richardson's Lovelace: Character and Prediction," in *Texas Studies in Literature and Language*. XIV (1972), pp. 53–75.

PAMELA

Type of work: Novel
Author: Samuel Richardson (1689–1761)
Type of plot: Sentimental romance
Time of plot: Early eighteenth century
Locale: England
First published: 1740–1741

    Generally considered the first modern English novel, Pamela, or, Virtue Rewarded, *fotlows the adventures of a young servant girl, forced by poverty to work in a nobleman's house, through her letters to her parents. The epistolary form allows for much introspection on Pamela's part, and her letters read more like private diary entries. Intended by Richardson to be taken as models of behavior for virtuous lower-class girls, the letters are divided into two sections: the first set,* Aggressive Chastity, *relates Pamela's harrowing experiences in defending her chastity against Mr. B—'s advances; the second,* Provocative Prudence, *depicts Pamela's life as the new wife of reformed Mr. B—, which position she has attained as the reward for her virtue.*

Principal Characters

Pamela Andrews, a virtuous servant girl of Lady B——, mistress of an estate in Bedfordshire. After the death of her mistress she intends to return home but is persuaded to stay by the son, Mr. B——, who promises to be a good master to her. Later she has cause to suspect his intentions, and after he makes a series of attempts on her virtue she determines to leave. The coach, however, deposits her at Mr. B——'s country estate, where she is held prisoner. She meets the local minister, Mr. Williams. She tries several times to escape. Finally Mr. B——, moved by her virtue, offers her an honorable marriage, and she accepts his proposal. Despite anonymous letters and suspicions of other love affairs, she remains faithful and eventually turns Mr. B—— into an honorable husband.

John and
Elizabeth Andrews, the parents of Pamela.

Mr. B——, the young squire who plots against Pamela's virtue, tries to seduce her, proposes to make her his mistress on carefully outlined terms, and then finally marries her.

Lady Davers, the daughter of Lady B——, who at first opposes her brother's marriage to a servant. She begins to sympathize with Pamela after reading the many letters the girl had written her parents, and she is finally won over completely by Pamela's beauty and virtue.

Mrs. Jervis, Mr. B——'s kind-hearted housekeeper. For a time she protects Pamela's honor. When Mr. B—— tries to intimidate her, she and Pamela determine to leave together.

Mrs. Jewkes, the villainous ex-prostitute caretaker of Mr. B——'s country estate. She tries to further her employer's plots against Pamela's virtue and keeps the girl a prisoner.

Mr. Williams, the country clergyman of

Lincolnshire who loves Pamela. Though the first proposal of marriage from him is part of Mr. B——'s scheme, he does seek to marry her. Discovered smuggling her letters out of the house, he is thrown into jail on a trumped-up charge. Eventually, when Mr. B—— repents, Mr. Williams performs the marriage ceremony and receives a permanent vicarage.

Sally Godfrey, a former sweetheart of Mr. B——, by whom he has a daughter. After her marriage Pamela offers to take the child under her own care.

The Daughter of Sally and Mr. B——.

Billy, the son of Pamela and Mr. B——.

A Countess, with whom Mr. B—— is philandering while Pamela is bearing his child. By reading some of Pamela's letters, she learns the punishment for those who depart from the path of virtue.

Mr. Longman, the steward of Mr. B——.

John, Mr. B——'s groom, who carries most of Pamela's letters to her parents, but keeps some for his master.

Robin, the coachman forced to take Pamela to Mr. B——'s country estate.

Nan, the rude servant who guards Pamela at Mr. B——'s estate.

Lady Jones, a neighbor who will give Pamela refuge if she succeeds in escaping from Mr. B——'s country estate.

Sir Simon Darnford and **Lady Darnford,** friends of Mr. B—— who want to help free Pamela.

Mrs. Towers, a neighbor who criticizes Pamela.

Mr. and Mrs. Brooks, neighbors.

Mrs. Arthur, another critical neighbor, who visits the new bride.

Sir Jacob Swynford, Mr. B——'s uncle. Prepared to dislike his nephew's humble bride, he is won over by Pamela's charm and virtue.

The Story

Pamela Andrews had been employed from a very young age as the servant girl of Lady B——, at her estate in Bedfordshire. Because she had grown very fond of her mistress, the letter to her parents telling of her ladyship's death expressed her deep sorrow. Her own plans were uncertain. But it soon became clear that Lady B——'s son wanted her to remain in his household. Taking her hand before all the other servants, he had said that he would be a good master to Pamela for his dear mother's sake if she continued faithful and diligent. Mrs. Jervis, the housekeeper, put in a friendly word as well, and Pamela, not wishing to be a burden upon her poor parents, decided to remain in the service of Mr. B——. Shortly, however, she began to doubt that his intentions toward her were honorable. And when, one day, he kissed her while she sat sewing in a summerhouse, she found herself in a quandary as to what to do.

Once again she discussed the situation with the good Mrs. Jervis, and decided to stay if she could share the housekeeper's bed. Mr. B—— was extremely annoyed at this turn of affairs. He tried to persuade Mrs. Jervis that Pamela was in reality a very designing creature who should be carefully watched. When he learned that she was writing long letters to her parents, telling them in great detail of his false proposals and repeating her determination to keep her virtue, he had as many of her letters intercepted as possible.

In a frightening interview between Mr. B——, Pamela, and Mrs. Jervis, he intimidated the housekeeper by his terrifying manner and told Pamela to return to her former poverty. After talking the matter over with her friend, however, Pamela decided that Mr. B—— had given up his plan to ruin her and that there was no longer any reason for her to leave. But another interview with Mr. B—— convinced her that she should return to her parents upon the completion of some household duties entrusted to her. When Mr. B—— discovered that she was indeed planning to leave, a furious scene followed, in which he accused her of pride beyond her station. That night he concealed himself in the closet of her room. When she discovered him, she threw herself on the bed and fell into a fit. Both Pamela and Mrs. Jervis served notice. In spite of Mr. B——'s threats on the one hand and his cajolings on the other, Pamela remained firm in her decision to return home. The housekeeper was reinstated in her position, but Pamela set out by herself in the coach Mr. B—— had ordered to return her to her parents.

What she had thought Mr. B——'s kindness was but designing trickery. Instead of arriving at her parents' humble home, Pamela now found herself a prisoner at Mr. B——'s country estate, to which the coachman had driven her. Mrs. Jewkes, the caretaker, had none of Mrs. Jervis' kindness of heart, and Pamela found herself cruelly confined. It was only by clever scheming that she could continue to send letters to her parents. She was aided by Mr. Williams, the village minister, who smuggled her mail out of the house. The young man soon confessed his love for Pamela and his desire to marry her. Pamela refused his offer, but devised with his help a plan to escape. Unfortunately, Mrs. Jewkes was too wily a jailer. When she suspected that the two were secretly planning for Pamela's escape, she wrote to Mr. B——, who was still in London. Pamela's persecutor, aided by his agents, contrived to have Mr. Williams thrown into jail on a trumped-up charge.

Although her plot had been discovered, Pamela did not allow herself to be discouraged. That night she dropped from her window into the garden. But when she tried to escape from the garden, she found the gate padlocked. Mrs. Jewkes discovered her cringing in the woodshed. From that time on her warder's vigilance and cruelty increased.

Mr. B—— at length arrived and frightened Pamela still further with his threats. With the help of Mrs. Jewkes, he attempted to force himself upon her, but opportunely Pamela was seized by fits. Mr. B—— expressed his remorse and promised never to attempt to molest her again. And now Pamela began to suspect that her virtue would soon be rewarded, for Mr. B—— proposed marriage to her. But as she was enjoying the thought of being Mrs. B——, an anonymous warning arrived, suggesting that she beware of a sham marriage. Pamela was greatly upset. At her request, a coach was called and she set out to visit her parents. On the way, however, letters arrived from Mr. B—— entreating her to return to him, and offering an honorable proposal of marriage.

Pamela returned immediately to Mr. B—'s hall, for in spite of all that had passed she found that she was in love with Mr. B—. He, in turn, was delighted with her beauty and goodness. She and Mr. B— were married by Mr. Williams before a few witnesses. Mr. Andrews, Pamela's father, was present and great was the rejoicing in the Andrews household when he returned and told of his daughter's virtue, and of the happiness it had brought her.

Pamela readily adapted herself to her new role as the wife of a gentleman. With typical virtue, she quickly forgave Mrs. Jewkes for her former ill-treatment. The only flaw in her married state was the fact that Lady Davers, Mr. B—'s sister, was angry with her brother because of his marriage to a servant girl. Pamela was alone when Lady Davers arrived. She so insulted Pamela that the poor girl fled to her husband for consolation. A terrible scene took place between Mr. B— and Lady Davers, but Pamela soon won the love and respect of that good woman when she showed her the letters she had written about her earlier sufferings.

One day Mr. B— told Pamela of a previous love affair with Miss Sally Godfrey and took her to see his daughter, who had been placed in a boarding-school in the neighborhood. Pamela liked the little girl and asked to have the pretty child under her care at some later date.

Mr. and Mrs. Andrews were pleased with Pamela's accounts of her happiness and of Mr. B—'s goodness to her. He gave the old people a substantial gift of money and thus enabled them to set themselves up in a small but comfortable business.

Lady Davers' correspondence with Pamela continued at a great length, and more and more she expressed her approval of Pamela's virtue and her disgust with her brother's attempts to dishonor her. During a visit she paid the young couple, Mr. B— expressed his regret for his earlier unmannerly conduct toward the one who had become his dearly beloved wife.

Mr. B—'s uncle, Sir Jacob Swynford, paid his nephew a visit, prepared to detest the inferior creature Mr. B— had married. But Pamela's charm, beauty, and virtue won his heart completely, and the grumpy old man left full of praises for his lovely niece.

At last Mr. B— and Pamela decided to leave the country and return to London. Although her husband was still as attentive and thoughtful as ever, Pamela began to suspect that he might be carrying on an intrigue with another woman. She was particularly distressed that she could not accompany him to the theater and other places of amusement as she was about to bear a child. The scene of the christening of their son was very gay, for besides the family, tenants from the estate arrived to express their joy that Mr. B— now had a son and heir.

But Pamela's suspicions after all had been justified. An anonymous note informed her that the business trip which Mr. B— had taken was in reality a journey to a neighboring city with a countess with whom he was having an affair. Pamela controlled her passions, and when Lord B— returned he was so overcome by this further evidence of her kindness and understanding that he begged her forgiveness and promised to remain faithful to her from that day on. Pamela made good use of the letters she had written to Lady Davers during this trying period by sending them to the countess that she might learn from them and turn away from the path of license.

True to her earlier wish, Pamela decided to take in Sally Godfrey's child and bring her up as a sister for her own son, Billy. Mr. B— was faithful to his resolve to devote himself only to his wife, and he spent the remainder of his days admiring and praising her virtue.

Critical Evaluation

Samuel Richardson has often been awarded the title "Father of the English Novel." Like most such titles, this one is an oversimplification of a complex issue, and one that has been particularly disputed by students of Richardson's contemporary Daniel Defoe, who is also justly noted for his important contributions to the genre. The importance of Richardson's position in the tradition of the novel, however, is undeniable, and is based on his redefinition of the form, through his success, in *Pamela,* in dealing with several of the major formal problems which Defoe and others had left unsolved.

The most significant of these problems was that of plot. Prior to the publication of *Pamela,* a novel was commonly defined as "a small tale, generally of love." Although this definition has more recently been applied to the novella, most of the sources in Richardson's era, notably Dr. Johnson's dictionary, construed it as referring to the novel. When *Pamela* appeared, it was considered a "dilated novel" because its subject matter was basically the single amorous episode which the short novels had previously emphasized. Yet its treatment was on a scale much closer to the romances of Defoe and Fielding, two authors who did not confront the definition problem in most of their works, which tended to deal with many episodes within a larger context. Such works, then, as *Moll Flanders* and *Tom Jones* fit more easily into the "romance" category under the eighteenth century definitions. It was Richardson who combined the scale of the romance and the scope of the traditional novel to form the basis of the form as we know it today. Richardson's use of the epistolary style—a style of which he was perhaps literature's foremost practitioner—facilitated the birth of the new form, although it causes some problems for modern readers.

Pamela's plot structure, based on a radically new concept in the novel form, is at once the work's major strength and weakness, as well as the subject of considerable controversy. Viewed in context with later novels, it appears awkward, contrived, and lacking in realism. Indeed, a major criticism of Richardson's novel concerns the question of how the major characters found the time in the midst of all of their adventures to be writing lengthy letters to one another. In a purely technical sense, perhaps the worst defect in the plot is that it is too long for its essential purpose, causing it to be static in movement and lacking in tension; it reaches a climax and resolution midway through the book, thus leaving hundreds of pages of dull and uneventful narrative. The account of Pamela's married life, serving as it does only to confirm her virtue in the eyes of the world, could have been trimmed considerably, thus enhancing the overall effect of the novel. As it is, the falling action of the novel, consisting of Mr. B's adultery and Pamela's forgiveness as well as the growing appreciation on the part of Mr. B. of his wife's virtue, is too unconvincing and sentimental.

The strength of the plot structure lies in Richardson's epistolary form which, its shortcomings notwithstanding, does convey a degree of realism. Letters are normally a means for the relation of one's common factual doings, and they presuppose an actual writer and an actual reader. Our preconceived notions concerning the normal functions of the mode make believable an actual maiden, an actual seducer, and an actual marriage. Richardson's manipulation of the machinery governing the epistles—the hidden pens and ink, the evasions and discoveries, and the secreting of letters in bosoms and underlinens—causes the effect to grow. The realism is further enhanced by the clustering and lingering effect which comes to surround each incident. An incident occurs and is reflected on, committed to paper, entrusted to a porter, and spied upon; it is either intercepted, or received, reflected upon, and responded to. The whole complex, repetitious effect, although it slows down the action, lends great credibility to the original incident.

Richardson's epistolary form, after establishing the necessary suspension of disbelief in readers regarding a servant girl who can read and write, also excuses logically much of Pamela's smooth and affected rhetoric; since a letter is an editing of life rather than life itself, the writer has an editorial option to tailor and refurbish experience. Thus Richardson, having posited a servant girl with a certain flair for writing, can justify a further suspension of disbelief, although sometimes not as much as the circumstances demand.

The weakest part of the plot structure in terms of realism is Richardson's handling of the sequence of incidents. The incidents in *Pamela,* while perhaps not disappointing our preconceived notions of drawing room and boudoir reality, are little more than interesting fits of manners and rarely reveal any depth of character or morals. These incidents are little more than stylistically balanced situations; outrages in the summer house are followed by contrition, and tearful farewells by triumphant reunions.

The same shallowness applies to some of Richardson's characters, who, being allegorical as demanded by the instructional premise of the novel, offer little depth of personality. Yet the heroine herself presents an interesting study; Pamela begins as the most fully allegorical figure and concludes by being the most fully human. Beginning in ignorance, she presents the prospect, particularly to readers steeped in Fielding, of becoming a satirical figure; yet she never does. Pamela is an incorruptibly good girl. What is interesting about her characterization is how the author converts us to accept the reality of his protagonist and her maidenly dilemma. He manages this by placing her in a crisis which is inherently genuine and appropriate to her way of life. He supplies her with neatly counterpoised groups of friends and enemies and fleshes out her vulnerability with an impressive strength and a striking ability to cope—a believable middle-class trait. The implied spectacle of her parents nervously hanging on from letter to letter adds further believability to the picture. Richardson also imbues Pamela with little vices which she realizes she has. Pamela, for example, knows that she is longwinded, prone to construe motives to her own advantage, and inclined to cling to praise and flattery. This realization of some of her own faults makes Pamela much more credible than a character who is merely symbolic and displays no insight into herself.

For all of Richardson's virtues and faults as a writer, it is his redefinition of the form of the novel that most makes him worth reading. *Pamela* was a radical departure from accepted concepts when it was first published, and in a sense it is a radical departure in our own day. While subsequent novelists learned from and modified Richardson's techniques, they for the most part drifted away from his epistolary form; while keeping his idea of treating a simple episode on a larger scale, they tended to follow the techniques developed by Fielding and Defoe. *Pamela* is thus as much of an anomaly today as it was in the eighteenth century. Yet it is a vital part of literary tradition and was instrumental in creating the novel as we know it now.

Bibliography

Allentuck, Marcia. "Narration and Illustration: The Problem of Richardson's *Pamela*," in *Philological Quarterly*. LI (1972), pp. 874–886.

Barker, Gerard A. "The Complacent Paragon: Exemplary Characterization in Richardson," in *Studies in English Literature, 1500–1900*. IX (Summer, 1969), pp. 503–519.

Cowler, Rosemary, Editor. *Twentieth Century Interpretations of* Pamela: *A Collection of Critical Essays*. Englewood Cliffs, N.J.: Prentice-Hall, 1969.

Donovan, Robert A. "The Problem of Pamela or, Virtue Unrewarded," in *Studies in English Literature, 1500–1900*. III (1963), pp. 377–395.

Doody, Margaret A. *A Natural Passion: A Study of the Novels of Samuel Richardson*. Oxford: Clarendon Press, 1974, pp. 14–98.

Erickson, Robert A. "Mother Jewkes, Pamela, and the Midwives," in *Journal of English Literary History*. XLIII (1976), pp. 500–516.

Folkenflik, Robert. "A Room of Pamela's Own," in *Journal of English Literary History*. XXXIX (1972), pp. 585–596.

Golden, Morris. *Richardson's Characters.* Ann Arbor: University of Michigan Press, 1963.

Guilhamet, Leon M. "From *Pamela* to *Grandison*: Richardson's Moral Revolution in the Novel," in *Studies in Change and Revolution: Aspects of English Intellectual History, 1640–1800.* Edited by Paul J. Dorshin. Menston, England: Scholar Press, 1972, pp. 191–210.

Kearney, Anthony M. "Richardson's *Pamela*: The Aesthetic Case," in *Review of English Literature.* VII (1966), pp. 78–90.

Kinkead-Weekes, Mark. *Samuel Richardson: Dramatic Novelist.* Ithaca, N.Y.: Cornell University Press, 1973, pp. 7–120.

Konigsberg, Ira. "The Dramatic Background of Richardson's Plots and Characters," in *PMLA.* LXXXIII (March, 1968), pp. 42–53.

McIntosh, Carey. "Pamela's Clothes," in *Journal of English Literary History.* XXXV (March, 1968), pp. 75–83.

Morton, Donald E. "Theme and Structure in *Pamela*," in *Studies in the Novel.* III (1971), pp. 242–257.

Muecke, D.C. "Beauty and Mr. B.," in *Studies in English Literature.* VII (1967), pp. 467–474.

Needham, Gwendolyn B. "Richardson's Characterization of Mr. B. and the Double Purpose in *Pamela*," in *Eighteenth-Century Studies.* III (1970), pp. 433–474.

Parker, Dorothy. "The Time Scheme of *Pamela* and the Character of B.," in *Texas Studies in Language and Literature.* XI (1969), pp. 695–704.

Reid, B.L. "Justice to *Pamela*," in *The Long Boy and Others.* Athens: University of Georgia Press, 1969, pp. 516–533.

Roussel, Roy. "Reflections on the Letter: The Reconciliation of Distance and Presence in *Pamela*," in *Journal of English Literary History.* XLI (1974), pp. 375–399.

Sharrock, Roger. "Richardson's *Pamela*: The Gospel and the Novel," in *Durham University Journal.* LVIII (1966), pp. 67–74.

Smidt, Kristian. "Character and Plot in the Novels of Samuel Richardson," in *Critical Quarterly.* XVII (1975), pp. 155–166.

Steeves, Harrison R. *Before Jane Austen: The Shaping of the English Novel in the Eighteenth Century.* New York: Holt, Rinehart and Winston, 1965, pp. 53–87.

Ten Harmsel, Henrietta. "The Villain-Hero in *Pamela* and *Pride and Prejudice*," in *College English.* XXIII (1961), pp. 104–108.

Wilson, Stuart. "Richardson's *Pamela*: An Interpretation," in *PMLA.* LXXXVIII (1973), pp. 79–91.

Wolff, Cynthia G.   *Samuel Richardson and the Eighteenth-Century Puritan Character.* Hamden, Conn.: Archon, 1972, pp. 58–73.

SIR CHARLES GRANDISON

Type of work: Novel
Author: Samuel Richardson (1689–1761)
Type of plot: Epistolary novel of manners
Time of plot: Eighteenth century
Locale: England
First published: 1753–1754

Sir Charles Grandison represents Samuel Richardson's ideal of manly virtue, the "just man made perfect." In his character the novelist deliberately and obviously attempts to offset the negative picture of the male he presented in Mr. B. (Pamela) and Lovelace (Clarissa). And perhaps he is intended as an idealized self-portrait. The artistic result, however, is dullness, the usual result of unalloyed virtue in literature.

Principal Characters

Sir Charles Grandison, an English baronet and the hero of a novel whose author, after writing two novels concerned with men who are rakes, was trying to present a picture of a truly virtuous character. The honorable Sir Charles rescues Harriet Byron from the clutches of Sir Hargrave Pollexfen and takes her to his country house as his sister. Though his family and friends favor his marriage to Harriet, he feels in honor bound to Lady Clementina della Porretta, who has a claim on his affection. When Lady Clementina finally refuses him, he feels free to ask for Harriet's hand.

Harriet Byron, a virtuous young woman of modest expectations. On a visit to London she is pursued by and refuses the attentions of Sir Hargrave Pollexfen. The enraged suitor attempts to abduct her and force a marriage. She is rescued by Sir Charles Grandison and taken to his home, where she falls in love with him. Realizing that Sir Charles regards her as a sister, she tries to subdue and hide her affection for him until he becomes free to declare his love for her and to win her hand.

Sir Hargrave Pollexfen, Harriet Byron's libertine suitor, from whom she is rescued by Sir Charles Grandison. After Sir Charles rescues him from the enraged family of a girl he has tried to seduce in France, Sir Hargrave begins to realize the evil of his ways. He reforms, and upon his death leaves his fortune to Sir Charles and Harriet Byron.

Lady Clementina della Porretta, an Italian beauty who is so in love with Sir Charles Grandison that his departure from Italy robs her of her reason, thus putting Sir Charles under an obligation which leaves him bound to her until a cure is effected and she finally refuses to marry him.

Charlotte Grandison and
Lady L., Sir Charles Grandison's sisters, on whom he bestows the benefits their late father was reluctant to give.

Mrs. Oldham, the paramour of Sir Charles Grandison's late father.
Lady Olivia, an Italian woman who is enamored of Sir Charles.

Emily Jervois, Sir Charles' young ward.

Mr. Greville, a suitor of Harriet Byron.

The Story

When Harriet Byron, a beautiful and virtuous English girl of modest expectations, left her aunt's home in rural Northamptonshire to visit in eighteenth century London, she left three men who loved her very much and various relatives
who feared that the social life of the city might offer moral pitfalls unknown to a
young and unsuspecting girl of virtue such as Harriet was. Having spent all her
life in the country, living with an aunt after her parents' deaths, Harriet was
excited at the prospect of the London visit. She went, too, with a happy heart, for
she had no one, despite her many admirers, that she was interested in marrying;
her suitors had not appealed strongly enough to her sentiments and mind in spite
of their respectable, if ardorous, attentions.

In London, where she had connections of a very respectable sort, Harriet was
invited to many homes and social events, and she met many wealthy suitors. One
of these was Sir Hargrave Pollexfen, who was determined not to accept a refusal.
When told by Harriet that he did not suit her fancy, Sir Hargrave became enraged and vowed he would have both the girl and revenge. He laid a plot to
abduct the girl from a masquerade ball and force her to marry him.

Sir Hargrave's plot almost succeeding, the experience was a horrible one for
Harriet. Fortunately for the girl, however, Sir Charles Grandison heard her
screams and rescued her from Sir Hargrave's clutches. Sir Charles took Harriet
to his country house, not far from London, where he and his sister invited Harriet
to remain as a guest, almost a member of the family. Sir Hargrave sent a challenge to Sir Charles, but the latter refused to fight a duel, insisting that no virtuous man, however brave and skilled, could become a duelist and retain his
virtue.

Harriet Byron soon fell in love with Sir Charles Grandison, who was, she realized, the very soul of honor and virtue, a man whose time was spent in carefully
managing his own affairs and in doing good for others. His father had died leaving his entire estate to Sir Charles, with no provision for the two daughters of the
family. When Sir Charles returned to England from the Continent to take over
his estate, he treated his sisters with all consideration and devotion. The oldest
received his permission for her to marry Lord L., a suitor frowned upon by her
father during his lifetime. Sir Charles also began to improve his estates and their
revenues so that he could set aside better marriage portions for both girls, something more than their father had been willing to do. Sir Charles befriended everyone who would accept his kindnesses, and he behaved always wisely and with
decorum. Even those persons who were prepared to dislike him found themselves
won over by his sympathetic, friendly, and yet dignified ways. Even to his father's
paramour, Mrs. Oldham, he behaved magnanimously, persuading the rest of the
family to view her as a misguided and miserable fellow human being.

Many women were in love with Sir Charles, including Harriet Byron, but no
one could ascertain whether he had any inclinations toward any particular
woman. But Harriet tried to hide her love for him and to subdue it, even though

many of Sir Charles' friends and relatives, including his sisters, favored the match. Sir Charles consistently referred to Harriet as a sister and behaved toward her with the same consideration he showed Charlotte Grandison and Lady L. Finally it became known that two Italian women he had met in his travels had won some favor from him and had some claim to him and his affections. One was Lady Olivia and the other was Lady Clementina della Porretta, whom he had met after saving her brother's life. Lady Clementina's family did not favor a marriage between their daughter and a Protestant Englishman, but the young woman was so enamored of Sir Charles that his departure from Italy unhinged her reason. Feeling a sense of responsibility to the lady and her family as the source of her misfortune, Sir Charles returned to Italy with English medical experts to try to effect a cure. Harriet Byron, believing that he would prefer Lady Clementina to her, began to prepare herself for news of his marriage to the Italian woman.

After she had recovered from her malady, however, Lady Clementina refused to marry Sir Charles, in spite of the fact that her family and he had been able to compromise over religious differences. Lady Clementina, a devout Roman Catholic, feared that she would be tempted by her love for Sir Charles and his virtue to leave her faith to become a Protestant. She asked to be free not to marry at all, since she could not marry him; her family hoped she would marry some other eligible man.

While he was still in Italy, an attempt was made on Sir Charles' life, almost certainly at the instigation of Lady Olivia, who had previously struck at him with a poniard after he had repulsed her addresses. After this incident Sir Charles felt himself free to pay his court where he would. He returned to England and immediately began his suit for Harriet Byron' hand, which he quickly won. In the meantime his sister Charlotte had married Lord G., and Harriet helped that impetuous and willful young woman to learn to bear properly the dignity of matrimony. Harriet's marriage to Sir Charles still faced some small obstacles. She had to learn to accept her suitor in new ways; she was shocked, for example, when he kissed her on the mouth instead of on the cheek. Harriet had to find a place in her heart, too, for Emily Jervois, Sir Charles' young ward. The young girl loved her guardian, and Harriet, aware of the girl's feelings, had to help her accept Harriet's marriage to Sir Charles. Another disturbance was caused by a former suitor of Harriet, Mr. Greville, who tried, while emotionally deranged, to fight a duel with Sir Charles.

Harriet Byron and Sir Charles were finally married. A short time later they were visited by Lady Clementina, who had run away from her home in Italy because of her parents' insistence that she marry. Through a compromise, Sir Charles managed to arrange a satisfactory agreement between the young woman and her family. Word came, too, of Sir Hargrave Pollexfen's death. Sir Hargrave, rescued in France by Sir Charles from the outraged relatives of a woman he had attempted to seduce, had discovered the evil of his ways. Wishing to make amends for the abduction and the attempted forced marriage to Harriet, Sir

Hargrave left his fortune to her and her husband. Even the mother of Emily Jervois was influenced to become a respectable and virtuous woman. Encouraged by Sir Charles' magnanimity and financial generosity, she interested herself in religion. Although that unfortunate woman had once looked on Sir Charles as her enemy and she and Mr. O'Hara, her one-time paramour and second husband, had attempted to force Emily into a degrading marriage with a rascal who had promised to share with them the girl's fortune that Sir Charles held in trust, they mended their dissolute ways and became sober, worthy persons.

Critical Evaluation

"Pot-boiler," a pejorative, twentieth century appelation directed at popular works without literary merit, has been applied unjustly to *Sir Charles Grandison*. Although the novel was deliberately written for popular consumption, it nonetheless has intrinsic literary qualities and holds an important place in the history of literature.

As a young man, Samuel Richardson, because he was literate at a time when many people were not, was often asked by young ladies to compose love letters for them. He later used those letters and other personal correspondence as bases for his novels, which were composed in the epistolary form, cast in an essentially first-person narrative. His first novel, *Pamela,* was published in 1740; the second, *Clarissa,* was published in 1747-1748. Both dealt with stories of virtuous women and brought him great acclaim. Thus it was by popular request that he wrote *Sir Charles Grandison,* a story of the ideal, virtuous man. In all three novels, Richardson used the epistolary form, as a simple and very personal way of narrating his tales; he has, in fact, been called the "father" of the English novel for having developed this narrative technique and for developing the novel of sensibility.

Richardson's sentimental portrayal of Sir Charles is as contrived as that of Pamela or Clarissa, since that approach appealed to his readers, and above all, Richardson sought to satisfy his readers. As a consequence, Sir Charles is a popular ideal rather than a real figure struggling with real-life problems. In an age of enlightenment, when rationality was supposed to overcome superstition, Sir Charles was an unrealistic figure, for he represented not what was, but what some believed ought to be. His idealistic motives and pure approach to life may have made him a popular hero representing what readers wanted to believe, but his staunch virginity and fidelity —especially in his social context—make him fundamentally incredible. The modern reader is struck with disbelief: no one in that time was so naïve, nor is anyone now. Yet *Pamela* and *Clarissa* enjoyed great popular success, and *Sir Charles Grandison* was only slightly less popular, because contradictions between ideal and real were not so fully recognized in the eighteenth century as they are in the twentieth.

In effect, *Sir Charles Grandison* contributed, like *Pamela* and *Clarissa,* to the development of the novel form, rather than to the body of enlightened thought. Still, the novel has compelling interest (who is immune to gossip?), and plot and characterization are paintstakingly nurtured to their melodramatic climax. Flaws notwithstanding, Richardson is, in the end, an effective novelist for capturing and holding our attention with a good story.

Bibliography

Ball, Donald. *Samuel Richardson's Theory of Fiction.* The Hague: Mouton, 1971.

Brophy, Elizabeth B. *Samuel Richardson: The Triumph of Craft.* Knoxville: University of Tennessee Press, 1974, pp. 76–90.

Cohen, Richard. "The Social-Christian and Christian-Social Doctrines of Samuel Richardson," in *Hartford Studies in Literature.* IV (1972), pp. 142–145.

Doody, Margaret A. *A Natural Passion: A Study of the Novels of Samuel Richardson.* Oxford: Clarendon Press, 1974, pp. 241–367.

Duncan-Jones, E.E. "The Misses Selby Steele," in *Times Literary Supplement (London).* (September 10, 1964), p. 845.

Eaves, T.C. Duncan and Ben D. Kimpel. *Samuel Richardson: A Biography.* Oxford: Clarendon Press, 1971, pp. 387–400.

Golden, Morris. *Richardson's Characters.* Ann Arbor: University of Michigan Press, 1963.

Guilhamet, Leon M. "From *Pamela* to *Grandison*: Richardson's Moral Revolution in the Novel," in *Studies in Change and Revolution: Aspects of English Intellectual History, 1640–1800.* Edited by Paul J. Dorshin. Menston, England: Scolar Press, 1972, pp. 194–198.

Kinkead-Weekes, Mark. *Samuel Richardson: Dramatic Novelist.* Ithaca, N.Y.: Cornell University Press, 1973, pp. 279–391, 420–423, 447–451.

Konigsberg, Ira. "The Dramatic Background of Richardson's Plots and Characters," in *PMLA.* LXXXIII (March, 1968), pp. 42–53.

————. *Samuel Richardson and the Dramatic Novel.* Lexington: University of Kentucky Press, 1968, pp. 48, 50–52, 65–69.

Levin, Gerald. "Character and Fantasy in Richardson's *Sir Charles Grandison*," in *Connecticut Review.* VII (1973), pp. 93–99.

McKillop, Alan D. *Critical Remarks on* Sir Charles Grandison, Clarissa, *and* Pamela. Los Angeles: Clark Memorial Library, 1950.

Smidt, Kristian. "Character and Plot in the Novels of Samuel Richardson," in *Critical Quarterly.* XVII (1975), pp. 155–166.

Wolff, Cynthia G. "The Problem of Eighteenth-Century Secular Heroinism," in *Modern Language Studies*. IV (1974), pp. 37–38.

————. *Samuel Richardson and the Eighteenth-Century Puritan Character*. Hamden, Conn.: Archon, 1972, pp. 174–229.

SIR WALTER SCOTT

Born: Edinburgh, Scotland (August 15, 1771)
Died: Abbotsford, Scotland (September 21, 1832)

Principal Works

NOVELS: *Waverley,* 1814; *Guy Mannering,* 1815; *The Antiquary,* 1816; *The Black Dwarf,* 1816; *Old Mortality,* 1816; *Rob Roy,* 1818; *The Heart of Midlothian,* 1818; *The Bride of Lammermoor,* 1819; *A Legend of Montrose,* 1819; *Ivanhoe,* 1820; *The Monastery,* 1820; *The Abbot,* 1820; *Kenilworth,* 1821; *The Pirate,* 1822; *The Fortunes of Nigel,* 1822; *Peveril of the Peak,* 1823; *Quentin Durward,* 1823; *St. Ronan's Well,* 1824; *Redgauntlet,* 1824; *The Betrothed,* 1825; *The Talisman,* 1825; *Woodstock,* 1826; *Chronicles of the Canongate,* 1927 *(The Two Drovers, The Highland Widow, The Surgeon's Daughter);* *The Fair Maid of Perth,* 1828; *Anne of Geierstein,* 1829; *Count Robert of Paris,* 1831; *Castle Dangerous,* 1831.

POEMS: *The Lay of the Last Minstrel,* 1805; *Marmion,* 1808; *The Lady of the Lake,* 1810; *The Vision of Don Roderick,* 1811; *The Bridal of Triermain,* 1813; *The Lord of the Isles,* 1815; *Rokeby,* 1815.

MISCELLANEOUS: *The Life and Works of John Dryden,* 1808; *The Life and Works of Jonathan Swift,* 1814; *The Life of Napoleon Buonaparte,* 1827.

In spite of physical handicaps Walter Scott lived a full, varied life and created an impressive body of writings. Stricken with infantile paralysis before he was two years old, and alternating between periods of physical vigor and serious ailments throughout his life, he loved and practiced outdoor sports for most of his sixty-odd years.

Born in Edinburgh, August 15, 1771, he was a product of the eighteenth century as well as of the romantic nineteenth. As a child he was a voracious reader and avid listener to tales and legends, particularly those of his native Scotland. His copious reading was stored in a retentive memory and used to advantage in his writings; and his interest in folklore led to his collection and publication of Scottish ballads. Although not a brilliant student, he was praised for his ability to enjoy and understand the Latin poets. He entered the University of Edinburgh in 1783, but after a year at college he suffered one of his severe illnesses and had to return home. He spent his convalescence with a sympathetic uncle, Captain Robert Scott, who encouraged his literary interests.

He studied law in his father's office; and in spite of a disinclination for the profession, he was admitted to the bar in 1792. He made use of his legal experiences in his novels, especially *Redgauntlet,* in which his friend William Clerk served as model for Darsie Latimer, and Scott himself for Allan Fairford. When he was twenty he cast his eye on a lovely fifteen-year-old girl, Williamina

Belsches. After an unsuccessful courtship of five years he lost her to a rival and indulged his sorrow for a time with melancholy self-dramatization out of keeping with his usual behavior.

In 1797, when the fear of a Napoleonic invasion seized Great Britain, Scott was the moving force in forming a volunteer home-guard unit, in which he held the position of quartermaster. In spite of his crippled leg he was a bold and expert horseman, and apparently was disappointed at not engaging Napoleon's forces. In the same year, on a tour of the Lake Country with his brother John and his friend Adam Ferguson, he met Charlotte Carpenter (Charpentier), daughter of a French royalist and ward of an English nobleman. This time his courtship was both short and successful, and he married his Charlotte on Christmas Eve, 1797. Their first child died in infancy, but four children reached maturity, two sons and two daughters.

In 1799 Scott was appointed Sheriff-depute of Selkirkshire; the position brought him a steady income and not-too-onerous duties. Seven years later he became Clerk of the Session in Edinburgh, adding to his steady income and increasing his routine labors considerably.

Although he translated for publication Gottfried Bürger's *Lenore* (1799) and Goethe's *Goetz von Berlichingen* (1799) and collected and edited—often revised—ballads in his *Minstrelsy of the Scottish Border* (1802–1803), he won his first recognition as a poet in 1805 with *The Lay of the Last Minstrel* and became a major literary figure in England with *Marmion* and *The Lady of the Lake*. His subsequent long poems added little to his reputation. Shortly after the publication of *The Lay of the Last Minstrel* he formed a partnership (Scott to be a silent partner) with the printer James Ballantyne, an old school friend. During his poetic career Scott completed two major works of scholarship, an eighteen-volume edition of Dryden and a nineteen-volume edition of Swift, either of which would have made a reputation for a professional scholar.

In 1814, with the anonymous publication of *Waverley*, Scott began a new literary career and his most illustrious, for he is now considered primarily a historical novelist, more than either poet or scholar. Scott gave reasons for not acknowledging the authorship of his novels; but at least one reason was a childish delight in mystification, a puckish joy in throwing dust into the public eye. Between 1814 and his death in 1832, he completed about thirty novels and novelettes, several long poems, a large mass of miscellaneous writings, and a nine-volume *Life of Napoleon*.

Scott was the first baronet created by George IV (1820). By this time he had bought acres of land and was sinking a fortune in Abbotsford. One friend who helped plan Abbotsford and stock its library was Daniel Terry, the actor-manager who produced dramatic versions of several of Scott's works, making an especial hit as Bailie Jarvie in *Rob Roy*. Scott's publishing ventures were in bad circumstances which grew worse; in 1826 Constable and Ballantyne failed. Instead of taking refuge in bankruptcy, Scott undertook to write himself and his colleagues out of debt. Few men have displayed more fortitude under adversity. To cap the material loss he suffered a severe spiritual one in the death of his beloved wife. His grief was profound, but he continued to write. In 1830, apparently as a result of his Herculean labors under stress, he suffered his first stroke of apoplexy. He recovered and continued work until recurring strokes paralyzed him and practically destroyed his mind. He died September 21, 1832, still in debt; but his son-in-law, John Gibson Lockhart, cleared the debts with the proceeds of his superb biography of the baronet.

Scott's merits as man and writer entitle him to a position much nearer his former reputation than he now holds. One of his admirers called him a combination of Shakespeare and Samuel Johnson. Those who think of him only as a cloak-and-sword romancer overlook his remarkable gift of creating comic characters and his broad view of human nature in all walks of life. He was greatly admired by Balzac and Dumas; and wise critics from Goethe to the present have been impressed with his humane wisdom.

Bibliography

There is no recent scholarly edition of Scott's works. The Border Edition of the *Waverley Novels*, 48 vols., 1892–1894, contains notes by Andrew Lang. John Gibson Lockhart's *Memoirs of the Life of Sir Walter Scott, Bart.*, 1837–1838, is basic; the definitive modern biography is Edgar Johnson, *Sir Walter Scott: The Great Unknown*, 1969. See also John Buchan (Lord Tweedsmuir), *Sir Walter Scott*, 1932; Sir Herbert Grierson, *Sir Walter Scott, Bart.*, 1938; Hesketh Pearson, *Sir Walter Scott*, 1954; F. R. Hart, *Scott's Novels*, 1966; David Daiches, *Sir Walter Scott and His World*, 1971; and Paul N. Landis, "The Waverly Novels, or a Hundred Years After," *Publications of the Modern Language Association*, LII (1937), 461–473.

THE HEART OF MIDLOTHIAN

Type of work: Novel
Author: Sir Walter Scott (1771–1832)
Type of plot: Historical romance
Time of plot: Early eighteenth century
Locale: Scotland
First published: 1818

Reputedly based on fact, The Heart of Midlothian *tells the story of a dairyman's daughter and her efforts to save her sister from being hanged on a charge of child murder. The narrative is exciting in the typical Scott style, and is filled with suspense, mystery, and romance. Many readers consider this Scott's greatest novel.*

Principal Characters

David Deans, a moderately prosperous Scottish farmer in the early 1700's. A vigorous, stern Presbyterian, he is hurt and stunned when his younger daughter is charged with child murder, and he finds comfort only in the devotion of his older daughter Jeanie, who indirectly gets him a more fertile farm while obtaining a pardon for her sister. Although David cannot wholly approve of Jeanie's fiancé, he is reconciled to the marriage.

Jeanie Deans, a rather plain and simple girl who shows much moral earnestness and courage when she refuses to lie to save her sister from a death sentence and then goes to London at great risk to present her case before the Queen. Her force and warmth impress the Duke of Argyle and the Queen, who obtain a pardon for her sister, give her father a better farm, and give her betrothed a good clerical position. As a result, she is able to marry, and eventually she bears three children.

Effie Deans, Jeanie's spoiled, pretty younger sister. When Effie's illegitimate child disappears, she is arrested and sentenced to hang for child murder. Released through the steadfast efforts of Jeanie, she marries her betrayer, the criminal known as Geordie Robertson,

and when he later acquires a title under his rightful name of George Staunton, she becomes a court beauty. Years after, she and her husband return to Scotland, where he is killed by a young outlaw who is really his long-lost son. Effie then retires to a convent.

Reuben Butler, Jeanie's betrothed, a sensible, educated, somewhat pedantic young minister. Unable to marry because of his impoverishment, his difficulties are cleared away when he gives Jeanie a hereditary claim on the Duke, is given a church on one of the Duke's estates, and earns the respect of David.

Geordie Robertson, in reality **George Staunton,** a reckless, profligate young man who seduces two girls but tries to redeem his past by offering to turn himself in as the leader of the Porteous riot in return for Effie's freedom. Jeanie, however, makes this offer unnecessary. After Effie has been pardoned he marries her and achieves a respectable life, first in the West Indies, later in the English court. When he willfully returns to seek his illegitimate son, the outlaw son kills him in a robbery attempt.

Meg Murdockson, a vicious old woman who serves as Effie's midwife, tries to destroy the child, and testifies that Effie killed the baby. Motivated by her desire for revenge because Robertson loves Effie instead of her own daughter, whom he had also seduced, she tries everything in her power to destroy Effie, including a murder attempt on Jeanie. Finally, after confessing her evil deeds, she is hanged as a witch.

John, Duke of Argyle, a skilled, honorable Scottish statesman in the court of King George II. He shows his generosity by giving Jeanie a hearing with the Queen and by aiding her father and Reuben Butler. He becomes a family friend.

The Laird of Dumbiedikes, a member of the gentry and Jeanie's clumsy suitor. He pays for Effie's defense and Jeanie's trip to London.

Madge Wildfire, Meg Murdockson's daughter, crazed after Robertson betrays her. She helps Jeanie escape Meg and is later harried to death by a mob.

Ratcliffe, the ex-criminal keeper of the Edinburgh jail. He treats Effie well and suggests to Jeanie that she seek a pardon from the Queen.

Queen Caroline, the touchy, powerful Queen who, affected by Jeanie's simplicity, secures her sister's pardon and gives Jeanie fifty pounds.

The Reverend Mr. Staunton, Robertson's righteous father. He shelters Jeanie after her escape from Meg Murdockson and gives her an escort to London.

The Whistler, Effie and Robertson's illegitimate son. After killing his father. he escapes to the wilds of America.

Bartoline Saddletree, a friend of the Deanses, a stupid, pompous, meddlesome lawyer who tries to take over Effie's case.

Mrs. Saddletree, his generous, motherly wife, who employs Effie as a servant during her pregnancy.

John Porteous, an officer who needlessly fired into a crowd of citizens at a hanging and was afterwards killed by a mob led by Robertson.

Andrew Wilson, Robertson's partner in crime, a smuggler hanged by Porteous.

Archibald, the Duke's groom of chambers, who escorts Jeanie back to Scotland.

Duncan of Knock, the brusque, lively protector of the Duke's estate on which David Deans is placed.

David,
Donald, and
Euphemia, Jeanie and Reuben Butler's three spirited children.

The Story

The first knowledge Jeanie Deans had that her sister Effie was in trouble came just a few moments before officers of justice arrived at the cottage to arrest Effie for child murder. They told Jeanie and her father, David Deans, that Effie had borne a male child illegitimately and had killed him or caused him to be killed soon after he was born. Effie admitted the birth of the child but refused to name her seducer. She denied that she had killed her baby, saying that she had fallen into a stupor and had recovered to find that the midwife who attended her had disposed of the child in some fashion unknown to Effie. In the face of the evidence, however, she was convicted of child murder and sentenced to be hanged. Jeanie might have saved her sister, for it was the law that if a prospective mother had told anyone of her condition she would not be responsible for her baby's death. But Jeanie would not lie, even to save her sister's life. Since there was no one to whom Effie had told her terrible secret, there was no defense for her, and she was placed in the Tolbooth prison to await execution.

Another prisoner in the Tolbooth was Captain John Porteous, who was awaiting execution for firing into the crowd attending the hanging of Andrew Wilson, a smuggler. Wilson's accomplice, Geordie Robertson, had escaped, and the officers feared that Robertson might try to rescue Wilson. For that reason, Porteous and a company of soldiers had been sent to the scene of the execution to guard against a possible rescue. Because Porteous had fired into the crowd without provocation, killing several people, he was to be hanged. But when his execution was stayed for a few weeks, a mob headed by Robertson, disguised as a woman, broke into the prison, seized Porteous, and hanged him. For that deed Robertson became a hunted man.

Meanwhile Jeanie Deans, who had refused to lie to save her sister, had not forsaken Effie. When she visited Effie in prison, she learned that Robertson was the father of her child. He had left her in the care of old Meg Murdockson, considered by many to be a witch, and it must have been Meg who had killed or sold the baby. Meg's daughter Madge had long before been seduced by Robertson and had lost her mind for love of him, and Meg had sworn revenge on any other woman Robertson might love. But proving the old woman's guilt or Effie's innocence was not possible, for Robertson had disappeared, and Meg swore that she had seen Effie coming back from the river after drowning the baby.

Jeanie, determined to save her sister, decided to walk to London to seek a pardon from the king and queen. She told her plans to Reuben Butler, a minister to whom she had long been betrothed. Reuben had not been able to marry her, for he had no position other than that of an assistant schoolmaster and his salary was too small to support a wife. Although he objected to Jeanie's plan, he was able to aid her when he saw that she could not be swayed from her purpose. Reuben's grandfather had once aided an ancestor of the present Duke of Argyle, and Reuben gave Jeanie a letter asking the duke's help in presenting Jeanie to the king and queen.

The journey to London was a long and dangerous one. Once Jeanie was captured by Meg Murdockson, who tried to kill her so that she could not save Effie. But Jeanie escaped from the old woman and sought refuge in the home of the Rev. Mr. Staunton. There she met the minister's son, George Staunton, and learned from him that he was Geordie Robertson, the betrayer of her sister. He admitted his responsibility to Effie, telling Jeanie that he had planned and executed the Porteous incident in order to rescue Effie from the prison. But she had refused to leave with him. He had tried many other schemes to save her, including an attempt to force from Meg the confession that she had taken the baby, but everything had failed. He told Jeanie that he had been on his way to give himself up in exchange for Effie's release when he fell from his horse and was injured. He told Jeanie to bargain with the Duke of Argyle, and as a last resort to offer to lead the authorities to Robertson in exchange for Effie's pardon. George promised not to leave his father's house until Effie was free.

Jeanie at last reached London and presented herself to the Duke of Argyle with Reuben's letter. The duke, impressed with Jeanie's sincerity and simplicity, arranged for an audience with the queen. She too believed Jeanie's story of Effie's misfortune, and through her efforts the king pardoned Effie, with the stipulation that she leave Scotland for fourteen years. Jeanie secured the pardon without revealing George Staunton's secret.

The duke was so impressed with Jeanie's goodness and honesty that he made her father the master of an experimental farm on one of his estates in Scotland, and he made Reuben the minister of the church. Jeanie's heart was overflowing with joy until she learned that Effie had eloped with her lover just three nights after her release from prison. No one knew where they were, as the outlaw's life was in constant danger because of his part in the Porteous hanging.

Reuben and Jeanie were married and were blessed with three fine children. They prospered in their new life, and Jeanie's only sorrow was her sister's marriage to George Staunton. She kept Effie's secret, however, telling no one that George was actually Robertson. After several years, George and Effie returned to London, George having inherited a title from his uncle, and as Sir George and Lady Staunton they were received in court society. Effie wrote secretly to Jeanie and sent her large sums of money which Jeanie put away without telling her husband about them. Even to him she could not reveal Effie's secret.

By chance Jeanie found a paper containing the last confession of Meg Murdockson, who had been hanged as a witch. In it Meg confessed that she had stolen Effie's baby and had given him to an outlaw. Jeanie sent this information to Effie, in London, and before long Effie, as Lady Staunton, paid Jeanie a visit. Effie had used a pretext of ill health to go to Scotland while her husband, acting on the information in Meg's letter, tried to trace the whereabouts of their son. Although it was dangerous for George to be in Scotland, where he might be recognized as Geordie Robertson, he followed every clue given in Meg's confession. In Edinburgh he met Reuben Butler, who was there on business, and secured an invitation to accompany Reuben back to the manse. Reuben, not knowing George's real identity, was happy to receive the Duke of Argyle's friend. Reuben, at that time, did not know that Effie was also a guest in his home.

As Reuben and George walked toward the manse, they passed through a thicket where they were attacked by outlaws. One, a young fellow, ran his sword through George and killed him. It was not until Reuben had heard the whole story of the Stauntons from Jeanie that he searched George's pockets and found there information which proved beyond doubt that the young outlaw who had killed George was his own son, stolen many years before. Because Effie was grief-stricken by George's death, Jeanie and Reuben thought it useless to add to her sorrow by revealing the identity of his assailant. Reuben later traced the boy to America, where the young man continued his life of crime until he was captured and probably killed by Indians.

Effie stayed with Reuben and Jeanie for more than a year. Then she went back to London and the brilliant society she had known there. No one but Jeanie and Reuben ever knew the secret of Effie and George. After ten years, Effie retired to a convent on the continent, where she spent her remaining years grieving for her husband and the son she had never known.

Reuben and Jeanie Butler, who had been so unavoidably involved in sordidness and crime, lived out their lives happily and carried their secret with them to the grave.

Critical Evaluation

Many critics have considered this novel Scott's best; but, although *The Heart of Midlothian* has received much praise, the reasons for its success are different from those of most of the Waverley series. The novel does not have the usual Gothic props of ruined abbeys, spectres, prophesizing old hags, or lonely windswept castles. Only one scene, where Jeanie Deans meets George Staunton at moonrise in Nicol Muschat's Cairn, is typical of wild, picturesque settings so frequent in Scott's fiction.

The plot is based upon authentic historical events; the Porteous Riot of 1736 in Edinburgh's famous Old Tolbooth prison, or as it was commonly called "the heart of Midlothian," sets the action on its course. But the story is not actually one of social history involving questions of justice. Nor is it a study of Scottish Presbyterianism. Long debates on both these issues take up major portions of the work, but Scott comes to no clear conclusions. These issues do not provide the unifying force that holds the story together.

A strong moral theme is the binding element, for most of the main protagonists are caught in dilemmas of conscience. Jeanie Deans must decide between telling a lie to save her sister Effie's life or speaking the truth and thereby condemning her to execution. Effie herself has the choice of attempting to live virtuously as she was taught or being faithful to her dissipated, criminal lover. Their father, stern David Deans, must decide whether to adhere to his Presbyterian principles or come to terms with the human condition and forgive Effie. George Staunton, alias Robertson, is forced either to follow his wild inclinations and stay with his desperate associates or to reform and assume responsibilities of position and inheritance. He must also confront his obligation to marry Effie, whom he has wronged. These varied dilemmas of conscience constitute the texture of the novel.

The heroine is the one strong character in the novel, but she differs strikingly from the usual Waverley heroine, who is tall, beautiful, exceedingly well bred, romantic and, of course, wealthy. Jeanie Deans is the unusual: a peasant heroine, plain in appearance, not trained in social deportment, and lacking a romantic, Gothic background to aid her. Perhaps the moral seriousness of *The Heart of Midlothian* plus the fact that Scott drew his heroine from the lower classes not only make the novel popular but also give it a coherence and unity unusual in his fiction.

In most of Scott's novels minor characters, who are largely drawn from Scottish rural life and humble occupations, are more real than upper-class figures. When dealing with them Scott has a more energetic and colorful style. Critics often remark that the strength of his work lies in such characters as Caleb Balderstone of *The Bride of Lammermoor,* Edie Ochiltree and Maggie Mucklebackit of *The Antiquary,* Callum Beg and Widow Flockhart of *Waverly.* Scott reproduces their speech faithfully and with obvious relish.

But in *The Heart of Midlothian,* although he still opposes the upper-class culture—with that of the lower and exploits resulting tensions, he elevates a dairyman's daughter to the status of heroine. And, in spite of the unyielding virtue of her character and the contrived situation in which she becomes involved, he not only makes her believable, but also enlists the somewhat skeptical, hesitant reader on her side. She has common sense, and the rough, matter-of-fact elements in her daily life leave no doubt that she will conquer all adverse forces to triumph in Effie's cause. The law of retribution is at work here as in Scott's other novels, but Providence has a fresh, indefatigable agent in Jeanie. It is interesting that she was Scott's own favorite heroine.

Believable, too, are several scenes in *The Heart of Midlothian,* particularly the Porteous Riot which opens the novel. Scott handles realistically the mob's capture of Tolbooth prison and the lynching of Captain Porteous. Another well constructed scene, and one which is moving, if sentimental, is that of Effie's trial. In such sections Scott tightens his control of character interaction and effects economy of language.

However, the entire account of Jeanie's journey to London to obtain from Queen Caroline Effie's pardon slows down the novel and fails to hold the reader's interest. And the last section of the work—almost an epilogue— though required by Scott's publisher, does not seem to be required by the story itself. Jeanie and Reuben with their children and old David Deans live out a mellowed existence in picturesque Roseneath; their rural domesticity is only enlivened by the reunion of Jeanie and her sister (now Lady Staunton) and George's murder by his and Effie's unrecognized son.

If some portions of the novel seem protracted and rather unexciting, still the whole is well-knit and more logical than much of Scott's fiction. Because Scott considered the function of the novel to furnish "solace from the toils of ordinary life by an excursion into the regions of imagination," he ordinarily was indifferent to technique; instead, he concentrated on subject matter. He stressed factual accuracy but felt that too much care in composition might destroy what he termed "abundant spontaneity." Following his own dicta, he wrote rapidly with disregard for planning and revision. He improvised with careless haste and his novels often suffer from poor style and construction. Critics have repeatedly faulted his work for improper motivation and lack of organic unity.

However, one does not get the impression from reading *The Heart of Midlothian* that the author wrote at his usual breakneck speed, casually assembling scenes and characters together without forethought. Motivation is more properly furnished, characterization consistent, and, as mentioned, the dilemmas of conscience are carried through logically. Scott has dispensed in this novel with excess supernatural escapades and the often flamboyant trappings of decadent nobility. He concentrates on the sincerity and integrity of his lower-class protagonists to effect a democratic realism new in the historical English novel, a genre he himself had invented.

Bibliography

Clements, Frances M. " 'Queens Love Revenge as Well as Their Subjects': Thematic Unity in *The Heart of Midlothian*," in *Studies in Scottish Literature.* X (1972), pp. 10–17.

Cockshut, A.O.J. *The Achievement of Walter Scott.* New York: New York University Press, 1969, pp. 171–192.

Craig, D. "*The Heart of Midlothian*: Its Religious Basis," in *Essays in Criticism.* VIII (April, 1958), pp. 217–225.

Cusac, Marian H. *Narrative Suggestion in the Novels of Sir Walter Scott.* The Hague: Mouton, 1969, pp. 32–36, 106–112.

Fisher, P.F. "Providence, Fate, and the Historical Imagination in Scott's *The Heart of Midlothian*," in *Nineteenth-Century Fiction.* X (1955), pp. 99–114.

Fiske, Christabel F. *Epic Suggestion in the Imagery of the Waverley Novels.* New Haven, Conn.: Yale University Press, 1940.

Fleishman, Avrom. *The English Historical Novel: Walter Scott to Virginia Woolf.* Baltimore: Johns Hopkins University Press, 1971, pp. 67–69.

Gordon, Robert C. *Under Which King? A Study of the Scottish Waverley Novels.* New York: Barnes & Noble, 1969, pp. 84–97.

Hart, Francis R. *Scott's Novels: The Plotting of Historic Survival.* Charlottesville: University of Virginia Press, 1966, pp. 127–149.

Hartveit, Lars. *Dream Within a Dream, a Thematic Approach to Scott's Vision of Fictional Reality.* New York: Humanities Press, 1974, pp. 22–71.

Hayden, John O. *Scott; The Critical Heritage.* New York: Barnes & Noble, 1970, pp. 165–176.

Hyde, William J. "Jeanie Deans and the Queen: Appearance and Reality," in

Nineteenth-Century Fiction. XXVIII (1973), pp. 86–92.

Johnson, Edgar. *Sir Walter Scott: The Great Unknown,* Volume I. New York: Macmillan, 1970, pp. 655–662.

Kettle, Arnold. *An Introduction to the English Novel,* Volume I. London: Hutchinson's, 1951, pp. 105–122.

Lauber, John. *Sir Walter Scott.* New York: Twayne, 1966, pp. 106–114.

Lynskey, Winifred. "The Drama of the Elect and the Reprobate in Scott's *Heart of Midlothian,*" in *Boston University Studies in English.* IV (1960), pp. 39–48.

Madden, William A. "The Search for Forgiveness in Some Nineteenth-Century English Novels," in *Comparative Literature Studies.* III (1966), pp. 139–153.

Marshall, W.H. "Point of View and Structure in *The Heart of Midlothian,*" in *Nineteenth-Century Fiction.* XVI (1961), pp. 257–262.

Mayhead, Robin. "*The Heart of Midlothian*: Scott as Artist," in *Essays in Criticism.* VI (July, 1956), pp. 266–277.

Pritchett, Victor S. *The Living Novel.* New York: Reynal & Hitchcock, 1947, pp. 63–68.

Van Ghent, Dorothy. *The English Novel.* New York: Rinehart, 1953, pp. 113–124.

Welsh, Alexander. *The Hero of the Waverley Novels.* New Haven, Conn.: Yale University Press, 1963, pp. 59–62, 127–148, 163–164.

IVANHOE

Type of work: Novel
Author: Sir Walter Scott (1771–1832)
Type of plot: Historical romance
Time of plot: 1194
Locale: England
First published: 1820

For a hundred and fifty years, Ivanhoe *has held its charm in the popular mind as the epitome of chivalric novels. Among its characters are two of the most popular of English heroes, Richard the Lion-Hearted and Robin Hood. It may not be Scott's greatest novel, but it is without doubt his most popular.*

Principal Characters

Cedric the Saxon, the rude, warlike master of Rotherwood, a small landholder during the reign of Richard I. Obstinately hoping for Saxon independence, he wishes his ward, Lady Rowena, to marry Athelstane of Coningsburgh, a descendant of the ancient Saxon kings, and he disinherits his son, Wilfred of Ivanhoe, for learning Norman customs. When Ivanhoe returns from the Crusades and falls wounded after winning the tournament at Ashby-de-la-Zouche, Cedric allows him to be cared for by strangers. Captured by Normans, Cedric is taken to Torquilstone Castle, but he escapes and helps the besiegers take the castle. In the end he becomes somewhat reconciled to the marriage of Ivanhoe and Rowena and with Norman rule under King Richard I.

Wilfred of Ivanhoe, the chivalrous, disowned hero, a Crusader. Returning home disguised as a pilgrim, he befriends a Jew, Isaac of York, and his daughter Rebecca on the way to the tournament at Ashby. After defeating his opponents in the tourney he reveals his true identity and faints from loss of blood while accepting the prize from Rowena. Captured with the Jew, along with Cedric and his party, he is cared for by Rebecca at Torquilstone and is rescued by the disguised King Richard. He repays Rebecca's kindness by defending her when she is accused of witchcraft. After Athelstane relinquishes his claim to Rowena, Ivanhoe marries her and enjoys prosperity under Richard's rule.

Lady Rowena, Cedric's beautiful ward. At Rotherwood she inquires of Ivanhoe's exploits from the disguised knight himself, becomes the tournament queen at his request, and learns his identity after he is declared victor. Seized by Norman knights, she is saved from the advances of a captor and the Torquilstone fire by the timely intervention of Richard, Cedric, and Robin Hood. Happy when Athelstane disclaims her, she weds Ivanhoe.

Isaac of York, an avaricious but kindly Jew. He supplies Ivanhoe with a horse and armor for the tournament and takes him off to be cared for after the knight has been wounded. Isaac is taken prisoner and about to be tortured for his gold when rescuers lay siege to the castle. He is set free but forced to pay a ransom. Learning of his daughter's abduction at the hands of haughty Sir Brian de Bois-Guilbert, he sends for Ivanhoe to rescue her. Sick of England, he and his daughter move to Spain.

Rebecca, the generous, lovely Jewess who returns Ivanhoe's payment for the horse and armor and nurses his wound. She is carried off by an enamoured Templar during the siege. Accused of witchcraft at Templar headquarters, she is rescued from burning by the exhausted Ivanhoe's defense.

Sir Brian de Bois-Guilbert (brē·än də bwä'-gēl·bĕr'), the fierce and passionate Templar who kidnaps Rebecca, deserts her because of Templar politics, and fights a fatal battle against her defender, Ivanhoe.

Richard the Lion-Hearted, an audacious, hardy king. Secretly returning to England, he saves Ivanhoe's life at the tournament and leads the siege of Torquilstone. After thwarting an ambush, he throws off his disguise of the "Black Sluggard" and claims his rightful throne.

Robin Hood (Locksley), the famed outlaw. He wins an archery contest, supports Richard during the siege of Torquilstone, and becomes a loyal subject of the restored King.

Athelstane of Coningsburgh (ath'əl-stān), the sluggish Saxon knight who half-heartedly woos Rowena and loses fights with Richard and Bois-Guilbert.

Maurice de Bracy, an ambitious Norman who captures Rowena; however, he possesses too much honor to pursue his designs on her.

Reginald Front de Boeuf (rĕ·zhē·nȧl' frôn' də bĕf'), the savage Norman who

seizes Isaac for his gold. He dies of a wound inflicted by Richard amid the flames of Torquilstone.

Prince John, Richard's haughty, unscrupulous brother, who has tried to usurp the throne with the aid of the Norman nobles.

Lucas de Beaumanoir (lü·kä' də bō·mȧ-nwȧr'), the bigoted, ascetic head of the Templars who presides over Rebecca's trial on a charge of witchcraft. His Order is disbanded by Richard because of treasonous activities and plotting against the King and the realm.

Philip and
Albert Malvoisin (ȧl·bĕr' mȧl·vwȧ·zȧn'), Templars executed by King Richard for treason.

Waldemar Fitzurse (vȧl·də·mȧr' fĭts·ẽrs'), Prince John's wily, aspiring follower, who is banished by Richard.

Aymer (ā'mẽr), the comfort-loving Prior of Jorvaulx, who is captured by Robin Hood and forced to pay a ransom.

Ulrica (ōōl·rē'kə), the Saxon hag who burns Torquilstone in order to be revenged on the Normans.

Gurth, Cedric's swineherd and Ivanhoe's loyal servant, who is given his freedom.

Wamba, Cedric's quick-witted jester; he helps Cedric escape Torquilstone by dressing him in a priest's robe.

Friar Tuck, Robin Hood's hefty, hearty follower, a hedge priest who treats Richard to a meal.

The Story

Night was drawing near when Prior Aymer of Jorvaux and the haughty Templar, Brian de Bois-Guilbert, overtook a swineherd and a fool by the roadside and asked directions to Rotherwood, the dwelling of Cedric the Saxon. The answers of these serfs so confused the Templar and the prior that they would have gone far afield had it not been for a pilgrim from the Holy Land whom they encountered shortly afterward. The pilgrim was also traveling to Rotherwood, and he brought them safely to Cedric's hall, where they claimed lodging for the night. The custom of those rude days afforded hospitality to all benighted travelers, and so Cedric gave a grudging welcome to the Norman lords.

There was a feast at Rotherwood that night. On the dais beside Cedric the Saxon sat his ward, the lovely Lady Rowena, descendant of the ancient Saxon princes. It was the old man's ambition to wed her to Athelstane of Coningsburgh, of the line of King Alfred. Because his son, Wilfred of Ivanhoe, had fallen in love with Rowena, Cedric had banished him, and the young knight had gone with King Richard to Palestine. None in the banquet hall that night suspected that the pilgrim was Ivanhoe himself.

Another traveler who had claimed shelter at Rotherwood that night was an aged Jew, Isaac of York. Hearing some orders the Templar muttered to his servants as the feast ended, Ivanhoe warned the old jew that Bois-Guilbert had designs on his moneybag or his person. Without taking leave of their host the next morning, the disguised pilgrim and Isaac of York left Rotherwood and continued on their way to the nearby town of Ashby de la Zouche.

Many other travelers were also on their way to the town, for a great tournament was to be held there. Prince John, Regent of England in King Richard's absence, would preside. The winner of the tournament would be allowed to name the Queen of Love and Beauty and receive the prize of the passage of arms from her hands.

Ivanhoe attended the tournament with the word *Disinherited* written upon his shield. Entering the lists, he struck the shield of Bois-Guilbert with the point of his lance and challenged that knight to mortal combat. In the first passage both knights splintered their lances but neither was unhorsed. At the second passage Ivanhoe's lance struck Bois-Guilbert's helmet and upset him. Then one by one Ivanhoe vanquished five knights who had agreed to take on all comers. When the heralds declared the Disinherited Knight victor of the tourney, Ivanhoe named Rowena the Queen of Love and Beauty.

In the tournament on the following day Ivanhoe was pressed hard by three antagonists, but he received unexpected help from a knight in black, whom the spectators had called the Black Sluggard because of his previous inactivity. Ivanhoe, because of his earlier triumphs during the day, was named champion of the tournament once more. In order to receive the gift from Lady Rowena, Ivanhoe had to remove his helmet. When he did so, he was recognized. He received the chaplet, his prize, kissed the hand of Lady Rowena, and then fainted from loss of blood. Isaac of York and his daughter, Rebecca, were sitting nearby, and Rebecca suggested to her father that they nurse Ivanhoe until he was well. Isaac and his daughter started for their home with the wounded knight carried in a horse litter. On the way they joined the train of Cedric the Saxon, who was still ignorant of the Disinherited Knight's identity.

Before the travelers had gone far, however, they were set upon and captured by a party led by three Norman knights, Bois-Guilbert, Maurice de Bracy, and Reginald Front de Boeuf. They were imprisoned in Front de Boeuf's castle of Torquilstone. De Bracy had designs upon Lady Rowena because she was an heiress of royal lineage. The Templar desired to possess Rebecca. Front de Boeuf hoped to extort a large sum of money from the aged Jew. Cedric was held for ransom. The wounded knight was put into the charge of an ancient hag named Ulrica.

Isaac and his daughter were placed in separate rooms. Bois-Guilbert went to Rebecca in her tower prison and asked her to adopt Christianity so that they might be married. But the plot of the Norman nobles with regard to their prisoners was thwarted by an assault on the castle by Richard the Lion-Hearted, The Black Sluggard of the tournament at Ashby, in company with Robin Hood and his outlaws. Ulrica aided the besiegers by starting a fire within the castle walls. Robin Hood and his men took the prisoners to the forest along with the Norman nobles. In the confusion, however, Bois-Guilbert escaped with Rebecca, and Isaac made preparation to ransom her from the Templar. De Bracy was set free and he hurried to inform Prince John that he had seen and talked with Richard. John plotted to make Richard his prisoner.

Isaac went to the establishment of the Knights Templar and begged to see Bois-Guilbert. Lucas de Beaumanoir, the grand master of the Templars, ordered Isaac admitted to his presence. Isaac was frightened when the grand master asked him his business with the Templar. When he told his story, the grand master learned of Bois-Guilbert's seizure of Rebecca. It was suggested that Bois-Guilbert was under a spell cast by Rebecca. Condemned as a witch, she was sentenced to be burned at the stake. In desperation she demanded, as was her right, a champion to defend her against the charge. Lucas de Beaumanoir agreed and named Bois-Guilbert champion of the Temple.

The day arrived for Rebecca's execution. A pile of wood had been laid around the stake. Rebecca, seated in a black chair, awaited the arrival of her defender. Three times the heralds called upon her champion to appear. At the third call a strange knight rode into the lists and announced himself as Rebecca's champion. When Bois-Guilbert realized that the stranger was Ivanhoe, he at first refused combat because Ivanhoe's wounds were not completely healed. But the grand master gave orders for the contest to begin. As everyone expected, the tired horse of Ivanhoe and its exhausted rider went down at the first blow, so that Ivanhoe's lance merely touched the shield of the Templar. Then to the astonishment of all, Bois-Guilbert reeled in his saddle and fell to the ground. Ivanhoe arose from where he had fallen and drew his sword. Placing his foot on the breast of the fallen knight, he called upon Bois-Guilbert to yield himself or die on the spot. There was no answer from Bois-Guilbert, for he was dead, a victim of the violence of his own passions. The grand master declared that Rebecca was acquitted of the charge against her.

At that moment the Black Knight appeared, followed by a band of knights and men-at-arms. It was King Richard, come to arrest Rebecca's accusers on a charge of treason. The grand master saw the flag of the Temple hauled down and the royal standard raised in its place.

King Richard had returned in secret to reclaim his throne. Robin Hood became his true follower. Athelstane relinquished his claims to Lady Rowena's hand so that she and Ivanhoe could be married. Cedric the Saxon, reconciled at last with his son, gave his consent, and Richard himself graced their wedding.

Isaac and Rebecca left England for Granada, hoping to find in that foreign land greater happiness than could ever be theirs in England.

Critical Evaluation

Scott himself wrote that he left the Scottish scenes of his previous novels and turned to the Middle Ages in *Ivanhoe* because he feared the reading public was growing weary of the repetition of Scottish themes in his books. Since he was fascinated with history all of his life, it was logical that Scott should turn to the past for subject matter. Many faults have been found with the historical facts of the book; Robin Hood, if he lived at all, belonged to a later century than that represented in the novel, and by the time of Richard I the distinction between Saxons and Normons had faded. But the thrilling story, the drama and action, still grip the reader, whatever liberties Scott took with history.

Scott's four great chivalric novels all possess similar structures in that they all focus on a moment of crisis between two great individuals, a moment which determines the survival of one of the opposed pair. In *Ivanhoe,* the symbolic contrast is between Richard the Lion-Hearted and his brother John. The struggle between these two helps to raise one of the principal questions of the novel: the decadence of chivalry. For generations of juvenile readers, *Ivanhoe* represented the glory of chivalric adventure, but actually Scott entertained serious doubts about the chivalric tradition. At several strategic points in *Ivanhoe,* passages occur which unequivocally damn the reckless inhumanity of romantic chivalry.

The novel is symmetrically designed in three parts, each reaching its climax in a great military spectacle. The first part ends with the Ashby tournament, the second with the liberation from the castle of Front de Boeuf, and the third with the trial by combat of Rebecca. The beginning chapters draw together all of the character groups for the tournament, Ivanhoe being present only as the mysterious palmer. The problem of seating at the tournament provides a sketch of the cultural animosities that divide the world of the novel.

Richard is the moral and political center of the book, and, therefore, the proper object of Ivanhoe's fidelity. The captive king does not appear until he fights the mysterious Black Knight during the second day of the tournament. He saves Ivanhoe and then disappears until the scene of his midnight feast with Friar Tuck. The reader's impression of him is of a fun-loving, heroic fighter. The friar thinks of him as a man of "prudence and of counsel." Richard possesses a native humanity and a love of life, as well as the heroic chivalric qualities. He is always ready to act as a protector of others.

John, by contrast, is an ineffectual ruler whose own followers despise him. His forces quickly disintegrate, his followers abandoning him for their own selfish ends. He is a petulant, stupid man, incapable of inspiring loyalty. It is inevitable that the historical climax of the novel should be the confrontation between Richard and John. The chivalric code has become completely corrupt in the England left to John's care. Both the narrator and the characters make clear that chivalry is no more than a mixture of "heroic folly and dangerous imprudence."

Rebecca speaks against chivalry, asking during the bloody siege of the castle if possession by a "demon of vainglory" brings "sufficient rewards for the sacrifice of every kindly affection, for a life spent miserably that yet may make others miserable?" (Rebecca is antichivalric, yet she is the most romantic character in the book, suggesting the traditional chivalric attitudes towards women.) The narrator speaks most sharply of the chivalric code at the end of the tournament: "This ended the memorable field of Ashby-de-la-Zouche, one of the most gallantly contested tournaments of that age; for although only four knights, including one who was smothered by the heat of his armour, had died upon the field, yet upwards of thirty were desperately wounded, four or five of whom never recovered. Several more were disabled for life; and those who escaped best carried the marks of the conflict to the grave with them. Hence it is always mentioned in the old records as the 'gentle and joyous passage of arms at Ashby.' "

An argument has been made that Scott's historical novels, such as *Ivanhoe* are inferior to his earlier novels based on his direct, personal knowledge of the Scottish customs and characters and land. But even in the historical novels, Scott's characters are colorful, full of vitality, and realized with amazing verisimilitude. Scott's knowledge of the past about which he was writing was so deep that he could draw upon it at will to clothe out his fictions. He did not find it necessary to research a novel such as *Ivanhoe* in order to write it; the historical lore was already part of him. Years before, at the time when he was beginning the Waverley series, he had written a study about chivalry. His prolific writing did not seem to exhaust his resources.

Sir Walter Scott was one of the most prolific writers in the history of British fiction; only Trollope could stand up against his record. Scott's novels were published anonymously, although their authorship came to be an open secret. His friends found it difficult to believe that he was the author of the novels, for he lived the life of a county magistrate and landowner, spending hours daily on these occupations, as well as entertaining lavishly and writing poetry and nonfiction works. His secret was that he would rise early and finish novel-writing before breakfast. In time, his compulsive working injured his health, and while he was writing *Ivanhoe,* he was tortured by a cramp of the stomach and suffered such pain that he could not physically hold the pen, but was forced to dictate much of the story.

Like many great novels, *Ivanhoe* betrays a complexity of attitude on the part of the author. Although much of the book makes clear Scott's severe view of the code of chivalry, beyond the antichivalric attitude the reader can see a definite attraction on Scott's part for the romantic traditions of the period. It is in Richard that Scott seems to instill the chivalric virtues, although his personality is not romantic. Through the characters of Rebecca and Rowena, Ivanhoe and Richard, Scott dramatized his ambivalent feelings about the chivalric period. The tension created through these mixed feelings, coupled with the dramatic (if historically inaccurate) story and the vast accumulation of detail as to costume and social customs and historical anecdotes, all worked together to create a novel which has remained popular for more than a hundred and fifty years. *Ivanhoe* is no longer considered as seriously as Scott's Scottish novels, but its achievement remains impressive.

Bibliography

Baker, Ernest A. *History of the English Novel,* Volume VI. London: Witherby, 1929, pp. 176–206.

Brewer, Wilmon. *Shakespeare's Influence on Sir Walter Scott.* Boston: Cornhill, 1925.

Buchan, John. *Sir Walter Scott.* London: Cassell, 1932, pp. 180–198.

Chandler, Alice. "Chivalry and Romance: Scott's Medieval Novels," in *Studies in Romanticism.* XIV (1975), pp. 191–194.

Cockshut, A.O.J. *The Achievement of Walter Scott.* New York: New York University Press, 1969, pp. 97–100.

Cusac, Marian H. *Narrative Structure in the Novels of Sir Walter Scott.* The Hague: Mouton, 1969, pp. 106–113, 118–119.

Duncan, Joseph E. "The Anti-Romantic in *Ivanhoe,*" in *Nineteenth-Century Fiction.* IX (March, 1955), pp. 293–300.

Fisch, Harold. *The Dual Image: The Figure of the Jew in English and American Literature.* New York: Ktav, 1971, pp. 59–62.

Fiske, Christabel F. *Epic Suggestion in the Imagery of the Waverley Novels.* New Haven, Conn.: Yale University Press, 1940.

Hart, Francis R. *Scott's Novels: The Plotting of Historic Survival.* Charlottesville: University of Virginia Press, 1966.

Hayden, John O. *Scott; The Critical Heritage.* New York: Barnes & Noble, 1970, pp. 177–184, 188–255.

Johnson, Edgar. *Sir Walter Scott: The Great Unknown*, Volume I. New York: Macmillan, 1970, pp. 736–746.

Lauber, John. *Sir Walter Scott*. New York: Twayne, 1966, pp. 125–126, 130–131.

Rosenberg, Edgar. "The Jew as Clown and the Jew's Daughter," in *From Shylock to Svengali: Jewish Stereotypes in English Fiction*. Edited by Edgar Rosenberg. Stanford, Calif.: Stanford University Press, 1960, pp. 73–115.

Simeone, William E. "The Robin Hood of *Ivanhoe*," in *Journal of American Folklore*. LXXIV (1961), pp. 230–234.

Tindall, William Y., Perry Miller and Lyman Bryson. *"Ivanhoe,"* in *Invitation to Learning: English and American Novels*. Edited by George D. Crothers. New York: Basic Books, 1966, pp. 81–88.

Welsh, Alexander. *The Hero of the Waverley Novels*. New Haven, Conn.: Yale University Press, 1963.

KENILWORTH

Type of work: Novel
Author: Sir Walter Scott (1771–1832)
Type of plot: Historical romance
Time of plot: 1575
Locale: England
First published: 1821

Scott spends much time in this historical novel establishing the setting and background for the slight action, and his immense knowledge and skill give these passages literary merit. As always in Scott's novels, the characters are well-portrayed and the story handled in a professional manner.

Principal Characters

Edmund Tressilian, an impoverished young gentleman, a friend of the Earl of Sussex and an unsuccessful suitor for Amy Robsart's hand. Generous, intelligent and honorable, he seeks to free Amy from Richard Varney, whom he believes to be her paramour. When Amy, secretly the wife of the Earl of Leicester, refuses to leave Cumnor Place, he tries to put his case before Queen Elizabeth. Supported by Amy's father and Sussex, he nonetheless makes a poor showing because of Varney's cleverness and his own desire to protect Amy. Accused later of cuckolding the Earl of Leicester, Tressilian is forced to duel with the Earl but is saved by the timely intervention of two friends. He clears himself before the Queen, though too late to save Amy from Varney's treachery.

Robert Dudley, the Earl of Leicester and master of Kenilworth Castle. Rivaled only by Sussex in Elizabeth's esteem, he has the advantage of appealing to her femininity. Knowing his marriage to Amy would spoil his chance for advancement, he keeps her at Cumnor Place under Varney's supervision. Basically noble, he is also quite gullible. When he tries to tell Elizabeth of his marriage, Varney convinces him Amy has been unfaithful. In a rage he orders Varney to kill her and fights a duel with Tressilian. On learning the truth he reveals his marriage and tries in vain to save Amy. He suffers the loss of his wife and temporary court disfavor.

Amy Robsart, Leicester's unfortunate wife. Deeply in love with him, she wants recognition as his lawful wife but hesitates to ruin his life at court. Imprisoned at Cumnor Place, she escapes with Tressilian's servant, Wayland Smith, to Kenilworth after Varney gives her a mild dose of poison. There she tries to see her husband and reveal her true identity, but she is deemed insane by Queen Elizabeth. Through Varney's scheme she is sent back to Cumnor Place and tricked into falling to her death. Lovely and honorable, she is also willful and tragic.

Richard Varney, Leicester's courtier and right-hand man, a cautious, charming, clever, imaginative person who is also ambitious and unscrupulous. He is instrumental in poisoning Sussex. Facing failure in his plans to keep Amy from interfering with Leicester's advance in royal favor, he persuades his master of her infidelity. He is captured after Amy's death and commits suicide in prison.

Michael Lambourne, a swashbuckling, unprincipled man of action in Varney's service and a participant in the plans to dispose of Amy. Varney's pupil in rascality, he tries to surpass his master and is killed for his efforts.

Queen Elizabeth, an extremely shrewd and skillful ruler, adept at playing court factions against one another but still capricious and feminine. Hot-tempered, vain, and jealous, she loses her self-control when Leicester reveals his marriage, and she threatens him with execution. She eventually forgives him and restores him to royal favor.

Wayland Smith, Tressilian's hardy friend and servant. A skilled smith and alchemist, he saves Sussex from poison, assists Amy to go to Kenilworth, and prevents Leicester from killing Tressilian in a duel.

Dickie Sludge (Flibbertigibbet), Wayland's swift, ugly, clever, elfish friend. He almost causes Tressilian's death by mischievously withholding Amy's letter to Leicester, but he redeems himself by delivering it in time.

Thomas Ratcliffe, the Earl of Sussex, the soldierly court opponent of Leicester. Poisoned under Varney's direction, he recovers and supports Tressilian.

Walter Raleigh, a Sussex courtier who wins Elizabeth's favor and is knighted. A friend of Tressilian, he assists at Varney's arrest.

Nicholas Blount, a soldierly, middle-aged courtier who becomes a court fool when knighted.

Dr. Demetrius Doboobie (Alasco), a villainous alchemist and astrologer serving Leicester. Used by Varney as a poisoner, he also dies accidentally of his own poison.

Anthony Foster, the keeper of Cumnor Place, a vulgar, ugly, puritanical and miserly person who serves as Amy's jailer. After her death he dies hiding in his gold room, unable to get out.

Janet Foster, his good-hearted daughter and Amy's maid. She aids Amy in her escape.

Sir Hugh Robsart, Amy's poor, senile father who encourages Tressilian to free her.

Master Michael Mumblazen, Sir Hugh's overseer, a rustic, generous person who supplies Tressilian with money for the purpose of thwarting Varney.

Giles Gosling, the Cumnor innkeeper who suggests that Tressilian put his case before Queen Elizabeth but then refuses to help Wayland.

Laurence Goldthred, a customer at Gosling's inn who wagers with Lambourne and later has his horse "borrowed" by Wayland.

Erasmus Holiday, a pretentious, pedantic schoolmaster who directs Tressilian to Wayland.

The Story

Michael Lambourne, who in his early youth had been a ne'er-do-well, had just returned from his travels. While drinking and boasting in Giles Gosling's inn, he wagered that he could gain admittance to Cumnor Place, a large manor where an old friend was now steward. It was rumored in the village that Tony Foster was keeping a beautiful young woman prisoner at the manor. Edmund Tressilian, another guest at the inn, went with Michael to Cumnor Place. As Tressilian had suspected, he found the woman there to be his former sweetheart, Amy Robsart, apparently a willing prisoner. At Cumnor Place he also encountered Richard Varney, her supposed seducer, and a sword fight ensued. The duel was broken up by Michael Lambourne, who had decided to ally himself with his old friend, Tony Foster.

Contrary to Tressilian's idea, Amy was not Varney's paramour but the lawful wife of Varney's master, the Earl of Leicester, Varney being only the go-between and accomplice in Amy's elopement. Leicester, who was a rival of the Earl of Sussex for Queen Elizabeth's favor, feared that the news of his marriage to Amy would displease the queen, and he had convinced Amy that their marriage must be kept secret.

Tressilian returned to Lidcote Hall to obtain Hugh Robsart's permission to bring Varney to justice on a charge of seduction. On his way there he employed as his manservant Wayland Smith, formerly an assistant to Dr. Doboobie, an alchemist and astrologer. Later he visited the Earl of Sussex, through whom he hoped to petition either the queen or the Earl of Leicester in Amy's behalf. While there, Wayland Smith saved Sussex's life after the earl had been poisoned.

When the earl heard Tressilian's story, he presented the petition directly to the queen. Confronted by Elizabeth, Varney swore that Amy was his lawful wife, and Leicester, who was standing by, confirmed the lie. Elizabeth then ordered Varney to present Amy to her when she visited Kenilworth the following week.

Leicester sent a letter to Amy asking her to appear at Kenilworth as Varney's wife. She refused. In order to have an excuse for disobeying Elizabeth's orders regarding Amy's presence at Kenilworth, Varney had Alasco, the former Dr. Doboobie, mix a potion which would make Amy ill but not kill her. This plan was thwarted, however, by Wayland Smith, who had been sent by Tressilian to help her. She escaped from Cumnor Place and with the assistance of Wayland Smith made her way to Kenilworth to see Leicester.

When she arrived at Kenilworth, the place was bustling in preparation for Elizabeth's arrival that afternoon. Wayland Smith took Amy to Tressilian's quarters, where she wrote Leicester a letter telling him of her escape from Cumnor Place and asking his aid. Wayland Smith lost the letter and through a misunderstanding he was ejected from the castle. Amy, disappointed that Leicester did not come to her, left her apartment and went into the garden. There the queen discovered her. Judging Amy to be insane because of her contradictory statements, she returned Amy to the custody of Varney, her supposed husband.

Leicester decided to confess the true story to the queen. But Varney, afraid for his own fortunes if Leicester fell from favor, convinced the earl that Amy had been unfaithful to him, and that Tressilian was her lover. Leicester, acting upon Varney's lies, decided that the death of Amy and her lover would be just punishment. Varney took Amy back to Cumnor Place and plotted her death. Leicester relented and sent Michael Lambourne to tell Varney that Amy must not die, but Varney killed Lambourne in order that he might go through with his murder of Amy. Leicester and Tressilian fought a duel, but before either harmed the other they were interrupted by Dickie Sludge, the child who had stolen Amy's letter. Reading it, Leicester realized that Amy had been faithful to him and that the complications of the affair had been caused by the machinations of Varney.

Leicester immediately went to the queen and told her the whole story. Elizabeth was angry, but she sent Tressilian and Sir Walter Raleigh to bring Amy to Kenilworth. Unfortunately, Tressilian arrived too late to save Amy. She had fallen through a trapdoor so rigged that when she stepped upon it she plunged to her death.

Tressilian and Sir Walter Raleigh seized Varney and carried him off to prison. There Varney committed suicide. Elizabeth permitted grief-strieken Leicester to retire from her court for several years but later recalled him and installed him once more in her favor. Much later in life he remarried. He met his death as a result of poison he intended for someone else.

Critical Evaluation

To a historical novelist like Sir Walter Scott, vivid and accurate settings were invaluable tools for summoning a past age before readers' eyes; but nowhere in his novels was the masterful use of place more central to theme and meaning than in *Kenilworth*. In this novel of love and intrigue in Elizabethan England, the moral statements dramatized through the story are buttressed by their association with either of the two places where all the major action occurs—Cumnor Place or Kenilworth; both places are described in highly-charged images and richly symbolic language. Cumnor Place is like a gilded prison. Decorated lavishly, its rooms sumptuously comfortable and filled with expensive finery, it is nevertheless designed as a place of detainment and hiding. In one vivid and eerie passage, Scott describes its specially designed oaken shutters and thick drapes, which allow the rooms to be ablaze with light without the slightest flicker showing to an observer on the outside. Leicester uses this strictly private place as the hiding place for his wife Amy Robsart, whose existence he wishes to keep secret from Queen Elizabeth; he also uses it as a place of escape and relief from court life for himself. He travels to Cumnor in disguise, and while there sheds the finery which identifies and validates him at court.

As opposed to Cumnor Place, Kenilworth is a thoroughly public manor house. With the entire court and nobility preparing for the royal entertainments, it exhibits all the pomp and splendor of a regal palace in its most concentrated form; it is literally exploding with feverish activity. The atmosphere at Kenilworth is one of unreality; in his initial picture of the place, Scott describes a row of guards, along the battlements, who are intended to represent King Arthur's knights—but uncannily, some are real men, some mere pasteboard figures, and it is impossible to distinguish from a distance which are which. A more sinister and frightening instance of the confusion between illusion and reality occurs when Elizabeth encounters Amy in the garden; unable to understand her muddled replies, the queen quickly assumes that Amy is one of the wandering actresses, planted throughout the grounds to pay her homage, who has forgotten her lines in embarrassment or fright.

Between these two places, the two major characters—Leicester and Amy—are torn, and close beside each of them throughout their trials are their personal servants, whose relationships with their master or mistress point up a major theme in the novel. This is the theme of the moral connection or interdependency between masters and their servants; a master, being responsible for his choice of servants, may be judged to a large extent by their attitudes and behavior. Thus, when Varney interviews Michael Lambourne as a prospective employee for himself—and, therefore, ultimately for Leicester —he is very pleased with Lambourne's list of desirable qualities in a courtier's servant, which includes "a close mouth" and "a blunt conscience." These are Varney's specifications exactly, to which are added cunning, greed, and consuming ambition. The proper scheme of things is turned topsy-turvy early in the story, in the symbolically prefigurative scene in which Varney persuades his master to disguise himself as a servant, while he impersonates the master. Leicester's moral guilt is clear when he recognizes his servant's true nature, yet keeps him in service; he calls Varney a devil, but he is a devil indispensable to the Earl's ambitious plans. In contrast to Leicester's and Varney's standards of a good servant are those of the admirable Tressilian, who warns Wayland Smith against knavery, pointing out that transgression committed "by one attending on me diminishes my honour." In addition to Wayland, Amy's maidservant offers another example of a loyal servant who reflects her mistress' worth; Janet Foster is totally devoted, even to the dangerous extreme of aiding her lady's escape from Cumnor Place in defiance of her father, Amy's jailer.

Bibliography

Brewer, Wilmon. *Shakespeare's Influence on Sir Walter Scott.* Boston: Cornhill, 1925, pp. 314–333, 445–447, 456–467.

Buchan, John. *Sir Walter Scott.* London: Cassell, 1932, pp. 231–233.

Cusac, Marian H. *Narrative Structure in the Novels of Sir Walter Scott.* The Hague: Mouton, 1969, pp. 44–45, 106–112.

Fiske, Christabel F. *Epic Suggestion in the Imagery of the Waverley Novels.* New Haven, Conn.: Yale University Press, 1940.

Hart, Francis H. *Scott's Novels: The Plotting of Historic Survival.* Charlottesville: University of Virginia Press, 1966, pp. 196–198, 203–210.

Johnson, Edgar. *Sir Walter Scott: The Great Unknown*, Volume I. New York: Macmillan, 1970, pp. 755–759.

Welsh, Alexander. *The Hero of the Waverley Novels*. New Haven, Conn.: Yale University Press, 1963, pp. 164–165, 220.

QUENTIN DURWARD

Type of work: Novel
Author: Sir Walter Scott (1771–1832)
Type of plot: Historical romance
Time of plot: 1468
Locale: France and Flanders
First published: 1823

This historical adventure, the first of Scott's novels to have a foreign setting, tells the story of a young Scotsman who must go abroad to seek his fortune in the service of a foreign king. The character of the hero Quentin is idealized as a younger son who must rely on his wits and bravery to survive and better himself.

Principal Characters

King Louis XI, sometimes disguised as Maître Pierre, a merchant, the wily, able monarch of France, rivaled in power by the hot-headed Duke of Burgundy. Gifted at Machiavellian politics, he schemes to weaken the Duke by placing, through marriage, a hostile nobleman in his territory. His plan in sending Isabelle, Countess de Croye, and her aunt to Liège is to have the outlawed Wild Boar of Ardennes waylay the ladies and marry one of them. Meanwhile he travels to Burgundy to bargain with the Duke and is imprisoned when the Duke learns of the uprising of his vassals at Liège. Louis barely escapes being killed, chiefly through diplomacy and luck. He assists the Duke in recapturing Liège and the two make a temporary truce.

Charles, the Duke of Burgundy, a rash, hasty-handed nobleman with bull-like courage but little intelligence in statecraft. Resentful of the assistance given by King Louis to the young Countess de Croye and her aunt, the Lady Hameline, he disregards the laws of hospitality and imprisons his royal guest. His temper explodes when he learns that the Wild Boar of Ardennes has led a revolt of the citizens of Liège, a city grown mutinous under the Duke's rule. Until his wrath is diverted against the outlaw he is on the verge of killing the King. His anger abates when Louis volunteers to assist him in retaking the city. The Duke vows that he will bestow the hand of the Countess de Croye on the man who will bring him the Wild Boar's head.

Quentin Durward, a stalwart young Scot. Of ancient lineage, he impresses disguised King Louis but later innocently brings the law down on himself when he cuts down the body of a Bohemian hanged by order of the monarch's provost marshal. He joins the Scottish Archers, the King's bodyguard, of which his uncle is a member. After he has shown his bravery by saving the King from a savage boar, he is chosen to escort the Countess de Croye and Lady Hameline, her aunt, to Liège. During the journey he thwarts the attempt of two court gallants to kidnap the Countess and an ambush set by the Wild Boar of Ardennes, and he delivers the ladies safely to the Bishop of Liège. When the Liègeois revolt, Quentin rescues the Countess at great risk to himself. The two are saved by a Burgundian nobleman and taken to the court of the Duke, where Quentin is instrumental in saving the King's life. At the recapture of Liège he fights with great gallantry and wins the Countess as his bride.

Isabelle, the Countess de Croye, a political pawn in the rivalry of King Louis and the Duke of Burgundy. When Quentin sees her first, she is disguised as Jacqueline, a peasant girl. Twice he saves her from the Wild Boar of Ardennes. The angry Duke offers her hand to the man who kills the outlaw. Quentin's uncle kills the Wild Boar but relinquishes his claim on the Countess to his gallant nephew.

Lady Hameline de Croye, the Countess Isabelle's silly, romantic, middle-aged aunt. Taken prisoner by the Wild Boar of Ardennes, she is compelled to marry him as part of his scheme to claim the estates of Croye.

William de la Marck, called **The Wild Boar of Ardennes,** a violent, treacherous outlaw. He attempts to capture the Countess de Croye, murders the Bishop of Liège, and seizes power in the city. He is killed by Ludovic Lesly when the troops of King Louis and the Duke of Burgundy storm Liège and put down the revolt of its citizens.

Ludovic Lesly, called **Le Balafré,** Quentin Durward's uncle, a cavalier in the King's Scottish Archers. He kills the Wild Boar of Ardennes but bestows the Countess de Croye on his nephew in order to perpetuate the family line.

Hayraddin Maugrabin, a Bohemian adventurer, the secret envoy of King Louis, and Quentin Durward's guide while escorting the Countess de Croye and her aunt to Liège. Although indebted to Quentin for cutting down the body of his hanged brother, he nevertheless tries to lead the young Scot into an ambush set by the Wild Boar of Ardennes. He also aids Lady Hameline in her attempt to deceive Quentin by disguising herself as the Countess during the uprising of the Liègeois. Before he is hanged, by order of the Duke of Burgundy, for impersonating a herald, Maugrabin reveals to Quentin the Wild Boar's plan to disguise his followers as French knights in order to create further dissension between the Duke and the King.

Count Philip de Crèvecoeur, the honorable ambassador sent by the Duke of Burgundy to deliver a list of that nobleman's grievances to King Louis. Later he rescues Quentin Durward and the Countess de Croye from pursuit by the Wild Boar of Ardennes and delivers them to the Duke's court.

Louis, Duke of Orleans, the unwilling prospective husband of King Louis' homely daughter, Joan. He tries to seize the Countess de Croye while she is traveling to Liège in the company of Quentin Durward.

The Count de Dunois, the accomplice of the Duke of Orleans in his attempt to kidnap the Countess de Croye. Dunois is King Louis' most valiant soldier.

Tristan l'Hermite, King Louis' provost marshal, a cruel, stupid ex-monk. He orders Quentin Durward seized and hanged for cutting down the body of Hayraddin Maugrabin's brother.

Oliver le Dain, also called **Oliver le Mauvais** and **Oliver le Diable,** King Louis' barber, groom of the chamber, and trusted adviser. He is a man of unscrupulous cunning.

John, Cardinal of Balue, a traitorous churchman, the secret enemy of King Louis.

Pavillon, the Syndic of Liège. He aids Quentin Durward and the Countess de Croye in their escape from the city after it has been seized by the Wild Boar of Ardennes.

Gertrude Pavillon, his daughter, saved from looting French soldiers by Quentin Durward during the recapture of Liège by French and Burgundian forces.

Louis of Bourbon, the murdered Bishop

of Liège, killed by the Wild Boar of Ardennes.

La Glorieux, the impertinent jester of the Duke of Burgundy.

Trois-Eschelles and
Petit André, the cruel hangmen of Tristan l'Hermite.

Carl Eberson, the son of the Wild Boar of Ardennes. Quentin Durward threatens to kill the lad in order to end the out-

law's butchery of his prisoners after the death of the Bishop of Liège.

Toison d'Or, the herald of the Duke of Burgundy. He unmasks Hayraddin Maugrabin who, calling himself Rouge Sanglier, pretends to be a herald dispatched to the Burgundian court by the Wild Boar of Ardennes.

Lord Crawford, the commander of the Scottish Archers, the King's bodyguard.

The Story

When Quentin Durward, a young Scottish gentleman, approached the ford of a small river near the castle of Plessisles-Tours, in France, he found the river in flood. Two people watched him from the opposite bank. They were King Louis XI in his common disguise of Maître Pierre, a merchant, and Tristan l'Hermite, marshal of France. Quentin entered the flood and nearly drowned. Arriving on the other side and mistaking the king and his companion for a respectable burgher and a butcher, he threatened the two with a drubbing because they had not warned him of the deep ford. Amused by the lad's spirit and daring, Maître Pierre took him to breakfast at a nearby inn to make amends. At the inn Quentin met a beautiful young peasant girl, Jacqueline. Actually, Jacqueline was Isabelle, Countess of Croye. Quentin tried to learn why the merchant, Maître Pierre, acted so much like a noble. He saw many other things which aroused his curiosity but for which he found no explanation.

Shortly afterward Quentin met Ludovic Lesly, known as Le Balafré, his maternal uncle, who was a member of King Louis' Scottish Archers. Le Balafré was exceedingly surprised to learn that Quentin could read and write, something which neither a Durward nor a Lesly had heretofore been able to do.

Quentin discovered the body of a man hanging from a tree. When he cut the man down, he was seized by two officers of Tristan l'Hermite. They were about to hang Quentin for his deed when he asked if there were a good Christian in the crowd who would inform Le Balafré of what was taking place. A Scottish archer heard him and cut his bonds. While they prepared to defend themselves from the mob, Le Balafré rode up with some of his men and took command of the situation, haughtily insisting that Quentin was a member of the Scottish Archers and beyond the reach of the marshal's men. Quentin had not joined the guards as yet, but the lie saved his life. Le Balafré took Quentin to see Lord Crawford, the commander of the guards, to enroll him. When the Scottish Archers were summoned to the royal presence, Quentin was amazed to see that Maître Pierre was King Louis.

Count Philip de Crèvecœur arrived at the castle to demand audience with the king in the name of his master, the Duke of Burgundy. When the king admitted de Crèvecœur , the messenger presented a list of wrongs and oppressions, committed on the frontier, for which the Duke of Burgundy demanded redress. The duke also requested that Louis cease his secret and underhand dealings in the towns of Ghent, Liège and Malines, and, further, that the king send back to Burgundy, under safeguard, the person of Isabelle, Countess of Croye, the duke's ward, whom he accused the king of harboring in secret. Dissatisfied with the king's replies to these demands, de Crèvecœur threw his gauntlet to the floor of the hall. Several of the king's attendants rushed to pick it up and to accept the challenge, but the king ordered the Bishop of Auxerre to lift the gauntlet and to remonstrate with de Crèvecœur for thus declaring war between Burgundy and France. The king and his courtiers then left to hunt wild boars.

During the chase Quentin Durward saved the king's life by spearing a wild boar when Louis slipped and fell before the infuriated beast. The king decided to reward Quentin with a special mission. He was ordered to stand guard in the room where the king entertained de Crèvecœur and others, and at a sign from the king Quentin was to shoot the Burgundian. But the king changed his mind; the signal was not given. Then the king made Quentin the personal bodyguard of Isabelle and her aunt, Lady Hameline, on their way to seek the protection of the Bishop of Liège.

En route to Liège the party was assaulted by the Count de Dunois and the Duke of Orleans. Quentin defended himself with great courage and received timely help from Lord Crawford, who arrived with a body of Scottish Archers. Lord Crawford made both men prisoners. The party's guide on the second half of the journey was Hayraddin Maugrabin, a Bohemian, whose brother it was whom Quentin had cut down earlier. Nothing untoward occurred until the small party reached Flanders. There Quentin discovered, by following Hayraddin, that a plot had been hatched to attack his party and carry off the women to William de la Marck, the Wild Boar of Ardennes. Quentin frustrated these plans by going up the left bank of the Maes instead of the right. He proceeded safely to Liege, where he gave over the women into the protection of the bishop at his castle of Schonwaldt. Four days later William de la Marck attacked the castle and captured it during the night. Lady Hameline escaped. In the bishop's throne room in the castle William de la Marck murdered the churchman in front of his own episcopal throne. Quentin, aroused by the brutality of William, stepped to the side of Carl Eberson, William's son, and placed his dirk at the boy's throat, threatening to kill the lad if William did not cease his butchery. In the confusion Quentin found Isabelle and took her safely from the castle in the disguise of the daughter of the Syndic of Liège. They were pursued by William's men, but were rescued by a party under Count de Crèvecœur, who conducted them safely to the court of the Duke of Burgundy at Peroune.

The king came to the castle of the Duke of Burgundy, asserting the royal prerogative of visiting any of his vassals. Disregarding the laws of hospitality, the duke imprisoned Louis and then held a council to debate the difficulties between France and Burgundy. Hayraddin appeared as a herald from William de la Marck, who had married the Lady Hameline. But Toison d'Or, the duke's herald, unmasked Hayraddin because he knew nothing of the science of heraldry. The duke released Hayraddin and set his fierce boar hounds upon him, but ordered the dogs called off before they tore Hayraddin to shreds. Then he ordered that Hayraddin be hanged with the proper ceremony.

The king and the duke also debated the disposal of Isabelle's hand and fortune. But she had fallen in love with Quentin and said that she preferred the cloister to any of the suggested alliances. The duke solved the problem, at least to his satisfaction, by declaring that Isabelle's hand would be given to the man who brought him the head of William de la Marck.

The king and the duke joined forces to assault Liège. Their combined forces gallantly besieged the city but were forced to go into bivouac at nightfall. That night William made a foray but was driven back into the city. Next day the forces of the king and the duke attacked once more, made breaches in the wall, and poured into the city. Quentin came face to face with William de la Marck, who rushed at him with all the fury of the wild boar for which he was named. Le Balafré stood by and roared out for fair play, indicating that this should be a duel of champions. At that moment Quentin saw a woman being forcibly dragged along by a French soldier. When he turned to rescue her, Le Balafré attacked de la Marck and killed him.

Le Balafré was announced as the man who had killed de la Marck, but he gave most of the credit to Quentin's valiant behavior and deferred to his nephew. While it was agreed that Quentin was responsible for de la Marck's death, there was still the question of his lineage, which the duke questioned. Indignant, Lord Crawford recited the pedigree of Quentin and thereby proved his gentility. Without more ado, Quentin and the Countess Isabelle were betrothed.

Critical Evaluation

Quentin Durward appeared when Sir Walter Scott's career as a novelist was nearly a decade old. Although Scott was still signing his novels "By the Author of Waverley," his authorship was by no means unknown. The "Wizard of the North" touched the familiar formulas of his fiction with an undeniable magic. With *Waverley* (1814) he had invented the historical novel, a new genre. This fictional treatment of the last of the Stuart uprisings in 1745, manifesting genuine insight into events "Sixty Years Since," had been solidly founded upon his knowledge of Scotland, its history, and its people. The author had perceived in the Jacobite-Hanoverian conflict the clash of two cultures at the very moment when the former was passing away forever and the other was just coming into being. He had made figures from history a part of his fiction, through them creating the tensions in which his fictitious characters were caught. This first novel established the pattern and theme for the serious historical novel, not only Scott's "Waverley Novels," but those of later writers such as James Fenimore Cooper.

Abounding in wealth and fame, his energies given also to public service, business, an estate in Scotland, an active social life, and other kinds of writing, Scott worked too hard and wrote too fast—one novel a year, sometimes two. With his tenth novel, *Ivanhoe* (1820), he sagaciously determined that his English reading public, after so many Scottish novels, would welcome a foray into English history. *Ivanhoe* became the talk of London, and his career gained new impetus. However, by 1823, his publisher, conscious of a waning popularity, advised Scott to turn to other kinds of writing. But the author boldly moved into the foreign territory of fifteenth century France and once again created a literary sensation—the reception of his new novel in Paris rivaled that of *Ivanhoe* in London. After *Quentin Durward,* Scott was recognized as a great writer both at home and abroad.

Today, *Quentin Durward* stands as a milestone in Scott's career rather than as a significant novel. His own remarks on the work contain casual apologies for his license with historical facts; some critics charge him with the worse fault of allowing superficial knowledge to make of *Quentin Durward* a mere costume romance rather than a serious historical novel. Others rate it simply as a good tale of adventure.

Nonetheless, *Quentin Durward* provides a good example of the conflict at the heart of Scott's best historical novels—the thematic clash between the old order and the new. The order which is passing away is the age of chivalry with its feudal system and its chivalric code. The age which is coming into being takes its traits from the leader who, rather than the titular hero, is the central character of the novel—King Louis XI of France. Louis is the antithesis of the chivalric ideal. Honor is but a word to him; he studies the craft of dissimulation. His unceremonious manners express contempt rather than knightly humility. He exercises the virtues of generosity and courtesy only with ulterior motives. Crafty and false, committed to his own self-interest, he is a complete Machiavellian.

If Louis is the chief representative of the new age, no one is a genuine survival of the old, despite noblemen who cling to a narrow concept of honor or imitate medieval splendor. Although Louis' principal rival, Charles of Burgundy, is his direct opposite, he is an inadequate symbol of chivalry. When Quentin says that he can win more honor under Charles's banner than under those of the king, Le Balafré counters with a description more accurate: "The Duke of Burgundy is a hot-brained, impetuous, pudding-headed, iron-ribbed dare-all." The decay of chivalry is epitomized in the hopelessness of Quentin's search for a leader who would keep his honor bright, and is confirmed by his ultimate conclusion that none of these great leaders is any better than the other. During the dramatic episode at Charles's court, when the king, ironically, is prisoner of his own vassal, the court historian, Des Comines, reminds Louis—who knows better than anyone else—that strict interpretation of the feudal law is becoming outdated while opportunity and power drive men to compromise and alter the old codes of chivalry.

Quentin Durward himself is the standard-bearer of the old order. Desiring to follow a man who will never avoid a battle and will keep a generous state, with tournaments and feasting and dancing with ladies, he lives upon ideas of brave deeds and advancement.

However, Quentin's ideals are impossible from the start. His rootlessness is symptomatic of the dying culture he reveres. His only real ties are with the mercenary band of Scottish Archers. Their weather-beaten leader Lord Crawford, one of the last leaders of a brave band of Scottish lords and knights, as well as Quentin's kinsman, the hideously scarred, almost bestial Le Balafré, serve as evidence that the glorious past is irrevocably past.

Moreover, though Quentin is introduced as a simple and naïve youth, he is not a rare survival of perfect chivalry. Equipped only with a rude mountain chivalry, he has his fair share of shrewdness and cunning. Far more politic than his experienced kinsman Le Balafré, this simple youth counsels Isabelle on the ways of telling half-truths with a skill which would credit Louis himself. Though it offends his dignity as a gentleman to accept money from a wealthy plebeian—ironically, King Louis in disguise—he immediately discerns that the simple maid of the little turret is far more attractive after she is revealed as Isabelle, Countess of Croye, a highborn heiress. Presented by the king with an unpleasant crisis—an order to be prepared to kill the noble Crèvecoeur from ambush—in which it would be "destruction in refusing, while his honor told him there would be disgrace in complying," Quentin chooses compliance.

Yet as an emblem of the future, Quentin is neither as contemptible as his wily king nor as foolish as his older comrades deem him. The venerable Lord Crawford defends him well when he argues: "Quentin Durward is as much a gentleman as the King, only as the Spaniard says, not so rich. He is as noble as myself, and I am chief of my name." Furthermore, the youthful squire successfully endures the perilous journey, the chivalric testing of a man, bravely and skillfully evading the snares of the wicked, from the literal traps in and around Louis' castle to the treacherous ambush planned by the king and the more horrible fate threatening him during the sack of Schonwaldt. Thus only partially valid is Crèvecoeur's ironic description of Quentin's trials as a pleasant journey full of heroic adventure and high hope. Crèvecoeur's capitulation at the end is more just: "But why should I grudge this youth his preferment? Since, after all, it is sense, firmness, and gallantry which have put him in possession of Wealth, Rank, and Beauty!"

In the characterization of both Quentin and Louis, Scott dramatizes the ambiguities which afflict a time of transition. Louis, lacking any real sense of moral obligations, nevertheless understands the interests of France and faithfully pursues them. Detested as too cautious and crafty, he nonetheless exhibits a coolness before the wrath of Charles that far outshines the brave deeds of arms which Quentin values. If Quentin too passively drifts into the service of Louis, he can summon courage enough to defy the king, and principle enough to support the king in adversity—even at the cost of telling a little falsehood and the risk of sacrificing his life.

Scott in this novel, as in others, vividly depicts the various ways in which men cope with a world of changing values, where as Crèvecoeur's speech jocularly implies, sense and firmness have replaced gallantry, and wealth and rank have toppled beauty in the scale of things. It is this view of reality which seems most characteristic of the author: he is, like Quentin, most certainly a Romantic, idealizing the glories of a legendary time; but he understands the practical demands of a present reality and the value of a Louis or of a shrewd and brave youth like Quentin Durward.

WAVERLEY

Type of work: Novel
Author: Sir Walter Scott (1771–1832)
Type of plot: Historical romance
Time of plot: 1745
Locale: England and Scotland
First published: 1814

In this historical romance treating Prince Charlie and the Scottish national cause, Scott attempted to pay tribute to his people by demonstrating their high degree of civilization. In the person of Fergus Mac Ivor we find not only intellect and sentiment, but also formal, courtly manners.

Principal Characters

Edward Waverley, a young British officer who holds his commission in the army of George II of England during the bloody days in 1745 when Charles Edward, the Pretender, is trying to gain the British throne. Through a set of circumstances, he learns of the young Pretender's cause at first hand; he is Charles' guest, lives for a time with some of his supporters, and swears allegiance to him. Though charged with treason and stripped of his commission, he finally regains favor with the King, inherits his father's fortune, and marries the woman of his choice.

Fergus Mac Ivor Vich Ian Vohr, a very famous clan chieftain who supports Prince Charles' bid for the throne. He is bluff and hearty, formal and courtly, a good politician. When the rebellion fails, he is executed for his crimes against the crown, and the power of the Highland clans is broken.

Prince Charles Edward Stuart, the Pretender, who, having arrived in Scotland from his exile in France, rallies Highlanders to his cause. He reflects his French court training in the polished, civil manner he shows all those about him. He is ruined when his forces are scattered at the Battle of Culloden.

Sir Cosmo Comyne Bradwardine, a Scottish nobleman and a Jacobite who introduces Edward to the forces marshaled under Prince Charles. Rose Bradwardine, the Baron's daughter, finally marries Edward.

Evan Dhu Maccombich, a Highlander in the service of Fergus Mac Ivor. He guides Edward through the Jacobite camp and introduces him to the famous Scottish chief. Maccombich is executed when the revolt fails.

Donald Bean Lean, a Highland bandit faithful to Mac Ivor and the Pretender. He rescues Edward from his English captors when the young officer is being taken to Stirling Castle to stand trial for treason.

Flora Mac Ivor, Fergus' sister, who is attracted to Edward but whose ardor for him cools. When the revolt fails, she enters a Catholic convent in France.

Rose Bradwardine, Edward's beloved and Sir Cosmo Comyne Bradwardine's daughter. Like her father, she is an ardent Jacobite. After the defeat at Culloden she marries Edward.

Richard Waverley, Edward's father, who, for political advantage, swears loyalty to King George II. Unfortunate political maneuvers ruin him. When he dies, Edward inherits the family wealth.

Sir Everard Waverley, a Jacobite who is Edward's uncle and Richard Waverley's brother. It is at Waverely-Honour, the family's ancestral home, that Edward receives much of his education in the political and social issues of the day.

Colonel Gardiner, Edward's military superior while the young man holds a commission in George II's dragoons.

Davie Gellatley, Baron Bradwardine's servant, a good storyteller who helps fire Edward's interest in the Jacobite cause.

Alice, Donald Bean Lean's daughter, who is in love with Evan Dhu Maccombich.

The Story

The English family of Waverley had long been known for its Jacobite sympathies. In the year 1745, Waverley-Honour, the ancestral home of the family, was a quiet retreat for Sir Everard Waverley, an elderly Jacobite. His brother, Richard Waverley, seeking political advantage in London, had sworn loyalty to the king.

Edward Waverley, the son of Whig Richard, divided his time between his father and his Uncle Everard at Waverley-Honour. On that great estate Edward was free to come and go as he pleased, for his tutor Pembroke, a devout dissenter, was often too busy writing religious pamphlets to spend much time in the education of his young charge. When Edward became old enough, his father obtained for him a commission in the army. Shortly afterward he was ordered to Scotland to join the dragoons of Colonel Gardiner. Equipped with the necessary articles of dress, accompanied by a retinue of men who had been selected by Sir Everard, and weighed down by the dissenting tomes of Pembroke, Edward left Waverley-Honour in quixotic fashion to conquer his world.

He had been instructed by Sir Everard to visit an old friend, Sir Cosmo Comyne Bradwardine, whose estate was near the village of Tully-Veolan in the Scottish Lowlands. Edward, soon after his arrival at the post of Colonel Gardiner, obtained a leave in order to go to Tully-Veolan. There he found Sir Everard's friend both cordial and happy to see him. The few days spent at Tully-Veolan convinced Edward that Scotland was a wilder and more romantic land than his native England. He paid little attention to Rose Bradwardine, the baron's daughter, his youthful imagination being fired by the songs and dances of Davie Gellatley, the baron's servant, and by tales about the Scottish Highlanders and their rude ways. At Tully-Veolan he was also confronted by a political issue that had been but an idealistic quarrel in his former existence; these Scottish people were Jacobites, and Edward ostensibly was a Whig royalist because of his father's politics and his own rank in the army of Hanoverian George II of England.

During his stay at Tully-Veolan an event occurred which was to change Edward's life. It began with the unexpected arrival of Evan Dhu Maccombich, a Highlander in the service of the renowned clan chieftain, Fergus Mac Ivor Vich Ian Vohr, a friend of the baron's. His taste for romantic adventure having been aroused, Edward begged another extension of his leave in order to accompany

Evan Dhu into the Highlands. In those rugged hills Edward was led to the cave that sheltered the band of Donald Bean Lean, an outlaw who robbed and plundered the wealthy Lowlanders. Staying with the bandit only long enough to discover the romantic attachment between Donald's daughter Alice and Evan Dhu, Edward again set out into the hills with his cheerful young guide. His curiosity had been sufficiently whetted by Evans' descriptions of Fergus Mac Ivor and his ancient castle deep in the Highland hills at Glennaquoich.

The welcome that Mac Ivor extended to Edward was open-handed and hearty. No less warm was the quiet greeting which Flora, Fergus Mac Ivor's sister, had for the English soldier. Flora was a beautiful woman of romantic, poetic nature, and Edward found himself before long deeply in love with the chieftain's sister. Mac Ivor himself seemed to sanction the idea of a marriage. That union could not be, however, for Flora had vowed her life to another cause—that of placing Charles, the young Stuart prince, upon the throne of England. At Edward's proposal of marriage, Flora advised him to seek a woman who could attach herself wholeheartedly to his happiness; Flora claimed that she could not divide her attentions between the Jacobite cause and marriage to one who was not an ardent supporter of Charles Edward Stuart.

Edward's stay at Glennaquoich was interrupted by letters carried to him by Davie Gellatley from Tully-Veolan. The first was from Rose Bradwardine, who advised him that the Lowlands were in a state of revolt. Her father being absent, she warned Edward not to return to Tully-Veolan. The other letters informed him that Richard Waverley had engaged in some unfortunate political maneuvers which had caused his political downfall. On the heels of this news came orders from Colonel Gardiner, who, having heard reports of Edward's association with traitors, was relieving the young officer of his command. Repulsed by Flora and disgraced in his army career, Edward resolved to return to Waverley-Honour. He equipped himself suitably for the dangerous journey and set out toward the Lowlands.

Because of armed revolt in Scotland and the linking of the Waverley name with the Jacobite cause, Edward found himself under arrest for treason against King George. The dissenting pamphlets of Pembroke which he carried, his stay in the Highlands, and the company he had kept there were suspicious circumstances which made it impossible for him to prove his innocence. Captured by some of the king's troopers, he was turned over to an armed guard with orders to take him to Stirling Castle for trial on a charge of treason.

But the friend of Fergus Mac Ivor Vich Ian Vohr was not to be treated in such a scurvy manner. On the road a quick ambush rescued Edward from his captors, and he found himself once again in the hands of some Highlanders whom he was able to recognize as a party of Donald Bean Lean's followers. Indeed, Alice once appeared among the men to slip a packet of letters to him, but at the time he had no opportunity to read the papers she had given him so secretively.

A few days' journey brought Edward to the center of Jacobite activities at Holyrood, the temporary court of Charles Edward Stuart, who had secretly crossed the Channel from France. There Edward Waverley found Fergus Mac Ivor awaiting him. When the Highlander presented Edward to Prince Charles, the Pretender welcomed the English youth because of the name he bore. The prince, trained in French courts, was a model of refinement and courtesy. His heartfelt trust gave Edward a feeling of belonging, after he had lost his commission, his cause unheard, in the English army. When Charles asked him to join in the Scottish uprising, Edward assented. Mac Ivor seemed quite happy about Edward's new allegiance. When the young Englishman asked about Flora, Mac Ivor explained that he had brought her along to the prince's court so that he could make use of her graces in gaining a political foothold when the battle was won. Edward resented this manner of using Flora as bait, but soon he perceived that the court of the Pretender functioned very much like the French court where Charles and his followers had learned statecraft. Mac Ivor pressed Edward to continue his courtship of Flora. The sister of Mac Ivor, however, met his advances coldly. In the company of the Highland beauty was Rose Bradwardine, whose father had also joined the Stuart cause.

Accepted as a cavalier by the women who clustered around the prince and under the influence of the Pretender's courtly manners, Edward soon became a favorite, but Mac Ivor's sister persisted in ignoring him. He began to compare the two women, Rose and Flora, the former gaining favor in his eyes as he watched them together.

The expedition of the Pretender and his Highlanders was doomed to failure. As they marched southward to England, they began to lose hope. The prince ordered a retreat to Scotland. Many of the clansmen were killed at the disastrous battle of Culloden. The survivors escaped to the Highlands, to spend their days in hiding from troops sent to track them down. A few were fortunate enough to make their way in safety to France.

Edward managed to get away and to find a friend who helped him to steal back to Scotland, where he hoped to find Rose Bradwardine. So far Edward had cleared himself of the earlier charges of treachery and desertion, which had been the initial cause of his joining the Pretender. It had been Donald Bean Lean who had deceived Colonel Gardiner with a false report of Edward's activities. The letters Alice had slipped to him had conveyed that information to Edward. Now he hoped to escape to France with Rose and wait for a pardon from England. Richard Waverley had died and Edward had inherited his fortune.

Fergus Mac Ivor and Evan Dhu Maccombich were executed for their crimes against the crown, and the power of the Highland clan was broken. Flora entered a Catholic convent in France, the country in which she had been reared. Edward Waverley and Rose were married after Edward was certain of his pardon. They returned to Tully-Veolan, where the baron's estate was awaiting its heirs.

Critical Evaluation

When *Waverley* appeared in 1814, it was immediately popular. One reason, of course, was the widespread conjecture about the mystery of the author, since Scott had published this first novel anonymously. Both in Scotland and in England literary individuals and laymen alike speculated as to its authorship.

Another reason for its extreme popularity was the fact that in *Waverley* Scott had literally created a new genre: the historical novel. Until its publication, Gothic novels were the vogue with all their paraphernalia of trap doors, vampires, ruined castles, and the like. Though their locales were often medieval, these novels were not accurate in historical setting or detail. *Waverley*, based on Scott's extensive reading of pamphlets, letters, diaries, personal interviews with survivors, and other material bearing on the Jacobite Rebellion of 1745, was a new literary form. This was fairly recent and valid history; the reading public felt close to the events, and so the recorded details of Edward Waverley's participation in the uprising were exciting and vivid. Scott sacrificed accuracy for picturesque effects, but he thought this justified because history for him was a dramatic process, the very evolution of a culture. He usually concentrated on history of the relatively recent past, particularly Scottish history.

One might think the regional dialects of Scotland would have proved a serious barrier to the English reading public, but quite the opposite was true. They loved the colorful Highland characters about whom they knew little and whose language was strange. If some remarked a glossary should have been included with *Waverley* for English readers, nevertheless they persevered and were so caught up with the romance and newness of the thing, it continued a sensation.

A third reason for its wide, enthusiastic reception was the fact that it was extravagantly romantic: escape literature at its best. The wild adventures of Waverley; the rugged glens of the Highlands with their inaccessible caves, foaming cataracts, somber forests; primitive bardic songs of the Northern tribes, as well as their striking dress; the beautiful if improbable heroines Flora Mac Ivor and Rose Bradwardine; melodrama of battle and testing of gentlemen's honor; and, of course, "Bonnie Prince Charlie" the Pretender, who drew out the heroic in stout Highland hearts—all the uncritical, avid reader could wish for.

The fact that Scott wrote the novel "with almost unbelievable speed"— the last two volumes in a mere three weeks, prevented him from developing his characters or constructing a tightly knit or well-developed plot. He was a careless writer, and in spite of the merits of his style and dramatic presentation, one finds much that is faulty.

The hero, Edward Waverley, is passive and colorless. He is projected into the Jacobite cause with Fergus Mac Ivor's clan, not by conscious choice or intense sympathy for it, but by outside forces that thrust him forward. He extricates himself from the embroilment by contrived means. He is attracted to Fergus' sister Flora, mainly because of her beauty and the romantic setting in which she moves; but without soul-searching or much great passion, he settles, after several rebuffs from Flora, upon Rose Bradwardine, whom he had not seriously considered. Edward does not grow inwardly but changes according to external circumstances. Although Fergus is decisive, logical, and far more real, his actions are predictable; no one is surprised that his single-minded purpose leads to his death.

It is the Scots villagers, Mac Ivor's retainers and other humble people like Callum Beg, Widow Flockhart, and Farmer Williams, who come to life dramatically. Scott is at his best with these minor characters; their speech, their actions ring true. The reader wonders why he could not bring this validity to his upper-class heroes and heroines, who often conduct themselves woodenly and speak in stilted Latinate diction—even in moments of great passion.

The novel generally lacks descriptive detail, especially color words. Scott had great opportunity for this: for example, the Highland feast at Ian nan Chaistel's hall, the ball at Holyrood Castle, the battle at Preston. But of what must have been brilliant plaids, dirks and daggers in their ornamental sheaths, and gaily dressed bagpipers Scott says nothing. Prince Edward's court at Holyrood was an occasion for a glittering display of color in dress and setting, but the author merely speaks vaguely of its "liveliness and elegance" and states "the general effect was striking." And as for the military spectacle of Preston, Scott, intrigued with the action and emotion, cannot bring it to life before the reader's eyes. After Fergus cries "Forward, sons of Ivor or the Camerons will draw the first blood!" and they rush "on with a tremendous yell," Scott states laconically, "The rest is well known." Most of the battle action from this point on deals only with Colonel Gardiner's death. But considering the speed at which Scott dashed off his novels, he had no time to spend on small details of picturesque language and setting. Still this would have greatly enriched their texture.

The manner in which Waverley clears himself of charges of treason and desertion, inherits great wealth, and marries Rose is narrated by the author in long passages which reveal subterfuges, motives, and transactions that were not part of the novel's organic unity and about which the reader was not apprised. This type of *deus ex machina* procedure prohibits thematic coherence and is distracting to the intelligent reader.

It is easy today to see the novel's structural faults. But there was enough conflict between romance and reality to satisfy Scott's contemporary audience, sufficient history to render the work real to them. And his portrayal of Highland manners and customs was thorough. Herein lies *Waverley's* importance. It was the first of Scott's whole series drawn from these materials and so heralded a new genre for the eighteenth and nineteenth centuries.

Bibliography

Baker, Ernest A. *History of the English Novel*, Volume VI. London: Witherby, 1929, pp. 122–143.

Buchan, John. *Sir Walter Scott*. London: Cassell, 1932.

Clipper, Lawrence J. "Edward Waverley's Night Journey," in *South Atlantic Quarterly*. LXXIII (1974), pp. 541–553.

Cockshut, A.O.J. *The Achievement of Walter Scott*. New York: New York University Press, 1969, pp. 107–128, 155–157.

Cusac, Marian H. *Narrative Structure in the Novels of Sir Walter Scott*. The Hague: Mouton, 1969.

Daiches, David. "Scott's Achievement as a Novelist," in *Nineteenth-Century Fiction*. VI (September, 1951), pp. 90–95.

Devlin, David D. *The Author of* Waverley: *A Critical Study of Walter Scott*. Lewisburg, Pa.: Bucknell University Press, 1971, pp. 56–80.

—————. "Scott and History," in *Scott's Mind and Art*. Edited by A. Norman Jeffares. London: Oliver and Boyd, 1969, pp. 78–80, 89–91.

Fiske, Christabel F. *Epic Suggestion in the Imagery of the Waverley Novels*. New Haven, Conn.: Yale University Press, 1940.

Gordon, Robert C. *Under Which King? A Study of the Scottish Waverley Novels*. New York: Barnes & Noble, 1969, pp. 11–25.

Gordon, S. Stewart. "*Waverley* and the 'Unified Design,' " in *Journal of English Literary History*. XVIII (June, 1951), pp. 107–122.

Hahn, H.G. "Historiographic and Literary: The Fusion of Two Eighteenth-Century Modes in Scott's *Waverley*," in *Hartford Studies in Literature*. VI (1974), pp. 243–267.

Hart, Francis R. *Scott's Novels: The Plotting of Historic Survival*. Charlottesville: University of Virginia Press, 1966.

Hartveit, Lars. *Dream Within a Dream, a Thematic Approach to Scott's Vision of Fictional Reality*. New York: Humanities Press, 1974, pp. 72–118.

Hayden, John O. *Scott; The Critical Heritage*. New York: Barnes & Noble, 1970, pp. 67–84.

Hennelly, Mark M. "*Waverley* and Romanticism," in *Nineteenth-Century Fiction*. XXVIII (1973), pp. 194–209.

Iser, Wolfgang. *The Implied Reader: Patterns of Communication in Prose Fiction from Bunyan to Beckett*. Baltimore: Johns Hopkins University Press, 1974, pp. 81–100.

Johnson, Edgar. *Sir Walter Scott: The Great Unknown*, Volume I. New York: Macmillan, 1970, pp. 520–530.

Kiely, Robert.   *The Romantic Novel in England.* Cambridge, Mass.: Harvard University Press, 1972, pp. 136–154.

Lauber, John.   *Sir Walter Scott.* New York: Twayne, 1966, pp. 48–66.

Raleigh, John H.   "*Waverley* and *The Fair Maid of Perth*," in *Some British Romantics.* Edited by James V. Logan, John E. Gordon and Northrop Frye. Columbus: Ohio State University Press, 1966, pp. 235–266.

————.   "*Waverley* as History; or 'Tis One Hundred and Fifty-Six Years Since,' " in *Novel.* IV (1970), pp. 14–29.

Welsh, Alexander.   *The Hero of the Waverley Novels.* New Haven, Conn.: Yale University Press, 1963.

Williams, Ioan.   *The Realist Novel in England: A Study in Development.* London: Macmillan, 1974, pp. 25–40.

MARY WOLLSTONECRAFT GODWIN SHELLEY

Born: London, England (August 30, 1797)
Died: Bournemouth, England (February 1, 1851)

Principal Works

NOVELS: *Frankenstein*, 1818; *Valperga*, 1823; *The Last Man*, 1826; *Lodore*, 1835; *Falkner*, 1837.
TRAVEL SKETCHES: *The Journal of a Six Weeks' Tour*, 1814; *Rambles in Germany and Italy*, 1844.

Authorship of *Frankenstein* was not the only claim to distinction possessed by Mary Wollstonecraft Shelley. The daughter of a radical philosopher and an early feminist, the wife of an unconventional boy genius, she early came to know life as something of a roller-coaster; and her masterpiece of fictional horror was only one of the more important incidents in an existence heavily underscored with drama.

The future novelist and mate of Percy Bysshe Shelley was born in London, August 30, 1797, the child of William Godwin and Mary Wollstonecraft. Bereaved of her mother almost immediately, she was reared in a bewildering clutter of family which included a stepmother, a stepbrother, a stepsister, a half-brother, and a half-sister. As Mary grew up she increasingly idolized her dead mother, for whose loss she was inclined to blame herself. The depth of this feeling was one of the important factors in her girlhood, the other being the atmosphere of intellectual discussion and debate which enveloped her father and his many visitors.

One of these visitors was a twenty-one-year-old youth whose mental accomplishments had made quite an impression upon William Godwin. The impression darkened when, a month before her seventeenth birthday, Mary Godwin eloped with Percy Bysshe Shelley, casually disregarding the fact that he was already in possession of a wife. More than two years passed before the suicide of Harriet Shelley allowed Shelley and Mary to legalize their marriage. All evidence available points to a reasonably happy union, though Mary's mind, clear and penetrating as it was, experienced times of bafflement in dealing with the unpredictable Shelley. On the other hand, Mary sometimes succumbed to periods of melancholy, which the death of her first three children did much to deepen.

Frankenstein was written in the Shelleys' first Italian days, during their companionship with Byron. So remarkable an achievement is it, especially for a girl of twenty, that it undoubtedly owes much of its sustained quality to the intellectual stimulation provided by the Shelley circle. The author's only novel to attain permanent reputation, it is an appealing combination of strangeness and reality, skillful in its plot structure and enlivened by sharp character contrasts. Published in 1818, *Frankenstein* was an immediate sensation; and its repeated dramatizations have given its title the familiarity of a household word. Other novels of

Mary Shelley were to follow, but the author never regained the touch that would lift her fiction above the level of mediocrity. After Shelley's death, his widow's life became a struggle to secure bread and ensure the proper education of the only surviving Shelley child, Percy Florence. Nevertheless, *The Last Man* is interesting for its expression of Mary Shelley's liberal social and political views, and *Lodore* has the fascination of a veiled autobiography.

After her husband's death, Mary refused various offers of marriage: among her suitors were Shelley's friend Trelawny, John Howard Payne and—reportedly, at least—Washington Irving. After the death of Sir Timothy Shelley in 1844, her financial situation became somewhat easier. One of the disappointments of her later years was the discovery that she lacked the strength to complete a long-planned biography of her husband. She died on February 1, 1851, at the age of fifty-three, and was buried at Bournemouth.

Bibliography

There is no edition of Mary Shelley's works. Frederick L. Jones has edited *The Letters of Mary W. Shelley*, 2 vols., 1944, and *Mary Shelley's Journal*, 1947. The standard biography is Mrs. Julian Marshall, *The Life and Letters of Mary Wollstonecraft Shelley*, 2 vols., 1889. Other more recent and less formal studies are R. G. Grylls, *Mary Shelley, A Biography*, 1938; Muriel Spark, *Child of Delight*, 1951; Elizabeth Nitchie, *Mary Shelley, Author of "Frankenstein,"* 1953; and Eileen Bigland, *Mary Shelley*, 1959. See also W. E. Peck, "The Biographical Element in the Novels of Mary Wollstonecraft Shelley," *Publications of the Modern Language Association*, XXXVI (1923), 196–219.

FRANKENSTEIN

Type of work: Novel
Author: Mary Godwin Shelley (1797–1851)
Type of plot: Gothic romance
Time of plot: Eighteenth century
Locale: Europe
First published: 1817

Victor Frankenstein, a brilliant inventor, actually succeeds in creating life. His creature, animate but lacking all human graces, is alone and scorned by mankind. Bitterly he accuses his creator and threatens to murder at will unless Victor creates a mate for him. Victor does, but in a moment of conscience, he destroys her. The monster avenges himself by strangling Victor's bride. Following the creature in an attempt to destroy him, Victor dies of exposure at the North Pole. The story hints in part at the possible dangers inherent in the pursuit of pure science; it also portrays the injustice of a society which persecutes such outcasts as Victor's creature.

Principal Characters

Victor Frankenstein, a native of Geneva who early evinces a talent in natural science. Having concluded his training at the university at Ingolstadt, he works until he discovers the secret of creating life. He makes a monster from human and animal organs found in dissecting rooms and butcher shops. The Monster brings only anguish and death to Victor and his friends and relatives. Having told his story, he dies before his search for the Monster is complete.

The Monster, an eight-foot-tall synthetic man endowed by its creator with human sensibilities. Rebuffed by man, it turns its hate against him. Its program of revenge accounts for the lives of Frankenstein's bride, his brother, his good friend, and a family servant. Just after Victor dies, the Monster appears and tells the explorer that Frankenstein's was the great crime, for he had created a man devoid of friend, love, or soul.

Robert Walton, an English explorer who, on his ship frozen in a northland sea of ice, hears the dying Frankenstein's story and also listens to the Monster's account of, and reason for, its actions.

Elizabeth Lavenza, Victor's foster sister and later his bride, who is strangled by the Monster on her wedding night.

William, Victor's brother, who is killed by the Monster while seeking revenge on its creator.

Henry Clerval, Victor's friend and a man of science who is killed by the Monster to torment Frankenstein.

Justine Moritz, a family servant tried and condemned for William's murder.

The Story

Walton was an English explorer whose ship was held fast in polar ice. As the company looked out over the empty ice field, they were astonished to see a sledge drawn by dogs speeding northward. The sledge driver looked huge and mis-shapen. That night an ice floe carried to the ship another sledge, one dog, and a man in weakened condition. When the newcomer learned that his was the second sledge sighted from the ship, he became much agitated.

Walton was greatly attracted to the man during his convalescence, and as they continued fast in the ice, the men had leisure to get acquainted. At last, after he had recovered somewhat from exposure and hunger, the man told Walton his story.

Victor Frankenstein was born of good family in Geneva. As a playmate for their son, the parents had adopted a lovely little girl of the same age. Victor and Elizabeth grew up as brother and sister. Much later another son, William was born to the Frankensteins.

Victor early showed promise in the natural sciences. He devoured the works of Paracelsus and Albertus Magnus, and thought in his ignorance that they were the real masters. When he grew older, his father decided to send Victor to the university at Ingolstadt. There he soon learned all that his masters could teach him in the fields of natural science. Engaged in brilliant and terrible research, he stumbled by chance on the secret of creating life. Once he had that knowledge he could not rest until he had employed it to create a living being. By haunting the butcher shops and dissecting rooms, he soon had the necessary raw materials. With great cunning he fashioned an eight-foot monster and endowed him with life.

But as soon as he had created his monster, he was subject to strange misgivings. During the night the monster came to his bed. At the sight of that horrible face, he shrieked and frightened the monster away. The horror of his act prostrated him with a brain fever. His best friend, Henry Clerval, arrived from Geneva and helped to nurse him through his illness. He was unable to tell Clerval what he had done.

Terrible news came from Geneva. William, Victor's young brother, was dead by the hand of a murderer. He had been found strangled in a park, and a faithful family servant, Justine, had been charged with the crime. Victor hurried to Geneva.

At the trial Justine told a convincing story. She had been looking for William in the countryside and, returning after the city gates had been closed, had spent the night in a deserted hut. But she could not explain how a miniature from William's neck came to be in her pocket. Victor and Elizabeth believed the girl's story, but in spite of all their efforts Justine was convicted and condemned.

Depressed by these tragic events, Victor went hiking over the mountainous countryside. Far ahead on the glacier, he saw a strange, agile figure that filled him with horrible suspicions. Unable to overtake the figure, he sat down to rest. Suddenly the monster appeared before him. The creature demanded that Victor listen to his story.

When he left Victor's chambers in Ingolstadt, everyone he met screamed and ran away. Wandering confusedly, the monster finally found shelter in an abandoned hovel adjoining a cottage. By great stealth he remained there during daylight and at night sought berries for food. Through observation he began to learn the ways of man. Feeling an urge to friendship, he brought wood to the cottage every day. But when he attempted to make friends with the cottagers, he was repulsed with such fear and fury that his heart became bitter toward all men. When he saw William playing in the park, he strangled the boy and took the miniature from his neck. Then during the night he came upon Justine in the hut and put the picture in her pocket.

Presently the monster made a horrible demand. He insisted that Victor fashion a mate for him who would give him love and companionship. The monster threatened to ravage and kill at random if Victor refused the request. But if Victor agreed, the monster promised to take his mate to the wilds of South America where they would never again be seen by man. It was a hard choice but Victor felt that he must accept.

Victor left for England with his friend Clerval. After parting from his friend he went to the distant Orkneys and began his task. He was almost ready to animate the gross mass of flesh when his conscience stopped him. He could not let the two monsters mate and spawn a race of monsters. He destroyed his work.

The monster was watching at a window. Angered to see his mate destroyed, he forced his way into the house and warned Victor that a terrible punishment would fall upon the young man on his wedding night. Then the monster escaped by sea. Later, to torment his maker, he fiendishly killed Clerval.

Victor was suspected of the crime. Released for lack of evidence, he went back to Geneva. There he and Elizabeth were married. Although Victor was armed and alert, the monster got into the nuptial chamber and strangled the bride. Victor shot at him, but he escaped again. Victor vowed eternal chase until the monster could be killed.

That was Victor's story. Weakened by exposure, he died there in the frozen North, with Elizabeth, William, Justine, and Clerval unavenged. Then to the dead man's cabin came the monster, and Walton, stifling his fear, addressed the gigantic, hideous creature. Victor's was the greater crime, the monster said. He had created a man, a man without love or friend or soul. He deserved his punishment. So saying, the monster vanished over the ice field.

Critical Evaluation

The best remembered novel of "Gothic Terror," *Frankenstein* superficially resembles Ann Radcliffe's *The Mysteries of Udolpho* (1794), Matthew Gregory Lewis' *The Monk* (1796), and Charles Robert Maturin's *Melmoth the Wanderer* (1820). Like these romances of suggested or actual physical horror, Mary Shelley's novel is steeped in sentimental melancholy. Unlike most Gothic novels, however, *Frankenstein: or, The Modern Prometheus* is at least partially philosophical and offers a scientific rather than supernatural explanation for the horror.

Indeed, for its serious ideas the novel more closely resembles *St. Leon* (1799) by Mary Shelley's father, William Godwin. As an illustration of the humanitarian philosophy of Jean Jacques Rousseau, *Frankenstein* shows the destructive results of undeveloped affection. The Creature (who is at the time of his composition a "monster" only to the fearful and ignorant) craves but is denied ordinary human tenderness. Rejected as a man, he becomes a vengeful monster. Although he is given vital existence by science, he is never fully alive. Victor Frankenstein's science (or rather pseudo-science of vitalism, a belief in the "vital spark") is unable to produce a creature capable of attracting love. Instead, his scientific genius creates death—a theme that appears rarely in nineteenth century literature, but is a major one in the twentieth century.

Readers familiar with the motion picture adaptations of *Frankenstein* popular during the 1930's—or, indeed, with the more accurate version produced by Christopher Isherwood and Don Bachardy for television in the 1970's—are likely to be surprised when they come upon Mary Shelley's novel. Not only is the book considerably richer in details, fuller in its development of minor characters, and more complicated in plot structure than later adaptations and parodies; it also treats the Creature from a significantly different point of view. Contrary to the popular stereotypes of the Frankenstein monster, he is articulate and, at least in the beginning, quite sympathetic. His revenge, though excessive, is motivated. From a modern reader's assessment, he is a monster too sentimental to be wholly frightening. Yet *Frankenstein,* for all its appeal to modern readers, represents the culmination of a tradition of nineteenth century Gothic horror on the one hand, and sentimentalism on the other. Given a different philosophical orientation, much of that horror is bound to be misunderstood. What is remarkable, to be sure, is that so much survives.

Bibliography

Adams, Richard P. "Hawthorne: The Old Manse," in *Tulane Studies in English.* VIII (1958), pp. 115–151.

Bloom, H. "*Frankenstein*, or the New Prometheus," in *Partisan Review.* XXXII (Fall, 1965), pp. 611–618.

Buchen, Irving H. "*Frankenstein* and the Alchemy of Creation and Evolution," in *Wordsworth Circle.* VIII (1977), pp. 103–112.

Cude, Wilfred. "Mary Shelley's Modern Prometheus: A Study in the Ethics of Scientific Creativity," in *Dalhousie Review.* LII (1972), pp. 212–225.

Dunn, Richard J. "Narrative Distance in *Frankenstein*," in *Studies in the Novel.* VI (1974), pp. 408–417.

Dussinger, John A. "Kingship and Guilt in Mary Shelley's *Frankenstein*," in *Studies in the Novel.* VIII (1976), pp. 38–55.

Hill, John M. "*Frankenstein* and the Physiognomy of Desire," in *American Imago*. XXXII (1975), pp. 335–358.

Hirsch, Gordon D. "The Monster Was a Lady: On the Psychology of Mary Shelley's *Frankenstein*," in *Hartford Studies in Literature*. VII (1975), pp. 116–153.

Joseph, Gerhard. "Frankenstein's Dream: The Child as Father of the Monster," in *Hartford Studies in Literature*. VII (1975), pp. 97–115.

Levine, George. "*Frankenstein* and the Tradition of Realism," in *Novel*. VII (Fall, 1973), pp. 14–30.

Mays, Milton A. "*Frankenstein*—Mary Shelley's Black Theodicy," in *Southern Humanities Review*. III (1969), pp. 146–153.

Micklewright, F.H. Amphlett. "The Noble Savage in Mary Shelley's *Frankenstein*," in *Notes and Queries*. CXCI (July 27, 1946), p. 41.

Nelson, Lowry, Jr. "Night Thoughts on the Gothic Novel," in *Yale Review*. LII (Winter, 1963), pp. 236–257.

Palmer, D.J. and R.E. Dowse. "*Frankenstein*: A Moral Fable," in *Listener*. LXVIII (August 23, 1962), pp. 281–284.

Philmus, Robert M. "*Frankenstein*; or, Faust's Rebellion Against Nature," in *Into the Unknown: The Evolution of Science Fiction from Francis Godwin to H.G. Wells*. Edited by Robert M. Philmus. Berkeley: University of California Press, 1970, pp. 82–90, 99, 102.

Pollin, Burton R. "Philosophical and Literary Sources of *Frankenstein*," in *Comparative Literature*. XVII (1965), pp. 97–108.

Prescott, F.C. "*Wieland* and *Frankenstein*," in *American Literature*. II (May, 1930), pp. 172–173.

Preu, James A. "The Tale of Terror," in *English Journal*. XLVII (May, 1958), pp. 243–247.

Rieger, James. "Dr. Polidori and the Genesis of *Frankenstein*," in *Studies in English Literature, 1500–1900*. III (1963), pp. 461–472.

Robinson, Charles E. "Mary Shelley and the Roger Dodsworth Hoax," in *Keats-Shelley Journal*. XXIV (1975), pp. 20–28.

Schug, Charles. "The Romantic Form of Mary Shelley's *Frankenstein*," in *Studies in English Literature, 1500–1900*. XVII (Autumn, 1977), pp. 607–619.

Spark, Muriel. "Mary Shelley: A Prophetic Novelist," in *Listener*. XLV (February 22, 1951), pp. 305–306.

Spatt, Hartley S. "Mary Shelley's Last Men: The Truth of Dreams," in *Studies in the Novel*. VII (1975), pp. 526–537.

Swingle, L.J.   "Frankenstein's Monster and Its Romantic Relatives: Problems in Knowledge in English Romanticism," in *Texas Studies in Literature and Language.* XV (Spring, 1973), pp. 51–65.

Tannenbaum, Leslie.   "From Filthy Type to Truth: Miltonic Myth in *Frankenstein*," in *Keats-Shelley Journal.* XXVI (1977), pp. 101–113.

TOBIAS SMOLLETT

Born: Dalquhurn, Scotland (March, 1721)
Died: Antignano, Italy (September 17, 1771)

Principal Works

NOVELS: *Roderick Random,* 1748; *Peregine Pickle,* 1751; *Ferdinand, Count Fathom,* 1753; *Sir Launcelot Greaves,* 1760–1762; *The Expedition of Humphry Clinker,* 1771.

TRANSLATIONS: *Gil Blas,* 1749; *Don Quixote,* 1755; *The Works of Voltaire,* 1761–1769.

MISCELLANEOUS: *A Complete History of England,* 1757–1758; *The Reprisal,* 1757; *The Modern Part of an Universal History,* 1759–1766; *A Continuation of the Complete History of England,* 1760–1761; 1765; *Travels in France and Italy,* 1766; *The Present State of All Nations,* 1768–1769; *The Adventures of an Atom,* 1769.

Tobias Smollett, born in March, 1721, at Dalquhurn near Bonhill, Scotland, had the ill fortune in his own time and today to be in competition with Henry Fielding. The result is that Smollett's moon has been obscured by Fielding's sun. This is a great pity, for, despite the unattractive behavior of many of his characters and the general brutality of his novels, there is much pleasure to be found in the pages of Smollett.

A poor and hot-tempered Scot, Smollett was a real-life replica of one of his own literary creations. After study at Glasgow University, he went to London to seek his fortune. After a hitch in the navy as surgeon's mate, he remained for a time in the West Indies, where he fell in love with Nancy Lascelles, daughter of a Jamaica planter, whom he later married. In 1744 he was back in London doctoring and writing. His first novel, *Roderick Random,* was a picaresque work which strung together a series of episodes through which the hero ultimately finds love and wealth. Many readers have been repelled by Roderick's selfishness and coarseness; but, as in all of Smollett's novels, there is a plentitude of delight to be found in the minor characters, who are treated as humorous types. Lieutenant Tom Bowling, eccentric sea dog, and Morgan, a Welsh surgeon, are two such figures. Because of his interest in naval life, Smollett has been called the father of the nautical novel. The picture of shipboard life and the account of the disastrous attack on Cartagena in *Roderick Random* are among the earliest literary protests against naval abuses.

Peregrine Pickle, his next novel, mined the vein of *Roderick Random.* Again, a young man with roguish tendencies achieves security after a series of adventures and amours. Commodore Hawser Trunnion, Smollett's finest picture of an old salt, graces this novel. *Ferdinand, Count Fathom,* published in 1753, is a novel remarkable chiefly for the baseness of its hero, a thoroughly villainous ingrate who is made to undergo an unconvincing reformation. This was followed by *Sir Launcelot Greaves*, a lackluster imitation of *Don Quixote*.

Then in the year of his death Smollett published *The Expedition of Humphry Clinker*, at once his masterpiece and his happiest book. This epistolary novel employs a trip through the British Isles as the framework for the exhibition of a brilliant set of humor characters. Chief among them is Matthew Bramble, a kind-hearted man who unsuccessfully tries to hide his goodness behind a gruff manner. Bramble is accompanied by his sister Tabitha, a grotesque virago who finally succeeds in marrying Lieutenant Obadiah Lismahago, a terrible-tempered Scot. The novel takes its title from a starveling whom Bramble befriends and who turns out to be Bramble's natural son. The episode of the discovery of Humphry's identity is unsurpassed in the English novel.

In addition to his novels, Smollett labored prodigiously at a number of literary projects in which he was sometimes the coördinator of the work of several hack writers. He translated *Gil Blas*, *Don Quixote*, and *The Works of Voltaire*. He edited *The Critical Review* (1756–1763), *The British Magazine* (1760–1767), and *The Briton* (1762–1763). He also wrote or edited a group of multiple-volume works: *A Complete History of England*, *A Continuation of the Complete History of England*, *A Compendium of Voyages* (1756), *The Modern Part of an Universal History*, and *The Present State of All Nations*. In the field of poetry he wrote "The Tears of Scotland" (1746?, 1753), "Advice, a Satire" (1746), "Reproof, a Satire" (1747), and "Ode to Independence" (1773). Smollett was very ambitious for a stage success; after the failure of his tragedy *The Regicide* (1749) he enjoyed a small hit with a farce, *The Reprisal*.

Ill health sent Smollett abroad, and out of his trips came *Travels in France and Italy*, a curious mixture of laughter and anger. *The Adventures of an Atom* is a scurrilous political satire in which events attributed to Japan stand for occurrences in England.

It is difficult to avoid the conclusions that despite his obvious lapses in taste Tobias Smollett possessed one of the most remarkable talents in all of English literature. He died at Antignano, near Leghorn, Italy, on September 17, 1771.

Bibliography

The *Letters* were edited by Lewis M. Knapp in 1971. The most authoritative study of Smollett is Lewis M. Knapp's *Tobias Smollett; Doctor of Men and Manners*, 1949. See also Lewis Melville, *The Life and Letters of Tobias Smollett*, 1927; Lewis M. Kahrl, *Tobias Smollett, Traveler-Novelist*, 1945; F. W. Boege, *Smollett's Reputation as a Novelist*, 1947; also Howard S. Buck, *A Study in Smollett, Chiefly "Peregrine Pickle,"* 1925; Louis L. Martz, *The Later Career of Tobias Smollett*, 1942; and Rufus Putney, "The Plan of *Peregrine Pickle*," *Publications of the Modern Language Association*, LX (1945), 1051–1065. Of importance is *Bicentennial Essays*, edited by G. S. Rousseau, 1971.

HUMPHRY CLINKER

Type of work: Novel
Author: Tobias Smollett (1721–1771)
Type of plot: Social satire
Time of plot: Mid-eighteenth century
Locale: England, Scotland, Wales
First published:1771

An epistolary novel, full of life and continually amusing, Humphry Clinker *offers a picture of a somewhat eccentric eighteenth century family and of the society in which it moved. It is considered a masterpiece of English humor.*

Principal Characters

Matthew Bramble, a Welsh bachelor who, while traveling in England and Scotland, keeps track of his affairs at Brambleton Hall through correspondence with Dr. Richard Lewis, his physician and adviser. Bramble, an eccentric and a valetudinarian, writes at great length of his ailments—the most pronounced being gout and rheumatism—and gives detailed accounts of his various attacks. With the same fervor that he discusses personal matters—health and finances—he launches into tirades on laws, art, mores, funeral customs, and the social amenities of the various communities he and his party pass through on their travels. As various members of the entourage become attracted to one another and are married, and the group plans to return to Brambleton Hall, Bramble senses that his existence has been sedentary. In his new-found interest of hunting, he changes from an officious, cantankerous attitude toward the affairs of others. He writes Lewis that had he always had something to occupy his time (as he has in hunting), he would not have inflicted such long, tedious letters on his friend and adviser.

Tabitha Bramble, his sister. A fussy old maid, she is the female counterpart of her brother in telling her correspondents of the annoyances of everyday life. Hers is a more personal world than her brother's, people being of more importance than ideas and things. With little likelihood of a change in interests, Tabitha does return home a married woman.

Jerry Melford, the nephew of Matthew and Tabitha, whose letters to a classmate at Cambridge, where Jerry is regularly a student, give a more objective account of incidents of travel and family. With the articulateness of the scholar and the verve of youth, Jerry describes the lighter side of everyday happenings. In his final correspondence, he admits to his friend that in the midst of matrimonial goings-on he has almost succumbed to Cupid. However, fearing that the girl's qualities—frankness, good humor, handsomeness, and a genteel fortune—may not be permanent, he passes off his thought as idle reflections.

Lydia Melford, his sister. The recipient of her letters, Miss Letitia Willis, is the object of Jerry's "idle reflections." Lydia, just out of boarding school, is concerned in her letters with the styles and movement of the young in various stops the party makes. Her primary concern, however, is with the presence or absence of young men. Lydia, it is learned, is carrying on a correspondence with a young actor, with Miss Willis acting as a go-between. A duel between the young man and Jerry is averted, but he continues to show up at various stages of the journey in various disguises. Lydia marries him after he has proved himself a young man of rank and wealth.

Winifred (Win) Jenkins, the maid, and the fifth of the letter writers whose correspondence makes up the story. Her correspondent is another servant at Brambleton Hall. Winifred's spelling exceeds all other known distortions of the English language. She sees people riding in "coxes," visits a zoo where she sees "hillyfents," looks forward to getting back "huom," and closes her letters with "Yours with true infection." But such ineptness does not hamper her personal achievements; able to make herself attractive, she is won by the natural son of Matthew Bramble. In the last letter in the book, Win makes her position clear to her former fellow servant, for she plans to return home as a member of the family rather than as a domestic. She reminds her correspondent that "Being, by God's blessing, removed to a higher spear, you'll excuse my being familiar with the lower servants of the family; but as I trust you'll behave respectful, and keep a proper distance, you may always depend upon the good will and purtection of Yours W. Loyd."

Humphry Clinker, the country youth later revealed as Matthew Loyd, the illegitimate son of Matthew Bramble. Clinker, a poor, ragged ostler, is taken on the trip by Bramble after a clumsy coachman has been dismissed. Clinker proves to be the soul of good breeding, a devout lay preacher, and a hero in saving Bramble from drowning. Quite by accident he hears Bramble addressed as Matthew Loyd, at which time Clinker produces a snuff box containing proof of his parentage. Bramble explains his having used the name Loyd as a young man for financial reasons and accepts Clinker as his son when "the sins of my youth rise up in judgment against me." Clinker, under his legal name, marries Winifred Jenkins.

George Dennison, the young actor who successfully follows the party in pursuit of Lydia's hand. George has masqueraded as an actor, Wilson, to avoid an unwelcome marriage being forced on him by his parents. His status in rank and wealth are proved by his father's and Bramble's recognition of each other as former classmates at Oxford.

Lieutenant Obadiah Lismahago, a Scottish soldier who joins the party at Durham. Lismahago's shocking stories of the atrocities he suffered as a captive of the American Indians entertain the party and win the devotion of Miss Tabitha. Lismahago's manner of doing things is best illustrated by his wedding present to Tabitha: a fur cloak of American sables, valued at eighty guineas.

Mr. and Mrs. Dennison, country gentry and George Dennison's parents.

The Story

Squire Matthew Bramble was an eccentric and skeptical gentleman with large estates in Wales. With him lived his sister, Miss Tabitha Bramble, a middle-aged maiden of high matrimonial hopes that were greater than her expectations. Painfully afflicted with the gout, the squire set out for Bath to try the waters, but with few hopes of their healing properties. With him went his sister; her servant, Winifred Jenkins; his own manservant; and, at the last minute, his niece and nephew, Lydia and Jerry Melford.

The young Melfords were orphans and Squire Bramble's wards. Lydia had been in boarding school, where, unfortunately, she had fallen in love with an actor—a circumstance Squire Bramble hoped she would soon forget among the gay and fashionable gatherings at Bath. Her brother, who had just finished his studies at Oxford, had tried to fight a duel with the actor, but an opportunity to defend his sister's honor had not presented itself to his satisfaction.

On the way to Bath a Jewish peddler made his way into Squire Bramble's lodgings on the pretext of selling glasses, and in a whisper made himself known to Lydia as George Wilson, the strolling player. The lovesick girl ordered Winifred Jenkins to follow the actor and talk with him. The maid came back in a great flurry. He had told her that Wilson was not his real name, that he was a gentleman, and that he intended to sue for Lydia's hand in his proper character. But, alas, the excited maid had forgotten Wilson's real name. There was nothing for poor Lydia to do but to conjecture and daydream as the party continued on toward Bath.

Arriving at Bath without further incident, the party entered the gay festivities there with various degrees of pleasure. Tabitha tried to get proposals of marriage out of every eligible man she met, and the squire became disgusted with the supposed curative powers of the waters which were drunk and bathed in by people with almost any infirmity in hopes of regaining their health. Lydia was still languishing over Wilson, and Jerry enjoyed the absurdity of the social gatherings. In an attempt to lighten his niece's spirits, Squire Bramble decided to go on to London.

They had traveled only a short way toward London when the coach accidentally overturned and Miss Tabitha's lapdog, in the excitement, bit the squire's servant. Miss Tabitha made such loud complaint when the servant kicked her dog in return that the squire was forced to discharge the man on the spot. He also needed another postilion, as Miss Tabitha declared herself unwilling to drive another foot behind the clumsy fellow who had overturned the coach. The squire hired a ragged country fellow named Humphry Clinker to take the place of the unfortunate postilion, and the party went on to the next village.

Miss Tabitha was shocked by what she called Humphry's nakedness, for he wore no shirt. The maid added to the chorus of outraged modesty. Yielding to these female clamors, the squire asked about Humphry's circumstances, listened to the story of his life, gruffly read him a lecture on the crimes of poverty and sickness, and gave him a guinea for a new suit of clothes. In gratitude Humphry refused to be parted from his new benefactor and went on with the party to London.

In London they were well entertained by a visit to Vauxhall Gardens as well as by several public and private parties. Squire Bramble was disconcerted by the discovery that Humphry was a preacher by inclination, and had begun giving sermons in the manner of the Methodists. Miss Tabitha and her maid were already among Humphry's followers. The squire attempted to stop what he considered either hypocrisy or madness on Humphry's part. Miss Tabitha, disgusted with her brother's action, begged him to allow Humphry to continue his sermons.

The family was shocked to learn one day that Humphry had been arrested as a highway robber, and was in jail. When the squire arrived to investigate the case, he discovered that Humphry was obviously innocent of the charge against him, which had been placed by an ex-convict who made money by turning in criminals to the government. Humphry had made a fine impression on the jailer and his family and had converted several of his fellow prisoners. The squire found the man who supposedly had been robbed and got him to testify that Humphry was not the man who had committed the robbery. In the meantime Humphry preached so eloquently that he kept the prison taproom empty of customers. When this became evident he was hurriedly released, and Squire Bramble promised to allow him to preach his sermons unmolested.

Continuing their travels north after leaving London, the party stopped in Scarborough, where they went bathing. Squire Bramble undressed in a little cart which could be rolled down into the sea, so that he was able to bath nude with the greatest propriety. When he entered the water, he found it much colder than he had expected and gave several shouts as he swam away. Hearing these calls from the squire, Humphry thought his good master was drowning, and rushed fully clothed into the sea to rescue him. He pulled the squire to shore, almost twisting off his master's ear, and leaving the modest man shamefaced and naked in full view upon the beach. Humphry was forgiven, however, because he had meant well.

At an inn in Durham, the party made the acquaintance of Lieutenant Lismahago, who seemed somewhat like Don Quixote. The lieutenant, regaling the company with tales of his adventures among the Indians of North America, quite captured the heart of Miss Tabitha. Squire Bramble was also charmed with the crusty conversation of the retired soldier, and made plans to meet him later on in their journey. The group became more and more fond of Humphry as time went on, especially Winifred. After a short and frivolous flirtation with Jerry's part-time valet, she settled down to win Humphry as a husband.

The party continued its trip through Scotland. In Edinburgh Lydia fainted when she saw a man who looked like Wilson, an action which showed her uncle that she had not yet forgotten the affair. After visiting several parts of Scotland and enjoying the most gracious hospitality everywhere, they continued by coach back to England. As they were traveling south, Lieutenant Lismahago rejoined the party and Miss Tabitha renewed her designs on him.

Just outside Dumfries the coach was overturned in the middle of a stream. Jerry and Lismahago succeeded in getting the women out of the water after a struggle, and Humphry staged a heroic rescue of the squire, who had been caught in the bottom of the coach. They found lodgings at a nearby inn until the coach could be repaired. While all were gathered in the parlor of a tavern, Squire Bramble was accosted by an old college friend named Dennison, a successful farmer of the county. Mr. Dennison had known the squire only as Matthew Lloyd, a name he had taken for a while in order to fulfill the terms of a will. When Humphry heard his master called Lloyd, he rushed up in a flutter of excitement and presented the squire with certain papers he had always carried with him. These papers proved that Humphry was the squire's natural son. In a gracious way, Squire Bramble welcomed his offspring, and presented him to the rest of his family. Humphry was overcome with pleasure and shyness. Winifred was afraid that his discovery would spoil her matrimonial plans, but Humphry continued to be the mild religious man he had been before.

The squire was also surprised to learn that the actor who had called himself Wilson was really Dennison's son, a fine proper young man who had run away from school and become an actor only to escape a marriage his father had planned for him long before. He had told his father about his love for Lydia, but Dennison had not realized that the Mr. Bramble who was her uncle was his old friend Matthew Lloyd. Now the two young lovers were brought together for a joyous reunion.

Lieutenant Lismahago was moved to ask for Miss Tabitha's hand in marriage, and both the squire and Miss Tabitha eagerly accepted his offer. The whole party went to stay at Mr. Dennison's house while preparations were being made for the marriage of Lydia and George. The coming marriages prompted Humphry to ask Winifred for her hand, and she also said yes. The three weddings were planned for the same day.

George and Lydia were a most attractive couple. The lieutenant and Tabitha seemed to be more pleasant than ever before. Humphry and Winifred both thanked God for the pleasures He saw fit to give them. The squire planned to return home to the tranquility of Brambleton Hall and the friendship of his invaluable doctor there.

Critical Evaluation

Humphry Clinker is considered by many critics to be the best of Tobias Smollett's works. First published in the very year of the author's death, the lively novel was written while Smollett was, like his character Matthew Bramble, in retirement seeking recovery from his failing health. Despite the novel's artful treatment of the effect of health on the individual's mentality, *Humphry Clinker* caters delightfully to the tastes of its eighteenth century audience. It focuses primarily on travel, distant societies, and manners since eighteenth century readers thrived on novels of the exotic. Smollett, however, lent that same exotic excitement to the travels of Bramble and his party as they made their excursion through England, Scotland, and Wales. Smollett combined, then, his audience's thirst for the remote with their increasing desire to learn more of history and social structure, particularly their own.

The structure of *Humphry Clinker* is at first glance deceptively simple. It is an epistolary novel, a genre very popular during its time, and as such, it lends itself readily to a straightforward, chronological structure. Dates and locations are given with every letter; even directions are given about where the author will be to receive an answer by return mail. Yet it is not the passing of time that is important for, during any particular period of time, nothing really changes; no one's opinions metamorphose from one point to another. Lydia continues to love "Wilson"; Jerry continues to despise him; Tabitha continues to struggle for masculine attention; Clinker continues to devote himself to a humble way of life; and Matthew Bramble continues to reaffirm above all else a distinct social division. Instead, action is of prime importance. Although there appears to be a tremendous change of orientation toward life at the conclusion of the novel, there is not. The social structure, having been tampered with by chance, has been rectified, and all continue to love and despise as before, now that the labels of the objects have been returned to normal.

Another characteristic of the structure is its semblance of the picaresque. Although it is quite clear that the novel fulfills many of the requirements of the picaresque novel—it is episodic and treats various levels of society—one is asked to question, who is the picaro? He is not the titular hero, who actually appears long after the novel is under way. The "picaro," then, is Bramble. Bramble is a particular type of picaro who appeared often in the eighteenth century. He is not a criminal, loose in his morals, nor is he an anti-hero; he is a reflection of the author, Smollett himself. Most important of all, Smollett-Bramble is a moralizer.

Bramble's moralizing is Smollett's avenue for displaying one of the novel's unifying features—humor. Above all, Smollett-Bramble is a special kind of moralizer—an idealist. According to Bramble's view of humanity, society is to be separated into strict social classes. The classes give society order, and through order men are essentially safe from the many bothersome problems which could prevent them from pursuing the style of life to which they feel entitled. Such is the latent subject of the majority of Bramble's letters to his dear Dr. Lewis. But the ironic and humorous vehicle for these moralistic treatises is his encounters with the oddest assortment of "originals." Although, for the most part, they concur with Bramble's views of society, socially they are not what they seem. Sons of refined blood appear to be lowly; people of adequate means conduct themselves only with the richest of tastes; worthy gentlemen are treated ill by life and reduced to poor, nearly inescapable circumstances. Most of Bramble's acquaintances are eccentrics and as such they are "humorous" in the true sense of the word. Each has a master passion that he fervently pursues, often to ludicrousness. And Bramble, in his effort to comprehend them in a magnanimous manner, is equally humorous—the conflict between his head and his heart is never resolved, and his endearing desire to help everybody is obviously his own master passion.

Humor, in *Humphry Clinker,* eventually lends itself to satire, and at this task Smollett is at least partially successful. Unfortunately Smollett's satire is often against personal enemies, and one of his faults is that his allusions are too obscure to be appreciated. But one means through which his more appreciable satire is executed is that of opposites. Town *versus* country, commoner *versus* gentleman are both opposite extremes which at first appear to have one side clearly preferable to the other. But one soon sees that Smollett does not present his reader with logical alternatives when opposites are in conflict. We know, for example, that the characters have common views of propriety because of their actions and, especially, their verbalized reactions. But the result when the reader tries to reconstruct what these guidelines are, is elusive. What are they based on? And what really are the consequencs if they are ignored? Although we know that the commodities used in pursuit of propriety are good favor, a good name, and money, it is difficult to see what it is these commodities secure when put to use.

Above all, what makes *Humphry Clinker* the successful novel it is, is Smollett's reaffirmation of the genuine emotional response. Bramble is a man of sensitivity to his physical and social surroundings and experiences. He is tempted, for example, to believe that his trip through Scotland is a glimpse into the ideal way of life he has been both proselytizing and searching for. However, Bramble senses that modernization threatens Scotland with the laziness and complacency that consume England. In addition, Smollett emphasizes how a man's character is shaped by his experiences and emotional responses, by anticipating the very responses a reader might have to such a travel novel. But most important, Bramble's solitary reflections imply that the most intense and meaningful emotions a person might have are those he does not feel obligated to verbalize. In this way Smollett's characters are safe from both our pity and our ridicule.

Bibliography

Auty, Susan G. "Smollett and Sterne and Animal Spirits: *Humphry Clinker*," in *The Comic Spirit of Eighteenth-Century Novels*. Port Washington, N.Y.: Kennikat, 1975, pp. 158–179.

Baker, Sheridan. "*Humphry Clinker* as Comic Romance," in *Essays on the Eighteenth Century Novel*. Edited by Robert Donald Spector. Bloomington: Indiana University Press, 1965. pp. 154–164.

Boucé, Paul-Gabriel. *The Novels of Tobias Smollett*. London: Longmans, 1976, pp. 191–251, 279–285, 335–340.

Copeland, Edward. "*Humphry Clinker*: A Comic Pastoral Poem in Prose?," in *Texas Studies in Language and Literature*. XVI (1974), pp. 493–501.

Donovan, Robert A. *The Shaping Vision: Imagination in the English Novel from Defoe to Dickens.* Ithaca, N.Y.: Cornell University Press, 1966, pp. 118–139.

Duncan, Jeffrey L. "The Rural Ideal in Eighteenth Century Fiction," in *Studies in English Literature, 1500–1900.* VIII (1968), pp. 520–523.

Evans, David L. "*Humphry Clinker*: Smollett's Tempered Augustanism," in *Criticism.* IX (1967), pp. 257–274.

Gassman, Byron. "The Economy of *Humphry Clinker*," in *Tobias Smollett Bicentennial Essays Presented to Lewis M. Knapp.* Edited by G.S. Rousseau and P.-G. Boucé. New York: Oxford University Press, 1971, pp. 155–168.

Giddings, Robert. *The Tradition of Smollett.* London: Methuen, 1967, pp. 140–150.

Graham, W.H. "Smollett's *Humphry Clinker*," in *Contemporary Review.* CLXXVI (1949), pp. 33–38.

Grant, Damian. *Tobias Smollett: A Study in Style.* Totowa, N.J.: Rowman and Littlefield, 1977.

Iser, Wolfgang. *The Implied Reader: Patterns of Communication in Prose Fiction from Bunyan to Beckett.* Baltimore: Johns Hopkins University Press, 1974, pp. 57–80.

Kahrl, George Morrow. *Tobias Smollett, Traveler-Novelist.* Chicago: University of Chicago Press, 1945, pp. 119–147.

Karl, Frederick R. "Smollett's *Humphry Clinker*: The Choleric Temper," in *A Reader's Guide to the Development of the English Novel in the 18th Century.* London: Thames and Hudson, 1975, pp. 183–204.

Knapp, Lewis M. *Tobias Smollett, Doctor of Men and Manners.* Princeton, N.J.: Princeton University Press, 1949, pp. 288–296, 321–323.

McKillop, Alan D. *The Early Masters of English Fiction.* Lawrence: University of Kansas Press, 1956, pp. 170–181.

Martz, Louis L. *The Later Career of Tobias Smollett.* New Haven, Conn.: Yale University Press, 1942, pp. 124–180.

Park, William. "Fathers and Sons: *Humphry Clinker*," in *Literature and Psychology.* XVI (1966), pp. 166–174.

Paulson, Ronald. "Satire in the Early Novels of Smollett," in *Journal of English and Germanic Philology.* LIX (July, 1960), pp. 381–402.

Preston, Thomas R. *Not in Timon's Manner: Feeling, Misanthropy, and Satire in Eighteenth Century England.* University: University of Alabama Press, 1975, pp. 107–120.

Rothstein, Eric. *Systems of Order and Inquiry in Later Eighteenth Century Fiction.* Berkeley: University of California Press, 1975, pp. 109–153.

Sekora, John. *Luxury: The Concept in Western Thought, Eden to Smollett.* Baltimore: Johns Hopkins University Press, 1977, pp. 215–295.

Siebert, Donald T., Jr. "The Role of the Senses in *Humphry Clinker*," in *Studies in the Novel.* VI (1974), pp. 17–26.

Spector, Robert D. *Tobias George Smollett.* New York: Twayne, 1968, pp. 127–135.

Warner, John M. "Smollett's Development as a Novelist," in *Novel.* V (1972), pp. 158–161.

PEREGRINE PICKLE

Type of work: Novel
Author: Tobias Smollett (1721–1771)
Type of plot: Picaresque romance
Time of plot: Early eighteenth century
Locale: England and the continent
First published: 1751

Following the misadventures of Peregrine, a rascally hero whose follies, extravagances, and practical jokes sometimes approach villainy, this picaresque novel reveals the chicaneries of Smollett's time. The author satirizes with wit and humor the manners and morals of early eighteenth century English life.

Principal Characters

Peregrine Pickle, called **Perry** in his younger days, a headstrong, rebellious young man. Bitterly disliked by his mother in his childhood, Peregrine is adopted by his godfather, a retired naval officer who lavishes money on his young ward, educates him, saves him from a love affair regarded as imprudent, and sends him traveling on the Continent. Although wealthy after his benefactor's death, Peregrine suffers reverses caused by his extravagance, his delight in practical jokes, and his foolhardiness in writing satires on public officials after he has stood unsuccessfully for Parliament and has been reduced to near penury. Thrown into prison, and without influential friends, he nevertheless refuses the hand and fortune of Emilia Gauntlet, with whom he is in love. He is saved by an inheritance from his father, marries Emilia, and settles down to the life of a country squire. Peregrine Pickle is developed beyond Smollett's other title characters. On his travels he is thrown with intellectuals, the associations leading to lengthy discussions on political, cultural, philosophical matters. He is also given to foolhardy and sometimes licentious behavior.

Commodore Hawser Trunnion, Peregrine's godfather and benefactor. An old sea dog, Trunnion keeps his house—called the garrison—like a ship; his speech is sharp and salty with naval jargon. His maintenance of a ship's atmosphere makes for much of the comedy in the novel.

Thomas Pipes, Trunnion's companion and servant, retired from the sea. He becomes a companion to Peregrine when he is sent to school and on his travels. Loyal to the young man, Pipes rescues his wayward master from many scrapes.

Lieutenant Jack Hatchway, the Commodore's one-legged companion. Like Pipes, he often shows up when Peregrine needs help. Hatchway's most opportune appearance comes when Peregrine is in Fleet Prison after his arrest for writing the political satires.

Emilia Gauntlet, called **Emy** by her family, Peregrine's sweetheart, whom he meets while he is attending Winchester School. The recurrent meetings of these two, tempered by quarrels and avowals of devotion, are for much of the story secondary in importance to Peregrine's pursuit of other women. Eventually Peregrine offers her his hand and Emilia accepts.

Godfrey Gauntlet, her brother. After a brief period of animosity, during which he worsts Peregrine in a duel, he becomes a devoted friend on learning that Peregrine is his secret benefactor. Peregrine, in his prosperous days, had anonymously provided funds for Godfrey and had used his influence to secure Godfrey's captaincy in the navy.

Gamaliel Pickle, Peregrine's father, the soul of humbleness, and the butt of his wife's ill temper. He is happy to see his son taken by Trunnion, away from the meanness of his wife. Whether unwittingly or not, Gamaliel wins the final victory over his wife; he dies intestate and his money goes to Peregrine, his first-born son.

Sally Appleby, Gamaliel's termagant wife. Left unprovided for at the death of her husband, she is forced to live on an allowance from Peregrine.

Grizzle Pickle, Gamaliel's sister and his housekeeper until he marries Sally. Refusing to be subjugated by her sister-in-law, Grizzle finds escape when she becomes Mrs. Trunnion. Her death brings sadness to Peregrine, who has considered her more a mother than an aunt.

Gam Pickle, Peregrine's young brother. His mother's favorite child, Gam conspires with his mother in her scheming. Their hatred for Peregrine is shown in their plot to have him murdered. Godfrey Gauntlet, mistaken for Peregrine, suffers from their machinations. Gam faces a dismal future when he is ordered away from the property with his mother, after Peregrine inherits his father's estate.

Julia Pickle, Peregrine's sister and the youngest of the children, who also suffers her mother's ill will. Sympathetic to Peregrine, she is taken in and cared for by Grizzle Trunnion.

Layman Pallet, an English traveler whom Peregrine meets at the Palais Royal in Paris. In addition to his discussion on art and the other aspects of sophistication which he lends to the story, he is pictured, almost in burlesque and in raucous circumstances, trying to seduce a woman in a party traveling to Ghent.

The Doctor, Pallet's traveling companion. His knowledge as a connoisseur of foods and wines adds to the tone of the story, stressing Peregrine's sophistication.

Cadwallader Crabtree, an eccentric old man whom Peregrine meets when he returns to London. Posing as a fortune-teller, he allows Peregrine to learn many women's secrets.

Deborah Hornbeck, the attractive wife of an English traveler in Paris. Her elopement with Peregrine threatens to become an international incident. The British ambassador sends Deborah back to her husband. After the second affair with her, Peregrine is put into prison. Freed, he is given three days to leave Paris.

Lady Vane, a notorious lady of quality. Her memoirs, which make up a sizable section of the novel, tell of her many lovers.

Amanda, a young woman traveling to Ghent. Peregrine's efforts to seduce her are exceeded in comedy only by Pallet's simultaneous activities with her traveling companion.

Jolter, a teacher at Winchester School, hired by Trunnion to act as Peregrine's traveling companion on the Continent. In this role he is called the Governor.

Miss Sophy, Emilia Gauntlet's cousin, who helps Peregrine in his affair with Emilia.

A Young Female Beggar, whom Peregrine encounters on the road to London. In Pygmalion-like manner, he buys her fashionable gowns and teaches her polite phrases in order to pass her off as a lady; however, her gaucherie causes him to lose friends because of his gross prank.

Sir Steady Steerwell, the Minister of Public Affairs and the subject of the satire which sent Peregrine to the Fleet Prison.

Charles Clover, Julia Pickle's husband, who informs Peregrine of his father's death. A young justice of the peace, he averts any plan Gam and his mother may have in forging a will after Gamaliel Pickle dies intestate.

Cecilia Gauntlet, Emilia's mother. She reprimands Peregrine for his conduct toward her daughter. Later she is much in favor of her son-in-law.

Mr. Sackbut, the curate, who plots with Gam and Sally to murder Peregrine.

Morgan, a Welsh surgeon identified as

Dr. Morgan, a character in Smollett's earlier novel, "Roderick Random."

Benjamin Chintz, a merchant who repays with interest a loan of seven hundred pounds while Peregrine is in Fleet Prison. The repayment marks the reversal of Peregrine's bad fortune.

Jennings and
Jumble, Peregrine's teachers, against whom, as a youngster, he rebels because of their hypocrisy.

Hadgi, Peregrine's valet on his travels. Peregrine befriends him after the party has returned to England and Hadgi is out of Peregrine's employ.

The Story

Mr. Gamaliel Pickle was the son of a prosperous London merchant who at his death bequeathed his son a fortune of no small degree. Later, having lost a part of his inheritance in several unsuccessful ventures of his own, Mr. Pickle prudently decided to retire from business and to live on the interest of his fortune rather than risk his principal in the uncertainties of trade. With his sister Grizzle, who had kept his house for him since his father's death, he went to live in a mansion in the country.

In the region to which he retired, Mr. Pickle's nearest neighbor was Commodore Hawser Trunnion, an old sea dog who kept his house like a seagoing ship and who possessed an endless list of quarterdeck oaths he used on any occasion against anyone who offended him. Other members of his household were Lieutenant Hatchway, a one-legged veteran, and a seaman named Tom Pipes.

Shortly after he had settled in his new home Mr. Pickle met Miss Sally Appleby, daughter of a gentleman in a nearby parish, and after a brief courtship the two were married. Before long Mr. Pickle discovered that his wife was determined to dominate him completely. Peregrine was the oldest son of that ill-starred union. During her pregnancy Mrs. Pickle took such a dislike to Grizzle that she tried in every way possible to embarrass and humiliate her sister-in-law. Realizing that she was no longer wanted in her brother's household, Grizzle began a campaign to win the heart of old Commodore Trunnion.

Ignoring his distrust of women in general, she won out at last over his obstinacy. The wedding was not without humor, for on his way to the church the commodore's horse ran away with him and carried him eleven miles with a hunting party. Upset by his experience, he insisted that the postponed ceremony be performed in his own house. The wedding night was also not without excitement when the ship's hammocks in which the bride and groom were to sleep collapsed and catapulted them to the floor. The next morning, wholly indifferent to her husband's displeasure, Mrs. Trunnion proceeded to refurnish and reorganize the commodore's house according to her own notions.

In order to silence his protests, Mrs. Trunnion conceived the idea of pretending to be pregnant. But the commodore's hopes for an heir were short-lived; his wife employed her ruse only to make herself absolute mistress of the Trunnion household. Lacking an heir of his own, the gruff but kindly old seaman turned his attention to young Peregrine Pickle, his nephew and godson. Peregrine was an unfortunate child. While he was still very young, his mother had taken an unnatural and profound dislike to him, and the boy was often wretched from the harsh treatment he received. Weak-willed Mr. Pickle, under the influence of his wife, did little to improve that unhappy situation. As a result, Peregrine grew into a headstrong, rebellious boy who showed his high spirits in all kinds of pranks that mortified and irritated his parents. Sent away to school, he rebelled against his foolish and hypocritical teachers, and at last he wrote to the commodore asking that he be removed from the school. Feeling pity for the boy and admiring his spirit of independence, the commodore took him out of school and adopted him as his son and heir.

When Peregrine's pranks and escapades became more than his indulgent uncle could stand, the boy was sent to Winchester School, with Pipes accompanying him as his servant. Aware of his uncle's kindness, Peregrine studied and made steady progress until he met Miss Emilia Gauntlet and fell in love with her. Emilia was visiting in Winchester; her own home was in a village about a day's journey away. So great was Peregrine's infatuation that soon after she had returned home he ran away from school and took lodgings in the village in order to be near her. His absence having been reported by the school authorities, Hatchway was sent to look for him. The boy was summoned to attend his uncle, who was alarmed by his heir's interest in a penniless girl. Peregrine's mother grew even more spiteful and his father disowned him for his youthful folly. Indignant at the parents' harsh treatment of their son, the commodore sent Peregrine to Oxford to continue his studies. There he encountered Emilia again and renewed his courtship. Because he hoped to make a good match for his nephew, the commodore attempted to end the affair by sending Peregrine on a tour of the continent. Aware of his uncle's purpose in sending him abroad, Peregrine visited Emilia before his departure and vowed eternal devotion.

Shortly thereafter, warned by the commodore that his reckless behavior would lead only to disaster, Peregrine set out for France. Faithful Pipes went with him as his servant and he was also accompanied by a mentor who was supposed to keep a check on Peregrine's behavior. All efforts in that direction were fruitless. Peregrine had barely set foot on French soil before he made gallant advances to Mrs. Hornbeck, the wife of a traveling Englishman. In Paris he encountered the lady again and eloped with her, an escapade that ended when the British ambassador intervened to send the lady back to her husband. On one occasion Peregrine was imprisoned by the city guard. At another time he fought a duel with a musketeer as the result of an amorous adventure. He quarreled with a nobleman at a masked ball and was sent to the Bastille in company with an artist friend. After Pipes had discovered his whereabouts and had secured his release, Peregrine was ordered to leave France within three days.

On his way back to England, Peregrine became embroiled with a knight of Malta, quarreled with Pipes, and was captivated by a lady he met in a carriage. Shortly afterward he lost his carriage companion and resumed his earlier affair with Mrs. Hornbeck. Her husband interposed and once more Peregrine was thrown into prison. After his release the travelers proceeded to Antwerp and from there to England. His uncle, who still retained his affection for his wayward nephew, received him with great joy.

On his return Peregrine called on Emilia, whom he found indifferent to his attentions. He wasted no time in pining over a lost love but continued to disport himself in London and Bath, until he was called home by the final illness of his uncle. The old commodore was buried according to his own directions and he was remembered with great affection and respect by his nephew. To Peregrine his uncle willed a fortune of thirty thousand pounds and his house. After a vain attempt to reach a friendly understanding with his parents, Peregrine left the house to the tenancy of Hatchway and returned to London.

As a handsome, wealthy young bachelor, he indulged in extravagance and dissipation of all kinds. After exaggerated reports of his wealth had been circulated, he was pursued by matchmaking mothers whose efforts merely amused him but whose designs gave him entrance into the houses of the fashionable and the great.

Meeting Emilia again, he began the same campaign to win her that had been successful with his other light and casual loves. Disappointed in his attempts to seduce her, he took advantage of the confusion attending a masquerade ball to try to overcome her by force. He was vigorously repulsed, and her uncle denied him the privilege of seeing Emilia again.

He became the friend of a notorious lady of quality who gave him a copy of her memoirs. The woman was Lady Vane, whose affairs with many lovers had created a great scandal in London.

Peregrine had a friend named Cadwallader who assumed the character of a fortune-teller and magician. In that way Peregrine was able to learn the secrets of the women who came to consult Cadwallader. Having acquired a reputation as a clever man and a wit, Peregrine used his knowledge to advance his own position.

Grizzle Trunnion died and Peregrine attended her funeral. On the road he met a vulgar young female beggar whom he dressed in fashionable clothes and taught a set of polite phrases. It amused him to introduce the girl into his own fashionable world. When his contemptuous joke was at last exposed, he lost many of his fine friends.

Peregrine now decided to retrench. He cut down his foolish expenses and made loans at a good rate of interest. He was persuaded to stand for Parliament. This decision was taken after he had met Emilia at her sister's wedding and he had begged the sister to intercede for him. But his political venture cost more money than he had expected. Having lost the election, he was for the first time in his life faced with the need for mature reflection on himself and his world.

His affairs went from bad to worse. A mortgage that he held proved worthless. A friend for whom he had endorsed a note defaulted. Reduced at last to complete ruin, he tried to earn money by writing translations and satires. He was again thrown into jail after the publication of a satire directed against an influential politician.

His old friends, Hatchway and Pipes, remained loyal to him in his adversity. Each brought his savings to the Fleet prison and offered them to Peregrine, but he refused to accept their aid. It was his intention to earn money for his release by his writing or else starve in the attempt.

About that time Emilia's brother, Captain Gauntlet, learned that he had been promoted to his rank largely through Peregrine's services in the days of his prosperity. Discovering Peregrine's plight, he set about to relieve his benefactor. Peregrine had an unexpected bit of luck when one of his debtors returned a loan of seven thousand pounds. Emilia, having inherited ten thousand pounds, offered the money and her hand to Peregrine. Touched by her generosity and forgiveness, he reluctantly refused to burden her with his debts and degradation.

Peregrine was saved at last by the death of his father, who died intestate. Legal heir to his father's fortune, he was able to leave Fleet prison and take immediate possession of his estate. Having settled an allowance upon his mother, who had gone to live in another part of the country, Peregrine hastened to ask for Emilia's hand in marriage. With his bride he settled down to lead the life of a country squire.

Critical Evaluation

The second of Smollett's novels, *Peregrine Pickle,* appeared only three years after *Roderick Random.* It is twice the length of that first work, and, in the opinion of most modern critics, about half as interesting. Certainly there is plenty of sportive comedy and wry wit as Perry forays, picaro-fashion, across the Continent and then through England. But midway in the novel the adventures begin to pall, if only because of their repetitiveness and simple accretion.

This is a strangely uneven book—even for Smollet, who is often capable of marked fluctuations in his artistry. The tone is one of unnerving harshness, of a satire verging near insolence. In a similar vein, its action, as many readers have noted, is often gratuitously violent, despite Smollett's obvious concern with exposing the violence of eighteenth century London life. And its picaresque hero seems at times incredibly disparate as a moral agent. Admittedly, this—or a version of this—is characteristic of Roderick Random, Tom Jones, and a host of similar figures, but one cannot avoid feeling that Smollett too often rubs out the spot of nobility in his hero. The net effect is that of a book occasionally out of control and a hero gone with it.

But there is also much to recommend the novel; and although it was not received with the same success as *Roderick Random,* Smollett's audience clearly enjoyed reading it. Much of the satire takes up predictable subjects: French gallantry and customs, the popularized Grand Tour, politics—both national and international—female vanity, polite adultery, and especially Roman Catholicism. Much of it, too, is very topical, as in the case of the physician whom Perry meets—almost surely a caricature of the poet Mark Akenside—and the ignoramus Pallet, who is thought by some to represent William Hogarth. There is also the very long interpolation entitled "The Memoirs of a Lady of Quality," which recounts the amorous adventures of Frances Viscount Vane. However forbidding the length, then, *Peregrine Pickle* does contain a number of pointed and amusing episodes.

Bibliography

Allen, Walter E. *The English Novel.* London: Phoenix House, 1954, pp. 67–68.

Auty, Susan G. "Smollett and Sterne and Animal Spirits: *Peregrine Pickle,*" in *The Comic Spirit of Eighteenth-Century Novels.* Port Washington, N.Y.: Kennikat, 1975, pp. 103–119.

Baker, Ernest A. *The History of the English Novel,* Volume IV. New York: Barnes & Noble, 1950, pp. 208–215.

Boucé, Paul-Gabriel. *The Novels of Tobias Smollett.* London: Longmans, 1976, pp. 124–142.

Elton, Oliver. *Survey of English Literature, 1730–1780,* Volume I. New York: Macmillan, 1928, pp. 204–208.

Evans, David L. "*Peregrine Pickle*: The Complete Satirist," in *Studies in the Novel.* III (1971), pp. 258–274.

Giddings, Robert. *The Tradition of Smollett.* London, Methuen, 1967, pp. 129–159.

Grant, Damian. *Tobias Smollett: A Study in Style.* Totowa, N. J.: Rowman and Littlefield, 1977.

Jeffrey, David K. "Smollett's Irony in *Peregrine Pickle,*" in *Journal of Narrative Technique.* VI (1976), pp. 137–146.

Kahrl, George Morrow. *Tobias Smollett, Traveler-Novelist.* Chicago: University of Chicago Press, 1945, pp. 28–50.

Knapp, Lewis M. *Tobias Smollett, Doctor of Men and Manners.* Princeton, N.J.: Princeton University Press, 1949, pp. 116–129, 318.

McKillop, Alan D. *The Early Masters of English Fiction.* Lawrence: University of Kansas Press, 1956, pp. 157–164.

Marshall, Percy. *Masters of the English Novel.* London: Dennis Dobson, 1962, pp. 69–71.

Paulson, Ronald. "The Pilgrimage and the Family: Structures in the Novels of Fielding and Smollett," in *Tobias Smollett: Bicentennial Essays Presented to Lewis M. Knapp.* Edited by G.S. Rousseau and P.-G. Boucé. New York: Oxford University Press, 1971, pp. 57–78.

————. *Satire and the Novel in Eighteenth Century England.* New Haven, Conn.: Yale University Press, 1967, pp. 180–187.

Piper, William Bowman. "The Large Diffused Picture of Life in Smollett's Early Novels," in *Studies in Philology.* LX (January, 1963), pp. 45–56.

Putney, Rufus. "The Plan of *Peregrine Pickle*," in *PMLA.* LX (December, 1945), pp. 1051–1065.

Preston, Thomas R. *Not in Timon's Manner: Feeling, Misanthropy, and Satire in Eighteenth-Century England.* University: University of Alabama Press, 1975, pp. 78–85.

Rousseau, G.S. "Pineapples, Pregnancy, Pica, and *Peregrine Pickle*," in *Tobias, Smollett: Bicentennial Essays Presented to Lewis M. Knapp.* Edited by G.S. Rousseau and P.-G. Boucé. New York: Oxford University Press, 1971, pp. 79–109.

Spector, Robert D. *Tobias George Smollett.* New York: Twayne, 1968, pp. 61–86.

Stevick, Philip. "Smollett's Picaresque Games," in *Tobias Smollett: Bicentennial Essays Presented to Lewis M. Knapp.* Edited by G.S. Rousseau and P.-G. Boucé. New York: Oxford University Press, 1971, pp. 111–130.

Warner, John M. "Smollett's Development as a Novelist," in *Novel.* V (1972), pp. 152–155.

RODERICK RANDOM

Type of work: Novel
Author: Tobias Smollett (1721–1771)
Type of plot: Picaresque romance
Time of plot: Eighteenth century
Locale: England
First published: 1748

Influenced by Le Sage's Gil Blas. *Tobias Smollett's first novel is a vigorous picaresque in which he sends his intrepid hero, Roderick Random, on a series of adventures which include such disparate settings as London high society and the naval battle of Cartagena. Smollett's narrative is strident and inventive, his caricatures are vivid and hilarious, and his prose is strong and direct.*

Principal Characters

Roderick Random, familiarly called **Rory,** a reckless and restless young man whose experiences parallel to a certain extent those of Smollett himself. Rory's mother dies when he is born, and his father, disinherited by his family because he had married a poor relation and a domestic, leaves England. Random, libertine and unscrupulous, goes through all the stages of the eighteenth century picaresque hero. As a boy, he is mistreated by alienated relatives; he is befriended and educated (in medicine) by a sympathetic one. His life is a series of assumed identities, leading to whirlwind courtships and attempted marriages to a number of wealthy women. Robbed by a rascally friar in France, he enlists in the army of King Louis XIV. When things seem to be going too well or too badly for Random, an antagonist or a protagonist appears to change the course of his life. Sea voyages and escapades in foreign countries seem to be Random's plight, until in Buenos Aires he meets a wealthy English trader who proves to be his father. After a series of events making for an unsettled, nomadic life, Random is established, happily married, on his father's estate, from which he was evicted as a youngster. Although he often acts without scruples Random is a likable and in the end a personable young man.

Tom Bowling, Random's uncle, lieutenant aboard H.M.S. "Thunder." Appearing early in the story, he becomes Random's benefactor. His first move is to get Random away from mean relatives and into school. As unsettled as his nephew, Bowling fights duels on sea and land, is robbed, loses and regains command of ships, suffers at the hands of ingrates he has befriended. Always the old salt, especially in avoiding interference in others' personal affairs, he makes his will in favor of Random and goes to sea again after seeing his young relative comfortable financially and happy maritally.

Hugh Strap, a schoolmate of Random. Like Bowling, Strap appears propitiously now and again to save Random from disaster or death. At times Strap's good deeds lead to further involvements for his friend. Strap, the imaginative, romantic figure, curries favor of a French nobleman to gain employment and an inheritance from his master. As the moneyed M. d'Estrapes, he grooms Random as a fine gentleman so that the scapegrace can make a wealthy marriage in England. His kindnesses are repaid when Random comes into money and acquaints Strap with the latter's wife to be.

Narcissa, the niece of the eccentric bluestocking to whom Random hires out as a footman. Narcissa falls in love with Random and he with her. Despite her relatives' and fate's working against her and Random, the beautiful, clever Narcissa remains faithful to him, avoids marriage with any of her many suitors, and in the end becomes his wife.

Don Roderigo, the wealthy English trader whom Random meets in Buenos Aires. Don Roderigo, who has made a fortune through the favors of a Spanish grandee, proves to be Random's father. Don Roderigo buys his paternal estate from a debt-ridden heir, and the Random family settles once more in Scotland.

Nancy Williams, a prostitute to whom Random gives medical care after she is taken ill on the street. Their recurring contacts lead to Miss Williams' becoming Narcissa's attendant. She marries Strap.

The Squire, Narcissa's drunken, foxhunting brother. His disposition is best described by his aunt, who refers to him as the Savage. The Squire's chief function in the plot is to contend against Random and to urge his sister toward other suitors.

Sir Timothy Thicket, one of Narcissa's suitors, whom Random beats with a cudgel for forcing his attentions on Narcissa.

Melinda Goosetrap, a young woman of fortune whom Random courts. He fails in his suit because Melinda's mother sees through his disguise as a person of means. Melinda even wins at cards with Random as he is trying to get some of her money through gambling. She exposes him when she finds him pursuing other wealthy girls.

Miss Snapper, a witty, wealthy, deformed young woman also courted by Random after he saves her and her mother from highwaymen. He neglects her after meeting Narcissa in Bath.

Lord Quiverwit, another of Narcissa's suitors, favored by her brother. Random defeats him in a duel.

Lieutenant Crampley, the commander of the "Lizard," one of the ships on which Random serves. Crampley appears to hound Random in an effort to right an old wrong.

Jack Ratlin,
Thomson, and
Captain Oakhum, members of ships' crews. They are representative of the many individuals involved in Random's experiences.

Launcelot Crab, the surgeon who lends Random money. Crab is only one of innumerable doctors, on land and at sea, who affect Random's fortunes.

Banter,
Chatwell, and
Bragwell, three of the wide circle of young men, in London and Bath, who are friends or foes of Random.

Mrs. Sagely, a kind old woman who befriends and takes care of Random after he has been seriously injured in a fight.

An Eccentric Blue-Stocking Lady, Narcissa's aunt, whom Mrs. Sagely persuades to hire Random as a footman. Random's employer, an authoress of sorts, takes to Random because of his interpretation of her writing. She offsets some of the Squire's antagonism throughout Random's pursuit of Narcissa.

Frère Balthazar, a Scottish priest, referred to as the **Capuchin.** As in much eighteenth century writing, the Capuchin is a debauched churchman. Among his misdeeds is the theft of Random's money, a loss which forces him to enlist in the French army.

The Story

Although Roderick Random came from a wealthy landowning family of Scotland, his early life was one of vicissitudes. Roderick's father had married a servant in the Random household, and for that reason he had been disowned without a penny. Soon after Roderick's birth his mother died. When his father disappeared, heartbroken, the grandfather was prevailed upon to send the lad to school for the sake of the family's reputation.

At school Roderick was the butt of the masters, although a great favorite with the boys his own age. His whippings were numerous, for he could be used as a whipping boy when something had gone wrong and the real culprit could not be determined. In Roderick's fourteenth year, however, there was a change in his fortunes. His mother's brother, Tom Bowling, a lieutenant in the navy, came to visit his young nephew.

Lieutenant Bowling remonstrated with his nephew's grandfather over his treatment of Roderick, but the old man was firm in his refusal to do anything beyond what necessity dictated for the offspring of the son whom he had disinherited. When the grandfather died, he left Roderick nothing. Tom Bowling sent the lad to the university, where Roderick made great progress. Then Tom Bowling became involved in a duel and was forced to leave his ship. This misfortune cut off the source of Roderick's funds and made it necessary for him to leave the university.

Casting about for a means of making a livelihood, Roderick became a surgeon's apprentice. He proved to be so capable that before long his master sent him to London with a recommendation to a local member of Parliament, who was to get Roderick a place as surgeon's mate in the navy

Securing a place on a man-of-war was a difficult task. To keep himself in funds, Roderick worked for a French chemist in London. In the shop he met Miss Williams, with whom he fell in love, but much to his chagrin he discovered one day that she was a prostitute trying to better her fortune. Soon afterward Roderick was accused of stealing and was dismissed by his employer. While he was leading a precarious existence, waiting for his navy warrant, he learned that Miss Williams lived in the same lodging-house. He won the everlasting gratitude of the young woman by acting as her doctor while she was ill.

One day, while walking near the Thames, Roderick was seized by a press-gang and shanghaied aboard the man-of-war *Thunder*, about to sail for Jamaica. Roderick, who had found friends on the ship, was made a surgeon's mate.

The voyage to Jamaica was a terrible one as the commanding officer, Captain Oakhum, was a tyrant who came very close to hanging Roderick and another surgeon's mate because one of the ship's officers claimed he had heard them speaking ill of both the surgeon and the captain. Thinking that Roderick's Greek notebook was a military code, the captain threatened again to hang him as a spy.

After seeing action against the Spanish at Cartagena, Roderick secured a billet as surgeon's mate aboard the *Lizard*, a ship returning to England with dispatches.

On the way the captain died and Lieutenant Crampley, an officer who greatly disliked Roderick, took command of the ship. Crampley, being a poor officer, ran the ship aground off the Sussex coast. The crew robbed and tried to kill Roderick when they reached the shore, but an old woman befriended him, cured him of his wounds, and found him a place as footman with a spinster gentlewoman who lived nearby.

Roderick spent several months in her service. He found his way into his employer's goodwill by his attention to his duties and by showing a knowledge of literature, even to the extent of explaining passages from Tasso's Italian poetry to her. The spinster had a niece and a nephew living with her. Narcissa, the niece, was a beautiful girl of marriageable age to whom Roderick was immediately attracted. Her brother, a drunken, fox-hunting young squire, was determined that she should marry a wealthy knight in the neighborhood.

One day Roderick prevented the girl's brutal suitor from forcing his attentions on her and beat the man severely with a cudgel. While he was deliberating on his next move, he was taken prisoner by a band of smugglers who for their own safety carried him to Boulogne in France. There Roderick found his uncle, Tom Bowling, and assured him that he would be safe if he returned to England, for the man Bowling believed he had killed in a duel was very much alive.

Roderick set out for Paris in company with a friar who robbed him one night and left him penniless. Meeting a band of soldiers, Roderick enlisted in the army of King Louis XIV and saw service at the battle of Dettingen. After the battle his regiment went into garrison and Roderick unexpectedly met a boyhood companion, Strap, who was passing as Monsieur D'Estrapes and who was friendly with a French nobleman. Strap befriended Roderick and secured his release from onerous service as a private in the French army.

Strap and Roderick schemed for a way to make their fortunes and finally hit upon the idea of setting up Roderick as a wealthy gentleman. They hoped that he would marry, within a short time, some wealthy heiress.

The two men went to Paris, where Roderick bought new clothes and became acquainted with the ways of a man about town. Then they went to London. There Roderick quickly became acquainted with a group of young men who were on the fringe of fashionable society.

Roderick's first attempt to become intimate with a rich woman was a dismal failure, for she turned out to be a woman of the streets. On the second attempt he met Melinda, a young woman of fortune, who won many pounds from him at cards and then refused to marry him because he did not have an independent fortune of his own. Finally one of Roderick's friends told him of a cousin, Miss Snapper, who was a wealthy heiress. The friend promised that he would help Roderick in his suit in return for Roderick's note for five hundred pounds, due six months after the marriage.

Falling in with this suggestion, Roderick immediately started out for Bath in company with the young woman and her mother. On the way he saved them from

being robbed by a highwayman, a deed which established him in the good graces
of both mother and daughter. At Bath, Roderick squired the young woman about
day and night. Although she was crippled and not good-looking, the thought of
her fortune was greater in his mind than her appearance. Besides, she was an
intelligent and witty young woman.

All went well with the plan until Roderick caught sight of Narcissa, the young
girl he had known while he was employed as a footman by her aunt. Realizing
that he was in love with her, he promptly deserted Miss Snapper.

Narcissa soon revealed to Roderick that she returned his love. The young
squire, her brother, had no objections to Roderick because he thought that Random was a wealthy man. Unfortunately Roderick's former love, Melinda, arrived
in Bath and caught the attention of Narcissa's brother. At a ball she spread evil
reports about Roderick because he had left her. The result was that Roderick first
fought a duel with Lord Quiverwit, one of Narcissa's admirers, and then saw his
Narcissa spirited away by her brother. The only thing that kept Roderick's hope
alive was the fact that he knew Narcissa loved him and that her maid, the Miss
Williams whom Roderick had long before befriended, was eternally grateful to
him and would help him in any way which lay in her power.

Returning to London, Roderick again met his uncle, Tom Bowling, who had
been appointed to take a merchant ship on a mysterious trip. He proposed to take
Roderick with him as ship surgeon, and he gave Roderick a thousand pounds with
which to buy goods to sell on the voyage. He also made out a will leaving all his
property to Roderick in case he should die.

The mysterious trip proved to be a voyage to the Guinea Coast to pick up
Negro slaves for the Spanish American trade. The slaves and the cargo, including
the goods shipped by Roderick, were sold at a handsome profit. While their ship
was being prepared for the return voyage, Roderick and his uncle spent several
weeks ashore, where they were entertained by people they met and with whom
they did business. One of their acquaintances was a rich Englishman known as
Don Rodrigo, who invited them to visit him on his estate. During their stay it was
discovered that the man was Roderick's father, who had gone to America to make
his fortune after having been disinherited because of his marriage to Roderick's
mother.

The voyage back to England was a happy one. Roderick was full of confidence,
for he had made a small fortune out of the voyage and had expectations of quite a
large fortune from the estates of his father and his uncle. He immediately paid
his addresses to Narcissa, who accepted his offer of marriage in spite of her
brother's opposition. They were married shortly afterward and went to live in
Scotland on the Random estate, which Roderick's father had bought from his
bankrupt elder brother.

Critical Evaluation

Roderick Random is without doubt among the most adventure-ridden episodic novels of the eighteenth century. Innumerable incidents befall Roderick as he roams in every conceivable direction on land and sea, driven by necessity and survival. It is, then, a novel written in the best picaresque tradition with a hero who is at once roguish and (to a point) virtuous, resilient in the face of adversity yet often despairing, honorable in some matters but underhanded in a great many others. He is by turns whimsical, deliberate, sensitive, vengeful, petulant, gracious, and whatever else Smollett finds occasion for him to be. Structurally *Roderick Random* also fits easily into the picaresque tradition, not only in the obvious influence of Le Sage's *Gil Blas,* noted by Smollett in his preface, but also in its plot deficiencies. There are several such weaknesses—most of them sudden, unconvincing turns in the narrative—which betray the picaresque fondness for overemphasizing action and character.

Today the novel is most often read for two things: its glittering wit and its caustic social satire. There are many delightful touches in the book (the repartee of Miss Snapper, for example) which show off Smollett's comic skills and these, added to the author's ribaldry, make for great fun at times. But perhaps the most engaging parts of the novel are its scenes of London life: the card sharps, the wags, the floozies and fops, the poverty, the stench, the cruelty. We meet every imaginable species of human creature from prissy lords and lavender-trousered ship captains to lascivious priests and penitent whores. As a result Smollett depicts not just the sins of a sin-worn world but also the need to match good nature with plain animal cunning. Part of the controlling idea in *Roderick Random* is that education is best obtained, albeit harshly, not in schoolrooms but in city streets.

This theme is a favorite of eighteenth century British fiction. Fielding's *Tom Jones,* published just a year after *Roderick Random,* is a well-known reiteration of it; Tom, like Roderick, lacks wisdom and self-control (the age would have called it prudence), hence, he is repeatedly victimized by individuals with a crueler nature than his own. In Smollett's book we see the same pattern: a young man with a basically "good nature" (to echo Fielding) forced into a world of duplicity where his kindness and trust are manipulated by others. Thus the "knavery of the world," as Smollett dubs it, everywhere demands that the hero learn to be worldly-wise; the difficulty is to do this without destroying one's fundamental goodness. Often we see Roderick on the verge of such destruction. He is ungracious to his faithful friend Strap; he is at times unconscionably cruel in his schemes for revenge; he gravitates too easily toward unsavory rakes (Banter is a good example) and is himself tainted with affectation. But the point is that he remains good at heart and in the end is "rewarded" with Narcissa much as Tom Jones, having gained *prudentia,* is allowed to possess "Sophia."

It can be said, then, that the novel employs its main character as a moral *exemplum* for preaching and illustrating the traditional values of the age, among them temperance, virtue, fortitude, and honesty. It can also be said that the book's emphasis on sensibility reinforces the efficacy of human goodness, for if the reader is moved to applaud virtue and hate vice, to upbraid the hero's ingratitude despite his attractiveness, then Smollett has in large part proved his point.

Even a quick reading of the novel makes it plain how much Smollett relies on the theme of disguise to develop not only the concept of prudence but also a number of other concerns. One notable example is clothing imagery (it abounds in the book) in such scenes as Beau Jackson's appearance before the medical examiners. Wildly costumed as an old duffer, Jackson is a literal application of the adage that "the clothes make the man." He is found out, naturally, and thereby Smollett prepares us for one of the dominant themes of the novel. Simply, that theme argues that pretension, subterfuge, and hypocrisy are all penetrable. With experience and a sharp eye an individual can see through them.

The question to be asked, then, is: "What individual?" And the answer usually offered up by eighteenth century writers is: "The satirist." It is a commonplace observation that the satirist strips away the coverings of things, that after creating disguises for his characters he tears them away in order to reveal what lies beneath. In the case of Smollett this is unquestionably so. The clothing imagery fits well with his satiric purposes, for everywhere his intent is to bare our moral as well as our physical natures. Also, an understanding of this commonplace in part elucidates Smollett's dislike of "Romance" and other such writings. His attack on romance in the preface owes much to the satiric spirit which prevailed in the Augustan age, for there are few modes so different in philosophy as the romantic and the satiric. Romances—or "novels" as they were often called in Smollett's day—are in a sense departures from this world; they are fantasies, unrealities, idealizations. Satire, on the other hand, is fully committed to the world as it is; thus, it both eschews the improbable and dissolves the apparently real in order to plummet life's deepest recesses.

It should also be mentioned that *Roderick Random,* Smollett's first novel, is interesting simply for its biographical and historical inclusions. Smollett was himself a surgeon, therefore as one might expect the book offers plenty of commentary on eighteenth century medical practices. He also served in the Royal Navy as a surgeon's mate, was present at the disastrous attack upon Cartagena (this is discussed at length in the novel), and so had a first-hand knowledge of seamanship as well as medicine. Lastly, the story of Molopoyn, which occurs near the end of the book, is a thinly disguised account of Smollett's endeavors to promote his tragedy, *The Regicide.*

Bibliography

Allen, Walter E. *The English Novel.* London: Phoenix House, 1954, pp. 65–67.

Alter, Robert. *Rogue's Progress: Studies in the Picaresque Novel.* Cambridge, Mass.: Harvard University Press, 1964, pp. 58–79.

Baker, Ernest A. *The History of the English Novel,* Volume IV. New York: Barnes & Noble, 1950, pp. 201–208.

Bjornson, Richard. "The Picaresque Hero as Young Nobleman: Victimization and Vindication in Smollett's *Roderick Random,*" in *The Picaresque Hero in European Fiction.* Madison: University of Wisconsin Press, 1977, pp. 228–245.

Boucé, Paul-Gabriel. *The Novels of Tobias Smollett.* London: Longmans, 1976, pp. 100–124, 266–271.

Brooks, Douglas. *Number and Pattern in the Eighteenth Century Novel: Defoe, Fielding, Smollett and Sterne.* London: Routledge and Kegan Paul, 1973, pp. 123–127.

Elton, Oliver. *Survey of English Literature, 1730–1780,* Volume I. New York: Macmillan, 1928, pp. 204–208.

Fredman, Alice Green. "The Picaresque in Decline: Smollett's First Novel," in *English Writers of the Eighteenth Century.* Edited by John H. Middendorf. New York: Columbia University Press, 1971, pp. 189–207.

Grant, Damian. *Tobias Smollett: A Study in Style.* Totowa, N.J.: Rowman and Littlefield, 1977.

Kahrl, George Morrow. *Tobias Smollett, Traveler-Novelist.* Chicago: University of Chicago Press, 1945, pp. 12–27.

Knapp, Lewis M. *Tobias Smollett, Doctor of Men and Manners.* Princeton, N.J.: Princeton University Press, 1949, pp. 93–103, 317–318.

McCullough, Bruce W. *Representative English Novelists: Defoe to Conrad.* New York: Harper, 1946, pp. 61–68.

McKillop, Alan D. *The Early Masters of English Fiction.* Lawrence: University of Kansas Press, 1956, pp. 147–157.

Marshall, Percy. *Masters of the English Novel.* London: Dennis Dobson, 1962, pp. 64–69.

Paulson, Ronald. *Satire and the Novel in Eighteenth Century England.* New Haven, Conn.: Yale University Press, 1967, pp. 167–180.

Piper, William Bowman. "The Large Diffused Picture of Life in Smollett's Early Novels," in *Studies in Philology.* LX (January, 1963), pp. 45–56.

Preston, Thomas R. *Not in Timon's Manner: Feeling, Misanthropy, and*

Satire in Eighteenth-Century England. University: University of Alabama Press, 1975, pp. 73–78.

Spector, Robert D.   *Tobias George Smollett.* New York: Twayne, 1968, pp. 39–60.

Stevick, Philip.   "Smollett's Picaresque Games," in *Tobias Smollett: Bicentennial Essays Presented to Lewis M. Knapp.* Edited by G.S. Rousseau and P.-G. Boucé. New York: Oxford University Press, 1971, pp. 111–130.

Warner, John M.   "Smollet's Development as a Novelist," in *Novel.* V (1972), pp. 150–152.

LAURENCE STERNE

Born: Clonmel, Ireland (November 24, 1713)
Died: London England (March 18, 1768)

Principal Works

NOVEL: *The Life and Opinions of Tristram Shandy, Gent.*, 1759–1767.

TRAVEL MISCELLANY: *A Sentimental Journey through France and Italy*, 1768.

SATIRE: *A Political Romance*, 1759.

SERMONS: *The Sermons of Mr. Yorick*, 1760–1769.

LETTERS AND JOURNALS: *Letters from Yorick to Eliza*, 1773; *Sterne's Letters to His Friends on Various Occasions*, 1775; *Letters of the Late Rev. Mr. Sterne to His Most Intimate Friends*, 1775; *Journal to Eliza*, 1904.

Laurence Sterne, the most delightfully eccentric of English novelists, was born in Clonmel, Ireland, on November 24, 1713, the son of an Irish woman and an ensign in the English army whose regiment had just been transferred to Ireland from Dunkirk. Though his parentage was undistinguished, Sterne's father came from an old family in Yorkshire, where a great-grandfather had been an archbishop. A childhood spent in the rigors of camp-following undoubtedly had a harmful effect on the novelist's frail constitution; but the experience provided him with details of barracks life and campaign reminiscences that ultimately enriched his great novel with such authentic creations as Uncle Toby and Corporal Trim.

Between 1723 and 1731, the year of his father's death, Sterne was in school at Halifax, Yorkshire. In 1733, after two years of idleness at Elvington, he was enrolled as a sizar in Jesus College, Cambridge, through the gruding benevolence of relatives. At Cambridge he indulged in the easy, convivial university life of the time. Not surprisingly he discovered an incapacity for mathematics and a contempt for formal logic. Nevertheless, he did considerable reading, developing a deep admiration for John Locke, whose philosophy was to be the most important single influence on his thinking. He also formed a close friendship with John Hall-Stevenson, later the hypochondriac author of *Crazy Tales* (1762). Cambridge granted Sterne a B.A. in 1737 and an M.A. in 1740.

As a matter of expediency rather than religious conviction, he took holy orders. He was ordained deacon in 1737 and inducted into the vicarage of Sutton on the Forest in 1738. Two years later he received a prebendal stall in the York Cathedral. In 1744 he acquired the parish of Stillington, near Sutton.

In 1741, after a "sentimental" courtship he married the homely but well-connected Elizabeth Lumley. A daughter, Lydia, was born in 1747. The Sternes, however, were never really compatible. Not only was Mrs. Sterne ill-tempered but she also suffered aberrations which, according to gossip, were not allayed by her husband's "small, quiet attentions" to various ladies. Actually, there is evidence that Sterne treated his wife with commendable patience. And though he was not averse to paying attention to other women, his philandering was chiefly sentimental—as was, for example, his affair with Catherine ("Kitty") Fourmantelle, a singer from London who came to York in 1759.

In Sutton, Sterne spent twenty years of relative obscurity, serving two parishes with some conscientiousness, unsuccessfully farming his glebe, and making occasional trips to York to preach his turn in the cathedral or to dabble in diocesan politics. He found amusement in hunting, skating, fiddling, and painting, as well as in social gatherings at Newburgh Priory, the seat of Lord Fauconberg, and in the ribald carousals of the "Demoniacks" at Hall-Stevenson's Skelton Castle. He later immortalized his role of "hetero-clite parson" in his portrait of Yorick.

In 1759 his participation in local church politics produced a satire called *A Political Romance* (later renamed *The History of a Good Warm Watch-Coat*). Though all but a few copies were burned to prevent embarrassment to the diocese, its success among Sterne's friends gave him the impetus to embark on *Tristram Shandy*, the first two volumes of which came out in York in December of the same year. Introduced to London through the enthusiasm of David Garrick, the novel so impressed the capital with its whimsicality, eccentric humor, and indecorum that it was immediately successful. In fact, when Sterne journeyed down to London in the spring of 1760, he found himself a social lion. Never had the city seen such a witty, hedonistic priest whose lustrous eyes and ebulliently secular conversation so enchantingly belied his black garb, his pale face, thin body, and hollow chest.

But disapprobation soon followed success. Literary men like Walpole, Goldsmith, and Richardson condemned the book for various evils ranging from tediousness to indecency; and a flood of hostile articles, pamphlets, and bad imitations poured from the press. When the author brought out the first two volumes of the *Sermons of Mr. Yorick* (1760), the comminatory chorus grew—chiefly because the title bore the name of "a *Jester*. . . . in an obscene romance."

Returning to Yorkshire, Sterne received from Lord Fauconberg the living of Coxwold, to which "sweet retirement" he moved his family. Here for the rest of his life his home was a rambling gabled house that he called Shandy Hall. In January, 1761, he was again in London to see two more volumes of *Tristram Shandy* published. Though the critical reception was now unfavorable, the books sold well. Sterne returned to Coxwold, completed two more volumes, and was back in November for their publication. This time his reputation soared again. The story of Le Fever, Trim's animadversions on death, and Uncle Toby's campaigns had won universal applause.

Weakened by a serious hemorrhage from chronically weak lungs, Sterne set out for France in 1762 in a "race with death." Recovering in Paris, he was brilliantly lionized by the cream of French intellectual society. He later settled with his family in Toulouse. Back in Coxwold in 1764, he completed volumes seven and eight of *Tristram Shandy*, including an account of his tour through France and the affair of Uncle Toby and the Widow Wadman. These came out in January, 1765. Two more volumes of sermons followed in January, 1766.

Once again on the Continent in 1766, Sterne had a "joyous" winter in France and Italy. Though hemorrhages were becoming more frequent, he returned during the year to his desk in Coxwold, and by January, 1767, he was on hand in London for the appearance of the ninth volume of *Tristram Shandy*. During this winter he indulged in his famous sentimental affair with Eliza Draper, the young wife of an official of the East India Company, for whom he kept the *Journal to Eliza* after her departure for Bombay.

Late in February, 1768, Sterne brought out *A Sentimental Journey through France and Italy*. Its triumphant reception he was permitted to enjoy only briefly. An attack of influenza that developed into pleurisy proved more than his disease-wracked body could bear. He died in London on March 18, 1768, and was buried at St. George's, Hanover Square.

Sterne's work, like his life, is marked with a refreshing unconventionality. Though the *Sermons* (1760–1769) lack religious conviction and orginality of material, they preach a warm benevolence and a comfortable morality in a style that can be at once graceful and dramatic. *A Sentimental Journey*—in which Sterne substituted his traveler's sentimental adventures for the conventional accounts of nations, peoples, and memorable sights in travel books—is a nearly perfect small masterpiece.

The humor of *Tristram Shandy* is plainly in the tradition of Rabelais, Cervantes, and Swift; and its borrowings range from Robert Burton to miscellaneous curiosa. Superficially, the novel may seem merely like an engaging hodge-podge full of tricks, including black, marbled, and blank pages, omitted chapters, unorthodox punctuation and typography, and numerous digressions. But *Tristram Shandy* is far from planless. By insisting on the importance of opinions about action rather than on that of action itself Sterne opened unexplored avenues into the inner lives of his superbly ingratiating characters and achieved a new architectonic principle based on the mind as Locke had illuminated it in the *Essay on Human Understanding*. At the same time he achieved a new concept of time in fiction, a fascinating awareness of the life process itself, and a fresh concept of comedy based on the idea of individual isolation in a world where each person is a product of his own peculiar association of ideas.

Bibliography

The standard edition is the *Life and Works of Laurence Sterne*, edited by Wilbur L. Cross, 12 vols., 1904. See also *Letters*, edited by L. P. Curtis, 1935; and *Tristram Shandy*, edited by James A. Work, 1940. The standard biography is Wilbur L. Cross, *The Life and Times of Laurence Sterne*, 2 vols., 1929. Other full-length biographical and critical studies include Walter Sichel, *Sterne: A*

Study, 1910; Lodwick Hartley, *This is Lorence*, 1943; L. V. Hammond, *Sterne's "Sermons of Mr. Yorick,"* 1946; E. N. Dilworth, *The Unsentimental Journey of Laurence Sterne*, 1948; and Arthur H. Cash and John M. Stedman, eds., *The Winged Skull* (essays by various hands), 1971.

See also Edward Wagenknecht, *Cavalcade of the English Novel*, 1943; Walter Allen, *The English Novel*, 1954; Herbert Read, The Sense of Glory, 1929; Virginia Woolf, "The 'Sentimental Journey' " in *The Second Common Reader*, 1932; W. B. C. Watkins, "Yorick Revisited," in *Perilous Balance*, 1939; Theodore Baird, "The Time-Scheme of Tristram Shandy and a Source," *Publications of the Modern Language Association*, LI (1936), 803–820; Walter L. Myers, "O, the Hobby Horse," *Virginia Quarterly Review*, XIX (1943), 268–277; Lodwick Hartley, "Tristram and the Angels," *College English*, IX (1947), 62–69; Louis D. Rubin, Jr., "Joyce and Sterne: A Study in Affinity," *Hopkins Review*, III (1950), 1–15; and Wayne Booth, "Did Sterne Complete Tristram Shandy?" *Modern Philology*, XLVIII (1951), 172–183.

A SENTIMENTAL JOURNEY

Type of work: Novel
Author: Laurence Sterne (1713–1768)
Type of plot: Novelized autobiography
Time of plot: 1760's
Locale: France
First published: 1768

Sterne called his book A Sentimental Journey Through France and Italy, *but the title of this unconventional mixture of autobiography, travel impressions, and fiction is misleading, because he died before writing the Italian segment. Sentimental, as the title implies, outrageous and eccentric in its humorous effects, the novel entertains the reader with delightful accounts and observations of whatever enters the author's mind.*

Principal Characters

Mr. Yorick, the Sentimental Traveler. He reacts with exaggerated sensibility to the many, mainly humorous sentimental adventures of which he is a collector in his travels.

La Fleur, Yorick's servant, a boy accomplished at flute playing and love-making.

Madame de L——, a fellow traveler whom Yorick meets in Calais. He hopes that she will travel to Paris with him and is heartbroken that she must return to Belgium.

Madame de R——, a lady living in Paris. Madame de L—— gives Yorick a letter of introduction to her.

Count de B——, a Frenchman enthusiastic about everything English. He mistakes Yorick for the character in "Hamlet" and, greatly pleased to meet so famous a person, presents him with a passport naming him the King's Jester. Later the Count and his friends entertain Yorick at many parties while he is in Paris.

Count L——, the brother of Madame de L——. He comes to take her back to Belgium, just as Yorick's acquaintance with her is ripening.

Maria, an unhappy girl who wanders about the country grieving for her dead father. Yorick sees her in Moulines and sheds a few tears with her.

The Story

With all the different kinds of travelers, the Idle Travelers, the Inquisitive Travelers, the Travelers of Necessity, the Simple Travelers, and the rest, Mr. Yorick felt no kinship. He was a Sentimental Traveler. As such, he collected sentimental adventures as other tourists collected postcards of the points of interest they visited. Mr. Yorick had started his journey because a man had asked him, with a sneer, if he had ever been in France. Yorick had just made some statement on the French and did not like being answered so tartly merely because he did not have first-hand experience. The same evening he packed some clothes and left by boat for Calais.

While he was having supper at an inn in Calais, a poor monk approached him and begged alms for his monastery. Yorick rebuffed him with caustic and witty remarks. A little later Yorick saw the monk talking with an attractive woman who was also staying at the inn. Afraid the monk might tell her how rudely he had behaved, Yorick approached the couple, apologized to the monk, and offered his shell snuffbox to him as a peace offering. Having made friends with the monk and the lady, Yorick planned to ask the lady to travel with him to Paris. Her name, he learned, was Madame de L—.

Proposing to make the trip to Paris in a private carriage, Yorick invited the lady to go with him to look over some of the vehicles for sale in a nearby courtyard. Their admiration of each other grew with unusual rapidity. Before Yorick had a chance to ask her to travel with him, however, she was called away by a message that her brother, Count L—, had arrived. He had come to take her back to Belgium with him. Yorick was brokenhearted.

In parting, Madame de L— asked Yorick to visit her in Belgium if he passed through that country. She also gave him a letter of introduction to a good friend in Paris, Madame de R—.

The next day Yorick set off in a small carriage for Paris. His baggage fell out of the chaise several times, and he had a most uncomfortable trip to Montriul. There an innkeeper suggested he needed a servant, and Yorick saw that the man was quite right. He hired a young boy named La Fleur, whose greatest accomplishments were playing the flute and making love to the girls. La Fleur was delighted at the prospect of traveling around Europe with a generous and unpredictable English milord; his only sadness on leaving home was the necessity to say goodbye to all his village sweethearts. Yorick was pleased with the lad's quickness and wit, as he was sure that the young Frenchman would be equal to any emergency arising along the way.

The first problem the travelers met on their journey was a dead ass lying in the middle of the road. The horses refused to pass the carcass, and La Fleur's horse threw him and ran away. Proceeding to the next town, they met and talked with the owner of the poor dead beast. He had taken the ass with him from Germany to Italy and was very unhappy at its death, not so much because the beast had been a help to him, but because he felt sure that the ass had loved him dearly and had been a good friend to him for many years.

In Paris, Yorick went to the opera. A quotation from Shakespeare popping into his mind, he suddenly decided to go and buy the works of that writer. He went into a bookstore and found a set on the counter. Unfortunately they were not for sale, but had been sent to be re-bound for Count de B—, a great lover of English authors and Englishmen. In the shop Yorick saw a most attractive young girl who, he decided, must be a chambermaid. When she left the shop, he followed her and began a conversation about the book she had bought. Yorick was surprised and pleased to discover that the young girl belonged to the household of Madame de R—. He told her to inform her mistress that he would call the next day.

On returning to his rooms, Yorick learned from La Fleur that the police wanted to see him. In his rush out of England he had forgotten to get a passport, and he had overlooked completely the fact that England and France were at war. Since he did not wish to be put in jail, he decided that he would have to get a passport. But he did not know how these matters were arranged in France. Madame de R— was the only person in Paris to whom he carried a letter of introduction, and he did not want to bother the lady about the matter. The only other chance of help was from Count de B—, who at least liked Englishmen.

It took Yorick some time to get in to see the count, but when he did the count was most polite. As an amusing way to introduce himself, Yorick opened one of the volumes of Shakespeare, which had just been sent from the bookseller's. Turning to *The Tragedy of Hamlet* and pointing to the passage about the jester Yorick, he said that was his name, The count was overcome with pleasure at meeting so famous a person, and Yorick could say nothing that would change the count's mind. The count left the room and did not return for a long while. When he did, he presented Mr. Yorick with a passport which called him the King's Jester. Realizing that he could not correct the mistake without losing his passport, Yorick thanked the count and returned to his rooms.

The next day Madame de R—'s chambermaid called to see why Mr. Yorick had not visited her mistress as he had promised. Yorick explained about the passport and asked her to present his apology. Some hours later, after the girl had gone, the manager of the hotel came in and objected to Yorick's having young ladies in his room. In order to keep from being evicted from the hotel. Yorick had to buy some lace from a young woman. He suspected that the manager pocketed most of the profits from such sales.

On Sunday La Fleur appeared in a fine suit of clothes which he had bought second-hand. He asked if he might be allowed to have the day off, as he had been able to make friends with a young woman he would like to see again that day. Yorick asked him to bring some food before he left for the day. Wrapped about the butter, which La Fleur brought with Yorick's dinner, was a piece of paper which bore on it some old printing. Yorick became interested in the story it told and spent the whole day translating the faded characters to read the story of a luckless notary. But he was never to know the ending of the tale, for La Fleur had used the rest of the paper to wrap up a bouquet for his new ladylove.

Yorick had a fine time at parties to which he was invited by Count de B— and the count's friends. He agreed with everyone to whom he talked, and made no remarks of his own, and so he was thought the finest wit in Paris. After several minor sentimental adventures, Yorick and La Fleur set out to travel through southern France. At Moulines, Yorick stopped to see Maria, a poor unhappy girl who wandered about the country grieving for her dead father. He had heard of the girl from his old friend, Mr. Toby Shandy, who had met her several years before. Yorick sat down on a rock with Maria and, moved by her purity and sadness, shed a few tears with her.

Before ascending Mount Taurira, Yorick stopped and had dinner with a pleasant peasant family. That night he was forced to stay in a roadside inn. There was only one room in the inn, and Yorick had to share it with a French lady and her maid. In the room there were two large beds standing beside each other and, in a closet connected to the room, a cot. After much deliberation, the lady and Yorick took the big beds and sent the maid into the closet. Yorick had to promise to stay in his bed all night, and not to say a word. Unable to sleep, both Yorick and the lady began talking. Afraid that something untoward might occur, the maid came out of the closet and, unseen, stood between the two beds. Yorick stretched out his hand. With this sentimental gesture Sterne ended abruptly the story of his sentimental journey.

Critical Evaluation

Both in form and apparent subject, *A Sentimental Journey* follows in the tradition of the "grand tour" novel. The assemblage of scenes and persons, the escapades on the road, the cultural adjustments required of an Englishman abroad, the things to be learned and the places to be visited—this was common, enjoyable reading matter for an eighteenth century audience.

However, Sterne's "grand tour" sports a delightful touch of irreverence. Its hero, Yorick, is not a typical young gentleman matriculating into a peripatetic finishing school but a low-key picaro buffeted by impulse and whimsy. Thus his "travelling" is apparently random. Unplanned, untimed, it accords perfectly with his sole principle, which, it seems, is to have no principle whatever except obedience to natural affections, his growing sensibility, and his often unseemly passion. He prefers *filles de chambre* to cathedrals, a pretty face to a gallery portrait. With a free-flowing nature, then, he does not seek improvement through a travel plan; he prefers to stumble over it in following his heart. And the point made by Sterne is this: a benevolent nature, trusted to, rarely errs in promoting human goodness.

"Sentiment" and a host of attendant words such as "good nature," "sensibility," and "affections" were all terms with particular significance in Sterne's day. The so-called "doctrine of sensibility," popularized by the late seventeenth century Latitudinarian divines, urged an inherent goodness in man, a "sense" of moral absolutes which expresses itself in acts of charity and social benevolence. Championed philosophically by the third Earl of Shaftesbury (in his *Characteristicks of Men, Manners, Opinions, Times,* 1711) and in fiction by Henry Fielding, this emphasis on good nature ran counter to the often equally influential tradition represented by Thomas Hobbes (*Leviathan,* 1651) and Bernard Mandeville (*The Fable of the Bees,* 1714), a tradition which urged self-interest as the basis of all human action. These are the two forces which collide in *A Sentimental Journey* as Sterne explores what it means to be a good man.

The glance at Hobbes we see revealed in several characters: the huge oaf who purposefully blocks the view of a dwarf, the postilion who thrashes his horses, and even Yorick himself at the start of the novel when he refuses charity to a monk. Yet this "natural" cruelty—as Hobbes would have it—is set against the virtues of a larger number of characters: the old French officer who assists the dwarf, the mourner who laments his dead animal, and of course the enlightened Yorick whom later we see guiding the unfortunate Maria. On the one hand Sterne recognizes only too well man's divided nature, in which good and evil are deeply intertwined, yet on the other hand he wants to insist that the "deeper affections," the "eternal fountain of our feelings," as Yorick says, are a primary impulse of inordinate strength.

Beneath the surface, *A Sentimental Journey* is something of an allegory, a type of metaphorical trek in which Yorick (hence the reader) discovers the primacy of human feeling. It is a journey into sentiment. It is a discovery of sentiment. It is a travel not just through space and time but into sensibility itself, which is the common bond of all humanity. True, the book is an outrageous comedy—and it is wise not to forget this. Its famous ending ("When I stretched out my hand, I caught hold of the fille de chambre's—") and the mixed motives of its characters should remind us that Sterne wrote for delight as much as for instruction. But the comedy ought not to obscure a more serious intent in the book. There is a delicate line separating love from lust, Sterne argues, if only because the "web of kindness" has "threads of love and desire . . . entangled with the piece." The temptation, too often, is to rent the whole web (as Yorick says) by drawing out the former, with the result that man becomes merely heartless and cold. Instead, one ought to excuse occasional moral lapses in the interest of fostering greater love, for it is love alone that characterizes man in his best moments. This is the main point of Sterne's delightful Aristophanic fragment on the town of Abdera: there literature succeeds in making the most profligate town devoted to Cupid. It is equally the point of Yorick's amorousness and of his belief that, once rekindled at Love's flame, he is all generosity and good will again. It underlies his celebration of freedom (in volume II), La Fleur's Casanovan conquests, the Count de B's encomium on the fair sex, and, unforgettably, the French officer's noble lesson that mutual toleration teaches us mutual love.

One might also say that it underlies Sterne's prose style inasmuch as we, like Yorick, are sentimental travelers. The associative drift of the narrative precludes expectation; it demands instead that the reader allow himself to be taken wherever his sensibility wishes to go. Simply, the novel demands to be read less with the head and more with the heart. Many of the scenes, for example, are unabashed tearjerkers. And clearly Sterne plays on our elementary sense of justice—our *feeling* for what is right and wrong—in order to score his points. In an intriguing way, then, *A Sentimental Journey* is not merely about a grand tour but is itself a grand tour. It is an education in the consistency of human nature, not its diversity. It is, like Euripides before Abdera, Sterne before the world.

Bibliography

Alvarez, A. "The Delinquent Aesthetic," in *Hudson Review*. XVIX (Autumn, 1966), pp. 590–600.

Auty, Susan G. "Smollett and Sterne and Animal Spirits: *A Sentimental Journey*," in *The Comic Spirit of Eighteenth Century Novels*. Port Washington, N.Y.: Kennikat, 1975, pp. 147–158.

Baker, Ernest A. *The History of the English Novel*, Volume IV. New York: Barnes & Noble, 1950, pp. 261–268.

Brissenden, R.F. *Virtue in Distress: Studies in the Novel of Sentiment From Richardson to Sade*. London: Macmillan, 1974, pp. 218–242.

Cash, Arthur H. *Sterne's Comedy of Moral Sentiments: The Ethical Dimension of the Journey*. Pittsburgh: Duquesne University Press, 1965.

Cross, Wilbur. *The Life and Times of Laurence Sterne*, Volume II. New Haven, Conn.: Yale University Press, 1929, pp. 138–159.

Dilworth, Ernest N. *The Unsentimental Journey of Laurence Sterne*. New York: King's Crown Press, 1948, pp. 80–107.

Fluchère, Henri. *Laurence Sterne: From Tristram to Yorick: An Interpretation of* Tristram Shandy. New York: Oxford University Press, 1965, pp. 367–399.

Jefferson, D.W. *Laurence Sterne*. London: Longmans, Green, 1954, pp. 25–31.

Hartley, Lodwick. "Sentimentalist or Jester?—*A Sentimental Journey*," in *Laurence Sterne in the Twentieth Century: An Essay and a Bibliography of Sternean Studies, 1900–1965*. Chapel Hill: University of North Carolina Press, 1966, pp. 35–42.

Koppel, Gene. "Fulfillment Through Frustration: Some Aspects of Sterne's Art of the Incomplete in *A Sentimental Journey*," in *Studies in the Novel*. II (1970), pp. 168–172.

Piper, William Bowman. *Laurence Sterne*. New York: Twayne, 1965, pp. 91–112.

Putney, Rufus. "The Evolution of *A Sentimental Journey*," in *Philological Quarterly*. XIX (1940), pp. 349–369.

————. "Laurence Sterne: Apostle of Laughter," in *The Age of Johnson: Essays Presented to Chauncey Brewster Tinker*. New Haven, Conn.: Yale

University Press, 1949, pp. 158–170. Reprinted in *Eighteenth Century English Literature: Modern Essays in Criticism.* Edited by James L. Clifford. New York: Oxford University Press, 1959, pp. 274–284.

Smitten, Jeffrey R. "Spatial Form as Narrative Technique in *A Sentimental Journey*," in *Journal of Narrative Technique.* V (1975), pp. 208–218.

Stedmond, John M. *The Comic Art of Laurence Sterne: Convention and Innovation in* Tristram Shandy *and* A Sentimental Journey. Toronto: University of Toronto Press, 1967, pp. 143–165.

Stout, G.D., Jr. "Yorick's *Sentimental Journey*: A Comic *Pilgrim's Progress* for the Man of Feeling," in *Journal of English Literary History.* XXX (December, 1963), pp. 395–412.

White, F. Eugene. "Sterne's Quiet Journey of the Heart: Unphilosophic Projection of Enlightened Benevolence," in *Enlightenment Essays.* II (1971), pp. 103–110.

Woolf, Virginia. "The *Sentimental Journey*," in *The Common Reader: Second Series.* New York: Harcourt, Brace, 1932, pp. 80–88.

TRISTRAM SHANDY

Type of work: Novel
Author: Laurence Sterne (1713–1768)
Type of plot: Humorous sensibility
Time of plot: 1718–1766
Locale: Shandy Hall in England
First published: 1759–1767 (published in several books)

The Life and Opinions of Tristram Shandy. Gentleman *blends Rabelaisian prankishness, sound psychological insight, sensibility, neoclassic common sense, and much irreverent nonsense in a comic masterwork remarkable for its technical inventiveness.*

Principal Characters

Tristram Shandy, the narrator and ostensible hero of this literary farrago devoted to some details of his early life, his father's opinions and eccentricities, his uncle's passion for the reënactment of Marlborough's military campaigns, and assorted oddities of mind and conduct. His mother having incurred some time before the expense of a needless trip to London for a lying-in, Tristram, according to the terms of his parents' marriage contract, is born at Shandy Hall on November 5, 1718. Various misfortunes befall him early in life: a broken nose, crushed by the doctor's forceps at birth; the wrong name, Tristram instead of Trismegistus, when he is christened by a stupid young curate; and the loss of his member, a heavy sash having fallen while he was relieving himself through an open window. Though crushed by these irreparable accidents, his father still insists that the boy shall have a proper education, and to this end Mr. Shandy writes a "Tristra-paedia" in imitation of the "Cyro-paedia" designed for the training of Cyrus the Great, as set forth in the pages of Xenophon. Except for a few scattered hints, the reader learns almost nothing about Tristram's later life. Sterne devotes most of the novel to reporting humorous incidents and the sayings of the other characters.

Walter Shandy, Tristram's father, a crotchety retired turkey merchant who possesses an immense stock of obscure information gained by reading old books collected by his ancestors. As the result of his reading, he takes delight in lengthy discussions on unimportant topics. A man of acute sensibilities, alert to the minor pricks and vexations of life, he has developed a drollish but sharp manner of peevishness, but he is so open and generous in all other ways that his friends are seldom offended by his sharpness of tongue. He suffers from sciatica as well as loquacity.

Mrs. Shandy, a good-natured but rather stupid woman. Typical is her interruption of the moment of Tristram's conception on the first Sunday of March, 1718, by asking her husband if he has remembered to wind the clock. "I dare say" and "I suppose not" in agreement with Mr. Shandy are her most brilliant remarks in conversation.

Toby Shandy, called **My Uncle Toby,** a retired army captain who had been wounded in the groin during the siege of Namur in 1698. Now retired to the country, he spends most of his time amid a large and complicated series of miniature fortifications and military emplacements on the bowling green behind

Shandy Hall. There he follows with all the interest and enthusiasm of actual conflict the military campaigns of the Duke of Marborough on the Continent. Occasionally forced into conversations with his brother, as on the night of Tristram's birth, he escapes the flood of Mr. Shandy's discourse by whistling "Lillibullero" to himself. Completely innocent on the subjects of women and sex, he is pursued by a neighbor, the Widow Wadman, whose intentions are matrimonial and whose campaign on the old soldier's heart is as strategically planned as his own miniature battles.

Widow Wadman, a buxom woman who lays siege to Uncle Toby's bachelor life and begs him to show her the exact spot where he was wounded. Eventually he indicates on a map the location of Namur. Her question kills her chance of a proposal when Corporal Trim tells his embarrassed master what the widow really wants to know.

Corporal Trim, the faithful and loquacious servant of Uncle Toby. He helps his master enact mimic battles on the bowling green.

Susannah, a vain and careless maid. Supposed to tell the curate to christen the sickly baby Trismegistus, after the minor philosopher admired by Mr. Shandy, she arrives on the scene so out of breath that she can say only that the name is Trissomething, and the curate decides that the child is to be called Tristram. He is pleased because that is his own name.

Parson Yorick, a mercurial and eccentric clergyman completely innocent of the ways of the wicked world. He is in the habit of speaking his mind plainly, often to the discomfiture or resentment of the man toward whom his remarks are directed. Once a lover of fine horses, he rides about the countryside on a nag that would disgrace Don Quixote. The reason is that his good horses were always spavined or wind-broken by anxious fathers who borrowed the animals to ride for a midwife. At the end of the novel he de-

clares that the closing anecdote is a Cock and Bull story, "and one of the best of its kind, I ever heard." As Tristram relates, the epitaph on the clergyman's tombstone is a simple, brief inscription: Alas, poor YORICK!

Dr. Slop, a squat, bungling country doctor, the author of a book on midwifery. For a fee of five guineas, this "man-midwife" sits in the back parlor of Shandy Hall and listens to Mr. Shandy hold forth on various topics, including a treatise on oaths, while a midwife is attending Mrs. Shandy upstairs. When called in to assist at the birth, his forceps permanently flatten Tristram's nose.

Obadiah, the outdoors servant at Shandy Hall, an awkward, good-natured fellow.

Jonathan, Mr. Shandy's dull-witted coachman.

Le Fever, a poor lieutenant who falls sick while traveling to rejoin his regiment in Flanders. When Corporal Trim, who has visited the dying man at the village inn, reports to Uncle Toby that the poor fellow will never march again, the old soldier is so moved that he swears one of his rare oaths while declaring that Le Fever shall not die. The recording angel, making a note of the oath, drops a tear on the word and blots it out forever.

Tom, Corporal Trim's brother, who marries the widow of a Jew in Lisbon.

A Negress, a friend of Tom Trim, who motivates a discussion on slavery.

Mrs. Bridget, Widow Wadman's maid, ambitious to marry Corporal Trim.

Eugenius, the friend and adviser of Parson Yorick. He witnesses the clergyman's dying moments.

Master Bobby Shandy, Tristram's older brother, whose death at an early age is reported. His sudden death gives Corporal Trim a good opportunity to provide the servants of Shandy Hall with a dramatic illustration—he drops his hat

—of man's mortality, the fact that he can be here one moment and gone the next. Trim's action causes Susannah, who has been thinking of the gown that may become hers when her mistress goes into mourning, to burst into tears.

The Story

Tristram Shandy, in telling the story of his earliest years, always believed that most of the problems of his life were brought about by the fact that the moment of his conception was interrupted when his mother asked his father if he had remembered to wind the clock. Tristram knew the exact date of his conception, the night between the first Sunday and the first Monday of March, 1718. He was certain of this date because, according to his father's notebook, Mr. Shandy set out immediately after this date to travel from Shandy Hall up to London. Before this date Mr. Shandy had been seriously inconvenienced by an attack of sciatica.

Another complication of Tristram's birth was the marriage settlement of his parents. According to this settlement, quoted in full by Tristram, Mrs. Shandy had the privilege of going to London for her lying-in. But, if Mrs. Shandy were to put Mr. Shandy to the expense of a trip to London on false pretenses, then the next child was to be born at Shandy Hall. The circumstance of a needless trip to London having occurred some time before, Mr. Shandy stoutly insisted that Tristram should be born at Shandy Hall, the birth to be in the hands of a country midwife, rather than in those of a London doctor.

On the night of Tristram's birth, his father and his Uncle Toby were sitting in the living room engaged in one of their interminable discussions and debates. Informed by Susannah, the maid, that Mrs. Shandy was about to be delivered of a child, they sent for the mid-wife. As an extra measure of safety, they sent also for Dr. Slop, a bungling country practitioner whom Mr. Shandy admired because he had written a five-shilling book on the history of midwifery. While the midwife attended Mrs. Shandy, the doctor would, for a fee of five guineas, drink a bottle of wine in the back parlor with Mr. Shandy and his brother, Toby.

Uncle Toby, who had been called the highest compliment ever paid human nature, had been a soldier until he was wounded during the siege of Namur in 1695. The wound, the exact position of which was to play such a large part in Tristram's story later on, forced him to retire to the country. There at the suggestion of his faithful servant, Corporal Trim, he had built, on a bowling green behind Shandy Hall, a large and complicated series of model fortifications and military emplacements. Uncle Toby's entire time was spent playing soldier and thinking about this miniature battlefield. It was his hobbyhorse, and he rode it continually with the greatest of pleasure. Mr. Shandy was not at all taken with his brother's hobby and had to keep him from discussing it by violent interruptions so that he could himself continue, or start, one of his long and detailed digressions on obscure information.

As the two brothers sat awaiting the arrival of the midwife and her rival, Dr. Slop, Mr. Shandy made a rhetorical question of the subject of Mrs. Shandy's preference for a midwife rather than a male doctor. Uncle Toby suggested naïvely that modesty might explain her choice. This innocent answer led Mr. Shandy into a long discussion of the nature of women, and of the fact that everything in the world has two handles. Uncle Toby's innocence, however, always made it impossible for him to understand such affairs.

Dr. Slop, with his bag of tools, finally arrived. The midwife was already in attendance when he went up to see about the birth of the child. Meanwhile, to pass the time, Corporal Trim read a sermon aloud. Dr. Slop, in attending Mrs. Shandy, unfortunately mistook Tristram's hip for his head. In probing with his large forceps, he flattened what Tristram always referred to as his nose. This mistake Tristram blamed essentially on the affair of the winding of the clock mentioned earlier. This, and a later incident concerning the falling of a window sash when Tristram, still a little boy, was relieving himself through a window, brought about a problem in his anatomy which he mentioned often in his story of his life.

Between Tristram's birth and almost immediate baptism, Mr. Shandy entertained the company with a long story he had translated from the Latin of the old German writer, Slawkenbergius, a tale telling of the adventures of a man with an especially long nose. By the time Mr. Shandy had recovered from the bad news of the accident with the forceps, and had asked about his child, he learned that it was very sickly and weak; consequently he summoned Mr. Yorick, the curate, to baptize the child immediately. While rushing to get dressed to attend the ceremony, Mr. Shandy sent word to the parson by the maid, Susannah, to name the child Trismegistus, after an ancient philosopher who was a favorite of Mr. Shandy. Susannah forgot the name, however, and told Mr. Yorick to name the child Tristram. This name pleased the old man because it happened to be his own as well. When Mr. Shandy, still half unbuttoned, reached the scene, the evil had been done. Despite the fact that Mr. Shandy thought correct naming most important, his child was Tristram, a name Mr. Shandy believed the worst in the world. He lamented that he had lost three-fourths of his son in his unfortunate geniture, nose, and name. There remained only one fourth—Tristram's education.

Tristram managed to give a partial account of his topsy-turvy boyhood between many sidelights on the characters of his family. Uncle Toby continued to answer most of his brother's arguments by softly whistling *Lillibullero*, his favorite tune, and going out to the little battlefield to wage small wars with his servant, Corporal Trim. The next important event in the family was the death of Master Bobby, Tristram's older brother, who had been away at Westminster school. To this event Mr. Shandy reacted in his usual way by calling up all the philosophic ideas of the past on death and discoursing on them until he had adjusted himself to the new situation. The tragic news was carried to the kitchen staff and Susannah, despite a desire to show grief, could think of nothing but the wonderful wardrobe of dresses she would inherit when her mistress went into mourning. The vision of all Mrs. Shandy's dresses passed through her mind. Corporal Trim well demonstrated the transitory nature of life by dropping his hat, as if it had suddenly died, and then making an extremporaneous funeral oration.

After many more digressions on war, health, the fashions of ancient Roman dress, his father's doubts as to whether to get Tristram a tutor, and whether to put him into long trousers, Tristram proceeded to tell the history of his Uncle Toby, both in war and in love. Near Shandy Hall lived the Widow Wadman, who, after laying siege to Uncle Toby's affections for a long period, almost got him to propose marriage to her. But the gentle ex-soldier, who literally would not kill a fly, finally learned the widow's purpose when she began to inquire so pointedly into the extent and position of his wound. First he promised the widow that he would allow her to put her finger on the very spot where he was wounded, and then he brought her a map of Namur to touch. Uncle Toby's innocence balked her real question until Corporal Trim finally told his master that it was the spot on his body, not the spot on the surface of the world where the accident took place, that was the point of the Widow Wadman's interest. This realization so embarrassed the old man that the idea of marriage disappeared from his mind forever. Tristram concluded his story with Parson Yorick's statement that the book had been one of the cock and bull variety, the reader having been led a mad, but merry, chase through the satirical and witty mind of the author.

Critical Evaluation

This masterpiece of eighteenth century narrative was written by a man who never reconciled his sentimental nature with his roguish tendencies, and who never tried to reconcile them. Sterne was educated at Jesus College, Cambridge, where he met John Hall-Stevenson, a young aristocrat who shared and encouraged his taste for erotic subjects and exaggeration. After taking holy orders, Sterne received, through family connections, an ecclesiastical appointment in Sutton; but he was temperamentally completely unsuited for the clerical, pastoral life. In fact, the only part of religion he mastered was sermon-writing and, at that, he excelled. Eventually he turned his pen to miscellaneous journalism in York periodicals. In 1759, *A Political Romance* appeared, including many elements that would characterize his Shandean masterpiece: allegory, levels of meaning, verbal fanfare, whimsical use of scholastic learning, profanity, and great stylistic versatility.

But it was the appearance of the first two volumes of *Tristram Shandy* that made Sterne an instant celebrity, despite the immediate denunciation of Johnson, Richardson, Walpole, Goldsmith, and other literary establishment figures who condemned Sterne's iconoclastic style and frankly mercenary attitude for both ethical and artistic reasons. Sterne characterized the first part of his life's work as "taking on, not only the weak part of the sciences in which the true part of Ridicule lies, but everything else which I find laugh-at-able." The reader soon discovers that Sterne finds *everything* laughable, his comic vision as universal, and as detailed, as that of Rabelais and Cervantes, whose works influenced Sterne's very strongly. Like Rabelais' *Gargantua* and *Pantagruel,* moreover, Sterne's is a work held together only by the unswerving and exuberant force of the author's own personality. " 'Tis a picture of myself," he admitted; indeed it is impossible to distinguish the profane minister from the "alleged" narrator, young Tristram—just as Rabelais makes his narrator Alcofibras tangible only when it suits his whim.

Tristram Shandy has also been called "a prolonged conversation" between Sterne and his reader, a conversation in which acquaintance becomes familiarity and, then, an enduring friendship. For this friendship to occur, however, the reader must accept certain ground rules and be willing to adopt a role he rarely embraces so willingly as he does here. In his endless comments to the reader (who is sometimes addressed in the plural, sometimes in the singular, sometimes as "your worship," sometimes as "Madam"), Sterne scolds us for wanting to know everything at once (Book 1, Chapter 4), asks us to help him sell his "dedication" (1:9), assures us that our company (of Sterne-readers) will swell to include all the world and all time, and dismisses our objections with a mad swirl of his pen. He tells us he is quite aware that some will understand and others will not; indeed the varying forms of address to the reader indicate his astute consciousness of the variety of his audience. He says the "cholerick" reader will toss the book away, the "mercurial will laugh most heartily at it," and the "saturnine" will condemn it as fanciful and extravagant. Like Cervantes he is not interested (or so he claims) in apologizing for his work, or for himself. We either take him, or leave him. So at the very beginning, as he begins one of his great digressions, he warns the strict reader that to continue may annoy him—only the curious need pass through the narrative line into this first of many excursions with him. "Shut the door," he directs the first kind of reader; if we pass through it with him, we realize the door is never opened again. Only the reader who is willing to let "anything go" will remain on speaking terms with this most quixotic, irrepressible author.

The work itself, alternately characterized by Tristram as "vile" and as "rhapsodic," defies structural analysis. Sterne makes his formal principles clear from the beginning: "not to be in a hurry," but to follow every new thought in whatever direction it may beckon until he loses track of his starting point and has to flip back the pages to find his place; "to spend two years discussing one," just as Tristram's mental and emotional autobiography reflects his father's *Tristrapaedia* (the gargantuan work of pedagogy which takes so long in the writing that Tristram grows up before he can start following its directives); and "in writing what I have set about, [to] shall confine myself neither to his [Horace's] rules, nor to any man's rules that ever lived." Sterne would have understood T. S. Eliot's dictum, "Immature poets borrow, mature poets steal." He not only steals—whether it is the actual music of Uncle Toby's "Lilliburlero" or a medieval French theological tract on baptism—but also openly admits and boasts of his theft. Yet the boast is itself misleading since, as Shakespeare did with North's Plutarch, Sterne subtlely but most effectively alters his thieveries to fit the chaotic image of his own work. At one point, in discussing the nature of digressions, Sterne characterizes that work as "digressive, and . . . progressive too—and at the same time." Digressions, he continues, are "the sunshine" of a writer's art, the very stuff of literary and fictional vitality. Life itself, in the ultimate reading, is nothing but a diverting digression for Sterne; the role of the author, as he embraces it, is to make that essential human digression as diverting, as complicated, as emotionally and intellectually rich, as possible.

The greatness of his comic wit lies in its indefatigable mastery of making one detail relevant to another, a detail from Tristram's unfortunate life immediately provoking in "my father" a pointed consideration of Saxo Grammaticus' Danish history or causing Uncle Toby to expound its relationship to the siege of Navarre. Reading *Tristram Shandy* is an education in the esoteric and picayune minutiae of forgotten scholarship at the same time that it is a parody of the irrelevance of scholarship (also following closely in the spirit of Rabelais). By the time we close even the first volume we are convinced of the validity of Sterne's point of departure: Epictetus' statement that, "Not actions but opinions of actions are the concern of men." In other words, it is not what happens to us that matters, but what we think of what happens to us. The relationship between the Shandean world and the real world is a very close, in fact a promiscuous, relationship; it is defined by Sterne's deliberate blurring of the line between fictional and real events, but also by his thematic insistence on the interdependence of thought, feeling, and action. Thought without emotion, he would say, is futile; but feeling without reason is equally sterile. All of the elements in human life, love, war, business, theology, religion, science, trade, medicine, are treated in an epic comprehensiveness and everything is shown to be related absolutely to everything else. The texture of the style, however, is not the reassuring predictability of epic; instead, it is a formal collage of typographical caprice, gestures, dramatic devices, soliloquies, offhand obscenity, serious and mock-serious treatises— all mixed together extemporaneously and punctuated orally. Sterne is like a magician juggling more balls than anyone can see, but who never loses control because his magic is as unflagging as it is electric. More than any other work of his century, Sterne's is a monument to the complexity, vitality, and *sprezzatura* of the mind.

Bibliography

Alter, Robert. "Sterne and the Nostalgia for Reality," in *Partial Magic: The Novel as a Self-Conscious Genre*. Berkeley: University of California Press, 1975, pp. 30–56.

Battestin, Martin C. *The Providence of Wit: Aspects of Form in Augustan Literature and the Arts*. Oxford: Clarendon Press, 1974, pp. 241–269.

Brissenden, R.F. *Virtue in Distress: Studies in the Novel of Sentiment from Richardson to Sade*. London: Macmillan, 1974, pp. 187–217.

Cash, Arthur H. *Laurence Sterne: The Early and Middle Years*. London: Methuen, 1975, pp. 278–297.

Cross, Wilbur. *The Life and Times of Laurence Sterne*, Volume I. New Haven, Conn.: Yale University Press, 1929, pp. 173–206, 229–266.

Donovan, Robert A. *The Shaping Vision: Imagination in the English Novel from Defoe to Dickens*. Ithaca, N.Y.: Cornell University Press, 1966, pp. 89–117.

Drew, Elizabeth A. *The Novel: A Modern Guide to Fifteen English Masterpieces*. New York: Norton, 1963, pp. 75–94.

Dyson, A.E. "Sterne: "The Novelist as Jester," in *Critical Quarterly*. IV (Winter, 1962), p. 309–320.

Goodin, George. "The Comic as a Critique of Reason: *Tristram Shandy*," in *College English*. XXIX (December, 1967), pp. 206–223.

Holtz, William V. *Image and Immortality: A Study of Tristram Shandy*. Providence, R.I.: Brown University Press, 1970.

Jefferson, D.W. "*Tristram Shandy* and the Tradition of Learned Wit," in *Essays in Criticism*. I (1951), pp. 225–248. Reprinted in *Laurence Sterne: A Collection of Critical Essays*. Edited by John Traugott. Englewood Cliffs, N.J.: Prentice-Hall, 1968, pp. 148–167.

Kettle, Arnold. *An Introduction to the English Novel*, Volume I. London: Hutchinson's, 1951, pp. 81–87.

Lanham, Richard A. Tristram Shandy: *The Games of Pleasure*. Berkeley: University of California Press, 1973.

Lehman, Benjamin H. "Of Time, Personality, and the Author: A Study of *Tristram Shandy*," in *Studies in the Comic, University of California Studies in English*. VIII (1941), pp. 233–250. Reprinted in *Laurence Sterne: A Collection of Critical Essays*. Edited by John Traugott. Englewood Cliffs, N.J.: Prentice-Hall, 1968, pp. 21–33. Also reprinted in *Essays on the Eighteenth Century Novel*. Edited by Robert Donald Spector. Bloomington: Indiana University Press, 1965, pp. 165–184.

McKillop, Alan D. *Early Masters of the English Novel*. Lawrence: University of Kansas Press, 1956, pp. 182–219.

McMaster, J. "Experience to Expression: Thematic Character Contrasts in *Tristram Shandy*," in *Modern Language Quarterly*. XXXII (March, 1971), pp. 42–57.

New, Melvyn. *Laurence Sterne as Satirist: A Reading of* Tristram Shandy. Gainesville: University of Florida Press, 1970, pp. 73–205.

Piper, William Bowman. *Laurence Sterne.* New York: Twayne, 1965, pp. 19–87.

Price, Martin. *To the Place of Wisdom: Studies in Order and Energy from Dryden to Blake.* New York: Doubleday, 1964, pp. 312–341.

Rothstein, Eric. *Systems of Order and Inquiry in Later Eighteenth Century Fiction.* Berkeley: University of California Press, 1975, pp. 62–108.

Russell, H.K. "*Tristram Shandy* and the Technique of the Novel," in *Studies in Philology*. XLII (1945), pp. 581–593.

Stedmond, John M. *The Comic Art of Laurence Sterne: Convention and Innovation in* Tristram Shandy *and* A Sentimental Journey. Toronto: University of Toronto Press, 1967, pp. 3–131.

Traugott, John. *Tristram Shandy's World.* Berkeley: University of California Press, 1954.

Van Ghent, Dorothy. "On *Tristram Shandy*," in *The English Novel: Form and Function.* New York: Rinehart, 1953, pp. 83–98.

Watt, Ian. "Introduction," in *The Life and Opinions of Tristram Shandy, Gentleman.* Boston: Houghton Mifflin, 1965, pp. vii–xxxv.

ROBERT LOUIS STEVENSON

Born: Edinburgh, Scotland (November 13, 1850)
Died: Apia, Samoa (December 3, 1894)

Principal Works

NOVELS: *Treasure Island,* 1883; *Prince Otto,* 1885; *The Strange Case of Dr. Jekyll and Mr. Hyde,* 1886; *Kidnapped,* 1886; *The Merry Men,* 1887; *The Black Arrow,* 1888; *The Master of Ballantrae,* 1888; *The Wrong Box,* 1889 (with Lloyd Osbourne); *The Wrecker,* 1892 (with Lloyd Osbourne); *Catriona,* 1893 [*David Balfour*]; *The Ebb-Tide,* 1894 (with Lloyd Osbourne); *Weir of Hermiston,* 1896 (unfinished); *St. Ives,* 1897 (completed by Arthur Quiller-Couch).

SHORT STORIES AND SKETCHES: *The New Arabian Nights,* 1882; *More New Arabian Nights,* 1885 (with Mrs. Stevenson); *Island Nights' Entertainments,* 1892.

TRAVEL SKETCHES AND IMPRESSIONS: *An Inland Voyage,* 1878; *Travels with a Donkey,* 1879; *The Silverado Squatters,* 1883; *Across the Plains,* 1892; *The Amateur Emigrant,* 1895; *In the South Seas,* 1896.

POEMS: *A Child's Garden of Verses,* 1885; *Underwoods,* 1887; *Ballads,* 1890.

ESSAYS AND STUDIES: *Virginibus Puerisque,* 1881; *Familiar Studies of Men and Books,* 1882; *Memories and Portraits,* 1887; *Father Damien,* 1890.

Robert Louis (Balfour) Stevenson, born in Edinburgh on November 13, 1850, has achieved fame by his romantic life nearly as much as by his romantic fiction, for his life displays the same dualism between romantic adventure and grim reality that the discerning reader finds in much of his writing. Stevenson's brief forty-four year life was a nearly constant journey in search of adventure and relief from the agonies of tuberculosis, with which he was afflicted from early childhood. His father, Thomas Stevenson, a successful Edinburgh lighthouse engineer, hoped for a law career for his only son; but, though Robert did study to be a barrister, he soon commenced a life of traveling that took him to Switzerland, France, the United States, and, finally, the South Seas. In each place Stevenson found adventure; and when he did not find it ready-made, he created it for himself out of his teeming imagination.

Although Stevenson is best known for his fiction, he was a prodigious essayist. The vivid impressions made by the places he visited are found recorded in such brilliant travel sketches and essays as *An Inland Voyage,* which tells of a canoeing trip through Belgium and France, and *Travels with a Donkey in the Cévennes,* which deals with his journeys in southern France. In these books Stevenson shows his fine eye for color and vivid impressions, that sort of sensitivity that was to add so much to the popularity of his fiction.

He had always been ambitious to write and had prepared himself laboriously for a literary career. His famous statements about how he copied the style of great writers such as Lamb, Hazlitt, Defoe, and Hawthorne, and about how he was always writing, polishing, and correcting are evidence of this ambition. So, too, is the delicate, precise, but rich style that his fiction achieves.

Stevenson fell in love with Mrs. Fanny Osbourne in France and went to California in 1879 to marry her after she had secured a divorce from her husband. This trip caused a break with Stevenson's family, who were opposed to the alliance, and he suffered many hardships until he acquired a measure of fame and prosperity with the publication of his first major work, *Treasure Island*, written chiefly for the entertainment of his stepson, Lloyd Osbourne. This most famous and loved of adventure stories demonstrated Stevenson's ability at colorful narration and his technique of using a relatively minor character as observer and narrator. *Kidnapped* was immediately popular, but it never attained the following of *Treasure Island*. A striking contrast to these tales of romantic adventure is *The Strange Case of Dr. Jekyll and Mr. Hyde*, perhaps the most famous of all Stevenson's fiction; this grim story of dual personality is moralistic and filled with Stevenson's concern for ethical problems.

Again in search of improved health, Stevenson left California and traveled in the United States, his longest stay being in Saranac Lake, a health resort in the Adirondacks. He stayed there during 1887–1888. While at Saranac Lake he wrote *The Master of Ballantrae*, a tale of the Jacobite struggle, the same subject dealt with in the earlier *Kidnapped*. In *The Black Arrow* he went farther back in time to the Wars of the Roses; this book contains a lively picture of late medieval times.

In a final desperate effort to regain his health, Stevenson moved to the South Seas and settled on the island of Samoa. There he found a serenity that encouraged his literary efforts. He was considered a truly great man by the natives, and he took an active interest in Samoan politics. In his last years he was very productive, turning out *The Wrecker* with Lloyd Osbourne, his stepson, and *David Balfour*, a sequel to *Kidnapped* but a more able literary performance.

Stevenson died suddenly of apoplexy on December 3, 1894, leaving unfinished his *Weir of Hermiston*, the work that is generally regarded as his masterpiece. In this fragment Stevenson manifests the culmination of his constant efforts to improve his style and displays again his conviction that the romance of life is, to the individual, more real than what critics and other materialistic novelists of his period were praising as detached objectivity. Criticism is still sharply divided over the whole body of his work, but he holds a firm place in the favor of all children and of all adults who believe that romance is a valid part of life.

Bibliography

Complete editions of Stevenson's works are the Swanston Edition, 25 vols., 1911–1912, with an introduction by Andrew Lang, and the Tusitala Edition, 35 vols., 1923–1924. There is also the *Collected Poems*, edited by J. Adam Smith,

1950. Sir Sidney Colvin has edited the *Letters* in 4 vols., 1911. The standard bibliography is by W. F. Prideaux, *A Bibliography of the Works of Robert Louis Stevenson*, 1903, revised by F. V. Livingston, 1917. Good biographies are J. C. Furnas' *Voyage to Windward*, 1951; and Charles Neider's edition of *Our Samoan Adventure*, 1955, which includes a previously unpublished three year diary and rare photographs. See also Dennis Butts, *R. L. Stevenson*, 1966. Important critical works are Frank Swinnerton, *Robert Louis Stevenson: A Critical Study*, 1923; J. A. Steuart, *Robert Louis Stevenson: Man and Writer. A Critical Biography*, 2 vols., 1924; David Daiches, *Robert Louis Stevenson*, 1946, *Stevenson and the Art of Fiction*, 1951; Robert Kiely, *Robert Louis Stevenson and the Fiction of Adventure*, 1964; and Edwin M. Eigner, *Robert Louis Stevenson and the Romantic Tradition*, 1966. Informative essays include H. W. Garrod's "The Poetry of Robert Louis Stevenson" in his *The Profession of Poetry*, 1929, and "The Poetry of Stevenson" in *Essays Presented to Sir Humphrey Milford*, 1948.

DR. JEKYLL AND MR. HYDE

Type of work: Novelette
Author: Robert Louis Stevenson (1850–1894)
Type of plot: Fantasy
Time of plot: Nineteenth century
Locale: London
First published: 1886

This classic romantic adventure and fantasy has steadily maintained its popularity ever since it was first published in 1886. Based upon the dual personalities of a single man representing beauty and beast, Stevenson's understanding of human nature and his mastery of English prose provide the story with subtle values as an illustration of man's dual nature.

Principal Characters

Dr. Henry Jekyll, a London physician who leads a double life. He concocts a drug to change his personality at times to conform to his evil side. To protect himself, he then makes a will leaving his money to the incarnation of his other personality, Edward Hyde. Finally, after the medicine to restore his original personality has run out, he kills himself while in the person of Hyde.

Edward Hyde, the evil side of Dr. Jekyll, a trampler of children and the murderer of Sir Danvers Carew.

Dr. Hastie Lanyon, an intimate friend of Jekyll, who was once present at one of the transformations and who leaves a written description of it, to be opened after Jekyll's death.

Sir Danvers Carew, a kindly old man murdered by Hyde for the joy of doing evil.

Poole, Dr. Jekyll's servant, who vainly seeks the rare drug for the restorative needed by his master.

Mr. Utterson, Jekyll's lawyer, who holds, unopened, Lanyon's letter.

Richard Enfield, who has witnessed Hyde's cruelty and wants an investigation to learn why Hyde is Jekyll's heir.

The Story

Mr. Richard Enfield, and his cousin, Mr. Utterson, a lawyer, were strolling according to their usual Sunday custom when they came upon an empty building on a familiar street. Mr. Enfield told that some time previously he had seen an ill-tempered man trample down a small child at the doorway of the deserted building. He and other indignant bystanders had forced the stranger, who gave his name as Hyde, to pay over a sum of money for the child's welfare. Enfield remembered the man Hyde with deep loathing.

Utterson had reasons to be interested in Hyde. When he returned to his apartment he reread the strange will of Dr. Henry Jekyll. The will stipulated that in the event of Dr. Jekyll's death all of his wealth should go to a man named Edward Hyde.

Utterson sought out Hyde, the man whom Enfield had described, to discover if he were the same who had been named heir to Dr. Jekyll's fortune. Suspicious of Utterson's interest, Hyde became enraged and ran into his house. Questioned, Dr. Jekyll refused to discuss the matter, but insisted that in the event of his death the lawyer should see to it that Mr. Hyde was not cheated out of his fortune. The lawyer believed that Hyde was an extortioner who was getting possession of Dr. Jekyll's money and who would eventually murder the doctor.

About a year later Hyde was wanted for the wanton murder of a kindly old man, Sir Danvers Carew, but he escaped before he could be arrested. Dr. Jekyll presented the lawyer and the police with a letter signed by Hyde, in which the murderer declared his intention of making good his escape forever. He begged Dr. Jekyll's pardon for having ill-used his friendship.

About this time Dr. Lanyon, who had been for years a great friend of Dr. Jekyll, became ill and died. Among his papers was a letter addressed to Utterson. Opening it, Utterson discovered an inner envelope also sealed and bearing the notice that it was not to be opened until after Dr. Jekyll's death. Utterson felt that it was somehow associated with the evil Hyde, but he could in no way fathom the mystery.

One Sunday Enfield and Utterson were walking again in the street where Enfield had seen Hyde mistreating the child. They now realized that the strange deserted building was a side entrance to the house of Dr. Jekyll, an additional wing used as a laboratory. Looking up at the window, they saw Dr. Jekyll sitting there. He looked disconsolate. Then his expression seemed to change, so that his face took on a grimace of horror or pain. Suddenly he closed the window. Utterson and Enfield walked on, too overcome by what they had seen to talk further.

Not long afterward Utterson was sitting by his fireside when Poole, Dr. Jekyll's manservant, sought entrance. He related that for a week something strange had been going on in Dr. Jekyll's laboratory. The doctor himself had not appeared. Instead, he had ordered his meals to be sent in and had written curious notes demanding that Poole go to all the chemical houses in London in search of a mysterious drug. Poole was convinced that his master had been slain and that the murderer, masquerading as Dr. Jekyll, was still hiding in the laboratory.

Utterson and Poole returned to Dr. Jekyll's house and broke into his laboratory with an ax. Entering, they discovered that the man in the laboratory had killed himself by draining a vial of poison just as they broke the lock. The man was Edward Hyde.

They searched in vain for the doctor's body, certain it was somewhere about after they discovered a note of that date addressed to Utterson. In the note Dr. Jekyll said he was planning to disappear, and he urged Utterson to read the note which Dr. Lanyon had left at the time of his death. An enclosure contained the confession of Henry Jekyll.

Utterson returned to his office to read the letters. The letter of Dr. Lanyon described how Dr. Jekyll had sent Poole to Dr. Lanyon with a request that Dr. Lanyon search for some drugs in Dr. Jekyll's laboratory. Hyde had appeared to claim the drugs. Then, in Dr. Lanyon's presence, Hyde had taken the drugs and had been transformed into Dr. Jekyll. The shock of this transformation had caused Dr. Lanyon's death.

Dr. Jekyll's own account of the horrible affair was more detailed. He had begun early in life to live a double life. Publicly he had been genteel and circumspect, but privately he had practiced strange vices without restraint. Becoming obsessed with the idea that people had two personalities, he reasoned that men were capable of having two physical beings as well. Finally, he had compounded a mixture which transformed his body into the physical representation of his evil self. He became Hyde. In his disguise he was free to haunt the lonely, narrow corners of London and to do the darkest acts without fear of recognition.

He tried in every way to protect Hyde. He cautioned his servants to let him in at any hour; he took an apartment for him, and he made out his will in Hyde's favor. His life proceeded safely enough until he awoke one morning in the shape of Edward Hyde and realized that his evil nature had gained the upper hand. Frightened, he determined to cast off the nature of Hyde. He sought out better companions and tried to occupy his mind with other things. However, he was not strong enough to change his true nature. He finally permitted himself to assume the shape of Hyde again, and on that occasion Hyde, full of an overpowering lust to do evil, murdered Sir Danvers Carew.

Dr. Jekyll renewed his effort to abandon the nature of Hyde. Walking in the park one day, he suddenly changed into Hyde. On that occasion he had sought out his friend Dr. Lanyon to go to his laboratory to obtain the drugs which would change him back to the personality of the doctor. Dr. Lanyon had watched the transformation with horror. Thereafter the nature of Hyde seemed to assert itself constantly. When his supply of chemicals had been exhausted and could not be replenished, Dr. Jekyll, as Hyde, shut himself up in his laboratory while he experimented with one drug after another. Finally, in despair, as Utterson now realized, he killed himself.

Critical Evaluation

The gothic Novel in England enjoyed its heyday in the eighteenth century. In this sense, Robert Louis Stevenson's *Dr. Jekyll and Mr. Hyde* is but a late appendage to a popular trend. In terms of content and style, however, it is in the mainstream of that highly popular genre. The novel has predilections for the far and remote, the marvelous and abnormal. It is an escape from reality, emphasizing intuition over reason and impulse over rationality. Like most romantic novels, it values impulsive, childlike, savage, or peasant behavior as uncorrupted by civilized ways. It is transcendental, grotesque, and bizarre while maintaining a sensitive approach to nature, beauty, and women. It is anti-intellectual and Rousseauistic in philosophy, but it is notable for being remote, simple, and democratic while focusing on the supernatural.

The central feature of *Dr. Jekyll and Mr. Hyde* is its theme of duality. Two personalities—opposite and antagonistic—mesh within one body, a psychological insight which, in its time, was remarkably prescient. Dr. Jekyll, an essentially good man, was fascinated by the idea of evil. As a research scientist, he pursued the idea to the point of developing a drug which would alter his conscious state from an intrinsically good person to a fundamentally bad one. Taking the drug, he developed a dual personality, combining the extremes of good and evil. The evil self emerged as the violent Mr. Hyde. This schizophrenia persisted until the "bad" Mr. Hyde overcame "good" Dr. Jekyll to become the dominant personality of the two—at which time it became apparent that Mr. Hyde would have to be annihilated—by then a solution both inevitable and desirable.

The process of transformation was alchemic, tainted with witchcraft. This touch of the occult—a distinct Gothic feature—rescued the novel from the banal, and elevated it to the realm of genuine Gothic horror. Alchemy, witchcraft, and the occult were to earlier ages what technology—especially the computer—is to the present day: a threat to the status quo and comfortable assumptions. The occult and technology are usually treated in like manner: with awe and apprehension. *Dr. Jekyll and Mr. Hyde* continues to fascinate readers—as well as motion picture audiences—for just those qualities of verisimilitude, fear, and hostility. The novel ultimately succeeds by terrifying us, for who among us does not contain the potential for developing that split personality of good and evil which the protagonist so vividly portrays. It is Stevenson's almost mystical capacity in language and characterization to evoke reader identification with his protagonist which accounts for the powerful impact of his novel.

Bibliography

Aring, Charles D. "The Case Becomes Less Strange," in *American Scholar*. XXX (Winter, 1960–1961), pp. 67–78.

Borowitz, Albert. *Innocence and Arsenic: Studies in Crime and Literature*. New York: Harper & Row, 1977, pp. 26–32.

Briggs, Julia. *Night Visitors: The Rise and Fall of the English Ghost Story*. Salem, N.H.: Faber and Faber, 1977, pp. 52–75.

Brown, John Mason. "R.L.S. and *Dr. Jekyll*," in *Saturday Review of Literature*. XXXIV (December 1, 1951), pp. 30–33.

Egan, Joseph J. "The Relationship of Theme and Art in *The Strange Case of Dr. Jekyll and Mr. Hyde*," in *English Literature in Transition*. IX (1966), pp. 28–32.

Eigner, Edwin M. *Robert Louis Stevenson and Romantic Tradition.* Princeton, N.J.: Princeton University Press, 1966, pp. 143–164.

Girling, H.K. "The Strange Case of Dr. James and Mr. Stevenson," in *Wascana Review.* III (1968), pp. 65–79.

Guerard, Albert J. *Stories of the Double.* Philadelphia: Lippincott, 1967, pp. 8–10.

Hellman, George S. "R.L.S. and the Streetwalker," in *American Mercury.* XXXVIII (1936), p. 344.

Hennessy, James Pope. *Robert Louis Stevenson.* New York: Simon and Schuster, 1974, pp. 207–210.

James, Henry. *Partial Portraits.* London: Macmillan, 1905, pp. 169–171.

Keppler, C.F. *The Literature of the Second Self.* Tucson: University of Arizona Press, 1972, pp. 8–9.

Kiely, Robert. *Robert Louis Stevenson and the Fiction of Adventure.* Cambridge, Mass.: Harvard University Press, 1965, pp. 208–210.

Masood, Rahila. "The Appeal of Stevenson," in *Venture.* I (March, 1960), pp. 38–57.

Miyoshi, Masso. "Dr. Jekyll and the Emergence of Mr. Hyde," in *College English.* XXVII (1966), pp. 470–474, 479–480.

Philmus, Robert M. *Into the Unknown: The Evolution of Science Fiction from Francis Godwin to H.G. Wells.* Berkeley: University of California Press, 1970, pp. 90–99.

Rogers, Robert. *A Psychoanalytic Study of the Double in Literature.* Detroit: Wayne State University Press, 1970, pp. 93–94.

Saposnik, Irving S. *Robert Louis Stevenson.* New York: Twayne, 1974, pp. 88–101.

————. "The Anatomy of *Dr. Jekyll and Mr. Hyde,*" in *Studies in English Literature, 1500–1900.* XI (1971), pp. 715–731.

Stern, Gladys Bronwyn. *Robert Louis Stevenson.* London: Longmans, Green, 1952, p. 19.

Stone, Donald D. *Novelists in a Changing World; Meredith, James, and the Transformation of English Fiction in the 1880's.* Cambridge, Mass.: Harvard University Press, 1972, pp. 55–56.

BRAM STOKER

Born: Dublin, Ireland (1847)
Died: London, England (April 20, 1912)

Principal Work

NOVEL: *Dracula*, 1897.

Born in Dublin, Ireland, in 1847, Bram (Abraham) Stoker, famous for his sensational novel, *Dracula*, was a sickly child, so weak that he was unable to stand up alone until the age of seven. He outgrew his childhood weakness, however, and became a champion athlete while at Dublin University, from which he was graduated in 1867. For the next ten years he drudged away as an Irish civil servant. From 1871 to 1876 Stoker served as an unpaid drama critic for the Dublin *Mail*, work which won for him the friendship of Henry Irving, the actor. As a result of their friendship, Stoker served as Irving's manager for many years.

After touring America with Irving, Stoker wrote a series of lectures about life in the United States to deliver to English audiences. The success of the lectures when printed in pamphlet form caused Stoker to consider other kinds of writing. *Dracula* appeared in 1897. Negligible as literature, the book is really no more than a *tour de force* combining werewolves, vampires, hypnotism, and unhappy spirits. It is horrifying, and yet it is compelling, and it has achieved notoriety, if not fame, as a novel, a stage play, and several motion picture versions. The work represents a late nineteenth century development of the earlier Gothic novel, and its marked success stimulated other authors to imitate the type. Other works by Stoker worth noting are *The Jewel of Seven Stars* (1904), a novel; and *Personal Reminiscences of Henry Irving* (1906), the latter recording Stoker's life with Irving and with the Lyceum Theatre. During his last years Stoker was also on the literary staff of the London *Telegraph*. He died in London on April 20, 1912.

Bibliography

The only biographical study is Harry Ludlam, *A Biography of Dracula: The Life Story of Bram Stoker*, 1962. An excellent study of the Gothic novel and its writers is Dorothy Scarborough, *The Supernatural in Modern English Fiction*, 1917.

DRACULA

Type of work: Novel
Author: Bram Stoker (1847–1912)
Type of plot: Horror romance
Time of plot: Nineteenth century
Locale: Transylvania and England
First published: 1897

This work is a classic of the gothic novel genre, and its principal character, Count Dracula, the vampire, continues to live on in contemporary entertainment media. Utilizing the rhetorical device of letters and diaries, and staging scenes full of gothic horror such as mysterious gloomy castles and open graves at midnight, the overall effect of the novel is one of excitement, realism, and horror.

Principal Characters

Count Dracula, a vampire. A corpse during the day, he comes to life at night. He has lived for centuries by sucking blood from living people. He pursues his victims in many harrowing episodes, and is pursued in turn from England to Rumania. There his body, in transport home to his castle, is overtaken and a stake driven through the heart, making it permanently dead.

Jonathan Harker, an English solicitor. He goes to Castle Dracula to transact business with the Count, whose nocturnal habits and total absence of servants puzzle Harker. Harker finds himself a prisoner in the castle, comes one day upon Dracula's corpse, and is occasionally victimized by the vampire. Then the coffin-like boxes are carried away and Harker finds himself left alone, still a prisoner. Later, after he has escaped, he is able to throw light on certain strange happenings in England.

Mina Murray, Harker's fiancée. She joins in the pursuit of Dracula; in a trance, she is able to tell the others that Dracula is at sea, on his return voyage.

Lucy Westenra, a lovely friend whom Mina visits at the time of Harker's trip to Rumania. She is the repeated victim of Dracula, now in England, who appears sometimes in werewolf guise. Finally she dies and becomes a vampire also.

Dr. Van Helsing, a specialist from Amsterdam called to aid the failing Lucy. His remedies are effective, but a fatal attack comes after he leaves; he then returns to England to still her corpse as well as to hunt Dracula.

Dr. Seward, Lucy's former suitor, who attends her during her illness. Until he makes a midnight visit to her empty tomb, he does not believe Van Helsing's advice that the dead girl's soul can be saved only if a stake is driven through her heart.

Arthur Holmwood, a young nobleman and Lucy's fiancée. As he kisses the dying Lucy, her teeth seem about to fasten on his throat. He goes with Seward and Van Helsing to the empty tomb and joins them in tracking down Dracula.

The Story

On his way to Castle Dracula in the province of Transylvania, in Rumania, Jonathan Harker, an English solicitor, was apprehensive. His nervousness grew when he observed the curious, fearful attitude of the peasants and the coachman after they learned of his destination. He was on his way to transact business with Count Dracula, and his mission would necessitate remaining at the castle for several days.

Upon his arrival at the castle, Harker found comfortable accommodations awaiting him. Count Dracula was a charming host, although his peculiarly blood-less physical appearance was somewhat disagreeable to Harker's English eyes. Almost immediately Harker was impressed with the strange life of the castle. He and the count discussed their business at night, as the count was never available during the daytime. Although the food was excellent, Harker never saw a servant about the place. While exploring the castle, he found that it was situated high at the top of a mountain with no accessible exit other than the main doorway, which was kept locked. He realized with a shock that he was a prisoner of Count Dracula.

Various harrowing experiences ensued. While Harker half dozed in the early morning hours, three phantom women materialized and attacked him, attempting to bite his throat. Then the count appeared and drove them off, whispering fiercely that Harker belonged to him. Later Harker thought he saw a huge bat descending the castle walls but the creature turned out to be Count Dracula. In the morning Harker, trying frantically to escape, stumbled into an old chapel where a number of coffin-like boxes of earth were stored. Beneath the cover of one which Harker opened lay the count, apparently dead. In the evening, how-ever, the count appeared as usual, and Harker demanded that he be released. Obligingly the count opened the castle door. A pack of wolves surrounded the entrance. The count, laughing hysterically, left poor Harker a prisoner in his room.

The next day Harker, weak and sick from a strange wound in his throat, saw a pack cart loaded with the mysterious boxes drive from the castle. Dracula was gone and Harker was alone, a prisoner with no visible means of escape.

In England, meanwhile, Harker's fiancée, Mina Murray, had gone to visit her beautiful and charming friend, Lucy Westenra. Lucy was planning to marry Arthur Holmwood, a young nobleman. One evening, early in Mina's visit, a storm blew up and a strange ship was driven aground. The only living creature aboard was a gray wolflike dog. The animal escaped into the countryside.

Soon afterward Lucy's happiness began to fade because of a growing tendency to sleepwalk. One night Mina followed her friend during one of her spells and discovered Lucy in a churchyard. A tall, thin man who was bending over Lucy disappeared at Mina's approach. Lucy, on waking, could remember nothing of the experience, but her physical condition seemed much weakened. Finally she grew so ill that Mina was forced to call upon Dr. Seward, Lucy's former suitor.

Lucy began to improve under his care, and when Mina received a report from Budapest that her missing fiancé had been found and needed care, she felt free to end her visit.

When Lucy's condition suddenly grew worse, Dr. Seward asked his old friend, Dr. Van Helsing, a specialist from Amsterdam, for his professional opinion. Van Helsing, examining Lucy thoroughly, paused over two tiny throat wounds which she was unable to explain. Van Helsing was concerned over Lucy's condition, which pointed to unusual loss of blood without signs of anemia or hemmorhage. She was given blood transfusions at intervals, and someone sat up with her at night. She improved but expressed fear of going to sleep at night because her dreams had grown so horrible.

One morning Dr. Seward fell asleep outside her door. When he and Van Helsing entered her room, they found Lucy ashen white and in a worse condition than ever. Quickly Van Helsing performed another transfusion; she rallied, but not as satisfactorily as before. Van Helsing then secured some garlic flowers and told Lucy to keep them about her neck at night. When the two doctors called the next morning, Lucy's mother had removed the flowers because their odor might bother her daughter. Frantically Van Helsing rushed to Lucy's room and found her in a coma. Again he administered a transfusion and her condition improved. She said that with the garlic flowers close by she was not afraid of nightly flapping noises at her window. Van Helsing sat with her every night until he felt her well enough to leave. After cautioning her always to sleep with the garlic flowers about her neck, he returned to Amsterdam.

Lucy's mother continued to sleep with her daughter. One night the two ladies were awakened by a huge wolf that crashed through the window. Mrs. Westenra fell dead of a heart attack and Lucy fainted, the wreath of garlic flowers slipping from her neck. Seward and Van Helsing, who had returned to England, discovered her half-dead in the morning. They knew she was dying and called Arthur. As Arthur attempted to kiss her, Lucy's teeth seemed about to fasten on his throat. Van Helsing drew him away. When Lucy died, Van Helsing put a tiny gold crucifix over her mouth, but an attendant stole it from her body.

Soon after Lucy's death several children of the neighborhood were discovered far from their homes, their throats marked by small wounds. Their only explanation was that they had followed a pretty lady. When Jonathan Harker returned to England, Van Helsing went to see him and Mina. After talking with Harker, Van Helsing revealed to Dr. Seward his belief that Lucy had fallen victim to a vampire, one of those strange creatures who can live for centuries on the blood of their victims and breed their kind by attacking the innocent and making them vampires in turn. The only way to save Lucy's soul, according to Van Helsing, was to drive a stake through the heart of her corpse, cut off her head, and stuff her mouth with garlic flowers. Dr. Seward protested violently. The next midnight Arthur, Dr. Seward, and Van Helsing visited Lucy's tomb and found it empty. When daylight came they did as Van Helsing had suggested with Lucy's corpse, which had returned to its tomb.

The men, with Mina, tried to track down Dracula in London, in order to find him before he victimized anyone else. Their object was to remove the boxes of sterilized earth he had brought with him from Transylvania so that he would have no place to hide in the daytime. At last the hunters trapped Dracula, but he escaped them. By putting Mina into a trance Van Helsing was able to learn that Dracula was at sea, and it was necessary to follow him to his castle. Wolves gathered about them in that desolate country. Van Helsing drew a circle in the snow with a crucifix and within that magic enclosure the travelers rested safely. The next morning they overtook a cart carrying a black box. Van Helsing and the others overcame the drivers of the cart and pried open the lid of Dracula's coffin. As the sun began to set, they drove a stake through the heart of the corpse. The vampire was no more.

Critical Evaluation

Legend is inextricably twined with Bram Stoker's novel *Dracula,* for the novel is based on the legend. It is impossible to separate the two: the reader will inevitably supply legendary associations between the lines of the novel. But more often than not, everyone tends to forget that both legend and novel were based on reality. This is not to say, of course, that vampires do or did roam Transylvania or elsewhere. However, the prototype for the Dracula legend was a verifiable historical figure, Prince Vlad Tepes, ruler of Transylvania and Walachia (now Rumania) in the mid-fifteenth century. Tepes— nicknamed "The Impaler"— earned a bloody reputation by spearing his victims (some 100,000 of them in a six to ten-year reign, so it is reported) on wooden sticks, a tactic which served to deter domestic criminals and potential outside invaders alike. He assumed the name Dracula—variously interpreted as "son of the dragon" and "son of the devil"—as a further reminder of his vicious tendencies. But the subjects of his small kingdom were convinced that such blood lust could be found only in a human vampire. Hence, Vlad Tepes, self-proclaimed Dracula, was the basis for the legend which Stoker captured so well.

Vampirism has been traced by historians, studied by scholars, embellished by artists and writers, and feared by the superstitious. And although vampirism has, in Western culture, been associated mainly with the Transylvania region of Eastern Europe, the vampire phenomenon in one form or another is attested in all parts of the world from ancient times onward. Outside of Europe, the vampire has appeared in the ancient cultures of the Middle East and the Mediterranean, in China as well as throughout Asia, in several African cultures, and in Aztec civilization and later in Mexico. Some references are in allegedly official reports and in religious works on demonology; others occur in folklore and in literature, drama, painting, and sculpture. Clearly, the vampire was no nineteenth century European invention, but the Romantic obsession with Gothic horror certainly stimulated a spate of vampiric literature, among its other supernatural preoccupations. A short story, "The Vampyre," by John Polidori, was published in 1819. The melodrama *Les Vampires,* by Charles Nodier and Carmouche, was first produced in Paris in 1820. *Varney the Vampire, or The Feast of Blood* (authorship is disputed; either John Malcolm Rymer or Thomas Peckett Prest), a long novel, appeared in 1847. And Joseph Sheridan Le Fanu's redoubtable "Carmilla" first saw print in 1871. But it was Stoker's *Dracula,* published in 1897, that surpassed them all and remains the paragon of vampire stories even today.

Drawing primarily upon European sources, Stoker produced a terrifyingly credible tale by eliminating the inconsistencies and the contradictions common to legendary matter. Wisely avoiding some of the more outlandish explanations of vampirism, for example, Stoker portrayed the trait as transmitted from vampire to victim, who in turn became a vampire, and so on. But to evade straining credulity, Stoker required prolonged contact between vampire and victim before the victim was irrevocably enlisted in the ranks. Thus, Jonathan Harker, whose sustenance of Count Dracula was brief, recovered with no lasting ill effects. But Lucy Westenra was literally drained and consequently became a vampire herself. As a result—and given the perilous circumstances—Van Helsing was compelled to restrain forcibly Lucy's erstwhile fiancé Arthur from giving her a deathbed kiss on her frothing fanged mouth. Stoker also conceded the vampire's power to exercise a species of demonic possession, without physical contact, as the affliction of Mina Murray Harker illustrates.

In like manner, Stoker employed only the most conventional techniques for repelling vampires: garlic and the crucifix. And the requirements for vampire survival were equally simplified from the vast complexity of alternatives which accumulated in the legend. Stoker limited his vampires to nocturnal acvtivity; mandated, of course, the periodic sucking of blood (allowing for moderate stretches of hibernation or abstinence); insisted upon daylight repose in a coffin filled with Transylvania soil; and claimed vampiric invulnerability to ordinary human weapons.

Finally, Stoker's methods for the total annihilation of vampires were similarly conventional, without resort to esoteric impedimenta. He stipulated that a wooden stake be driven through the vampire's heart (although Dracula himself was dispatched with a bowie knife); that the vampire's head be cut off; and the vampire's mouth be stuffed with garlic flowers. Again the inconsistency of these remedies accounts for much of the impact of Stoker's horror story.

In fact, Stoker's recounting of the vampire legend has become the "standard version" in Western culture. Short stories and novels have spun off from the Stoker novel—all distinctly imitative and inferior; attempted sequels have been likewise unsatisfactory, never rising above the level of cheap journalism.

A number of theatrical and film adaptations have been mounted. But the classic stage and screen performances of Bela Lugosi, based upon Stoker's *Dracula,* have never been equaled. Lugosi's 1932 portrayal of Dracula still spellbinds motion-picture audiences as no other production has been able to do. And in this atmosphere of at least semi-credulity, reported sightings of vampiric activity—much like reported sightings of flying saucers or unidentified flying objects—continue to the present.

In the meanwhile, Vlad Tepes's castles in Walachia and the Carpathians have been refurbished by the Rumanian government as tourist attractions, and the historical Dracula is being hailed as a national hero who strove to upgrade the moral fiber of his subjects. Thus, in many ways, Stoker's Dracula lives on to influence the present as powerfully—albeit in a different manner— as he influenced the past.

Bibliography

Bentley, C.F. "The Monster in the Bedroom: Sexual Symbolism in Bram Stoker's *Dracula,*" in *Literature and Psychology.* XXII (1972), pp. 27–34.

Bierman, Joseph S. "*Dracula*: Prolonged Childhood Illness, and the Oral Triad," in *American Imago.* XXIX (1972), pp. 186–198.

Copper, Basil. *The Vampire in Legend, Fact and Art.* Secaucus, N.J.: Citadel Press, 1974, pp. 72–90.

Fry, Carrol L. "Fictional Conventions and Sexuality in *Dracula,*" in *Victorian Newsletter.* XLII (1972), pp. 20–22.

Hennelly, M.M., Jr. "*Dracula*: The Gnostic Quest and Victorian Wasteland," in *English Literature in Transition.* XX (1977), pp. 13–26.

Kirtley, Bacil F. "Dracula, the Monastic Chronicles and Slavic Folklore," in *Midwest Folklore.* VI (1956), pp. 133–139.

MacGillivray, Royce. "*Dracula*: Bram Stoker's Spoiled Masterpiece," in *Queen's Quarterly.* LXXIX (1972), pp. 518–527.

McNally, Raymond T. and Radu Florescu. *In Search of Dracula; A True Story of Dracula and Vampire Legends.* Greenwich, Conn.: New York Graphic Society, 1972, pp. 160–163, 176–181.

Massey, Irving. *The Gaping Pig; Literature and Metamorphosis.* Berkeley: University of California Press, 1976, pp. 98–114.

Nandris, G. "The Historical Dracula: The Theme of His Legend in the Western and in the Eastern Literatures of Europe," in *Comparative Literature: Matter and Method.* Edited by Alfred Owen Aldridge. Urbana: University of Illinois Press, 1969, pp. 109–143.

Richardson, Maurice. "The Psychoanalysis of Ghost Stories," in *Twentieth Century.* CLXVI (December, 1959), pp. 419–431.

Ronay, Gabriel. *The Truth About Dracula*. New York: Stein and Day, 1972, pp. 53–60, 166–170.

Roth, Phyllis A. "Suddenly Sexual Women in Bram Stoker's *Dracula*," in *Literature and Psychology*. XXVII (1977), pp. 113–121.

Wasson, Richard. "The Politics of *Dracula*," in *English Literature in Transition*. IX (1966), pp. 24–27.

Weissman, J. "Women and Vampires: *Dracula* as a Victorian Novel," in *Midwest Quarterly*. XVIII (July, 1977), pp. 392–405.

JONATHAN SWIFT

Born: Dublin, Ireland (November 30, 1667)
Died: Dublin (October 19, 1745)

Principal Works

SATIRICAL FICTION: *A Tale of a Tub*, 1704; *Travels into Several Remote Nations of the World ... by Lemuel Gulliver*, 1726 [*Gulliver's Travels*].

ESSAYS AND TRACTS: *A Discourse on the Dissensions between the Nobles and Commons in Athens and Rome*, 1701; *The Battle of the Books*, 1704; *The Sentiments of a Church of England Man*, 1708; *An Argument against Abolishing Christianity*, 1708; *A Project for the Advancement of Religion*, 1709; *The Conduct of the Allies*, 1711; *The Public Spirit of the Whigs*, 1714; *The Drapier Letters*, 1724; *A Modest Proposal for Preventing the Children of Poor People of Ireland from Being a Burden to Their Parents*, 1729.

POEMS: *Petition to Frances*, 1700; *Miscellanies*, 1708–1711; *Cadenus and Vanessa*, 1713; *On Poetry: A Rhapsody*, 1733; *Verses on the Death of Dr. Swift, Written by Himself*, 1739.

Jonathan Swift, with perhaps the keenest mind and sharpest tongue in an age marked by intellectual brilliance, was a mass of contradictions. Dedicated to the ideals of rationality and common sense, he approached the irrational in his contempt for man's failure to live up to his ideal; profoundly distrustful of all "enthusiasm" or fanaticism, he was himself something of an enthusiast in his glorification of "pure reason"; possessed of one of the clearest and most direct styles in the English language, the subtleties of his irony were misunderstood in his own and later ages.

Although biographical details will never adequately explain either the genius or the contradictions of a man like Swift, the combination of extreme pride and a position of dependence on the favors of the rich or powerful does throw some light on the persistent dissatisfaction with life as it is that colors almost all his work. Born in Dublin on November 30, 1667, the son of an impecunious Englishman who had settled in Ireland, Swift was educated at Trinity College with the aid of a wealthy uncle. In 1688 he left Ireland and became secretary to Sir William Temple at Moor Park, Surrey. Temple was not a congenial master, and Swift chafed to be independent in the more exciting world of London. It was the cultured Sir William, however, who gave polish to the somewhat uncouth young man, and introduced him into his own world of wit and polite learning, and it was in his behalf that Swift entered the controversy over the relative merits of the "ancients" and the "moderns" in his *Battle of the Books*. In this brilliant example of neo-classical mock-heroic prose, Swift pours out his contempt on the self-righteous complacency of modern criticism and poetry. During this same period (1696–1698) Swift, on his own behalf, wrote *A Tale of a Tub*, a burlesque history of the Church in which his genius first revealed itself in its full force. Just as important as his tale of the degradation of the Church through selfishness and fanaticism are the numerous digressions on moral, philosophical, and literary subjects. It was also at Moor Park that Swift first met Esther Johnson, possibly Temple's illegitimate daughter, the "Stella" of his later life.

In 1694, dissatisfied with Moor Park, Swift returned to Ireland, where he was ordained an Anglican priest, but after a dreary year in an Irish parish he was back in England. Between 1708 and 1714 he was in London, and during that period he achieved his greatest triumphs, social, literary, and political. He quickly became familiar with the literary lights of the age, Steele, Addison, Pope, Gay, and Arbuthnot. He wrote pieces for Steele's *Tatler*, and entered Church controversies with such essays as his brilliantly ironic *Argument to prove that the Abolishing of Christianity in England, may . . . be Attended with some inconveniences.* In 1710, partly from hopes of personal advancement, and partly through a passionate interest in defending the prerogatives of the Church, Swift switched his allegiance from the Whig to the Tory party. This move won him the enmity of Whigs such as Addison and Steele, but gained him even more powerful friends in Robert Harley and Henry St. John, leaders of the new Tory ministry. Swift's political writing, in the Tory *Examiner* (which he edited briefly, from 1710–1711) and in pamphlets attacking Robert Walpole and the Duke of Marlborough, was a powerful aid to the Tory administration in its attempts to discredit the Whig "war party." For his untiring labors Swift hoped, and expected, to be rewarded with ecclesiastical preferment, perhaps a bishopric. But the memories of men who have risen to high places are notoriously short. Finally, in 1713, Swift was made Dean of St. Patrick's Cathedral, Dublin—virtually exiled from England. When the Tory ministry collapsed in 1714, all hope ended, and Swift returned to Ireland for good, disillusioned and bitter. Probably the best picture of Swift's mind during this period of political writing, as well as of the behind-the-scenes intrigue of London politics, is to be found in the charming and frank letters which make up the *Journal to Stella* (1766–1768), his correspondence with his protégée and friend, Esther Johnson. This was also the period in which Esther Vanhomrigh, whom he had met in London, followed him to Ireland. The "Vanessa" of his poem *Cadenus and Vanessa*, she died in 1723.

Bitter as he was, Swift's energy and wit could not long be stifled, and he turned his talents to defending Irish political and economic interests against the English. In such pamphlets as *The Drapier's Letters*, in which he protests against the circulation of debased coinage in Ireland, or his ironic masterpiece, *A Modest Proposal*, in which he suggests that for the Irish to sell their infants as food is their only defense against economic starvation by England, Swift not only continued his war with the Whig administration, but won the love and respect of all Ireland. During this period (1721–1725), he also worked intermittently on his greatest and best-known work, *Travels into Several Remote Nations of the World*, better known to us today as *Gulliver's Travels*.

Gulliver's Travels, Swift's final word on man and human nature, is a witty and at times vitriolic comment on man's abuse and perversion of his God-given reason. Books I and II, the account of the voyages to Lilliput and Brobdingnag, deal with the corruption of practical reason, as it operates in the social and political worlds. Books III and IV are concerned with theoretical reason, either in its misuse, as among the Laputans or in the Academy of Lagado, or in its ideal application among the Houyhnhnms. Swift's brutal characterization of man as a despicable Yahoo (Book IV) has led many readers to feel that the intensity of his misanthropy destroys the validity of his work as satire. But bitter as Swift was at man's failure to live up to his ideal of rationality and common sense, the very fact that he wrote *Gulliver's Travels* suggests his recognition of the existence of such a goal, or at least his hope that man could be stimulated to reach it. For those who can rise above the smug satisfaction of having read *Gulliver's Travels* as a children's classic, Swift's satire and irony can scarcely help producing a serious reevaluation of the principles by which we live.

Swift's health had never been good, and by 1740 mental decay had seriously weakened his mind. In 1742 guardians were appointed for him since he was on the verge of insanity. He died in Dublin on October 19, 1745.

Bibliography

The basic edition is the Dublin edition of the *Works*, published by George Faulkner, 4 vols., 1735, with later editions edited by John Hawkesworth, 12 vols., 1755; Sir Walter Scott, 19 vols., 1814; and Temple Scott, Bohn Classical Library, 12 vols., 1897–1908. The standard modern edition of the *Prose Works* is edited by Herbert Davis, 14 vols., 1939–1968. The *Poems* have been edited by Harold Williams, 3 vols., 1937. There are three important collections of letters: Swift's *Correspondence*, edited by F. Elrington Ball, 6 vols., 1910–1914; *Vanessa and Her Correspondence with Jonathan Swift*, edited by Alexander M. Freeman, 1921; and *The Letters of Swift to Charles Ford*, edited by David Nichol Smith, 1935. A useful one-volume edition of selections is *The Portable Swift*, edited by Carl Van Doren, 1948.

The standard biography is Sir Henry Craik, *The Life of Jonathan Swift*, 2 vols., 1894, but this is being supplanted by Irvin Ehrenpreis, *Swift: The Man, His Works, and the Age*, Vol. I, 1962, Vol. II, 1967. The best critical study is Richard Quintana, *The Mind and Art of Jonathan Swift*, 1936. For additional biographical and critical studies see Carl Van Doren, *Swift*, 1930; W. B. C. Watkins, *Perilous Balance*, 1939; G. Wilson Knight, *The Burning Oracle*, 1939; R. W. Jackson, *Swift and His Circle*, 1945; R. C. Churchill, *He Served Human Liberty*, 1946; Herbert Davis, *The Satire of Jonathan Swift*, 1947; Evelyn Hardy, *The Conjured Spirit*, 1949; and J. M. Bullit, *Jonathan Swift and the Anatomy of Satire*, 1953. The *Correspondence* has been edited by Harold Williams, 5 vols., 1963–1965.

The literature on *Gulliver's Travels* is extensive. See W. A. Eddy, *Gulliver's Travels: A Critical Study*, 1923; A. E. Case, *Four Essays on Gulliver's Travels*, 1945; Harold Williams, *The Text of Gulliver's Travels*, 1952; H. M. Dargan,

"The Nature of Allegory as Used by Swift," *Studies in Philology*, XIII (1916), 159–179; J. B. Moore, "The Role of Gulliver," *Modern Philology*, XXV (1928), 469–480; Samuel Kliger, "The Unity of *Gulliver's Travels*," *Modern Language Quarterly*, VI (1945), 401–415; Edward Stone, "Swift and the Horses: Misanthropy or Comedy," *ibid.*, X (1949), 367–376; Ellen D. Leyburn, "Certain Problems of Allegorical Satire in *Gulliver's Travels*," *Huntington Library Quarterly*, XIII (1950), 161–189; H. D. Kelling, "Some Significant Names in *Gulliver's Travels*," *Studies in Philology*, XLVIII (1951), 413; K. M. Williams, "Gulliver's Voyage to the Houyhnhnms," *English Literary History*, XVIII (1951), 275–286; Irvin Ehrenpreis, "Swift and Satire," *College English*, XIII (1952), 309–312; and H. D. Kelling, "*Gulliver's Travels*: A Comedy of Humours," *University of Toronto Quarterly*, XXI (1952), 362–375.

Edith Sitwell's novel, *I Live Under a Black Sun*, 1938, is based on the life of Swift.

GULLIVER'S TRAVELS

Type of work: Simulated record of travel
Author: Jonathan Swift (1667–1745)
Type of plot: Social satire
Time of plot: 1699–1713
Locale: England and various fictional lands
First published: 1726–1727

One of the masterpieces of satire among the world's literature, Gulliver's Travels is written in the form of a travel journal divided into four sections, each of which describes a different voyage of ship's physician Lemuel Gulliver. In each section he visits a different fantastical society—Lilliput, Brobdingnag, Laputa, and Houyhnhnmland—and records the facts and customs of the country. Through Gulliver's adventures and observations, Swift aims his at times savage satire against the English people generally and the Whigs particularly, against various political, academic, and social institutions, and against man's constant abuse of his greatest gift, reason.

Principal Character

Lemuel Gulliver, a surgeon, sea captain, traveler and the narrator of these travel accounts, the purpose of which is to satirize the pretentions and follies of man. Gulliver is an ordinary man, capable of close observation; his deceptively matter-of-fact reportage and a great accumulation of detail make believable and readable a scathing political and social satire. On his first voyage he is shipwrecked at Lilliput, a country inhabited by people no more than six inches tall, where pretentiousness, individual as well as political, is ridiculed. The second voyage ends in Brobdingnag, a land of giants. Human grossness is a target here. Moreover, Gulliver does not find it easy to make sense of English customs and politics in explaining them to a king sixty feet high. On Gulliver's third voyage pirates attack the ship and set him adrift in a small boat. One day he sees and goes aboard Laputa, a flying island inhabited by incredibly abstract and absent-minded people. From Laputa he visits Balnibari, where wildly impractical experiments in construction and agriculture are in progress. Then he goes to Glubbdubdrib, the island of sorcerers, where he is shown apparitions of such historical figures as Alexander and Caesar, who decry the inaccuracies of history books. Visiting Luggnagg, Gulliver, after describing an imaginary immortality of constant learning and growing wisdom, is shown a group of immortals called Struldbrugs, who are grotesque, pitiable creatures, senile for centuries, but destined never to die. Gulliver's last journey is to the land of the Houyhnhnms, horse-like creatures in appearance, possessed of great intelligence, rationality, restraint, and courtesy. Dreadful human-like creatures, called Yahoos, impart to Gulliver such a loathing of the human form that, forced to return at last to England, he cannot bear the sight of even his own family and feels at home only in the stables.

The Story

Lemuel Gulliver, a physician, took the post of ship's doctor on the *Antelope*, which set sail from Bristol for the South Seas in May, 1699. When the ship was wrecked in a storm somewhere near Tasmania, Gulliver had to swim for his life. Wind and tide helped to carry him close to a low-lying shore where he fell, exhausted, into a deep sleep. Upon awaking, he found himself held to the ground by hundreds of small ropes. He soon discovered that he was the prisoner of humans six inches tall. Still tied, Gulliver was fed by his captors; then he was placed on a special wagon built for the purpose and drawn by fifteen hundred small horses. Carried in this manner to the capital city of the small humans, he was exhibited as a great curiosity to the people of Lilliput, as the land of the diminutive people was called. He was kept chained to a huge Lilliputian building into which he crawled at night to sleep.

Gulliver soon learned the Lilliputian language, and through his personal charm and natural curiosity he came into good graces at the royal court. At length he was given his freedom, contingent upon his obeying many rules devised by the emperor prescribing his deportment in Lilliput. Now free, Gulliver toured Mildendo, the capital city, and found it to be similar to European cities of the time.

Learning that Lilliput was in danger of an invasion by the forces of the neighboring empire, Blefuscu, he offered his services to the emperor of Lilliput. While the enemy fleet awaited favorable winds to carry their ships the eight hundred yards between Blefuscu and Lilliput, Gulliver took some Lilliputian cable, waded to Blefuscu, and brought back the entire fleet by means of hooks attached to the cables. He was greeted with great acclaim and the emperor made him a nobleman. Soon, however, the emperor and Gulliver fell out over differences concerning the fate of the now helpless Blefuscu. The emperor wanted to reduce the enemy to the status of slaves; Gulliver championed their liberty. The pro-Gulliver forces prevailed in the Lilliputian parliament; the peace settlement was favorable to Blefuscu. But Gulliver was now in disfavor at court.

He visited Blefuscu, where he was received graciously by the emperor and the people. One day, while exploring the empire, he found a ship's boat washed ashore from some wreck. With the help of thousands of Blefuscu artisans, he repaired the boat for his projected voyage back to his own civilization. Taking some little cattle and sheep with him, he sailed away and was eventually picked up by an English vessel.

Back in England, Gulliver spent a short time with his family before he shipped aboard the *Adventure*, bound for India. The ship was blown off course by fierce winds. Somewhere on the coast of Great Tartary a landing party went ashore to forage for supplies. Gulliver, who had wandered away from the party, was left behind when a gigantic human figure pursued the sailors back to the ship. Gulliver was caught in a field by giants threshing grain that grew forty feet high. Becoming the pet of a farmer and his family, he amused them with his humanlike behavior. The farmer's nine-year-old daughter, who was not yet over forty feet high, took special charge of Gulliver.

The farmer displayed Gulliver first at a local market town. Then he took his little pet to the metropolis, where Gulliver was put on show to the great detriment of his health. The farmer, seeing that Gulliver was near death, sold him to the queen, who took a great fancy to the little curiosity. The court doctors and philosophers studied Gulliver as a quaint trick of nature. He subsequently had adventures with giant rats the size of lions, with a dwarf thirty feet high, with wasps as large as partridges, with apples the size of Bristol barrels, and with hailstones the size of tennis balls.

Gulliver and the king discussed the institutions of their respective countries, the king asking him many questions about Great Britain that Gulliver found impossible to answer truthfully without embarrassment.

After two years in Brobdingnag, the land of the giants, Gulliver escaped miraculously when a large bird carried his portable quarters out over the sea. The bird dropped the box containing Gulliver and he was rescued by a ship which was on its way to England. Back home, it took Gulliver some time to accustom himself once more to a world of normal size.

Soon afterward Gulliver went to sea again. Pirates from a Chinese port attacked the ship. Set adrift in a small sailboat, Gulliver was cast away upon a rocky island. One day he saw a large floating mass descending from the sky. Taken aboard the flying island of Laputa, he soon found it to be inhabited by intellectuals who thought only in the realm of the abstract and the exceedingly impractical. The people of the island, including the king, were so absent-minded they had to have servants following them to remind them even of their trends of conversation. When the floating island arrived above the continent of Balnibari, Gulliver received permission to visit that realm. There he inspected the Grand Academy, where hundreds of highly impractical projects for the improvement of agriculture and building were under way.

Next Gulliver journeyed by boat to Glubbdubdrib, the island of sorcerers. By means of magic, the governor of the island showed Gulliver such great historical figures as Alexander, Hannibal, Caesar, Pompey, and Sir Thomas More. Gulliver talked to the apparitions and learned from them that history books were inaccurate.

From Glubbdubdrib, Gulliver went to Luggnagg. There he was welcomed by the king, who showed him the Luggnaggian immortals, or Struldbrugs—beings who would never die.

Gulliver traveled on to Japan, where he took a ship back to England. He had been away for more than three years.

Gulliver became restless after a brief stay at his home, and he signed as captain of a ship which sailed from Portsmouth in August, 1710, destined for the South Seas. The crew mutinied, keeping Captain Gulliver prisoner in his cabin for months. At length, he was cast adrift in a long boat off a strange coast. Ashore, he came upon and was nearly overwhelmed by disgusting half-human, half-ape creatures who fled in terror at the approach of a horse. Gulliver soon discovered, to his amazement, that he was in a land where rational horses, the Houyhnhnms, were masters of irrational human creatures, the Yahoos. He stayed in the stable-house of a Houyhnhnm family and learned to subsist on oaten cake and milk. The Houyhnhnms were horrified to learn from Gulliver that horses in England were used by Yahoo-like creatures as beasts of burden. Gulliver described England to his host, much to the candid and straightforward Houyhnhnm's mystification. Such things as wars and courts of law were unknown to this race of intelligent horses. As he did in the other lands he visited, Gulliver attempted to explain the institutions of his native land, but the friendly and benevolent Houyhnhnms were appalled by many of the things Gulliver told them.

Gulliver lived in almost perfect contentment among the horses, until one day his host told him that the Houyhnhnm Grand Assembly had decreed Gulliver either be treated as an ordinary Yahoo or be released to swim back to the land from which he had come. Gulliver built a canoe and sailed away. At length he was picked up by a Portuguese vessel. Remembering the Yahoos, he became a recluse on the ship and began to hate all mankind. Landing at Lisbon, he sailed from there to England. But on his arrival the sight of his own family repulsed him; he fainted when his wife kissed him. His horses became his only friends on earth.

Critical Evaluation

When Jonathan Swift created the character of Lemuel Gulliver as his narrator for *Gulliver's Travels*, he developed a personality with many qualities admired by an eighteenth century audience, and still admired by readers today. Gulliver is a decent sort of person, hopeful, simple, fairly direct, and full of good will. He is a scientist, a trained doctor; and, as any good scientist should, he loves detail. His literal-minded attitude makes him a keen observer of the world around him. Furthermore, he is, like another famous novel character of the eighteenth century—Robinson Crusoe—encouragingly resourceful in emergencies. Why is it, then, that such a seemingly admirable, even heroic character, should become, in the end, an embittered misanthrope, hating the world and turning against everyone, including people who show him kindness?

The answer lies in what Swift meant for his character to be, and Gulliver was certainly not intended to be heroic. Readers often confuse Gulliver the character and Swift the author, but to do so is to miss the point of *Gulliver's Travels*. The novel is a satire, and Gulliver is a mask for Swift the satirist. In fact, Swift does not share Gulliver's values: his rationalistic, scientific responses to the world and his belief in progress and the perfectibility of man. Swift, on the contrary, believed that such values were dangerous to mankind, and that to put such complete faith in the material world, as scientific Gulliver did, was folly. As Swift's creation, Gulliver is a product of his age, and he is designed as a character to demonstrate the great weakness underlying the values of the "Age of Enlightenment," the failure to recognize the power of that which is irrational in man.

Despite Gulliver's apparent congeniality in the opening chapters of the novel, Swift makes it quite clear that his character has serious shortcomings, including blindspots about human nature and his own nature. Book III, the least readable section of *Gulliver's Travels,* is in some ways the most revealing part of the book. In it Gulliver complains, for example, that the wives of the scientists he is observing run away with the servants. The fact is that Gulliver —himself a scientist—gives little thought to the well-being of his own wife. In the eleven years covered in Gulliver's "travel book," Swift's narrator spends a total of seven months and ten days with his wife.

Thus, Gulliver too is caught up in Swift's web of satire in *Gulliver's Travels.* Satire as a literary form tends to be ironic; the author says the opposite of what he means. Consequently, we can assume that much of what Gulliver observes as good, and much of what he thinks and does, is the opposite of what Swift thinks.

As a type of the eighteenth century, Gulliver exhibits its major values: belief in rationality, in the perfectibility of man, in the idea of progress, and in the Lockean philosophy of the human mind as a *tabula rasa,* or blank slate, at the time of birth, controlled and developed entirely by the differing strokes and impressions made on it by the environment. Swift, in contrast to Gulliver, hated the abstraction that accompanied rational thinking; he abhorred the rejection of the past that resulted from a rationalistic faith in the new and improved; and he cast strong doubts on man's ability to gain knowledge through reason and logic.

The world Gulliver discovers during his travels is significant in Swift's satire. The Lilliputians, averaging not quite six inches in height, display the pettiness and the smallness Swift detects in much that motivates human institutions, such as church and state. It is petty religious problems that lead to continual war in Lilliput. The Brobdingnagians continue the satire in Part Two by exaggerating man's grossness through their enlarged size. (Swift divided human measurements by a twelfth for the Lilliputians and multiplied the same for the Brobdingnagians.)

The tiny people of Part One and the giants of Part Two establish a pattern of contrasts which Swift follows in Part Four with the Houyhnhnms and the Yahoos. The Yahoos, "their heads and breasts covered with a thick hair, some frizzled and others lank," naked otherwise and scampering up trees like nimble squirrels, represent the animal aspect of man when it is viewed as separate from the rational. The Houyhnhnms, completing the other half of the split, know no lust, pain, or pleasure. Their rational temperaments totally rule their passions, if they have any at all. The land of the Houyhnhnms is a Utopia to Gulliver, and he tells the horse-people that his homeland is unfortunately governed by Yahoos.

But what is the land of the Houyhnhnms really like, how much a Utopia? Friendship, benevolence, and equality are the principal virtues there. Decency and civility guide every action. As a result, each pair of horses mates to have one colt of each sex; after that, they no longer stay together. The marriages are exacted to insure nice color combinations in the offspring. To the young, marriage is "one of the necessary actions of a reasonable being." After the function of the marriage has been fulfilled—after the race has been propagated—the two members of the couple are no closer to each other than to anybody else in the whole country. It is this kind of "equality" that Swift satirizes. As a product of the rational attitude, such a value strips life of its fullness, denies the power of emotion and instinct, subjugates all to logic, reason, the intellect, and makes all dull and uninteresting—as predictable as a scientific experiment.

By looking upon the Houyhnhnms as the perfect creatures, Gulliver makes his own life back in England intolerable:

> I . . . return to enjoy my own speculations in my little garden at Redriff; to apply those excellent lessons of virtue which I learned among the Houyhnhnms; to instruct the Yahoos of my own family as far as I shall find them docible animals; to behold my figure often in a glass, and thus if possible habituate myself by time to tolerate the sight of a human creature. . . .

When Gulliver holds up rational men as perfect man, and when he cannot find a rational man to meet his ideal, he concludes in disillusionment that mankind is totally animalistic, like the ugly Yahoos. In addition to being a satire and a parody of travel books, *Gulliver's Travels* is an initiation novel. As Gulliver develops, he changes; but he fails to learn an important lesson of life, or he learns it wrong. His naïve optimism about progress and rational man leads him to bitter disillusionment.

It is tragically ironic that Swift died at the age of seventy-eight after three years of living without his reason, a victim of Ménière's disease, dying "like a rat in a hole." For many years he had struggled against fits of deafness and giddiness, symptoms of the disease. As a master of the language of satire, Swift remains unequaled, despite his suffering and ill health. He gathered in *Gulliver's Travels,* written late in his life, all the experience he had culled from both courts and streets. For Swift knew people, and, as individuals, he loved them. But, when they changed into groups, he hated them, satirized them, stung them into realizing the dangers of the herd. Gulliver never understood this.

Bibliography

Barzun, Jacques. *Energies of Art: Studies of Authors, Classics and Modern.* New York: Harper & Row, 1956, pp. 81–100.

Bloom, Allan. "An Outline of *Gulliver's Travels*," in *The Writings of Jonathan Swift.* Edited by Robert A Greenberg and William Bowman Piper. New York: Norton, 1973, pp. 648–661.

Carnochan, W.B. *Lemuel Gulliver's Mirror for Man.* Berkeley: University of California Press, 1968, pp. 1–181.

Davis, Herbert J. *The Satire of Jonathan Swift.* New York: Macmillan, 1947, pp. 79–106.

Dyson, Anthony Edward. *The Crazy Fabric: Essays in Irony.* New York: St. Martin's, 1965, pp. 1–13.

Eddy, William A. Gulliver's Travels, *A Critical Study.* Princeton, N.J.: Princeton University Press, 1923.

Ehrenpreis, Irvin. *Literary Meaning and Augustan Values.* Charlottesville: University of Virginia Press, 1974, pp. 94–109.

Ewald, William Bragg. *The Masks of Jonathan Swift.* Cambridge, Mass.: Harvard University Press, 1954, pp. 125–162.

Horrell, Joseph. "What Gulliver Knew," in *Sewanee Review.* LI (Autumn, 1943), pp. 476–504. Revised and reprinted in *Swift: A Collection of Critical Essays.* Edited by Ernest Tuveson. Englewood Cliffs, N.J.: Prentice-Hall, 1964, pp. 55–70.

Hunting, Robert. *Jonathan Swift.* New York: Twayne, 1967, pp. 92–114.

Kelling, Harold D. "*Gulliver's Travels*: A Comedy of Humours," in *University of Toronto Quarterly.* XXI (July, 1952), pp. 362–375.

Milburn, Daniel J. *The Age of Wit, 1650–1750.* New York: Macmillan, 1966, pp. 120–152.

Monk, Samuel H. "The Pride of Lemuel Gulliver," in *Sewanee Review.* LXIII (1955), pp. 48–71. Partly reprinted in *Twentieth Century Interpretations of* Gulliver's Travels: *A Collection of Critical Essays.* Edited by Frank Brady. Englewood Cliffs, N.J.: Prentice-Hall, 1968, pp. 70–79.

Newman, Bertram. *Jonathan Swift.* London: Allen and Unwin, 1937, pp. 300–319.

Piper, William Bowman. "The Sense of *Gulliver's Travels*," in *Rice University Studies.* LXI (Winter, 1975), pp. 75–106.

Price, Martin. *To the Palace of Wisdom: Studies in Order and Energy from Dryden to Blake.* New York: Doubleday, 1964, pp. 179–203. Partly reprinted in *Twentieth Century Interpretations of* Gulliver's Travels: *A Collection of*

Critical Essays. Edited by Frank Brady. Englewood Cliffs, N.J.: Prentice-Hall, 1968, pp. 89–95.

Quintana, Ricardo.   *The Mind and Art of Jonathan Swift*. London: Methuen, 1953, pp. 287–327.

Rawson, Claude J.   *Gulliver and the Gentle Reader: Studies in Swift in Our Times*. London: Routledge and Kegan Paul, 1973, pp. 1–32.

Ross, John F.   "The Final Comedy of Lemuel Gulliver," in *Studies in the Comic, University of California Publications in English*. VIII (1941), pp. 175–196. Reprinted in *Swift: A Collection of Critical Essays*. Edited by Ernest Tuveson. Englewood Cliffs, N.J.: Prentice-Hall, 1964, pp. 71–89.

Sutherland, William O.S.   *The Art of the Satirist: Essays on the Satire of Augustan England*. Austin: University of Texas Press, 1965, pp. 108–125.

Taylor, Dick, Jr.   "Gulliver's Pleasing Visions: Self-Deception as Major Theme in *Gulliver's Travels*," in *Tulane Studies in English*. XII (1962), pp. 7–61.

Tilton, John W.   *"Gulliver's Travels* as a Work of Art," in *Bucknell Review*. VIII (December, 1959), pp. 246–259.

Tuveson, Ernest.   "Swift: The View from Within the Satire," in *The Satirist's Art*. Edited by H. James Jensen and Malvin R. Zirker. Bloomington: Indiana University Press, 1972, pp. 70–85.

Ward, David.   *Jonathan Swift: An Introductory Essay*. London: Methuen, 1973, pp. 121–183.

Williams, Kathleen.   *Jonathan Swift and the Age of Compromise*. Lawrence: University of Kansas Press, 1958, pp. 154–209.

WILLIAM MAKEPEACE THACKERAY

Born: Calcutta, India (July 18, 1811)
Died: London, England (December 24, 1863)

Principal Works

NOVELS: *Catherine*, 1839–1840; *The History of Samuel Titmarsh and the Great Hoggarty Diamond*, 1841; *Barry Lyndon*, 1844; *Vanity Fair*, 1847–1848; *Pendennis*, 1848–1850; *Henry Esmond*, 1852; *The Newcomes*, 1853–1855; *The Virginians*, 1857–1859; *The Adventures of Philip*, 1861–1862; *Denis Duval*, 1864.

SKETCHES: *The Paris Sketch Book*, 1840; *Comic Tales and Sketches*, 1841; *The Irish Sketch Book*, 1843; *The Book of Snobs*, 1848; *Sketches and Travels in London*, 1856.

CHRISTMAS STORY: *The Rose and the Ring*, 1854.

LECTURES AND ESSAYS: *The English Humorists of the Eighteenth Century*, 1851; *The Four Georges*, 1855; *Roundabout Papers*, 1864.

William Makepeace Thackeray was born at Calcutta, India (where his father was in the service of the East India Company), on July 18, 1811, and died in London on December 24, 1863. At least until 1859, when George Eliot's *Adam Bede* appeared, he was Dickens' only possible rival as the leading Victorian novelist.

Thackeray's father, Richmond Thackeray, died in 1815; his mother thereafter married Captain Henry Carmichael-Smyth, who became the original of Colonel Newcome. In 1822 the boy was sent to the Charterhouse School, whence he proceeded to Trinity College, Cambridge, which he left without taking a degree. He studid law in a desultory fashion and wandered about Weimar and Paris dabbling in art. In 1833, through a combination of folly and ill luck, he lost most of his considerable fortune. His first thought was to make his living as an artist (he later illustrated his own writings), but he soon turned instead to literature.

Thackeray began his career by burlesquing popular contemporary novelists whose work he considered mawkish, absurd, or morally vicious, for *Fraser's Magazine*; the most important outcome of these labors was his *Catherine*, in which he attacked the vogue of the story of crime. A more important enterprise, *Barry Lyndon*, was an eighteenth century rogue story, importantly influenced by Thackeray's admiration for Fielding's *Jonathan Wild*; but the writer did not really catch the public fancy until he published *Vanity Fair* in 1847–1848. From then until the end, though his sales always ran far behind those of Dickens, his reputation was secure. In the 1850's he made two lecture tours in America; from 1860 to 1862 he edited *The Cornhill Magazine*. His domestic happiness was clouded by the insanity of his Irish wife, Isabella Shaw (whom he married in 1836, and who outlived him by many years); in his relations with his daughters he showed all the tenderness of which his kindly, but in some ways weak, nature was capable.

Thackeray was at once a cynic and a sentimentalist. The judgments he makes of his characters are often uncertain and conventional, but he portrays them with a vivid realism which in his time seemed shocking in English fiction. Many of his most successful characters are, in one way or another, rogues. "The Art of Novels," he declared, "*is* to represent Nature; to convey as strongly as possible the sentiment of reality. . . ." The heightening and idealism proper to "a tragedy or a poem or a lofty drama" he ruled out. Not by this alone was he differentiated from Dickens but also by his upper-class point of view, his lack of Dickens' enthusiasm, vitality, and inexhaustible sympathy, and by his more bookish, elegant style. His world, in its main aspects, comprises Mayfair and Bohemia. Though the two great writers did not fail to appreciate each other, Dickens was inclined to resent his rival's somewhat superior and aristocratic air toward "the art that he held in trust." Thus the tone of careless ease in Thackeray's writing is an important element in his charm, but it also indicates an important limitation.

His major novels are few in number and make up a comparatively small portion of the twenty-five odd volumes of his collected works. Probably the most brilliant are *Vanity Fair*, a stunning panorama of a corrupt upper- and middle-class society around the Waterloo crisis, with a heroine, Becky Sharp, who has been for a hundred years the most celebrated female rogue in English fiction, and *Henry Esmond*, a novel in the form of a memoir, presenting Jacobitish and other intrigues in an eighteenth century London in some ways more congenial to Thackeray's mind and spirit than his own time. *Henry Esmond's* cool, autumnal elegance and perfect distinction of style place it forever in the aristocracy of the world's great novels. It has, too, in Beatrix Esmond, one of the most subtly and completely portrayed of all heroines of fiction. *Pendennis* is an attempt to use for fiction the materials of Thackeray's own life in the manner and spirit of Fielding's *Tom Jones*. The *Newcomes*, a family novel covering three generations, is a wider-scoped *Vanity Fair*. *The Virginians* gives us Esmond's grandsons in the American Revolution and in London. These are all major novels. But *The Adventures of Philip* is only a minor *Pendennis*, and *Denis Duval*, a brilliant adventure story, which represents for Thackeray a frank capitulation to romance which he unfortunately did not live to finish.

Thackeray's achievement, like that of his master Fielding, is central in the development of the English novel. Though he had neither Scott's imagination nor Dickens' brilliance, he had an unerring sense of the scope and direction of fiction. After a hundred years he still deserves to be called one of our very greatest realists.

Bibliography

The most significant modern contribution to Thackeray biography and criticism is Gordon N. Ray's *The Letters and Private Papers of William Makepeace*

Thackeray, 4 vols., 1945–1946, prepared with the cooperation of the Thackeray family. Ray's *The Buried Life*, 1952, a major critical study, uses this material; and his *Thackeray: The Uses of Adversity*, 1955, and *Thackeray: The Age of Wisdom*, 1958, now make up the definitive biography. Lionel Stevenson, *The Showman of Vanity Fair*, 1947, was the last important book prepared without access to Ray's documents.

Among the books published before the *Letters and Private Papers*, the most useful are the writings of Thackeray's daughter, Lady Ritchie, especially *Chapters from Some Unwritten Memoirs*, 1894; and *Thackeray and His Daughter*, 1924. See also Lewis Melville, *The Life of William Makepeace Thackeray*, 2 vols., 1899; and Malcolm Elwin, *Thackeray: A Personality*, 1932. Miriam M. H. Thrall's *Rebellious Fraser's*, 1934, is important for Thackeray's apprenticeship. More recent biographies include John W. Dodds, *Thackeray: A Critical Portrait*, 1941; Geoffrey Tillotson, *Thackeray the Novelist*, 1954; John A. Sutherland, *Thackeray at Work*, 1974; and John Carey, *Thackeray: Prodigal Genius*, 1977.

Although little of the early criticism of Thackeray still has modern relevance, two exceptions are George Saintsbury, *A Consideration of Thackeray*, 1931; and Lord David Cecil, "William Makepeace Thackeray," in *Early Victorian Novelists*, 1934. Recent criticism includes Lambert Ennis, *Thackeray: The Sentimental Cynic*, 1950; John Young T. Greig, *Thackeray: A Reconsideration*, 1950; Geoffrey Tillotson and Donald Hawes, *Thackeray: The Critical Heritage*, 1968; M. G. Sundell, ed., *Twentieth Century Interpretations of Vanity Fair: A Collection of Critical Essays*, 1969; Juliet McMaster, *Thackeray: The Major Novels*, 1971; Barbara Hardy, *The Exposure of Luxury: Radical Themes in Thackeray*, 1972; and Jack P. Rawlins, *Thackeray's Novels: A Fiction That Is True*, 1974.

Useful special studies include Robert Stanley Forsythe, *A Noble Rake, the Life of Charles, Fourth Lord Mohun, Being a Study in the Historical Background of Thackeray's "Henry Esmund"*, 1928; and Robert Bledsoe, "*Pendennis* and the Power of Sentimentality," in *Publications of the Modern Language Association*, XVI (1978), 871–883.

BARRY LYNDON

Type of work: Novel
Author: William Makepeace Thackeray (1811–1863)
Type of plot: Picaresque romance
Time of plot: Eighteenth century
Locale: England, Ireland, and Europe
First published: 1843

From the first boastful paragraph to the last petulant complaint against his wife's deceit, Redmond Barry in his narrative constantly exposes himself as a man of the basest tendencies. Given to murder, adept at winning at cards, a skillful and deceitful wooer, he is a thoroughly corrupt scoundrel in the pattern of Fielding's Jonathan Wild.

Principal Characters

Redmond Barry, later **Redmond Barry Lyndon,** after his marriage. The boastful and petulant narrator of this picaresque novel set in the eighteenth century, he is a corrupt bully. Throughout his many adventures, he behaves with consistent dishonor. Suffering from delirium tremens, he dies in the Fleet Prison.

The Widow Barry, his mother, who was deprived of wealth and estates by relatives. She devotes herself to the rearing of her son until his Uncle Brady persuades her to let him take the boy to Brady Castle. Much later, after Barry's marriage, Widow Barry lives with her son and aids him in his nearly successful attempt to drive his wife mad.

Lady Honoria Lyndon, who holds the former Barry lands. Immediately upon learning of her husband's death, Barry begins an underhanded and relentless courtship which at last wears down her resistance. So brutal a husband is he that Lady Lyndon's natural haughtiness is thoroughly subdued. Kept virtually a prisoner by Barry and his mother, she is almost driven mad before her former suitor and her indignant relatives contrive to free her from Barry's custody.

Lord Bullingdon, Lady Lyndon's son and heir. Barry does his best to deplete Lord Bullingdon's future property in order to live in style and to provide for his own son, who will have no rights of inheritance. Lord Bullingdon is driven by his stepfather to run off to fight the rebels in America. He is reported killed but shows up again just in time to keep his weak-willed mother from succumbing once more to her now estranged husband.

Bryan Lyndon, the son of Lady Lyndon and Barry, a boy overindulged by his father. Thrown from his horse, he is killed. His mother's anguish over his death causes a report that she is mad.

Uncle Brady, who invites the young Barry to Castle Brady and treats him kindly.

Nora Brady, Barry's cousin. He falls in love with her when he is fifteen and she twenty-four. In a fit of jealousy, and with characteristic selfishness, Barry fights a duel with the man she loves and whom her family wants her to marry.

Captain John Quinn, loved by Nora. Believing he has wounded Quinn, Barry flees to Ireland. Later he finds that the dueling pistols were loaded with tow and that Captain Quinn, far from dead, is married to Nora.

Mrs. Fitzsimons, a highway robbery victim whom Barry befriends on the road to Dublin. Visiting at her castle, he attempts to make a lavish impression. When his money is gone, his host and hostess are glad to see him leave.

Chevalier Balibari, suspected of being an Austrian agent by the Prussians. Having deserted from the British Army to the Prussians, Barry, now in Berlin, is sent to spy on Balibari, whom he discovers to be his own father's brother, Barry of Ballybarry, now an elderly gambler. Barry, in disguise, leaves the Prussian service and goes to Dresden with this uncle.

Countess Ida, a wealthy heiress whom Barry dislikes but courts.

Chevalier De Magny, the fiancé of Countess Ida. Barry wins from him, in gambling, all his possessions, including his claim to the hand of Countess Ida. Involvement in a court intrigue, however, foils the matrimonial scheme when Barry is forced to leave the duchy.

Lord Charles Lyndon, the husband of Lady Honoria Lyndon. Barry becomes acquainted with them at a spa and resolves to marry Lady Lyndon as soon as the sickly Lord Lyndon is dead.

Lord George Poynings, Lady Lyndon's former suitor, who helps in freeing her from Barry's custody.

Mick Brady, Barry's cousin. He persecutes young Barry during the latter's stay in Brady Castle.

Mrs. Brady, the wife of Uncle Brady. She hates Barry.

Frederick the Great, of Prussia. He sends Barry to spy on the Chevalier Balibari.

The Duke of X——, at whose court Barry pursues the Countess Ida.

The Story

Deprived of wealth and estates by relatives, Widow Barry devoted herself to the careful rearing of her son Redmond. Uncle Brady took a liking to the lad and asked the widow for permission to take the child to his ancestral home, Brady Castle. There Barry was treated kindly by his uncle. One of his cousins, Mick, persecuted him, however, and Mrs. Brady hated him.

Aggressive by nature, Barry invited animosity; his landless pride in his ancestral heritage led him into repeated neighborhood brawls until he had fought every lad in the area and acquired the reputation of a bully. At fifteen he fell in love with twenty-four-year-old Nora Brady, who was in love with Captain John Quinn, an Englishman. Deeply in debt, Uncle Brady hoped that Nora would marry the captain, who had promised to pay some of the old man's debts. Thoroughly unscrupulous and lacking in appreciation for his uncle's kindness, Barry, in a fit of jealousy, insulted Quinn and wounded him in a duel.

Believing the captain dead, Barry hurriedly set out on the road to Dublin. On the way he befriended a Mrs. Fitzsimons, the victim of a highway robbery. She took him to her castle, where Barry spent some of his own money in a lavish attempt to create a good impression. When he had lost all his money through high living and gambling, Mrs. Fitzsimons and her husband were glad to see him leave.

Barry next took King George's shilling and enlisted for a military expedition in Europe. Boarding the ship, a crowded and filthy vessel, he learned that Captain Quinn had not died after all, for the pistols had been loaded only with tow, but had married Nora Brady.

Detesting service in the British Army, Barry deserted to the Prussians. At the end of the Seven Years' War he was garrisoned in Berlin. By that time he was known as a thorough scoundrel and a quarrelsome bully. Sent by Frederick the Great to spy on the Chevalier Balibari, suspected of being an Austrian agent, Barry learned that the officer was his own father's brother, Barry of Ballybarry. This elderly gentleman actually made his way by gambling, rising and falling in wealth as his luck ran. When the gambler decided to leave Berlin, Barry, eager to escape from Prussian service, disguised himself and fled to Dresden. There he joined his uncle, who was high in favor at the Saxon court.

Barry, living like a high-born gentleman, supported himself by operating a gambling table. At the court of the Duke of X— he pursued Countess Ida, one of the wealthiest heiresses in the duchy. Disliking the countess personally but greatly admiring her fortune, he ruthlessly set about to win her from her fiancé, the Chevalier De Magny. Gambling with the hapless man, Barry won from him all he possessed. At last De Magny agreed to play for the hand of Countess Ida, and lost. Barry's scheme might have succeeded if he had not become involved in a court intrigue. He was forced to leave the duchy.

Roaming through all the famous cities of Europe, Barry acquired a wide reputation as a skillful gambler. At Spa he met Lord Charles and Lady Honoria Lyndon who held the former Barry lands, and he decided to marry Lady Lyndon following the death of her husband, who was very ill. A year later, hearing that Lord Charles had died at Castle Lyndon, in Ireland, he set out to woo Lady Honoria. Employing numerous underhanded devices, which included blackmail, bribery, dueling, and intimidation, Barry forced himself upon Lady Lyndon, who at first resisted his suit. But Barry persecuted the lady relentlessly, bribing her servants, spying on her every move, paying her homage, and stealing her correspondence. When she fled to London to escape his persistent attentions, he followed her. At last he overcame her aversion and objections, and she agreed to become his wife. Adding her name to his own, he became Barry Lyndon, Esq.

Although she was haughty and overbearing by nature, Lady Lyndon soon yielded to the harsh dominance of her husband, who treated her brutally and thwarted her attempts to control her own fortune. After a few days of marriage the Lyndons went to Ireland, where he immediately assumed management of the Lyndon estates. Living in high fashion, he spent money freely in order to establish himself as a gentleman in the community. When Lady Lyndon attempted to protest, he complained of her ill temper; if she pleaded for affection, he called her a nag. The abuse he showered upon her was reflected in the way he used her son, Lord Bullingdon, who, unlike his mother, did not submit meekly to Barry's malice.

The birth of Bryan Lyndon added to Barry's problems. Since the estate was entailed upon Lord Bullingdon, young Bryan would have no rights of inheritance to Lady Lyndon's property. To provide for his son, Barry sold some of the timber on the estates, over the protests of Lord Bullingdon's guardian. Barry gave the money so obtained to his mother, who used it to repurchase the old Barry lands, which Barry intended to bequeath to his son. Barry himself was actively despised in the community, but through foul means and cajolery he won a seat in Parliament and used his victory to triumph over his enemies.

Barry made no attempt to disguise his contempt and disgust for his wife, who under his profligacy had become petulant. When she rebelled against his conduct, he threatened to remove Bryan from her; she was subdued many times in this manner. Little Bryan was completely spoiled by his father's indulgence. Barry contrived also to rid himself of his stepson, who finally obliged him by running off to America to fight against the rebels. Barry's enemies used Lord Bullingdon's flight to slander the Irish upstart, and the young man's legal guardians continued their efforts to curb the wasteful dissipation of Lady Lyndon's wealth, which was dwindling under Barry's administration. In the end Barry's unpopularity caused him to lose his seat in Parliament.

Heavily in debt, he retired to Castle Lyndon. When Lord Bullingdon was reported killed in America, young Bryan became heir to the estates. Soon afterward the boy died when thrown from his horse. His death caused Lady Lyndon such anguish that a report spread that she was mad. Barry and his mother, now the mistress of Castle Lyndon, treated Lady Lyndon shabbily. Keeping her virtually a prisoner, spying on her every move, and denying her intercourse with her friends, they did almost drive her mad. Under the necessity of signing some papers, she tricked Barry into taking her to London. There he was trapped by Lord George Poynings, Lady Lyndon's former suitor, and her indignant relatives, gathered to free the unhappy woman from his custody.

Offered the alternative of going to jail as a swindler or of leaving the country with an annuity of three hundred pounds, he chose the latter. Later he returned secretly to England and nearly succeeded in winning back his weak-willed wife. His attempt was foiled, however, by Lord Bullingdon, who reappeared suddenly after he had been reported dead. Barry was thrown into the Fleet Prison, where, suffering from delirium tremens, he died.

Critical Evaluation

Published three years before *Vanity Fair, The Luck of Barry Lyndon: A Romance of the Last Century,* as it was titled in serial presentation, is a minor masterpiece of classic comedy, embodying many of the same concerns with sham, materialistic values, and egoism found in Thackeray's later major novel. The twentieth century reader will recognize the anti-hero type as many of Thackeray's contemporaries did not. For Barry, the appealing rogue, is true to his own code and values, reprehensible as they might seem. His autobiography, cast in the vehicle of adult remembrance of some forty years of his life, shows Thackeray's skillful handling of time and imaginative creation of picaresque episodes so that Barry may ingenuously, naïvely, and yet arrogantly, reveal his own vices and ambiguous virtues.

Readers who admit to an ambivalent delight in *Vanity Fair's* picara, Becky Sharp, will recognize the psychology of Barry, a man whose vigor, daring, and self-concern vividly emerge far beyond mere revelations of eighteenth century life. Thackeray is much more than a social historian. The three-part arrangement of the novel permits the reader to view Barry in adolescence and first love in Ireland, then abroad in English and Prussian military service, gambling in Europe, and the return to England in a marital conquest after his martial and monetary luck. In the tradition of Defoe, Smollett, and Fielding, Thackeray provides a picaro who can reveal the tawdriness of empire and gaming as well as reflect on the kinds of truths by which all people deceive themselves. Readers of Hardy's *Tess of the d'Urbervilles* recognize Barry's longing for place and position—for his rightful aristocratic heritage—distorted though such longing may be, along with his ruthless manipulation of others, especially women, to gain his goal.

In *Barry Lyndon,* Thackeray provides a deftly compressed, imaginative re-creation of a past age. But ultimately what gives the "romance" far more substance than that offered by the usual historical novel is the skillfully sustained self-revelation of a man true to false values.

Bibliography

Anisman, Martin J. "Introduction," in *The Luck of Barry Lyndon.* New York: New York University Press, 1970.

Colby, Robert A. "*Barry Lyndon* and the Irish Hero," in *Nineteenth-Century Fiction.* XXI (1966), pp. 109–130.

Dodds, John Wendell. *Thackeray: A Critical Portrait.* New York: Oxford University Press, 1941, pp. 72–75.

Greig, John Young. *Thackeray: A Reconsideration.* London: Oxford University Press, 1950, pp. 41–43.

McMaster, Juliet. *Thackeray: The Major Novels.* Toronto: University of Toronto Press, 1971, pp. 187–191.

Matthews, James Brander. *The Historical Novel, and Other Essays.* New York: Scribner's, 1901, pp. 152–162.

Ray, Gordon N. *Thackeray: The Uses of Adversity, 1811–1846.* New York: McGraw-Hill, 1955, pp. 339–347.

Saintsbury, George. *A Consideration of Thackeray.* New York: Russell and

Russell, 1968, pp. 93–97.

Tillotson, Geoffrey. *Thackeray the Novelist.* Cambridge: Cambridge University Press, 1954, pp. 212–215.

Wheatley, James H. *Patterns in Thackeray's Fiction.* Cambridge: Massachusetts Institute of Technology, 1969, pp. 49–53.

Whibley, Charles. *William Makepeace Thackeray.* New York: Dodd, 1903, pp. 62–76.

HENRY ESMOND

Type of work: Novel
Author: William Makepeace Thackeray (1811–1863)
Type of plot: Historical romance
Time of plot: Late seventeenth, early eighteenth centuries
Locale: England and the Low Countries
First published: 1852

One of the great English historical novels, Henry Esmond *is notable both for its accurate reproduction of the speech, manners, traditions, and historical events of late 1600's and early 1700's, and for its fascinating characterizations, especially that of the bewitching coquette, Beatrix. Thackeray was inspired by his low regard for the average historian of his day to write this novel, which he intended as a model of how history ought to be presented. He continued the story of Henry's descendants in America in another novel,* The Virginians.

Principal Characters

Henry Esmond, an orphan believed to be the illegitimate son of the late Thomas Esmond, Lord Castlewood. He is seen first as a grave, observant boy and later as an intelligent, level-headed young man. The novel, though narrated in the third person, takes the form of his memoirs, beginning when he is twelve years old and continuing until his early manhood and marriage. A lonely boy under the guardianship of his kinsman, Francis Esmond, Viscount Castlewood, Henry spends his adolescence at the Castlewood estate. The untimely death of Viscount Castlewood, fatally wounded in a duel, leads to Henry's discovery that he is the true heir to the Castlewood title. This secret he continues to keep out of affection for his kinsman's widow and her children. For years he believes himself in love with his beautiful cousin, Beatrix Esmond, and for her sake he becomes involved in a Jacobite plot to secure the English throne for James, the young Stuart Pretender, at the time of Queen Anne's death. When events prove that he has been deceived in both Beatrix and the Stuart exile, he realizes that the real object of his affection is Rachel Esmond,

the youthful mother of Beatrix. With her he emigrates to America, leaving her son Frank in possession of the title and the Castlewood estate.

Francis Esmond, Viscount Castlewood, a hard-living, pleasure-seeking nobleman, the amiable, though hardly devoted, guardian of young Henry Esmond. Having aided in concealing the secret of Henry's birth, he repents the injustice done the boy and on his deathbed reveals that Henry is the true heir to the Castlewood title.

Rachel Esmond, the Viscount's much younger wife, a quiet, attractive woman whose loyalty to her husband never fails, even when he begins to neglect her for drinking and gambling with his reckless, pleasure-loving London friends. Her chief fault, a tendency to possessiveness, is displayed first toward the Viscount and later toward Henry Esmond, whom she marries after the plot to put James Stuart on the throne of England has failed.

Beatrix Esmond, the beautiful and lively daughter of Francis and Rachel Castlewood. As fickle and unstable as she is fascinating, lovely but ambitious and scheming, she accepts Henry Esmond's attentions when no more suitable admirer is at hand. Her affair with James, the Stuart Pretender, finally reveals to Henry her true nature.

Frank Esmond, the sturdy, unimaginative younger brother of Beatrix Esmond. He is, by virtue of Henry Esmond's sacrifice, the eventual successor to the lands and title wrongly held by his father, the former Viscount.

Father Holt, Henry Esmond's tutor in boyhood. The priest secretly acts as a Jacobite spy, helping to prepare the way for the return of the Stuart Pretender.

Lord Mohun, a London rake with designs on Rachel Esmond. He kills her husband in a duel.

The Duke of Hamilton, an impetuous young nobleman engaged to marry Beatrix Esmond. He is killed in a duel in which he fatally wounds Lord Mohun.

The Duke of Marlborough, the famous military commander-in-chief. During his campaigns of 1702-1704 Henry Esmond sees service as a soldier in France and Spain.

General John Webb, the officer to whom Henry Esmond serves as aide-de-camp. Webb becomes involved in a bitter controversy with the Duke of Marlborough.

Richard Steele, an early friend of Henry Esmond. Steele is presented as a henpecked husband and lovable scapegrace; his status as a literary man is only lightly accented.

Joseph Addison, a leading Whig of the period as well as a prominent man of letters.

The Story

Henry Esmond grew up at Castlewood. He knew there was some mystery about his birth and he dimly remembered that long ago he had lived with weavers who spoke a foreign tongue. Thomas Esmond, Viscount Castlewood, had brought him to England and turned him over to Father Holt, the chaplain, to be educated. That much he learned as he grew older.

All was not peace and quiet at Castlewood in those years, when his lordship and Father Holt were engaged in a plot for the restoration of the exiled Stuart king, James II. When James attempted to recover Ireland for the Stuarts, Thomas Esmond rode off to his death at the battle of the Boyne. His widow fled to her dower house at Chelsea. Father Holt disappeared. Henry, a large-eyed, grave-faced twelve-year-old boy, was left alone with servants in the gloomy old house.

There his new guardians and distant cousins, Francis and Rachel Esmond, found him when they arrived to take possession of Castlewood. The new Viscount Castlewood, a bluff, loud-voiced man, greeted the boy kindly enough. His wife was like a girl herself—she was only eight years older than Henry—and Henry thought her the loveliest lady he had ever seen. With them were a little daughter, Beatrix, and a son, Frank, a baby in arms.

As Henry grew older he became more and more concerned over the rift he saw coming between Rachel Esmond and her husband, both of whom he loved because they had treated him as one of the immediate family in the household at Castlewood. It was plain that the hard-drinking, hard-gambling nobleman was wearying of his quiet country life. After Rachel's face was disfigured by smallpox, her altered beauty caused her husband to neglect her even more. Young Beatrix also felt that relations between her parents were strained.

When Henry was old enough, he went to Cambridge, sent there on money left Rachel by a deceased relative. Later, when he returned to Castlewood on a vacation, he realized for the first time that Beatrix was exceptionally attractive. Apparently he had never really noticed her before. Rachel, for her part, had great regard for her young kinsman. Before his arrival from Cambridge, according to Beatrix, Rachel went to Henry's room ten times to see that it was ready.

Relations between Rachel and the viscount were all but severed when the notorious Lord Mohun visited Castlewood. Rachel knew her husband had been losing heavily to Mohun at cards, but when she spoke to the viscount about the bad company he was keeping, he flew into a rage. He was by no means calmed when Beatrix innocently blurted out to her father, in the company of Mohun, that that gentleman was interested in Rachel. Jealous of another man's attentions to the wife he himself neglected, the viscount determined to seek satisfaction in a duel.

The two men fought in London, where the viscount had gone on the pretext of seeing a doctor. Henry, who suspected the real reason for the trip, went along, for he hoped to engage Mohun in a fight and thus save the life of his beloved guardian. The viscount, however, was in no mood to be cheated out of an excuse to provoke a quarrel. He was heavily in debt to Mohun and thought a fight was the only honorable way out of his difficulties. Moreover, he knew Mohun had written letters to Rachel, although, as the villain explained, she had never answered them. They fought, and Mohun foully and fatally wounded the viscount. On his deathbed the viscount confessed to his young kinsman that Henry was not an illegitimate child, but the son of Thomas, Lord Castlewood, by an early marriage, and the true heir to the Castlewood title. Henry Esmond generously burned the dying man's confession and resolved never to divulge the secret.

For his part in the duel Henry Esmond was sent to prison. When Rachel visited Henry in prison, she was enraged because he had not stopped the duel and because he had allowed Mohun to go unpunished. She rebuked Henry and forbade him to return to Castlewood. When Henry left prison he decided to join the army. For that purpose he visited the old dowager viscountess, his stepmother, who bought him a commission.

Henry's military ventures were highly successful, and won for him his share of wounds and glory. He fought in the campaign of the Duke of Marlborough against Spain and France in 1702 and in the campaign of Blenheim in 1704. Between the two campaigns he returned to Castlewood, where he was reconciled with Rachel. There he saw Frank, now Lord Castlewood, and Beatrix, who was cordial toward him. Rachel herself cautioned Henry that Beatrix was selfish and temperamental and would make no man happy who loved her.

After the campaign of 1704 Henry returned to his cousins, who were living in London. To Henry, Beatrix was more beautiful than ever and even more the coquette. But he found himself unable to make up his mind whether he loved her or Rachel. Later, during the campaign of 1706, he learned from Frank that the ravishing Beatrix was engaged to an earl. The news put Henry in low spirits because he now felt she would never marry a poor captain like himself.

Henry's affairs of the heart were put temporarily into the backgrond when he came upon Father Holt in Brussels. The priest told Henry that while on an expedition in the Low Countries, Thomas Esmond, his father, had seduced the young woman who was Henry's mother. A few weeks before his child was born Thomas Esmond was injured in a duel. Thinking he would die, he married the woman so that her child would be born with an untainted name. But Thomas Esmond did not die, and when he recovered from his wounds he deserted his wife and married a distant kinswoman, the dowager viscountess, Henry's stepmother.

When Henry returned to Castlewood, Rachel informed him she had learned his secret from the old viscountess and consequently knew that he, not Frank, was the true heir. For the second time Henry refused to accept the title belonging to him.

Beatrix's interest in Henry grew after she became engaged to the Duke of Hamilton and learned that Henry was not illegitimate in birth but the bearer of a title her brother was using. Henry wanted to give Beatrix a diamond necklace for a wedding present, but the duke would not permit his fiancée to receive a gift from one of illegitimate birth. Rachel came to the young man's defense and declared before the duke, her daughter, and Henry the secret of his birth and title. Later the duke was killed in a duel with Lord Mohun, who also met his death at the same time. The killing of Rachel's husband was avenged.

The Duke of Hamilton's death gave Henry one more chance to win Beatrix's heart. He threw himself into a plot to put the young Stuart pretender on the throne when old Queen Anne died. To this end he went to France and helped to smuggle into England the young chevalier whom the Jacobites called James III, the king over the water. The two came secretly to the Castlewood home in London, the prince passing as Frank, the young viscount, and there the royal exile saw and fell in love with Beatrix.

Fearing the results of this infatuation, Lady Castlewood and Henry sent Beatrix against her will to Castlewood. When a report that the queen was dying swept through London, the prince was nowhere to be found. Henry and Frank made a night ride to Castlewood. Finding the pretender there, in the room used by Father Holt in the old days, they renounced him and the Jacobite cause. Henry realized his love for Beatrix was dead at last. He felt no regrets for her or for the prince as he rode back to London and heard the heralds proclaiming George I, the new king.

The prince made his way secretly back to France, where Beatrix joined him in his exile. At last Henry felt free to declare himself to Rachel, who had grown very dear to him. Leaving Frank in possession of the title and the Castlewood estates, Henry and his wife went to America. In Virginia he and Rachel built a new Castlewood, reared a family, and found happiness in their old age.

Critical Evaluation

Critical reaction to *Henry Esmond* is as varied as reader reaction to the characters themselves. What Thackeray attempted to do was to offset contemporary charges of his "diffusiveness" by providing a well-integrated novel, sacrificing profitable serial publication to do so. He concluded that *Henry Esmond* was "the very best" he could do. Many critics have agreed with him. Others, however, remain loyal to the panoramic social vision and ironic authorial commentary of the earlier *Vanity Fair*. What makes evaluation of *Henry Esmond* so variable?

Short of a full history of cycles and fashions in fiction, certain features may illustrate the problems. First is the narrative point of view. Thackeray cast *Henry Esmond* in the form of a reminiscential memoir—an old man recounts his earlier life, describing it from the vantage point of a later time and distancing it further with third-person narration. The occasional use of "I" suggests the involved narrator, either at emotional highpoints or moments of personal reflection. The distancing in time is increased by Esmond's daughter's Preface, wherein Rachel Esmond Warrington not only "completes" certain details of the plot but also suggests the ambiguities in characterization of her own mother, Rachel, and of her stepsister, Beatrix. Readers of Henry James may react favorably to this early use of a central intelligence whose point of view, limited not omniscient, can suggest the disparities between appearance and reality. They may also welcome the shifting interpretations readers themselves can form of the "reliability" of the narrator. Is Esmond providing a framework within which to reveal only the exemplary, vindicating himself consciously, or is he recollecting as honestly as the self can permit, with the reader knowing more than he at many points?

Another point of contention involves the historical setting of the novel, which purports to be a historical romance. Thackeray casts the novel in the early eighteenth century and attempts to catch the flavor of the Augustan Age, its military conflicts, its waverings between Church of England and Catholicism, and the problems of its monarchs, William, Queen Anne, George II, and the Stuart Pretender. Most readers laud Thackeray's adept handling of the technical problem of suggesting the language and manners of that earlier time without lapsing into linguistic archness or sending readers to glossaries. It is, then, praised by many as a polished example of the historical romance and relished as many relish Scott or Stevenson—for its adventure and its depiction of society, at least those levels that Thackeray chooses to treat. For as with *Vanity Fair,* he is less concerned with portrayal of the lackeys than of the masters, primarily the newly arrived and still aspiring scions of society. Their foibles were his special target.

Yet for others the novel's fascination lies in its domestic realism. Commentators find much to explore in the rendering of the marriage conventions. Lord and Lady Castlewood, new heirs to Castlewood, befriend the supposedly illegitimate Henry Esmond and gradually reveal the strained bonds which hold their marriage together. Esmond, as narrator, takes sides with Rachel, seeing the husband as carousing, unfaithful, not too intelligent. Readers, however, can also realize, despite the analysis of "domestic tyranny," that Rachel's purity and coldness might lead the husband not only to drink but to other fleshly delights. Devoted Henry Esmond may lament the waste of such a fine woman, but the reader perceives in the dramatic scenes that Rachel, who began by worshiping her husband, is also quite capable of both restrictive possessiveness and emotional repression.

Historical romance, novel of domestic manners—*Henry Esmond* also illustrates a favorite nineteenth century form, the *bildüngsroman,* or novel of development and education, which is also represented in such popular contemporary examples as *David Copperfield* and *Great Expectations.* Henry Esmond remembers his childhood vaguely, a time spent with poor weavers, a foreign language. Brought to Castlewood, he is treated with favor by Lord Castlewood but kept in place as a page. It is only with the death of Lord Castlewood that Henry receives any emotional response, this from the new heirs—and most especially from Rachel, Lady Castlewood. Thackeray carefully distances Esmond to be eight years younger than Rachel and eight years older than her daughter Beatrix. Esmond's growth is the principal subject but readers are also aware of the young son Frank and of Beatrix, both children who are alternately spoiled and then emotionally isolated from Rachel. The much sought after but "loveless" Beatrix reveals how isolated she was made to feel by the possessive nets her mother cast over the father and then over the seemingly favored brother. Momentarily consoling Esmond, Beatrix shows the motivation for her romantic conquests so that readers understand her complexity and ambivalence though Esmond may choose not to do so.

As Esmond progresses through Cambridge, through imprisonment following a duel fatal to Lord Castlewood, through military campaigns, through the loss of one idol after another and on to a slow knowledge of the way of the world, the reader watches for his "present" age to come closer to his recollected past. The reader watches for his insight to develop, for memory and maturity to coincide. Whether or not Esmond achieves that wholeness is yet another point for critics and readers to ponder.

Esmond has virtuously denied himself his birthright as legitimate heir to Castlewood so that young Frank may assume the title and Rachel and Beatrix can stay ensconced in society, but some might think Henry revels in the self-sacrifice. He has also chosen to believe that Beatrix will admire him for military daring and political plotting. Thus when the Stuart Pretender misses a chance for the throne in order to secure an amorous chance with Beatrix, Esmond loses two idols at once. "Good" Henry Esmond is settled at the end of the novel on a Virginia plantation in the New World, his marriage to the widowed Rachel compressed into two pages. All ends happily, except for those strange overtones and even stranger suggestions in the Preface by the daughter of this autumnal marriage. She reminds us that Esmond was writing for a family audience, that his role had been carefully established, and that she, Rachel Esmond Warrington, like Beatrix, had also suffered from her mother's possessiveness and jealousy.

Ultimately, then, what the modern reader may enjoy most is the psychological penetration into love bonds which Thackeray provides through the "unreliable" narrator. Dramatic irony permits the reader more knowledge than Esmond permits himself. And as readers circle back in their own memories to the daughter's Preface, the whole range of interrelationships and the ambivalences of human affairs unfold. The characters, in short, remain fascinating puzzles long after the historical details fade. Emotional life, the subtleties of rejection and acceptance, time rendered both precisely and in psychological duration—these are the elements which will continue to tantalize readers of *Henry Esmond*.

Bibliography

Brogan, Howard O. "Rachel Esmond and the Dilemma of the Victorian Ideal of Womanhood," in *Journal of English Literary History*. XIII (1946), pp. 223–232.

Brown, John Macmillan. *Esmond, A Study*. Christchurch, New Zealand: Whitcome and Tombs, 1904.

Dodds, John Wendell. *Thackeray: A Critical Portrait*. New York: Oxford University Press, 1941, pp. 160–178.

Donovan, Robert A. *The Shaping Vision: Imagination in the English Novel from Defoe to Dickens*. Ithaca, N.Y.: Cornell University Press, 1966, pp. 193–205.

Edgar, Pelham. *The Art of the Novel From 1700 to the Present Time*. New York: Macmillan, 1933, pp. 109–116.

Ennis, Lambert. *Thackeray: The Sentimental Cynic*. Evanston, Ill.: Northwestern University Press, 1950, pp. 176–182.

Fleishman, Avrom. *The English Historical Novel: Walter Scott to Virginia Woolf*. Baltimore: Johns Hopkins University Press, 1971, pp. 127–148.

Greig, John Young. *Thackeray: A Reconsideration.* London: Oxford University Press, 1950, pp. 154–166.

Harden, Edgar F. "Esmond and the Search for Self," in *Yearbook of English Studies.* III (1973), pp. 181–195.

Hardy, Barbara N. *The Exposure of Luxury: Radical Themes in Thackeray.* London: Owen, 1972.

————. "Memory and Memories," in *Tellers and Listeners: The Narrative Imagination.* London: Athlone, 1975, pp. 56–101.

Iser, Wolfgang. *The Implied Reader: Patterns of Communication in Prose Fiction from Bunyan to Beckett.* Baltimore: Johns Hopkins University Press, 1974, pp. 123–135.

Lukács, Georg. *The Historical Novel.* London: Merlin Press, 1962, pp. 201–206. Reprinted in *Thackeray: A Collection of Critical Essays.* Edited by Alexander Welsh. Englewood Cliffs, N.J.: Prentice-Hall, 1968, pp. 121–126.

McMaster, Juliet. *Thackeray: The Major Novels.* Toronto: University of Toronto Press, 1971, pp. 87–125, 204–207.

Rawlins, Jack P. *Thackeray's Novels: A Fiction That Is True.* Berkeley: University of California Press, 1974, pp. 187–233.

Ray, Gordon N. *Thackeray: The Age of Wisdom, 1847–1863.* New York: McGraw-Hill, 1958, pp. 175–194.

Saintsbury, George. *A Consideration of Thackeray.* New York: Russell and Russell, 1968, pp. 192–200.

Tilford, John E., Jr. "The Love Theme of *Henry Esmond*," in *PMLA.* LXVII (September, 1952), pp. 684–701. Reprinted in *Thackeray: A Collection of Critical Essays.* Edited by Alexander Welsh. Englewood Cliffs, N.J.: Prentice-Hall, 1968, pp. 127–146.

————. "The Unsavoury Plot of *Henry Esmond*," in *Nineteenth-Century Fiction.* XII (September, 1957), pp. 148–153.

————. "The Untimely Death of Rachel Esmond," in *Nineteenth-Century Fiction.* XII (1957), pp. 148–153.

Wheatley, James H. *Patterns in Thackeray's Fiction.* Cambridge: Massachusetts Institute of Technology, 1969, pp. 106–109.

Whibley, Charles. *William Makepeace Thackeray.* New York: Dodd, 1903, pp. 180–193.

Williams, Ioan. *The Realist Novel in England: A Study in Development.* London: Macmillan, 1974, pp. 156–168.

Worth, George J. "The Unity of *Henry Esmond*," in *Nineteenth-Century Fiction.* XV (March, 1961), pp. 345–353.

THE NEWCOMES

Type of work: Novel
Author: William Makepeace Thackeray (1811–1863)
Type of plot: Social criticism
Time of plot: Early nineteenth century
Locale: England
First published: 1853–1855

The Newcomes *is a family chronicle in which Thackeray demonstrates the evil effects of such nineteenth century social conventions as parental marriage choices, the over-indulgence in the accumulation of wealth, and the worldliness of the upper classes. Many consider Colonel Newcome to be Thackeray's most perfect fictional gentlemen, and the notion of the true gentleman is central to the ideals of social behavior Thackeray is attempting to illustrate.*

Principal Characters

Colonel Thomas Newcome, the son of Thomas Newcome, Esq., and his first wife Susan. Always rebellious as a boy, he left home and went to India, where he distinguished himself in the Bengal Cavalry and in service with the East India Company. During his career he married and fathered a son, Clive. When Mrs. Newcome died, the small boy was sent to England to be educated. Later, after he had acquired a considerable fortune, Colonel Newcome returned to England to rejoin his son. Their fortunes prospered, and the father tried to give his son a happy life. Honest, naïve, tenderhearted, he acts always for the best, but his affairs turn out badly. Eventually his fortune is dissipated by the failure of the great Bundlecund Banking Company in which he has invested his money, his daughter-in-law's, and funds some friends had entrusted to him. He spends his last days in poverty and at the mercy of a domineering old widow, the mother of his daughter-in-law. Always mindful of his son's happiness, the Colonel tries for years to guide Clive's life, but he succeeds only in involving the young man with the wrong wife and settling him in a business career which he does not en-

joy. At the time of his death the Colonel is a pensioner in the Hospital of Grey Friars.

Clive Newcome, the Colonel's son, a young man with considerable artistic ability. His charming manner endears him to a great many friends, including his cousin, Ethel Newcome, but because Clive is not of noble birth her mother and grandmother do not approve of the match. Clive marries another young woman whom his father cherishes, but the union is a failure because a domineering mother-in-law presides over the Newcome household. Clive changes from the carefree boy that he once was to a bitter young man estranged for a time from his devoted father, whom he blames for much of his misery. At the end of the story Clive is a widower with a small son; the reader is left with the impression that he will marry Ethel Newcome.

Ethel Newcome, the beautiful, spirited daughter of Colonel Newcome's half brother Brian. Her mother, Lady Ann Newcome, is descended from an aristocratic family, and it is the hope of her grandmother, Lady Kew, that Ethel will marry well. Ethel is especially fond of Colonel Newcome. She is also attracted to Clive, but the energy of her grandmother in pushing her into society blinds her to her cousin's attentions. Haughty and high-spirited, Ethel rejects several offers of marriage and ends up taking charge of the children of her selfish, brutal brother Barnes. Estranged from the Colonel and Clive because she has belittled her cousin's intentions, she develops into a serious, self-sacrificing spinster; but at the end of the story she turns over a part of the Newcome fortune to her uncle and cousin, and the reader is left anticipating her subsequent marriage to Clive.

James Binnie, Colonel Newcome's friend in the Indian service, a man of great humor, good sense, and intelligence. He, his widowed sister, Mrs. Mackenzie, and her daughter Rosa live with the Colonel and Clive. He leaves his fortune to his niece when he dies; this is some of the money that the Colonel invests in the Bundlecund Banking Company. Fortunately, Binnie dies before his friend goes bankrupt and his sister turns into a shrew.

Rosa Newcome, called **Rosey,** the daughter of Mrs. Mackenzie, a shy, pretty girl when she and her mother come to live with the Newcomes and her uncle, James Binnie. Always anxious to please, Rosey has no life of her own, for she is completely overwhelmed by her domineering mother. Never truly in love with Clive because she lacks the maturity capable of a woman's love for her husband, she turns more and more against him after their marriage. She dies in childbirth without having known any real happiness.

Mrs. Mackenzie, called the **Campaigner,** the widowed sister of James Binnie and a vigorous, good-humored, but domineering person at the beginning of the story. She is particularly possessive of her daughter Rosey, who marries Clive Newcome. After their money has been lost through Colonel Newcome's unwise investments, she turns into a termagant and a domestic terror. She torments the Colonel because of his misfortunes, becomes more and more possessive of Rosey, and makes life miserable for Clive.

Thomas Newcome, Esq., the father of Thomas, Brian, and Hobson Newcome, a poor man who, through industry and thrift, created a prosperous banking establishment. Truly in love with his first wife, who dies soon after the birth of their son Thomas, he marries a second time but is never really happy thereafter.

Susan Newcome, the first wife of Thomas Newcome, Esq. She is pretty but penniless, and she dies young, in childbirth.

Sophia Althea Newcome, the stepmother of young Thomas Newcome and mother of the twins, Brian and Hobson. An efficient businesswoman, she influences her husband in his banking business. Rigid and domineering, she never cares for her stepson and is happy when he goes off to India. Before her death, however, she requests that he inherit some of her money; this is the sum that Ethel Newcome turns over to Colonel Newcome and her cousin Clive.

Sir Brian Newcome, the half brother of Colonel Newcome and the twin of Hobson. He is a neat, bland, smiling banker whose external appearance masks his selfish, ambitious nature. Never fully aware of his half brother's virtues, Brian does not entertain him until after he learns of the Colonel's wealth after his return to England.

Lady Ann Newcome, Sir Brian's wife, the daughter of haughty old Lady Kew. Pleasant but rather flighty, she entertains a more aristocratic set than does her sister-in-law, Mrs. Hobson Newcome. She is kind to Colonel Newcome and Clive, though she cannot approve the idea of the young man's marriage to her daughter Ethel.

Hobson Newcome, Sir Brian's twin brother, a portly, red-whiskered country squire. Never really comfortable with his wife's intellectual and artistic friends, he tolerates them as long as they do not interfere with his agricultural pursuits.

Mrs. Hobson Newcome, a fat, pretty woman fond of artistic people. She never fails to hint that this interest makes her superior to her sister-in-law, of whom she is jealous. She has affection for Clive and believes that she deals generously and gracefully with Colonel Newcome.

Barnes Newcome, Sir Brian's oldest son, a hypocritical dandy who conceives a great dislike for Colonel Newcome and his cousin Clive. The father of two children by one of the village girls, he marries Lady Clara Pulleyn. Their marriage is a dreadful one because he tortures his wife mentally and treats their children abominably. Finally Lady Clara leaves him and Ethel Newcome cares for the abandoned children. Barnes stands against his uncle in an election and loses to him, but Colonel Newcome's bankruptcy prevents his serving in Parliament.

Lady Clara Pulleyn, later Barnes Newcome's wife, a pretty, sad girl whose marriage was arranged by her parents. She leads a miserable life, even after she has been divorced from her brutal husband and has married Jack Belsize; there is always the shadow of her former life between them.

The Hon. Charles Belsize, called Jack Belsize by his friends, later **Lord Highgate,** in love with Lady Clara Pulleyn. On one occasion, in Switzerland, he creates a scandalous scene because of his jealousy of Barnes Newcome. Lady Clara flees to him when she deserts her husband, and after her divorce they are married.

Lord Kew, called Frank, Ethel Newcome's cousin and Jack Belsize's good friend, an open-hearted, honorable young man who sincerely loves Ethel. She refuses his suit after the scandal of her brother's family life and divorce is made public.

Lady Kew, Lady Ann Newcome's aristocratic mother. Insulting and overbearing, she runs the affairs of her family and arranges their marriages.

Lady Julia, Lady Kew's older daughter, completely dependent on her mother and forced to take the fierce old woman's abuse.

Lady Walham, Lord Kew's mother, a long-suffering victim of her mother-in-law's domineering ways.

George Barnes, Lord Kew's younger brother.

Lady Henrietta Pulleyn, Lady Clara's sister. She marries Lord Kew after Ethel Newcome has rejected him.

Sarah Mason, Susan Newcome's housekeeper and companion, never forgotten by Colonel Newcome. He supports her throughout most of her life and tries to do so even after he has gone bankrupt.

Martha Honeyman, Clive Newcome's aunt and his guardian during his boyhood in England, a soft-spoken woman who dearly loves her charge. Thrifty and careful, she is constantly alarmed by the spendthrift ways of Charles, her clergyman brother.

Charles Honeyman, Martha's clergyman brother and Colonel Newcome's brother-in-law. Fond of gambling and the wine bottle, he wastes much of the money that the Colonel gives him. Later he goes to India and becomes a popular clergyman there. Though appearing humble and meek in manner, he is actually cunning and selfish.

Mr. Ridley, Charles Honeyman's landlord.

Mrs. Ridley, his wife, a good woman who befriends Colonel Newcome.

John James Ridley, called J. J., their son and Clive Newcome's good friend. A talented boy, he becomes a successful artist and is elected to the Royal Academy. When Clive is in financial difficulties, J. J. buys several of his friend's paintings.

Arthur Pendennis, Clive Newcome's friend and an editor of the "Pall Mall Gazette." He narrates the story of the Newcomes, and he and his wife are always ready to help Colonel Newcome and Clive in their troubles.

Laura Pendennis, his wife. She becomes fond of Ethel Newcome and tries to promote the affair between Clive and his cousin. Never able to tolerate Rosey Newcome, Laura is not surprised when Clive's marriage proves unhappy.

Larkins, the Pendennises' servant.

George Warrington, co-editor of the "Pall Mall Gazette" and a friend of Clive Newcome and Arthur Pendennis.

The Marquis of Farintosh, a gossipy, fashionable young man whom Lady Kew selects as an eligible suitor for Ethel Newcome's hand. Ethel rejects his offer.

Lady Glenlivat, Lord Farintosh's mother.

Todhunter and
Henchman, toadies to Lord Farintosh.

The Duc d'Ivry, a sixty-year-old French nobleman.

Madame la Duchesse d'Ivry, his wife, much younger than her husband; a poetess and a patroness of the arts. She is responsible for a duel between Lord Kew and hot-tempered Monsieur de Castillones.

Antoinette, their daughter.

Monsieur de Castillones, Lord Kew's rival for the favors of the Duchesse d'Ivry. He wounds Lord Kew, but not fatally, in a duel.

The Comte de Florac, later the Duc d'Ivry, a French aristocrat of ancient lineage and a gentleman of the old school.

Madame de Florac, his wife, for many years secretly in love with Colonel Newcome.

Vicomte Paul de Florac, also the Prince de Montcontour, their son, an exuberant young Frenchman, a friend of Clive Newcome and Lord Kew.

Madame la Princesse de Montcontour, nee Higgs, of Manchester, Paul de Florac's English wife, a good-hearted, garrulous woman of wealth and ungrammatical speech.

Miss Cann, an artist, a tenant of the Ridleys and a friend of Clive Newcome and J. J. Ridley.

Fred Bayham, another tenant of the Ridley's, a boisterous old school friend of Charles Honeyman, whom he loves to bait. He is a favorite among the poor people of Newcome when he campaigns for the election of Colonel Newcome to Parliament.

Mr. Gandish, an artist, the head of the art school where Clive Newcome and J. J. Ridley study.

Charles Gandish, his son.

Mrs. Irons, the housekeeper of Colonel Newcome and James Binnie. Jealous of Mrs. Mackenzie, she does not get along with that domineering woman.

Mr. Sherrick, a wine merchant and a friend of the Honeymans. Because he had invested money in the Bundlecund Banking Company, he is one of those whom Colonel Newcome feels he must repay.

Mrs. Sherrick, his wife, a former opera singer.

Miss Sherrick, their daughter.

Rowland and
Oliver, the lawyers in the divorce suit of Lady Clara and Barnes Newcome.

Horace Fogey,

Sir Thomas de Boots, and
Charles Heavyside, friends of Barnes
Newcome and members of the fashionable London club of which he is a member.

John Giles, Esq., the brother-in-law of
Mrs. Hobson Newcome, a poor relation.

Louisa Giles, his wife.

Mademoiselle Lebrun, the French governess to the children of the Hobson
Newcomes.

Hannah Hicks, Martha Honeyman's devoted servant, who assists her mistress
in the operation of a seaside lodging
house.

Sally, another servant in the Honeyman

lodging house, a pretty girl but not efficient.

Captain Gobey, a friend whom Colonel
Newcome, James Binnie, and the Mackenzies meet on the Continent.

Captain Hobey, another friend from the
Continent, a suitor of Rosey Mackenzie.

Tom Potts, a hatter in Newcome and
editor of the local paper; he hates Barnes
Newcome.

Dr. Quackenboss, a society doctor who
attends Rosey Newcome.

Miss O'Grady, the governess of the
daughter of the Duc and Duchesse
d'Ivry.

The Story

Colonel Thomas Newcome's late wife had a sister and a brother. The sister,
Miss Honeyman, ran a boarding-house in Brighton, where little Alfred and Ethel
came with their mother, Lady Ann, for a vacation. There Colonel Newcome and
Clive had also arrived for a visit. Mr. Honeyman lived in another house in
Brighton, where the keeper's young son, John James Ridley, delighted in drawing
pictures from the story-books which he found in Mr. Honeyman's room. While
Clive, who aspired to be an artist, delighted in Ridley's drawings, Ethel became
extremely fond of the colonel and his unaffected mannerisms. The colonel's great
love for children caused him to be a favorite with all the Newcome youngsters,
but it was fair-haired little Ethel who won the colonel's heart with her simple,
adoring ways and her sincerity.

Colonel Newcome bought a house in London, where he lived with Clive and
Mr. James Binnie, the colonel's friend. Clive was given a tutor, but the young
man neglected his studies to sketch everything he saw and everyone he knew. If
the colonel was disappointed by Clive's choice of career, he said nothing, but
allowed Clive to attend art school with his friend Ridley. Clive was becoming a
kind, generous and considerate young man. The colonel himself was satisfied that
his son was growing up to be the fine man that the retired officer wished him to
be. He spent a great deal of money fitting up a well-lighted studio for Clive in a
house not far from his own. Meanwhile Mr. Binnie had taken a fall from a horse
and was laid up in bed. Binnie's widowed half-sister, Mrs. Mackenzie, and her
daughter, Rosey, came to stay with the bedridden Binnie in the colonel's house.

After a time the colonel found himself financially embarrassed. Realizing that
he could no longer live on his income in London, he planned to return to India

until he reached a higher grade in the army. Then with the increased pension he could afford to retire in London.

Ethel Newcome grew into a beautiful and charming young lady, and the colonel dreamed of a match between Ethel and Clive, but Lady Ann placed an early prohibition on such a match. She told her brother-in-law that Ethel had been promised to Lord Kew, a relative of Lady Kew, Lady Ann's mother. The other Newcomes thought that Rosey Mackenzie would be a fine wife for Clive.

After Colonel Newcome had returned to India, leaving Clive with a substantial income, Clive and Ridley, now a successful artist, went to Baden. There Clive met Ethel and the other Newcome children vacationing without the dampening presence of Lady Ann or her aristocratic mother. Ethel and Clive enjoyed a short period of companionship and innocent pleasure, and Clive fell in love with his beautiful cousin. When Lady Ann and Lady Kew arrived, Clive was warned that he must not press his suit with Ethel any longer, for Ethel must marry in her own station of life. Clive was reminded that the family had assumed him to have found in Miss Rosey Mackenzie a woman of his own social level. Bitterly Clive took his leave and went to Italy with Ridley.

Ethel, beginning to rebel against the little niche that had been assigned to her in society, defied social custom and defended Clive against the charges her brother Barnes repeatedly hurled at him. Finally she broke her engagement to young Lord Kew. When Clive learned of the broken betrothal, he returned to England to press his own suit once more.

In London Clive had little time for his art. He was fast becoming a favorite in London society, whose fashionable hostesses thought him the only son of a wealthy officer in India. Against the wishes of her grandmother, Lady Kew, Ethel arranged frequent meetings with Clive, and at last Clive proposed marriage. But Ethel sadly explained that she would not inherit Lady Kew's fortune unless she married properly. Ethel claimed that her younger brothers and sisters were in need of the money, for after her father's death Barnes Newcome had selfishly kept the family fortune for himself. Meanwhile Lady Kew was wooing Lord Farintosh for Ethel.

After three years' absence Colonel Newcome returned to London. During his absence the colonel had amassed a large fortune for his son, and armed with this wealth Colonel Newcome went to Barnes with a proposal of marriage between Ethel and Clive. Barnes was polite but non-committal. Shortly afterward Lady Kew announced Ethel's engagement to Lord Farintosh. Then, suddenly, Lady Kew died, leaving her immense fortune to Ethel, whose only concern was that the money should go to her younger brothers and sisters.

Barnes' marriage to Lady Clara Pulleyn had never been happy. Soon after they were married he had begun to mistreat his wife, who at last decided that she could no longer stand his bullying treatment. She ran off with her first lover, leaving her small children behind. The shock of the scandal and the subsequent divorce opened Ethel's eyes to dangers of loveless marriages. Realizing that she could never be happy with Lord Farintosh because she did not love him, she broke her second engagement.

Ethel retired from her former social life to rear Barnes' children. Clive, meanwhile, had succumbed to the wishes of Mr. Binnie and his own father. Before the news of Ethel's broken engagement with Lord Farintosh had reached the colonel and his son, Clive had married sweet-faced Rosey Mackenzie.

Clive's marriage was gentle but bare. The colonel was Rosey's chief protector and her greater admirer. Clive tried to be a good husband, but inwardly he longed for more companionship. Once he admitted to his father that he still loved Ethel.

The elder Thomas Newcome married his childhood sweetheart, who died after bearing him one son, named for his father. Thomas remarried, and his second wife bore two sons, Brian and Hobson. Young Thomas proved to be a trial to his stepmother. When he was old enough, he went to India where he later became a colonel. He married and had a son, Clive, whom he loved with a passion far beyond the normal devotion of a father. Having lost his mother, little Clive was sent to England to begin his education.

Brian and Hobson Newcome had inherited their mother's wealthy banking house. Brian married Lady Ann, who was well-known in London for her lavish parties. When little Clive had spent about seven years in England, his impatient father crossed the ocean to join him. He expected to receive a warm welcome from his two half-brothers, Brian and Hobson. Much to the colonel's bewilderment, the bankers received him politely but coldly and passed on the responsibility of entertaining him to young Barnes, Brian's son, a youthful London swell and a familiar figure at the city's clubs.

The colonel had been handling the family income very unwisely since his return from India. Shortly after the birth of Clive's son, Thomas, an Indian company in which the colonel had heavy investments failed, and he went bankrupt. Clive, Rosey, and Colonel Newcome were now nearly penniless. Rosey's mother, Mrs. Mackenzie, descended upon them, and in a few months she began ruling them with such tyranny that life became unbearable for the colonel. With the help of some friends he retired to a poorhouse and lived separated from his beloved son. Clive faithfully stayed with Rosey under the forceful abuse of his mother-in-law. He was able to make a meager living by selling his drawings.

When Ethel learned of the pitiful condition of the old colonel, whom she had always loved, and of Clive's distress, she contrived a plan whereby she was able to give them six thousand pounds without their knowing that it came from her. Rosey had been very ill. One night Ethel visited Clive, and Mrs. Mackenzie raised such an indignant clamor that Rosey was seriously affected. She died the following day. The colonel, broken in spirit, also grew weaker from day to day, and soon afterward he too died.

Clive had never lost his love for Ethel through all the years of his unfortunate marriage to Rosey. Many months after the death of his wife, he went once more to Baden with little Thomas. There it was said, by observers who knew the Newcomes, that Clive, Ethel, and little Tommy often were seen walking together through the woods.

Critical Evaluation

"I am about a new story," Thackeray wrote an American friend shortly after his first visit to the United States (1852-1853), "but don't know as yet if it will be any good. It seems to me I am too old for story-telling. . . . " Although at forty-three Thackeray was certainly not in his dotage, he had already behind him the success of *Vanity Fair* (1847-1848), *Pendennis* (1849-1850), and *Henry Esmond* (1852), his strength seemed to ebb, and to his friends he had the physical appearance of an old man broken in health. Nevertheless, he needed money ($20,000 was his estimate) so he began writing *The Newcomes,* often in ill health, throughout various places in Italy, Germany, and Switzerland, and published the novel serially, the first number in October 1853, the last in August 1855. Extensive even by Victorian standards, *The Newcomes* is a typical mid-nineteenth century family chronicle, detailed with cogent observation of manners and morals. Above all, in spite of its gentle comedy, it satirizes human follies that Thackeray particularly scorned: snobbery, greed, and misguided romantic idealism.

The chronicle is narrated by Arthur Pendennis, an older friend of Clive Newcome, who purports to "edit" the memoirs of "a most respectable family." At first a mere spokesman for the author, Pendennis gradually becomes a character in his own right, participating in, as well as commenting upon, the action. Prudish, smug, and whimsical, Pendennis provides an ironical insight into the other characters. His admiration for Colonel Newcome ("so chivalrous, generous, good looking") is uncritical to the point that it becomes amusing. Moreover, his fulminations upon folly, especially in the famous parody of moral anecdotes in Chapter 1, ring hollow at last, in view of the narrator's own punctilious regard for class and status, his social snobbery, his moralizing.

Typical of Thackeray's fiction, the heroes and heroines of the novel (Colonel Thomas Newcome, his son Clive, and Ethel and Rosey) are true-blue, the villains (Barnes Newcome, Lady Kew, and Mrs. Mackenzie) quite dastardly. Yet even some of the unpleasant characters are redeemed, not always convincingly, by the author's pity. Barnes Newcome, the Colonel's longtime nemesis, is humiliated in the family election, promises to mistreat his wife no longer, and finally comes to terms with Clive. The cold-hearted Lady Kew leaves the bulk of her estate to Ethel. And Ethel herself, psychologically the most interesting personality in the book, develops from a charming but calculating young lady to a woman capable of self-sacrifice and deepest love.

Unlike Rosey—simple, innocent, but vacuous—Ethel is sophisticated and clever. Her virtue, tested in life, is consequently earned. She becomes a worthy mate for Clive, and the tender author promises his readers that the couple will be both happy and wealthy.

As for Clive, he must also earn the reader's approval. Spoiled by his doting father, he makes the most of his good looks, his modest talents as an artist, and the honorable reputation of his family. Yet his young manhood is wasted in prodigality. Thwarted in his desire to marry Ethel, he chooses as second best the sweet but dull Rosey Mackenzie, then chafes at the restraints of wedlock. Nevertheless, like Ethel, he is educated by life, learns his limitations, and grows in self-respect. In Chapter 68, the emotional climax of the novel, Clive and his father come to regard each other as equals, man to man, without recriminations but with mutual respect and affection. Clive comes into his own as a person of worth, a gentleman.

Indeed, *The Newcomes* is a social novel of manners that teaches the Victorian reader how to recognize and, if possible become, a true gentleman (or gentle-lady). Colonel Newcome, the epitome of English gentility, may be a triumph of Grundyism—provincial morality—but the character is probably a bore to most modern readers. Too nearly perfect—that is to say, too proper, innocent, and augustly virtuous—his very rectitude becomes a subject for unconscious satire. As a matter of fact, some of Thackeray's reviewers detected in the author's creation of the Colonel an element of cynicism; one reviewer for *The Times*, London, went so far as to attack the book on the grounds of "morality and religion." But Thackeray's avowed intention was certainly not to satirize the true gentleman and his outmoded virtues. Rather, it was to expose the parvenu, the snob, the ingrate. He ridicules the upstart middle class, especially Anglo-Indian, society: ill-bred, vulgarly assertive, graspingly materialistic.

Above all, the thrust of Thackeray's satire is toward women rather than men. Barnes Newcome is a rascal, to be sure, but not a fool. However, Thackeray's obnoxious women manipulate their men, lead them into folly, either through their aggressiveness or their simpering, smiling domestic tyranny. "Theirs is a life of hypocrisy," concludes Pendennis, speaking for his author; and their chief wile is flattery. Even Ethel, the virtuous and clever heroine, does not wholly escape Thackeray's censure. When he criticizes her for prolonging her romance with Clive, he lays her weakness to a fault of her sex, rather than to a personal folly, and thereby partly "excuses" her. As for Rosey, Clive's unfortunate wife, she never transgresses the social prohibitions but is, like Amelia of *Vanity Fair,* a foolish innocent, to be protected and cherished like a pet. Her opposite is her mother, Mrs. Mackenzie, a tigress when cornered, truly a mean and fearful specimen of womankind.

Nevertheless, the reader's final impression of *The Newcomes* is not one of abrasive social satire, no matter how archly Thackeray pursues the objects of his chastisement. Rather it is one of reconciliation. At the end of the novel, Ethel and Clive are reunited. The good Colonel Newcome dies nobly as he had lived, a scene that is touching in its restrained dignity. And the reader hopes that the Newcome family, in spite of human folly, will endure. To Thackeray that hope, "Fable-land," is the harmless anodyne to the pain of living.

Bibliography

Dodds, John Wendell. *Thackeray: A Critical Portrait.* New York: Oxford University Press, 1941, pp. 192–210.

Fraser, Russell A. "Sentimentality in Thackeray's *The Newcomes*," in *Nineteenth-Century Fiction.* IV (December, 1949), pp. 187–196.

Grieg, John Young. *Thackeray: A Reconsideration.* London: Oxford University Press, 1950, pp. 170–178.

Hardy, Barbara. *The Exposure of Luxury: Radical Themes in Thackeray.* London: Owen, 1972, pp. 146–155, 168–171.

Howells, William Dean. *Heroines of Fiction*, Volume I. New York: Harper, 1901, pp. 215–220.

McMaster, Juliet. *Thackeray: The Major Novels.* Toronto: University of Toronto Press, 1971, pp. 87–125, 204–207.

Olmsted, John. " 'The Steps of a Good Man': Thackeray's Colonel Newcome," in *Cithara.* XVI (May, 1977), pp. 77–89.

Rawlins, Jack P. *Thackeray's Novels: A Fiction That Is True.* Berkeley: University of California Press, 1974, pp. 91–111.

Ray, Gordon N. *Thackeray: The Age of Wisdom, 1847–1863.* New York: McGraw-Hill, 1958, pp. 236–249. Reprinted in *Thackeray: A Collection of Critical Essays.* Edited by Alexander Welsh. Englewood Cliffs, N.J.: Prentice-Hall, 1968, pp. 147–160.

Saintsbury, George. *A Consideration of Thackeray.* London: Oxford University Press, 1931, pp. 208–220.

Sutherland, J.A. *Thackeray at Work.* London: Athlone, 1974, pp. 74–85.

Wheatley, James H. *Patterns in Thackeray's Fiction.* Cambridge: Massachusetts Institute of Technology, 1969, pp. 114–119.

Whibley, Charles. *William Makepeace Thackeray.* New York: Dodd, 1903, pp. 194–216.

VANITY FAIR

Type of work: Novel
Author: William Makepeace Thackeray (1811–1863)
Type of plot: Social satire
Time of plot: Early nineteenth century
Locale: England and Europe
First published: 1847–1848

Thackeray's most famous novel, Vanity Fair *is intended to expose social hypocrisy and sham. Moralistic and sentimental, the work also has redeeming strengths: its panoramic sweep—especially the scenes of the battle of Waterloo— and its creations of lifelike characters, chief among them Becky Sharp.*

Principal Characters

Rebecca Sharp, called **Becky,** an intelligent, beautiful, self-centered, grasping woman whose career begins as an orphaned charity pupil at Miss Pinkerton's School for girls and continues through a series of attempted seductions, affairs, and marriages which form the background of the novel. Unscrupulous Becky is the chief exponent of the people who inhabit Vanity Fair—the world of pretense and show—but she is always apart from it because she sees the humor and ridiculousness of the men and women of this middle-class English world where pride, wealth, and ambition are the ruling virtues.

Amelia Sedley, Becky Sharp's sweet, good, gentle schoolmate at Miss Pinkerton's School. Although married to George Osborne, who subsequently dies in the Battle of Waterloo, Amelia is worshiped by William Dobbin. Amelia does not notice his love, however, so involved is she with the memory of her dashing dead husband. Eventually some of Amelia's goddess-like virtue is dimmed in Dobbin's eyes, but he marries her anyway and transfers his idealization of women to their little girl, Jane.

Captain William Dobbin, an officer in the British Army and a former schoolmate of George Osborne at Dr. Swishtail's school. He idolizes Amelia Sedley, George's wife, and while in the background provides financial and emotional support for her when she is widowed. After many years of worshiping Amelia from afar, he finally marries her.

George Osborne, the dashing young army officer who marries Amelia despite the fact that by so doing he incurs the wrath of his father and is cut off from his inheritance. George, much smitten with the charms of Becky Sharp, slips a love letter to Becky on the night before the army is called to the Battle of Waterloo. He is killed in the battle.

George Osborne, called **Georgy,** the small son of Amelia and George.

Captain Rawdon Crawley, an officer of the Guards, the younger son of Sir Pitt Crawley. He marries Becky Sharp in secret, and for this deception his aunt cuts him out of her will. Charming but somewhat stupid, he is a great gambler and furnishes some of the money on which he and Becky live precariously. He lets Becky order their life, and even though she flirts outrageously after they are married, he does not abandon her until he discovers her in an intimate scene with the Marquis of Steyne. He dies many years later of yellow fever at Coventry Island.

Rawdon Crawley, the son of Rawdon and Becky. He refuses to see his mother in her later years, though he gives her a liberal allowance. From his uncle he inherits the Crawley baronetcy and estate.

Joseph Sedley, called Jos, Amelia's fat, dandified brother whom Becky Sharp attempts unsuccessfully to attract into marrying her. A civil servant in India, the Collector of Boggley Wollah, Jos is rich but selfish and does nothing to rescue his father and mother from bankruptcy. Persuaded by Dobbin, finally, to take some family responsibility, he supports Amelia and her son Georgy for a few months before Dobbin marries her. For a time he and Becky travel on the Continent as husband and wife. He dies at Aix-la-Chapelle soon after Amelia and Dobbin's marriage. His fortune gone from unsuccessful speculations, he leaves only an insurance policy of two thousand pounds, to be divided between Becky and his sister.

Sir Pitt Crawley, a crusty, eccentric old baronet who lives at Queen's Crawley, his country seat, with his abused, apathetic second wife and two young daughters, Miss Rosalind and Miss Violet. Immediately after Lady Crawley's death Sir Pitt proposes marriage to Becky. His offer reveals her secret marriage to Rawdon Crawley, his younger son. Later, grown more senile than ever, Sir Pitt carries on an affair with his butler's daughter, Betsy Horrocks, much to the disgust of his relatives. He eventually dies, and his baronetcy and money go to Pitt, his eldest son.

Miss Crawley, Sir Pitt's eccentric sister, a lonely old maid. Imperious and rich, she is toadied to by everyone in the Crawley family and by Becky Sharp, for they see in her the chance for a rich living. She finally is won over by young Pitt Crawley's wife, Lady Jane, and her estate goes to Pitt.

Pitt Crawley, the older son of Sir Pitt Crawley. A most proper young man with political ambitions, he marries Lady Jane Sheepshanks, and after his brother's secret marriage so endears himself to Miss Crawley, his rich, domineering aunt, that he gains her money as well as his father's.

Lady Jane, Pitt Crawley's wife. Like Amelia Sedley, she is good, sweet, and kind, and is, above all else, interested in her husband's and their daughter's welfare.

The Reverend Bute Crawley, the rector of Crawley-cum-Snailby and Sir Pitt's brother. His household is run by his domineering wife.

Mrs. Bute Crawley, who dislikes Becky Sharp because she recognizes in her the same sort of ambition and craftiness that she herself possesses. Mrs. Bute fails in her plans to gain Miss Crawley's fortune.

James Crawley, the son of the Bute Crawleys. For a time it looks as if this shy, good-looking young man will win favor with his aunt, but he ruins his prospects by getting very drunk on his aunt's wine and later smoking his pipe out the window of the guest room. Miss Crawley's maid also discovers that James has run up a tremendous bill for gin (to which he treated everyone in the local tavern in one of his expansive moods) at the local inn, and this fact combined with his smoking tobacco puts an end to the Bute Crawleys' prospects of inheriting Miss Crawley's money.

Horrocks, Sir Pitt Crawley's butler.

Betsy Horrocks, the butler's daughter and old Sir Pitt's mistress. She is done out of any inheritance by the interference of Mrs. Bute Crawley.

Mr. John Sedley, the father of Amelia and Joseph, a typical middle-class English merchant of grasping, selfish ways. After his failure in business his family is forced to move from Russell Square to a cottage kept by the Clapps, a former servant of the Sedleys. Never able to accept his poverty, Mr. Sedley spends his time thinking up new business schemes with which to regain his former wealth.

Mrs. John Sedley, the long-suffering wife of Mr. Sedley, and mother of Amelia and Joseph. She, like her daughter, is a sweet woman. Her only expression of wrath in the entire story comes when she turns upon Amelia after her daughter has criticized her for giving little Georgy medicine that has not been prescribed for him.

John Osborne, George Osborne's testy-tempered father, provincial, narrow, and mean. Never forgiving his son for marrying the penniless Amelia Sedley, Mr. Osborne finally succeeds in getting the widow to give up her adored Georgy to his care. Amelia regains her son, however, and when he dies Mr. Osborne leaves to his grandson a legacy of which Amelia is the trustee.

Jane,
Maria, and
Frances Osborne, George's sisters, who adore their young nephew. Maria finally marries Frederick Bullock, Esq., a London lawyer.

Mr. Smee, Jane Osborne's drawing teacher, who tries to marry her. Mr. Osborne, discovering them together, forbids him to enter the house.

Lord Steyne, Lord of the Powder Closet at Buckingham Palace. Haughty and well-borne and considerably older than Becky, he succumbs to her charms. Her husband discovers them together and leaves her.

Wirt, the Osbornes' faithful maid.

Mrs. Tinker, the housekeeper at Queen's Crawley.

Lord Southdown, Lady Jane Crawley's brother, a dandified London friend of the Rawdon Crawleys.

Miss Briggs, Miss Crawley's companion

and later Becky Sharp's "sheepdog." She fulfills Becky's need for a female companion so that the little adventuress will have some sort of respectability in the eyes of society.

Bowles, Miss Crawley's butler.

Mrs. Firkins, Miss Crawley's maid. Like the other servants, she is overwhelmed by the overbearing old lady.

Charles Raggles, a green grocer, at one time an assistant gardener to the Crawley family. Having saved his money, he has bought a green grocer's shop and a small house in Curzon Street. Becky and Rawdon live there for a time on his charity, for they are unable to pay their rent.

Lord Gaunt, the son of Lord Steyne. He goes insane in his early twenties.

Major O'Dowd, an officer under whom George Osborne and William Dobbin serve. He is a relaxed individual, devoted to his witty and vivacious wife.

Mrs. O'Dowd, the Irish wife of Major O'Dowd. She is an unaffected, delightful female who tries to marry off her sister-in-law to William Dobbin.

Glorvina O'Dowd, the flirtatious sister of Major O'Dowd. She sets her cap for Dobbin, but because she is only "frocks and shoulders," nothing comes of the match. She marries Major Posky.

General Tufto, the officer to whom Rawdon Crawley at one time serves as aide-de-camp. He is a typical army man with a mistress and a long-suffering wife.

Mrs. Tufto, his wife.

Mrs. Bent, his mistress.

Dolly, the housekeeper to the Rawdon Crawleys in London. She is the one who fends off tradesmen when they come to demand their money.

Mrs. Clapp, the landlady of the Sedleys after their move from Russell Square.

Polly Clapp, a young former servant of the Sedleys. She takes Dobbin to meet Amelia in the park after the former's ten-year absence in the Indian service.

Mary Clapp, another daughter of the Clapps and Amelia's friend.

Lady Bareacres, a snobby old aristocrat who cuts Becky socially in Brussels. Later Becky has her revenge when she refuses to sell her horses to the old woman so that she may flee from Napoleon's invading army.

Lady Blanche Thistlewood, Lady Bareacres' daughter and a dancing partner of George Osborne when they were very young.

Mr. Hammerdown, the auctioneer at the sale of the Sedley possessions.

Major Martindale,
Lieutenant Spatterdash, and
Captain Cinqbars, military friends of Rawdon Crawley who are captivated by his charming wife.

Tom Stubble, a wounded soldier who brings news of the Battle of Waterloo to Amelia Sedley and Mrs. O'Dowd. They care for him until he regains his health.

Mr. Creamer, Miss Crawley's physician.

Miss Pinkerton, the snobbish mistress of the academy for girls at which Amelia Sedley and Becky Sharp met. She dislikes Becky intensely.

Miss Jemima Pinkerton, the silly, sentimental sister of the elder Miss Pinkerton. She takes pity on Becky and tries to give her the graduation gift of the academy, a dictionary, but Becky flings it into the mud as her coach drives off.

Miss Swartz, the rich, woolly-haired mulatto student at Miss Pinkerton's School. Because of her immense wealth she pays double tuition. Later the Crawley family tries to marry off Rawdon to her, but he has already married Becky.

Mr. Sambo, the Sedley's colored servant.

The Reverend Mr. Crisp, a young curate in Chiswick, enamored of Becky Sharp.

Miss Cutler, a young woman who unsuccessfully sets her cap for Joseph Sedley.

Mr. Fiche, Lord Steyne's confidential man. After Becky's fortunes have begun to decline, he tells her to leave Rome for her own good.

Major Loder, Becky's escort in the later phases of her career.

The Story

Becky Sharp and Amelia Sedley became good friends while they were students at Miss Pinkerton's School for girls. It was proof of Amelia's good, gentle nature that she took as kindly as she did to her friend, who was generally disliked by all the other girls. Amelia overlooked as much as she could the evidences of Becky's selfishness.

After the two girls had finished their education at the school, Becky accompanied her friend to her home for a short visit. There she first met Joseph Sedley, Amelia's older brother Jos, who was home on leave from military service in India. Jos was a shy man, unused to women, and certainly to women as designing and flirtatious as Becky. His blundering and awkward manners did not appeal to many women, but Becky was happy to overlook these faults when she compared them with his wealth and social position. Amelia innocently believed that her friend had fallen in love with her brother, and she discreetly tried to further the romance.

To this end she arranged a party at Vauxhall, at which Becky and Jos, along with Amelia and her admirer, George Osborne, were present. There was a fifth member of the group, Captain Dobbin, a tall, lumbering fellow, also in service in India. He had long been in love with Amelia, but he recognized how much more suitable for her was the dashing George Osborne. But all the maneuvering of the flirtatious Becky and the amiable Amelia was not sufficient to corner Jos, who drank too much punch and believed that he had made a silly figure of himself at the party. A day or so later a letter delivered to the Sedley household announced that Jos was ill and planned to return to India as soon as possible.

Since there was no longer any reason for Becky to remain with the Sedleys, she left Amelia, after many tears and kisses, to take a position as governess to two young girls at Queen's Crawley. The head of the household was Sir Pitt Crawley, a cantankerous old man renowned for his miserliness. Lady Crawley was an apathetic soul who lived in fear of her husband's unreasonable outbursts. Deciding that she would have nothing to fear from her timid mistress, Becky spent most of her time ingratiating herself with Sir Pitt and ignoring her pupils. Becky also showed great interest in Miss Crawley, a spinster aunt of the family, who was exceedingly wealthy. Miss Crawley paid little attention to Sir Pitt and his children, but she was fond of Rawdon Crawley, a captain in the army and a son of Sir Pitt by a previous marriage. So fond was she of her dashing young nephew that she supported him through school and paid all his gambling debts with hardly a murmur.

During Becky's stay, Miss Crawley visited Sir Pitt only once, at a time when Rawdon was also present. The handsome young dragoon soon fell prey to Becky's wiles and followed her about devotedly. Becky also took care to ingratiate herself with the holder of the purse strings. Miss Crawley found Becky witty and charming, and did not attempt to disguise her opinion that the little governess was worth all the rest of the Crawley household put together. And so Becky found herself in a very enviable position. Sir Pitt was obviously interested in her, as was his handsome son. Miss Crawley insisted that Becky accompany her back to London.

Becky had been expected to return to her pupils after only a short stay with Miss Crawley. But Miss Crawley was taken ill and she refused to allow anyone but her dear Becky to nurse her. Afterward there were numerous other excuses to prevent the governess from returning to her duties. Certainly Becky was not unhappy. Rawdon Crawley was a constant caller, and a devoted suitor for Becky's hand. When the news arrived that Lady Crawley had died, no great concern was felt by anyone. But a few days later Sir Pitt himself appeared, asking to see Miss Sharp. Much to Becky's surprise, the baronet threw himself at her feet and asked her to marry him. Regretfully, she refused his offer. She was already secretly married to Rawdon Crawley.

Following this disclosure, Rawdon and his bride left for a honeymoon at Brighton. Old Miss Crawley, chagrined and angry, took to her bed, changed her will, and cut off her nephew without a shilling. Sir Pitt raved with anger.

Amelia's marriage had also precipitated a family crisis. Her romance with George had proceeded with good wishes on both sides until Mr. Sedley, through some unfortunate business deals, lost most of his money. Then George's snobbish father ordered his son to break his engagement to a penniless woman. George, whose affection for Amelia was never stable, was inclined to accept this parental command. But Captain Dobbin, who saw with distress that Amelia was breaking her heart over George, finally prevailed upon the young man to go through with the marriage, regardless of his father's wishes. When the couple arrived in Brighton for their honeymoon, they found Rawdon and Becky living there happily in penniless extravagance.

Captain Dobbin also arrived in Brighton. He had agreed to act as intercessor with Mr. Osborne. But his hopes of reconciling father and son were shattered when Mr. Osborne furiously dismissed Captain Dobbin and took immediate steps to disown George. Captain Dobbin also brought the news that the army had been ordered to Belgium. Napoleon had landed from Elba. The Hundred Days had begun.

In Brussels the two couples met again. George Osborne was infatuated with Becky. Jos Sedley, now returned from India, and Captain Dobbin were also stationed in that city, Captain Dobbin in faithful attendance upon neglected Amelia. Everyone was waiting for the next move Napoleon would make, but in the meantime the gaiety of the Duke of Wellington's forces was widespread. The Osbornes and Crawleys attended the numerous balls. Becky, especially, made an impression upon military society and her coquetry extended with equal effect from general to private. The fifteenth of June, 1815, was a famous night in Brussels, for on that evening the Duchess of Richmond gave a tremendous ball. Amelia left the party early, brokenhearted at the attentions her husband was showing Becky. Shortly after she left, the men were given orders to march to meet the enemy. Napoleon had entered Belgium, and a great battle was impending.

As Napoleon's forces approached, fear and confusion spread through Brussels, and many of the civilians fled from the city. No so Amelia or Becky. Becky was not alarmed, and Amelia refused to leave while George was in danger. She remained in the city some days before she heard that her husband had been killed. Rawdon returned safely from the battle of Waterloo. He and Becky spent a gay and triumphant season in Paris, where Becky's beauty and wit gained her a host of admirers. Rawdon was very proud of the son she bore him.

Amelia, too, had a child. She had returned to London almost out of her mind with grief, and only after her son was born did she show any signs of rallying.

When Becky grew bored with the pleasures of Paris, the Crawleys returned to London. There they rented a large home and proceeded to live well on nothing a year. By this time Becky was a past master at this art, and so they lived on a grander scale than Rawdon's small winnings at cards would warrant. Becky had become acquainted with the nobility of England, and had made a particular impression on rich old Lord Steyne. At last all society began to talk about young Mrs. Crawley and her elderly admirer. Fortunately Rawdon heard nothing of this ballroom and coffee house gossip.

Eventually, through the efforts of Lord Steyne, Becky achieved her dearest wish, presentation at Court. Presented along with her was the wife of the new Sir Pitt Crawley. The old man had died, and young Sir Pitt, his oldest son and Rawdon's brother, had inherited the title. Since then friendly relations had been established between the two brothers. If Rawdon realized that his brother had also fallen in love with Becky, he gave no sign, and he accepted the money his brother gave him with good grace. But more and more he felt himself shut out from the gay life that Becky enjoyed. He spent much time with his son, for he realized that the child was neglected. Once of twice he saw young George Osborne, Amelia's son.

Amelia struggled to keep her son with her, but her pitiful financial status made it difficult to support him. Her parents had grown garrulous and morose with disappointment over their reduced circumstances. At length Amelia sorrowfully agreed to let Mr. Osborne take the child and rear him as his own. Mr. Osborne still refused to recognize the woman his son had married against his wishes, however, and Amelia rarely saw the boy.

Rawdon was now deeply in debt. When he appealed to Becky for money, she told him that she had none to spare. She made no attempt to explain the jewelry and other trinkets she bought. When Rawdon was imprisoned for a debt, he wrote and asked Becky to take care of the matter. She answered that she could not get the money until the following day. But an appeal to Sir Pitt brought about Rawdon's release, and he returned to his home to find Becky entertaining Lord Steyne. Not long afterward Rawdon accepted a post abroad, never to return to his unfaithful, designing wife.

Amelia's fortunes had now improved. When Jos Sedley returned home, he established his sister and father in a more pleasant home. Mrs. Sedley having died, Jos resolved to do as much as he could to make his father's last days happy. Captain Dobbin had returned from India and confessed his love for Amelia. Although she acknowledged him as a friend, she was not yet ready to accept his love. It was Captain Dobbin who went to Mr. Osborne and gradually succeeded in reconciling him to his son's wife. When Mr. Osborne died, he left a good part of his fortune to his grandson, appointing Amelia as the boy's guardian.

Amelia, her son, Captain Dobbin, and Jos Sedley took a short trip to the continent. This visit was perhaps the happiest time in Amelia's life. Her son was with her constantly, and Captain Dobbin was a devoted attendant. Eventually his devotion was to overcome her hesitation and they were to be married.

At a small German resort they encountered Becky once more. After Rawdon left her, Becky had been unable to live down the scandal of their separation. Leaving her child with Sir Pitt and his wife, she crossed to the continent. Since then she had been living with first one considerate gentleman and then another.

When she saw the prosperous Jos, she vowed not to let him escape as he had before. Amelia and Jos greeted her in a friendly manner, and only Captain Dobbin seemed to regard her with distrust. He tried to warn Jos about Becky, but Jos was a willing victim of her charms.

Becky traveled with Jos wherever he went. Although she could not get a divorce from Rawdon, Jos treated her as his wife, and in spite of Captain Dobbin's protests he took out a large insurance policy in her name. A few months later his family learned that he had died while staying with Becky at Aix-la-Chapelle. The full circumstances of his death were never established, but Becky came into a large sum of money from his insurance. She spent the rest of her life on the continent, where she assumed the role of the virtuous widow and won a reputation for benevolence and generosity.

Critical Evaluation

When we call Thackeray's characters in *Vanity Fair* "life-like," we are milking that term for a subtler meaning than it usually conveys. His people are not true to life in the sense of being fully rounded or drawn with psychological depth. On the contrary, we sometimes find their actions too farcical to be human: Jos Sedley's ignominious flight from Brussels after the battle of Waterloo; or too sinister to be credible: the implication that Becky poisons Jos to collect his insurance is totally out of keeping with what we have learned about her in the previous sixty-six chapters. She may be a selfish opportunist, but she is no murderess. Thackeray's characters *are* "life-like" if we think of "life" as a typological phenomenon; when we shrug our shoulders and say "that's life," we are indulging in a kind of judgment on the human race which is based on types, not individuals; on the common failings of all men and women, not on the unique goodness or evil of some. Insofar as we share one another's weaknesses we are all represented in *Vanity Fair*. Our banality levels us all. That is the satirical revelation that *Vanity Fair* provides; that is the way in which its characters are "life-like."

Thackeray's general approach is comic satire; his method is that of the theatrical producer, specifically, the puppeteer. In his prologue he calls himself the "Manager of the Performance" and refers to Becky, Amelia, and Dobbin as puppets of varying "flexibility . . . and liveliness." Critics usually interpret this offhanded way of referring to his principal characters as a vindication of his own intrusions and asides; as a reminder to the reader that he, the author, is as much involved in the action as any of his characters. But we should probably take a harder look at his metaphor: he is a puppeteer because he must be one; *because* his people are puppets, someone must pull the strings. The dehumanized state of Regency and early Victorian society comes to accurate life through the cynical vehicle of Thackeray's puppeteering. Sentimentality and hypocrisy, closely related social vices, seem interchangeable at the end of the novel when Thackeray gathers all the remaining puppets: Amelia and Dobbin, a "tender little parasite" clinging to her "rugged old oak," and Becky, acting out her new-found saintliness by burying herself "in works of piety" and "having stalls at Fancy Fairs" for the benefit of the poor. "Let us shut up," concludes Thackeray, "the box and the puppets, for our play is played out."

Despite the predictability of all the characters' puppet-like behavior, they often exhibit just enough humanity to make their dehumanization painful. Thackeray wants us to feel uncomfortable over the waste of human potential in the vulgar concerns of *Vanity Fair*. George Osborne lives like a cad, is arrogant about his spendthrift ways, unfaithful to his wife, and dies a hero, leading a charge against the retreating French at Waterloo. We are left with the impression that the heroism of his death is rendered irrelevant by the example of his life. Such satire is demanding in its moral vision precisely because it underscores the price of corruption: honor becomes absurd.

Rawdon Crawley's love for his little son slowly endows the father with a touch of decency, but he is exiled by the "Manager of the Performance" to Coventry Island where he dies of yellow fever "most deeply beloved and deplored." Presumably the wastrel, separated from his son, dies in a position of duty. Or are we to pity him for having been forced, by his financial situation, to accept the position at Coventry as a bribe from Lord Steyne? Thackeray is elusive; again, the suggestions of pathos are touched on so lightly they hardly matter. The indifference itself is *Vanity Fair's* reward. For all his jocularity and beef-eating familiarity, the "Manager of the Performance" sets a dark stage. *Vanity Fair* is colorful enough: the excitement at Brussels over Waterloo, the gardens at Vauxhall, the Rhine journey; but it is a panoply of meritricious and wasteful human endeavor. And we really do not need Thackeray's moralizing to convince us of the shabbiness of it all.

Astonishing is the fact that despite the novel's cynicism, it also has immense vitality. We sense the very essence of worldliness in its pages, and who can deny the attractiveness of *Vanity Fair?* Bunyan made that perfectly clear in *Pilgrim's Progress,* and Thackeray simply updates the vision. What was allegory in Bunyan becomes realism in Thackeray; the modern writer's objectivity in no way detracts from the alluring effect achieved by Bunyan's imaginary Vanity Fair. Bunyan still operates in the Renaissance tradition of Spenserian façade; evil traps man through illusion, as exemplified in the trials of the Knight of the Red Crosse. Thackeray drops the metaphor of illusion, and shows us corruption bared—and still it is attractive.

Becky Sharp is described as "worldliness incarnate" by Louis Kronenberger, but the reader cannot deny her charms. Thackeray calls his book "A Novel Without a Hero," but we and Thackeray know better. Becky's pluck and ambition are extraordinary; her triumph is all the more impressive because of the formidable barriers of class and poverty she has to scale.

When she throws the Johnson dictionary out of the coach window on leaving Miss Pinkerton's academy, we cannot help but thrill to her refusal to be patronized; her destructive and cruel manipulations of the Crawleys have all the implications of a revolutionary act. Thackeray actually emphasizes Becky's spirit and power by making virtuous Amelia so weak and sentimental. Although we are tempted to see this as a contradiction of Thackeray's moral intention, we must remember that he understood very clearly that true goodness must be built on strength: "clumsy Dobbin" is Thackeray's somewhat sentimental example. The human tragedy is that most men and women cannot reconcile their energies with their ideals; that in a fallen world of social injustices, we must all sin in order to survive. It is ironic that precisely because Becky Sharp is such an energetic opportunist, we almost believe her when she says "I think I could have been a good woman if I had 5000 a year."

Bibliography

Alter, Robert. "The Self-Conscious Novel in Eclipse," in *Partial Magic: The Novel as a Self-Conscious Genre.* Berkeley: University of California Press, 1975, pp. 84–137.

Cecil, David. *Early Victorian Novelists: Essays in Revaluation.* London: Constable, 1934, pp. 79–91.

Dodds, John Wendell. *Thackeray: A Critical Portrait.* New York: Oxford University Press, 1941, pp. 107–136.

Drew, Elizabeth A. *The Novel: A Modern Guide to Fifteen English Masterpieces.* New York: Norton, 1963, pp. 111–126.

Dyson, Anthony Edward. "*Vanity Fair:* An Irony Against Heroes," in *Critical Quarterly.* VI (Spring, 1964), pp. 11–31. Reprinted in *The Crazy Fabric: Essays in Irony.* New York: St. Martin's, 1965, pp. 72–95. Also reprinted in *Twentieth-Century Interpretations of* Vanity Fair: *A Collection of Critical Essays.* Edited by M.G. Sundell. Englewood Cliffs, N.J.: Prentice-Hall, 1969, pp. 73–90.

Fraser, Russell R. "Pernicious Casuistry: A Study of Character in *Vanity Fair*," in *Nineteenth-Century Fiction.* XII (September, 1957), pp. 137–147.

Greig, John Young Thomson. *Thackeray: A Reconsideration.* London: Oxford University Press, 1950, pp. 102–117.

Halperin, John. *Egoism and Self-Discovery in the Victorian Novel: Studies in the Ordeal of Knowledge in the Nineteenth Century.* New York: Burt Franklin, 1974, pp. 33–45.

Hardy, Barbara. *The Exposure of Luxury: Radical Themes in Thackeray.* London: Owen, 1972.

Kettle, Arnold. *An Introduction to the English Novel*, Volume I. London: Hutchinson's, 1951, pp. 156–170. Reprinted in *Twentieth Century Inter-*

pretations of Vanity Fair: *A Collection of Critical Essays.* Edited by M.G. Sundell. Englewood Cliffs, N.J.: Prentice-Hall, 1969, pp. 13–26.

Knoepflmacher, Ulrich Camillus. *"Vanity Fair*: The Bitterness of Retrospection," in *Laughter and Despair: Readings in Ten Novels of the Victorian Age.* Berkeley: University of California Press, 1971, pp. 50–83.

Loofburow, John. "Form, Style, and Content in *Vanity Fair,*" in *Thackeray and the Form of Fiction.* Princeton, N.J.: Princeton University Press, 1964, pp. 73–91. Reprinted in *Twentieth Century Interpretations of* Vanity Fair: *A Collection of Critical Essays.* Edited by M.G. Sundell. Englewood Cliffs, N.J.: Prentice-Hall, 1969, pp. 91–106.

McMaster, Juliet. *Thackeray: The Major Novels.* Toronto: University of Toronto Press, 1971, pp. 1–49, 191–195.

Paris, Bernard J. *A Psychological Approach to Fiction: Studies in Thackeray, Stendhal, George Eliot, Dostoevsky, and Conrad.* Bloomington: Indiana University Press, 1974, pp. 71–132.

Rawlins, Jack P. *Thackeray's Novels: A Fiction That Is True.* Berkeley: University of California Press, 1974, pp. 1–35.

Ray, Gordon N. *Thackeray: The Uses of Adversity, 1811–1846.* New York: McGraw-Hill, 1955, pp. 384–426.

Saintsbury, George. *A Consideration of Thackeray.* London: Oxford University Press, 1931, pp. 164–176.

Stevens, Joan. "Thackeray's *Vanity Fair,*" in *Review of English Studies.* VI (January, 1965), pp. 19–38.

Sutherland, J.A. *Thackeray at Work.* London: Athlone, 1974, pp. 11–44.

Taube, Myron. "The Character of Amelia and the Meaning of *Vanity Fair,*" in *Victorian Newsletter.* XVIII (1960), pp. 1–8.

Tillotson, Kathleen Mary. *Novels of the Eighteen-Forties.* Oxford: Clarendon Press, 1954, pp. 224–256. Reprinted in *Thackeray: A Collection of Critical Essays.* Edited by Alexander Welsh. Englewood Cliffs, N.J.: Prentice-Hall, 1968, pp. 65–86. Also reprinted in *Twentieth Century Interpretations of* Vanity Fair: *A Collection of Critical Essays.* Edited by M.G. Sundell. Englewood Cliffs, N.J.: Prentice-Hall, 1969, pp. 40–54.

Van Ghent, Dorothy. "On *Vanity Fair,*" in *The English Novel: Form and Function.* New York: Holt, Rinehart, and Winston, 1953, pp. 139–152. Reprinted in *Twentieth Century Interpretations of* Vanity Fair: *A Collection of Critical Essays.* Edited by M.G. Sundell. Englewood Cliffs, N.J.: Prentice-Hall, 1969, pp. 27–39.

Wheatley, James H. *Patterns in Thackeray's Fiction.* Cambridge: Massachusetts Institute of Technology, 1969, pp. 56–93.

Whibley, Charles. *William Makepeace Thackeray.* New York: Dodd, 1903, pp. 90–120.

Williams, Ioan. *Thackeray.* New York: Arco, 1969, pp. 57–76.

ANTHONY TROLLOPE

Born: London, England (April 24, 1815)
Died: Harting, England (December 6, 1882)

Principal Works

THE CHRONICLES OF BARSETSHIRE: *The Warden*, 1855; *Barchester Towers*, 1857; *Doctor Thorne*, 1858; *Framley Parsonage*, 1861; *The Small House at Allington*, 1864; *The Last Chronicle of Barset*, 1867.

POLITICAL NOVELS: *Can You Forgive Her?*, 1864; *Phineas Finn, the Irish Member*, 1869; *The Eustace Diamonds*, 1873; *Phineas Redux*, 1874; *The Prime Minister*, 1876; *The Duke's Children*, 1880.

IRISH NOVELS: *The Macdermots of Ballycloran*, 1847; *The Kellys and the O'Kellys*, 1848; *Castle Richmond*, 1860; *The Landleaguers*, 1883.

NOVELS OF SOCIETY: *The Bertrams*, 1859; *Orley Farm*, 1862; *Rachel Ray*, 1863; *The Belton Estate*, 1866; *He Knew He Was Right*, 1869; *The Vicar of Bullhampton*, 1870; *The Way We Live Now*, 1875; *Is He Popenjoy?*, 1878; *Dr. Wortle's School*, 1881.

SHORT STORIES: *Tales of All Countries*, 1861, 1863; *Lotta Schmidt and Other Stories*, 1867; *An Editor's Tales*, 1870; *Why Frau Frohmann Raised Her Prices and Other Stories*, 1882.

MEMOIRS: *Autobiography*, 1883.

Anthony Trollope's father, Thomas Anthony Trollope, was an eccentric barrister who lost his wealth in wild speculations; his mother, Frances Trollope, kept the family together by fleeing to Belgium to escape creditors and by writing a total of 114 volumes, mostly novels. Her best-known work today is *Domestic Manners of the Americans* (1832), a caustic and grossly exaggerated account of the America she observed on an unsuccessful trip to Cincinnati in 1823 to set up a great bazaar. Since his older brother, Thomas Adolphus, was also a writer, Anthony was following a well-established family tradition.

According to his posthumous *Autobiography*, Trollope was born in London on April 24, 1815; he grew into an ungainly, oafish, and unpopular boy who spent miserable and friendless years at Harrow and Winchester, where he learned nothing. When he was nineteen, he sought work in London, first as a clerk and then as a civil servant with the Post Office. He hated his work and his lonely life in the city, and seven years later accepted with relief an appointment as traveling postal inspector in Ireland (1841–1859). Later his duties carried him on brief trips to all the continents of the world. In Ireland, Trollope's pleasant experiences with genial country people and an exhilarating landscape developed his confidence and optimism.

He married Rose Haseltine and at the age of thirty began to write, his first novels beings inspired by the ruins of an Irish mansion. His early works were failures, but he persevered under difficult conditions until his fourth book, *The Warden*, found a responsive audience in 1855. This "scene from clerical life," its setting the episcopal establishment of Barchester, presents a detailed account of the day to day events of provincial life in Victorian England. Its sequel, *Barchester Towers*, with its incorrigible comic character, Bertie, was so successful that it was followed by four other novels on the same theme, the whole group constituting the perennially popular "Chronicles of Barsetshire." During this same period, Trollope also wrote other novels, the best of which are *The Three Clerks* (1858), an autobiographical account of the English civil service, and *Orley Farm*, a work which combines a plot involving a forged will with genre pictures of family life in the country.

In 1867, now confident of his powers, Trollope resigned from the Post Office and became interested in politics. He stood as Liberal candidate for Parliament in 1868 but was defeated. Nevertheless, he cut an impressive bearded figure, chatting in the London literary clubs and riding to the hounds in Southern England. All these interests are faithfully embodied in a series sometimes called the "Parliamentary Novels," among them *Phineas Finn*, *Phineas Redux*, *The Prime Minister*, and *The Duke's Children*. But Trollope could not compete with Disraeli in this field (just as he was unable to compete with Dickens in depicting city life among the lower and middle classes), and despite their appealing portraits of political life and character, his Parliamentary series was not widely read.

Trollope continued to turn out novel after novel—social manners, mild satires, histories, romances, travelogues, and even, in *The Fixed Period* (1882), a futuristic work about life in 1980. A curiously interesting work is the story of an erring woman, in *Can You Forgive Her?*—a novel as close as he ever came to modern realism. Despite the fact that he wrote some sixty novels in all, it cannot be said of Trollope that he made the world his stage. He surveys generally a rather narrow scene, usually rural and provincial, peopled by mild villains and tame heroes. No powerful philosophical or social conviction charges his writing, and no keen analysis of human psychology opens the inner beings of his characters. "A novel," he said, "should give a picture of common life enlivened by humor and sweetened by pathos." In this endeavor Trollope succeeded so completely that Henry James said of him, "His great, his inestimable merit was a complete appreciation of the usual." He died of paralysis at Harting, Sussex, on December 6, 1882.

Trollope's posthumously published *Autobiography* disappointed his admirers and dampened his reputation, for he candidly confessed (as Arnold Bennett was to do a half-century later) that he wrote 250 words per minute, completing eight to sixteen pages a day. He is said to have earned some £70,000 from his writings. Despite the fact that he was not an inspired writer, he amused a whole generation with pleasant tales, the best of which have considerable value as sociological insights into a mellow and tranquil age now forever past.

Bibliography

Readers have a choice of two excellent modern biographies of Anthony Trollope, James Pope-Hennessy's comprehensive *Anthony Trollope*, 1971; and Lord C. P. Snow's briefer but cogent *Trollope: His Life and Art*, 1975; these studies supersede the still useful Michael Sadleir, *Anthony Trollope: A Commentary*, 1927. The author's *An Atuobiobiography*, 2 vols., 1883, has been re-issued in 1974. Other important older source studies include Thomas Adolphus Trollope, *What I Remember*, 3 vols., 1887–1889 (re-issued 1973); and Thomas Sweet Escott, *Anthony Trollope: His Works, Associations, and Literary Originals*, 1913. For additional biography see Hugh Walpole, *Anthony Trollope*, English Men of Letters Series, 1928; Beatrice C. Brown, *Anthony Trollope*, 1950; Bradford A. Booth, *Anthony Trollope*, 1958; Peter Edwards, *Anthony Trollope*, 1969; Alice G. Fredman, *Anthony Trollope*, 1971; and Arthur Pollard, *Anthony Trollope*, 1978.

Among the earlier critical studies of importance see Henry James, *Partial Portraits*, 1888; S. van B. Nichols, *The Significance Anthony Trollope*, 1925; and Lord David Cecil, *Early Victorian Novelists*, 1935. For recent criticism see W. G. and J. T. Gerould, *A Guide to Trollope*, 1948; A. O. J. Cockshut, *Anthony Trollope: A Critical Study*, 1955; Robert M. Polhemus, *The Changing World of Anthony Trollope*, 1968; Donald Smalley, *Anthony Trollope, The Critical Heritage*, 1969; Ruth apRoberts, *Trollope, Artist and Moralist*, 1971; David Skelton, *Anthony Trollope and His Contemporaries: A Study in the Theory and Conventions of Mid-Victorian Fiction*, 1972; John M. Hardwick, *A Guide to Anthony Trollope*, 1974; John W. Clark, *The Language and Style of Anthony Trollope*, 1975; Joan M. Cohen, *Form and Realism in Six Novels of Anthony Trollope*, 1976; Spenser V. Nichols, *The Significance of Anthony Trollope*, 1977; James R. Kincaid, *The Novels of Anthony Trollope*, 1977; John Halperin, *Trollope and Politics: A Study of the Pallisers and Others*, 1977; P. D. Edwards, *Anthony Trollope, His Art and Scope*, 1978; R. C. Terry, *Anthony Trollope: The Artist in Hiding*, 1978; and Robert Tracy, *Trollope's Later Novels*, 1978.

More specialized studies include John T. Wildman, *Anthony Trollope's England*, 1940; Lucy P. Stebbins and Richard P. Stebbins, *The Trollopes: The Chronicle of a Writing Family*, 1945; Marcie Muir, *Anthony Trollope in Australia*, 1949; and W. O. Chadwick, *The Victorian Church*, 2 vols., 1966–1970. For insight into the upper class of Victorians see Lady Gwendoline Cecil, *Life of Robert, Marquis of Salisbury*, 4 vols., 1921–1932. For ongoing Trollope scholarship, see *Nineteenth Century Fictions* (formerly *The Trollopian*). In particular see numbers by John H. Hagan, 1958–1959; Jerome Thale, 1960; David A. Aitken, 1966–1974; and Roger L. Slaker, 1973.

BARCHESTER TOWERS

Type of work: Novel
Author: Anthony Trollope (1815–1882)
Type of plot: Social satire
Time of plot: Mid-nineteenth century
Locale: "Barchester," an English cathedral town
First published: 1857

This sequel to The Warden *is probably the best-known of the novels in the Barsetshire series. Barchester Towers is a story of clerical intrigue centering on the power struggle between an obnoxious and imperious bishop's wife and her scheming, sneaking chaplain. Trollope's fine irony of tone, and his delightful characterizations create a light and purely entertaining novel unburdened by social comment or philosophical questioning.*

Principal Characters

Eleanor Bold, younger daughter of the Reverend Septimius Harding, the "Warden," and wealthy widow of John Bold. She lives with her baby son and her sister-in-law, Mary Bold. Much of the novel revolves around Eleanor's choice of one of her three suitors: Mr. Slope, Bertie Stanhope, and Mr. Arabin. Throughout a large portion of the novel, most of her ecclesiastical friends and relatives assume that she will choose Mr. Slope.

Dr. Proudie, the clergyman who becomes Bishop of Barchester after the death of Archdeacon Grantly's father. Dr. Proudie is a vain but weak man, dominated by his wife and by Mr. Slope. Although all Barchester expects him to offer the wardenship of Hiram's Hospital to Mr. Harding, Dr. Proudie allows Mr. Slope's chicanery to gain the appointment for Mr. Quiverful.

Mrs. Proudie, the aggressive and domineering wife of the Bishop of Barchester. She attempts to control Barchester by championing evangelical and Low Church causes, awarding church patronage, and manipulating people through the offices of Mr. Slope. She antagonizes the established ecclesiastical society in Barchester.

The Rev. Obadiah Slope, the Bishop's chaplain. An evangelical clergyman, Mr. Slope antagonizes most of the chapter with his initial fiery sermon at Barchester Cathedral. He first acts as Mrs. Proudie's agent, but, after he supports the claims of Mr. Harding in an attempt to gain favor with Eleanor Bold, Mrs. Proudie scorns him. Unable to win favor or Eleanor or the post of Dean of Barchester, he returns to London.

The Rev. Theophilus Grantly, the Archdeacon of Barchester and rector of Plumstead Episcopi. He strongly supports the claims of Harding, his father-in-law, to be reinstated as warden of Hiram's Hospital. When the nearby living of St. Ewold's becomes vacant, he goes to Oxford to obtain the post for the Reverend Francis Arabin. He also fears that his sister-in-law, Eleanor Bold, will marry the Low Churchman, Slope.

Susan Grantly, wife of Archdeacon Grantly and the elder daughter of Mr. Harding. She generally follows her husband, but attempts to mitigate his anger at her sister.

The Rev. Septimus Harding, former Warden of Hiram's Hospital. He desires his former charge but is denied it through the machinations of Mr. Slope and Mrs. Proudie, who make his appointment conditional on his assuming extra duties and administering evangelical Sunday Schools. Later he is offered the Deanship of Barchester Cathedral, but he refuses the post because of his advanced age.

The Rev. Francis Arabin, a scholarly High Church clergyman from Oxford who is brought into the living at St. Ewold's to strengthen forces against Bishop Proudie and Mr. Slope. He eventually becomes Dean of Barchester and marries Eleanor Bold.

Dr. Vesey Stanhope, holder of several livings in the Barchester area who has spent the preceding twelve years in Italy. He is summoned to Barchester by Dr. Proudie, through Slope, but has little interest in the political or ecclesiastical affairs of Barchester.

Mrs. Stanhope, his wife, interested chiefly in dress.

Charlotte Stanhope, the oldest daughter of the Stanhopes, who manages the house and the rest of the family with efficiency and intelligence. She, a friend of Eleanor Bold, urges her brother to propose to Eleanor.

La Signora Madeline Vesey Neroni, nee Stanhope, the great beauty of the Stanhope family who has been crippled in a short, disastrous marriage to a brutal Italian. Although confined to her sofa, she attracts men easily. One of her victims is Mr. Slope, whose hypocrisy she exposes, but she is sufficiently generous to encourage Eleanor to marry Mr. Arabin.

Ethelbert Stanhope (Bertie), the amiable son of the Stanhopes, who has dabbled in law, art, and numerous religions. His family wishes to settle him with Eleanor and her money, but Bertie's proposal fails and he is sent back to Carrara by his father.

Mr. Quiverful, the genial clergyman and father who is persuaded to accept the preferment at Hiram's Hospital in addition to his living at Puddingdale.

Mrs. Letty Quiverful, his wife and the mother of fourteen children, who begs Mrs. Proudie to bestow the preferment at Hiram's Hospital on her husband.

Miss Thorne of Ullathorne, the member of an old family at St. Ewold's who gives a large party at which both Mr. Slope and Bertie Stanhope propose to Eleanor. Miss Thorne, however, favors Arabin and invites both Arabin and Eleanor to stay until the engagement is settled.

Wilfred Thorne, Esq., of Ullathorne, the younger brother of Miss Thorne, a bachelor, and an authority on tradition and geneology.

Dr. Gwynne, Master of Lazarus College, Oxford, the man instrumental in securing the Deanship for Mr. Arabin.

Olivia Proudie, the daughter of the Proudies, briefly thought to be engaged to Mr. Slope.

Mary Bold, the sister-in-law and confidante of Eleanor Bold.

Johnny Bold, the infant son of Eleanor and the late John Bold.

Griselda Grantly, the pretty daughter of Archdeacon Grantly.

Dr. Trefoil, Dean of Barchester Cathedral, who dies of apoplexy.

The Bishop of Barchester, the father of Archdeacon Grantly. He dies at the very beginning of the novel.

Dr. Omicron Pi, a famous doctor from London.

The Story

At the death of Bishop Grantly of Barchester, there was much conjecture as to his successor. Bishop Grantly's son, the archdeacon, was ambitious for the position, but his hopes were deflated when Dr. Proudie was appointed to the diocese. Bishop Proudie's wife was of Low Church propensities. She was also a woman of extremely aggressive nature, who kept the bishop's chaplain, Obadiah Slope, in constant tow.

On the first Sunday of the new bishop's regime, Mr. Slope was the preacher in the cathedral. His sermon was concerned with the importance of simplicity in the church service and the consequent omission of chanting, intoning, and formal ritual. The cathedral chapter was aghast. For generations the services in the cathedral had been chanted; the chapter could see no reason for discontinuing the practice. In counsel it was decreed that Mr. Slope never be permitted to preach from the cathedral pulpit again.

The Reverend Septimus Harding, who had resigned because of conscientious scruples from his position as warden of Hiram's Hospital, now had several reasons to believe that he would be returned to his post, although at a smaller salary than that he had drawn before. But when Mr. Slope, actually Mrs. Proudie's mouthpiece, told him that he would be expected to conduct several services a week and also manage some Sunday Schools in connection with the asylum, Mr. Harding was perturbed. Such duties would make arduous a preferment heretofore very pleasant and leisurely.

Another change of policy was effected in the diocese when the bishop announced, through Mr. Slope, that absentee clergymen should return and help in the administration of the diocese. Dr. Vesey Stanhope had for years left his duties to his curates while he remained in Italy. Now he was forced to return, bringing with him an ailing wife and three grown children, spinster Charlotte, exotic Signora Madeline Vesey Stanhope Neroni, and ne'er-do-well Ethelbert. Signora Neroni, separated from her husband, was an invalid who passed her days lying on a couch. Bertie had studied art and had been at times a Christian, a Mohammedan, and a Jew. He had amassed some sizable debts.

The Proudies held a reception in the bishop's palace soon after their arrival. Signora Neroni, carried in with great ceremony, quite stole the show. She had a fascinating way with men and succeeded in almost devastating Mr. Slope. Mrs. Proudie disapproved and did her best to keep Mr. Slope and others away from the invalid.

When the living of St. Ewold's became vacant, Dr. Grantly made a trip to Oxford and saw to it that the Reverend Francis Arabin, a High Churchman, received the appointment. With Mrs. Proudie and Mr. Slope advocating Low Church practices, it was necessary to build up the strength of the High Church forces. Mr. Arabin was a bachelor of about forty. The question arose as to what he would do with the parsonage at St. Ewold's.

Mr. Harding's widowed daughter, Mrs. Eleanor Bold, had a good income and was the mother of a baby boy. Mr. Slope had his eye on her and attempted to interest Mrs. Bold in the work of the Sunday Schools. At the same time he asked Mr. Quiverful, of Puddingdale, to take over the duties of the hospital. Mr. Quiverful's fourteen children were reasons enough for his being grateful for the opportunity. But Mrs. Bold learned how her father felt over the extra duties imposed upon him, and she grew cold toward Mr. Slope. In the end, Mr. Harding decided that he simply could not, at his age, undertake the new duties. So Mr. Quiverful, a Low Churchman, was granted the preferment, much to Mrs. Proudie's satisfaction.

Mr. Slope was not the only man interested in Mrs. Bold. The Stanhope sisters, realizing that Bertie could never make a living for himself, decided that he should ask Mrs. Bold to be his wife.

Meanwhile Mr. Slope was losing favor with Mrs. Proudie. That he should throw himself at the feet of Signora Neroni was repulsive to Mrs. Proudie. That he should be interested in the daughter of Mr. Harding, who refused to comply with her wishes, was disgraceful.

The Thornes of Ullathorne were an old and affluent family. One day they gave a great party. Mrs. Bold, driving to Ullathorne with the Stanhopes, found herself in the same carriage with Mr. Slope, whom by this time she greatly disliked. Later that day, as she was walking with Mr. Slope, he suddenly put his arm around her and declared his love. She rushed away and told Charlotte Stanhope, who suggested that Bertie should speak to Mr. Slope about his irregularity. But the occasion for his speaking to Mr. Slope never arose. Bertie himself told Mrs. Bold that his sister Charlotte had urged him to marry Mrs. Bold for her money. Naturally insulted, Mrs. Bold was angered at the entire Stanhope family. That evening, when Dr. Stanhope learned what had happened, he insisted that Bertie go away and earn his own living or starve. Bertie left several days later.

The Dean of Barchester was beyond recovery after a stroke of apoplexy. It was understood that Dr. Grantly would not accept the deanship. Mr. Slope wanted the position but Mrs. Proudie would not consider him as a candidate. When the dean died, speculation ran high. Mr. Slope felt encouraged by the newspapers, which said that younger men should be admitted to places of influence in the church.

After Bertie had gone, Signora Neroni wrote a note asking Mrs. Bold to come to see her. When Mrs. Bold entered the Stanhope drawing-room, Signora Neroni told her that she should marry Mr. Arabin. With calculating generosity she had decided that he would make a good husband for Mrs. Bold.

Meanwhile, Mr. Slope had been sent off to another diocese, for Mrs. Proudie could no longer bear having him in Barchester. And Mr. Arabin, through Oxford influences, was appointed to the deanship—a victory for the High Churchmen. With Mr. Slope gone, the Stanhopes felt safe in returning to Italy.

Miss Thorne asked Mrs. Bold to spend some time at Ullathorne. She also contrived to have Mr. Arabin there. It was inevitable that Mr. Arabin should ask

Mrs. Bold to be his wife. Dr. Grantly was satisfied. He had threatened to forbid the hospitality of Plumstead Episcopi to Mrs. Bold if she had become the wife of a Low Churchman. In fact, Dr. Grantly was moved to such generosity that he furnished the deanery and gave wonderful gifts to the entire family, including a cello to his father-in-law, Mr. Harding.

Critical Evaluation

As a young man, Anthony Trollope, son of a ne'er-do-well barrister of good family, seemed destined to further the decline of the family. An undistinguished student in two distinguished public schools, he had no hopes for university or career. His mother persuaded a family friend to find work for him in the London Post Office where his performance as a clerk was to be rated as "worthless." Indeed, the burdens of the family fell upon his indefatigable mother, who had converted a family business failure in Cincinnati, Ohio, into a literary career with her satiric study *Domestic Manners of Americans* (1832). Like his mother, the son found his way after a change of scenery. When the Post Office sent him to the south of Ireland to assist in a postal survey, his career in the postal service began to advance, he married happily, and he began to write.

Success as a novelist came when the Post Office sent Trollope to survey southwest England. A midsummer visit to the beautiful cathedral town of Salisbury produced the idea for *The Warden* (1855) and, more importantly, furnished the outlines for a fictional county, Barsetshire, which is as impressive as Hardy's Wessex or Faulkner's Yoknapatawpha. When he returned in *Barchester Towers* to the milieu of *The Warden,* which had been a modest success, he achieved resounding success. Afterwards he was to write four more novels in the series known as the Barsetshire Novels, set in the chiefly agricultural county with its seat of Barchester, a quiet town in the West of England, noted for its beautiful cathedral and fine monuments, but hardly for its commercial prosperity. Thus at middle age began the career of one of the most prolific of the Victorians and, until his last years, one of the most popular.

In his own day Trollope was admired as a realist. He himself was delighted with Hawthorne's appraisal that his novels were "just as real as if some giant had hewn a great lump out of the earth and put it under a glass case, with all its inhabitants going about their daily business, and not suspecting that they were being made a show of." Today Trollope's novels are generally viewed as comic works. Instead of merely being people going about their daily affairs, Trollope's characters are in the grip of a firmly controlled irony.

The irony which Trollope perceives in the affairs of the men of Barchester arises from discrepancies between the ideals they uphold and the means by which they uphold their ideals. A layman with no special knowledge of the

Church of England, Trollope vividly depicts the internecine war which breaks out between the party of the new Bishop of Barchester and that of the former Bishop's son, Archdeacon Grantly. Both parties intend to preserve the integrity of the Church. However, the Church is vested in buildings, furnishings, livings; and these clergymen fight for power over the appurtenances, the worldly forms of the Church spiritual.

Barchester Towers consists of a number of subplots, all of which are related to the ecclesiastical power struggle. Since buildings, furnishings, and livings are occupied by human beings, the clerics who guard the Church must also dispose of the lives of men. The subplots involve characters who become mere objects in a dispute over power—for example, Mr. Harding and the Quiverfuls in the competition for wardenship of Hiram's Hospital, or Eleanor Bold in the rivalry of two clergymen for her hand in marriage. Episodes not directly related to the ecclesiastical battles serve to underscore them: as in the parallel between the rivalry of Mrs. Lookaloft and Mrs. Greenacre and the absurd ploys of the higher orders that abound in the novel.

The main conflicts of the novel are those which engage the high and the mighty of Barchester. The strength of Trollope's satire lies in his refusal to oversimplify the motives of these worldlings of the Church or to deny them sincerity in their defense of the Church. Even as Slope genuinely believes Grantly and his type to be the enemies of religion, so also does the Archdeacon honestly believe that Slope is the kind who could well ruin the Church of England.

One of Trollope's devices for deflating these militant clerics is to treat their wars in the mock heroic vein. After the first meeting between the Archdeacon and the Proudies, the author declares, "And now, had I the pen of a mighty poet, would I sing in epic verse the noble wrath of the Archdeacon." In time, Mrs. Proudie is ironically likened unto Juno, Medea, even Achilles, while the Archdeacon's extravagance in celebrating Eleanor Bold's marriage to his champion, Arabin, is suggestive of the glorious warrior returning from the fields with his spoils.

The reduction of martial glory is furthered by a recurrent analogy with games, underscoring the truth that Barchester's leadership is really concerned with social rather than spiritual or moral issues. Slope's major defeats arise from his indecorous behavior with Madeline Neroni, who is alert to every possible move. Worse, he underestimates his other opponent, Mrs. Proudie, and at the end he discovers that "Mrs. Proudie had checkmated him."

Human strife is incongruous with the idealized setting of peaceful Barchester, its venerable church and close, its rural villages round about, all endowed with a loveliness suggestive of the age-old pastoral tradition. The cathedral itself seems to judge the folly of its worldly champions. As the battles commence, Archdeacon Grantly looks up to the cathedral towers as if evoking a blessing for his efforts. However genial the comedy played out beneath the Barchester towers, the outcome is not without serious significance. For the ultimate result is the further separation of man from his ideals. In the end, the Bishop's wife finds that her "sphere is more extended, more noble, and more suited to her ambition than that of a cathedral city," while the Bishop himself "had learnt that his proper sphere of action lay in close contiguity with Mrs. Proudie's wardrobe." As Mr. Slope makes his ignominious final departure from the city, "he gave no longing lingering look after the cathedral towers." As for the Archdeacon, it is sufficient for him to "walk down the High Street of Barchester without feeling that those who see him are comparing his claims with those of Mr. Slope."

Despite the futility of its human strivings, *Barchester Towers* is a cheerful novel, not merely because the satire provokes laughter, but also because occasionally, briefly, the real and the ideal meet. Mr. Harding, for example, is too peaceable, too naïve, too reticent to be effective in the world. Nonetheless, when he is prompted by his dedication to simple justice to introduce Mr. Quiverful personally to his own former charges at Hiram Hospital, an action representing the union of his profession and practice, the consequence is greater than the act would suggest for it caused the Barchester world to treat Mr. Quiverful with more respect as he assumes his duties.

Quite appropriately, then, Trollope brings the novel to its close with pastoral serenity by offering a word of Mr. Harding, who functions not as a hero and not as a perfect divine, but as a good, humble man without guile.

Bibliography

Baker, Ernest A.   *The History of the English Novel*, Volume VIII. New York: Barnes & Noble, 1950, pp. 129–132.

Bankert, M.S.   "Newman in the Shadow of *Barchester Towers*," in *Renascence*. XX (1967–1968), pp. 153–161.

Booth, Bradford A.   *Anthony Trollope: Aspects of His Life and Art*. London: Edward Hulton, 1958, pp. 39–44.

Cadbury, William.   "Character and the Mock Heroic in *Barchester Towers*," in *Texas Studies in Literature and Language*. V (1963–1964), pp. 509–519.

Fredman, Alice Green.   *Anthony Trollope*. New York: Columbia University Press, 1971, pp. 14–16.

Hennedy, Hugh L.   "Trollope on Reform and Change: *Barchester Towers*," in *Unity in Barsetshire*. The Hague: Mouton, 1971, pp. 37–55.

Kincaid, James R.   "*Barchester Towers* and the Nature of Conservative Comedy," in *Journal of English Literary History*. XXXVII (December, 1970), pp. 595–612.

————. *The Novels of Anthony Trollope*. Oxford: Clarendon Press, 1977, pp. 101–113.

Knoepflmacher, Ulrich Camillus. *Laughter and Despair: Readings in Ten Novels of the Victorian Age*. Berkeley: University of California Press, 1971, pp. 3–49.

Krieger, Murray. "Postscript: The Naive Classic and the Merely Comic," in *The Classic Vision: The Retreat from Extremity in Modern Literature*. Baltimore: Johns Hopkins University Press, 1971, pp. 221–252.

Kronenberger, Louis. "*Barchester Towers*," in *The Polished Surface: Essays in the Literature of Worldliness*. New York: Knopf, 1969, pp. 217–232.

Pickering, Samuel F., Jr. "Trollope's Poetics and Authorial Intrusion in *The Warden* and *Barchester Towers*," in *Journal of Narrative Technique*. III (1973), pp. 131–140.

Polhemus, Robert M. *The Changing World of Anthony Trollope*. Berkeley: University of California Press, 1968, pp. 35–50.

Sadleir, Michael. *Trollope: A Commentary*. New York: Farrar, Straus, 1947, pp. 169–176.

Saintsbury, George. "Trollope Revisited," in *The Collected Essays and Papers of George Saintsbury, 1875–1920*. Volume II. London: J.M. Dent, 1923, pp. 326–329.

Shaw, W. David. "Moral Drama in *Barchester Towers*," in *Nineteenth-Century Fiction*. XIX (June, 1964), pp. 45–54.

Taylor, Robert H. "On Rereading *Barchester Towers*," in *Princeton University Library Chronicle*. XV (1953–1954), pp. 10–15.

Walpole, Hugh. *Anthony Trollope*. New York: Macmillan, 1928, pp. 47–51.

The Barsetshire Novels

Escott, T.H.S. *Anthony Trollope: His Work, Associates and Literary Associations*. London: John Lane, 1913, pp. 101–116.

Hennedy, Hugh L. "The Series: Essentially Clerical," in *Unity in Barsetshire*. The Hague: Mouton, 1971, pp. 125–138.

Kincaid, James R. "The Barsetshire Chronicle," in *The Novels of Anthony Trollope*. Oxford: Clarendon Press, 1977, pp. 92–142.

Knox, Ronald A. "The Barsetshire Novels," in *Literary Distractions*. London: Sheed and Ward, 1958, pp. 134–144.

Quiller-Couch, Sir Arthur. "Anthony Trollope: The Barsetshire Novels," in *Charles Dickens and Other Victorians*. Cambridge: Cambridge University Press, 1925, pp. 219–234.

Sherman, Theodore A. "The Financial Motif in the Barsetshire Novels," in

College English. IX (1947–1948), pp. 413–419.

Walpole, Hugh. *Anthony Trollope*. New York: Macmillan, 1928, pp. 63–81.

DOCTOR THORNE

Type of work: Novel
Author: Anthony Trollope (1815–1882)
Type of plot: Domestic realism
Time of plot: Mid-nineteenth century
Locale: "Barsetshire," England
First published: 1858

This third novel in the Barchester Series continues the mixture of sentiment, humor, romance, and fidelity to human nature and experience of Trollope's chronicle of clerical and country life. The usual Trollopian theme of making money and a successful marriage is portrayed against the background of an English country estate and the life connected with it. Trollope's chief value lies in his authentic depiction of middle-class country life in nineteenth century England, which reproduces better than that of any other writer of his time the manners and morals of the Victorian period.

Principal Characters

Dr. Thomas Thorne, the benevolent physician of Greshamsbury in East Barsetshire. He had adopted Mary, the illegitimate child of his brother and Mary Scatcherd, a village girl, after his brother was killed by Roger Scatcherd, Mary's brother, Dr. Thorne conceals Mary's identity until after she has inherited Roger Scatcherd's fortune. A humane man, Dr. Thorne is friendly with both the Scatcherds and with the aristocratic Greshams of Greshamsbury Park.

Mary Thorne, the niece of Dr. Thorne, unaware, until the end of the novel, of her illegitimate origin. She was brought up with the young Greshams at Greshamsbury Park and is in love with Frank Gresham, the heir. Although banished from Greshamsbury Park because Frank must marry money, Mary remains true to Frank. When she learns of her origin and her inheritance, she is able to marry Frank.

Frank Gresham, the young heir to Greshamsbury Park. Although his mother constantly insists on his need to marry a wealthy heiress, Frank never wavers in his devotion to Mary. Sent to win wealthy Miss Dunstable, Frank cannot overcome his innate honesty, despite family pressure.

Francis Newbold Gresham, the father of Frank and Squire of Greshamsbury. He has dissipated his family fortune in an unsuccessful attempt to regain his father's seat in Parliament. He has also sired ten children and watched his land gradually sold in order to pay his bills. Although kindly, he recognizes that his son must marry money in order to rebuild the family's holdings.

Lady Arabella De Courcy Gresham, wife of Squire Gresham and mother of Frank. A proud member of the De Courcy clan, she is ambitious for her son and eager to assert her lineage. She insists that Frank marry money and banishes Mary Thorne from her house.

Sir Roger Scatcherd, the poor stonemason who served six months in jail for killing Dr. Thorne's brother after he betrayed Mary Scatcherd. Through intelligence and industry, he becomes a wealthy railroad manufacturer. He is elected to Parliament, but later is unseated when an election fraud of which he is innocent is uncovered. Always fond of alcohol, he then drinks himself to death. His will leaves all his property to his son, and, in the event of his son's death, to his sister's child.

Lady Scatcherd, Sir Roger's loyal and patient wife. She is a good friend to Dr. Thorne and was once wet nurse to young Frank Gresham.

Louis Philippe Scatcherd, Sir Roger's only son and a drunkard. He is in love with Mary Thorne; rejected, he drinks himself to death. His early death brings the family fortune to Mary Thorne.

Countess Rosina De Courcy, sister-in-law of Lady Arabella, equally ambitious both politically and socially. She invites young Frank to Courcy Castle to give him his chance at an heiress.

Earl De Courcy, the owner of Courcy Castle and one of the principal Whig aristocrats of Barsetshire. He is completely overshadowed by his wife.

Lord Porlock, the oldest son and heir to Courcy Castle.

The Honourable George De Courcy, the second son, neither honorable nor wise.

The Honourable John De Courcy, the third son, a spendthrift.

Martha Dunstable, the wealthy heiress to a patent medicine fortune, accustomed to refusing importunate young men. Frank Gresham is expected to win her at Courcy Castle, and she is rather charmed by his naïve inability to be dishonest (she is ten years older than he). They become good friends and she gives him advice about Mary Thorne. The Honourable George proposes to her but is not accepted.

Augusta Gresham, the dutiful eldest daughter of the Squire of Greshamsbury, jilted by her fiancée, Mr. Moffat.

Mr. Moffat, a local member of Parliament, defeated by Sir Roger Scatcherd. He jilts Augusta Gresham when he realizes that the Greshams have less money than he has assumed.

Beatrice Gresham, the second daughter of the Squire of Greshamsbury and particular friend of Mary Thorne, later married to the Reverend Caleb Oriel.

The Reverend Caleb Oriel, the young rector of Greshamsbury, an adherent of High Church doctrine.

Patience Oriel, his sister, a close friend to Mary Thorne.

Lady Amelia De Courcy, eldest daughter of the De Courcys. She maintains rigorous standards of propriety and social caste.

Mortimer Gazebee, a hard-working and opportunistic young attorney of no family. He proposes to Augusta Gresham, who, on the advice of her cousin, Lady Amelia, rejects him. He later marries Lady Amelia.

Dr. Fillgrave, the Barchester physician who sometimes attends Sir Roger Scatcherd.

Harry Baker, a friend of Frank Gresham.

Mr. Nearthewinde, a Parliamentary agent.

Mr. Closerstil, another Parliamentary agent.

Mr. Romer, a barrister who manages Sir Roger Scratcherd's campaign for Parliament.

Mrs. Proudie, the aggressive wife of the Bishop of Barchester.

Mr. Reddypalm, a publican interested in politics.

The Duke of Omnium, owner of Gathe- rum Castle and the leading Whig aris- tocrat in the vicinity.

Fothergill, the Duke's agent.

Miss Gushing, a young lady in love with the Reverend Caleb Oriel; she later marries Mr. Rantaway.

Jonah (Joe), a brutal servant to Louis Philippe Scatcherd.

Mr. Bideawhile, a London attorney.

Lady Rosina De Courcy, Lady Margaretta De Courcy, and Lady Alexandrina De Courcy, younger daughters of the De Courcys.

The Story

Greshamsbury Park, in the county of Barsetshire, dominated the life of the surrounding countryside. Unfortunately, Greshamsbury's lord, Squire Gresham, was rapidly spending himself into poverty.

Most of his financial troubles resulted from the desire of his wife, Lady Ara- bella De Courcy Gresham, to get him into politics. The squire had inherited his father's seat in Parliament. He had lost favor, however, because of his Whig lean- ings. Barsetshire, overwhelmingly Tory, did not approve of Gresham's Whig friends or the fact that his wife's aristocratic family, the De Courcys, were ag- gressively Whig in sentiment. Having lost his seat in the Parliamentary elections, Gresham twice tried to regain it. These attempts were stimulated by his wife, who fancied being the wife of a member of Parliament. But Gresham was not successful, and he lost a great deal of money in financing his campaigns.

Consequently, when his son Frank came of age, Squire Gresham had not much to offer him in the way of financial security. Lady Arabella saw as their only hope the possibility of Frank's marriage to a wealthy heiress. That he might do such a thing seemed rather doubtful, however, for, much to the distress of his mother and her family, young Frank was highly enamored of Mary Thorne, niece of the local doctor. Frank and Mary had known each other all their lives, and Mary had been educated along with the young Greshams at Greshamsbury Park. Hers was an interesting history.

She had been brought to live with her uncle, Doctor Thorne, when she was a mere infant. The real circumstances of her birth—that she was the illegitimate child of Doctor Thorne's brother and Mary Scatcherd, a village girl—were known only to the doctor. Even Mary Scatcherd's brother Roger, who had killed his sister's betrayer, did not know that Doctor Thorne had adopted the child. Roger Scatcherd, a poor stonemason, had been sentenced to six months in prison for his crime. When his term was up, he was told that the child had died. Since the doctor stood in high favor with Squire Gresham and daily attended Lady Arabella, it was natural that his niece should visit the estate. Because she was an attractive child and near the age of the Gresham children, she soon took her lessons with them. By the time Frank was of age, Mary Thorne seemed part of the family. But Lady Arabella was determined that this was not to be the literal state of affairs; Mary had no money.

One of Squire Gresham's greatest misfortunes was the loss of a particularly choice part of his estate, land sold to pay off his numerous and most pressing debts. Doctor Thorne, acting as agent for the squire, found a buyer in Sir Roger Scatcherd, a wealthy baronet. Sir Roger was the former stonemason, who had prospered well after his jail term and was now the possessor of a title, a seat in Parliament, and a large fortune. Although he knew nothing of the existence of his sister's illegitimate child, Sir Roger was in close contact with Doctor Thorne. Sir Roger was a chronic alcoholic, and Doctor Thorne was often called on to attend him during his sprees.

To the Gresham family the loss of this piece of property was indeed a tragedy, for the sale greatly diminished the estate Frank would someday inherit. Nervously, Lady Arabella began to plan for the future of her family. Fortunately, one of the daughters was engaged to marry money, a politician who wanted the Gresham and De Courcy position and family connections. Another daughter would marry the local vicar and so would be assured of a respectable position, though one without much money. But Frank was his mother's real hope. If he could make a wealthy marriage, their troubles would be over. But Frank, in love with Mary Thorne, had no lofty matrimonial ambitions. Lady Arabella's family, to save him from an unfortunate romance, invited Frank to De Courcy Castle for a visit.

It was the Countess De Courcy's plan to make a match between Frank and Miss Dunstable, a family friend. Miss Dunstable was considered the wealthiest heiress in England, but she was wary and sharp-tongued. Mostly to humor his aunt, Frank pretended to woo the heiress, and to his surprise he found her rather good company. Miss Dunstable, ten years his senior and much more worldly-wise, soon uncovered his little plot. Thereafter they became the best of friends, and she acted as an adviser to Frank in his affair with Mary Thorne.

Meanwhile Sir Roger Scatcherd was in such poor health from excessive drinking that he decided to make his will, leaving everything to Louis Philippe, his equally alcoholic son. When Dr. Thorne learned the terms of the will, he told Sir Roger that Mary Scatcherd's child was still living. Sir Roger made her his second heir in the event of his son's death.

Otherwise matters were not going well for Mary. Lady Arabella, finding Frank's attachment for Mary unchanged, would not allow the girl to visit Greshamsbury. When Frank arrived home and became aware of the shabby treatment she had received, he was furious. But the family insisted that he had to marry wealth, particularly after his sister, who was to marry money, had been jilted.

Sir Roger was also in difficulties. Having discovered a fraud in his election, the committee unseated him, and the shock was too great for the old man. He went on one final drinking bout and died from the effects. Louis Philippe, having inherited the estate, also formed an attachment for Mary, but she remained true to Frank. Dr. Thorne's only hope for the happiness of Mary and Frank lay in the possible death of Louis Philippe. Meanwhile that young man was well on his way to fulfilling the doctor's half-wish. Having paid a visit to the squire for the purpose of foreclosing on some debts, Louis Philippe went on a drinking spree that rivaled any of his father's. Weak and very ill, he was finally sent home.

Soon afterward, in a stormy interview, Lady Arabella demanded that Mary end her engagement to Frank. Mary refused to break her promise, but she did ask the young man to release her because of the hopelessness of the situation in which they found themselves. Frank refused, insisting that they loved each other. Then it was that Louis Philippe died. Doctor Thorne jubilantly told Mary the news of her inheritance, news which opened the way for her marriage to Frank. With Mary now an heiress in her own right, not even the proud De Courcys could object to so excellent a match. For the first time in years an atmosphere of rejoicing hung over Greshamsbury Park.

Critical Evaluation

Third of the Barset novels, *Doctor Thorne* (1858) extends the range of *The Warden* (1855) and *Barchester Towers* (1857) beyond the confined world of ecclesiastical politics to the open countryside surrounding Grashamsbury. It is a sunny, leisurely fiction centering around the problems of romantic love. Like all of Trollope's important novels, *Doctor Thorne* shows how the affairs of love are crucially entangled with those of power. For the Victorians, power was seen to derive from the privileges of caste and money. And in *Doctor Thorne* the amorous couple cannot wed until they settle these two vexing matters to the satisfaction of their families. Trollope lets us know that his two attractive lovers—the sprightly Mary Thorne and her sturdy, faithful Frank Gresham—are destined to marry. In his first chapter, indeed, the writer intrudes: "I am too old now to be a hard-hearted author," so he promises the likelihood that Frank "may not die of a broken heart." But before this happy consummation can be reached, he places before his romantic lovers the main obstacles to their progress: those caused by caste and money.

From a modern reader's viewpoint, the obstacles—simply conventions of the Victorian novel—are difficult to apprehend. Trollope's was a restricted class society, in which individuals enjoyed only a limited freedom to break their inherited social barriers. For most Victorians, the sole opportunity to rise in class was to attain sufficient money—usually through a legacy or some chance windfall—to alter the conditions of one's original rank. As a test of class, then, two qualities had to be measured, blood (caste) and wealth. One's class was more or less fixed, inherited. Yet the lines of inheritance were not always very clear indications of blood, not even going back several generations, because each individual had to be judged on the basis of both maternal and fraternal family strains; and those blood-lines associated with rank or property were considered finer than those merely indicating good old stock. Of course, with money one could greatly improve his social caste. So money serves as the conventional means of attaining power in the Victorian novel.

Running throughout *Doctor Thorne* is the litany: "Frank must marry money." His family has blood, but the elder Gresham has unwisely squandered the source of the family wealth, landed property. The young man's problem, then, is to get money; that is, to marry money in order to restore the family's estate. But to the Victorians, money like blood signified caste. The most respectable money was seen to derive from properties of the old landed gentry; less respectable money could come from inheritance; and the least respectable money could come from labor. Sir Roger Scatcherd's wealth has been earned through his hard work, his mechanical genius, and his special managerial skills. Nevertheless, his money is suspect, vulgar. On the other hand, the de Courcys, aristocratic snobs of the purest but most lethargic blood, have pride in their money because they do not work for it. They judge money, almost as they judge blood, on the basis of its source. Yet money is money, and even money vulgarly acquired, like that of Miss Dunstable, is far better than none.

Trollope's Victorian audience appreciated the writer's fine discriminating sense of the social caste system. For them the class novel was educational as well as entertaining. They could learn by imitation the speech, manners, and affectations of gentility; above all, they could learn how to imitate the character of upper-class people. For character was believed to be a product of breeding. In *Doctor Thorne*, Trollope demonstrates his mastery of the types of character that could be studied and emulated. At the top of his social scale is the Duke of Omnium, nearly as wealthy as royalty and quite as proud. When the Duke (who is to figure prominently in the later Palliser novels) makes a brief appearance at the final wedding scene, he bestows upon the principals of the story the greatest social blessing they might hope to expect. Below him in rank, blood, and certainly wealth are the de Courcys of Courcy Castle; they are proud, stiff, unimaginative, acquisitive, and dull. Lady Arabella, the elder Gresham's wife, is a typical de Courcy in her narrow family pride; but the author pardons her faults to a degree, because she has motherly aspirations for her darling Frank. The Greshams, also old in blood but now reduced from their former land holdings, fall below the de Courcys. And quite below that family are the Thornes. Also of good old stock, they are landless, snubbed by the aristocratic Thornes of Ullathorne. Because Dr. Thorne, a genteel country doctor, works for a living, his rank on the social scale is consequently lower. Yet in his pride of blood, he feels greatly superior to Sir Roger, a parvenu without the honorable status of old blood but embarrassed with an excess of money.

For modern readers of *Doctor Thorne*, of course, the Victorian caste system may be appreciated as a convention of the novel. Along with other conventions governing romantic love—extended courtship of lovers, sexual reticence, and absolute parental authority—that of class can be viewed as a complicated game in which all the players know their rules perfectly well and have to maneuver as best they can within a very narrow range of action. Part of the pleasure of reading

Trollope is to play, along with the author, the game according to its strict rules. In fact, Trollope participates in the plot as a friend and guide to the reader, now commenting on the action, now speaking directly to his audience. Unlike the philosophical Thackeray or the moralistic George Eliot, Trollope speaks directly to the reader as a congenial, urbanely amused interpreter of the action. Following his example, his readers are expected to take part in the game as well, not so much passive observers as friends who wish their fictional acquaintances good fortune.

To maintain his genial tone, Trollope treats with gentle irony his characters' pretentions to elevated caste. We perceive that the de Courcys' pride in their blood is absurd. But isn't the Greshams' pride nearly as foolish? And what about the good Dr. Thorne, who is passionately proud of his family line? Trollope's attitude about this crucial matter is ambivalent. On the one hand, he shows us clearly that Mary Thorne, except for her tainted birth, is a perfect mate in every sense for Frank Gresham; in fact, she is surely the more industrious, more lively, and more patient of the pair. But can strength of character compensate for some supposed deficiency in family stock? Trollope never tests the question directly, for he finally bestows upon Mary the gift of an inheritance great enough to allow for any defect in blood. Yet the question persists. For Dr. Thorne, an otherwise sensible and honorable man, the answer is clear enough: without money, Mary is not worthy of Frank, because blood is the chief quality of class. Nevertheless, Trollope gives the reader scope to make an independent judgment. And that judgment is bound to be more liberal than Dr. Thorne's.

The most severe test for Dr. Thorne as a man of character is the way he handles the provisions of Sir Roger's will. As executor of the Scatcherd estate, he has obligations—however unpleasant—to guide the conduct of Sir Louis, the dissolute heir of the family fortune. By his actions Dr. Thorne proves that he is a gentleman, worthy of Sir Roger's trust, by counselling Louis to abstain from the alcohol that had killed his father. What makes Dr. Thorne's conduct the more admirable is his knowledge that, should the young man succumb to vice and die prematurely from his debauchery, Mary Thorne would inherit most of the great wealth of the estate. He loves Mary, would wish her happy, and could—with only a few words hinting about her possible great expectations as a legatee—inspire her with hopes for marrying Frank. Or a few words to his friend Gresham might smooth the way for the lovers. But Dr. Thorne maintains a stoical silence. Not until he is certain that the Scatcherd will is legally authentic and names his niece as heiress will be announce (with suitable suspense) the long-awaited good news.

On one level of interpretation, Dr. Thorne's reticence is admirable. He follows absolutely his code of action to allow Mary to make whatever decisions about a mate she wishes, without bending to her uncle's authority. But on another level of interpretation, the doctor's reticence is difficult to approve. By withholding until the last possible moment the information about Mary's fortune, he causes great suffering to his friends, and above all to Mary. Is he simply stubborn, as he seems to be when he denies Sir Roger's deathbed request, a modest enough satisfaction of blessing his sister's child? Or is he peevish, as when he prohibits Mary from visiting Lady Scatcherd, perhaps out of fear of some vulgar contamination with a woman of her class? Or has Dr. Thorne some deeper psychological reasons that might explain his curious reticence: secret incestuous feelings for Mary? Of course, the question is at best speculative. Trollope's surface investigation of Dr. Thorne's character does not permit a closer analysis of the uncle's motivation. For the modern reader, it is sufficient to accept Dr. Thorne's conduct as a test of his integrity. A man of character—of honor—he subdues his sentimental inclinations to lighten Mary's burdens by raising her hopes until he has perfect reason to do so.

More difficult for the modern reader to understand is the romantic motivation of the lovers. They are obviously well matched, have been childhood playmates, then adolescent affectionate friends. Now Trollope wants us to accept their developing passion as young adults. But he never really shows us the stages of the passion. Instead, he assumes that the handsome Frank will naturally love the beautiful Mary, and that the love will be returned. However, he separates the lovers throughout most of the novel, and when he joins them near the conclusion—with the money impediment out of the way—they seem at first as shy toward each other as we would expect them to be. On the other hand, the relationship between Frank and the plain but sensible Miss Dunstable has been presented with perfect realism to the reader. One of the most effective scenes of the novel is Miss Dunstable's rejection of Frank's callow marriage proposal. She gives him a splendid lesson in manners—one that Mary is never permitted to match. Small wonder that Miss Dunstable seems more nearly rounded a character than either Frank or Mary.

At his best, Trollope bends the conventions of the Victorian novel to treat with humor and gentle realism the true character of men and women. For example, when Sir Roger argues with Dr. Thorne about the deleterious effects of alcoholism, we know that the writer understands the human heart. Or, in the delightful Chapter 12, when Dr. Thorne confronts his rival, Dr. Fillgrave, at the Scatcherd mansion, we are prepared for a scene of high comedy that carries the conviction of truth. In many realistic touches throughout the novel, Trollope fulfills his early promise to the reader, to atone for any artistic faults "by straightforward, simple, plain story telling." Indeed, the writer was pleased with *Doctor Thorne*. In his *Autobiography,* he judged that the novel "has, I believe, been the most successful book I have ever written." Most modern readers would choose either *The Warden* or *Barchester Towers* for this honor; but surely *Doctor Thorne* holds a special place of affection among Trollope's admirers as the writer's most endearing love story.

Bibliography

Baker, Ernest A.   *The History of the English Novel*, Volume VIII. New York: Barnes and Noble, 1950, pp. 132–134.

Booth, Bradford A. *Anthony Trollope: Aspects of His Life and Art.* London: Edward Hulton, 1958, pp. 44–48.

Dixon, Sir Owen. "Sir Roger Scatcherd's Will, in Anthony Trollope's *Doctor Thorne*," in *Jesting Pilate, and Other Papers and Addresses.* Sydney, Australia: Law Book Company, 1965, pp. 71–81.

Hagan, John. "The Divided Mind of Anthony Trollope," in *Nineteenth-Century Fiction.* XIV (June, 1959), pp. 1–26.

Hennedy, Hugh L. "*Doctor Thorne*: Fairy Tale and Satire," in *Unity in Barsetshire.* The Hague: Mouton, 1971, pp. 56–70.

Kincaid, James R. *The Novels of Anthony Trollope.* Oxford: Clarendon Press, 1977, pp. 113–120.

Melada, Ivan. *The Captains of Industry in English Fiction, 1821–1871.* Albuquerque: University of New Mexico Press, 1970, pp. 166–171.

Polhemus, Robert M. *The Changing World of Anthony Trollope.* Berkeley: University of California Press, 1968, pp. 52–58.

Sadleir, Michael. *Trollope: A Commentary.* New York: Farrar, Straus, 1947, pp. 375–385.

Saintsbury, George. "Trollope Revisited," in *The Collected Essays and Papers of George Saintsbury, 1875–1920*, Volume II. London: J.M. Dent, 1923, pp. 330–331.

Walpole, Hugh. *Anthony Trollope.* New York: Macmillan, 1928, pp. 51–55.

Williams, Raymond. *The English Novel: From Dickens to Lawrence.* London: Chatto and Windus, 1970, pp. 84–86.

THE LAST CHRONICLE OF BARSET

Type of work: Novel
Author: Anthony Trollope (1815–1882)
Type of plot: Domestic realism
Time of plot: Mid-nineteenth century
Locale: "Barsetshire," England
First published: 1867

As in the other novels set in the shire of Barset, this last book in the series displays Anthony Trollope's genius for understanding both human wisdom and human ignorance. The gentler satire of the earlier Barsetshire stories is replaced by a criticism of materialism more cutting than usual for Trollope.

Principal Characters

The Rev. Josiah Crawley, "perpetual curate of Hogglestock," a poor parish. He is frequently unable to pay his bills from his meager living and Dean Arabin often gives him money he is shy about taking. On one occasion he pays a butcher's bill with a stolen check and is brought before a magistrate's court. The court decides on a full trial, for Crawley's explanation is vague and contradictory. In addition, Mrs. Proudie attempts to have him removed from his living. Finally, John Eames reaches Mrs. Arabin, traveling in Europe, who completely exonerates Crawley and explains the stolen check. Crawley later receives the more profitable living of St. Ewold's.

Grace Crawley, his daughter, in love with Major Henry Grantly. When Mr. Crawley is accused, Henry Grantly feels he must stick by Grace and, despite the fierce objection of his father, he proposes to her. Grace nobly refuses, but, after her father is cleared, she marries Henry.

Mrs. Mary Crawley, the self-sacrificing wife of Mr. Crawley who copes extremely well with his intransigence and eccentricity.

Bishop Thomas Proudie, Bishop of Barchester, a weak man who is harassed by his wife until he agrees to bring Mr. Crawley before a clerical commission.

Mrs. Proudie, wife of the Bishop, who believes it her mission to uphold the honor of the Church. She persecutes Crawley and shames her husband by insisting on attending all his conferences. She dies of a heart attack.

Major Henry Grantly, a retired officer and a widower with a small daughter. When his father opposes his plans to marry Grace Crawley, he is ready to sell his lodge and move to France.

Archdeacon Theophilus Grantly, Archdeacon and wealthy ecclesiastical power in Barchester. He opposes his son's marriage to Grace Crawley.

Susan Grantly, his wife, who tries to keep peace between her husband and son.

Francis Arabin, Dean of Barchester Cathedral, who has always befriended the Crawleys.

Eleanor Arabin, his wife, whose generosity in stuffing an additional twenty pounds into the envelope for Mr. Crawley inadvertently precipitates the events of the novel. When she hears of the trouble, she immediately returns to give evidence.

Lilian Dale (Lily), a friend of Grace Crawley previously jilted by Adolphus Crosbie. Although Crosbie's wife, Lady Alexandrina has died, Lily still refuses to allow Crosbie to court her again.

John Eames, now private secretary to Sir Raffle Buffle and the cousin of Grace Crawley. At his own expense, he goes to Italy to find Mrs. Arabin. Although in love with Lily, he barely extricates himself from the clutches of Madalina Demolines.

Bernard Dale, the heir of the Squire of Allington, Lily's cousin, who becomes engaged to Emily Dunstable.

Emily Dunstable, cousin of Mrs. Martha Dunstable Thorne, a wealthy heiress.

Mrs. Martha Dunstable Thorne, a jolly social woman who tries to give Henry Grantly the courage to remain loyal to Grace.

Dr. Thomas Thorne, her husband, who sides with the Crawleys.

Christopher Dale, the Squire of Allington, who is extremely fond of Grace Crawley.

Mrs. Mary Dale, Lily's mother, who invites Grace to stay at Allington after the magistrate's hearing.

Lady Julia de Guest, the constant benefactress of John Eames.

Lady Lufton, an aristocrat who constantly opposes Mrs. Proudie and befriends the Crawleys.

Lord Ludovic Lufton, a friend of the Crawleys whose check was originally stolen.

Lady Lucy Robarts Lufton, his wife, a friend of the Crawleys.

Mr. Soames, Lord Lufton's business agent who thought he had dropped the check at Hogglestock parsonage.

Adolphus Crosbie, now a widower, in debt to Gagebee, who would like to marry Lily Dale.

Lady Dumbello, the Marchioness of Hartletop, Griselda Grantly, daughter of the Archdeacon, who sides with her father in objecting to Henry's marriage to Grace.

The Rev. Septimus Harding, the aged father of Eleanor Arabin, with whom he lives, and Susan Grantly. A warm old man, he requests, on his deathbed, that Crawley be given the living at St. Ewold's.

Edith Grantly, daughter of Major Henry Grantly.

Mr. Thomas Toogood, the lawyer who defends Mr. Crawley.

The Rev. Caleb Trumble, the clergyman Mrs. Proudie sends to take over Mr. Crawley's parish.

The Rev. Dr. Mortimer Tempest, a rural dean and vicar of Silverbridge. He leads the clerical commission investigating the case and thinks that Crawley should be judged by the court before the Church decides about his living.

Miss Madalina Demolines, a young London lady who plots to marry John Eames and writes an anonymous note to Lily Dale.

Lady Demolines, willingly a partner in her daughter's schemes.

Sir Raffle Buffle, the pompous chairman of the Income Tax Office.

Mr. Fletcher, the butcher who received the stolen check.

Mr. Quiverful, a member of the clerical commission and warden of Hiram's Hospital. Mrs. Proudie appoints him to the commission.

The Rev. Caleb Oriel, rector of Greshamsbury and a member of the clerical commission at Mrs. Proudie's suggestion.

The Rev. Mark Robarts, vicar of Framley, a member of the clerical commission.

Mr. Kissing, a silly secretary in the Income Tax Office.

Mr. Peter Bangles, a wine merchant who finally marries Madalina Demolines.

The Story

In the community of Hogglestock the citizens were upset because Mr. Crawley, the curate, had been accused of stealing a check for twenty pounds. In Archdeacon Grantly's home, where there was concern lest Henry Grantly might marry Grace Crawley, the curate's schoolteacher daughter, feeling was high.

Bishop Proudie and his wife were set against the unfortunate Crawley. Mrs. Proudie, who exerted great power over her husband, persuaded the bishop to write a letter forbidding Mr. Crawley to preach in his church until the case should have been settled one way or another. Mr. Crawley refused the injunction. Mr. and Mrs. Proudie quarreled over the answer, and Mr. Proudie sent for Mr. Crawley to attend him in the bishop's palace at once. When Mr. Crawley arrived, he was hot and tired from walking. He repeated what he had stated in his letter and left the bishop and his wife amazed at his boldness.

Mr. Crawley was not kept from performing his duties on Christmas morning. Since he could not recall how he had come into possession of the money in question, he informed his wife that he had but two choices—either to go to jail or to bedlam.

At last Henry Grantly decided to ask Grace Crawley to marry him, even though he should be going against his parents' wishes. At the same time Lily Dale, Grace Crawley's friend, was being wooed by young John Eames, a clerk in the Income Tax Office in London and a suitor, once rejected, whom Lily's mother favored. Eames was the friend of a London artist named Conway Dalrymple, who was painting a portrait of Miss Clara Van Siever, a mutual friend, in the sitting-room of Mrs. Dobbs Broughton. Meanwhile the aged Mrs. Van Siever was engaged in forcing Dobbs Broughton to pay money he owed to her.

Not long afterward John Eames met Henry Grantly. Neither liked the other at first. John, meeting Lily in Lady Julia de Guest's home, where Grace was also a guest, discussed his unfavorable meeting with Henry Grantly in front of Grace. When Henry proposed to Grace, she refused him and returned home to be with her father during his trial. Lily told John that she planned to die an old maid, her heart having been broken by Adolphus Crosbie, a former suitor.

Mr. Toogood, a distant relative, was to defend Mr. Crawley. John Eames was brought into the Crawley case by Mr. Toogood, who wanted John to go to Florence and attempt to persuade Mr. Arabin, an influential clergyman, to come to Mr. Crawley's rescue. There was another reason why Arabin should return to England. Mrs. Arabin's father, Mr. Harding, was ailing and growing weaker each day.

Conway Dalrymple worked on Miss Van Siever's picture, which was still a secret from Dobbs Broughton, in whose house it was being painted. Although Broughton had ordered the artist out of his house, Mrs. Broughton wanted the picture painted, regardless of her jealous husband's reactions.

The clerical commission summoned by Bishop Proudie reached no decision concerning Mr. Crawley. It was resolved that nothing should be done until the civil courts had decided his case.

Archdeacon Grantly tried to engage the help of Lady Lufton to prevent the marriage of his son to Grace Crawley, but Lady Lufton refused. The archdeacon finally promised that he would no longer oppose the marriage if Mr. Crawley should be found innocent of any crime.

Dobbs Broughton was being pressed hard for money by old Mrs. Van Siever. Clara Van Siever was to marry Musselboro, Broughton's former partner. Dalrymple, still hoping to marry Clara, was putting the last touches to the canvas when Mrs. Van Siever entered the Broughton house. At her word he destroyed the portrait. Over Clara's objections, Mrs. Van Siever announced that her daughter was to marry Musselboro. After the Van Sievers left, Musselboro arrived with news that Dobbs Broughton had killed himself that morning. Clara and Dalrymple resolved to face Mrs. Van Siever's wrath together.

Mrs. Proudie continued her fight to have Mr. Crawley removed. After a quarrel between the bishop and Mrs. Proudie, she retired to her room and there died of a heart attack. True to the resolution imposed upon him by Mrs. Proudie before her death, Mr. Crawley preached a final sermon in his church and never again entered it as the curate.

On the continent John Eames learned from Mrs. Arabin the cause of Mr. Crawley's troubles. Mrs. Arabin, who had received the check from a tenant, had turned it over to Mr. Crawley without telling her husband, the dean, of the transaction. She had only recently heard of the charges and she was hurrying home to England to do what could be done to straighten out the matter. In the meantime Mr. Toogood traced the theft of the check to the tenant who had forwarded it to Mrs. Arabin.

Mr. Toogood and Henry Grantly took the good news to Mr. and Mrs. Crawley. When she heard their story, Mrs. Crawley, who had defended her husband from the beginning, broke into tears. The messengers had to explain the situation carefully to Mr. Crawley, who could not at first believe that his innocence was about to be proved. Then Mr. Harding, the aged incumbent in St. Ewold's, died. Archdeacon Grantly offered the living to Mr. Crawley as a recompense for all he had suffered. In midsummer Grace Crawley became Mrs. Henry Grantly.

John Eames did not marry Lily Dale after all, for Lily was unable to make her decision, but Dalrymple married Clara Van Siever as he had planned. Musselboro, who had lost Clara, proceeded to marry the widow of his old partner and thus Mrs. Broughton's sorrows were brought to an end.

Critical Evaluation

In this novel Trollope brings to a close the great Barsetshire series: *The Warden* (1855), *Barchester Towers* (1857), *Dr. Thorne* (1858), *Framley Parsonage* (1861), and *The Small House at Allington* (1864). The ecclesiastical and social controversies of the earlier novels are extended in *The Last Chronicle of Barset* to a satire of a society which is becoming increasingly materialistic. The Reverend Josiah Crawley represents the extreme rejection of worldly ambition; he is so absorbed in ministering to his poor parishioners that he literally cannot remember what became of a check for twenty pounds that passed through his hands. To be accused of stealing is the utmost irony for a man of Crawley's uncompromising integrity. His old friend Archdeacon Grantly is equally honest, but he lives "in the world," enjoying prosperity and good living. He is dismayed at his son Henry's desire to marry Crawley's penniless daughter instead of looking about for a more suitable match. Henry's sister Griselda had previously set an excellent example by marrying Lord Dumbello and thus bringing both wealth and title into the family. Trollope implies an ironic contrast between this loveless marriage of social ambition and the genuine attachment of Henry and Grace Crawley; and like Lady Lufton in *Framley Parsonage,* Archdeacon Grantly learns that he must at last give way or lose his son's affection.

The scenes in London in this novel emphasize the ugliness of materialistic society. In the dark world of the Dobbs Broughtons and Van Sievers, only the acquisition of money has any reality. The world of Barsetshire, for all its petty jealousies and minor skirmishing, seems sunlit compared with this urban world devoid of all moral values.

The Last Chronicle of Barset closes the Barsetshire series with the deaths of two memorable characters, Mrs. Proudie and the Reverend Harding. Bishop Proudie, the classically henpecked husband, at last asserts himself on the issue of Crawley's innocence, and the shock symbolically—and perhaps literally—brings on Mrs. Proudie's death. The Reverend Harding, the Warden of the first novel, represents the balanced character that Trollope sees as the ideal: he is as honest as Crawley, but gentle and affectionate where Crawley is stiff-necked and proud. With Harding's passing, the world of Barset also passes into irrevocable change.

Bibliography

Arthur, R. Anthony. "Authorial Intrusion as Art in *The Last Chronicle of Barset,*" in *Journal of Narrative Technique.* I (1971), pp. 200–206.

Baker, Ernest A. *The History of the English Novel.* Volume VIII. New York: Barnes & Noble, 1950, pp. 141–146.

Booth, Bradford A. *Anthony Trollope: Aspects of His Life and Art.* London: Edward Hulton, 1958, pp. 56–59.

Brown, Beatrice Curtis. *Anthony Trollope.* Denver: Alan Swallow, 1950, pp. 57–58.

Corsa, Helen Storm. " 'The Cross-Grainedness of Men': The Reverend Josiah Crawley—Trollope's Study of a Paranoid Personality," in *Hartford Studies in Literature.* V (1973), pp. 160–172.

Escott, T.H.S. *Anthony Trollope: His Work, Associates and Literary Associations.* London: John Lane, 1913, pp. 236–238.

Fredman, Alice Green. *Anthony Trollope.* New York: Columbia University Press, 1971, pp. 17–21.

Harvey, Geoffrey M. "The Form of the Story: Trollope's *The Last Chronicle of Barset*," in *Texas Studies in Literature and Language.* XVIII (Spring, 1976), pp. 82–97.

————. "Heroes in Barsetshire," in *Dalhousie Review.* LII (1972), pp. 458–468.

Hennedy, Hugh L. "Disgrace and Obedience in *The Last Chronicle of Barset*," in *Unity in Barsetshire.* The Hague: Mouton, 1971, pp. 105–124.

Kincaid, James R. *The Novels of Anthony Trollope.* Oxford: Clarendon Press, 1977, pp. 132–142.

Mizener, Arthur. "Introduction," in *The Last Chronicle of Barset.* Boston: Houghton Mifflin, 1964, pp. i–xv.

Page, Norman. "Trollope's Conversational Mode," in *English Studies in Africa.* XV (1972), pp. 33–37.

Polhemus, Robert M. *The Changing World of Anthony Trollope.* Berkeley: University of California Press, 1968, pp. 129–146.

Pope-Hennessey, James. *Anthony Trollope.* Boston: Little, Brown, 1971, pp. 272–277.

Priestly, J.B. "In Barsetshire," in *The Balconinny.* New York: Harper, 1930, pp. 152–159.

Saintsbury, George. "Trollope Revisited," in *The Collected Essays and Papers of George Saintsbury, 1875–1920,* Volume II. London: J.M. Dent, 1923, pp. 338–340.

Terry, R.C. *Anthony Trollope: The Artist in Hiding.* Totowa, N.J.: Rowman and Littlefield, 1977.

Thale, Jerome. "The Problem of Structure in Trollope," in *Nineteenth-Century Fiction.* XV (September, 1960), pp. 147–157.

Walpole, Hugh. *Anthony Trollope.* New York: Macmillan, 1928, pp. 63–67.

West, William A. "*The Last Chronicle of Barset*: Trollope's Comic Techniques," in *The Classic British Novel.* Edited by Howard M. Harper, Jr. and Charles E. Edge. Athens: University of Georgia Press, 1972, pp. 121–142.

ORLEY FARM

Type of work: Novel
Author: Anthony Trollope (1815–1882)
Type of plot: Domestic romance
Time of plot: Mid-nineteenth century
Locale: England
First published: 1862

In this lively and complicated story, Trollope calls into play all those elements which Victorian readers so enjoyed: a forged will, a false heir, a woman with a guilty secret, a chivalrous gentleman, romantic young love, a long court trial, expiation, and the defeat of villainy.

Principal Characters

Lady Mary Mason, the widow of Sir Joseph Mason, forty-five years her senior. After Sir Joseph's death her son Lucius was awarded Orley Farm by a codicil to his father's will. The codicil had been contested by Joseph Mason, Sir Joseph's son by an earlier marriage, but Lady Mason won the court case. Later a shady attorney, Dockwrath, angry at Lucius, digs up some papers that lead him to believe the codicil a forgery. He gets Joseph Mason to reopen the case. Lady Mason is befriended by Sir Peregrine Orme. When Sir Peregrine proposes, Lady Mason confesses that the codicil was, indeed, a forgery, her only means of gaining property for her son. Nevertheless, she also wins the second case. She then confesses to Lucius, who turns the property over to Joseph, and mother and son leave for Germany.

Lucius Mason, the son of Sir Joseph and Lady Mary Mason, educated in Germany. When he returns, he decides to establish Orley Farm as a working experiment for his agricultural theories. This project involves forcing Dockwrath off his small fields, and Dockwrath's ire precipitates the second court case. He proposes to Sophia Furnival, but she refuses him after he is no longer in control of Orley Farm.

Sir Peregrine Orme, the owner of The Cleeve, a wealthy and highly respected gentleman. Very chivalrous, he is willing to stand by his proposal to Lady Mason even after he knows she has forged the codicil.

Mrs. Edith Orme, the widowed daughter-in-law of Sir Peregrine Orme, who lives with him. Also loyal to Lady Mason, she accompanies her to court.

Peregrine Orme (Perry), the son of Mrs. Edith Orme and heir to The Cleeve. He proposes to Madeline Stavely, but is rejected.

Joseph Mason, owner of Groby Park in Yorkshire and older son of Sir Joseph Mason. He is a severe man, a county magistrate, but he is not unjust; he has always believed that his father intended to leave Orley Farm to him.

Mrs. Mason, his wife, an inhospitable, parsimonious woman.

Judge Stavely, a kind and perceptive judge who owns Noningsby. He is proud that his daughter has chosen an ugly, brilliant man rather than the suitable young Peregrine Orme.

Lady Stavely, his devoted wife, who cannot understand her daughter but finally gives her blessing to the marriage.

Madeline Stavely, their beautiful daughter, who chooses and waits for the penniless Felix Graham to win her parents' permission to propose.

Augustus Stavely, a friend of Felix Graham. He, like Lucius Mason, proposes to Sophia Furnival, but she puts him off.

Felix Graham, a brilliant and ugly young barrister who is the youngest lawyer taking Lady Mason's case. At first he is engaged to Mary Snow, a girl he befriends and is training to be his wife. He then breaks several bones while hunting at the Stavely's, is forced to remain at Noningsby, and falls in love with Madeline. He arranges another wedding for Mary Snow and marries Madeline himself.

Mr. Furnival, an attorney for Lady Mason and a member of Parliament. He suspects that Lady Mason is guilty, but remains loyal to her.

Mrs. Furnival, nee Kitty Blacker, his wife who is frequently left alone while he works. At one point, she suspects her husband is attached to Lady Mason and leaves him, but she later returns.

Sophia Furnival, their pretty daughter, who flirts her way into two proposals but accepts neither.

Samuel Dockwrath, a shady attorney who wants to be employed by Joseph Mason. His efforts are unsuccessful.

Mrs. Miriam Usbech Dockwrath, his wife, the mother of sixteen children.

Jonathan Usbech, Miriam's father and Sir Joseph's attorney. He was supposed to be ill at the time the codicil was drawn up and he died before the first trial.

John Kenneby, Sir Joseph's former clerk, who testifies that he had witnessed the signing of a document. Heckled by the attorneys at both trials, he acknowledges that he did not know the nature of the document he witnessed.

Mr. Moulder, a salesman of tea, coffee, and brandy, brother-in-law to John Kenneby.

Mrs. Mary Anne Moulder, Kenneby's sister, anxious to promote his marriage to a wealthy widow.

Mrs. Smiley, a widow who owns brick fields and is engaged to John Kenneby.

Bridget Bolster, a chambermaid who testifies at both trials.

Mr. Chaffanbrass, a seasoned attorney and a friend of Mr. Furnival, adept at breaking down witnesses.

Mr. Solomon Aram, an Old Bailey lawyer, also employed for Lady Mason.

Mr. Matthew Round, attorney for the firm of Round and Crook, employed by Joseph Mason.

Mr. Crabwitz, an old assistant in Mr. Furnival's office.

Miss Martha Biggs, the friend who wants Mrs. Furnival to join her in Red Lion Square when she contemplates leaving Mr. Furnival.

Mary Snow, the daughter of an engraver, engaged to Felix Graham, later married to Albert Fitzallen.

Albert Fitzallen, a worker in an apothecary shop, helped by Felix Graham.

Mr. Snow, an engraver, Mary's father, a habitual gin drinker.

Mrs. Thomas, who uncovers Mary's correspondence with Albert.

Mr. Green, the curate at Groby Park.

Mrs. Green, his wife, who receives patent steel furniture in bad condition from Mrs. Mason.

Mr. Slow and
Mr. Bideawhile, attorneys to Sir Peregrine Orme.

The Story

Sir Joseph Mason was nearing seventy when he married a second wife forty-five years his junior. Having been in turn merchant, alderman, mayor, and knight, he had by that time amassed a large fortune, out of which he purchased Groby Park, a landed estate in Yorkshire. This property he turned over to the son of his first marriage, Joseph Mason, Esq., who under his father's generous provision was able to lead the life of a country gentleman with as much magnificence as his mean, grasping nature would allow. Sir Joseph himself made his home at Orley Farm, a country residence not far from London. Joseph Mason had always been assured that the farm would go to him, as head of the family, at his father's death.

The baronet's second marriage was little more than an old man's attempt to find companionship and comfort in his declining years, and young Lady Mason, a quiet, sensible, clever woman, cheerfully accepted it as such. One son, Lucius, was born to them. Then Sir Joseph died suddenly, and when the time came to prove his will it was discovered that in an attached codicil he had bequeathed Orley Farm to his infant son. Joseph Mason, feeling that he had been deprived of property rightfully his, contested the codicil.

The Orley Farm Case, as it was called, had many complications. The will had been drawn up by Jonathan Usbech, Sir Joseph's attorney, but it, like the codicil, was in Lady Mason's handwriting, old Usbech having suffered from a gouty hand at the time. It had been witnessed by John Kennerby, Sir Joseph's clerk, and by Bridget Bolster, a housemaid. At the trial both swore that they had been called to their master's bedside and there, in the presence of Usbech and Lady Mason, had signed a document which all assumed had been the codicil. Lady Mason readily admitted that while she had asked nothing for herself she had wanted much for her child, and that before Usbech and Mr. Furnival, a barrister, she had often urged her husband to leave Orley Farm to little Lucius. Old Usbech having died in the meantime, she was unable to have her statement confirmed by him, but Mr. Furnival testified to the truth of her assertion.

The result was that Joseph Mason lost his case. The will and codicil having been upheld, Lady Mason and her son continued to live at Orley Farm and to enjoy its yearly income of eight hundred pounds. Joseph Mason retired to sulk at Groby Park. Miriam Usbech, old Jonathan's daughter, also benefited under the terms of the codicil to the extent of two thousand pounds, an inheritance she lost when she entrusted it to her husband, Samuel Dockwrath, a shady young attorney from the neighboring town of Hamworth. Relations between Usbech's daughter and the mistress of Orley Farm were always friendly. Because of Lady Mason, Dockwrath held at low rental two outlying fields on the estate.

Among the neighbors who had stood by Lady Mason during the trial was Sir Peregrine Orme of The Cleeve. Other members of his household were his daughter-in-law, Mrs. Orme, who was Lady Mason's best friend, and his grandson, namesake, and heir. Young Peregrine Orme and Lucius Mason were the same age. They had little else in common. Peregrine, educated at Harrow and Oxford, heir to a great estate, was a well-meaning but somewhat wild young man whose chief interests were fox hunting and rat-baiting. He was also in love with Madeline Stavely, lovely daughter of Judge Stavely of Noningsby. Lucius Mason, after a term at a German university, returned to Orley Farm with the plan of putting into practice methods of scientific farming he had learned abroad.

One of his first acts was to serve notice of his intention to repossess the fields leased to Dockwrath. An unpleasant interview between Lady Mason and the angry attorney followed. Concerned over Dockwrath's vague threats, she went to Sir Peregrine for advice, as she had gone on many occasions during the past twenty years. Sir Peregrine snorted with disgust over Lucius' agricultural theories and announced that he would bring the young man to his senses. Lucius went to dine at The Cleeve but refused to give up his plans. Sir Peregrine decided that the earnest young man was as conceited as he was stubborn.

In the meantime Dockwrath had been busy. Going through his father-in-law's papers, he learned that on the date carried by the codicil Sir Joseph had signed a deed of separation dissolving a business partnership between him and one Mr. Martock. Either two documents had been signed on that day, a possibility which the evidence at the trial made unlikely, or the codicil was a forgery. Armed with this information, Dockwrath went to Groby Park to confer with Joseph Mason. The upshot of that conference was Mason's decision to reopen the Orley Farm Case.

Dockwrath, hoping to advance himself in his profession, begged for an opportunity to handle the case, but the squire, aware of Dockwrath's reputation, told him to take his information to the firm of Round and Crook, reputable London lawyers who would be above suspicion. Mason did promise, however, that Dockwrath would be rewarded if Lady Mason were convicted and Orley Farm returned to its rightful owner. The Hamworth lawyer then went to London and offered his services to Round and Crook. They were willing to use him but only to collect information which might prove useful.

When Miriam Dockwrath carried to Orley Farm an account of her husband's activities, Lady Mason appealed to Sir Peregrine, her good friend, and Mr. Furnival, her attorney, for advice and help. Mr. Furnival, with the passing of time, had changed from a hard-working young barrister into a fashionable attorney with a weakness for port wine and lovely women. Lady Mason was still attractive, and so he comforted her more as a woman than as a client, assuring her that the Orley Farm Case, unappealed at the time, was not likely to be reviewed. Chivalrous Sir Peregrine was stirred to great indignation by what he considered the dastardly conduct of Joseph Mason, whom he had always disliked.

Lucius, hearing the news, was equally indignant and told his mother to leave the matter in his hands. Sir Peregrine and Mr. Furnival had difficulty in restraining him from acting rashly.

Actually, the outcome of the suit was more important to Lucius than he realized. He was in love with Sophia Furnival, daughter of his mother's attorney, but that prudent young woman intended to choose her husband with discretion. Another of her suitors was Adolphus Stavely, son of the distinguished jurist. She could afford to wait for the time being.

Meanwhile Peregrine's wooing of Madeline Stavely had fared badly, for Madeline had no interest in anyone except Felix Graham, a penniless young barrister. The judge, convinced that Graham would make his way in the world, silently approved his daughter's choice, but her mother, eager to see her daughter mistress of The Cleeve, grew impatient with her husband because of his refusal to speak up for young Orme.

There was some delay in determining grounds for a suit. The will having been upheld years before, it was felt that a charge of forgery was impossible after so long a time. Finally Round and Crook decided to prosecute for perjury, charging that in the previous trial Lady Mason had sworn falsely to the execution of the will.

When word came that Lady Mason would have to stand trial, Mrs. Orme invited her to stay at The Cleeve. This invitation, dictated by Sir Peregrine, was intended to show to the county the Ormes' confidence in their neighbor's innocence. But Sir Peregrine's chivalry did not stop there. At last he offered Lady Mason the protection of his name as well as his house, and she, almost overwhelmed by the prospect of the coming trial, promised to marry him.

Lucius and Peregrine were both opposed to the marriage, although Sir Peregrine reconciled his grandson in part by encouraging that young man in his own unsuccessful suit. Mr. Furnival became less gallant. Lady Mason's conscience, however, would not allow her to accept Sir Peregrine's offer. One night she went to him and confessed that she had forged the codicil in a desperate effort to keep the property for her son. Sir Peregrine, shocked by the news, was still determined to stand by her during the trial.

Mr. Furnival was shrewd. When he heard that his client was not to marry Sir Peregrine after all, he was convinced that the whole story had not been told. Suspecting her possible guilt, he hired the famous Mr. Chaffanbrass and his associate, Mr. Solomon Aram, noted criminal lawyers, to defend Lady Mason at the trial. Felix Graham was to act as a junior counsel for the defense.

The trial lasted for two days and part of another. The heckling attorneys so confused John Kennerby that his testimony was worthless. Bridget Bolster insisted, however, that she had signed only one document on that particular day. Even Mr. Chaffanbrass was unable to break down her story; the most damaging admission she made was that she liked an occasional glass of spirits. But Dockwrath was completely discredited, especially after Mr. Chaffanbrass forced him to admit his revengeful motives and Joseph Mason's promise to reward him for his services. At the end of the second day Lady Mason confessed her guilt to her son. The next morning he was not in court with her when the verdict was announced. Lady Mason was acquitted.

The jury's verdict was legal only, not moral. A few days later Mr. Furnival notified Joseph Mason that Lucius was transferring Orley Farm to his half-brother. Lucius himself was returning to Germany with his mother; later he hoped to become a farmer in Australia. Sir Peregrine went to see Lady Mason in London. Their farewell was gentle and sad on his part, final on hers. Dockwrath sued Joseph Mason to collect payment for his help and was completely ruined in the suit. Sophia Furnival decided that she could never be anything but a sister to Lucius. Madeline Stavely married her penniless barrister and lived more happily than her mother thought she deserved. Young Peregrine Orme eased his broken heart by shooting lions and elephants in central Africa.

Critical Evaluation

The narrative of *Orley Farm* proceeds with a leisurely pace seldom, if ever, found in modern novels. One of the charms of Trollope's long and richly detailed book is this lack of bustle. There seems to be time for everything in the Trollopian world. No troubles exist which cannot be postponed for a fortnight or six months. The legal technicalities and convolutions of the story are the least important parts of the novel to a modern reader. They are merely the framework upon which Trollope hangs his lively and vivid picture of mid-Victorian England. The characters are well drawn and amusing, but the reader has only mild interest as to who will triumph in the end. This kind of novel can be brought to a conclusion at almost any point (with all of the plot ends neatly tied up) or allowed to stretch on almost indefinitely.

Although the plot is not as thrilling as that of a Dickens or Wilkie Collins novel, and the social perceptions are not as profound as in a Thackeray story, and the moral problems are not handled with the philosophical insight of George Eliot, Trollope created an entire world in *Orley Farm* and his other great novels, and it is this achievement that his readers continue to treasure. Ordinary life is viewed with a gentle and endearing humor. For example, the alternating views of the Christmas festivities at the homes of the principal characters of *Orley Farm* give a delightful and vivid picture of traditional Victorian holiday customs through several social strata. The scene in the commercial room of the King's Head in which Mr. Kantwise demonstrates enthusiastically the merits of his new line of "Louey catorse" iron furniture is as funny today as when it was written. And equally humorous is the scene in which the parsimonious Mrs. Mason presents a damaged "new" set of the iron furniture to the open-mouthed curate and his wife. In scenes such as these (which usually have nothing to do with the plot) Trollope is at his best; and few authors have equaled the good-natured but sharp humor which seems to have been so effortlessly put on paper.

Trollope became notorious after the publication of his *Autobiography* for the deliberate method in which he wrote his novels. He rose regularly at

5:30 A.M. and wrote steadily for two hours and a half at the rate of 250 words every quarter of an hour. After the failure of his first books, he was proud of his ability at last to make money from his writing. Eventually, he made as much as thirty-five hundred pounds from a single novel and averaged nearly five thousand pounds a year. The poverty of his childhood and his mother's frantic scribbling to make ends meet seems to have been responsible for this calculated approach to his art. Yet, from the Barchester series on, his novels maintain an amazingly high quality, not suffering from his tremendous output. He was a professional writer and wrote "not because he had to tell a story, but because he had a story to tell." His craftsmanship was such that when he sat down each morning (Sundays included) he could write his story smoothly and well.

And he wrote with a humor which has endured to our own day. It is seldom forced and rarely emphasized; it seems to have come so naturally to Trollope that he hardly realized that he was permeating his novels with it. Almost incidentally, the everyday doings of life are tinged with Trollope's gentle, tolerant humor. It is far removed from the "black humor" of the twentieth century, but perhaps will outlast most such sophisticated literary fashions.

Nathaniel Hawthorne in 1860 paid Trollope this tribute: "Have you ever read the novels of Anthony Trollope? They precisely suit my taste—solid and substantial, written on the strength of beef and through the inspiration of ale, and just as real as if some giant had hewn a great lump out of the earth and put it under a glass case, with all its inhabitants going about their daily business, and not suspecting that they were being made a show of." It is this vitality and sense of authentic life that we today find so rewarding in Trollope's books; and *Orley Farm,* without heights of passion or depths of tragedy of extremes of farce, represents precisely this vision of real human beings captured as if by photography.

Although they are well drawn, the hero and heroine, Felix Graham and Madeline Stavely, are not the most prepossessing characters of *Orley Farm.* Far more interesting are Samuel Dockwrath, as he grubs around to find money to support his sixteen children, Mrs. Joseph Mason, as she stoops to ever more ridiculous attempts to save money and food even from her own family, Lucius Mason and his blind but idealistic games with scientific farming, and the magnificent old gentleman Sir Peregrine Orme, whose gallantry even leads him to propose marriage to a woman in need when he is well past seventy.

Trollope reveled in man's idiosyncrasies, but he admired the solid virtues which built the Empire. His pen spent more time sketching these human idiosyncrasies than in moralizing. The characters develop little, if at all; their personalities are full-blown from their first entrances. Yet the book does not suffer from this. Trollope's technique makes the most of each character's individuality without requiring growth or deep changes. His brightly colored scenes and clearly drawn characters moving through neat plots suggest the cinema, and it is quite true that his novels were the popular entertainment of their day.

Trollope's ability to keep a score of personal relationships aloft like balls in the air suggests the juggler's art as much as that of the novelist. Even minor characters in *Orley Farm,* such as the jealous Mrs. Furnival and the industrious young Mr. Crabwitz or Mary Snow, the would-be "moulded wife" of Felix Graham, are glimpsed in the midst of their own busy and (to them) important lives. They never give the impression of having been dragged into the scene to fill up space like so many film extras. It is this sense of the simultaneity of life on many different levels that gives the book its powerful feeling of reality. The chief difference between *Orley Farm* and real life is that the novel is never dull.

Bibliography

Adams, Robert M. *"Orley Farm* and Real Fiction," in *Nineteenth-Century Fiction.* VIII (June, 1953), pp. 27–41.

Booth, Bradford A. *Anthony Trollope: Aspects of His Life and Art.* London: Edward Hulton, 1958, pp. 192–195.

————. "Trollope's *Orley Farm*: Artistry Manqué," in *From Jane Austen to Joseph Conrad: Essays Collected in Memory of James T. Hillhouse.* Edited by Robert C. Rathburn and Martin Steinmann, Jr. Minneapolis: University of Minnesota Press, 1958, pp. 146–159.

Cockshut, A.O.J. *Anthony Trollope: A Critical Study.* London: Collins, 1955, pp. 164–168.

Cohen, Joan Mandel. *"Orley Farm*: Pain, Reality, and the Green World," in *Form and Realism in Six Novels of Anthony Trollope.* The Hague: Mouton, 1976, pp. 19–36.

Escott, T.H.S. *Anthony Trollope: His Work, Associates and Literary Associations.* London: John Lane, 1913, pp. 188–198.

Harvey, Geoffrey M. "Bulwer-Lytton and the Rhetorical Design of Trollope's *Orley Farm*," in *Ariel.* VI (1975), pp. 68–79.

Kincaid, James R. *The Novels of Anthony Trollope.* Oxford: Clarendon Press, 1977, pp. 78–82.

King, Margaret. "Trollope's *Orley Farm*: Chivalry versus Commercialism," in *Essays in Literature.* III (1976), pp. 181–193.

Newbolt, F. "Reg. vs. Mason," in *Nineteenth-Century Fiction.* XCV (February, 1924), pp. 227–236.

Polhemus, Robert M.   *The Changing World of Anthony Trollope.* Berkeley: University of California Press, 1968, pp. 76–88.

Pope-Hennessey, James.   *Anthony Trollope.* Boston: Little, Brown, 1971, pp. 244–248.

Saintsbury, George.   "Trollope Revisited," in *The Collected Essays and Papers of George Saintsbury, 1875–1920,* Volume II. London: J.M. Dent, 1923, pp. 333–334.

Terry, R.C.   *Anthony Trollope: The Artist in Hiding.* Totowa, N.J.: Rowman and Littlefield, 1977, pp. 140–143.

Walpole, Hugh.   *Anthony Trollope.* New York: Macmillan, 1928, pp. 126–130.

THE WARDEN

Type of work: Novel
Author: Anthony Trollope (1815–1882)
Type of plot: Domestic realism
Time of plot: Mid-nineteenth century
Locale: London and "Barchester," England
First published: 1855

The Warden, *the first of the Barchester novels, which concern British ecclesiastical life in the time of Queen Victoria, is a pleasant story, gently realistic in details, told in a leisurely manner. The plot is continued in* Barchester Towers.

Principal Characters

The Rev. Septimus Harding, a kind and gentle man who had been a minor canon near Barchester for many years. At the age of fifty, he had become precentor of Barchester Cathedral, a position which also included the wardenship of Hiram's Hospital. The latter was an alms house for twelve old men established by the will of John Hiram four centuries before. Through the efforts of John Bold, a local reformer, and the "Jupiter," a newspaper devoted to attacking the greed and power of the Church, Mr. Harding is accused of receiving too large an income from his management of the hospital. The legal issue is ambiguous and the almshouse has been well-managed, but Mr. Harding, distressed that others might question the justice of his position, resigns. All the legal and ecclesiastical officials, even John Bold himself, protest the resignation. After the suit has been dropped the Bishop offers the Warden a position as chaplain in the Bishop's house, but Mr. Harding refuses this charity and lives in poor lodgings in town, supported only by his tiny living near the Cathedral Close.

Eleanor Harding, the favorite and younger daughter of Mr. Septimus Harding. She is in love with John Bold. Fully cognizant of her father's sensitivity, she understands why he wants to resign his wardenship. In a scene which reveals their love for each other, she begs John Bold to drop the suit, as he does. She marries Bold, and her father frequently visits the couple.

The Rev. Theophilus Grantly, Archdeacon of Barchester and rector of Plumstead Episcopi. The son of the Bishop and the son-in-law of Mr. Harding, Archdeacon Grantly believes in "the sacred justice of all ecclesiastical revenues." Recognized as more worldly than his fellow churchmen, he insists that Mr. Harding take a strong stand against the lawsuit and the press, and he disapproves strongly of Eleanor's interest in John Bold.

Susan Grantly, the wife of Archdeacon Grantly and the older daughter of Mr. Harding. She joins her husband in trying to persuade her father to insist on the prerogatives of the Church.

Bishop Grantly, the father of Archdeacon Grantly. Over seventy, the bland, kindly Bishop of Barchester warmly supports Mr. Harding, but leaves most of the controversial campaigning to his son.

John Bold, a surgeon and town councilor, genuinely concerned with reform.

He honestly feels that John Hiram's will did not provide for the income the Warden receives, and he begins the action by instituting a lawsuit. When he is persuaded that the lawsuit has created more injustice than it has ameliorated, he willingly drops the charges.

Mary Bold, the older sister of John Bold. A kindly woman, she promotes the engagement of her brother to Eleanor Harding, her best friend.

John Bunce, the oldest of the beadsmen at Hiram's Hospital. He is entirely loyal to Mr. Harding.

Abel Handy, another beadsman at Hiram's Hospital, selfishly disloyal to Mr. Harding.

Tom Towers, a reporter for the "Jupiter." He maintains, in print, that Mr. Harding has unjustly received more money than Hiram's will intended. His attacks, originating from an anticlerical point of view, are both personal and unfair.

Sir Abraham Haphazard, an eminent Queens' Counsel and Attorney General. He is hired to defend Mr. Harding and is a conservative adherent of ecclesiastical privilege.

Mr. Finney, the solicitor hired by John Bold to collect evidence against the Warden. He gets most of the inmates of Hiram's Hospital to sign a petition protesting the management by promising them each one hundred pounds per year.

Doctor Pessimist Anticant, a Scots pamphleteer, one of whose moral and reforming pamphlets "exposes" Mr. Harding.

Mr. Popular Sentiment, a muckraking novelist whose work, "Almshouse," makes the clergyman a vicious monster depriving the old beadsmen of all sustenance.

Chadwick, the Bishop's steward and the man who farms John Hiram's estate.

Charles James Grantly, the oldest child of Archdeacon Grantly, an exact, careful boy.

Henry Grantly, the second and favorite son of Archdeacon Grantly, the most "brilliant" of the children.

Samuel Grantly, the sneaky, cunning child of Archdeacon Grantly.

Florinda and
Grizzel Grantly, daughters of Archdeacon Grantly.

The Story

At the age of fifty the Reverend Septimus Harding was appointed precentor of Barchester Cathedral, a position which carried with it the wardenship of Hiram's Hospital. This institution had for over four hundred years provided a home for twelve men in their old age, and as the income had grown to a considerable size, the warden and the steward received substantial yearly salaries. With his income of eight hundred pounds a year, Mr. Harding was able to provide comfortably for his younger daughter, Eleanor. His older daughter, Susan, was married to Dr. Grantly, archdeacon of the cathedral.

John Bold, a young physician with a small practice, turned his energies to reform. On investigation he discovered that the will of John Hiram, donor of the hospital, made no stipulation which would result in such a discrepancy as existed between the warden's and the steward's incomes and those of the twelve inmates, and he felt that his duty obliged him to bring this discrepancy to light. He en-

gaged the interest of a newspaper friend, Tom Towers, and the services of a solicitor named Finney. Finney explained the situation to the inmates and encouraged
them to think in terms of an annual income of one hundred pounds a year. Most
of them signed a petition addressed to the bishop, asking that justice be done.

The *Jupiter,* for which Towers worked, published editorials about the greedi-
ness of the church and unscrupulous clergymen. Mr. Harding was distressed. It
had never entered his head that he was living off an income not his by rights, and
he began to talk of resigning. Eleanor agreed that if her father were unhappy at
Hiram's Hospital, they would be better off at Crabtree Parva, a small parish
which belonged to Mr. Harding and which paid an annual income of fifty pounds.

Dr. Grantly, a worldly man, would not hear of Mr. Harding's resignation. He
insisted that the warden had an obligation to the church and to his fellow members of the clergy which required a firm stand against the laity and the press.
Besides, as he pointed out, the living at Crabtree Parva could not provide a suitable match for Eleanor.

Dr. Grantly came to the hospital and addressed the inmates. He told them
John Hiram had intended simply to provide comfortable quarters for old single
men who had no other homes. But Dr. Grantly's speech had little effect, except
on John Bunce and his two cronies. John Bunce, who was especially close to Mr.
Harding, served as a sub-warden of the old men. The others felt they had a right
to a hundred pounds a year.

When Eleanor saw how unhappy the whole affair made her father, she begged
him to resign. Finally she went to John Bold and begged him to give up the suit.
After promising to do anything he could for her, Bold declared his love. Eleanor,
who had hoped not to let matters go so far, confessed her love in return.

Bold went to see Dr. Grantly and told him that for reasons best known to
himself he was withdrawing the charges he had made. Dr. Grantly replied that he
did not think the defendants wished to have the suit withdrawn. He had been
advised that Mr. Harding and the steward were, in effect, servants, and so were
not responsible and could not be defendants in a suit.

Mr. Harding decided to go to London for a conference with Sir Abraham Haphazard, counsel for the defense. Eleanor had come home expecting to tell her
father all that Bold had told her, but she could not bring herself to discuss her
own affairs before those of the wardenship had been settled. Mr. Harding had
decided that he had no right to the income from Hiram's Hospital.

Bold also was going to London. When he arrived there, he went to Tom Towers
and asked him not to print any more editorials about the Barchester situation.
Towers said he could not be responsible for the attitude of the *Jupiter.* Bold then
went to the offices of his lawyer and told him to drop the suit. The lawyer sent
word to Sir Abraham.

Mr. Harding arrived in London and was given an appointment with Sir Abraham the next night at ten. Having explained his intention in a note to Dr.
Grantly, he was afraid that Dr. Grantly would arrive in London before he would

have a chance to carry out his plan. He left his hotel at ten in the morning and spent most of the day in Westminster Abbey in order to avoid Dr. Grantly. That night he told Sir Abraham that he must in all conscience resign his post as warden. When he returned to his hotel, he found Dr. and Mrs. Grantly waiting for him, but their arguments could not make the warden change his mind. Back in Barchester, he wrote a formal letter of resignation to the bishop and sent a copy to Dr. Grantly.

The bishop offered him a position as chaplain in his household. Mr. Harding declined the offer. Then it was suggested that a trade be effected between Mr. Harding and Mr. Quiverful of Puddingdale. Mr. Quiverful, who had ten children, would be glad to double his annual income and would be impervious to any attacks from the press. But this arrangement, too, met with opposition, for Puddingdale was too far from Barchester for Mr. Harding to attend to his duties as precentor at the cathedral.

As the time for Mr. Harding's departure from Hiram's Hospital drew near, he called in all the inmates and had a last talk with them. They were disturbed, even those who had petitioned the bishop, for they felt that they were being deprived of a friendly and sympathetic warden.

Mr. Harding took lodgings and was given a tiny parish at the entrance to the cathedral close. His daughter Eleanor married John Bold. So Mr. Harding's income continued to be ample for his needs. He dined frequently with the bishop and kept his cello at Eleanor's house, where he often went to make music. In short, Mr. Harding was not an unhappy man.

Critical Evaluation

The first in Trollope's series of novels about the provincial English clergy, *The Warden* enjoys the unique role of a pace setter; it is an indication of all that is to follow in plot, characterization, and theme. With Trollope we are always close to the simplicity and quiddity of actual life. The stories never tax our credulity; indeed they shower us with what Trollope designedly intended to be the *familiar*. His stories and people are within the possible experience of most of his readers, but his themes often challenge—with humor and subtlety—the moral and political assumptions of his time.

Behind Trollope's gossipy incursions into the domestic lives of the clergy lies a tough-minded purpose. In *The Warden,* for example, he is not only eavesdropping on the Grantlys but also relating a universal theme of great consequence, what Henry James described as "simply the history of an old man's conscience."

As the Reverend Septimus Harding grows steadily more uneasy at the idea of continuing to draw his high salary as warden at Hiram's Hospital, this "sweet and serious little old man" becomes an ethical giant who puts into the shadow the opportunistic Archdeacon, Dr. Grantly, and the legal establishment and parliament as well. He alone seems to grasp the significance of a moral principle; once he is determined to abide by it, he is invincible, for all his gentleness. Ironically, John Bold, whose "passion is the reform of all abuses," compromises his principles and withdraws his suit for love of Mr. Harding's daughter.

The cumulative effect of Mr Harding's stand is to make him a far greater "Warden" than he was in the first place. Trollope has him lose Hiram's Hospital only to become a symbolic guardian of the English conscience.

Bibliography

ApRoberts, Ruth. *The Moral Trollope.* Athens: Ohio University Press, 1971, pp. 34–42.

Best, G.F.A. "The Road to Hiram's Hospital: A Byway of Early Victorian History," in *Victorian Studies.* V (December, 1961), pp. 135–150.

Booth, Bradford A. *Anthony Trollope: Aspects of His Life and Art.* London: Edward Hulton, 1958, pp. 34–39.

Escott, T.H.S. *Anthony Trollope: His Work, Associates and Literary Associations.* London: John Lane, 1913, pp. 102–110.

Ganzel, Carol. "*The Times* Correspondent and *The Warden,*" in *Nineteenth-Century Fiction.* XXI (1966–1967), pp. 325–336.

Goldberg, M.A. "Trollope's *The Warden*: A Commentary on the 'Age of Equipoise,'" in *Nineteenth-Century Fiction.* XVIII (June, 1963), pp. 381–390. Reprinted in *The Victorian Novel: Modern Essays in Criticism.* Edited by Ian P. Watt. New York: Oxford University Press, 1971, pp. 337–346.

Haskin, Dayton. "Awakening Moral Conscience: Trollope as Teacher in *The Warden,*" in *Cithara.* XIII (1973), pp. 42–52.

Hawkins, Sherman. "Mr. Harding's Church Music," in *Journal of English Literary History.* XXIX (June, 1962), pp. 202–223.

Heilman, Robert B. "Trollope's *The Warden*: Structure, Tone, Genre," in *Essays in Honor of Esmond Linworth Marilla.* Edited by Thomas Austin Kirby and William John Olive. Baton Rouge: Louisiana State University Press, 1970, pp. 210–229.

Hennedy, Hugh L. "*The Warden*: Novel of Vocation," in *Unity in Barsetshire.* The Hague: Mouton, 1971, pp. 21–36.

Houston, Maude. "Structure and Plot in *The Warden,*" in *University of Texas Studies in English.* XXXIV (1955), pp. 106–113.

Kincaid, James R. *The Novels of Anthony Trollope.* Oxford: Clarendon Press, 1977, pp. 98–101.

Knox, Ronald. "Introduction to the Barsetshire Novels," in *The Warden*. London: Oxford University Press, 1952, pp. vii–xix.

Marshall, William H. *The World of the Victorian Novel*. New York: Barnes, 1967, pp. 322–336.

Polhemus, Robert M. *The Changing World of Anthony Trollope*. Berkeley: University of California Press, 1968, pp. 25–34.

Pope-Hennessey, James. *Anthony Trollope*. Boston: Little, Brown, 1971, pp. 146–149.

Saintsbury, George. "Trollope Revisited," in *The Collected Essays and Papers of George Saintsbury, 1875–1920*, Volume II. London: J.M. Dent, 1923, p. 326.

Terry, R.C. *Anthony Trollope: The Artist in Hiding*. Totowa, N.J.: Rowman and Littlefield, 1977, pp. 214–215, 246–247.

Tillotson, Geoffrey. "Afterword," in *The Warden*. New York: New American Library, 1964.

Walpole, Hugh. *Anthony Trollope*. New York: Macmillan, 1928, pp. 44–47.

HORACE WALPOLE

Born: London, England (September 24, 1717)
Died: London (March 2, 1797)

Principal Works

NOVEL: *The Castle of Otranto,* 1765.

LETTERS: *Letters,* edited by Peter Cunningham, 1857–1859 (9 vols.); *Letters,* edited by Mrs. Paget Toynbee, 1903–1905 (16 vols.); *The Yale Edition of Horace Walpole's Correspondence,* edited by W. S. Lewis, 1937 ff.

MEMOIRS: *Reminiscences,* 1805; *Memoirs of the Last Ten Years of the Reign of George II,* 1822; *Memoirs of the Reign of George III,* 1845; *Journal of the Reign of George III from 1771 to 1783,* 1859.

PLAY: *The Mysterious Mother,* 1768.

MISCELLANEOUS: *Aedes Walpolianae,* 1747; *A Catalogue of the Royal and Noble Authors of England,* 1758; *Anecdotes of Painting in England,* 1763–1771; *Historic Doubts on the Life and Reign of Richard III,* 1768.

Born in London, September 24, 1717, Horace (christened Horatio) Walpole was the son of Sir Robert Walpole, notorious British prime minister of the eighteenth century. At the age of ten Walpole was sent to Eton, where he formed friendships with boys like Thomas Ashton, Richard West, and Thomas Gray, who all became famous men. Following Eton came an academic career at King's College, Cambridge, from 1735 to 1739. Although he was supposed to enter upon a study of law after leaving the university, Walpole, in the company of Thomas Gray, made a lengthy tour of the Continent, visiting and finding delightful Paris, the Alps, Florence, and Rome. In Florence they met Horace Mann, the famous American who was destined to receive the largest number of Walpole's letters after the English dilettante became the most inveterate and voluminous writer of letters in English literary history.

Following his return to England, Walpole became a member of Parliament, serving from 1741 to 1768. In 1747 he acquired a small house in Twickenham, a residence to become famous as Strawberry Hill; famous as Walpole's home, as the center of the owner's enthusiasm for Gothic architecture and "ruins," as the home of the Strawberry Hill Press, and as a kind of park-museum-showplace. By his work on Strawberry Hill, Walpole—who was something of an expert in society, politics, literature, and painting—was to make a name for himself as a gardener and an architect. For twenty years the house was enlarged and given additional architectural features. The Strawberry Hill Press, which published Gray's great odes, also stimulated Walpole to publication. His *Fugitive Pieces in Verse and Prose* (1758) and his tragic drama, *The Mysterious Mother,* were printed there, although his famous *The Castle of Otranto*, which was published anonymously, was not.

In his second preface to *The Castle of Otranto*, Walpole said that his novel was written to revive the supernatural elements of the earlier French romances, adding some of the aspects of the sentimental novel of the eighteenth century in England. The supernatural elements were designed to provide terror for the readers; if they did at the time, they do so no longer, being regarded often by contemporary readers as merely slightly humorous. Perhaps the chief contribution Walpole made to fiction was a reliance on stage-set backgrounds. Later Gothic writers adopted them in an effort to provide a background against which the reader would accept anything that the novelist wished to include in the action, regardless of how absurd it might be.

Outside the realm of fiction, other facets of Walpole's life loom as much more important. His memoirs, covering the last half of the eighteenth century, were written in a conscious effort to be the historian of his own times. One set covers the reign of George III, and another set covers the last years of the reign of George II. Of even greater importance to the modern student of history is Walpole's tremendous correspondence. In his letters Walpole specialized. To Horace Mann, for example, went letters on politics, while to other selected recipients, he sent letters on other topics. A vast amount of information on the culture and affairs of England and the Continent is contained in the letters; they are a source of historical knowledge which is still far from measured, and they have been compared in value to a thousand of the "documentary" films of the twentieth century.

Walpole became the fourth Earl of Orford in 1791. He never married; perhaps too busy for domestic affairs. Mme. du Deffand, the famous French wit and bluestocking, was in love with him, and Mary Berry, a neighbor whose family was intimate with Walpole, seems to have been in love with him as well. Walpole's most famous aphorism is his statement, "Life is a comedy to those who think, a tragedy to those who feel." He died in London, March 2, 1797. The auction of his Strawberry Hill collection in 1842 was one of the most celebrated sales of the nineteenth century.

Bibliography

The standard modern biography is Robert W. Ketton-Cremer's *Horace Walpole: A Biography*, 1940 (reprinted 1966). For biography and criticism see also Austin Dobson, *Horace Walpole*, 1890; Dorothy M. Stuart, *Horace Walpole*, 1927; K. K. Mehrota, *Horace Walpole and the English Novel*, 1934; Montague Summers, *The Gothic Quest*, 1938; Hugh Honour, *Horace Walpole*, 1957; W. S. Lewis, *Horace Walpole*, 1960: Warren H. Smith, ed., *Horace Walpole: Writer, Politician, and Connoisseur*, (essays by various hands), 1967; and W. S. Lewis, "Horace Walpole Reread," *Atlantic Monthly*, CLXXVI (1945), 48–51.

THE CASTLE OF OTRANTO

Type of work: Novel
Author: Horace Walpole (1717–1797)
Type of plot: Gothic romance
Time of plot: Twelfth century
Locale: Italy
First published: 1764

This gothic novel, the first of the genre in English, is replete with all the stock character types, situations, and special effects associated with fiction of the haunted-castle-rattling-chain variety. The plot involves the evil Manfred's unlawful rule at Otranto and the eventual establishment, aided by numerous supernatural happenings, of the rightful heir, Theodore.

Principal Characters

Manfred, Prince of Otranto, a usurper. After Manfred's son is mysteriously killed on his wedding day, Manfred plans to divorce his wife and marry the promised bride himself, in order to have a male heir. After much frightening supernatural intervention, Manfred surrenders his claims to Otranto; he and his wife then enter neighboring convents.

Conrad, the fifteen-year-old son of Manfred. On his wedding day he is found crushed to death beneath a gigantic helmet.

Isabella, the daughter of the Marquis of Vicenza and the fiancée of Conrad. Manfred plans to marry her after Conrad's death, but she escapes him with the aid of the true heir to Otranto, whom she marries after Manfred's abdication.

Theodore, a young peasant and the true heir to Otranto. He is imprisoned and nearly executed by Manfred's order, but with both human and supernatural aid he triumphs, marrying Isabella and becoming the new Prince of Otranto.

Matilda, Manfred's daughter. She gives aid to Theodore. Learning that Theodore is in the chapel with a woman, the jealous Manfred goes there and stabs the woman, only to learn that he has killed his daughter Matilda.

Father Jerome, formerly Prince of Falconara, now a priest. Called to give absolution to the condemned Theodore, he discovers that Theodore is his own son, born before he entered the Church.

The Marquis of Vicenza, Isabella's father. Disguised as the **Knight of the Gigantic Sabre,** he comes to Otranto, bringing with him a huge sword carried by a hundred men. On its blade is written that only Manfred's blood can atone for the wrongs done to the family of the true heir. By betrothing the Marquis to Matilda, Manfred gets his consent to his own marriage with Isabella; but terrifying omens and warnings cause the Marquis to renounce Matilda.

Prince Alfonso the Good, formerly the ruler of Otranto. It was the helmet of his statue which crushed Conrad. His giant form appears to proclaim Theodore, the son of his daughter, heir to Otranto. He then ascends to Heaven.

St. Nicholas, who receives Prince Alfonso into Heaven.

The Story

Manfred, the prince of Otranto, planned to marry his fifteen-year-old son, Conrad, to Isabella, daughter of the Marquis of Vicenza. But on the day of the wedding a strange thing happened. A servant ran into the hall and informed the assembled company that a huge helmet had appeared mysteriously in the courtyard of the castle.

When Count Manfred and his guests rushed into the courtyard, they found Conrad crushed to death beneath a gigantic helmet adorned with waving black plumes. Theodore, a young peasant, declared the helmet was like that on a statue of Prince Alfonso the Good which stood in the chapel. Another spectator shouted that the helmet was missing from the statue. Prince Manfred imprisoned the young peasant as a magician and charged him with the murder of the heir to Otranto.

That evening Manfred sent for Isabella. He informed her that he intended to divorce his wife so that he himself might marry Isabella and have another male heir. Frightened, Isabella ran away and lost herself in the passages beneath the castle. There she encountered Theodore, who helped her to escape through an underground passage into a nearby church. Manfred, searching for the girl, accused the young man of aiding her. As he was threatening Theodore, servants rushed up to tell the prince of a giant sleeping in the great hall of the castle. When Manfred returned to the hall, the giant had disappeared.

The following morning Father Jerome came to inform Manfred and his wife that Isabella had taken sanctuary at the altar of his church. Sending his wife away, Manfred called upon the priest to aid him in divorcing his wife and marrying Isabella. Father Jerome refused, warning Manfred that heaven would have revenge on him for harboring such thoughts. The priest unthinkingly suggested Isabella might be in love with the handsome young peasant who had aided in her escape.

Manfred, enraged at the possibility, confronted Theodore. Although the young man did not deny having aided the princess, he claimed never to have seen her before. The frustrated Manfred ordered him to the courtyard to be executed, and Father Jerome was called to give absolution to the condemned man. But when the collar of the lad was loosened, the priest discovered a birthmark which proved the young peasant was Father Jerome's son, born before the priest had entered the Church. Manfred offered to stay the execution if the priest would deliver Isabella to him. At that moment a trumpet sounded at the gates of the castle.

The trumpet signaled the arrival of a herald from the Knight of the Gigantic Sabre, champion of Isabella's father, the rightful heir to Otranto. Greeting Manfred as a usurper, the herald demanded the immediate release of Isabella and the abdication of Manfred, or else the satisfaction of mortal combat. Manfred invited the Knight of the Gigantic Sabre to the castle, hoping through him to get permission to marry Isabella and keep the throne. The knight entered the castle with five hundred men at arms and a hundred more carrying one gigantic sword.

After a feast, during which the strange knight kept silence and raised his visor only to pass food into his mouth, Manfred broached the question of marrying Isabella, telling the knight he wished to marry again to insure himself an heir. Before he had finished, Father Jerome arrived with the news of Isabella's disappearance from the church. After everyone had gone to find Isabella, Matilda assisted Theodore to escape from the castle.

In the forest Theodore met Isabella and promised to protect her. Shortly thereafter they met the Knight of the Gigantic Sabre. Fearing the knight meant harm to Isabella, the young man overcame him in combat. Thinking himself about to die, the knight revealed to Isabella that he was her father in disguise.

They all returned to the castle. There Isabella's father confided to her that he had discovered the gigantic sword in the Holy Land. It was a miraculous weapon, for on the blade it was written that only the blood of Manfred could atone for the wrongs committed on the family of the true ruler of Otranto. Manfred returned to the castle, where he found Theodore dressed in armor. It seemed to Manfred that the young man resembled the prince whose throne Manfred had usurped.

Manfred still hoped to wed Isabella, and he craftily won her father's consent by betrothing that nobleman to Matilda. At that point a nearby statue dripped blood from its nose, an omen that disaster would follow those proposed marriages.

Manfred saw only two courses open to him. One was to surrender all claims to Otranto; the other was to go ahead with his plan to marry Isabella. In either case it appeared that fate was against his success. Nor did a second appearance of the giant in the castle ease the anxiety he felt. When news of the giant came to Isabella's father, he decided not to court disaster for himself by marrying Matilda or by permitting Manfred to marry his daughter. His resolution was increased when a skeleton in the rags of a hermit called upon him to renounce Matilda.

Hours later Manfred was told that Theodore was in the chapel with a woman. Jealous, he went to the chapel and stabbed the woman, who was his own daughter Matilda. Over the body of Matilda, Theodore announced that he was the true ruler of Otranto. Suddenly there appeared the giant form of the dead Prince Alfonso, who proclaimed Theodore to be the true heir. Then he ascended to heaven where he was received by St. Nicholas.

The truth was now made known. Theodore was the son of Father Jerome, then prince of Falconara, and Alfonso's daughter. Manfred confessed his usurpation and he and his wife entered neighboring convents. Theodore married Isabella and ruled as the new prince of Otranto.

Critical Evaluation

Horace Walpole's *The Castle of Otranto* is among the best-known, best-loved, and best-crafted novels of the Gothic genre in English. It is also one of the first. Gothic fiction was representative of the late eighteenth century rejection of the rational, realistic creed of Neo-Classicism, which asserted the superiority for literary purposes of things familiar and contemporary. This reaction was but a phase of the revival of interest in the recondite past, an interest which focused on medieval life and manifested itself in pseudo-scholarly antiquarianism, imitation Gothic castles, artificial ruins, balladry, and contrived narratives.

These narratives, permeated with fashionable melancholy, attempted to portray human conduct and sentiment with psychological realism while setting the action in remote and mysterious places and times. The emotional thrills of adventure thus provided the reader with an escape from humdrum existence. Hence, the villain was characteristically somber and restless. The heroine was beautiful, innocent, young, and sensitively perceptive; she waited dutifully to be rescued by a brave and courageous lover. The obligatory setting was a haunted castle, a cloister, or a ruined abbey, fortuitously furnished with underground passages, secret doors, and locked and unused rooms, and surrounded by wild and desolate landscape. The action inevitably included strange and deliberate crimes (often to the accompaniment of rattling chains and other inexplicable phenomena), incidents of physical violence, and emotional anguish orchestrated with supernatural manifestations. A strong erotic element usually underscored the plot. And any comic relief was, following Shakespeare's model, confined to servants. In a bogus historical setting, chronologically and geographically remote, novels of mystery and passionate emotion depicted the trials and misfortunes of sentimental love with an overlay of ghosts, prescience, and preternatural forces together with the titillating horror of violence and crime.

In the very forefront of this Gothic revival was *The Castle of Otranto,* whose author personally seemed ideally suited to his book (rather than the more usual obverse). Horace Walpole was a nobleman, respected for his antiquarian scholarship; he was also a fussy bachelor in precarious health, unable to join his peers in hunting, tippling, and wenching. He escaped the demands of this world by retreating into the past, psychologically as well as physically. He built himself a pseudo-Gothic retreat at Strawberry Hill where he displayed his collection of antiques and led an active fantasy life, imagining himself at one time a feudal lord and at another time a learned monk. Of an evening, he reportedly climbed his narrow Gothic staircase with his dog to his Gothic library to dream—possibly with the aid of opium—of the romantic past.

Out of such dreams *The Castle of Otranto* was spawned, illustrating two major themes in the Gothic novel. The story united a baroque view of architecture and sentiment in a repudiation of Neo-Classical ideals of proportion, balance, harmony, and ultimately narrow limitations. Thus the physical appearance of the Castle of Otranto was an exaggeration of genuine Gothic style, carrying the visual image to such excessive lengths that the structure bore hardly any resemblance to authentic examples of medieval Gothic architecture. Yet the effectiveness of the description is undeniable in the context of the novel. Likewise, the emotional overreaction of the characters—in defiance of all Neo-Classical canons of moderation—served a similar purpose: to transcend the mundane realities of common life on the wings of fancy. In the very uncommon life of this story, Walpole sought to liberate imagination and allow it to rove freely in what he characterized as "the boundless realms of invention . . . [thence] creating more interesting situations." Simultaneously (and without any sense of contradiction), Walpole claimed to strive for "naturalness" and "probability" in his character development. Yet fanciful setting and untrammeled emotion were the hallmarks of his—as well as many another—Gothic novel.

Nevertheless, Walpole employed supernatural devices—decidedly not natural or probable—to create the so-called interesting situations which he avowedly wanted to create. The totally immersed reader can, of course, become so wrapped up in the plot that inconsistencies escape notice. Thus, the plot itself is plausible even today, but the events surrounding it and somewhat precipitating it are more than a little suspect. The story opens with the ambiguous prophecy that "the castle and lordship of Otranto should pass from the present family, whenever the real owner should be grown too large to inhabit it." Intrigue thickens with Conrad's peculiar death and Manfred's frantic attempts to sire another heir. In due course, other supernatural manifestations intervene: two manservants see a strange apparition, which also appears to Bianca, Matilda's maid. Manfred's reasonable objections notwithstanding, these events very nearly unseat his reason. But even as Manfred argues with Hippolita to annul their marriage so that he can marry Isabella and produce an heir, three drops of blood fall from the nose of the statue of Alfonso, the original Prince of Otranto who won the principality through fraud and deceit. Manfred is thus given supernatural warning to desist from his wicked plan, but he is still undeterred. However, his intended new father-in-law also sees an apparition when he goes to the chapel to pray for guidance. In the end, after many such scenes of terror, violence, and bewilderment, the true heir of Otranto is unexpectedly discovered amid a thunderclap, a rattling of armor, and a disembodied pronouncement about legitimate succession.

All of these contrivances may strain the credulity of today's reader—but only in retrospect. For the chain of events is so enveloping that the act of reading suspends one's normal skepticism to such an extent that customary doubt and ordinary questions are held in abeyance. It is only after the fact that the reader begins to examine the logic and question the veracity of Walpole's highly convincing tale. And therein lies the art of the story.

Bibliography

Baker, Ernest A. *The History of the English Novel*, Volume V. New York: Barnes & Noble, 1950, pp. 178–179.

Beers, Henry A. "The Gothic Revival," in his *A History of English Romanticism in the Eighteenth Century*. New York: Holt, 1926, pp. 229–241.

Collins, Norman. "Major Minor Novelists (Johnson, Goldsmith, Walpole)," in his *Facts of Fiction*. New York: Dutton, 1933, pp. 82–103.

Dobson, Austin. *Horace Walpole: A Memoir*. London: Harper, 1910, pp. 163–167.

Elton, Oliver. *A Survey of English Literature, 1730–1780*, Volume I. New York: Macmillan, 1928, pp. 33–34.

Gwynn, Stephen. *The Life of Horace Walpole*. London: Thornton Butterworth, 1932, pp. 190–194.

Hogan, Charles Beecher. "The 'Theatre of Geo. 3,' " in *Horace Walpole: Writer, Politician, and Connoisseur*. Edited by Warren Hunting Smith. New Haven, Conn.: Yale University Press, 1967, pp. 237–240.

Honour, Hugh. *Horace Walpole*. London: Longmans, Green, 1957, pp. 17–21.

Kallich, Martin. *Horace Walpole*. New York: Twayne, 1971, pp. 92–104.

Ketton-Cremer, R.W. *Horace Walpole*. New York: Longmans, Green, 1940, pp. 211–219.

Kiely, Robert. *The Romantic Novel in England*. Cambridge, Mass.: Harvard University Press, 1972, pp. 27–42.

Lewis, W.S. *Horace Walpole*. New York: Pantheon, 1961, pp. 157–161.

————. "Introduction," in *The Castle of Otranto*. London: Oxford University Press, 1964, pp. vii–xvi.

Marshall, Roderick. *Italy in English Literature, 1755–1815: Origins of the Romantic Interest in Italy*. New York: Columbia University Press, 1934, pp. 245–246.

Mehrotra, Kewal Krishna. *Horace Walpole and the English Novel: A Study of the Influence of* The Castle of Otranto, *1764–1820*. Oxford: Blackwell, 1934.

Prew, James A. "The Tale of Terror," in *English Journal*. XLVII (May, 1958), pp. 243–247.

Quennell, Peter. "The Moon Stood Still on Strawberry Hill," in *Horizon*. XI (Summer, 1969), pp. 113–119.

Railo, Eino. *The Haunted Castle: A Study of the Elements of English Romanticism*. New York: Dutton, 1927.

Skilton, David. *The English Novel: Defoe to the Victorians.* New York: Barnes & Noble, 1977, pp. 59–61.

Steeves, Harrison Ross. *Before Jane Austen: The Shaping of the English Novel in the Eighteenth Century.* New York: Holt, Rinehart and Winston, 1965, pp. 243–271.

Stuart, Dorothy Margaret. *Horace Walpole.* New York: Macmillan, 1927, pp. 162–168.

Summers, Montague. *The Gothic Quest: A History of the Gothic Novel.* London: Fortune, 1936, pp. 179–187.

Varma, Devendra P. *The Gothic Flame.* London: Arthur Barker, 1957, pp. 42–73.

Wagenknecht, Edward C. "The Renascence of Wonder," in his *Cavalcade of the English Novel.* New York: Holt, 1943, pp. 112–114.

ALPHABETICAL LIST OF TITLES